COMMONPLACES

Working on an American Architecture

Brian Healy

Bikram Yoga

COMMONPLACES

Working on an American Architecture

Brian Healy

Introduction
Robert McCarter

Contributions
Brian Healy
Juhani Pallasmaa
Marlon Blackwell
Robert Campbell
Julian Bonder
Peter MacKeith
Edward Mitchell
Vladimir Belogolovsky

Editor
Oscar Riera Ojeda

OSCAR RIERA OJEDA
PUBLISHERS

We Have On This Earth
What Makes Life Worth Living.

Mahmoud Darwish

TABLE OF CONTENTS

Programming is the highest form of creativity...
it gives birth to form and culture...

Alvar Aalto

FOREWORD

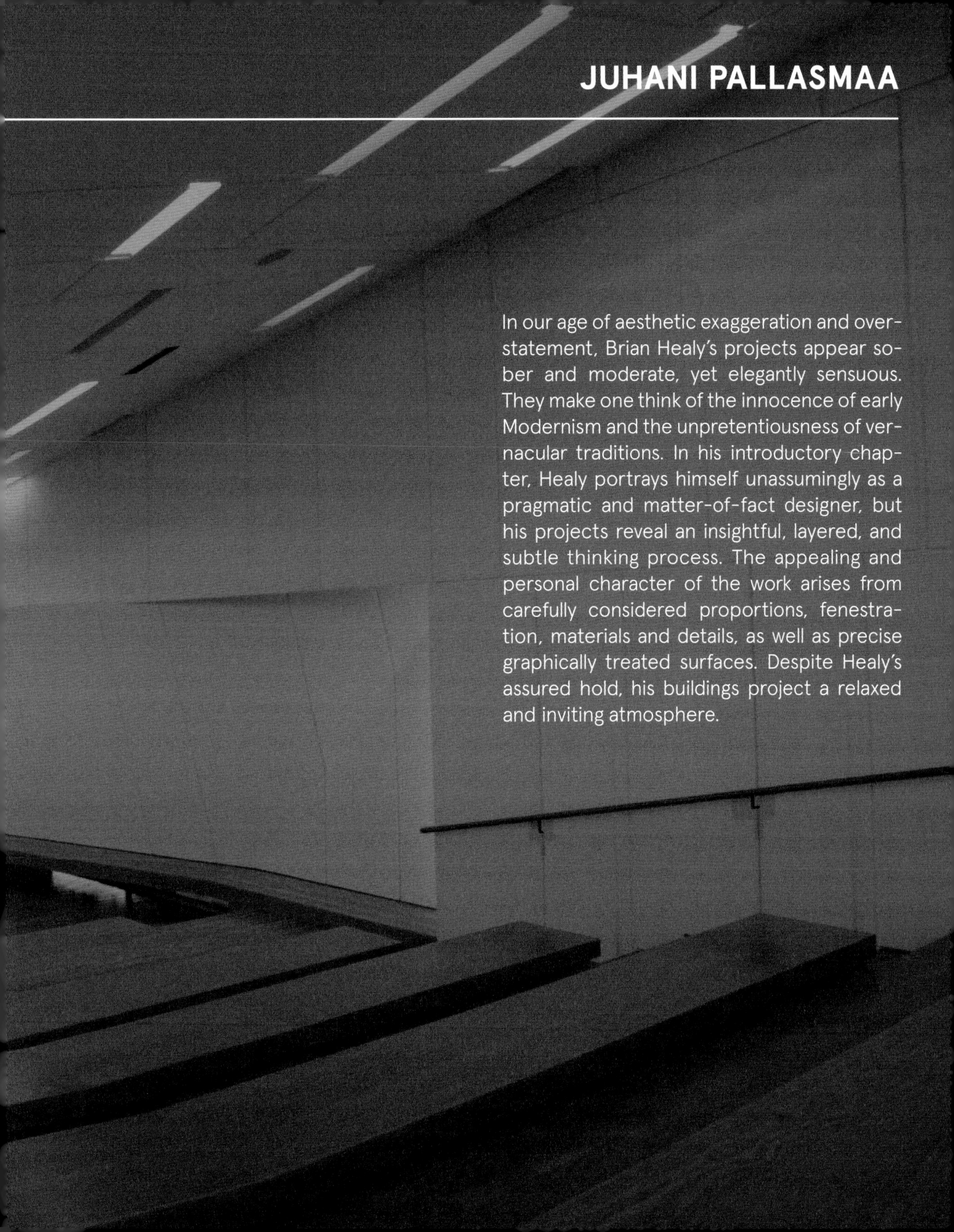

JUHANI PALLASMAA

In our age of aesthetic exaggeration and overstatement, Brian Healy's projects appear sober and moderate, yet elegantly sensuous. They make one think of the innocence of early Modernism and the unpretentiousness of vernacular traditions. In his introductory chapter, Healy portrays himself unassumingly as a pragmatic and matter-of-fact designer, but his projects reveal an insightful, layered, and subtle thinking process. The appealing and personal character of the work arises from carefully considered proportions, fenestration, materials and details, as well as precise graphically treated surfaces. Despite Healy's assured hold, his buildings project a relaxed and inviting atmosphere.

INTRODUCTION

We shall not cease from exploration
And the end of all our exploring
Will be to arrive where we started
And know the place for the first time.

Little Gidding – T. S. Eliot

ROBERT McCARTER

COMMON SENSE: TOWARD AN ARCHITECTURE BOTH POETIC AND PRACTICAL

Brian Healy is an architect who works within the modern American tradition. That is to say, he endeavors to engage the tradition of practice as exemplified by architects such as Louis Sullivan, Frank Lloyd Wright, and Louis I. Kahn. It takes considerable courage to engage the American tradition of practice today, in a time dominated by an obsessive emphasis on universal "globalization" and the parallel loss of local place, culture and identity. Yet, as the philosopher Paul Ricoeur stated sixty years ago, while universal civilization is available around the world and is desired by everyone, anywhere, there is no culture that is not local, that does not belong to a particular place. In his work, Healy endeavors to seek the essence of his discipline, architecture, as defined by its place and time — an American architecture, born of the commonplace and the vernacular, yet at the same time engaging the great works of our modern predecessors.

Early nineteenth century American artist and critic, Horatio Greenough, noted that "the mind of this country" had never been seriously applied to the subject of building, and that Americans tended to accept all their styles — of clothing, entertainment, and architecture — from Europe. Louis Sullivan, who practiced before and after the turn of the twentieth century, believed it was essential to evolve an appropriate American architecture, yet he warned against "grafting or transplanting" European forms onto the American continent. He believed, as had Ralph Waldo Emerson, that any true indigenous American architecture would develop on a regional basis, with variations dependent upon climate, landscape, and local building methods. From the outset of his over seventy-year career, Frank Lloyd Wright dedicated his life to the cause of developing "an American architecture," as he titled one of his late books, and today, more than sixty years after his death, Wright remains its most universally recognized practitioner.

Yet, architecture, modern or ancient, has never existed in the abstract, without being grounded in the concrete characteristics of a particular place and time. In his "thinking about an American architecture," and in his designs for various American contexts, Healy understands that the subject is, as always, unsettled, and that each generation, and each architect, must search for their own way of making an American architecture. In a time when we are incessantly told that we live in a "globalized" world and can no longer belong to, and draw our identity from, a particular place, the need for adaptations of modern architecture's universal liberative spatial concepts to local culture, climate and landscape, and a parallel integration of innovative and traditional construction technologies and materials, is more pressing than ever before. Where American architecture survives and exists as a living tradition today, it does so only as it is redefined, re-grounded, and reborn in the contemporary works of architects such as Healy.

Healy is part of the modern American tradition that employs an ethical definition of architecture — one determined by economical, functional, ecological, constructive, structural, material, aesthetic, experiential, social, and cultural principles — which values not what a building *looks* like, but what it is like *to live in*. Taken altogether, these principles directly affect our experience of inhabitation, which remains the ultimate measure of the quality of a work of architecture. This is a fundamentally integrated ideal of architecture, one that endeavors to build urban spaces, buildings, and interior rooms in such a way that, when inhabiting each, all of our senses are engaged in its experience. Healy sets himself the task of constructing places where we can truly dwell: places that allow what Aldo van Eyck called "homecoming"; places where the authenticity of our experience is made concrete and specific; places where what Healy has called the "resonant presence" of beauty becomes inextricably intertwined in our daily lives, ennobling and enriching our everyday rituals of inhabitation.

Here we should note Healy's regular and resolute use of the term "beauty," a refreshingly forthright advocacy of what he clearly believes is a critically important characteristic of experience — and yet a word that has, today, almost entirely vanished from our disciplinary vocabulary. Healy believes that beauty, despite its absence from recent architectural discourse, is nevertheless an essential characteristic of the American architecture that he admires, whether it be the commonplace vernacular of the barn or the exceptional design of Wright or Kahn. And, more importantly, he also understands that the beautiful, the poetic, and the more prosaic, practical aspects necessary to the everyday functioning of a building are in no way incompatible and are in fact mutually interdependent. Kahn suggested exactly such a reciprocal relation when he spoke of "the poetry of economy," alluding to the integrated nature of construction. The poetic and practical character of place-making is both modern and ancient in origin, as defined by the composer Igor Stravinsky in his *Poetics of Music*: "The exact meaning of poetics is the study of work to be done. The verb *poiein* from which the word is derived means nothing else but *to do* or *make* ... For [the classical philosophers] the single word *techne* embraced both the fine arts and the useful arts and was applied to the knowledge and study of the certain and inevitable rules of craft. That is why Aristotle's *Poetics* constantly suggest ideas regarding personal work, arrangements of materials, and structures."

This balance of the beautiful and poetic, and the functional and practical can be traced back to two experiences of Healy's childhood in Bucks County, Pennsylvania. The first are his memories of visiting the remarkable Mercer Museum in nearby Doylestown. This large, multi-level basilica-like space is densely packed with thousands of "early American domestic tools and vehicles" (as the museum describes its collection), housing "useful" things (as Healy describes them) from furniture and farm implements to boats and wagons, all of which are hung in the side aisles and central nave of this cathedral celebrating practical ingenuity and poetic elegance — and their fusion in the handcrafted artifact. Though separated from the houses and landscapes where they were originally put to use, the lessons of the "museum of useful things" are those of economy as an ethical imperative, minimal material used for maximal effect, and the understanding that, as the architect Brian MacKay-Lyons has said, "the vernacular is what you do when you cannot afford to fail." Imagined in their original working contexts — the early farmsteads of rural Pennsylvania — these "useful things" serve as a reminder that, at their foundation, architecture and agriculture are closely related ways of *cultivating* and *caring for* the earth.

The second experience came when, pedaling his bicycle through the cornfields at age thirteen, Healy discovered the home, studio and workshops of the internationally recognized wood master craftsman George Nakashima outside nearby New Hope. After knocking on the door and being invited inside to have tea with Nakashima on his first visit, Healy made a ritual of bicycling the ten miles to the Nakashima compound on weekends, where he was welcome to roam around what he would only much later learn was one of the foremost centers of contemporary wood-working craft. Of equal interest to Healy, who had been interested in art and architecture since a young age, was the fact that the workshops and artifacts were housed in a remarkable collection of buildings, including the main house and showroom, with their traditional Japanese detailing and modern plans, the thin-shell concrete hyperbolic paraboloid-roofed wood storage sheds, and the astonishing "Conoid" studio, with its thin-shell concrete roof, continuously folding vaults, and conoidal geometric transition across its section from flat to curved elevations (similar to the works of Gaudí in Barcelona) — all constructed in the 1950s. Nakashima's furniture marked a high-point in the fusion of traditional wood-working craft with modern design, and the buildings in his New Hope compound are a kind of catalog of modern and traditional construction techniques — all of which made the deepest impression on the young Healy. But it would only be many years later, when he was in the audience as Nakashima's work was presented in a university lecture, that Healy made the connection to the weekend visits of his childhood.

Above Brian Healy at Frank Lloyd Wright's Taliesin West

Above George Nakashima's Studio in New Hope, Pennsylvania

The relation between craft and culture embedded in both of these childhood experiences was reinforced by Healy's Yale professor, George Kubler's paradigm-shifting book, *The Shape of Time: Remarks on the History of Things* of 1962. Kubler proposes that history should be understood as the shape of time that engages with all human-made things, from crafts to architecture to art, as variations on themes in a continuously linked evolution of forms across time, and that history consists of those things that humans have made. In this Kubler is close to the eighteenth century philosopher Giambattista Vico, whose aphoristic motto was *Verum Ipsum Factum* — "we only know what we make," as Carlo Scarpa applied it to architectural education, and "we can only know what we and our kind have made," as Vico applied it to human history. Both Kubler and Vico's interpretations of history emphasize the continuity of culture as it is embodied in craft over the disruptive formal gestures disengaged from history and place that are typical of individual "inventions" (such as those of today's "star architects"). As evidenced in Healy's work, the rejection of spectacular self-referential "inventions" in favor of constructions characterized by cultural continuity, historical resonance and place enhancement — of working within the modern American tradition while simultaneously engaging the incremental modifications of craft and the vernacular — proves to be the approach that is more generative and supportive of community, and the mode of action that constructs the more enduring artifacts and places.

"We must endeavor to proceed like the Greeks: they invented nothing, but they transformed everything," the architect Viollet-le-Duc wrote in 1872. Building understood not as some form of "invention" but as the "transformation of reality" (as Álvaro Siza has said) is closely linked to what Wright called "the nature of materials," and Kubler states that the architect, artists and craftsman are all "*homo faber*, whose calling is to evoke a perpetual renewal of form in matter." Regarding the relation of materials to making, Kubler finds that the artist-craftsman "was bound to achieve his unconventional aim with conventional means." Kubler's definition of the craft-like character of architectural practice, and its profound implications for the culture and place for which it is made, find reinforcement in Kenneth Frampton's recent observation: "Despite the ubiquitous triumph of technological modernization, the practice of architecture is still to be more properly regarded as a craft, one that, at its full range, is dedicated to the significant mediation of the environment."

Healy's practice is grounded in a particularly American interpretation of the commonplace as the true purpose of architecture, and this extends through all scales from individual dwelling to communal multi-family housing to urban infrastructure. In thinking about our commonplaces — the places we hold in common — as examples of "places dedicated to the significant mediation of the environment," perhaps the most archetypal American place is the New England village green. Though today a public park, the Boston Common was, like all village greens, originally a "commonwealth," an open field for the communal grazing of farm animals belonging to those who lived in the community. In his recognition of the responsibilities of the urban building to its shared street, Healy indicates his understanding that the places we hold in common in the city also include "the street as a room of human agreement," as Kahn defined it, calling for the reinstatement of "the street where people live, learn, shop and work as the room [formed] out of community... The street is a community room."

This is high praise from Kahn, who believed that "the room is the beginning of architecture," and that "in a large room, the event [that takes place] is of commonality." Many of Healy's rooms for gathering, whether for religious ceremony or community meeting, celebration or performance, have the character of what are called the "common rooms" in convents, monasteries and Shaker villages — rooms where the individual members can come together and meet as equals, thereby embodying the community. Works of architecture, and the rooms they enclose and the streets they frame, are the most substantial and lasting things that we make and hold in common. Buildings also exercise a profound influence on the actions that take place within them, as Edward T. Hall noted in describing the power of rooms to engender both habitual use and embodied memory; "it is the mold into which a great deal of behavior is cast. It was this feature of space that the late Sir Winston Churchill referred to when he said: 'We shape our buildings and they shape us.' During the debate on restoring the House of Commons after the war, Churchill feared that departure from the intimate spatial pattern of the House, where opponents face each other across a narrow aisle, would seriously alter the patterns of government."

In Healy's buildings, we find that every element and space have both a *poetic* and a *practical* character. This is one of the most important attributes of the modern American architectural tradition that Healy has reengaged in his practice. In this way of working, the poetic experiences allowed by the building, the moments where beauty comes into "resonant presence," are the architect's claim to success, while the practical functioning of the building was, at least in Wright's time, taken entirely for granted as the minimal competence required to call oneself an architect. Yet today it is courageous to engage in such an ethical and integrated practice of architecture in a time that takes for granted the notion that, rather than constructing such poetic and practical places, architects specialize in providing evermore narrowly defined "products." Contemporary examples would include buildings that are *only* of a single program type, of the lowest possible cost, erected in the least time, ecologically "sustainable," socially "engaged," contextually "responsive," universally-applicable and repeatable, intentionally "banal" — or even buildings "designed" as spectacles to obtain publicity! In this, we should recall Wright's sharp reminder of the larger ethical responsibilities of our discipline; "The sins of architects are permanent sins."

Brian Healy is a good architect in that he knows his limits, and yet he holds himself and his work to the very highest of standards. He does so precisely because he knows that architecture directly affects people's lives, conditioning their everyday experiences, as well as requiring a significant percentage of the community's and the world's resources for its realization and continuing use. Rather than "star architects," with their artist's "boutique" ateliers and "signature" designs, or the corporate, "architecture as a business" offices, with their lowest-common-denominator "products," what the world needs more of today are good architects such as Healy — architects who do the right thing, who do what is appropriate (Kahn said: "I teach appropriateness. I don't teach anything else."), who act like architects and practice their discipline in an ethical manner, working for the betterment of society, culture, and everyday experience.

Yet today, this ethical charge given to architecture, and assumed by all good architects, is almost completely invisible to the dominant instruments of publicity, as are the built works of good architects. Again, this mode of practice demands considerable courage (some would say, foolhardiness), for we live in a time when the instruments of publicity are intimately related to the mechanisms of commission distribution. If one wishes to "get the job," the battle cry of both the American corporate practice and international "star architect" boutique, one's work must be *seen* by the instruments of publicity (as photographs of free-standing objects of aesthetic speculation), and recognized by the architecture "critics" (whose "reviews" rarely if ever involve actually *being there*). On the other hand, good architects are not particularly focused on gaining notice; they are, instead, like Healy, obsessed with making good architecture.

For Healy, this is simply a matter of common sense. In a time when architects invariably crave publicity and recognition, and, in order to gain this, they accentuate their work's supposed difference, inventiveness, and novelty, Healy has chosen to title this book *Commonplaces* — thus associating his work with the commonplace, with things we hold in common, with the common that underlies community, with the commonality that defines both place and our identity, and with the common sense that orders everyday life. Healy's embrace of common sense, rather than being a lowering of his standards (as might be suggested by contemporary instruments of publicity, incapable as they are of recognizing and appreciating the commonplace), is instead a setting of standards at the highest level possible for an architect: that is, the ethical responsibility to construct places that give dignity and bring beauty to the rituals of everyday life.

Like all the very best architects practicing today, Healy begins his designs from the realization that, here in the first quarter of the twenty-first century, all works of architecture, irrespective of whether their contexts are urban, suburban, or rural, must be conceived as appropriate *additions* to a pre-existing manmade place. This has come with the recognition by enlightened contemporary practitioners that, as a society and as a species, we can no longer afford the questionable luxury of building free-standing objects that take no cognizance of the needs of the community and the history of the place where they are set. And yet we live in a time when this still remains a depressingly typical practice among architects, particularly the more celebrated. On the other hand, Healy's works are invariably carefully fitted into their place, taking cognizance of both subtle and powerful patterns of inhabitation that have been inscribed into the earth over time. These are patterns that often work at widely varying scales, as well as overlap and obscure each other, so that, in the effort to engage them all in the design, Healy must unravel them and make each present as part of the larger order brought to the site by the design, a design which is itself necessarily understood as only a single step in the still unfolding history of the place.

For Healy, our need to have our own place is paramount, and his often-lonely search for an appropriate American architecture is essential to his making of new places today. While his work is inspired equally by the buildings of Frank Lloyd Wright and by what he calls "the well worn, the vernacular, and the commonplace," Wright's Usonian Houses are perhaps closest in spirit to Healy's buildings. Wright built hundreds of Usonian Houses between 1930 and 1959, the year of his death, and they share the characteristic of being at once commonplace and astonishing — and in this, they were without peer in contemporary American architecture. Many of Healy's works, like Wright's Usonian Houses, are modest designs, constructed of standardized materials, yet nevertheless providing the most remarkably rich range of experiences. Also, like Wright's Usonian Houses, Healy's buildings are deeply rooted to their sites, enclosing both interior and exterior space, and weaving their occupants into the local place. In what is without a doubt the highest compliment I can give him, I find Healy's buildings to be like Wright's Usonian Houses in that they are at once commonplace, allowing our homecoming, and deeply moving and enriching places to be. This arises from the fact that Healy's work embodies values we hold in common, the most important of which is integrity, as defined in Wright's statement: "What is needed most in architecture today is the very thing that is most needed in life — integrity. Just as it is in a human being, so integrity is the deepest quality in a building... The Usonian House, then, aims to be a *natural* performance, one that is integral to site; integral to environment; integral to the life of the inhabitants."

Healy is an optimistic architect, in that he believes that architecture, by employing Wright's (too little noted) measure of "human use and comfort," and by bringing the "resonant presence" of beauty to the spaces where everyday life takes place, can make the world a better place. Such a positive viewpoint is something that one would assume was essential to such a fundamentally constructive discipline as architecture, and yet we live in a time where the most recognized architects exhibit a fashionable form of cynicism. On the other hand, Healy pursues the particular form of satisfaction that comes from making a good building. In this, Healy's work exemplifies Wright's surprisingly modest definition of architecture as the "framework or background" for the events of daily life. For us to truly understand Healy's buildings, as with Wright's, they must not become the object of our attention, seen as photographs in publications. Rather, we must be inside them. It is in this experience of inhabitation that Healy's architecture excels, and his richly woven fabrics of complementary materials – light and heavy, thick and thin, vertical and horizontal, smooth and rough, immense and intimate – enclose us in precisely orchestrated layers of space and light, engaging all our senses in a fully embodied experience. If this essay is successful, it will inspire the reader to inhabit these places for themselves, experiencing what Wright called "the space within."

In the very first sentences of his Introduction that follows, Healy points out that, in the discourse surrounding contemporary architectural practice, we architects have effectively eliminated both passion and place from our collective consciousness. This is a provocative observation, yet one immediately senses the truth in it – which is typical of Healy's laconic yet insightful way of speaking about his work as an architect. Might this loss of both passion and place from architectural discourse, and, by implication, from contemporary architecture itself, not be directly connected to the loss of our common sense? Despite our world increasingly being defined as "globalized" in nature, and our concomitant expectations that everything should happen with ever greater rapidity, Healy's work indicates that the power of architecture, and its true task – requiring, I might note, both passion and patience from the architect – continues to be to anchor us to our place, to protect the authenticity of human experience, to remind us who we are, to give us a common sense of identity. This is an identity inextricably formed by and engaged in our particular place, in the place we share in common with others in our community – our commonplaces.

References:

Kenneth Frampton, "Critical Regionalism Revisited: Reflections on the Mediatory Potential of Built Form," in M. Umbach and B. Hüppauf, eds, *Vernacular Modernism* (Stanford: Stanford University Press, 2005).

Horatio Greenough, "Form and Function" (1853); reprinted in Lewis Mumford, ed., *Roots of Contemporary American Architecture* (New York: Dover, 1972).

Edward T. Hall, *The Hidden Dimension* (New York: Random House, 1966).

Brian Healy, "Poetics and Pavement," *Casas International: Brian Healy* (Madrid: Kliczkowski, 2000).

Louis I. Kahn, Robert McCarter, (London: Phaidon Press, 2005).

Louis I. Kahn: Writings, Lectures, Interviews, Alessandra Latour, ed. (New York: Rizzoli, 1991).

George Kubler, *The Shape of Time* (New Haven: Yale University Press, 1962).

The Work of MacKay-Lyons Sweetapple Architects: Economy as Ethic, Robert McCarter, (London: Thames & Hudson, 2017).

Nature Form and Spirit: The Life and Legacy of George Nakashima, Mira Nakashima, (New York: Abrams, 2003).

Paul Ricoeur, "Universal Civilization and National Cultures" (1961), *History and Truth* (Evanston: Northwestern University Press, 1965).

Alvaro Siza, Poetic Profession (Milan: Electa, 1986).

Igor Stravinsky, *Poetics of Music* (Cambridge, MA: Harvard University Press, 1942).

Louis Sullivan, "Characteristics and Tendencies of American Architecture" (1885), *Kindergarten Chats and Other Writings* (New York: Dover, 1979).

Aldo van Eyck, Robert McCarter, (New Haven: Yale University Press, 2015)

Eugene-Emmanuel Viollet-le-Duc, *Entretiens sur l'architecture (Lectures on Architecture*, 1872) (reprinted, New York: Dover, 1987)

Frank Lloyd Wright, *Frank Lloyd Wright: Collected Writings* (5 volumes), Bruce Brooks Pfeiffer, ed. (New York: Rizzoli, 1992-5).

Above George Nakashima's Studio in New Hope, Pennsylvania

Robert McCarter is a practicing architect, author, and Ruth and Norman Moore Professor of Architecture at Washington University in St. Louis since 2007. He previously taught at the University of Florida from 1991 to 2007, where he was founding Director of the School of Architecture; at Columbia University from 1986 to 1991; and at five other institutions, two of them international. During his 35 years in academia, including 17 years in leadership roles at three institutions, McCarter has taught at least one design studio every semester, and he has taught more than 1,800 students. He has had his own architectural practice since 1982, in New York, Florida and St. Louis, with 25 realized buildings. He is the author of two hundred essays, introductions and book chapters, as well as authoring twenty-three published books to date, including *Place Matters: The Architecture of WG Clark* (2019); *Grafton Architects* (2018); *The Work of MacKay-Lyons Sweetapple Architects: Economy as Ethic* (2017); *The Space Within: Interior Experience as the Origin of Architecture* (2016); *Marcel Breuer* (2016); *Steven Holl* (2015); *Aldo van Eyck* (2015); *Herman Hertzberger* (2015); *Local Architecture* (with Brian MacKay-Lyons, 2015); *Alvar Aalto* (2014); *Carlo Scarpa* (2013); *Understanding Architecture: A Primer on Architecture as Experience* (with Juhani Pallasmaa, 2012); *Wiel Arets: Autobiographical References* (2012); *Frank Lloyd Wright: Critical Lives* (2006); *Louis I. Kahn* (2005); *On and By Frank Lloyd Wright: A Primer on Architectural Principles* (2005); *William Morgan, Architect* (2002); and *Frank Lloyd Wright* (1997). McCarter also recently edited (with Karla Britton) the book, *Modern Architecture and the Lifeworld: Essays in Honor of Kenneth Frampton* (2020). Among other awards and honors, the curators of the 2018 Venice Biennale of Architecture selected McCarter as one of 71 International Exhibitors, and his exhibit in the Central Pavilion of the Giardini was entitled "Freespace in Place: Four Unrealized Modern Architectural Designs for Venice; Carlo Scarpa's *Quattro progetti per Venezia* Revisited"; and he was named one of the "Ten Best Architecture Teachers in the US" by *Architect* magazine in December 2009.

BACKGROUND

The river is within us, the sea is all about us.

The Dry Salvages – T.S. Eliot

BRIAN HEALY

CORNFIELDS, COASTLINES, AND SQUARES

I've tried to understand what America represents, and what an architecture could become within that understanding. I then tried to hold each of these architectures accountable to an inherent promise of a better life. Similar to other commonplace books, which since antiquity have compiled knowledge in communal records akin to scrapbooks, the content of this book traces forty years of trying to identify strategies for that architecture. It is a book of stories and recollections that hopes to engage other narratives - other approaches.

As an idea, America constantly changes without self-evident boundaries. Named by a cartographer in 1507, spanning more than five centuries and two continents, it presents the world with often contradictory aspirations of freedom and opportunity — promises not equitably distributed — but with a potential path for collective good. Architecture seems vast and expansive as well - equally challenging with its own need for broader inclusivity –but also not limited to a certain sect, concept of form or maker.

Architecture is more than a career and America is much more than a nation. They are not about geography or craft - but rather ambitious thoughts offering hope. The ideas seem as kindred spirits with an ethical imperative to explore each other as they evolve — to nurture each other while protecting both accommodation and shelter. They blur our definitions and challenge our vague concepts of boundaries. They are neither ideal nor perfect — they are both grainy and routine.

There are many things we never say as architects. We cloak our intentions in pedantic language that removes the passion and the place from our work. I have always wanted to be an architect, so my life and my work become inseparable. Everything I see is architectural and everything I do has spatial and social implications. For me, architecture is not made of intentions but of works. In its

Top left Detail from Waldseemuller Map of 1507. **Left** Cornfields coastlines + squares. **Above** Istanbul, Brian Healy.

very essence, architecture involves a renunciation of words and an engagement with the physical. It steps beyond ideas to become experiential. It begins with a desire to locate our place in the world and it leads to an engagement with aspiration, self-identity, and mystery. It makes concrete our most subtle emotions.

We have been bombarded with a refrain of an imminent singular global culture detached from both time and place. But local cultures need to be acknowledged and understood. Every encounter between a building and a person who visits it occurs at a particular time in a particular place. It is the real power of architecture, the power to connect us to where we are in the world. It cannot be any place. It is always some place.

For the past forty years, I have been trying to develop an understanding and language for an American architecture. To review that work is to revisit these scattered sites and crisscross the country in some mnemonic nod to days spent hitchhiking, or driving on long road trips. It is to encounter a string of memorable vernacular and historic structures, as well as the profound work by others across the centuries. The list is long and fortunately continues to grow. As with all construction, the projects bear the mark of many fingerprints — including those of my family, colleagues, and clients. Inevitably, the endeavor is less a matter of individual inspiration and more an honest acknowledgment that things could be done differently and that a different proposition could always be made.

OPEN ROADS

My family's home was the first of many neo-colonial wooden houses that were built in a field on Greene's Farm in Bucks County, Pennsylvania. For years, the house remained isolated, adrift in the field. It had no significant mooring to the land nor did it contribute to a definition of the place that the land was to become. · The field was adjacent to Pebble Hill Road, a rural route that connected us to town and other fields. Some of those fields were still being tended while others slowly gave way to roads, driveways and more houses. The road was lined with barns and fences, punctuated by bridges and overpasses, laced with billboards and power lines, and provided fleeting views to ponds and dams, farm houses and abandoned buildings. Unlike the neo-colonial houses, the road and the simple structures along it provided me with a vehicle for understanding a landscape in transition – from things familiar to those imagined. · I am still drawn to the beauty of these anonymous American structures; built in fields and cities and dependent on roads, sidewalks, and streets. Their beauty is wed to the realities of utility and experience rather than to symbolism or intention. The well-worn, the vernacular, and the commonplace represent a grounding: a forthright stance in the evolution of a place. In them, we sense things as they are even as they slip away and we are forced to imagine what they might become.

EMPTY SIDEWALKS

As we walked along Pebble Hill Road, a sidewalk would present itself to us just before we got into town. It was always empty at first. It was neglected and overlooked. But it was also the beginning of an adventure that would connect us to the majestic collection of places that Doylestown had to offer – Mercer Museum, Fonthill, the library, the movie theater, smoke shops, churches, and clubs. · When one understands the architecture of a place as the complex connection of spaces and materials – of sidewalks and streets – one becomes wary of heroics or monumental gestures. We move at a specific speed and our dimensions vary within small increments. Our experience is bound by the fences and the walls; the portals and apertures; the scale of things. These are the variables that I work with: the walls and openings within reach that relate directly to the human form. My work builds upon these small spaces – like sidewalks and porches – that are vital enough to become places in-between other places. · In a story, the narrative is captured in the telling: it is the selective details and descriptive moments that evoke a tone or mood. The plot is what actually happens, and a good plot can produce countless stories. I hope that my architecture suggests a multiplicity of tellings: that there are stories within the stories, and that the plot suggests narratives that are as complex and layered as the unfolding tales discovered wandering the streets of a small town.

From far left to right Alvaro Siza's Library at Aveiro, Portugal 1988-93; Composition with Color Planes, Piet Mondrian, 1914; Kitchen at the Monastery of Alcobaca, Portugal **Opposite page from left to right** Ipswich Bay; White Mountains in Jackson, New Hampshire; The Estate at Davis Neck

BIG ROOMS

Our house has a porch that is one of a string of porches that run along the coast of a small summer community on Cape Ann. They stand shoulder to shoulder with each other and each looks out beyond the street to face the distant sea. It is a perfect room – floating somewhere between the indoors and the outdoors — adrift between the sounds and smells of the waterfront and those of a domestic life. · The spaces we inhabit communicate — to ourselves and others — who we are and who we aspire to be. It is the possibility that people can project their own stories onto the architecture that drives me to model, remodel, draw, and build. If people claim and use the walls and windows that we leave for them, if they exploit the possible connections built into the section and the plan, then we have successfully created place. · Frank Lloyd Wright once observed that people are rooted in their homes just as plants are rooted in the soil. I still believe this observation to be true, although it's an increasingly complex truth. The legacy of restlessness is deeply embedded in American culture and our desire to establish roots is tempered with personal migrations which continually transform the landscape. The landscape that for Wright was unchanging and absolute and only needed to be revealed is for us constantly changing and inchoate. Its potential can only be suggested. · The primary focus of my work is on the connection of a building to these landscapes in transition. It is equally true whether urban or rural. I engage what is already there in an attempt to be a part of that place and a part of what that place is becoming. The connection is dependent on the relationship of the rooms within to the street outside, the articulation of the building components, along with the use of color with its temporal effects and natural sympathies to the existing palette of the site.

SMALL CITIES

I moved to Boston from New York City when I received a small residential commission on Cape Cod. I knew almost no one in Boston and — with little work — I began to explore her streets, neighborhoods, and parks as a form of post graduate study. It was there that I discovered the sounds of a contemporary city, and I have spent my entire professional life there discovering how architects can create modern work while still harmonizing with the old melodies of that place. Just as Louis Kahn recognized the city as the place of availabilities, Boston continues to show how a city can shape one's future as much as it speaks to the past. · Architecture never stands alone. It is intimately connected to place, land, and community. Housing, streets, and neighborhoods are the ground from which a city springs. Its inhabitants' stories unfold in the streets, sidewalks, neighborhoods, buses, and subways. Cities are defined by these connections just as strongly as by its buildings. The success of a building is locked to the life of the street and, therefore, great design can galvanize a neighborhood. · I believe that everything in our world is in flux: cities, fields, highways, and towns, constantly evolve and devolve. All these landscapes are in constant transition. Space only becomes relevant when used. When you see things this way, there is tremendous pressure on the side of the architect and community to write a solid plot, one that can spawn stories for the present, even as they anticipate that others will follow.

WORK

A man's work is nothing but this slow trek to rediscover, through the detours of art, those two or three great and simple images in whose presence his heart first opened.

Albert Camus

EDWARD MITCHELL

OF COMMON AND ORDINARY THINGS

Brian Healy and I met in New Haven on the Yale faculty about twenty years ago, but our most intense conversations and attempts at collaboration came about later between Boston and New Haven after he left. I was already a great admirer of his work, and remain so today. Our exchange of ideas was driven by a series of studios I was running on the river and port cities on the outskirts of Boston. Though rich in history these communities lacked a clear vision of their future. Brian toured me through several of the rugged coastal towns on the North Shore, introduced me to some colorful locals, taught me the differences in the variations of oysters in each small cove, and showed me several of the projects he has worked on in these area. I was, in turn, brought into conversations with many of the local community leaders, and he and I made some attempts at collaborating on projects, including the Florence Gray Community Center in the northern end of Newport, a vital area very unlike the touristic center of town, but one which also had its own history and a strong core group of people vested in their neighborhood.

I bring up the two cities of New Haven and Boston, though, to offer a contrast, specious though it may be, between two ideas represented by those city's respective public spaces that represent the shared ideas we both wrestle with and color how I understand Brian's work and the nature of our friendship. For the sake of argument, and we both enjoy a good argument, the New Haven Green stands for the abstract concept, the Boston Common the contested ground. Unreal and real, let us say.

New Haven is credited as the first planned city in the northern United States, recognizable by its nine square grid with the Green at the center. That configuration represented, for the city founders, an ideal based on biblical proportions referencing the Temple of Solomon. Geometry, one could argue, drew the contract with the divine before Colin Rowe understood the nine squares as a diagram of democracy and before John Hejduk used it as a base for abstract compositional experimentation. And let it also be acknowledged, in contradiction to my previous statement about the two cities, that "through the certain

Above Hannah Otis, sampler "View of Boston Common" c. 1750. Museum of Fine Arts, Boston

eye," in the words of Wallace Stevens whom we both admire, "Real and unreal are two in one: New Haven/ Before and after one arrives."

The Boston Common is a more complicated figure than the Green. As evidence, I offer two interesting image of the Common, one by Hannah Otis embroidered in 1750, the other a 1768 perspective by Christian Remick. Otis's embroidery lacks Remick's quiet tension. Its Arcadian landscape is a riot of people, plants, and animals moving in and out of the picture plane that compete for our visual attention. The architecture is folded into the landscape through the use of multiple perspectives. This Common is a world not quite "settled" into a stable and coherent form. Remick's depiction of the Common, is, as art historian Margaretta Lovell stated, "calmly factual" but filled with "personal turmoil and extraordinary public enmity." Each citizen in the Common remains a figure apart. However, in the middle band a group of British soldier drills on the green, there to enforce authority on an increasingly rebellious public. The architectures of this second image are ephemeral while the composition of the Common, reads like a temple. The trees in the foreground act as columns, the middle zone of activities is the inner space or sanctum, and the horizon is populated by walls and buildings which shelters and contains the sanctum of the Common like a roof.

Commons, or to volley back Brian Healy's title, "Commonplaces," are not common at all, but a collage of disparate actors, sometime in harmony, sometimes apart, assembling into and vying for a shared space. The Common's space, unlike the idealized New Haven Green, is not preordained by the diagram. It is not divine; it is a place of negotiation. Again, to misuse Stevens and mimic the dialectic reversal he performs in "An Ordinary Evening in New Haven", the Common more so than the Green, aspires to a world of "dark things" — birds, buildings, animals and people — the "crude collops" come together as one, in "a festival sphere." And the subjects who take their place and take part in that commonplace, the public festival sphere, are given voice. In taking one's place one speaks.

Above A prospective view of part of the commons by Sidney Lawton Smith after Christian Remick's 1768 watercolor.

Does architecture speak? Rowe and Hejduk made the architecture of the nine square a surrogate of the urban subject, though this was sometimes taken to hallucinatory extremes by Hejduk. I do not know what "poetry in architecture" means. Architecture is made up of things not words, and confusing the two catches us in the absurd play of signs. As subjects or becoming-subjects in space we interact with things and are only aware of space when it disrupts normal experience, when it has not settled into convention, when it is slightly uncomfortable. Architectural space interacts with the mind across cognitive breaks, and the design of these spaces is formed as variation between disjunctive ideas. In turn, we experience space, just as space is influence by us.

Acts of architecture, whether in drawing, model, or built structure, are both private concepts and public acts. While we may think of the concept, exemplified in the diagram, as the grammar of the discipline, and, therefore, the vehicle of a shared language, the irony is that the "language of architecture" is the private language of a priori conception. Form, based in geometry and diagram, is a private affair taking place in the mind which can influence and predetermines outcomes. But the making of things, even if executed by an individual, is inherently public. It takes place in a space and in time whether it be a sheet of paper, a table, or a site. And the completion of the act is in our shared perception and engagement with that act. The facts, such as they are of art or architecture, the material presence of the artifact, it can be said, refute solipsistic interpretation. What you see versus what I see is of little consequence. What we see together is where our common point of view coincides. This argument was once made by Rosalind Krauss relative to a new generation of post-conceptual artists. The same might be said of architecture. The negotiation between the real and unreal, between ideal and material fact, constitutes architecture's public territory. The architect moves between the modes of an inherited language and the activation of those ideas through the deployment of a palette of materials. And the act of making, then, takes place in time and in the moment of execution. Architecture, with its deferrals of drawing to building, is troubled with the delay of actions and the contract between its representations and its manifestations. This is inherent to the discipline. Many architects find ways to overcome this delay.

Noting those very complex negotiations, it should be mentioned that, like other significant architects, Brian is also a painter, and his drawings and models exhibit that tension between abstraction and material presence. When I say that his architecture is public, I mean that the activity of his architecture takes place not in the mind of the author, but in the temporal acts of making, the sustain of a building unfolding in time, and in the conscious address to an audience that is present in both a drawing and the cultivation of client.

I see traces of concepts (or precepts) in Brian's work – nine squares and four squares – particularly in the drawings, where the basic organization of a building program and his cubist compositional structures are most evident, and where the organizational concept, the plan, drives the idea; however, the buildings leave little trace of a didactic demonstration of order. And to steal from another poet – No ideas but in things. Walls are rarely abstract planes, conceptual placeholders. Instead the collisions of larger volumes resolve as and into things - bookshelves evolve into benches, ceilings fold into walls, floors rise into seats. Whether public or private programs, in projects like the Tree House, the Loveladies Beach House, the Sag Harbor House, the Darwin Martin Visitor's Center, and the Brookline Community Center, those things compete restlessly with one another and collide in the common spaces. These areas of the major intersection of volumes are both "calmly factual" but filled with "personal turmoil." I say this as a compliment. Brian is a restless agitator, he asks questions, he is not an "idea man."

While he was teaching in Cincinnati, Brian spoke to me about the importance of the exonarthex in the church, a problem he has worked on in several projects. The exonarthex is not part of the church proper, the sacred space of the altar where the mass takes place, but an extended threshold for the laity or common people. Brian and his work are more comfortable in the exo-narthex, among the common people and commonspaces, then in those sacred spaces, though there are hints of things most uncommon. And, to no surprise, in the Brookline Community Center he gives his clients of the chapel, primarily the children of the parish, a most sophisticated space. He cedes no common ground to the always fractious neighborhood of the local "People's Republic," by stooping to facile contextual architectural signs, but accommodates their daily pedestrian needs with a public bench on which to rest. And so, like Stevens's Professor Eucalyptus of New Haven who seeks the divine "with an eye that does not look beyond the object" the task for this architect is not "grim reality but reality grimly seen/And spoken in paradisal parlance new/And in any case never grim."

We are in difficult times. Our common public spaces are either vacuously generic, designed to offend no one, representing nothing – these are common things of the lowest order – or worse yet, perhaps, they are spaces of conflict and difference that separate us. We cannot hold a thing in common. Our solipsistic fictions and exhausted political and aesthetic ideals keep us apart. I prefer the "crude collops" of Healy's work and value the challenges set by a good friend and generous talent, and the heated but always productive conversations we have had together and with our students. Brian Healy has upheld and demonstrated for an amiably contested public space, as a teacher, an advocate, an artist, and as an architect. In his work, one can find, in Stevens's words, where "The commonplace became a rumpling of blazons."

Edward Mitchell is the Director of Architecture and Interior Design and Professor at the University of Cincinnati. Prior to his appointment he was Associate Professor at the School of Architecture, Yale University, where he served as Director of the Post Professional program and coordinated the post-professional and graduate studios in architecture and urbanism. His award-winning practice has been recognized by the Architectural League of New York and the Boston Society of Architects. His books include *A Train of Cities* and *Common Wealth*, studies done at Yale on the communities surrounding Boston.

PIER 7

Boston, Massachusetts

HYATT PLACE
LEGAL

PIER 7

Boston, Massachusetts

This proposal is intended as a replacement for Barge 8 at Pier 7 in South Boston for use as an new terminal for harbor play and adventure off the Seaport District. It consists of a mixed use program of a harbor cruise terminal, restaurant and professional office space in a four story 51,000 square foot structure. The building and adjacent harbor walk will be designed with a pile supported wharf structure of approximately 20,000 square feet that will invite the public into and around the site and - as importantly - will help augment educational programs sponsored by Save the Harbor. The final part of the program consists of the initial phase of a floating pier structure that will accommodate our tenant, the Charles Riverboat Company, and their fleet of cruise and touring vessels.

The building design recognizes and reinforces the edge of the Boston Marine Industrial Park by positioning itself lengthwise on a north/south axis, while allowing a significant view corridor from the Seaport District. The proposed structure is modern in concept but is designed to retain the image of an abstract vessel with exterior finishes carefully articulated to include materials that hark back to maritime materials.

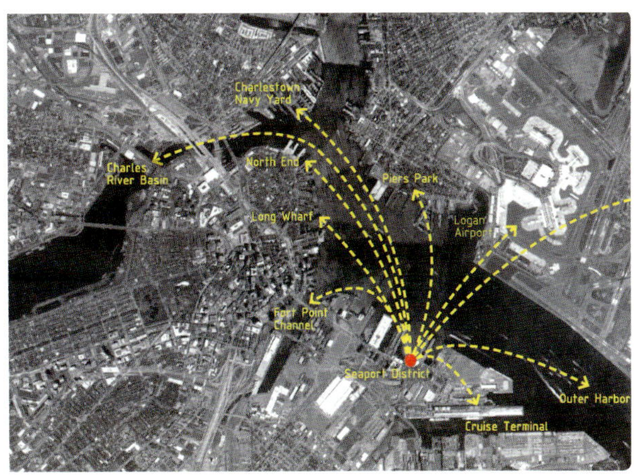
Charlestown Navy Yard
Charles River Basin
North End
Piers Park
Long Wharf
Logan Airport
Fort Point Channel
Seaport District
Outer Harbor
Cruise Terminal

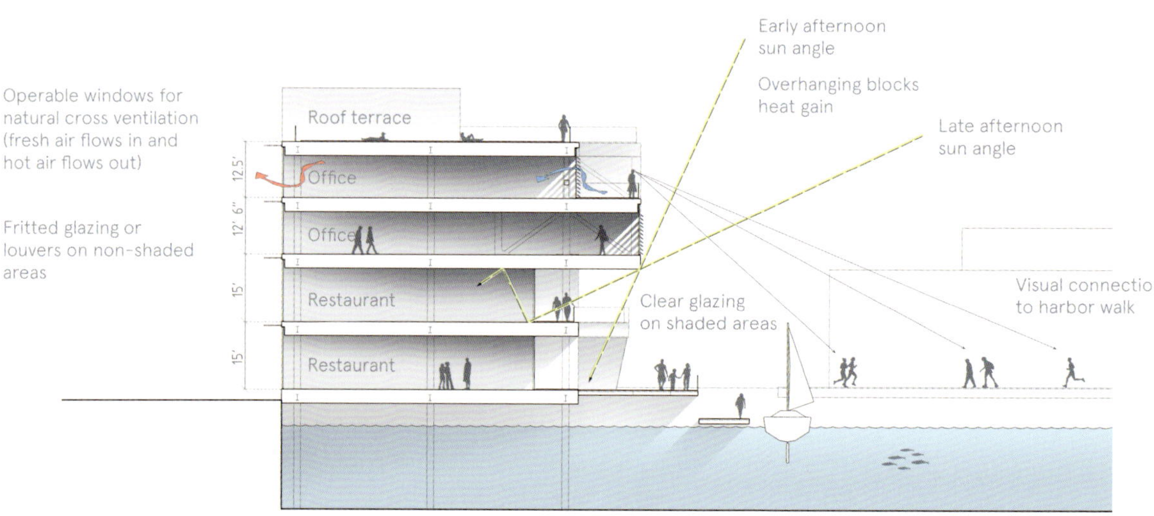
Early afternoon sun angle
Overhanging blocks heat gain
Late afternoon sun angle
Operable windows for natural cross ventilation (fresh air flows in and hot air flows out)
Fritted glazing or louvers on non-shaded areas
Roof terrace
Office
Office
Restaurant
Restaurant
12.5'
12' 6"
15'
15'
Clear glazing on shaded areas
Visual connection to harbor walk

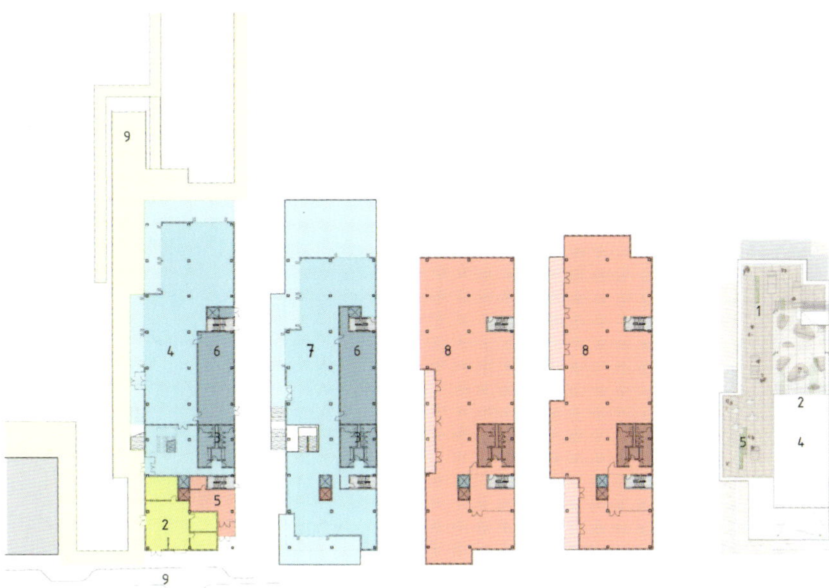

Level 1-5
1 Maritime
2 Tickets and retail
3 Lobby & public water closets
4 Restaurant 1
5 Elevator Lobby
6 Kitchen
7 Restaurant 2
8 Professional office space

Roof level
1 The porch
2 Public water closets
4 Mechanical
5 The platform

Plans — Level 1 — Level 2 — Level 3 — Level 4 — Roof level

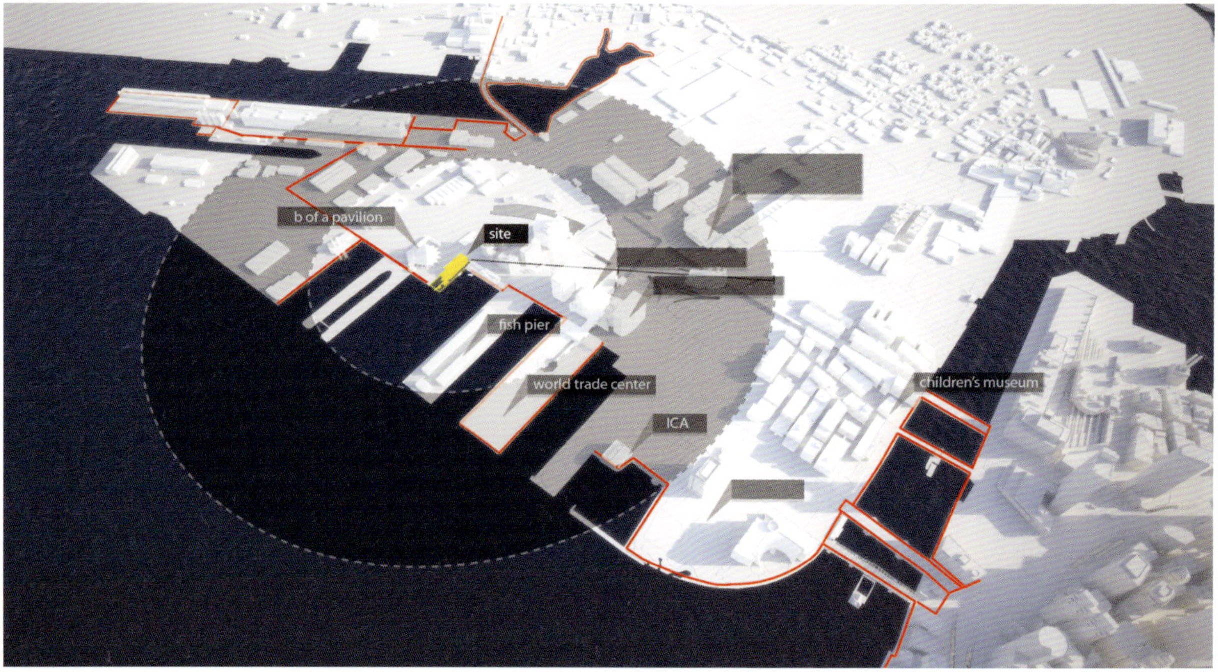
b of a pavilion
site
fish pier
world trade center
ICA
children's museum

Public space

Office space

Harbor walk

JACKSON FIRE

Jackson, New Hampshire

JACKSON FIRE

Jackson, New Hampshire

Jackson is a small village located in a valley just south of Mount Washington in the White Mountains of New Hampshire. The existing fire station — built in the 1960s — is outdated, does not meet current codes, and is incapable of receiving modern equipment such as current fire trucks. According, the village will demolish it and build a new station. This design imagines a new village common composed of the new station co-existing alongside the existing town hall and public library.

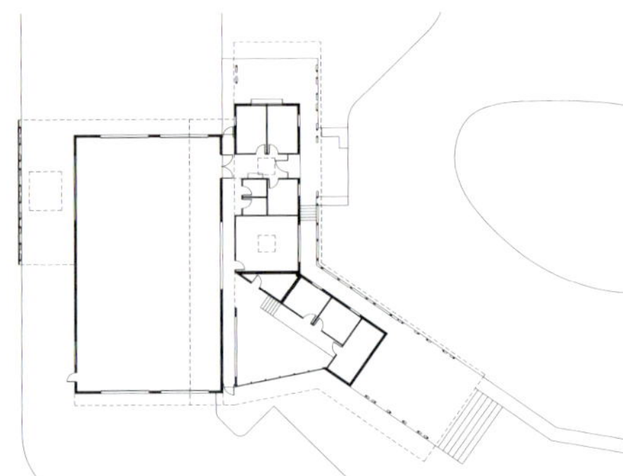

Plan

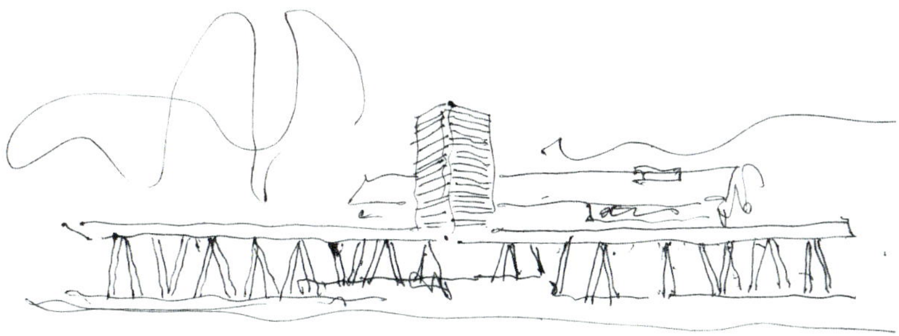

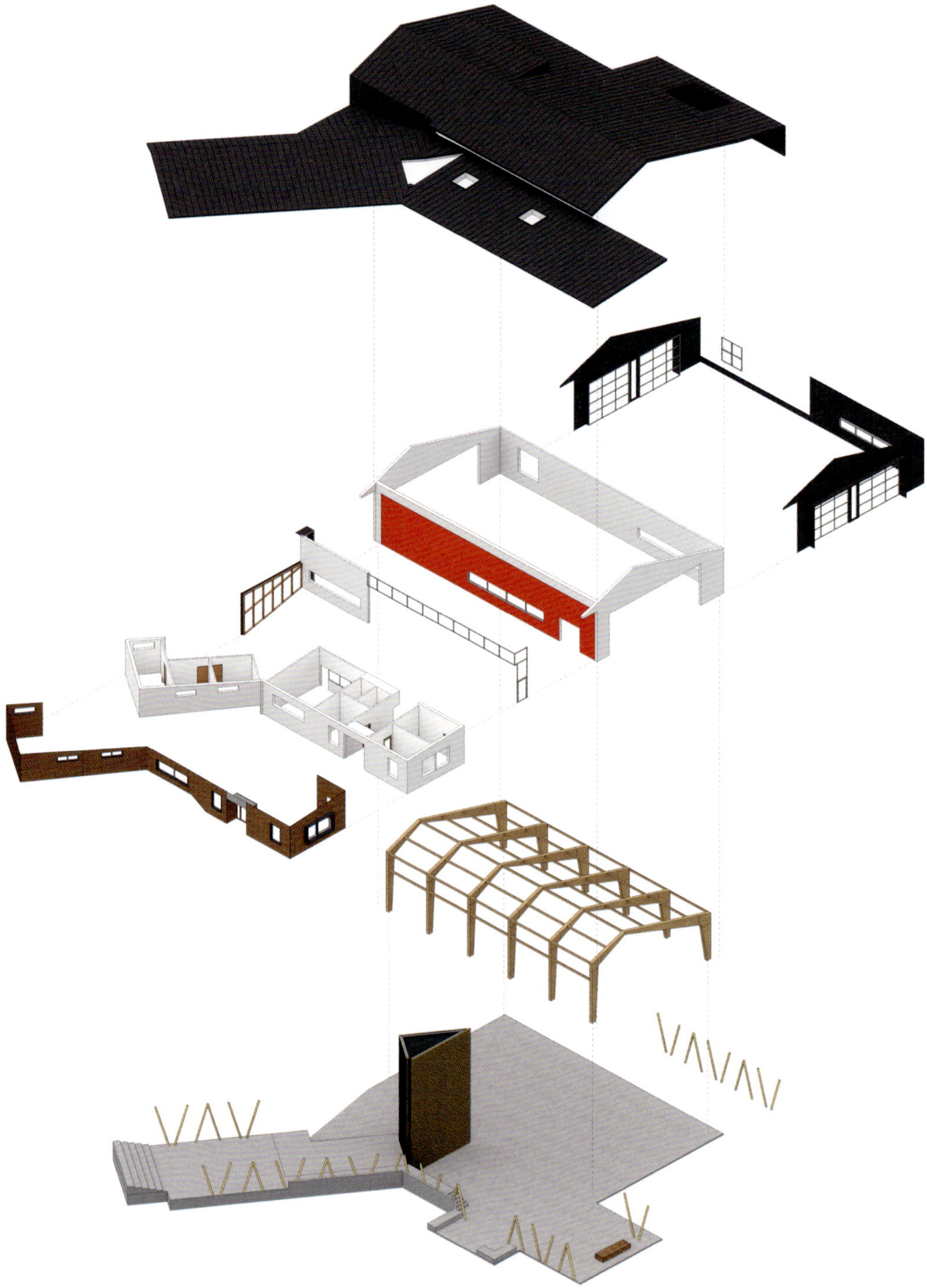

Exploded axonometric

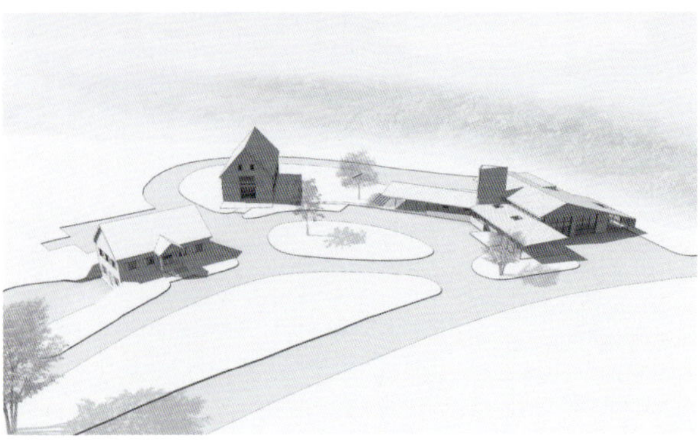

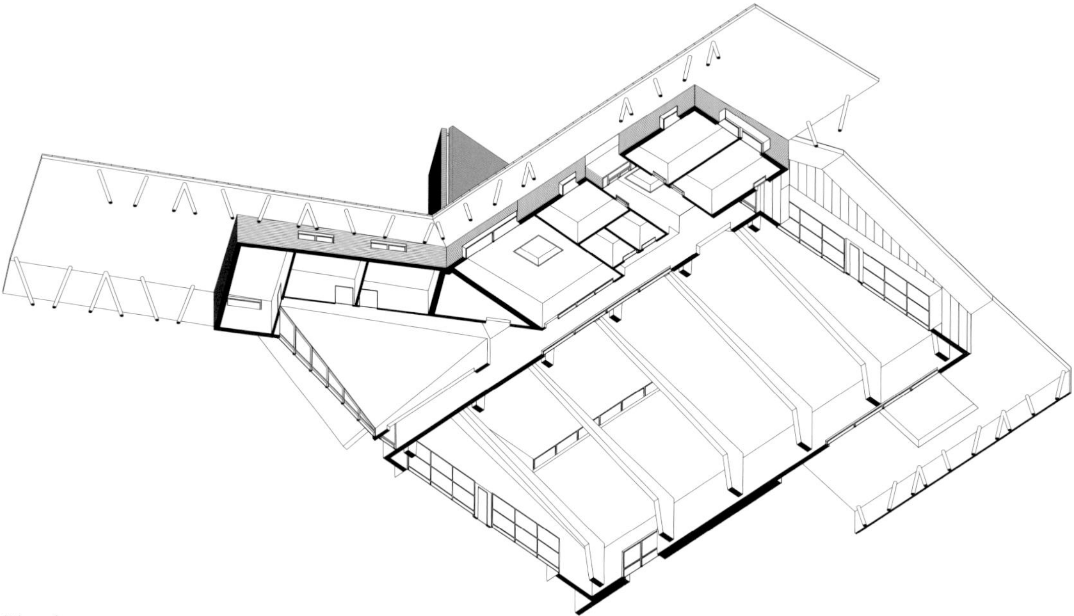

Worm's eye

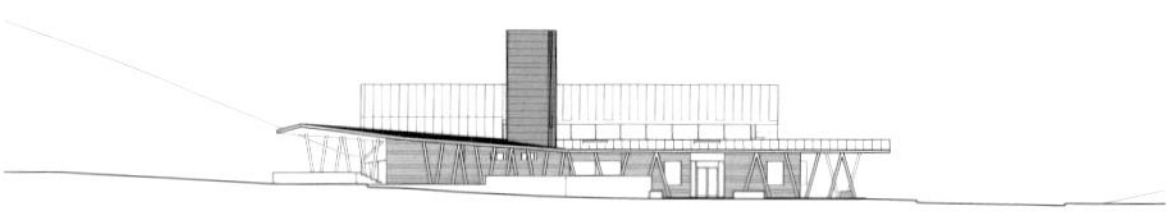

East elevation

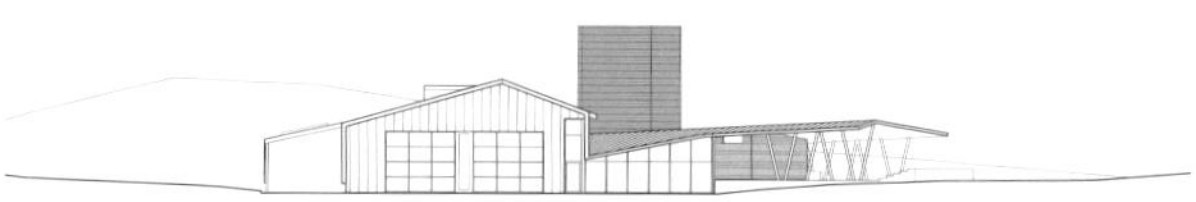

North elevation

South elevation

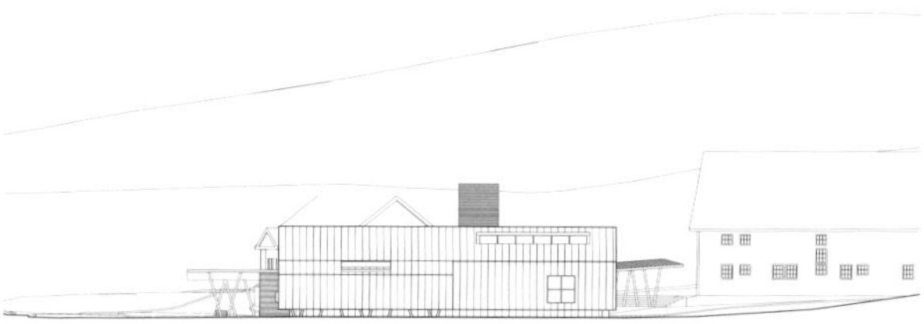

West elevation

ELLIS RIVER STUDIO

Jackson, New Hampshire

ELLIS RIVER STUDIO

Jackson, New Hampshire

The two acre compound is located in the village of Jackson, New Hampshire and contains three independent structures including this renovated cabin along the Ellis River. Just south of Mount Washington in the White Mountains, the river feeds into the Saco which flows into the North Atlantic along the Maine coastline. An abandoned structure used to sit on a bluff overlooking the river and was renovated to include a broad porch, tool shed, and stone terrace. Wooden steps lead down the twenty-five feet to the river for swimming and fishing. The cabin is wood frame clad in fir and cedar siding.

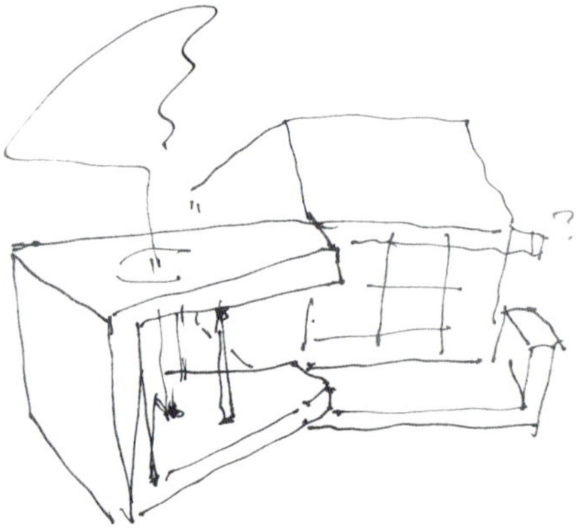

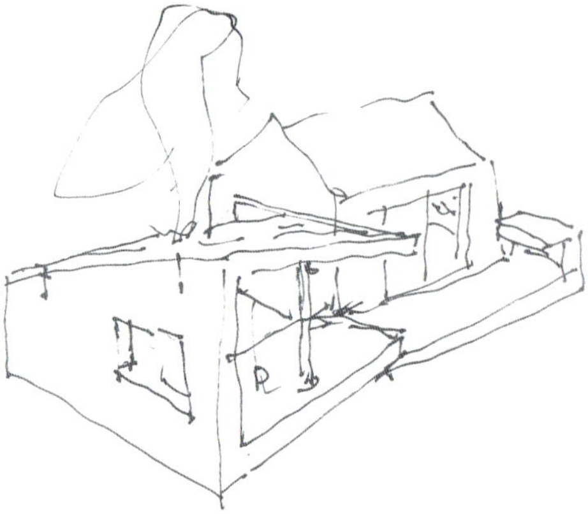

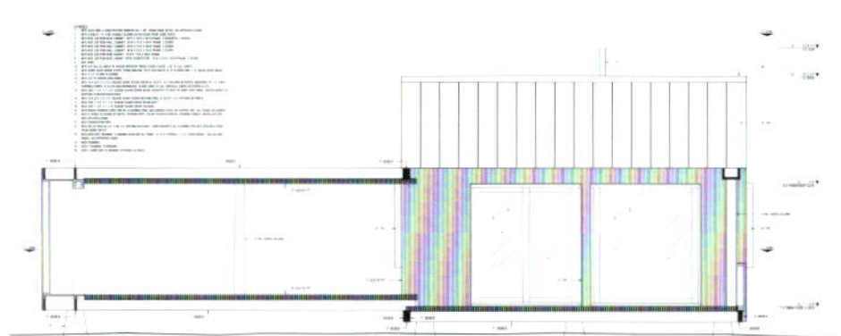

Longitudinal section

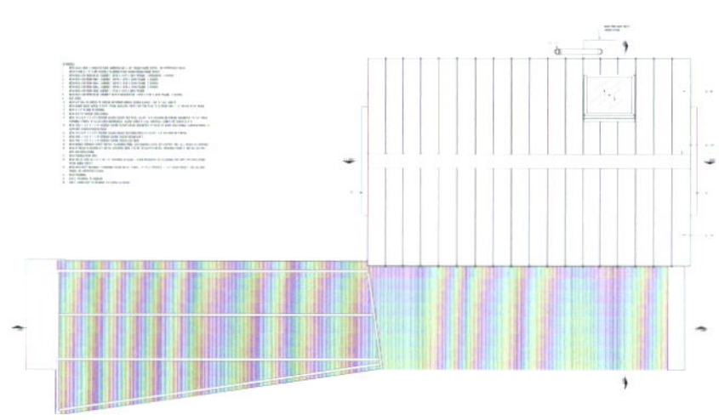

Roof plan

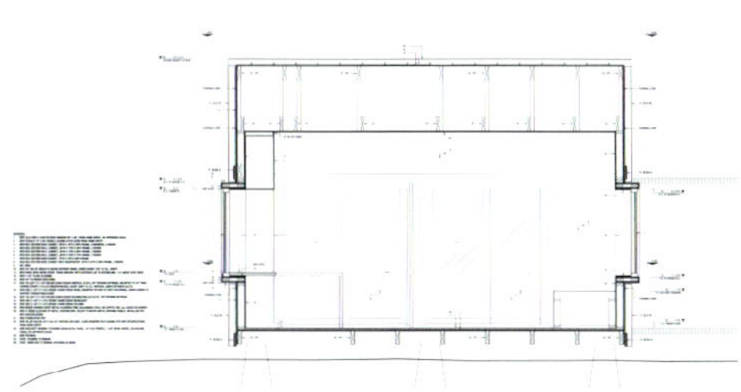

Longitudinal section

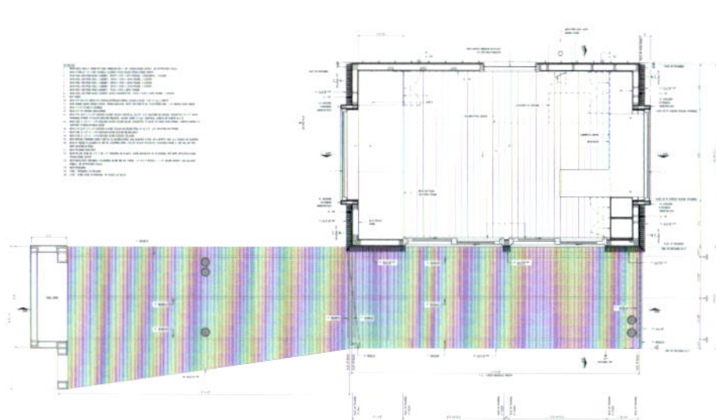

Floor plan

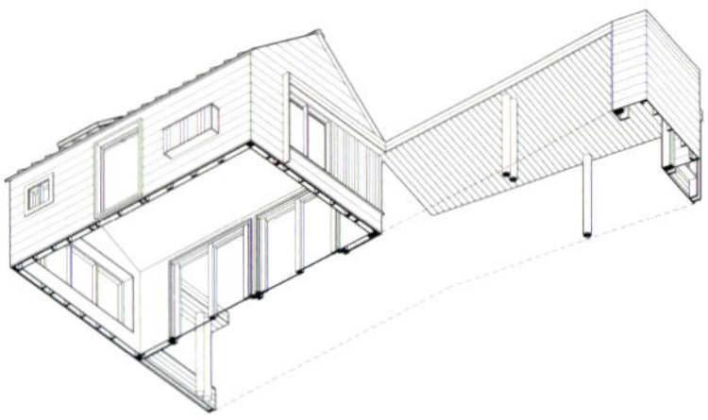

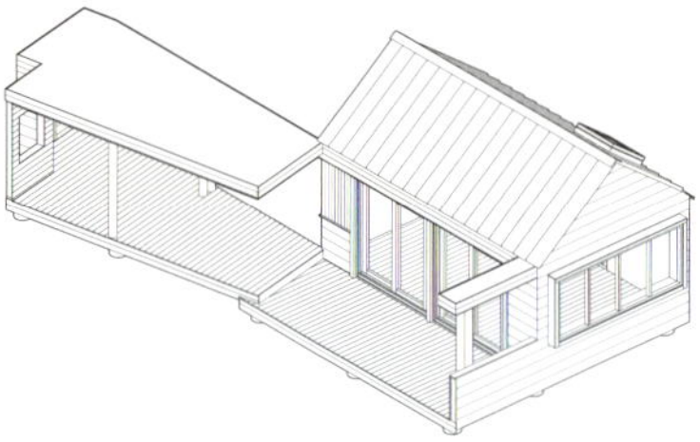

Worms eye

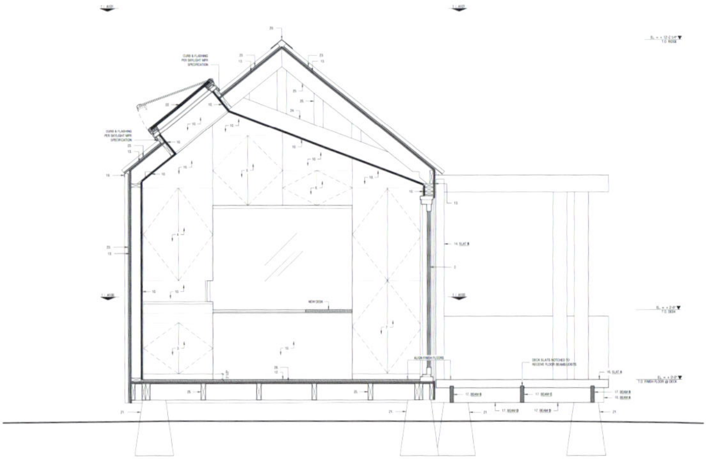

Transverse section

INNOVATION CENTER

Wentworth Institute of Technology
Boston, Massachusetts

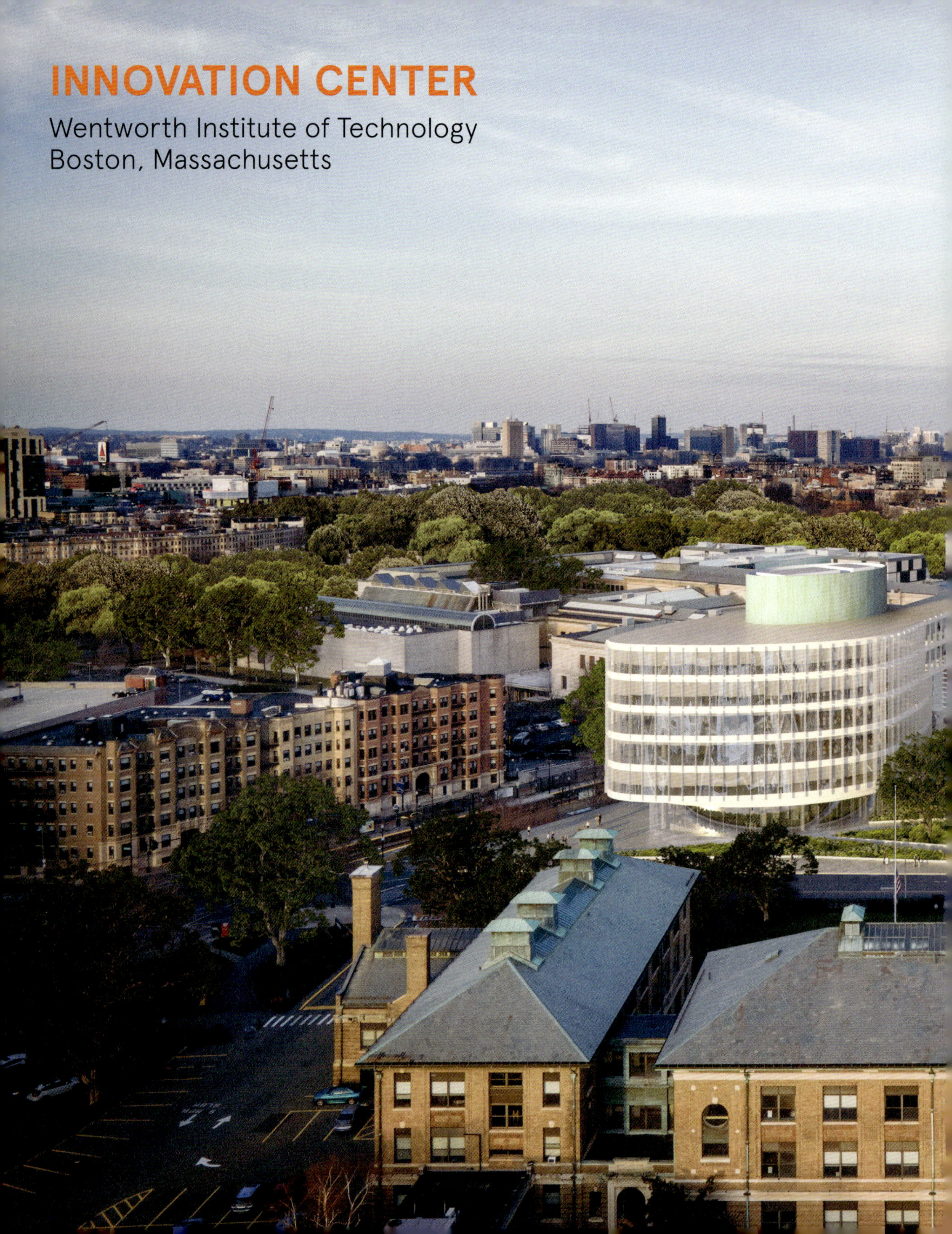

INNOVATION CENTER

Wentworth Institute of Technology
Boston, Massachusetts

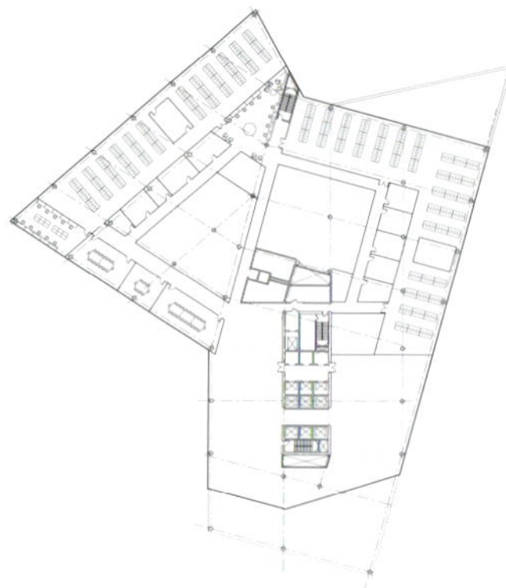

Lab planning

Wentworth Institute of Technology is in the process of developing Sweeney Field and, while at Perkins + Will, Healy led a team with Tim Marsters to develop the site into 630,772 square feet of building space in three interconnected buildings. The development plan will be anchored by the 78,000 square foot Wentworth Center for Innovation in Engineering & Technology at the corner of Huntington Avenue and Ruggles Street. This center would be fully occupied by Wentworth and the focus of this facility will be research and education in the area of applied research in engineering.

The goal of the center will be to take high impact initial discoveries and test them for their potential of product development. Given the breadth of Wentworth's engineering programs, this activity could include research in a wide range of areas from Biomedical to Mechanical Engineering. This center will be an important resource for the economy of Boston and will be of great interest to firms seeking to locate in Boston to collaborate with Wentworth and other leading institutions. The remainder of the facilities in the development would include 538,772 square feet of state of the art (non-institutional) R&D/office space and 14,000 square feet of first floor retail space.

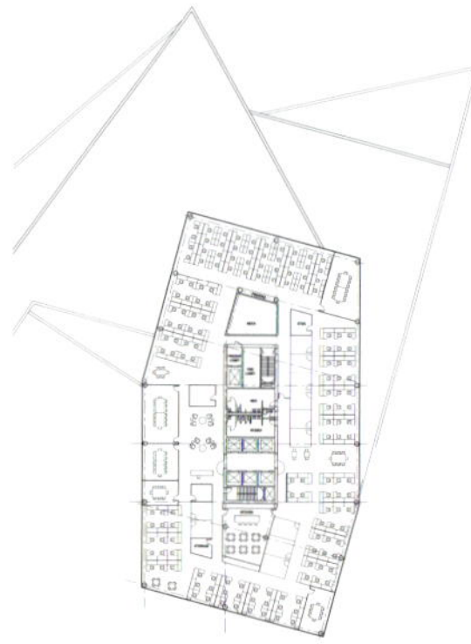

Office planning

The site planning acknowledges the existing pathways that cross the site connecting public transportation hubs and links Wentworth and Northeastern University to Huntington Avenue - Avenue of the Arts - and the Boston Museum of Fine Arts, and the Emerald Necklace to the northeast.

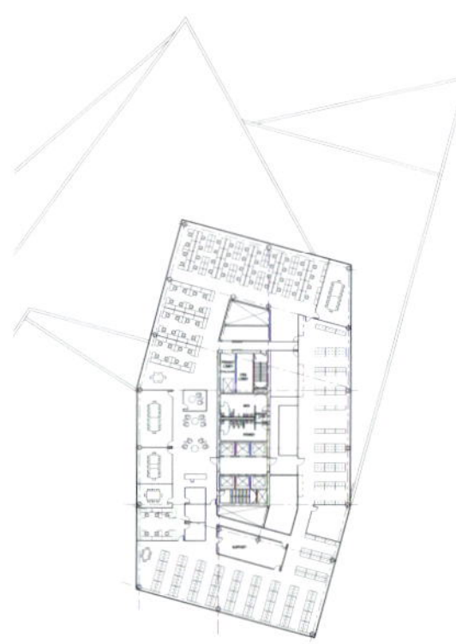

Lab planning

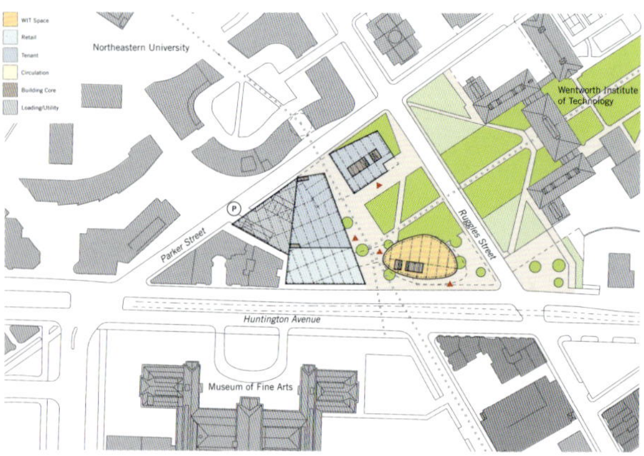

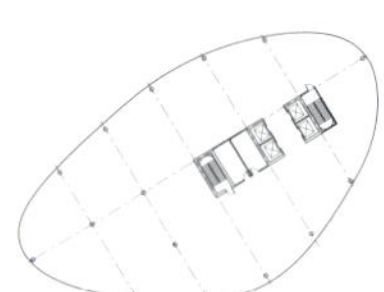

Plan of innovation hub

THE KAFE'
THE KAFE'

THE KAFE'
GELATO

+280'-0" T.O. Mech screen
+253'-0" Roof
+93'-0" Level 06 roof
+63'-0" Level 04 roof
+0'-0" Ground level
0 15 30 60 120

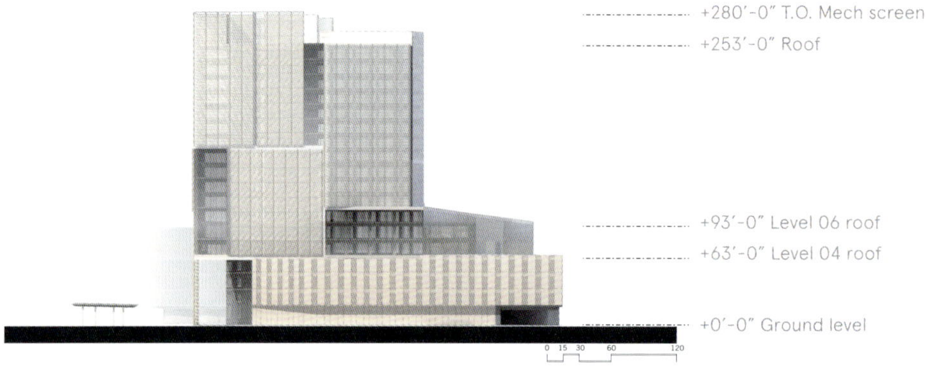
+280'-0" T.O. Mech screen
+253'-0" Roof
+93'-0" Level 06 roof
+63'-0" Level 04 roof
+0'-0" Ground level
0 15 30 60 120

+280'-0" T.O. Mech screen
+253'-0" Roof
+93'-0" Level 06 roof
+63'-0" Level 04 roof
+0'-0" Ground level
0 15 30 60 120

JACKSON LAB

Farmington, Connecticut

JACKSON SQUARE

Farmington, Connecticut

The Jackson Laboratory for Medical Genomics would be located in Farmington, Connecticut and consists of site development as well as the design of a LEED certified biomedical research facility of approximately 173,000 gross square feet with biomedical laboratories, computational/bio-informatics research laboratories, support space and core service facilities. It will also include a state of the art data center, common and collaboration space, conference and training facilities, office space, and general supporting administrative facilities and infrastructure.

Initially focusing on complex diseases and conditions like cancer, Parkinson's disease, Alzheimer's and amyotrophic lateral sclerosis (ALS), the Laboratory will also create one of the world's most definitive bioinformatics databases of individual whole genome sequences and correlate them with disease progression and responses to therapies. Gary Shaw led the effort at P+W with Healy in developing a series of schematic studies that explore the relationship of the program to the site and the potential for future growth for each lab. In that effort, they developed two options – Jackson Square and Jackson Ellipsis – each executed around the concept of a shared open courtyard facilitating and promoting cross-pollination of ideas. Jackson Square was predicated on a more extraverted presentation of the facility while Ellipsis focused inward.

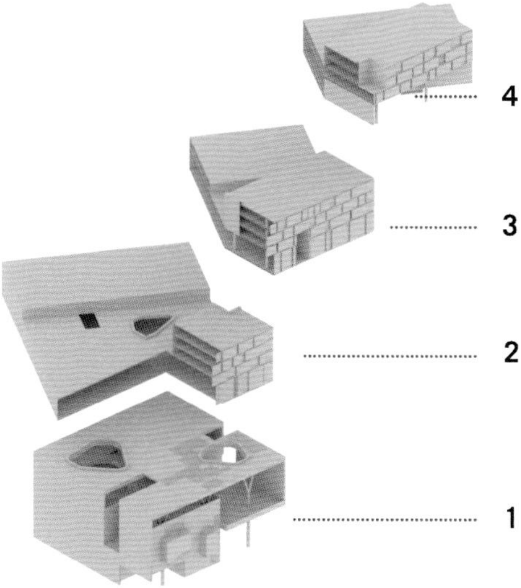

Building phases

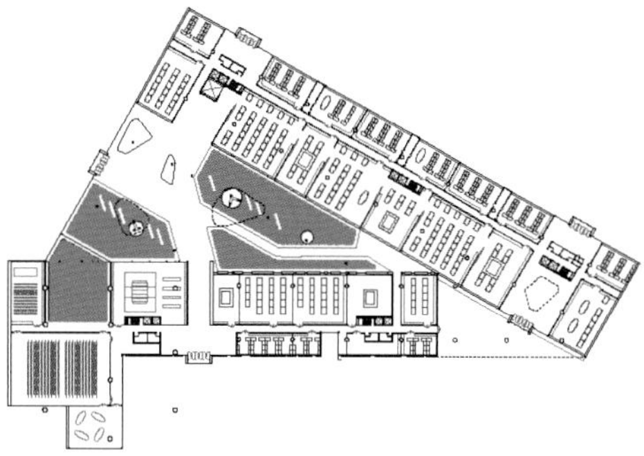

Ground floor plan

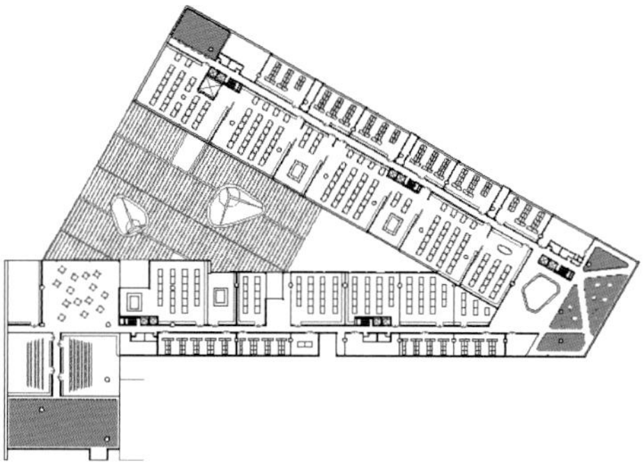

Second floor plan

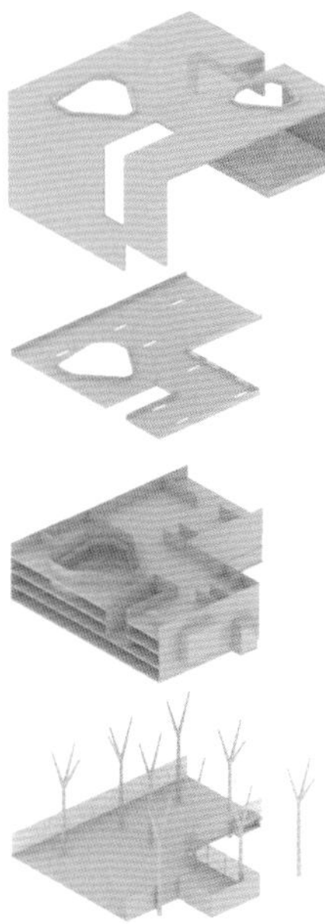

Axonometric view of building components

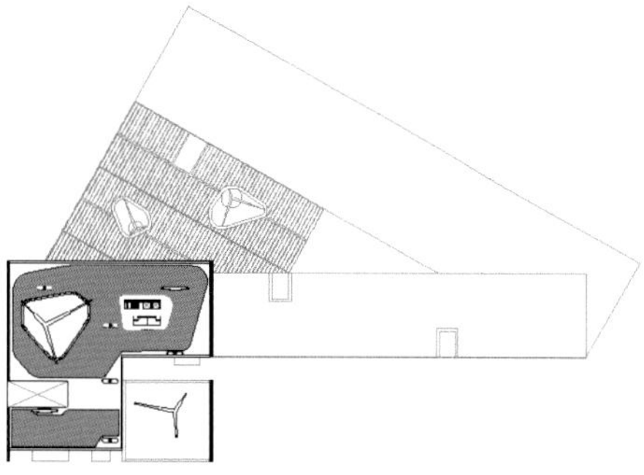

Roof plan

Building sections

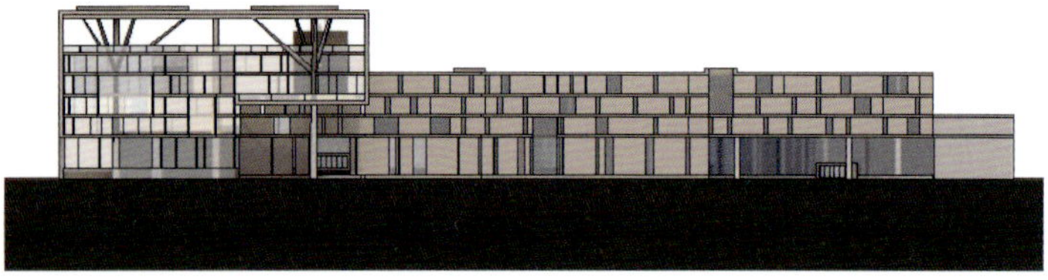

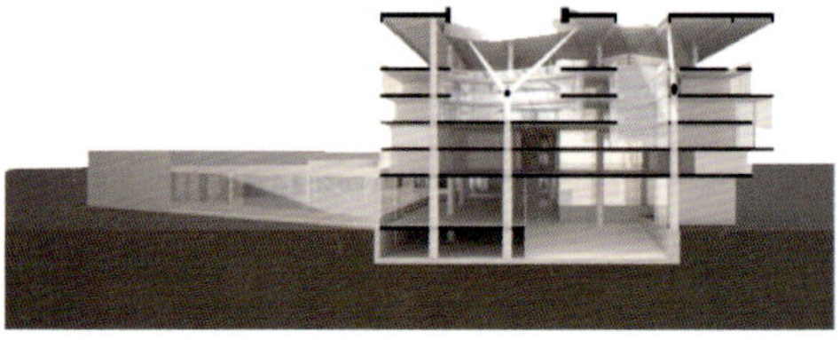

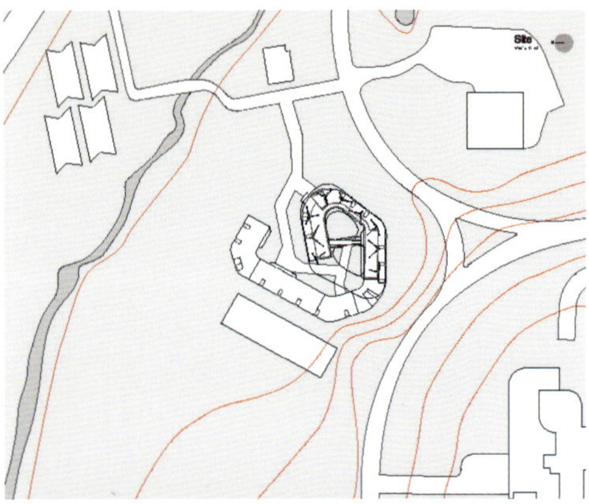

JACKSON ELLIPSIS

Farmington, Connecticut

Like Jackson Square, the Ellipsis alternative option will house research groups in Comparative Genetics and Bioinformatics/ Computational Biology utilizing both wet and dry labs. Both developed around the idea of a shared courtyard facilitating promoting the expansion and cross-pollination of evolving ideas and aspirations. Ellipsis further included a concept of a reflective cloister — or inward looking building with an ability to circumambulate, think, or converse – with a distinct outer shell protecting the internal workings — and energies — of those that will work and study there.

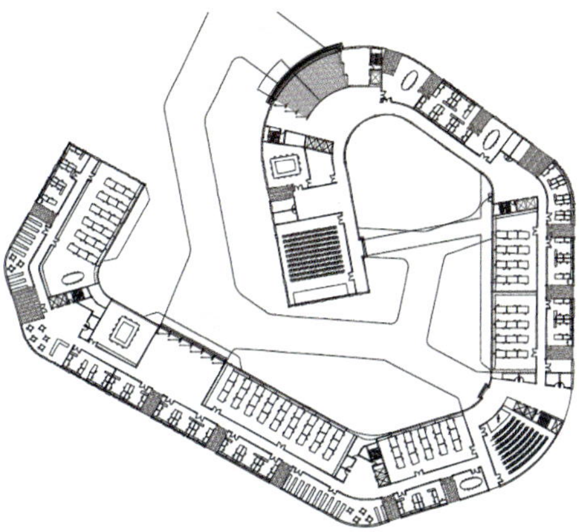

Ground floor plan

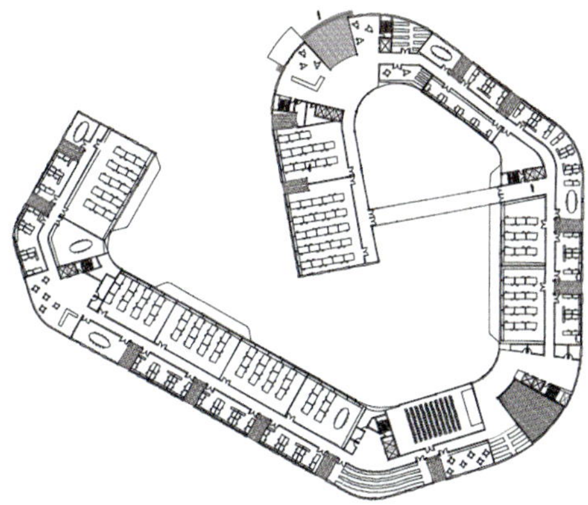

Third floor plan

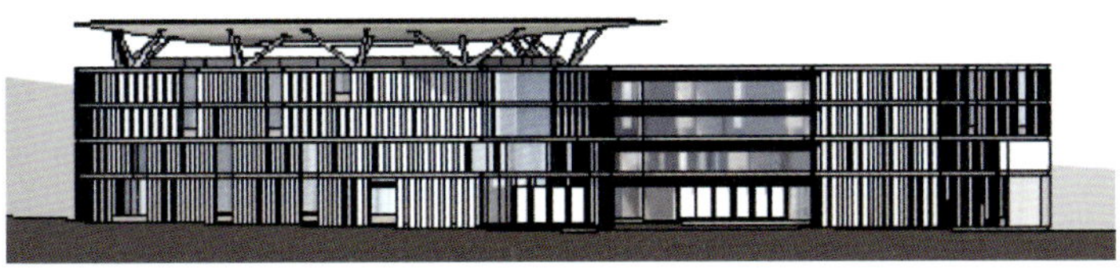

Elevation

View of main entry

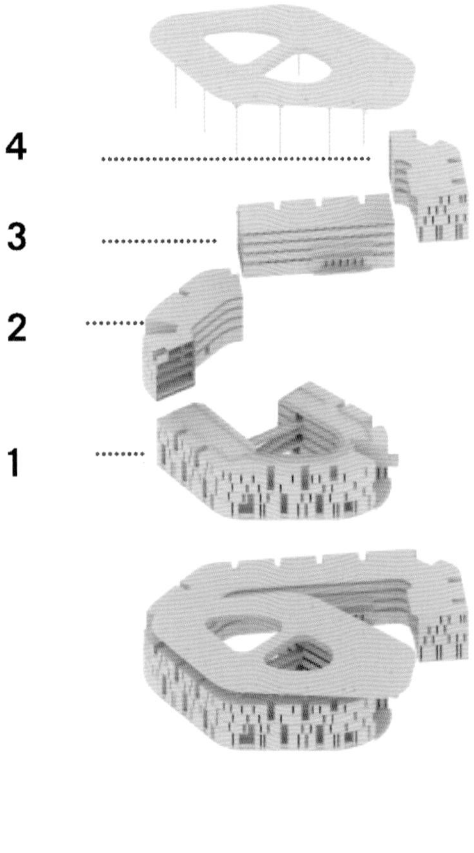

Building phases

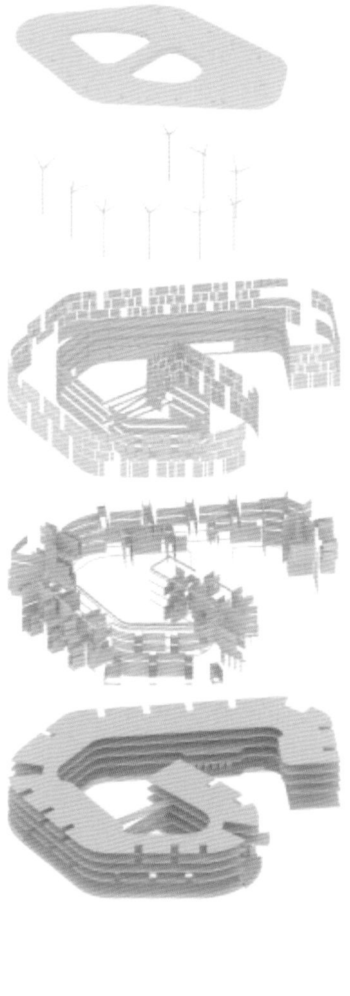

Axonometric view of building components

HARVARD SEAS

School of Engineering and Applied Science - Harvard University Cambridge, Massachsetts

The school requested the design and construction of a new multi-use building acting as a connector between Cruft and Pierce Halls while reinforcing the internal links across the school itself. In order to understand the options available to achieve this goal, five distinct approaches to the challenge were studied – along with their associated variations – to organize this addition connecting to Cruft but also creates a new localized, communal place within the school. Each scheme also acts to support a strong connection to the larger campus of Harvard University.

Because of the complexity of the building scales coming together at this intersection between SEAS and the myriad pathways of Harvard's campus – with the presence of Pierce and Cruft Halls, Oxford Street, the Law School Quad, and the master plan for the area – the design of the proposed facility needed to be as flexible as possible to maximize the site's potential and to provide opportunities for research and interaction between the students, faculty, and staff. Each option develops an environment that facilitates interior connections within the school while promoting an openness of adjacent exterior space.

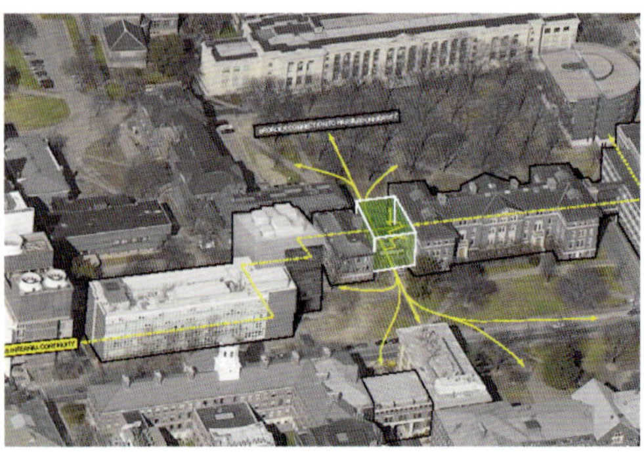

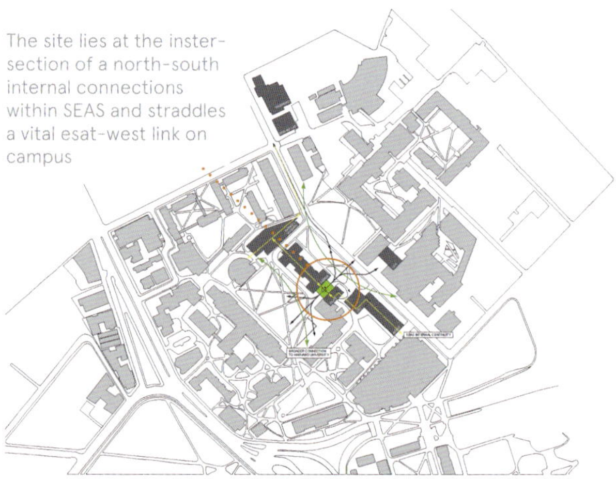

The site lies at the intersection of a north-south internal connections within SEAS and straddles a vital esat-west link on campus

Aerial view of site

Option A: new building as an addition to Cruft Hall with a vertical garden along Pierce Hall

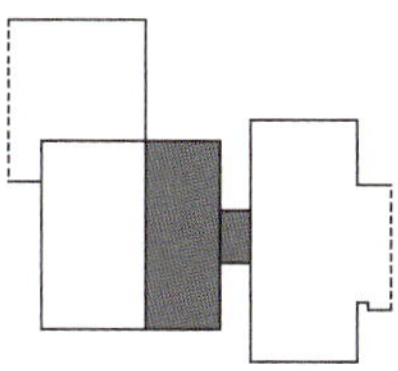

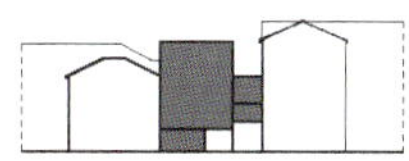

Addition to Cruft

Option B: new building as an addition to Pierce Hall with a vertical garden along Cruft Hall

Option C: new building as an infill structure with passage at grade and extensive green roof adjacent to the library in Pierce Hall

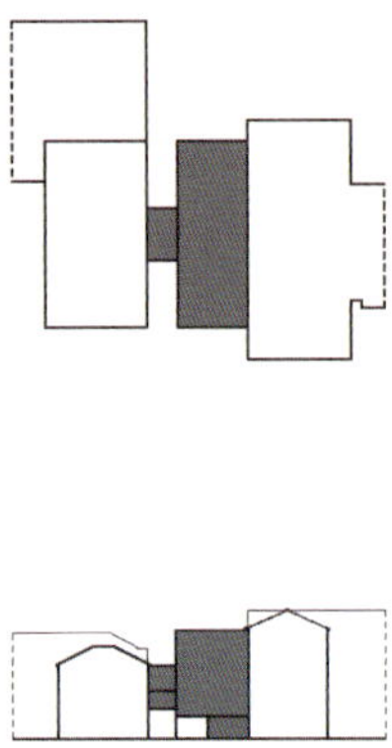

Addition to Pierce

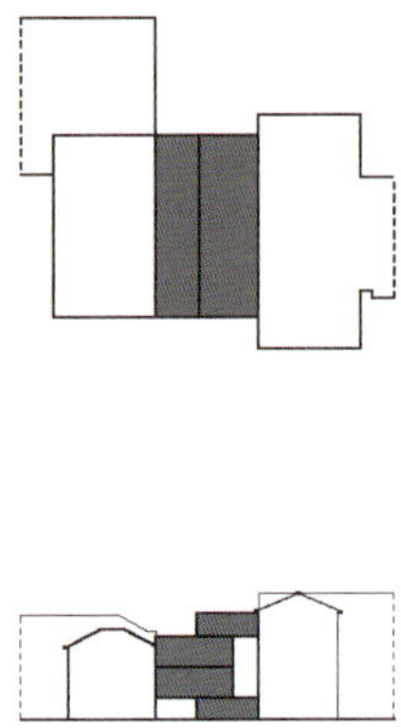

Infill

Option D: new building as a free-standing structure with twin vertical gardens along both Cruft and Pierce Halls

Option E: new building as a shell or semi-autonomous structure with twin vertical atriums along both Cruft and Pierce Hall

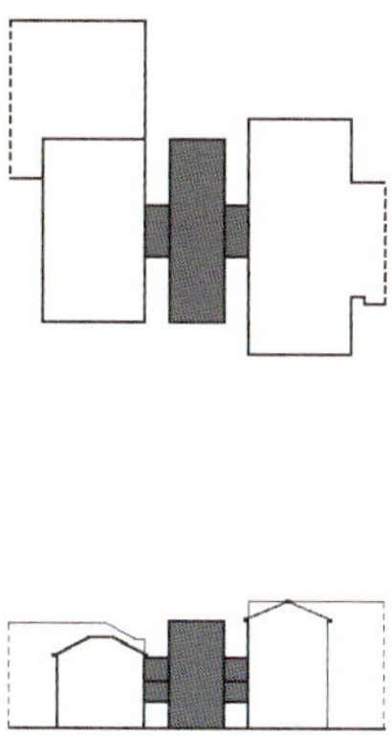

Freestanding

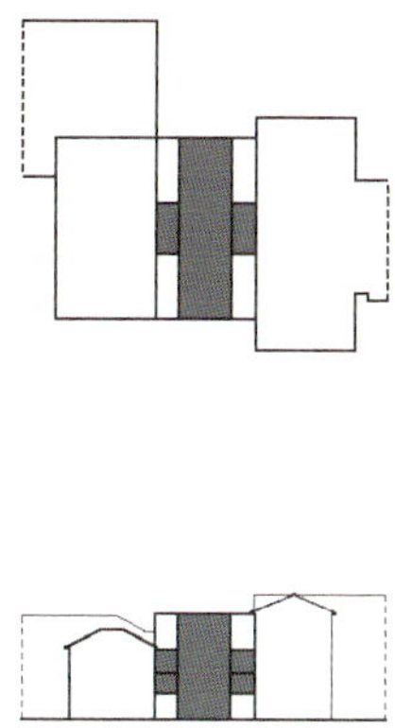

Shell

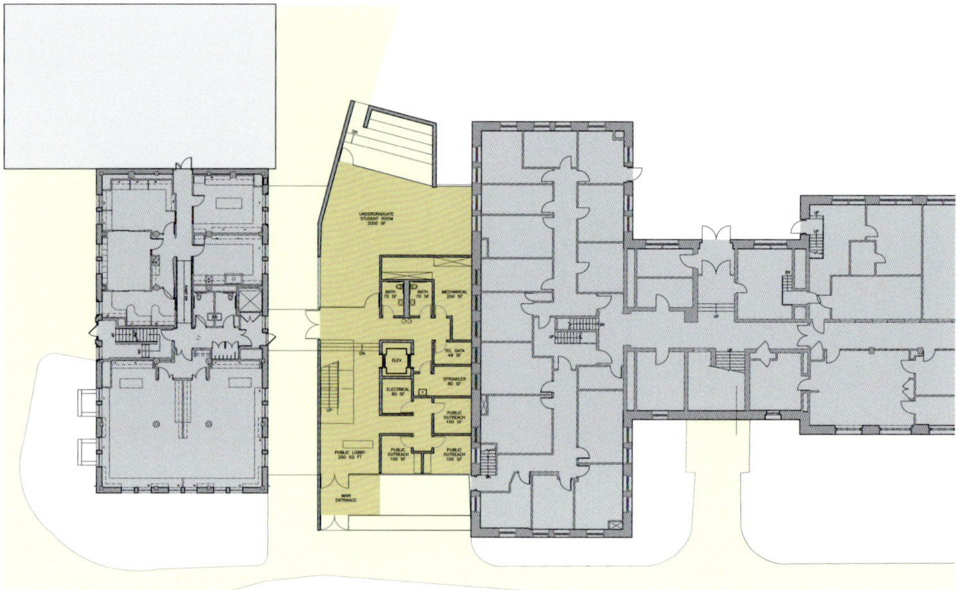

Cruft Hall — New multi-use building — Pierce Hall — Ground level floor plan

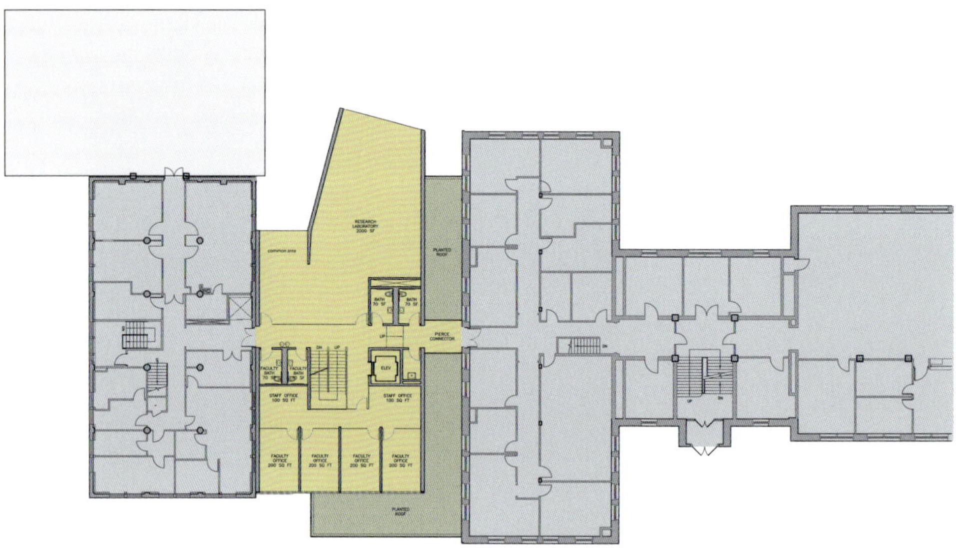

Cruft Hall — New multi-use building — Pierce Hall — Second level floor plan

New multi-use building — Cruft Pierce Connector – The School of Engineering and Applied Sciences, Harvard University, Cambridge, Massachusetts

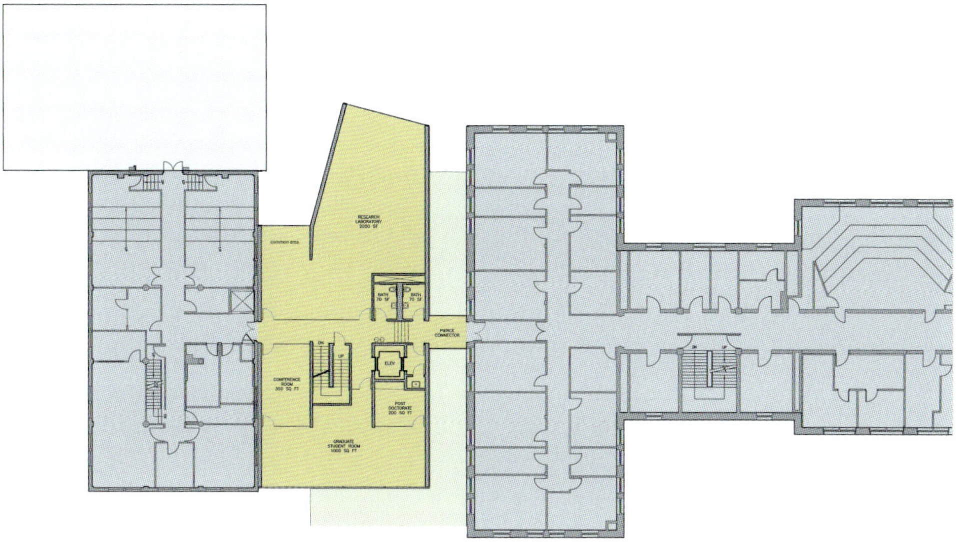

Cruft Hall | New multi-use building | Pierce Hall | Third level floor plan

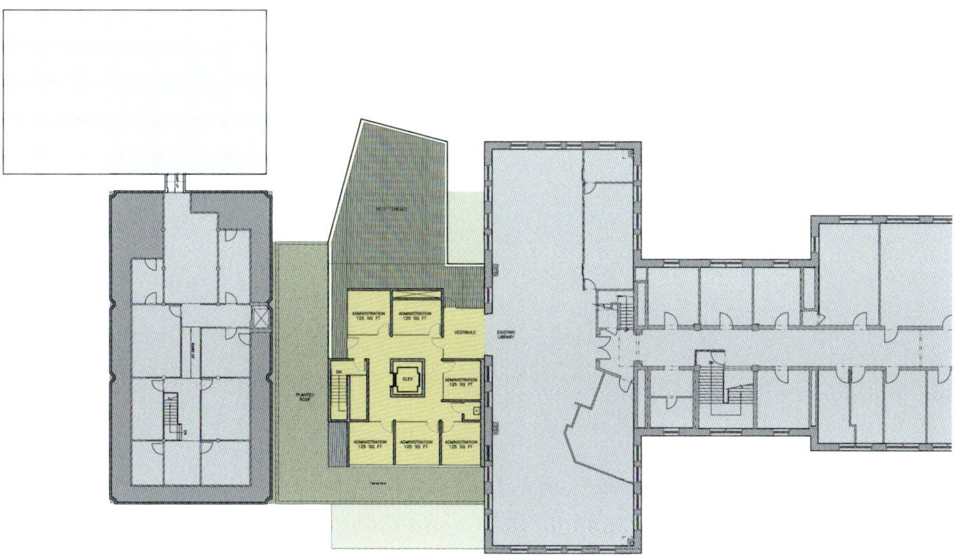

Cruft Hall | New multi-use building | Pierce Hall | Fourth level floor plan

E.M. KENNEDY INSTITUTE

Boston, Massachusetts

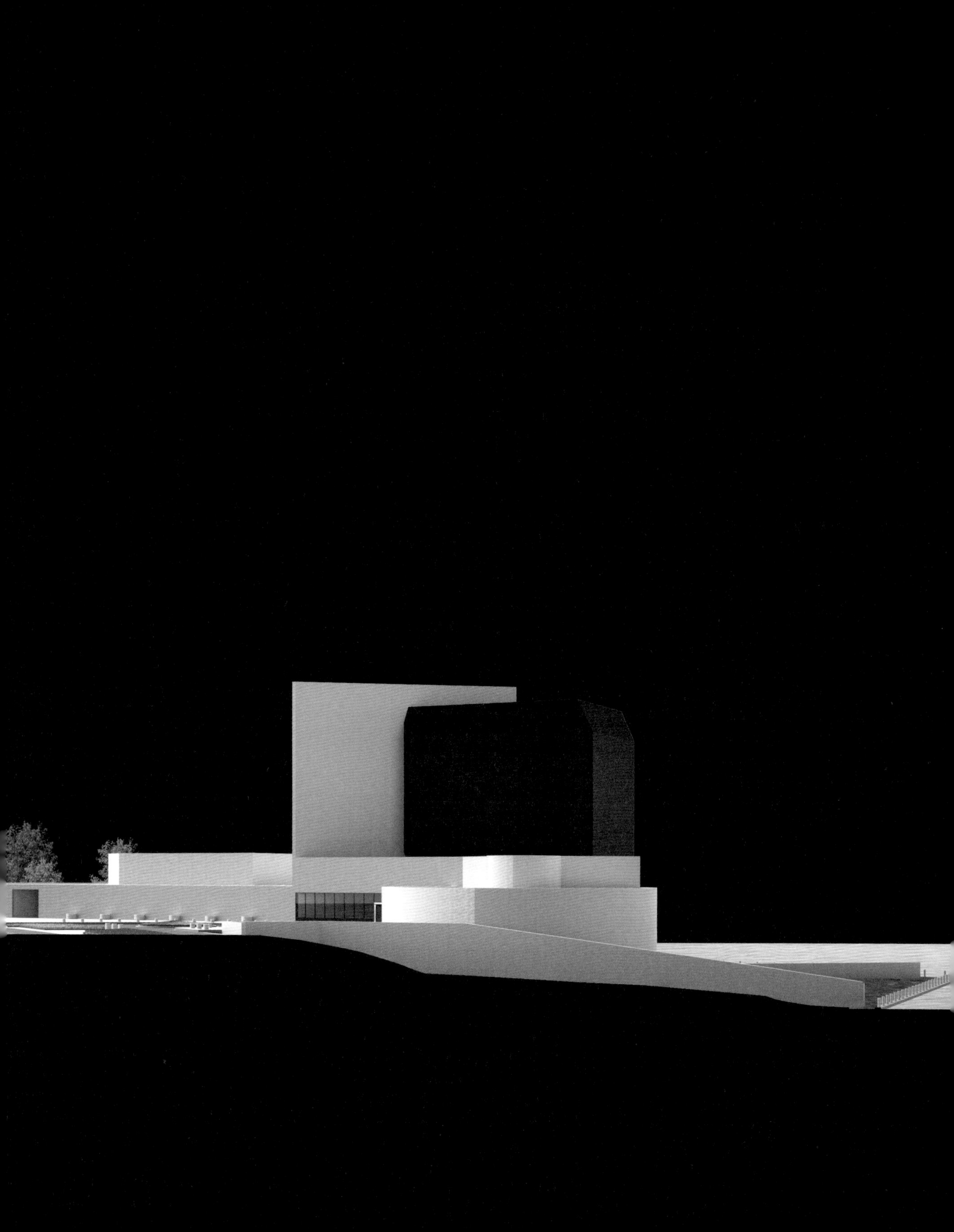

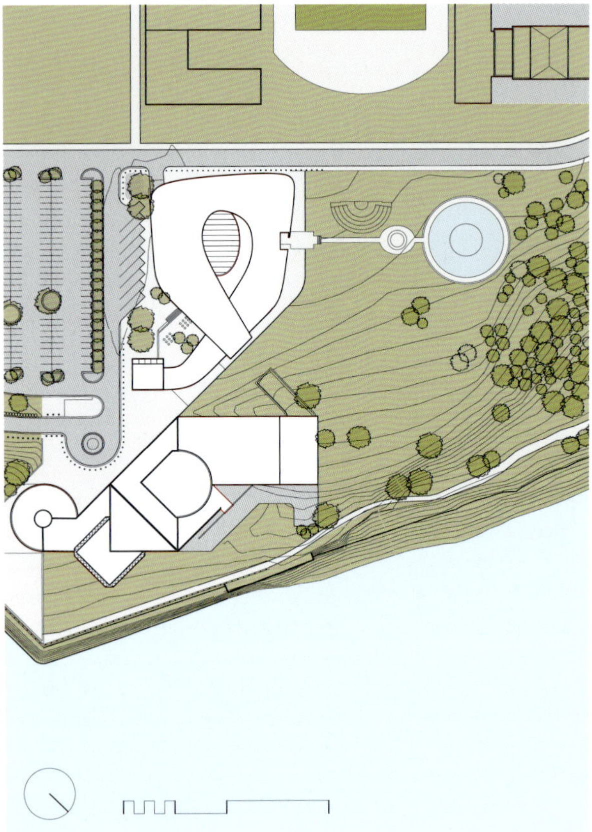

Site plan

E.M. KENNEDY INSTITUTE

E.M. Kennedy Institute for the Senate
University of Massachusetts
Boston, Massachusetts

'I am a part of all that I have met...
Tho much is taken, much abides...
That which we are, we are–
One equal temper of heroic hearts,
...strong in will
To strive, to seek, to find, and not to yield.'
Alfred, Lord Tennyson

Senator and Victoria Kennedy asked several architects to prepare and present their thoughts on a design for the Edward M. Kennedy Institute for the Senate that would be constructed directly adjacent to his brother's presidential library on Columbia Point. The land was donated by the University of Massachusetts with the intention that the new facility reinforce the master plan that UMass developed to reconnect the campus to the Boston Harbor. This new institute is intended to focus on civic education with a particular emphasis on the role of the United States Senate in shaping the nation's agenda.

The Institute for the Senate is a 60,000 sf educational facility with a full-scale replica of the United States Senate Chamber and interactive exhibitions of the history of the Senate and the contributions of Senator Kennedy. It will also house a library, classrooms, internet studio, offices, archives, cafeteria, and ceremonial reception areas.

The proposed design locks itself into the site providing an edge to Dan Kiley's landscape design and I.M. Pei's design for the John F. Kennedy Library. By doing so, the building also creates an open court shared with the entry to the Library and a new pedestrian passageway between the Library and a new park created on the campus of the University of Massachusetts. The Institute itself is defined by a continuous curving ramp that maps the evolution of the Senate. It begins in a pavilion on the entry court, envelops the replica of the Senate Chambers, and opens views to the park, to the campus, to Boston Harbor, and to the Boston skyline. The Senate Chambers lies at the heart of the building below a large translucent dome.

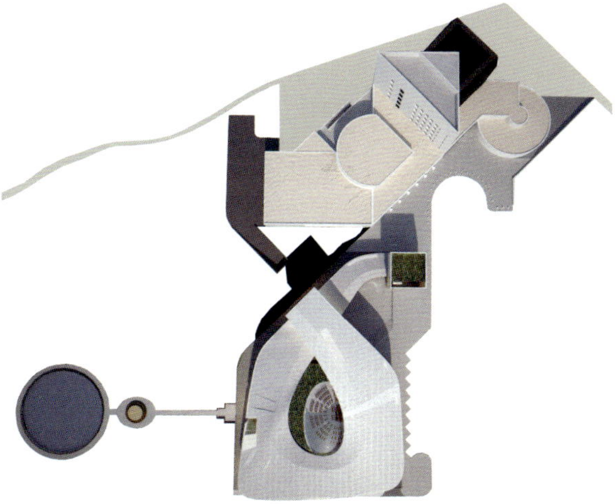

A round pool reflects the position of the rotunda of the Capital in Washington to the recreated Senate chambers

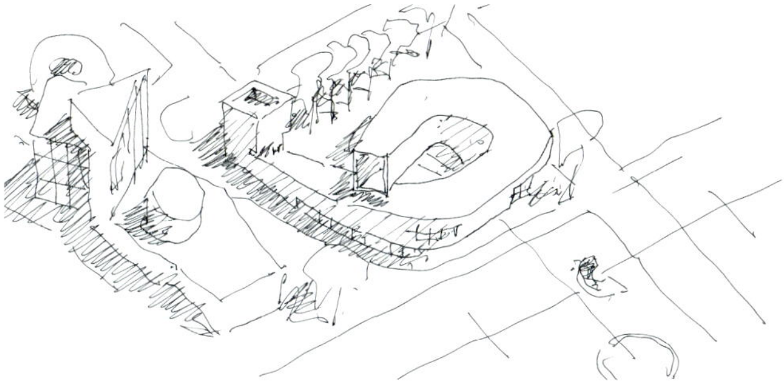

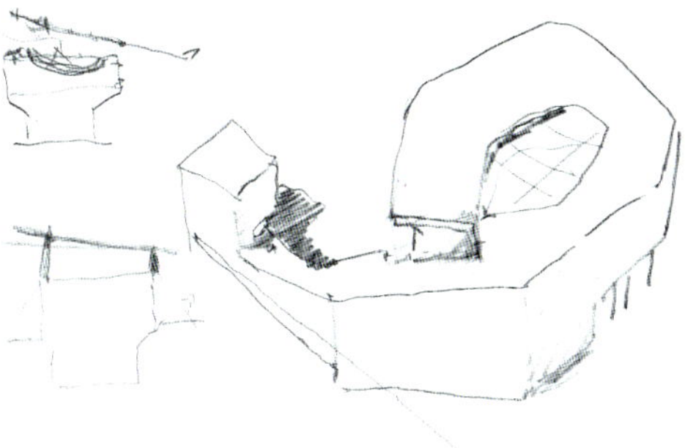

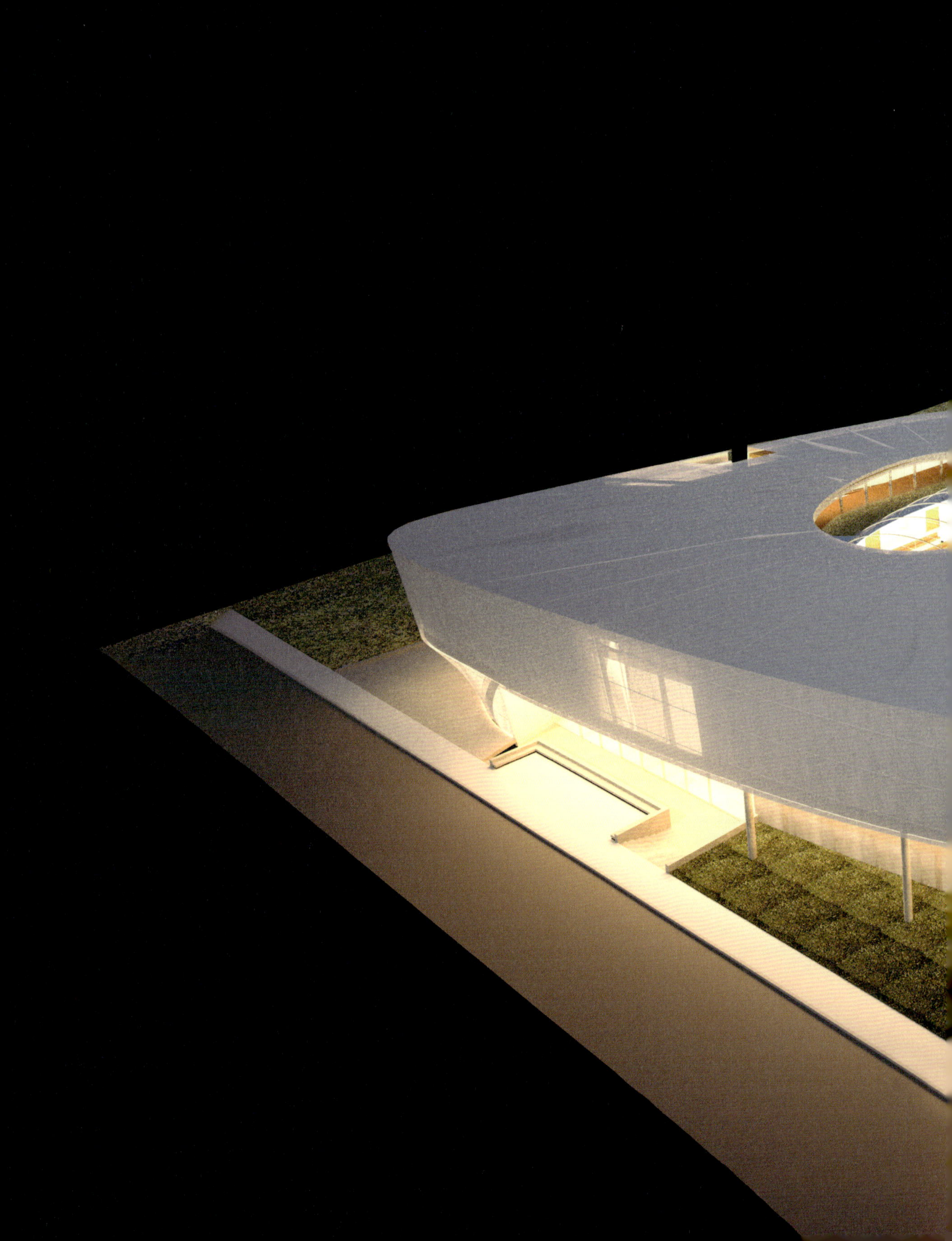

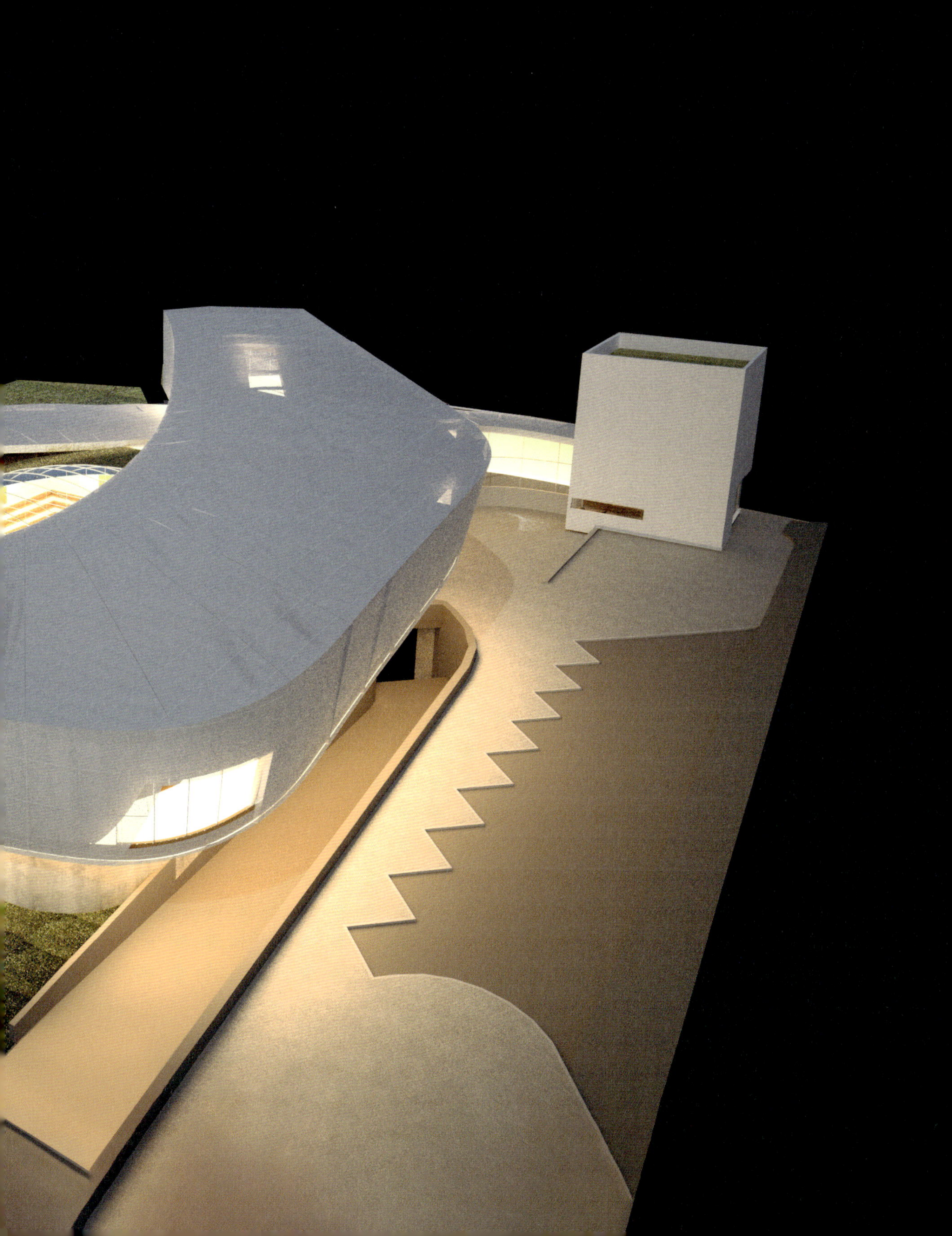

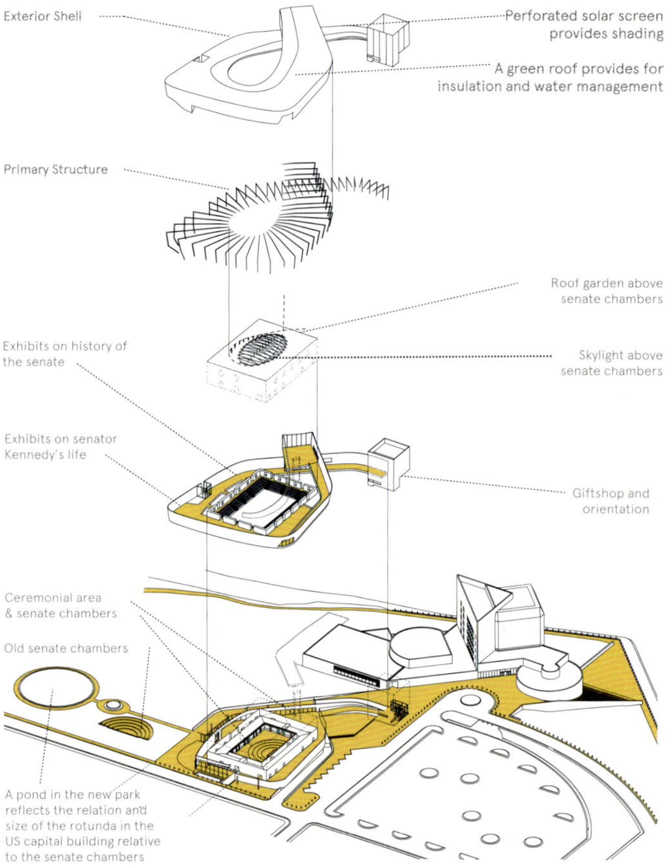

Exploded axonometric

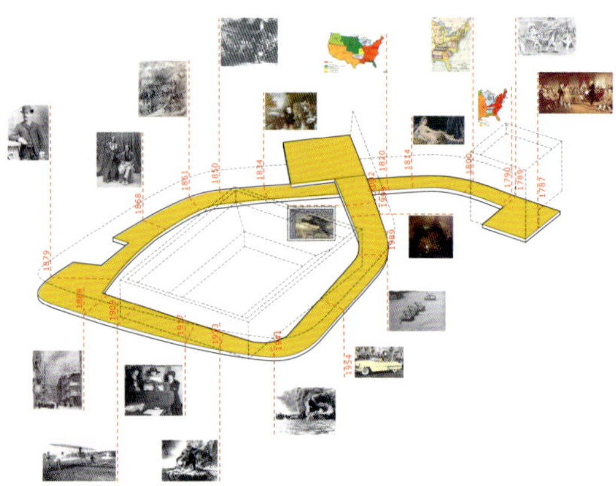

History of Senate

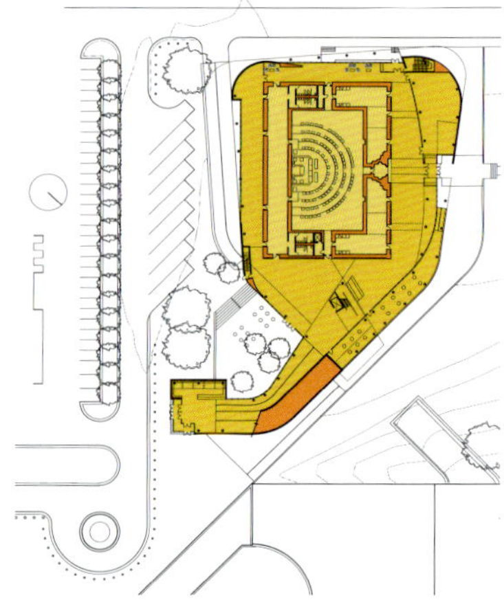

Grade floor plan

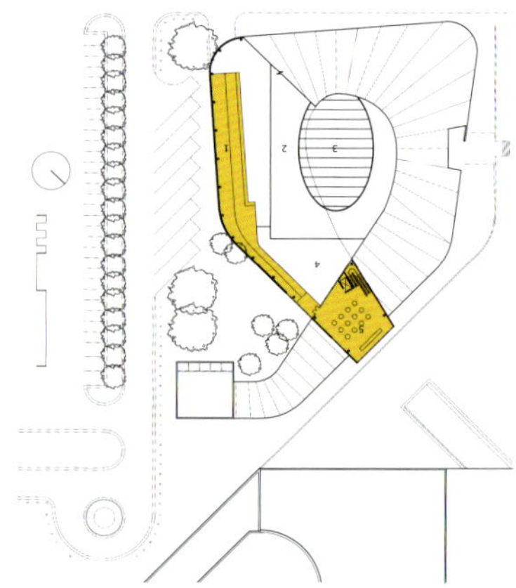

Mezzanine floor plan

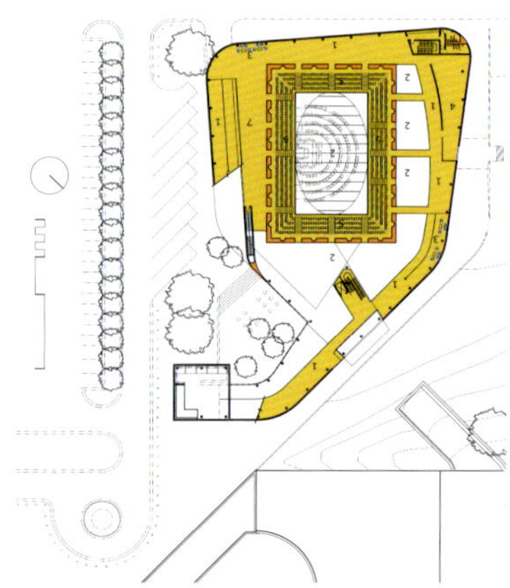

Upper level floor plan

INSTITUTE FOR
C-SPAN

1820
1814
ILLUSTRATED

CIVIC CENTER

Lake Elsinore, California

CIVIC CENTER

Lake Elsinore, California

Located right on I-15, Lake Elsinore is part of the inland empire that lies off the Pacific coast between Los Angeles and San Diego in southern California. In 2007, the City held an open competition to design a new Civic Center – including a city hall, library, business incubator, retail space, and a post office – to help revitalize the downtown area.

Our proposal establishes an open city square that anchors the south end of Main Street with direct connections to the existing City Park and a proposed promenade down to the Lake. This new cityscape complements the existing historic nature of Main Street while providing a catalyst for future development.

City Hall has an inner and outer skin that provides environmental protection from the sun and creates an animated nocturnal presence on the square. This shell encloses the City Council Chambers and Library and contains a series of balconies and roof terraces overlooking the lake. From these open spaces, one can view the city, the Ortega Mountains, the Cleveland National Forest, and the new public boardwalk and parks that spill down to the waterfront.

We deliberately occupied the perimeter of the block with the central public space containing a large reflecting pool connected to a series of open smaller pools. By providing a pedestrian friendly environment, the cultural and commercial opportunities of the Lake Elsinore Civic Center can be discovered through casual street encounters. It is our hope that this urban strategy will stimulate adjacent development on the blocks surrounding the Center, and continue to contribute to the rejuvenation of Lake Elsinore, Main Street, and the surrounding areas.

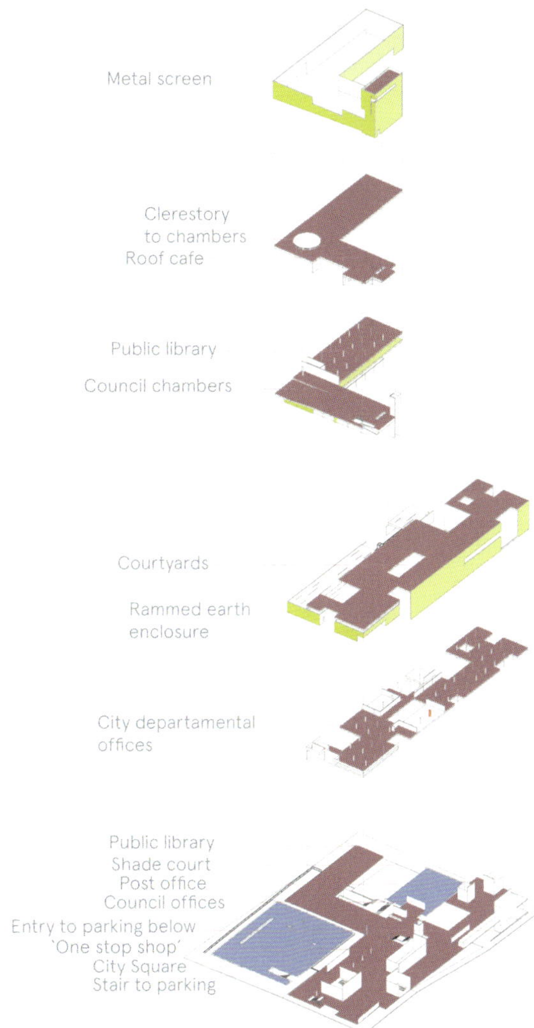

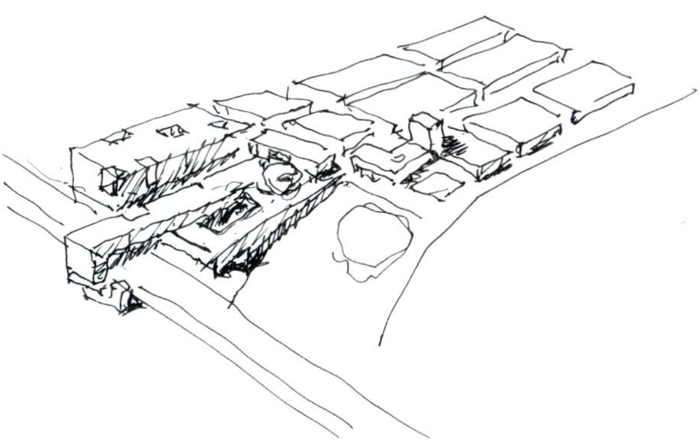

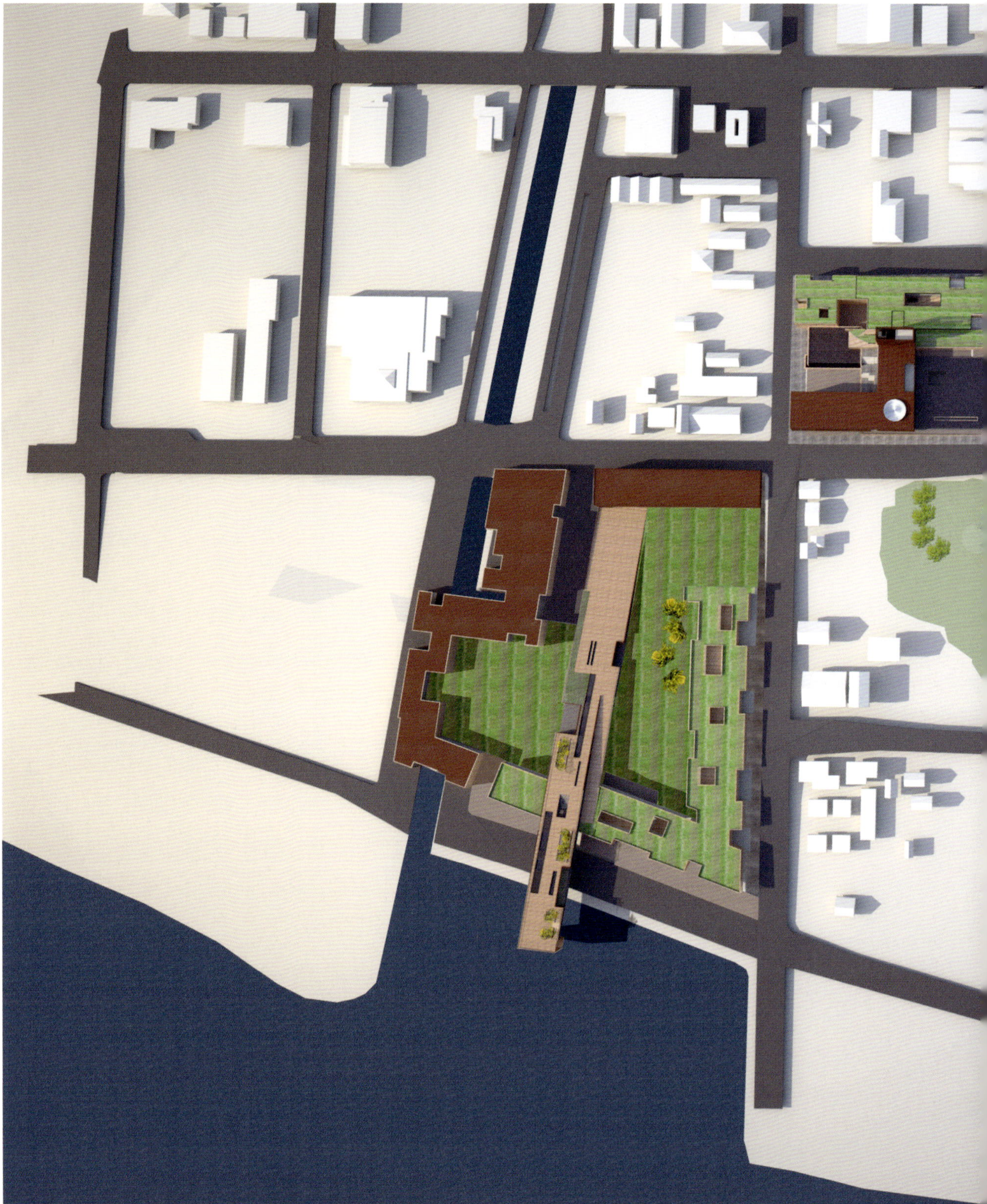

DOWNTOWN CROSSING

Boston, Massachusetts

DOWNTOWN CROSSING

Boston, Massachusetts

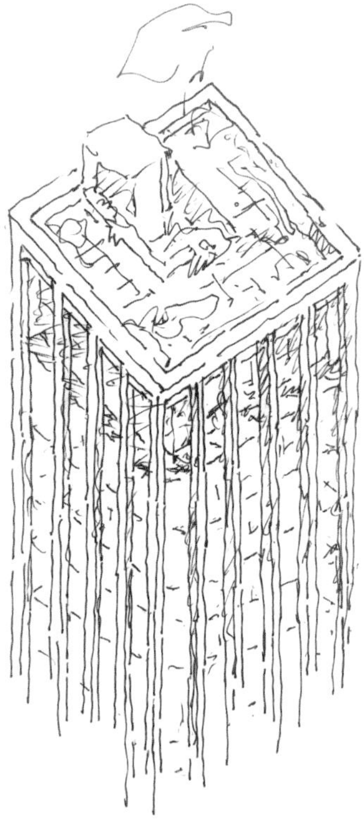

Downtown Crossing is a prominent shopping district located east of Boston Common, west of the Financial District, south of Government Center, and north of Chinatown and the old Combat Zone. It features numerous bars, restaurants, and retail shops, as well as large department stores and street vendors. An MBTA subway station lies in the center of the district.

The district gets its name from the intersection of Washington Street with Winter and Summer Streets. The district is a major pedestrian shopping area, with the area of Washington, Winter, and Summer streets surrounding the intersection closed to most vehicular traffic so that pedestrians may walk freely in the street.

This project is located at 30 Winter Street and includes the renovation and re-positioning of an existing tower to upgrade its services, redesign the streetscape, and add several floors to the top of the building. Existing exoskeletal columns were re-clad and extended to cap the tower with three open floors of office space with floor to ceiling glass walls and an exterior roof terrace overlooking Boston Common and the golden dome of the Massachusetts State House.

TD Bank
planet fitness
MUSIC HALL PL

LINCOLN STREET GARAGE

Boston, Massachusetts

LINCOLN STREET GARAGE

Boston, Massachusetts

The original building was a parking garage both shaped and programmed by the burgeoning car culture of Boston. Its arced plan perfectly described the curve of the on-ramp to the interstate. Built during the construction of the 'Skyway' (Boston's elevated highway, now underground) in 1956, the original two-story structure was proudly utilitarian. It used the thinnest steel stick members and a parsimonious section to accommodate the parking ramps and stairs. The enclosed office space was added to the top deck in 1973. Our charge was to re-examine the cladding, the mechanical systems, and use of the existing structure

We examined the most important views: the narrow view up from Chinatown between the densely packed brick warehouses, the view along Lincoln Street to consider the location and articulation of the entrance, and the building's presence on the surface road directly across from the main gate into Chinatown. The question was how to assert a presence from these three perspectives in a clear way, using new materials and a more articulated vocabulary.

By selectively adding and subtracting the skin around the steel skeleton, and designing two separate cladding systems, we could play off ideas of enclosure, screen, and volume. The interplay between skin and screen, frame and volume, allowing building to celebrate its utilitarian heritage while supporting a contemporary hybrid program.

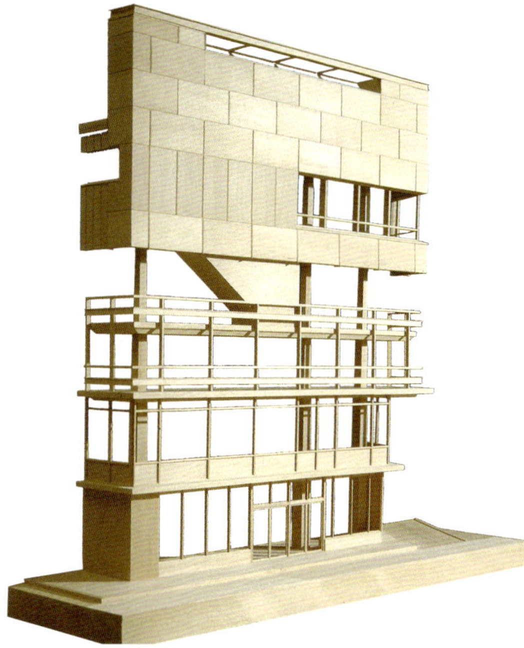

Study model of east facade

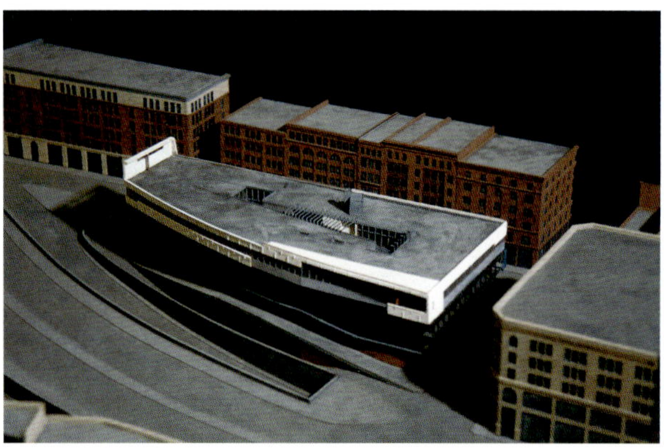

Aerial view of model along Central Artery

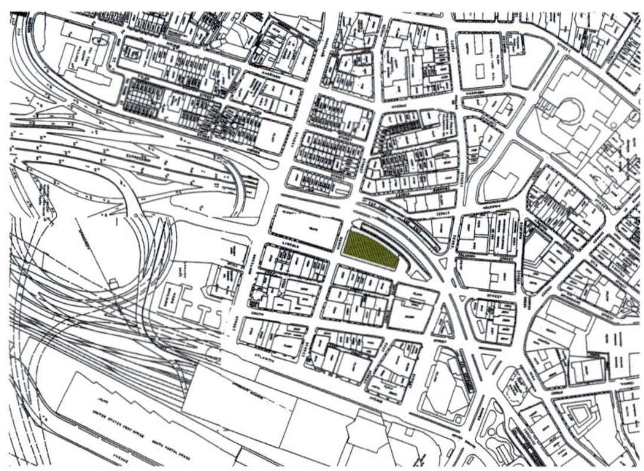

Site plan

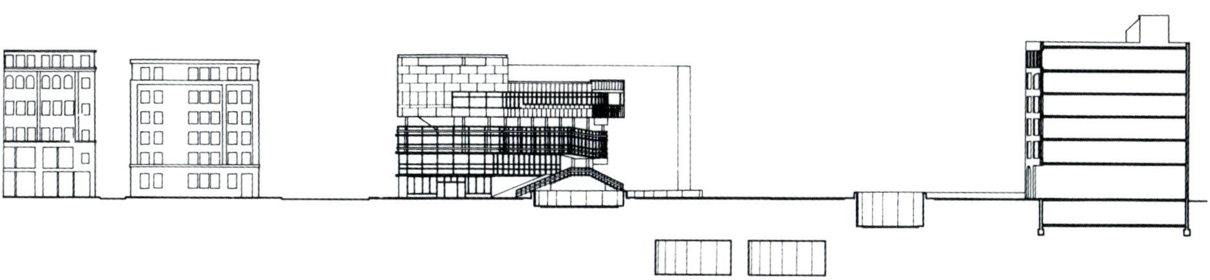

Section through Central Artery with elevation of Lincoln Street Garage

125

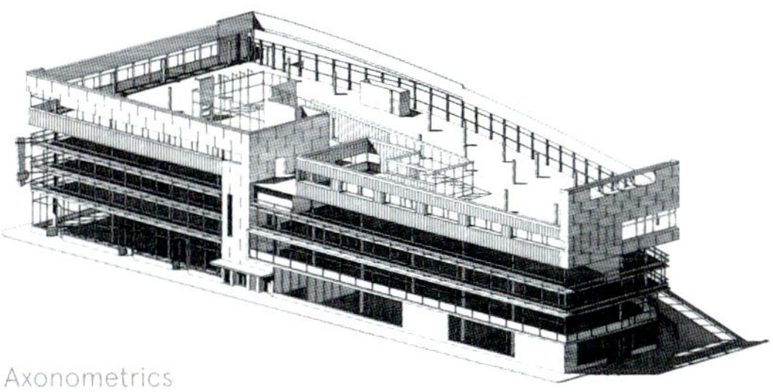

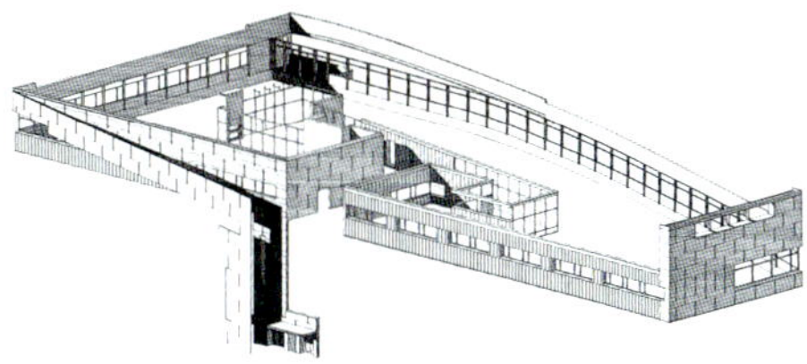

Axonometrics

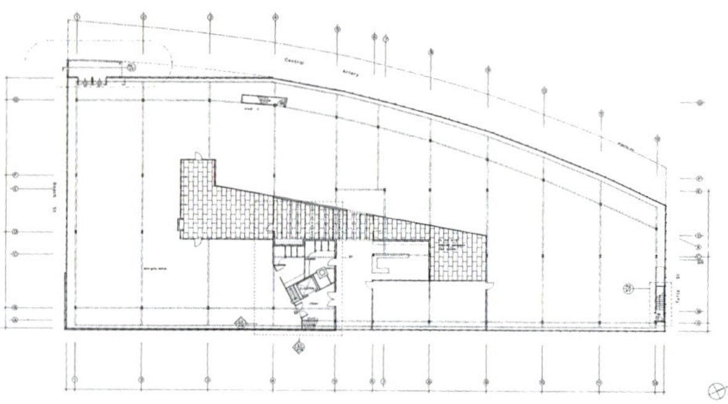

Fifth floor plan

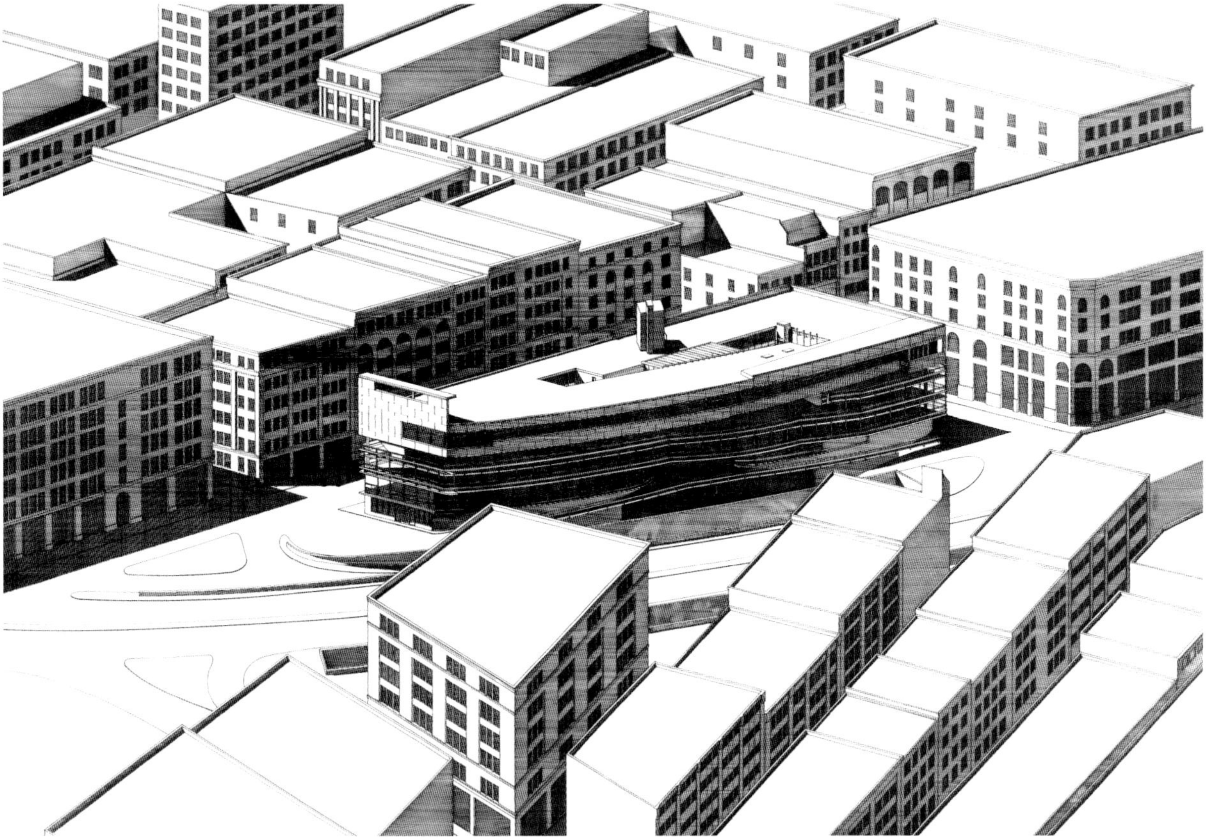

Aerial perspective

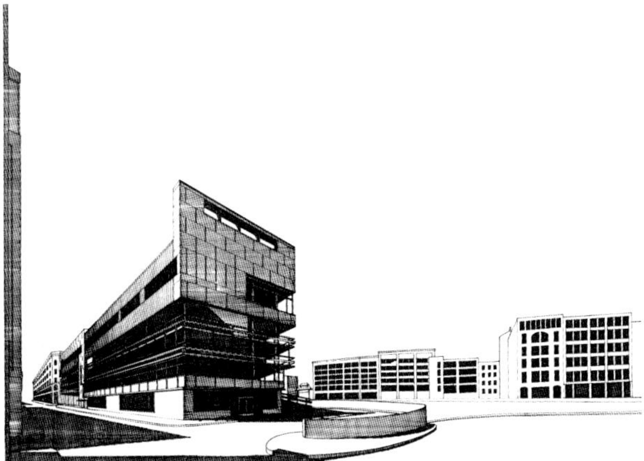

Perspective along Lincoln Street

Axonometric view

BOSTON FILM

Cambridge, Massachusetts

This small film company required temporary office and production space within sixty days on a limited budget. They chose 1,600 square feet on the seventh floor of an existing corporate building near Kendall Square in Cambridge. The existing conditions provide only one set of widows opposite the entry to bring natural light into the space. A series of plaster screens and wooden boxes obscure the light source and mediate between the corporate hallway and the external views of the industrial landscape behind MIT.

Axonometric views of common areas

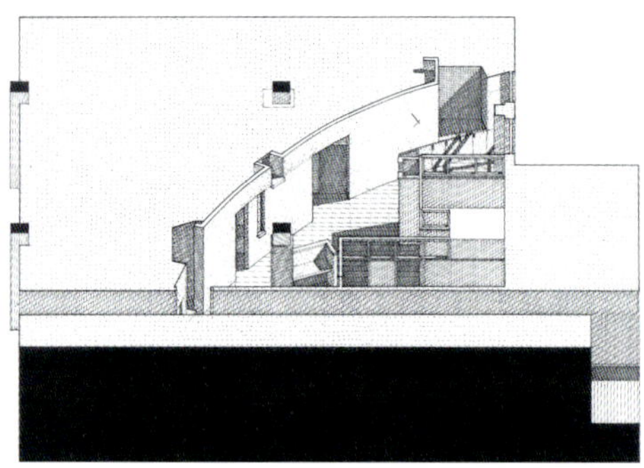

LEARN

When was it that the particles became
The whole man, that tempers and beliefs became
Temper and belief and that difference lost
Difference and were one? It had to be
In the presence of a solitude of the self,
An expanse and the abstraction of an expanse,
A zone of time without the ticking of clocks,
A color that moved us with forgetfulness.
When was it that we heard the voice of union?

Things of August – Wallace Stevens

educational facilities + civic venues

PETER MACKEITH

THREE ENCOUNTERS

I.

"*...The task of the present generation is to construct a history of things that will do justice both to meaning and being, both to the plan and to the fullness of existence, both to the scheme and to the thing...*"
George Kubler, *The Shape of Time*
Excerpted from the epigram of *Perspecta, The Yale Architectural Journal*, vol. 19. Brian Healy, editor / Nate McBride, co-editor.
1982: Cambridge, The MIT Press.

I met Brian Healy first as a persona of literary construction, through the reading of a sequence of deliberately solicited essays, in the pages of *Perspecta 19*, the 1982 volume of *The Yale Architectural Journal* that the then 25-year old Healy had conceived, shaped and edited, with the assistance of his classmate Nate McBride. Having just finished my first year in Yale's master of architecture program, that literary meeting through the school's venerable publication was perhaps predictable and perhaps inevitable. But at the time, and even now in retrospect, that meeting — imbued with creative and intellectual character — can be seen as simultaneously fortuitous, reassuring, and stimulating. And in the fullness of time, and with the benefit of multiple meetings with the editor of Perspecta 19 since that first encounter, I might even say that our 1982 meeting, in the black-and-white pages of Lorraine Wild's superb book design, so seemingly impersonal, insubstantial and remote, remains one of the most affecting and transformative encounters in my life and work in architectural culture.

The Brian Healy I encountered in *Perspecta 19*, in the space and duration of its 14 essays and 190 pages, reveals himself to be an ardent student of the breadth and depth of architecture, of its cultural responsibilities and its internal demands, of its metaphorical capability and its material presence, of its representational character and its rhetorical expressiveness. Indeed, I may understate the editor's vocation,

Previous spread Petajavesi Old Church, Petajavesi, Finland (church 1763 + bell tower 1821). **This spread first and second images** Aalto's Town Hall at Säynätsalo (1951) and Studio in Helsinki, Finland (1955). **This spread third and fourth images** Resurrection Chapel by Erik Bryggman, Turku, Finland (1940).

for the editor of *Perspecta 19*, this literary Healy, is surely more than the self-centered post-graduate student, but in fact the most passionate of public advocates for architecture's cultural role, for its historical complexity and its artistic ambitions. As I met the editor then, through the succession of essays and the symposium of voices he so skillfully assembled and moderated (and simply sequenced in alphabetical order!) — initially Raimund Abraham giving way to Rainer Crone, with an interlude provided by T. S. Eliot, then Fellows to Harries to Hedjuk ... and on to Kahn and Kubler, Pelli and Roche, our own current faculty Millard and Purves, and Richard Serra's declaratory voice in conclusion — I also encountered an expanding universe of ideas, resonant with the voices of my own experiences and previous education, but equally consciousness-altering and infinitely challenging.

A 2004 critique of *Perspecta 19* would describe it as "rather thoroughly dominated by phenomenological themes and imagery," a bittersweet assessment which reveals more of the critic's biases than those of the editor. The Brian Healy I met in 1982, possessed by a sense of architecture's gravity and poignancy, spoke to me and many others at that precise moment with forceful, appreciable intelligence and measured, deliberate emotion. The encounter with Brian Healy, the thoughtful, passionate editor of *Perspecta 19*, left me deeply moved, and moves me still.

II.

"In a story, the narrative is captured in the telling; it is the selective details and descriptive moments that evoke a tone or mood. The plot is what actually happens, and a good plot can produce countless stories. I am interested in an architecture that suggests an equivalent multiplicity of telling, and in plots that suggest narratives that are as complex and layered in people themselves. I look for the stories within stories. Architecture is made not of intentions but of works. In its very essence, it involves a renunciation of words and an engagement with the physical. As graduate students, you are developing ideas about

architecture and how architects can create environments that promote occupation. This studio focuses on the translation of the students' ideas into legible architectural form with an eye towards both its plot and narration."

Excerpt from *Advanced Design Studio Project Statement*, Fall 2005.
Brian Healy, Ruth and Norman Moore Visiting Professor
Graduate School of Architecture and Urban Design, Washington University in St. Louis.

I met Brian Healy again in the fall of 2005, not for the second time, but at that moment as a teacher, a constructor of design education, in his role as an invited visiting professor of practice at the School of Architecture at Washington University in St. Louis. More precisely, we met at the foot of the central terrazzo stair of Givens Hall, just inside the bronzed doors of that 1937 ascetically classical building for the School of Architecture, as he arrived for the semester. I met him then as associate dean of the School, as host and guide for his semester of studio instruction in the graduate curriculum, and as an observer of the studio as it was conceived and developed through the association with the twelve graduate students enrolled during the autumn months.

In making the appointment, the Dean of the School at that time, Cynthia Weese, and I had recruited a practitioner-educator of experience and accomplishment. Twenty years on from his editing of *Perspecta*, and having established his eponymous practice in 1986, Healy had built a practice of nationally recognized work, paralleled by a portfolio of faculty appointments across the breadth of American schools of architecture, including the significant graduate programs at Yale, Harvard and MIT. Our school, aspirant and ascendant, sought to challenge our graduate students by such an appointment – but also to remain consistent with our own identity, our own DNA, as a school committed to an ethos of architecture as constructed experience.

This was the Brian Healy I encountered and observed in 2005: an architect-educator not only committed empathetically to that institutional ethos, but moreover one utterly committed to the developing identities and voices of the twelve students with whom he worked over the course of the semester. The ambition of the studio he projected was clear from the start, as can be seen from the excerpted studio statement above, but the essential project is given even clarity from further elaboration: "The goal for the studio is to design and develop a building. The criteria for the evaluation of that building are the relationship of the building to the site; the quality of experience of both external and internal spaces; and the articulation of building components." These direct, even laconic, statements belie the intensity of the instructor's constant emphasis throughout the semester, best understood as an implicit imperative: a student in a professional program must commit mentally to the given project as a realistic proposition, to a design as an actual constructed reality, to a fundamental responsibility for the physical acts of making and inhabiting.

The work of the students, as I observed it in development, production and presentation over the course of that fall semester, achieved that desired depth, an accomplishment surely due to their commitment to the studio goals, but equally, due to the sure guidance of professor Healy. The Brian Healy I met in 2005, possessed by a sense of architecture's physicality and responsibility, spoke to me and twelve student-architects at that precise moment with forceful, appreciable intelligence and measured, deliberate emotion. The encounter with Brian Healy, the dedicated, supportive architect-educator, left me inspired in my work, and inspires me still.

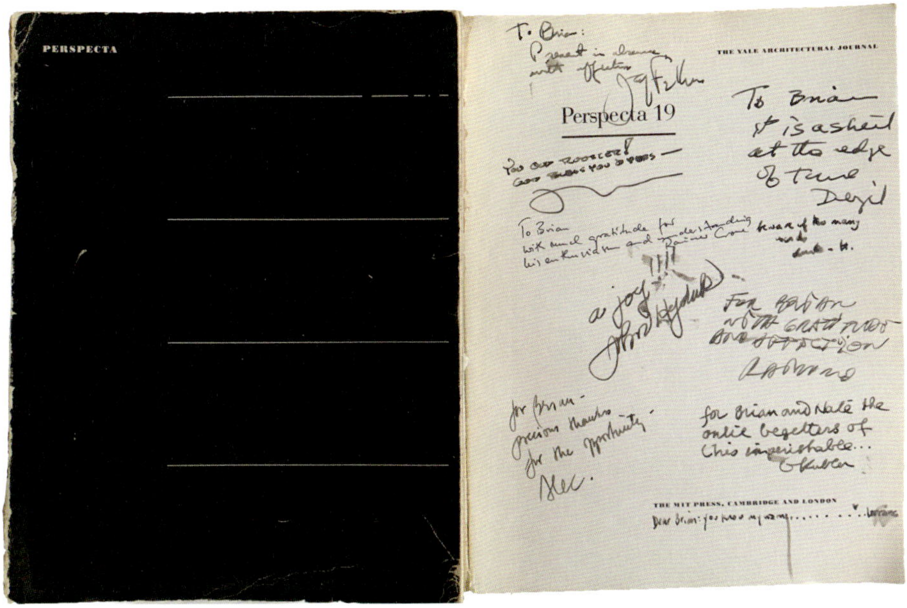

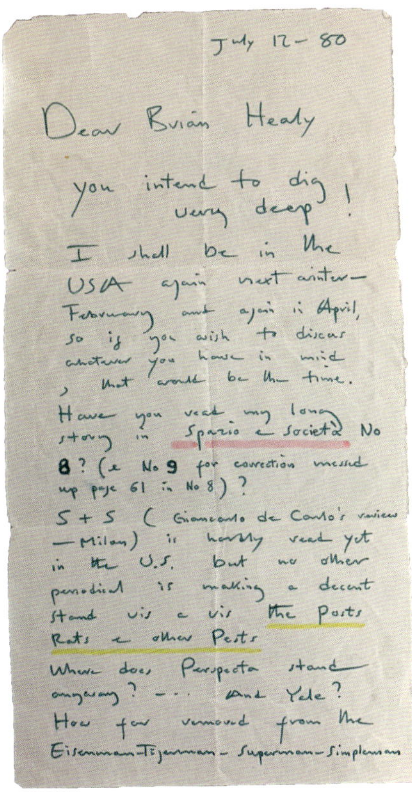
July 12 – 80

Dear Brian Healy

you intend to dig very deep!

I shall be in the USA again next winter — February and again in April, so if you wish to discuss whatever you have in mind, that would be the time.

Have you read my long story in Spazio e Società No 8? (& No 9 for correction messed up page 61 in No 8)?

S + S (Giancarlo de Carlo's review — Milan) is hardly read yet in the U.S. but no other periodical is making a decent stand vis a vis the Posts Rats & other Pests

Where does Perspecta stand anyway? ... And Yale? How far removed from the Eisenman-Tigerman-Superman-Simpleman

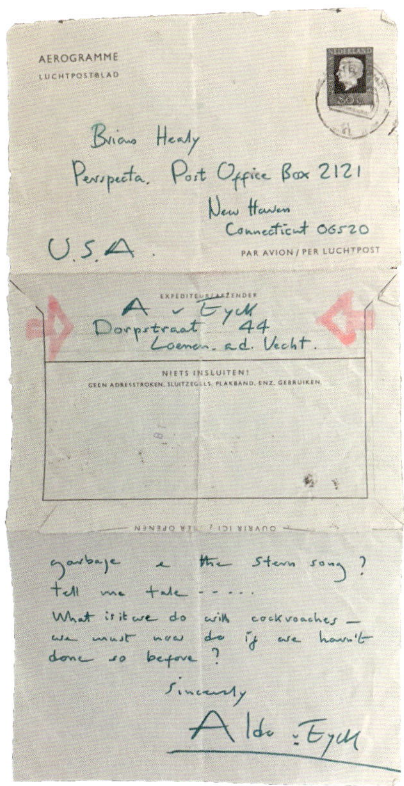
AEROGRAMME
LUCHTPOSTBLAD

Brian Healy
Perspecta Post Office Box 2121
New Haven
Connecticut 06520
U.S.A.

PAR AVION / PER LUCHTPOST

EXPEDITEUR/AFZENDER
A v Eyck
Dorpstraat 44
Loenen a.d. Vecht.

NIETS INSLUITEN!
GEEN ADRESSTROKEN, SLUITZEGELS, PLAKBAND, ENZ. GEBRUIKEN.

garbage & the Stern song? tell me tale....

What is it we do with cockroaches — we must now do if we haven't done so before?

Sincerely

Aldo v Eyck

Top Frontispiece of Perspecta 19 - signed by contributors. **Above left and right** Letter to Healy from Aldo van Eyck - 1980

Interlude

"Architecture has an ulterior motive, which always lurks, so to speak, around the corner. It is the only purpose of our houses. If we did not always carry this thought around with us all our houses would become simpler and more trivial and life would become ... would it be at all worth living? Each house, each product of architecture that is worthwhile as a symbol is an endeavor to show that we want to build an earthly paradise for people ... Architecture may not be able to save the world, but perhaps it can set a small example."
Alvar Aalto, 1957

I met Brian Healy again, soon after that educational encounter, in the summer of 2006, over the course of a ten-day excursion I had organized for a small group of American architects, an in-depth architectural tour coinciding with the Alvar Aalto Symposium in the central Finnish city of Jyväskylä. Besides Healy, the group included architects Marlon Blackwell, Wendell Burnette and Harry Weese, architectural educators Robert McCarter, Max Underwood and Cynthia Weese, and a rotating cast of Finnish architects and designers. We were three days into the intensive schedule, having already explored Helsinki and its environs, and were now venturing further into the rural and forested landscapes, and the full effect of the qualities of climate, light, landscape and built environment was beginning to take hold.

We arrived in the forest community of Säynätsalo, in the Paijanne lakelands, to spend our afternoon at the Town Hall designed by Alvar Aalto during the post-war years of 1948-1953. One of the most photographed of Aalto's works, and the one most often used to represent the Finnish architect's work in total, the red-brick architecture is centered around an elevated grassed courtyard, approached by a formal granite stair at one corner and a set of grassed terraces at another. The courtyard on a sunlit summer afternoon can be surprisingly intimate, calm, restful even ... an ideal setting for an open-air picnic lunch, a sketching session, deliberate or idle conversation, often a nap.

Architect Healy may have availed himself of all those activities, but as I encountered him, again and again, I found him in contemplation, by turns in delighted wonderment and in tactile appreciation. "This is all about being alive and being alert to being alive" he told me, continuing, "about the importance of community and the possibility of being a good community. In so many ways, it's about hope."

III.

"I am still drawn to the beauty of these anonymous American structures: built in both fields and cities and dependent on roads, sidewalks, and streets. Their beauty is wed to the realities of utility and experience rather than to symbolism or intention. The well-worn, the vernacular, and the commonplace represent a grounding, a forthright stance in the evolution of a place. In them, we sense things are they are, even as they slip away and we are forced to imagine what they might become."
Excerpt from *Commonplaces: Thinking about an American Architecture*, Brian Healy, 2007, p.15.

I meet Brian Healy again, now, in the distanced, remote modes we live and work in (circa 2020), in these pages depicting his built and projected works since 1986. I meet him as an architect of accomplishment and experience; in the "beforetimes (before 2020)" I have been fortunate to visit several of these built projects, and fortunate, too, to visit with the architect during the design process of several others, whether ultimately unbuilt or completed. The current *Commonplaces* book is, of course, an expanded edition of the 2007 publication, and is an occasion for reflection, at least. As the reader now knows, my encounters with Brian Healy have a near 40 year history; each of those meetings is, upon reflection, a meeting with, by turns, a student, an intellectual, an educator, a builder, a dreamer, a poet, a sole proprietor, a collaborator, an optimist, an artist ... and too, along the way, I have met him in his lives as a father, a son, a brother. The multiple dimensions of the author and architect portrayed in Commonplaces have been sketched with the broadest of pens — three encounters only — but in the spirit of Wallace Stevens, one of Healy's favorite poets, evocative of "thirteen ways of seeing (the architect)."

But this is a work-book, less than an autobiography, and the fundamental reflection merited is on the work itself, rather than its author. Here, too, that reflection can be understood as a laminate of multiple layers of identification and value. But the laminated reflection resolves itself into a singular comprehension, an aspiration, in fact, across multiple typologies, across attentiveness to latitude, site, climate and light, across constructional means and methods, across the built and the projected: the aspiration is, at least, a desire for an architecture of ideal ethical dimension, an authentic attitude of how to live, animating both individual and society. Each of the buildings displayed in *Commonplaces* posits such an existential, engaged vision of constructed community. Healy's architecture, insistent on the material, the spatial, the illuminated, the tactile, is bound together by an ambitious ethos, one proposing meaningful, purposeful, intimate places for people of all walks of life to live their lives with meaning and purpose. The encounter with Healy's work is propositional, stimulating, and challenging, for the moment when such a vision can no longer be proposed for an individual or for a society, the making of an authentic architecture becomes impossible.

How should we assess a society? Perhaps best by a society's care for its children, for its elderly, for the less advantaged, by its equitable provision of a full quality of life to all — and thus, ultimately, by its architecture, by its humane, social art. How should we assess an architect in that society? Perhaps best by that architect's cultivation of literacy, of education, and of physical and mental well-being — and thus, ultimately, by his or her commitment to architecture as a humane, social practice. The works of *Commonplaces* are evidence of Brian Healy's cultivation and commitment; the book is an encounter with an architect of uncommon sensitivity and substance.

Peter MacKeith is Dean and Professor of Architecture, Fay Jones School of Architecture and Design, University of Arkansas. He was Associate Dean and Associate Professor at the Sam Fox School of Design & Visual Arts, Washington University in St. Louis from 1999 to 2014, and has held previous academic and administrative appointments at Yale, the University of Virginia and the Helsinki University of Technology (now Aalto University). Editor of *Perspecta, The Yale Architectural Journal*, volume 24 (1988), and *The SOM Journal*, volumes 8 and 9 (2012-15), he has authored or edited twelve books, including *Encounters, Essays on Architecture*, volumes 1 and 2, by Juhani Pallasmaa. Since receiving a Fulbright Fellowship to Finland in 1990, MacKeith has worked as a liaison between Finland, the Nordic nations and the United States, through lectures, publications, exhibitions, and education. He is a Senior Fellow of the Design Futures Council and a Design Futures Council Educator of the Year (2017 and 2019). In 2014, the President of Finland recognized MacKeith as a Knight, First Class, of the Order of the Lion of Finland for his contributions to the advancement of Finnish architecture.

STUDENT CENTER

University of Massachusetts
Lowell, Massachusetts

STUDENT CENTER

University of Massachusetts
Lowell, Massachusetts

The University of Massachusetts – Lowell campus – is located in the urban downtown area of this central Massachusetts city with three distinctly separate campuses. In an effort to integrate the existing campuses into a single more unified campus, the university purchased the buildings and property of the former Saint Joseph's Hospital, located at the central point of the existing campuses. The site became the home of a new 140,000 square foot University Crossing – a vibrant new campus center – that acts as the campus center and identity for both the university and surrounding community incorporating dining, retail, and a broad range of student life support functions.

Led by Dana Anderson, Patrick and Janel had the organization and planning of this project well developed when Healy joined the team. Building on their design work, he focused – with James and Emily – on the design and development of a new wood screen – or tapestry – to animate the large open atrium and pay tribute to the history of the school that used to be named the Lowell Textile Institute.

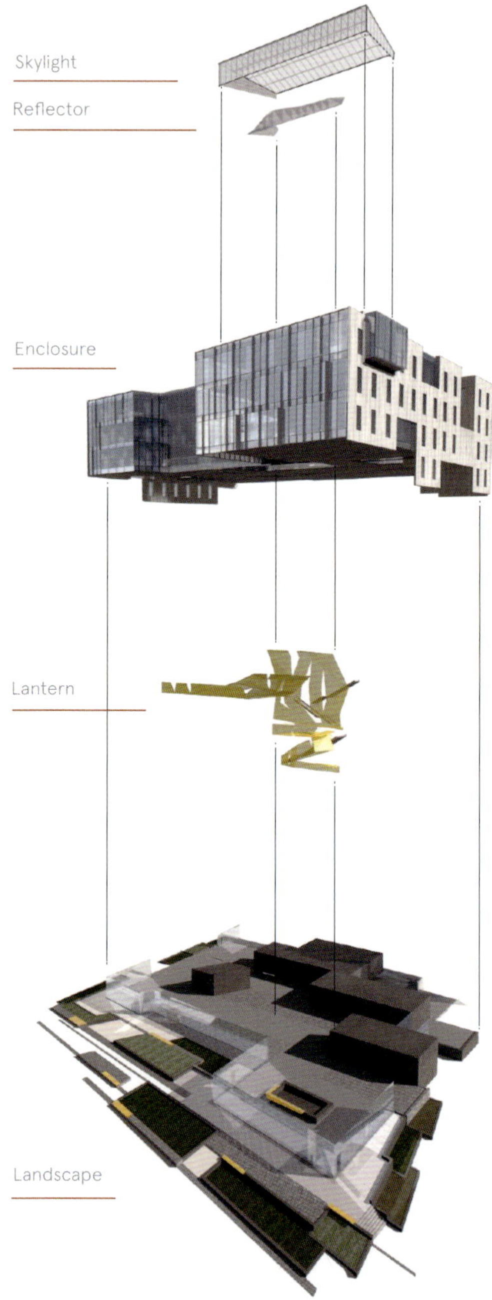

UNIVERSITY CROSSING
220 PAWTUCKET STREET
Crossroads
CAFE

REFLECTED LIGHT: A Backdrop for Student Life

When we designed a new student center for the University of Massachusetts at Lowell, we decided to organize it - and its ambitious social agenda — around a central, vertical atrium space. This interior space is the primary stage for the active theater of campus life. To animate that stage — and make its presence known — we set ourselves the challenge of inventing a dynamic new stage set or backdrop for the activities of that space. We wanted it to be a place for a variety of creative social interactions within the academic and adjacent communities of Lowell with a symbolic and unifying presence within the building and the campus. We also wanted this backdrop to develop its own character that changed across the day and the seasons and — so — decided to animate it with a calculated play of reflected light. These interactive and changing qualities then became the primary driver for the development of the atrium itself.

To achieve success with these goals, we needed a mechanism to study the light and calibrate its effects. We also needed to identify and understand contemporary computational tools that would allow its fabrication and installation. It is these elements, the process, and application that we submit as an illustration of the dynamic spirit of our design studio working with Paul Z and the lighting experts at LAM Partners.

Our case study for this atrium focuses on those tools and the methods needed to analyze, study, and accomplish the day lighting aspirations that define the space. More broadly, we attempt to address the challenges that many urban day lit buildings confront as deep or tall buildings on constrained sites. Building forms often seem to be driven by ideas that work counter to the ideal geometries of day lighting design. The depth of a building's floor plate, the orientation of the existing urban grid, the shadowing of existing site geometry, among other factors inform decisions that create unique design challenges when conceptualizing spaces inspired by daylight.

Within these challenges, we seek to identify the benefits to the building users and the broader environmental context by finding effective and innovative day lighting solutions. We hope to illustrate the potency of developing new design methodologies alongside the latest digital fabrication processes. We also hope to encourage the redefining of design and production methodologies through the cultivation of strong, interdisciplinary partnerships, the exploration of new computational and physical tools, and a willingness of all trades to explore the potential of new construction assemblies.

— Brian Healy

Rendering - Noon

Rendering - 2pm

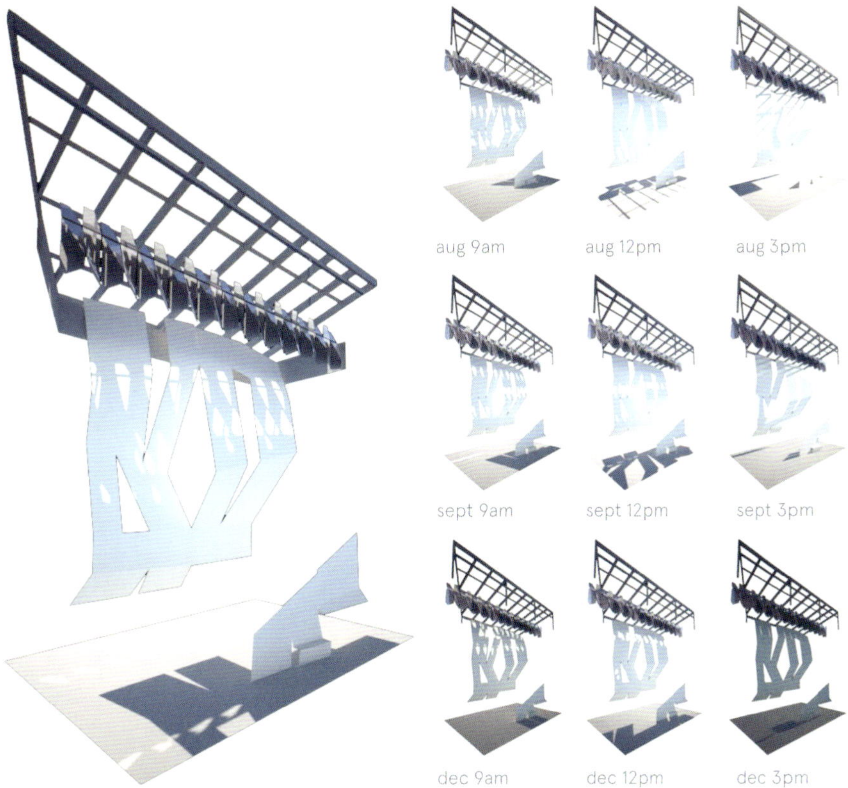

Surface normals can the be used to generate a faceted or curved sirface that reflects light in a way that can be simulated using rendering engines

UMASS LOWELL

UMASS LOWELL
UNIVERSITY CROSSING

Crossroads
Crossroads
CAFE
University Crossing
Admissions
Visitor Parking
University Police

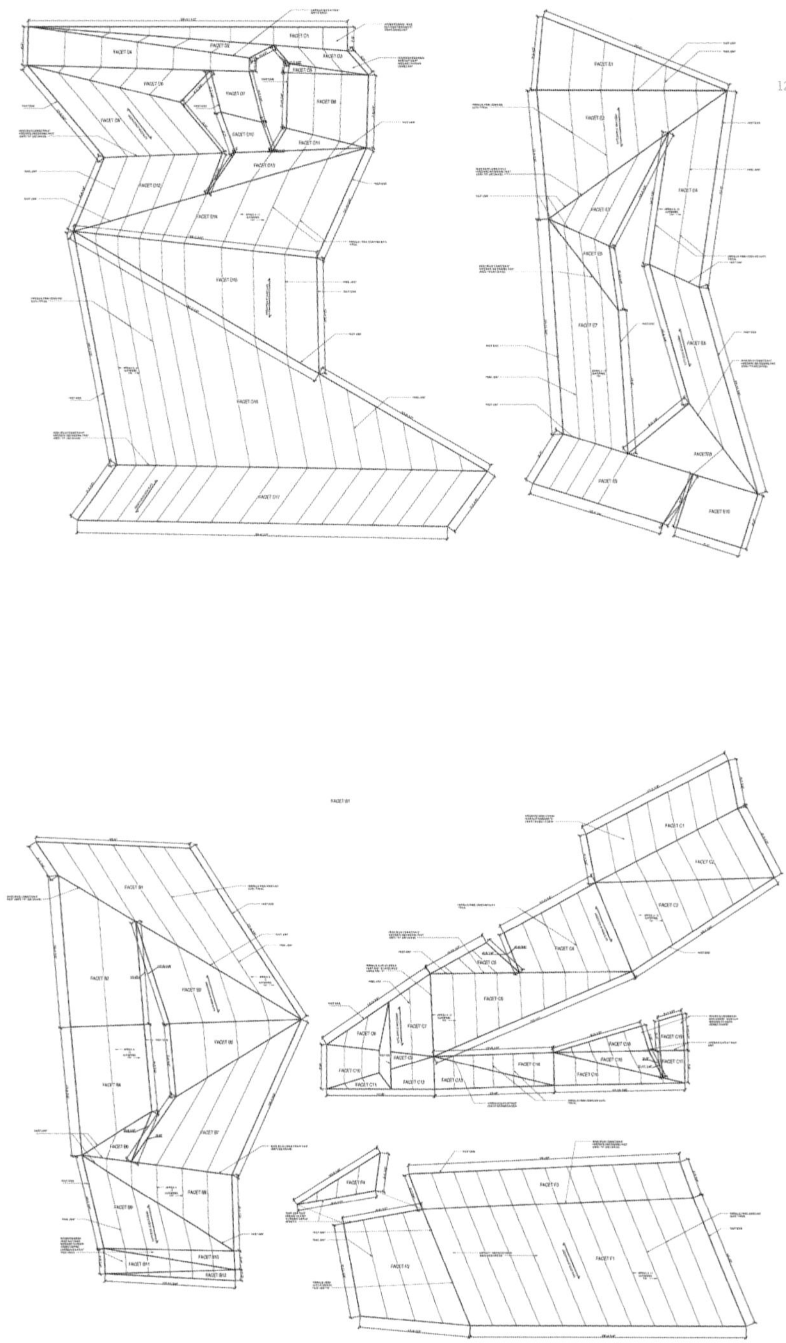

Working drawings

THE SOLUTION CENTER
INFORMATION

Interior visualization of lantern

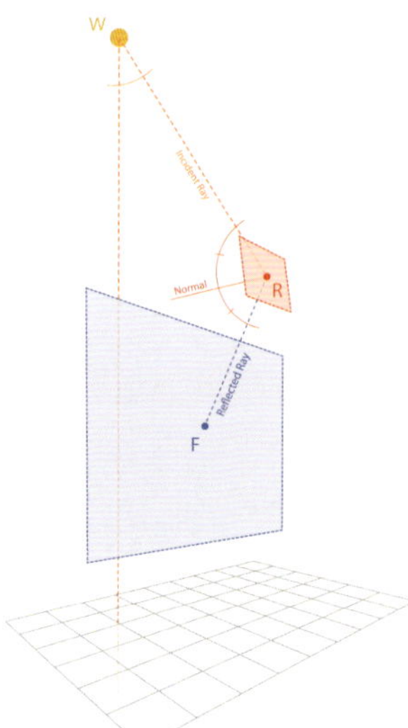

The normal of a reflective surface is derived from the incident solar vector and the focus (F) and reflector (R) points

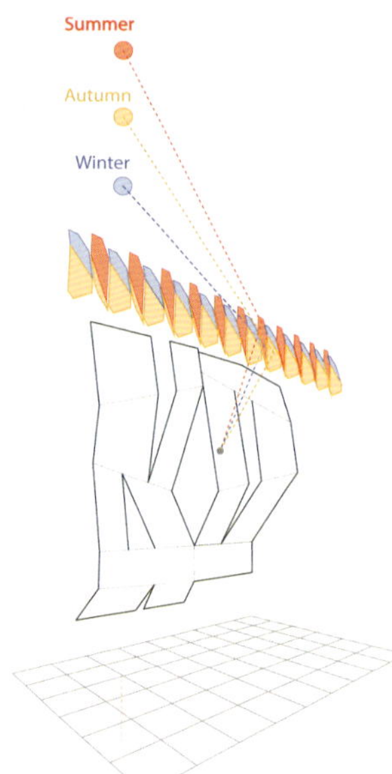

Multiple solar positions over the course of the day and year can be used to generate a series of surface normals

UNIVERSITY CROSSING
RIVER HAWK SHOP

Crossroads
CAFE

ENFOLD

Boston, Massachusetts

ENFOLD

Boston, Massachusetts

As part of the Social Responsibility Initiative at Perkins+Will, Kim Poliquin organized a team of colleagues at PW – along with Healy and volunteers from local architecture programs—to design and construct this temporary installation in Evan's Way Park – designed by Frederick Law Olmsted – directly across from the Stewart Gardner Museum.

ENfold was commissioned by the Fenway Alliance to commemorate the designation of the Fenway as Boston's first statewide Cultural District. The Fenway Alliance – the designated manager of the District – includes twenty-two institutions in the Fenway area, including the Boston Symphony Orchestra, the Museum of Fine Arts, MassArt, the Isabella Stewart Gardner Museum, and Berklee College of Music, among others.

Enfold was a translucent ribbon extending the length of the park. Its form was derived from the graceful canopy of trees that cover Evans Way. The installation served as an interactive backdrop to support formal – and informal – programming for the greater Fenway Community during September and October of 2012. It was a key component of a youth arts program at the Alliance's annual Opening Our Doors event.

At the opening ceremony, ENfold acted as an imaginative frame for musical performances including Afro-Brazil – a Brazilian drumming band, a tai chi exhibition, and numerous other artistic experiences. As the Fenway "opened its doors" to the entire extended community, the installation prompted new experiences with both nature and the arts.

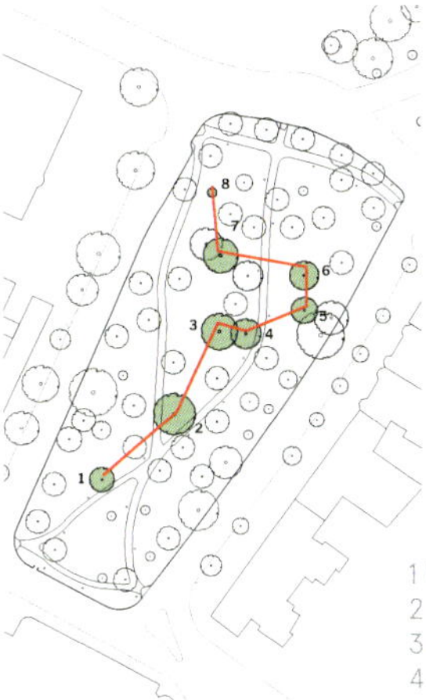

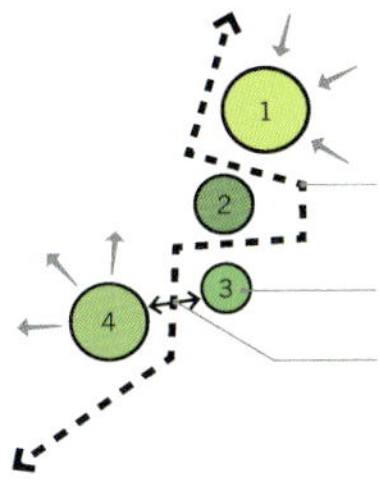

1 Workshop event space
2 Performance, theatre and film
3 Exercise martial arts and dance
4 Exhibition and showcase

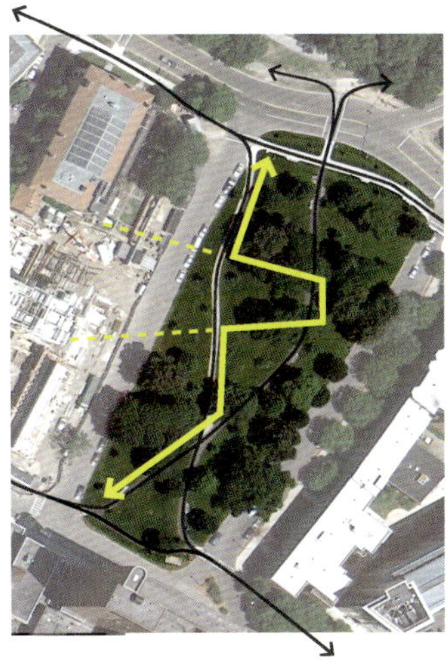

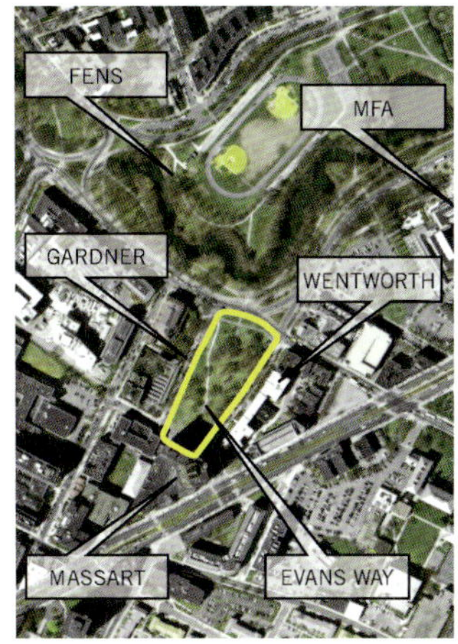

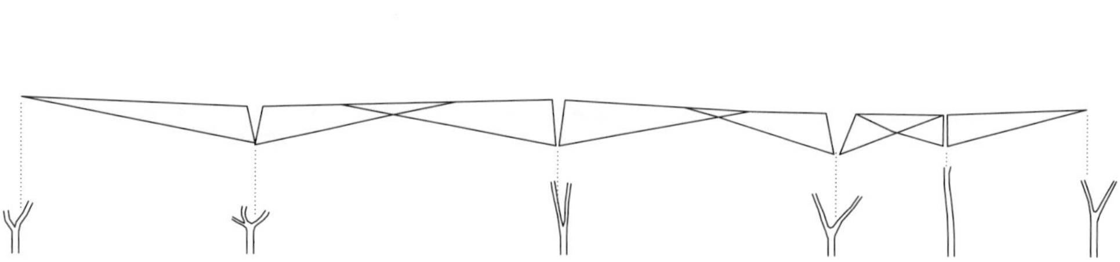

STADIUM ADDITIONS

University of Massachusetts
Amherst, Massachusetts

3

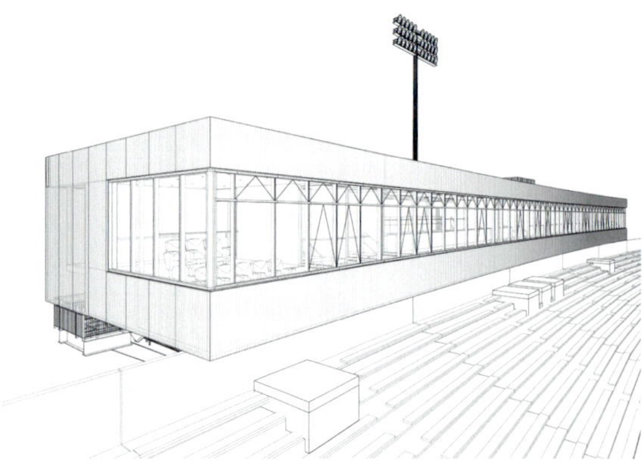

Press box perspective view from southeast

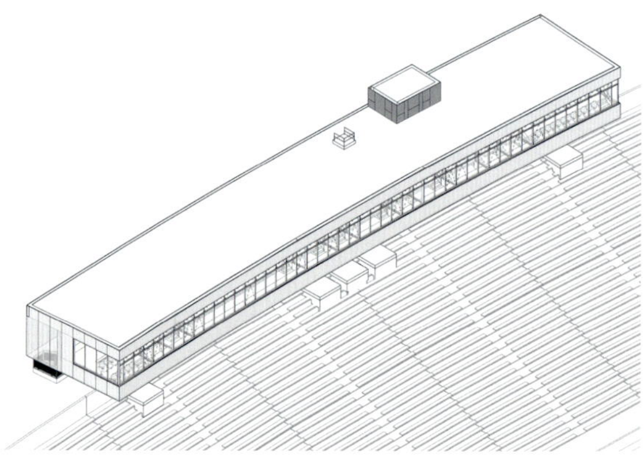

Press box axonometric view from southeast

STADIUM ADDITIONS

Press Box and Training Facility, University of Massachusetts Amherst, Massachusetts

Warren P. McGuirk Alumni Stadium is a 17,000 seat, multi-purpose stadium on the campus of the University of Massachusetts (UMASS) at Amherst. Designed by Gordon Bunshaft as primarily cast-in-place concrete with precast concrete seating risers, the stadium opened on September 25, 1965. It serves as the home to the UMASS Minutemen Men's Football and Women's Lacrosse teams and is also used for special campus events including commencement in the spring semester. The stadium, however, has not seen any major improvements since it was constructed. In 2012, UMASS Amherst, in conjunction with the University of Massachusetts Building Authority, engaged Perkins Will to design a new Football Training Facility and Press Box for the facility in response to an expanding football program at the university. Subsequently, David Dymecki — along with Healy and other PW colleagues — were asked to study various expansion options to increase the seating capacity, improve the overall infrastructure, and enhance the fan experience at the stadium site. The projects include: upgrading the exiting stadium structure to improve accessibility and add necessary toileting and concession outlets; adding south end-zone grandstands; creating an intermediate level over the existing or rebuilt east grandstand; adding a private club and suites; and adding an upper east grandstand to bring the stadium to 30,000 spectator seats. Actively complementing the new football performance center and press box, the stadium expansion will continue to elevate the growth and status of UMASS athletics.

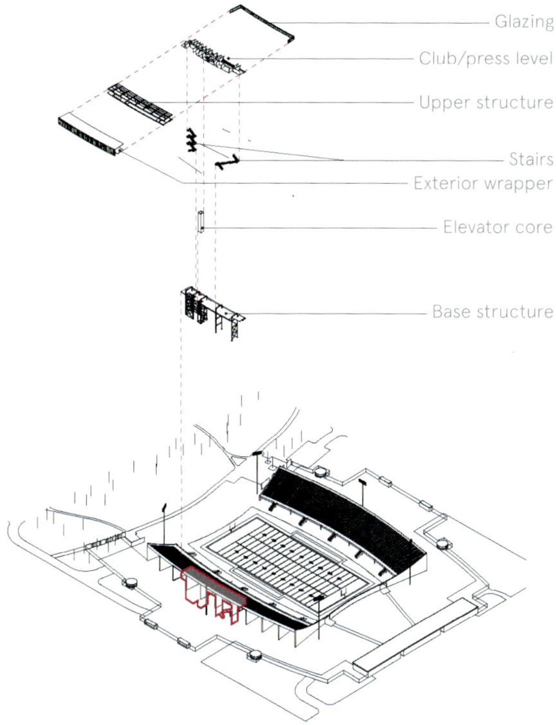

Exploded axonometric view of press box and stadium

Press box perspective view from northwest

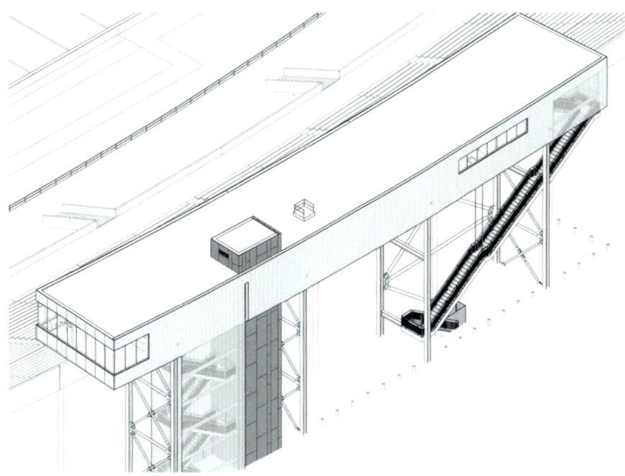

Press box axonometric view from northwest

3

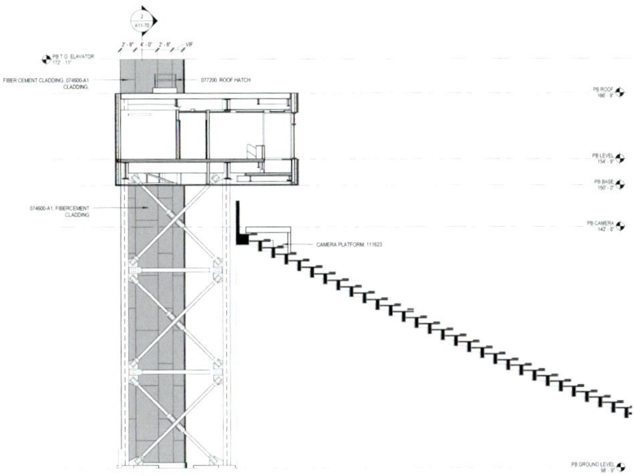

Press box elevator tower - South elevation

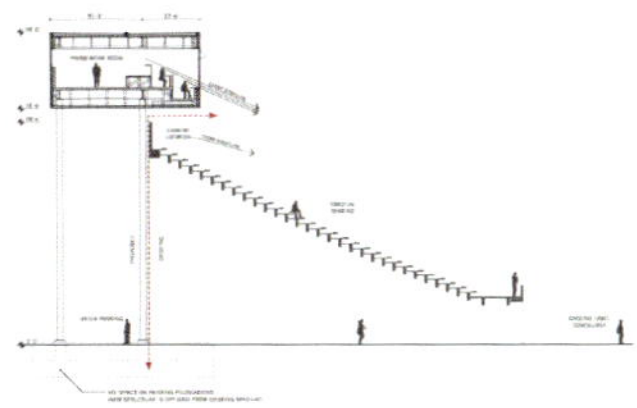

Building section through press box and bleachers

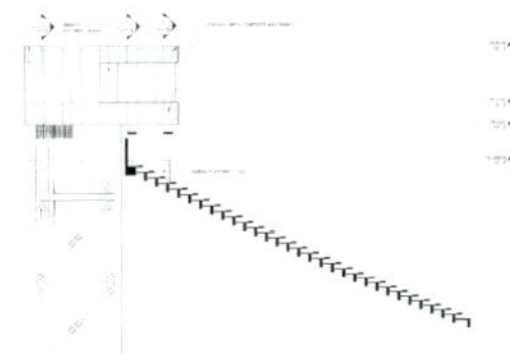

Press box - South elevation

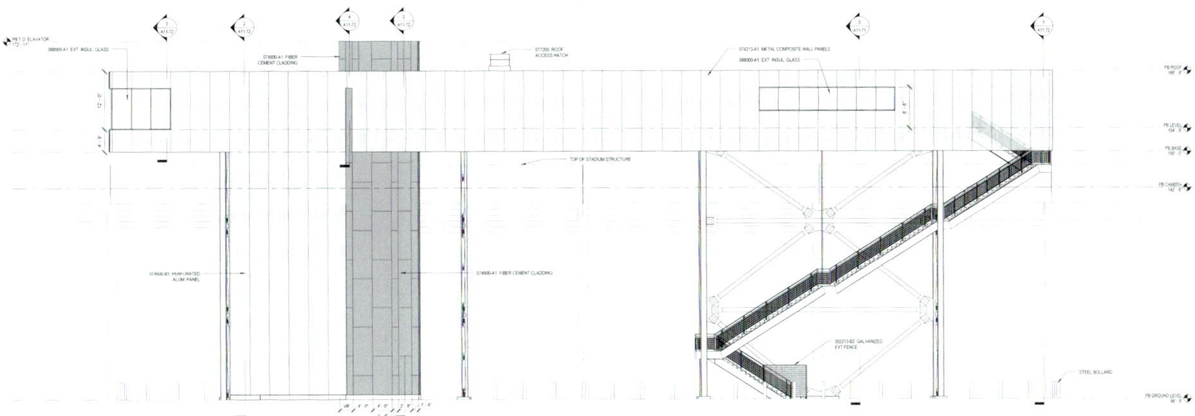

Press box - West elevation

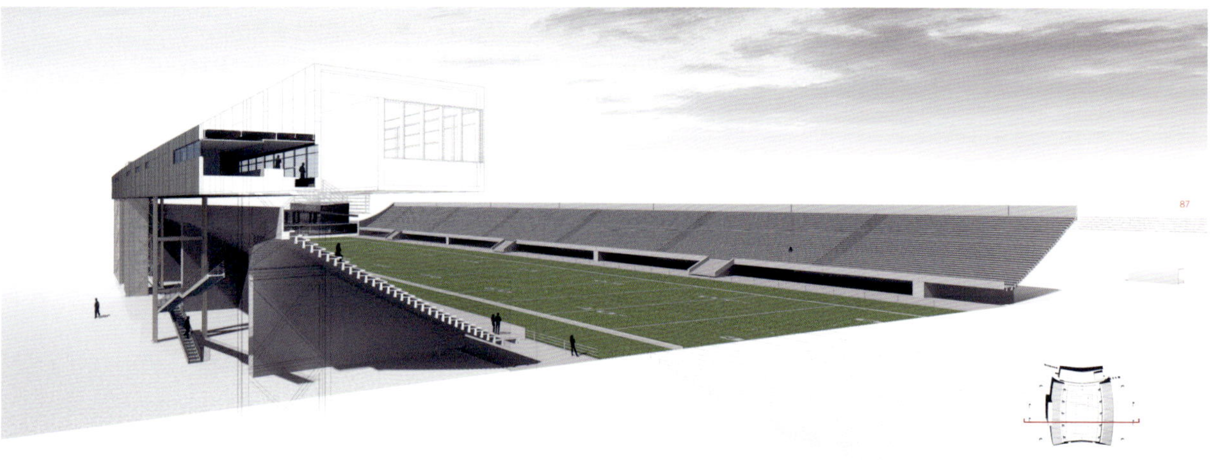

Site section through press box and stadium

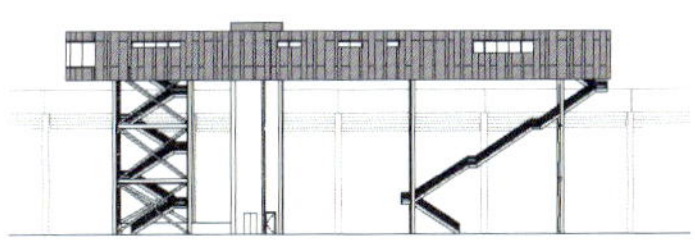

West elevation

View of new press box from southeast

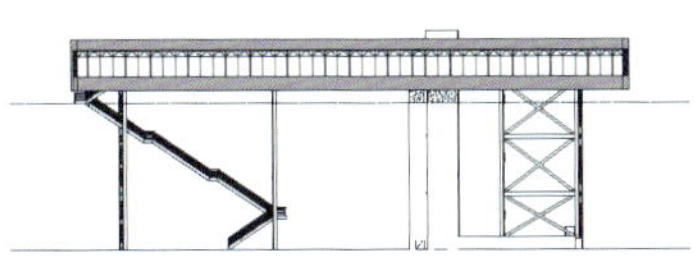

East elevation

View of new press box from east

Elevation

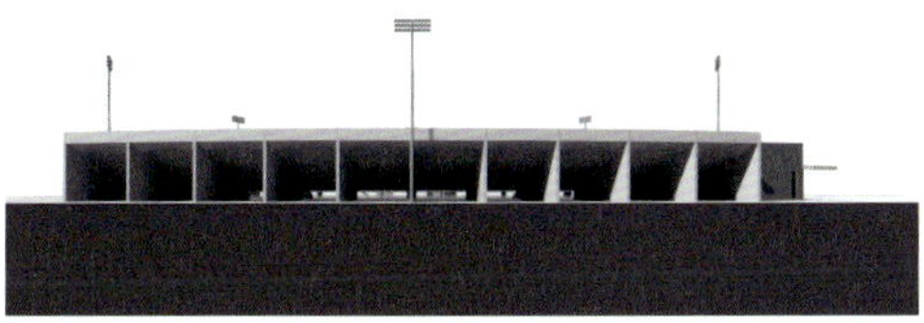

West elevation

UMASS

foundation

FOOTBALL PERFORMANCE CENTER

STOREFRONT INSTALLATION

Boston Architectural College
Boston, Massachusetts

Invited by Karen Nelson and Ted Landsmark, the project was a temporary installation of prototypical building components and models – made from rigid interlocking panels of wood and medium density fiber board – to explore the potential for creating new integral structural and spatial opportunities through digital design and fabrication processes. It is seen as a form of applied design research accepting the implication that these processes will allow architects greater control of building processes as we move from design to utility. It was erected in the McCormack Gallery of the Boston Architectural College in Boston, Massachusetts during the spring of 2009 and includes an extensive exhibition of our models, drawings, and support material.

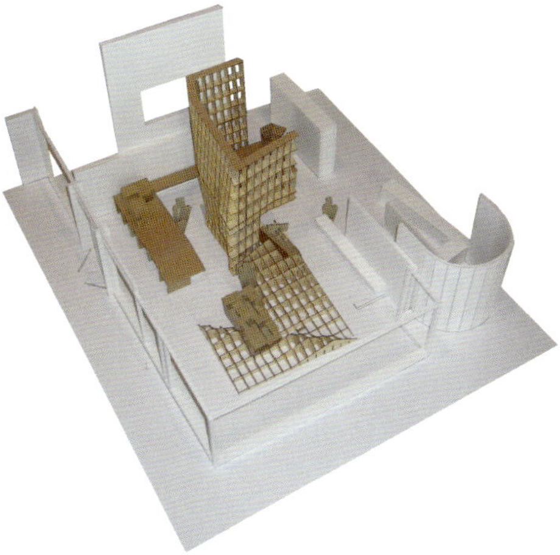

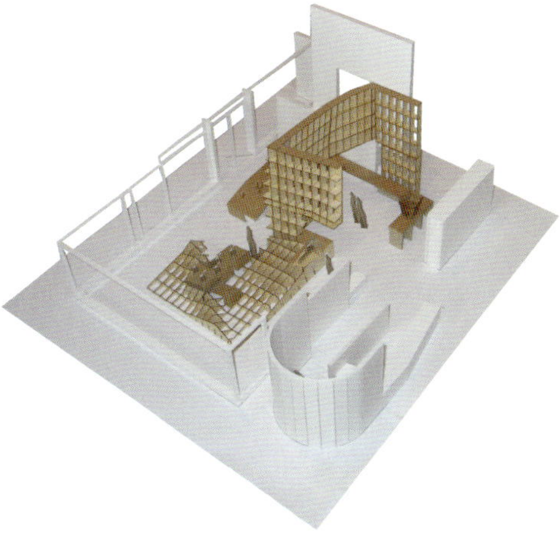

Commonplaces

Commonplaces

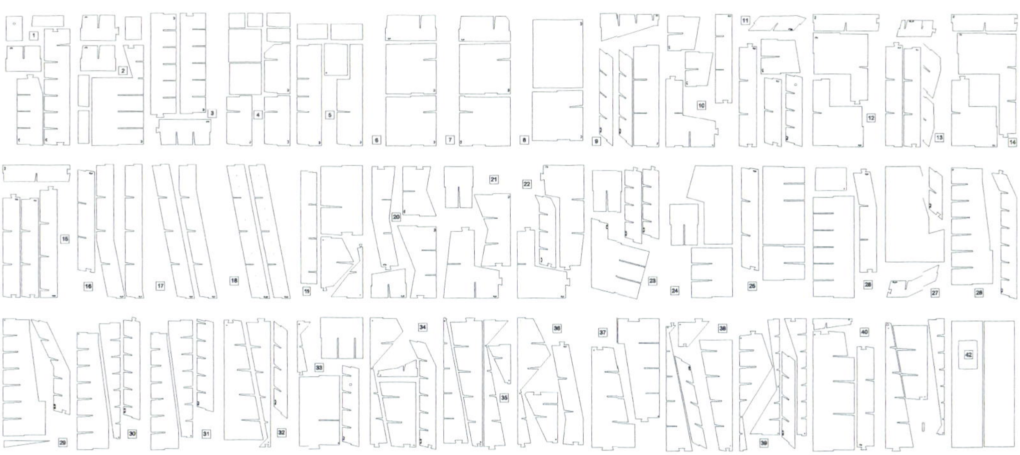

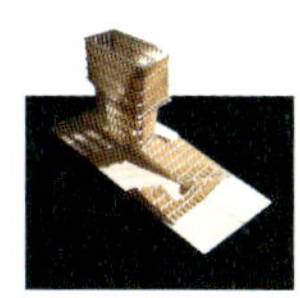

Study model of assembled components

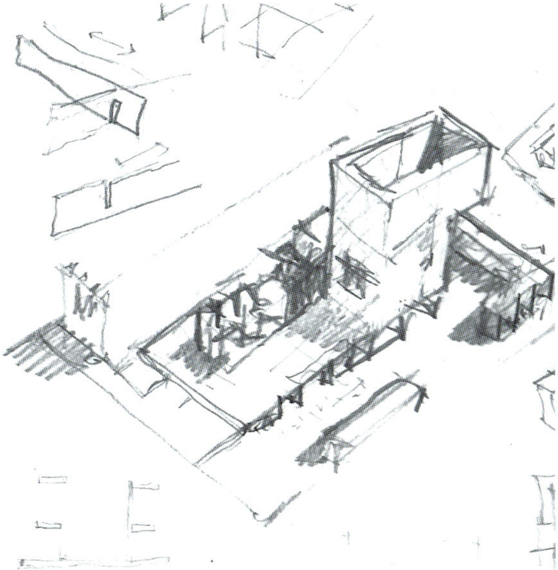

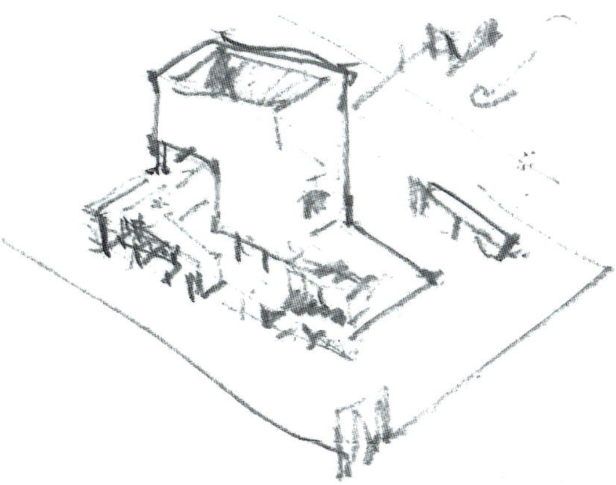

GRANT RECITAL HALL

Brown University
Providence, Rhode Island

GRANT RECITAL HALL

Brown University
Providence, Rhode Island

Grant Recital Hall was placed within the masonry shell of a small existing carriage house on Brown University's campus in Providence, Rhode Island. The building is adjacent to Orwig Hall which houses the school's Music Department on the east side of their campus. With just 135 seats, it is an intimate venue for the department's presentation of chamber music, electronic music, and smaller jazz combos.

The acoustic performance of the space was enhanced by exposing the entire volume of the original carriage house and inserting two distinct acoustic screens within the space.

The sidewalls of the hall were shaped with a plaster and wood scrim to modulate the sound within the space and conceal mechanical systems. A perforated bamboo screen surrounds the stage to allow for sound to either reverberate off the masonry shell or be absorbed by retractable felt banners behind the openings.

The specific progression through the spaces – along with improved sightlines – promote an interaction between the performers and the audience in both a classroom and performance setting. The recital hall is supported by a new entry, lobby and reception area, and musician's room.

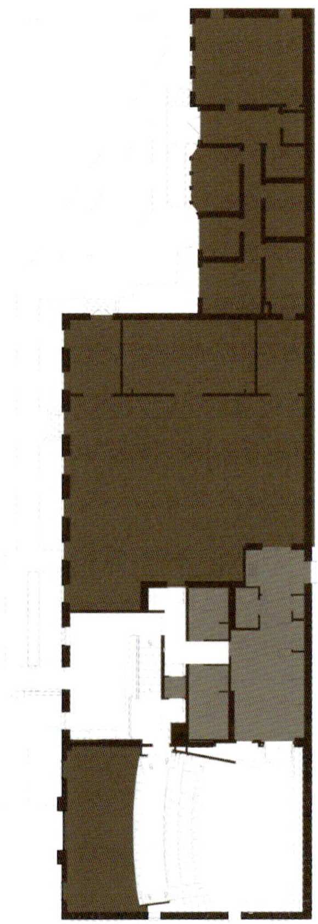

Second floor plan

GRANT RECITAL HALL
DINOSAUR ANNEX

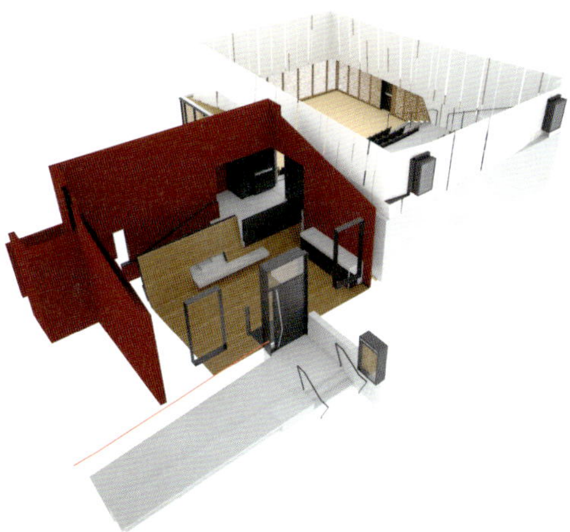

Acoustic shells

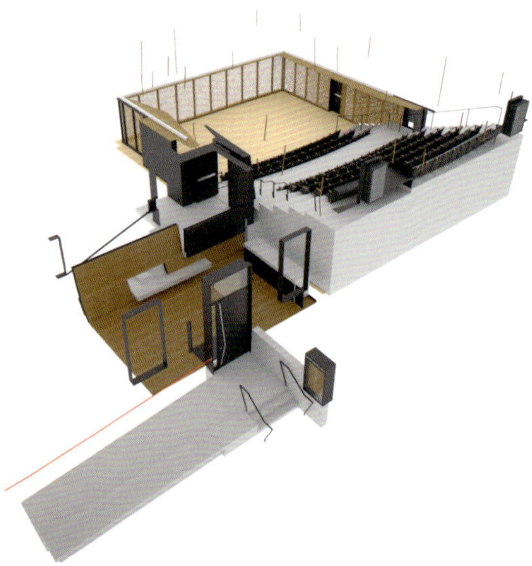

Entry sequence into grant hall

EXIT

EXIT

FULTON CONCERT HALL

Brown University
Providence, Rhode Island

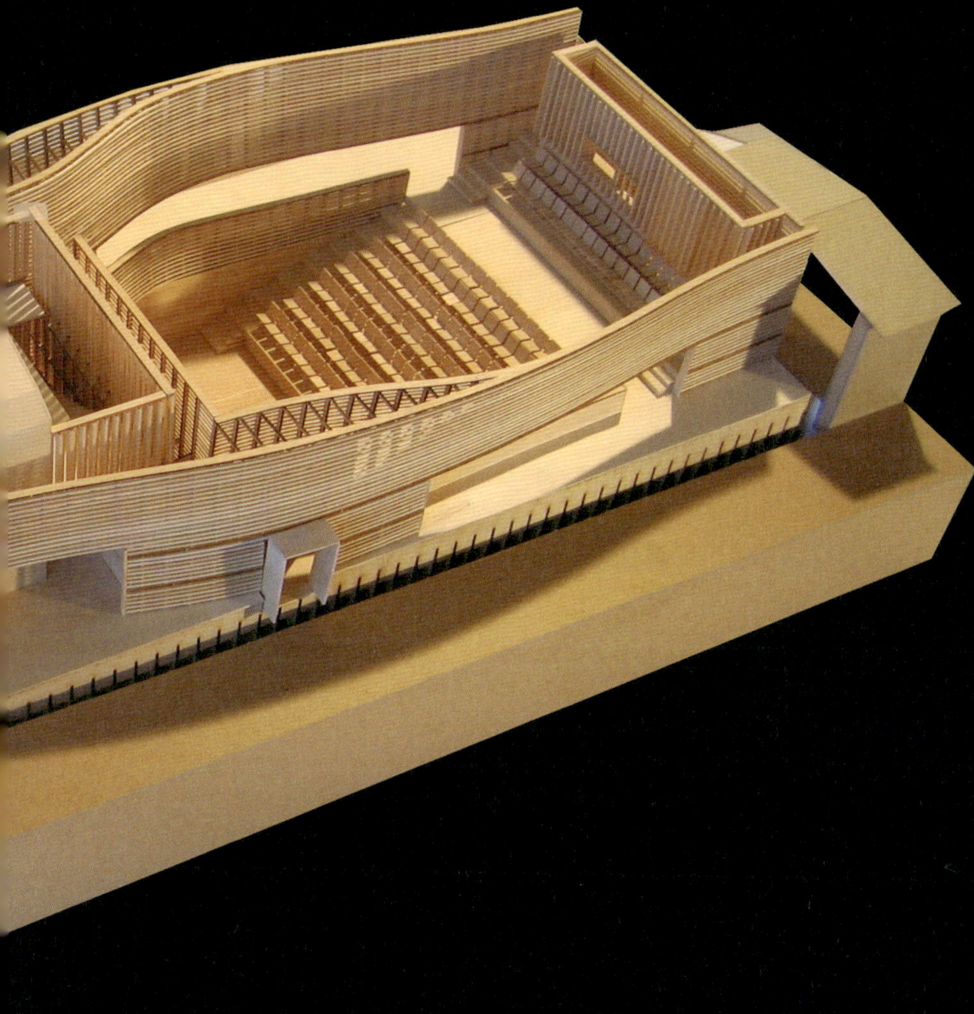

FULTON CONCERT HALL

Brown University
Providence, Rhode Island

While working on the adjacent Grant Recital Hall, the Music and Facilities Departments at Brown University requested a feasibility study for the conversion of Fulton Hall – a large rehearsal hall that is also located within a masonry carriage house on campus – into a new performance space.

Healy's team proposed that the new room be thought of as a 235-seat "acoustic instrument" inserted into the existing historically significant shell. The curved wooden slats serve as a sound baffle, reflector, and intermediary between the existing walls and the new space. Access and entry passage are then created between the old brick walls and new wood screens. The warmth of the wood and its sensuous curves would unfold behind this neoclassical facade, rewarding the audience with an acoustically refined hall combined with a rich visual experience. Storage and support for the performers are established behind the proposed stage with a new sound and AV booth in the rear of the space.

As with Grant Recital Hall and the Mill Center for the Arts, this project and acoustic study was done in collaboration with Kirkegaard Associates out of Chicago, Illinois.

Split walls / Muted shell

Site plan

Longitudinal section

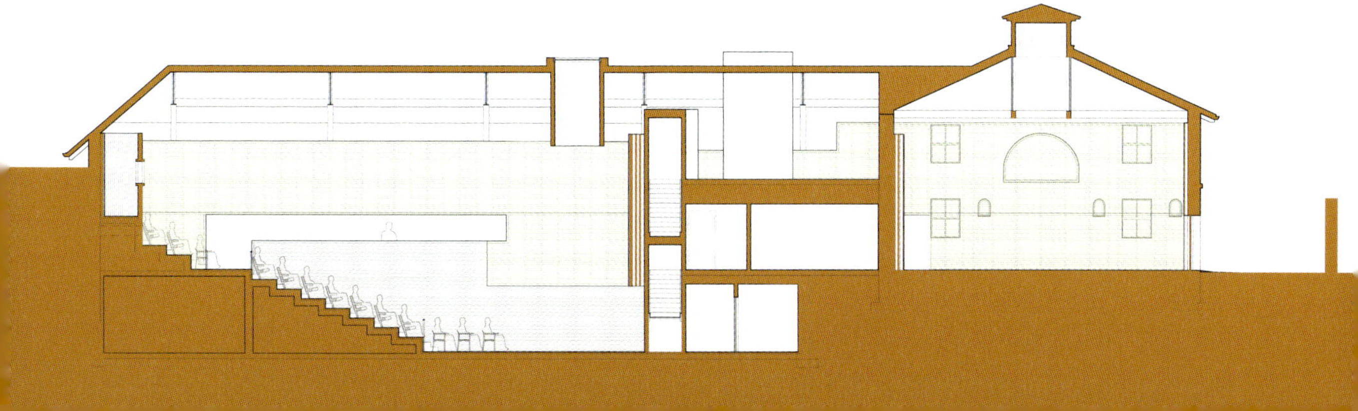

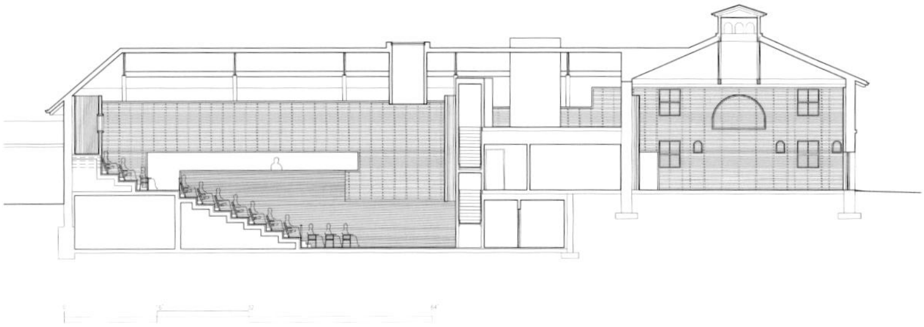

Longitudinal section

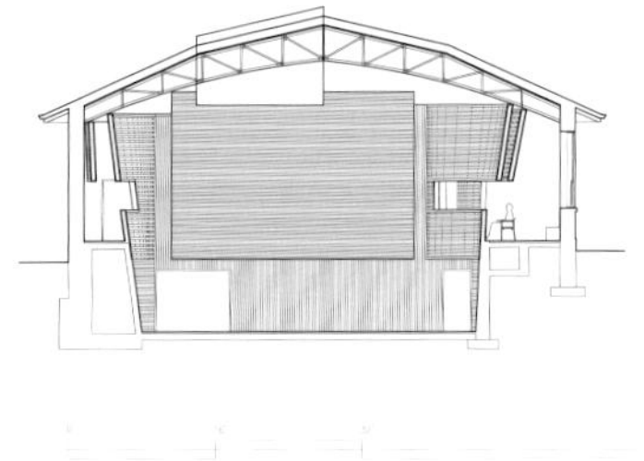

Cross section

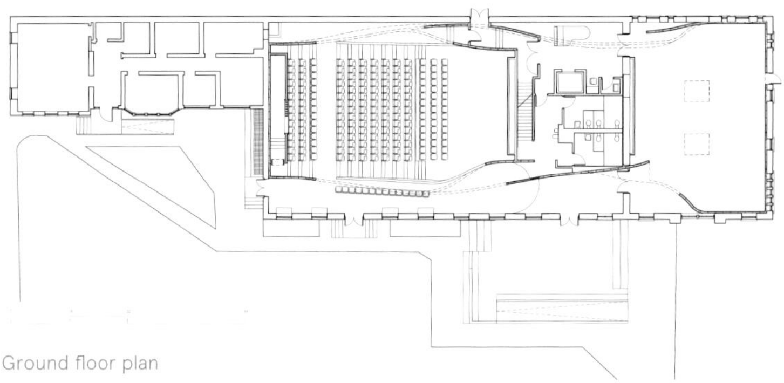

Ground floor plan

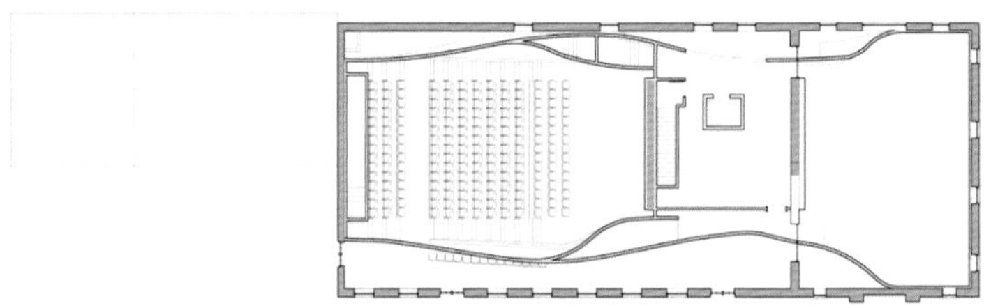

Upper level floor plan

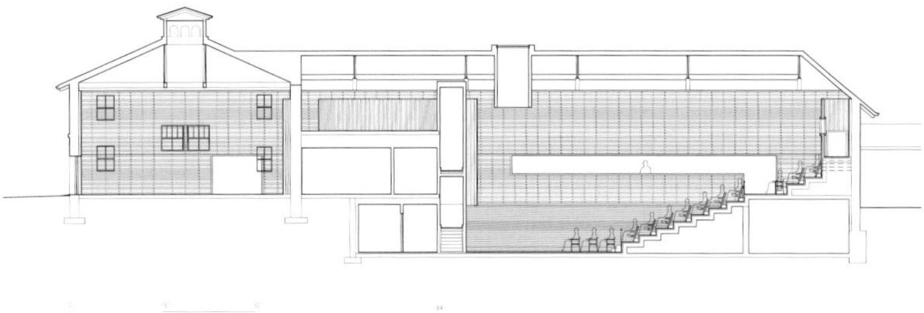

Longitudinal section

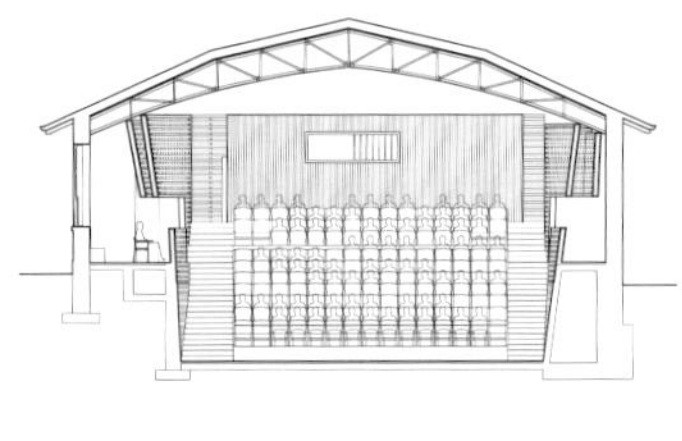

Cross section

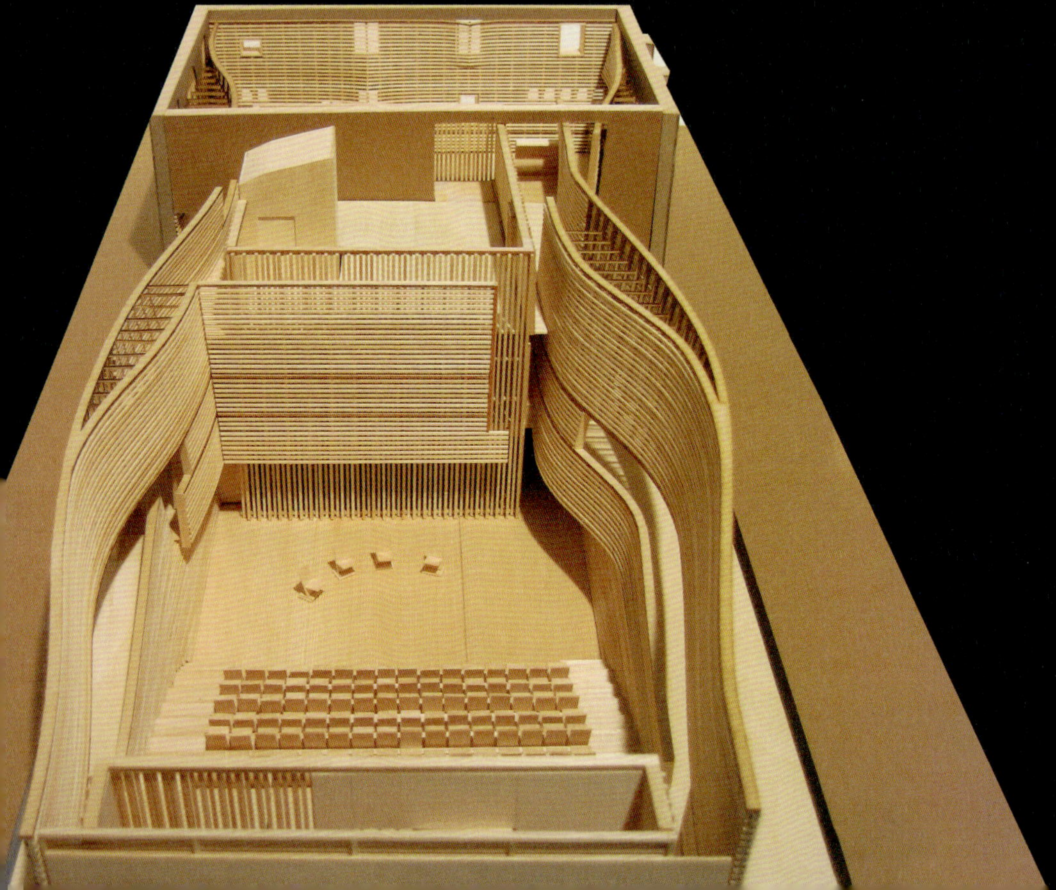

MILL CENTER FOR THE ARTS

Hendersonville, North Carolina

MILL CENTER FOR THE ARTS

Hendersonville, North Carolina

"Healy treated the entire complex as a single entity using a holistic aesthetic vision, coming together through a clear and bounded perimeter. At the heart of his design is the creation of this incredible public space. The lawn surrounding the Mill Center will serve as a cultural town square or green. The potential for this space in terms of use is incredible. It will serve as a formal connector to the community at large. The space echoes the undulating landscape of the surrounding hills and valleys through the buildings and walls, which Brian has beautifully articulated using various sized pieces of stone. The principle reference s both the strata of the natural landscape and the native architecture if the palace."
Ned Cramer – Design Jury Chair

"Brian has created a building, both modern and abstract, which in its beautiful and pure geometry echoes the civic pride represented by other buildings in town, namely the historic courthouse. This building is rooted in the landscape. It expresses Hendersonville's desire to respect the sense of place, by referencing the historic community, and to mark a place on the map by moving forward as a community. This is as vital today as it was at the origin of the town in the early nineteenth century. The building bridges time and place and retains a singular, iconic vision for the community. With its simple elegance, Brian Healy has delivered to the town of Hendersonville, a building which does a tremendous amount of work, while making it look effortless."
Design Jury Report

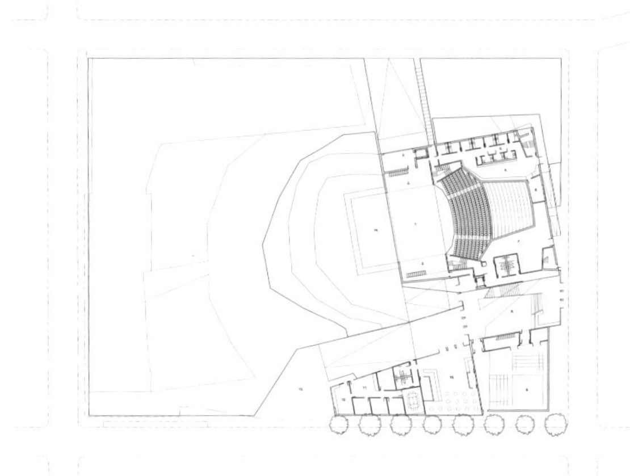

Ground floor plan

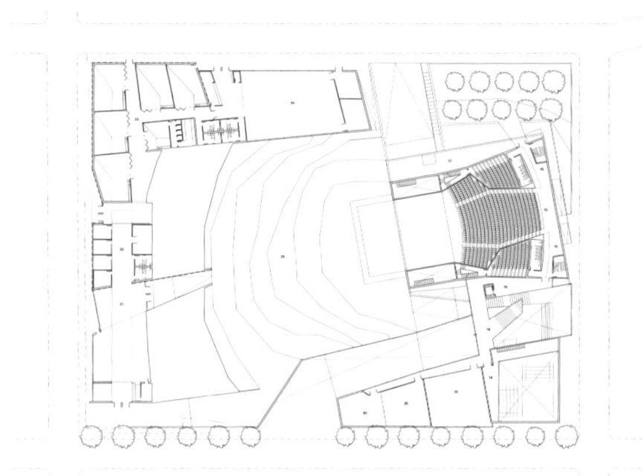

First floor plan

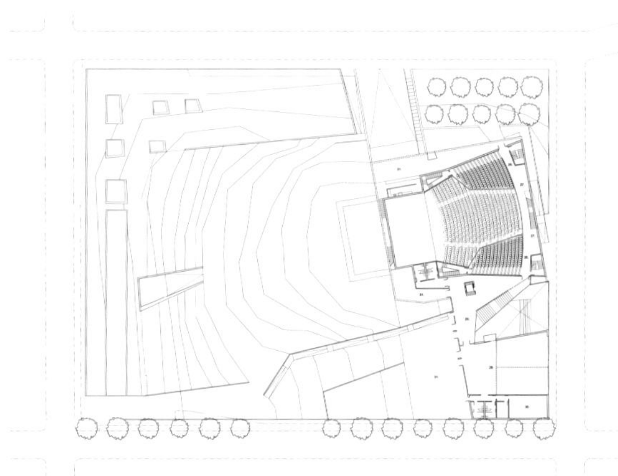

Second floor plan

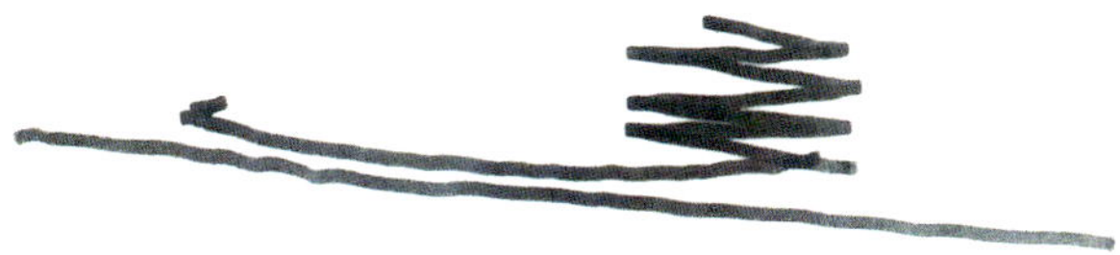

screen components
stone screen

We wanted to create a place — a strong common ground — where friends, family, artists, musicians, and all the residents of Henderson County could experience the energy of the performing and visual arts. Our design establishes an autonomous cityscape for the arts community within a single block in Hendersonville — complete with theaters, secluded arborways, a series of roof gardens, and an animated streetscape of retail, workshops, classrooms, and gallery spaces, all of which frame a grand, landscaped outdoor amphitheater.

We approached our design as an unraveling double membrane — an architectural metaphor for the transformation of the city from something opaque and dense to something lighter and translucent, revealing the deeper opportunities found in a culturally invested city. The main performance hall has inner and outer skins that conceal a hidden shell. This shell shapes the acoustics of the hall while the outer skins unravel toward the sky, revealing a spiral-like series of luminous ramps, balconies, stairs, and lounges. From these open spaces, theater goers can view the city, the mountains, and the verdant public amphitheater that rises from the central stage below.

When desirable, huge doors open the stage to the outdoor amphitheater so that performances can be enjoyed under the stars, as well as from within the theater itself. When the doors are closed, performances can be projected simultaneously onto the theater's façade, allowing anyone to bring a picnic, sit on the grass of our landscaped amphitheater, and enjoy the gifts of this vital arts community.

We believe that streets and sidewalks energize a city, so we deliberately occupied the entire perimeter of the block with inviting storefronts, generous entrances, and a wide, welcoming promenade off the Oklawaha Greenway that leads into our central public space.

—Brian Healy

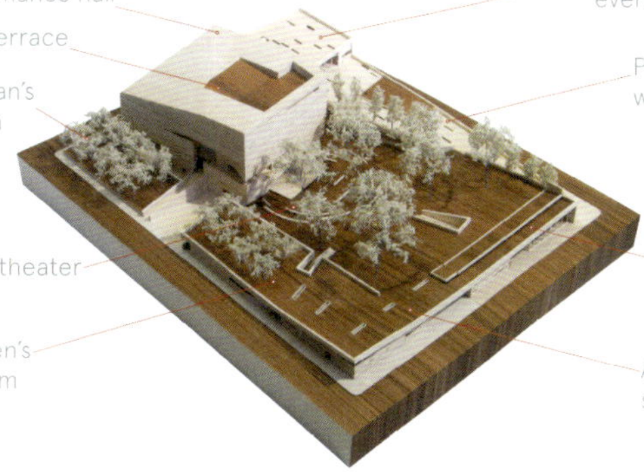

Northwest aerial

Southwest aerial

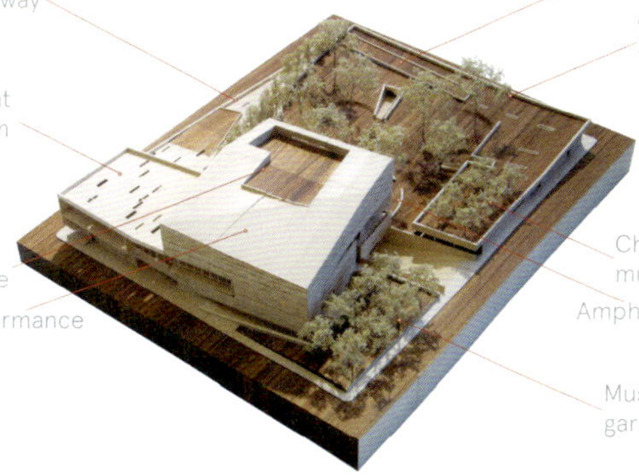

Northest aerial

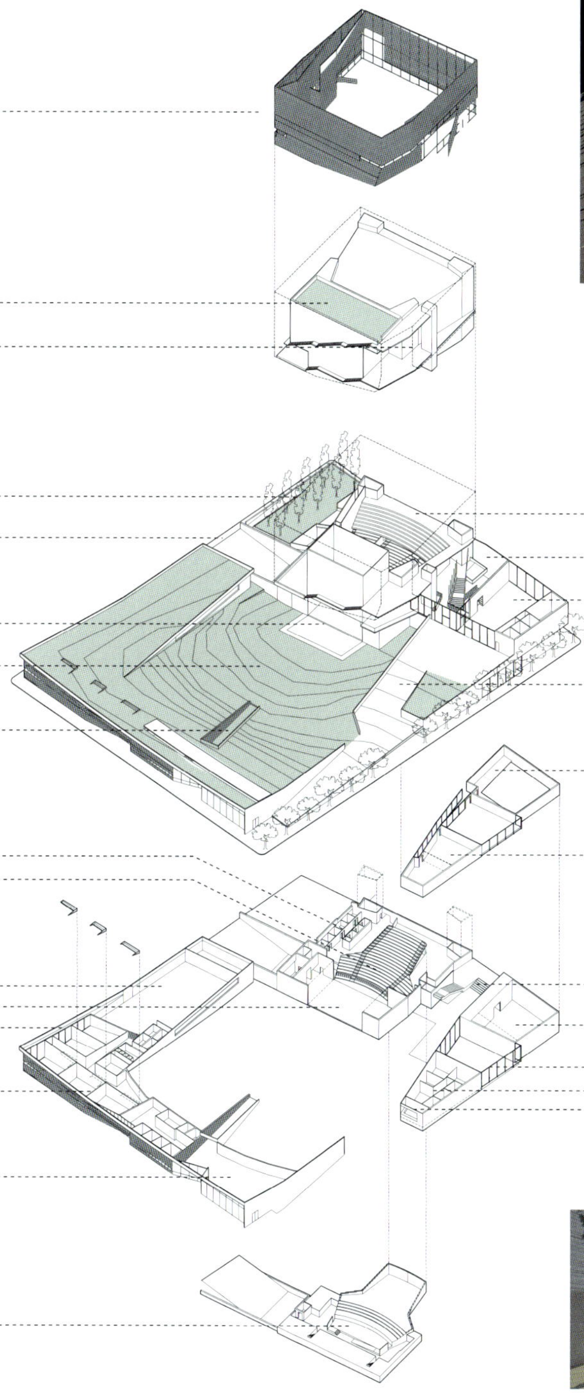

Enclosure for Main Hall
Roof Garden
Stairway to Roof Garden
Sculpture Court
Loading
Stage
Outdoor Amphitheater
Access from Art Gallery
Balcony of Main Hall
Main Lobby
Event Hall
Promenade from Greenway
Upper Level of Black Box
Classrooms
Musician's Rooms
Main Performance Seating
Childrens Museum
Stage
Art Classrooms
Art Studios
Art Gallery
Main Lobby
Black Box Theater
Cafeteria and Gift Shop
Administration
Box Office
Orchestra Pit

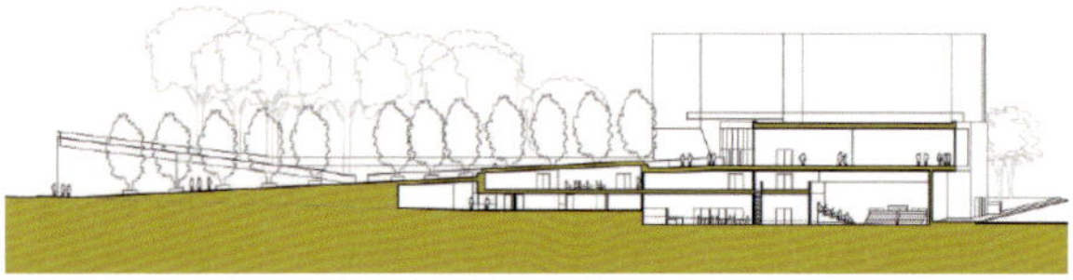

Section through box office - black box

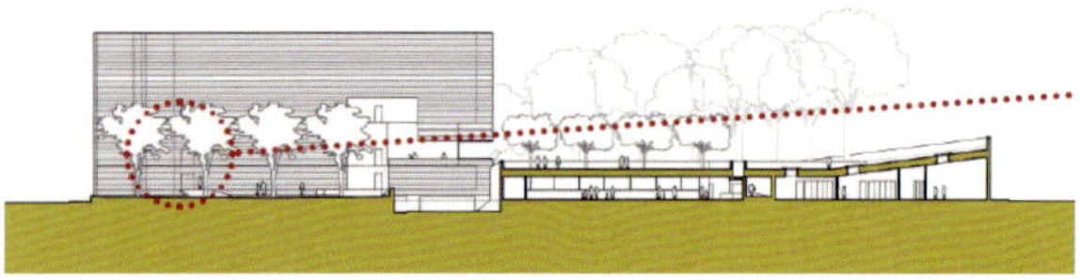

Section through children's museum

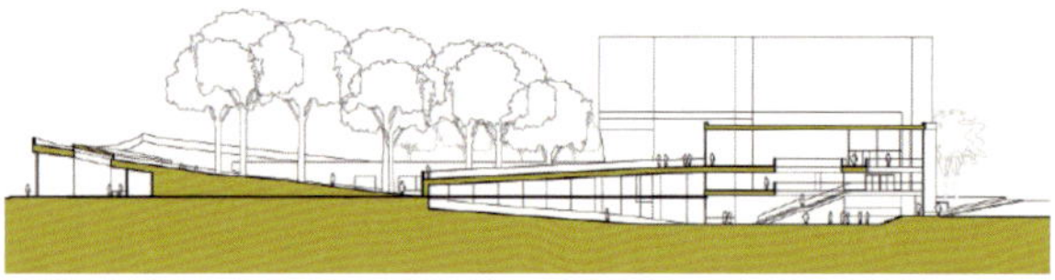

Section through ramp - lobby

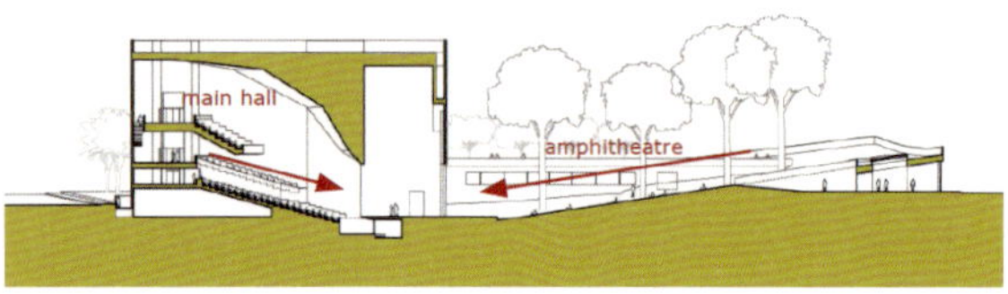

Stage open to interior and exterior seating

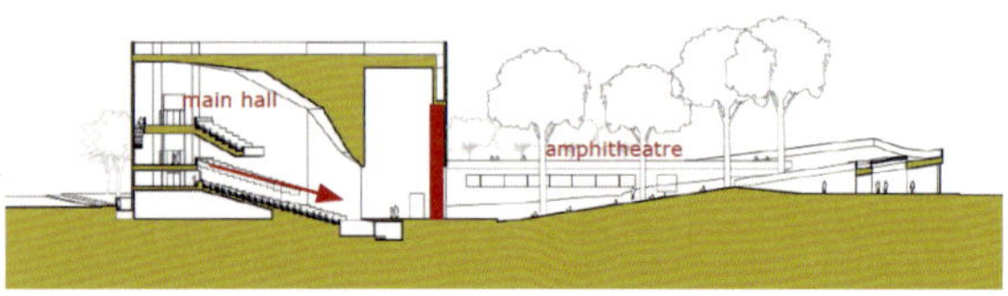

Stage open to interior seating

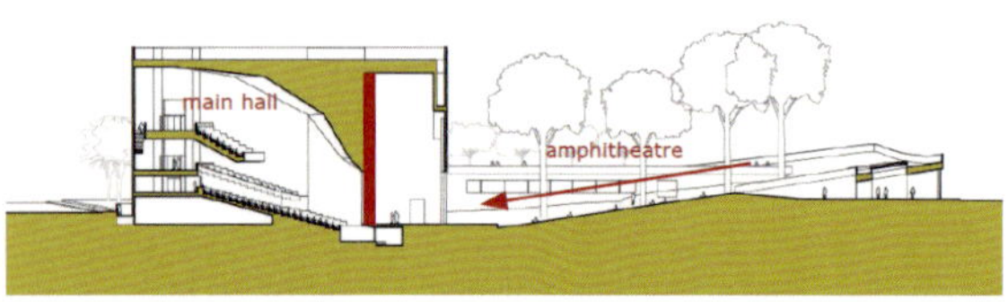

Stage open to exterior seating

ROSE KENNEDY GREENWAY

Boston, Massachusetts

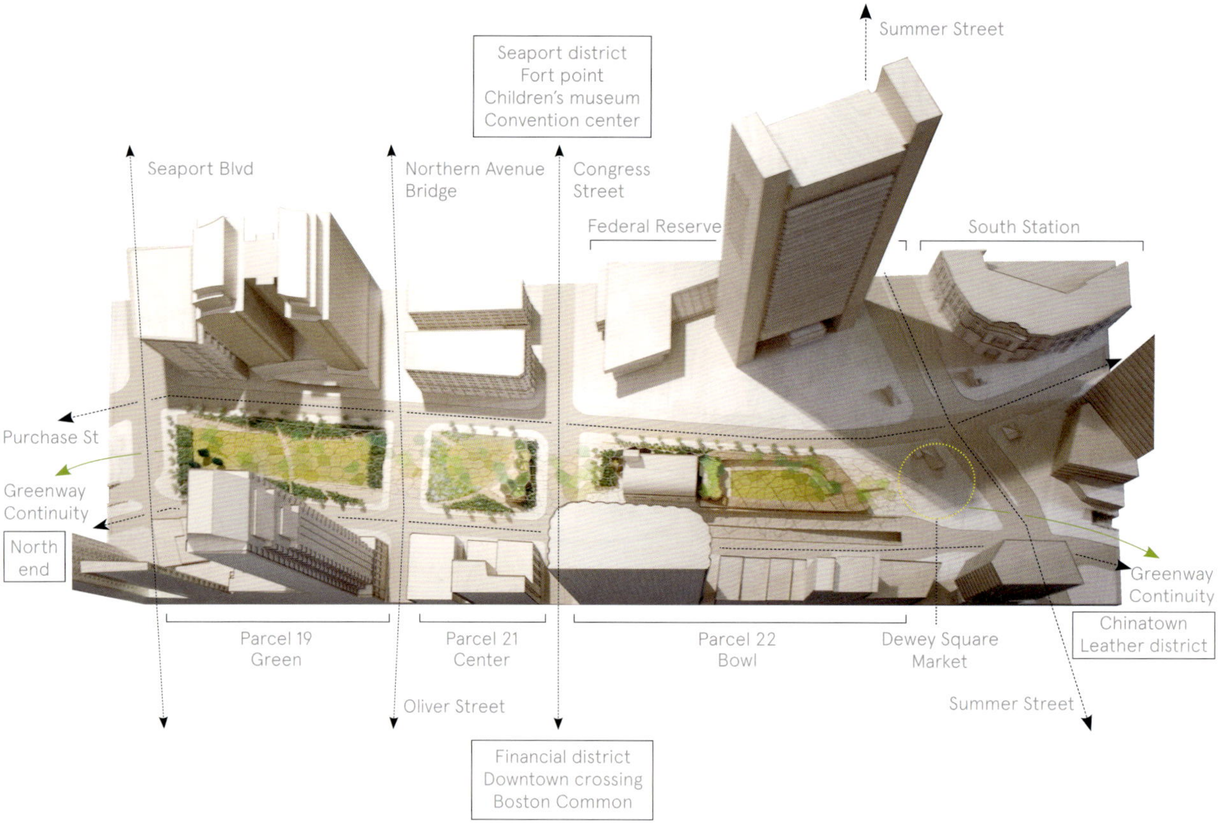

ROSE KENNEDY GREENWAY

Boston, Massachusetts

The Rose Fitzgerald Kennedy Greenway was created along the ground left behind when the Central Artery – an elevated highway that ran through downtown Boston for forty years – was placed underground as part of the 'Big Dig' initiative. This displacement created the potential for a new 27 acre greenway that meanders through Boston from Chinatown along the harbor's edge up to the North End. It also afforded an opportunity to re-connect neighbors and the city to its harbor.

In the Spring of 2007, The Greenway Conservancy asked Ed Schlossberg and Brian Healy to coordinate another design initiative called the Design Panel for Interim Programming, to study and create new possibilities for temporary programming on the three parcels adjacent to South Station and Dewey Square. Along with members of the Conservancy, they established a panel of professionals including Laura Solano, Meejin Yoon, Matt Johnson, Linda Wheelock, Matt Coogan, and John Fernandez to explore new capabilities for the sites that would be transient, environmentally alert, and able to promote broad social interaction for both citizens and visitors to Boston. They were asked to imagine a place rich with activities both day and night as well as appropriate for each of our New England seasons.

The proposals included a temporary stadium in front of South Station with ice skating in the winter and movie nights in the summer, an open farmer's market, a temporary information pavilion with a large open lawn for concerts, and a light cable net covering the entire site to provide periodic areas of shade and support the infrastructure necessary for performances and exhibitions.

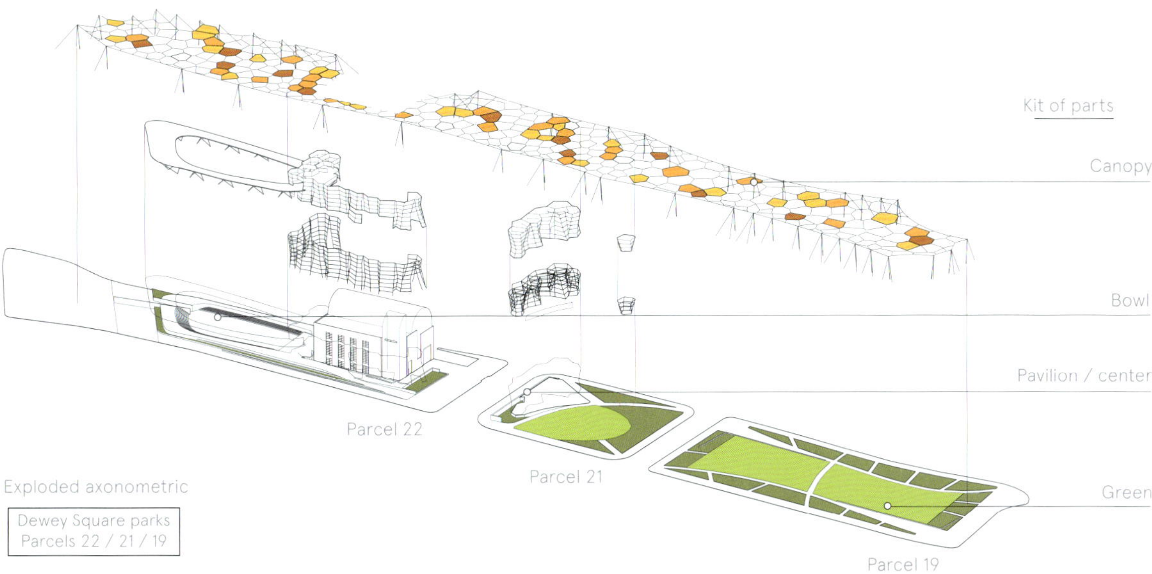
Kit of parts
Canopy
Bowl
Pavilion / center
Green
Parcel 22
Parcel 21
Parcel 19
Exploded axonometric
Dewey Square parks
Parcels 22 / 21 / 19

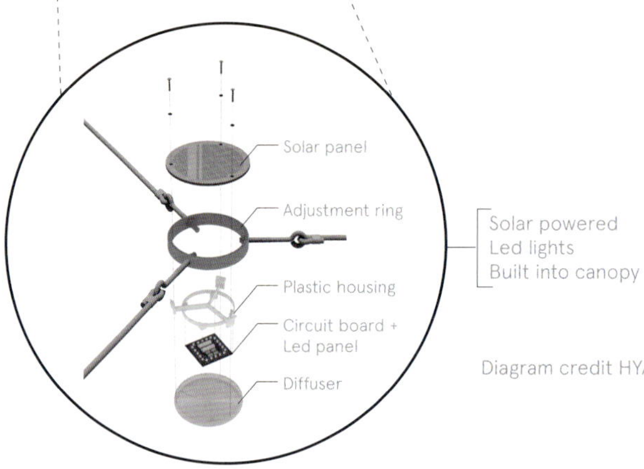

Diagram credit HYA

Sky down + ground up / Program variations through surface + canopy

Night aerial view of Dewey Square parks from Oliver street

Sporting events in the bowl

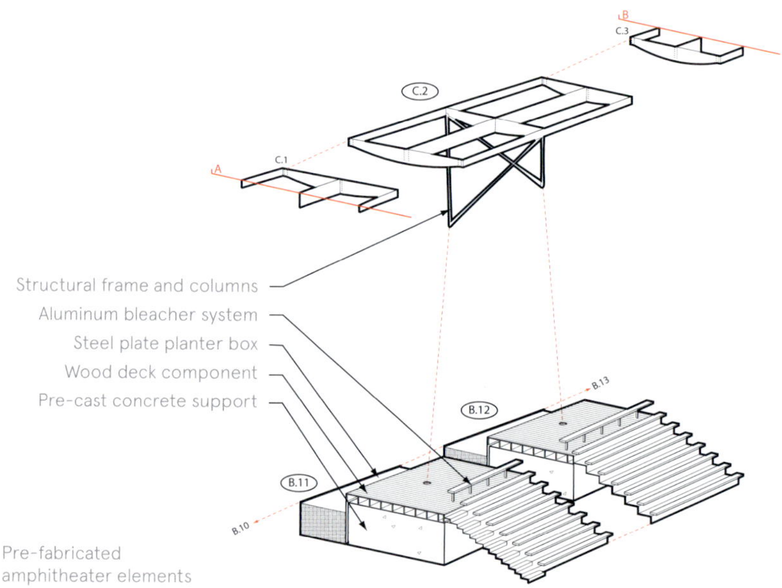

Pre-fabricated
amphitheater elements

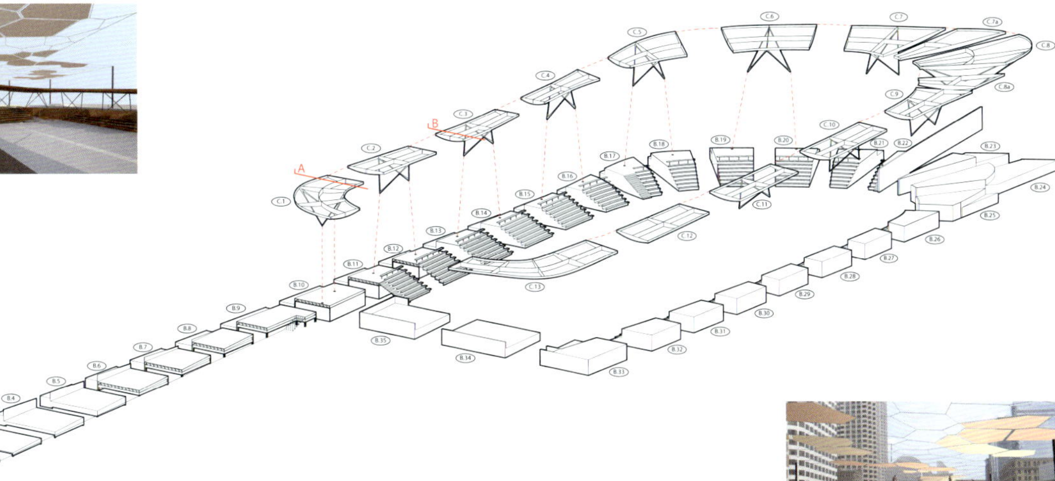

Layout of pre-fabricated pieces for amphitheater

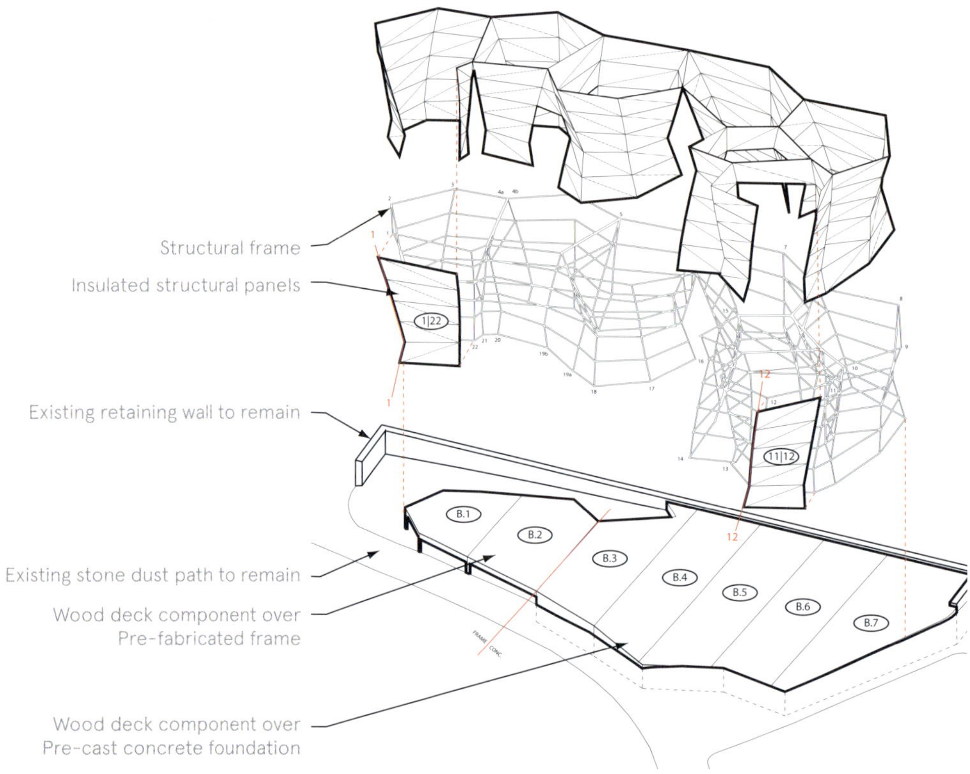

Pre-fabricated pavilion elements

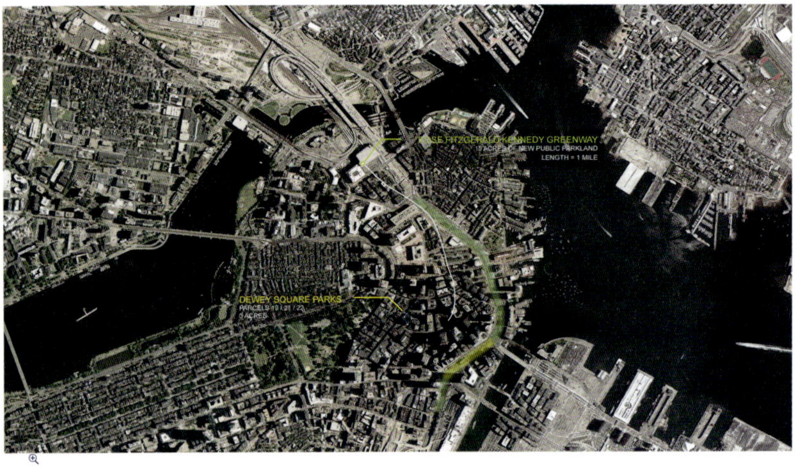

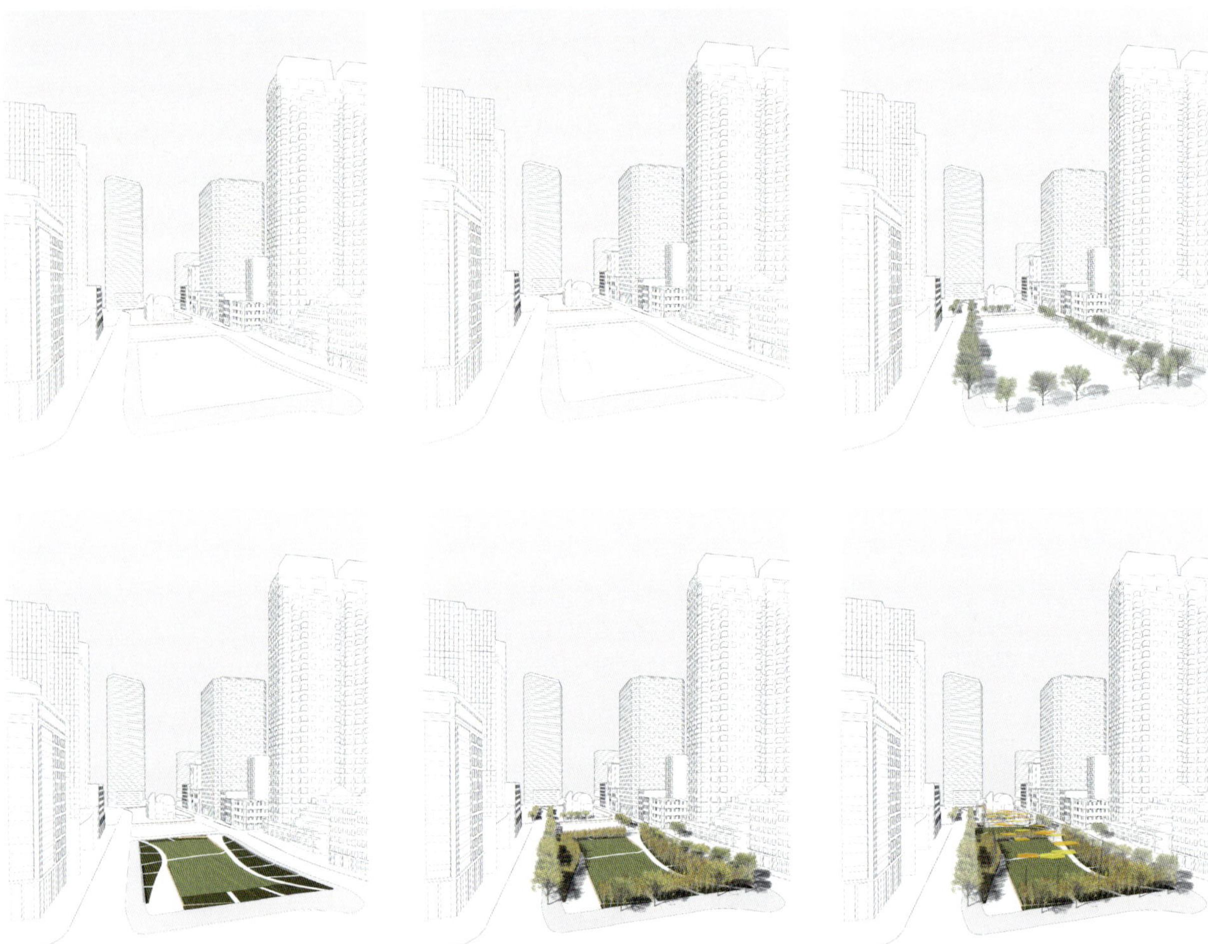

Site Development Diagrams

FLW VISITORS' CENTER

Frank Lloyd Wright's Darwin Martin House
Buffalo, New York

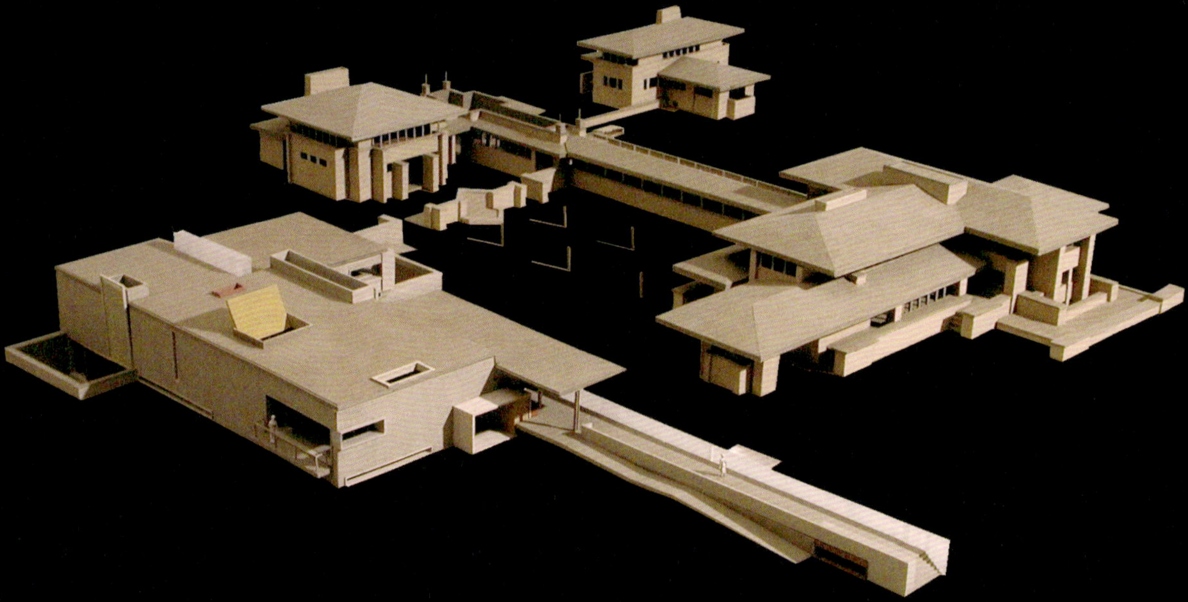

FLW VISITORS' CENTER

Frank Lloyd Wright's Darwin Martin House
Buffalo, New York

Our American architecture - homes, landscapes, workplaces, neighborhoods - was changed forever by what happened in Buffalo one hundred years ago. Frank Lloyd Wright's Martin House and Larkin Building sprang to life and seemed to leap across boundaries of social demarcation. These buildings were public and private, communal and individualistic, homespun and heroic.

Our present-day challenge — in considering the design of a Visitors' Center — is to extend this rich, multiform legacy beyond the insular Wasmuth plan into the myriad characteristics and seductions of the Martin House, we should incorporate another: an acknowledgement of life as it is now lived in the rejuvenated East Parkside neighborhood of Buffalo. By paying tribute to the present as well as the past, we can ensure that the restored Martin House Complex and its Visitors' Center continue to contribute to the unfolding evolution of the American landscape.

The vitality of a neighborhood is locked to the shared communal spaces of street and sidewalk. We propose a direct link to this public realm by extending the building out to engage the sidewalk. In doing so, we create a raised exterior terrace for gathering overlooking the historic entrance to the Martin House. This terrace becomes a place for relaxation and reflection; a stream of such contemplative spaces will wind through the Visitors' Center and spread across the entire campus. The Visitors' Center itself is conceived as a moment of repose to compliment the ongoing narrative of intense energy and constant motion which animates the Martin House.

—Brian Healy

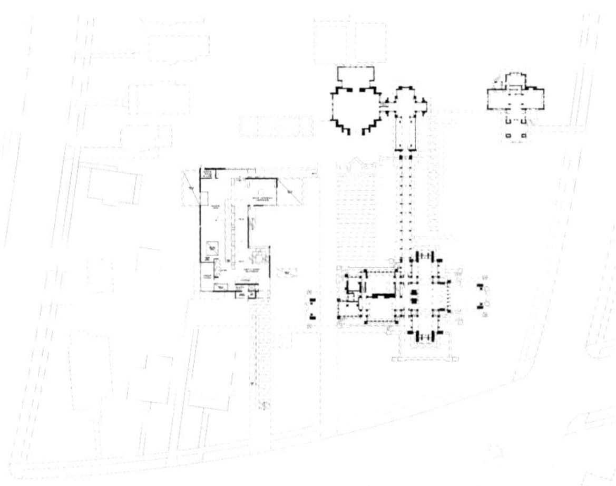

Site plan

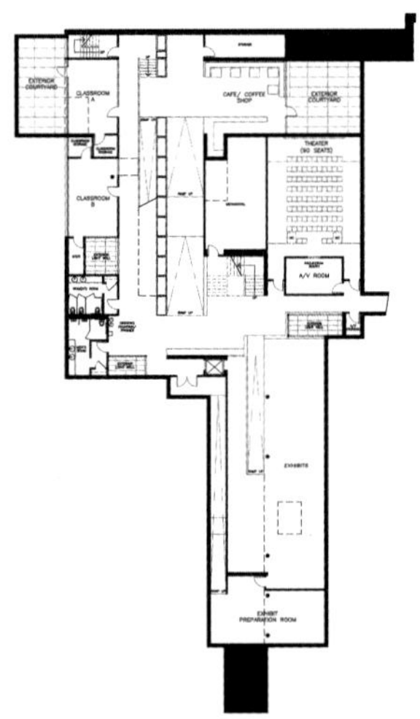

Lower level plan

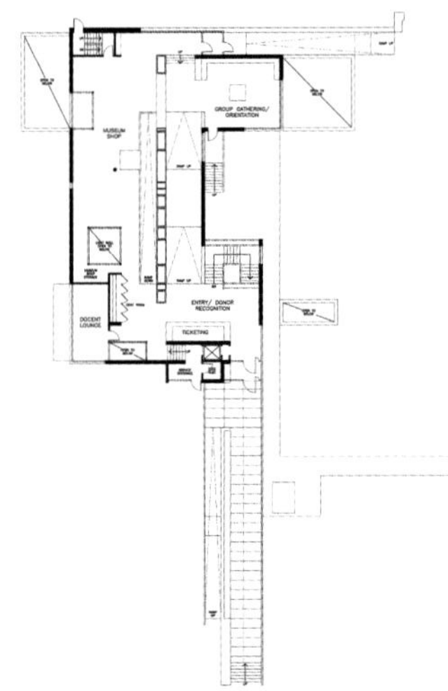

Ground level plan

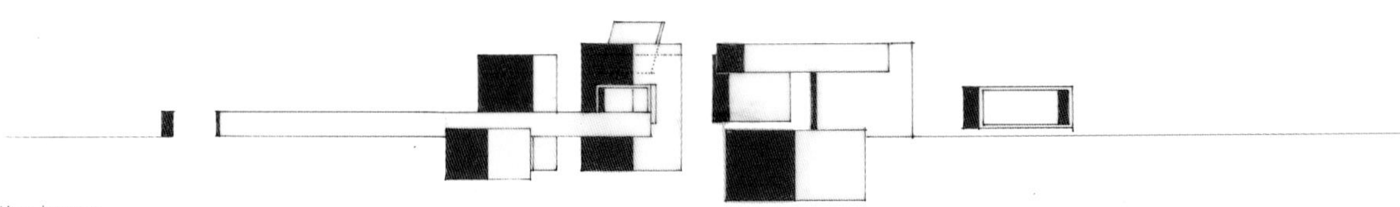

Floating boxes

Axonometrics

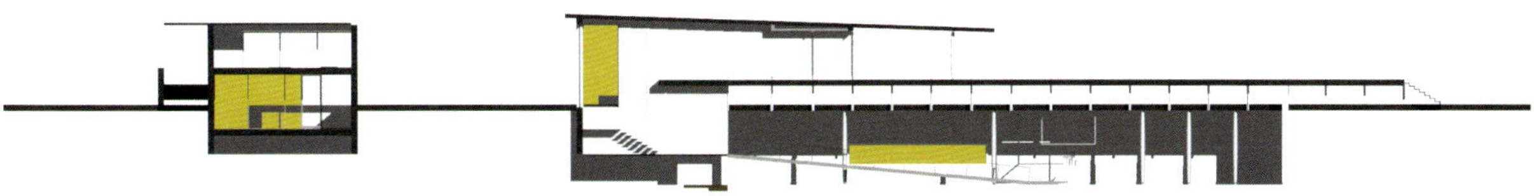

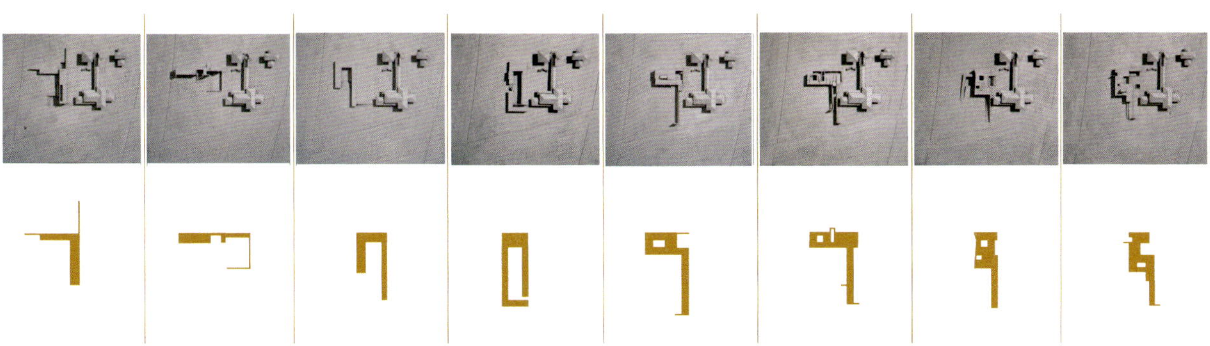

RURAL POOL HALL

Boone, North Carolina

RURAL POOL HALL

Boone, North Carolina

While at the MacDowell Art Colony in Peterborough, New Hampshire, Healy was asked by a fellow colonist asked to design a pool hall that could sponsor regional tournaments and serve as a social center for the community including teenagers in the afternoon and older citizens in the evening. The site was 3.6 acres of agricultural land on a highway transforming itself from a rural route into a commercial strip.

The artifacts of different periods of development can be found along the highway — barns, motels, billboards, impromptu churches, and service garages — and they provide a palette ripe for interpretation. This was another highway that could offer a syntax to connect our new building to the site's agrarian past, as well as its suburban future. Like each of its neighbors, the building stands alone — in a field — set back from the road. Unlike them, this building's form and its signage are hybridized: they are part urban, part rural. A basic rural shed provides the main volume for the pool hall but it is interrupted by more blunt urban forms: flat-roofed volumes topped by a prominent sign, reminiscent of a steeple or billboard.

This hybridization continues inside with the multi-leveled section. While many buildings in this rural environment have the luxury of spreading out to accommodate their program on a single level, we introduced a more dense sectional quality that provides opportunities for dynamic programmatic overlap.

Both the section and form of the building set up differing narratives about the ways the pool hall can be used throughout the day. Even the light — from midday to night — turns the spaces from outward in. During the day, the shed feels light and lofty. At night, selective lighting focuses moments within each space, so one moves between the shadows around the illuminated moments.

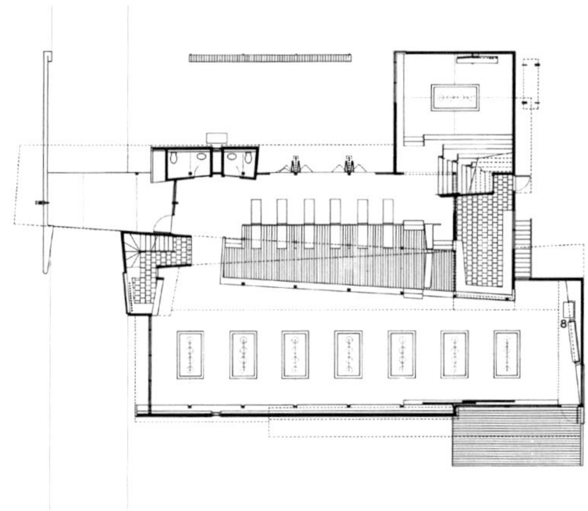

Ground floor plan

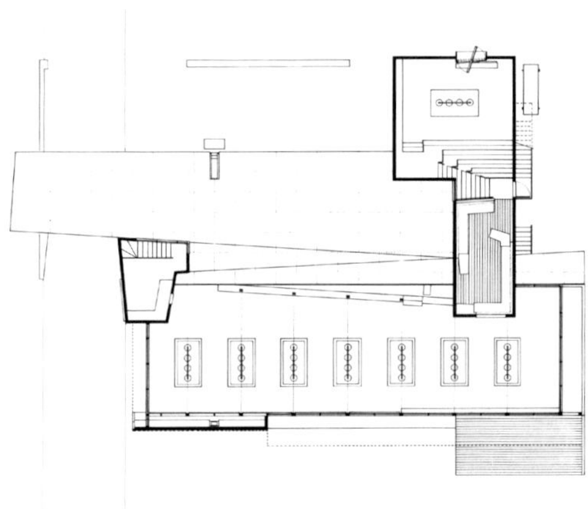

Upper level floor plan

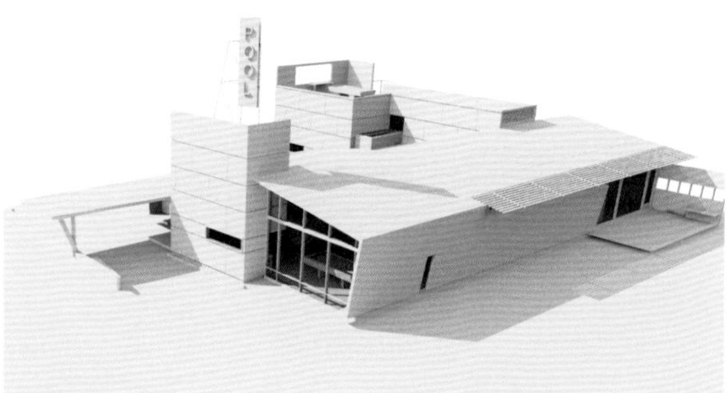

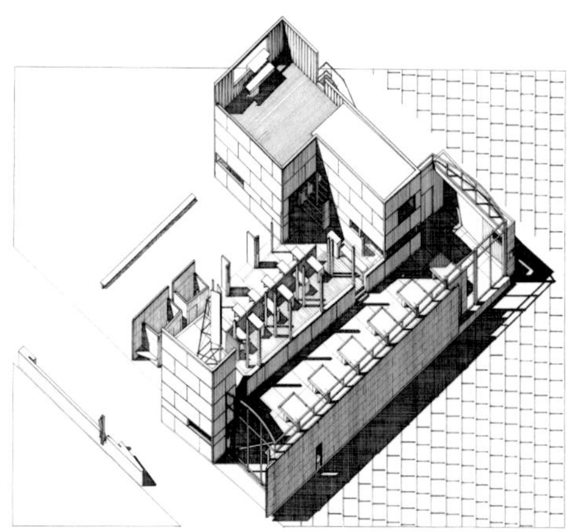

POOL

URBAN PREP SCHOOL

Boston, Massachusetts

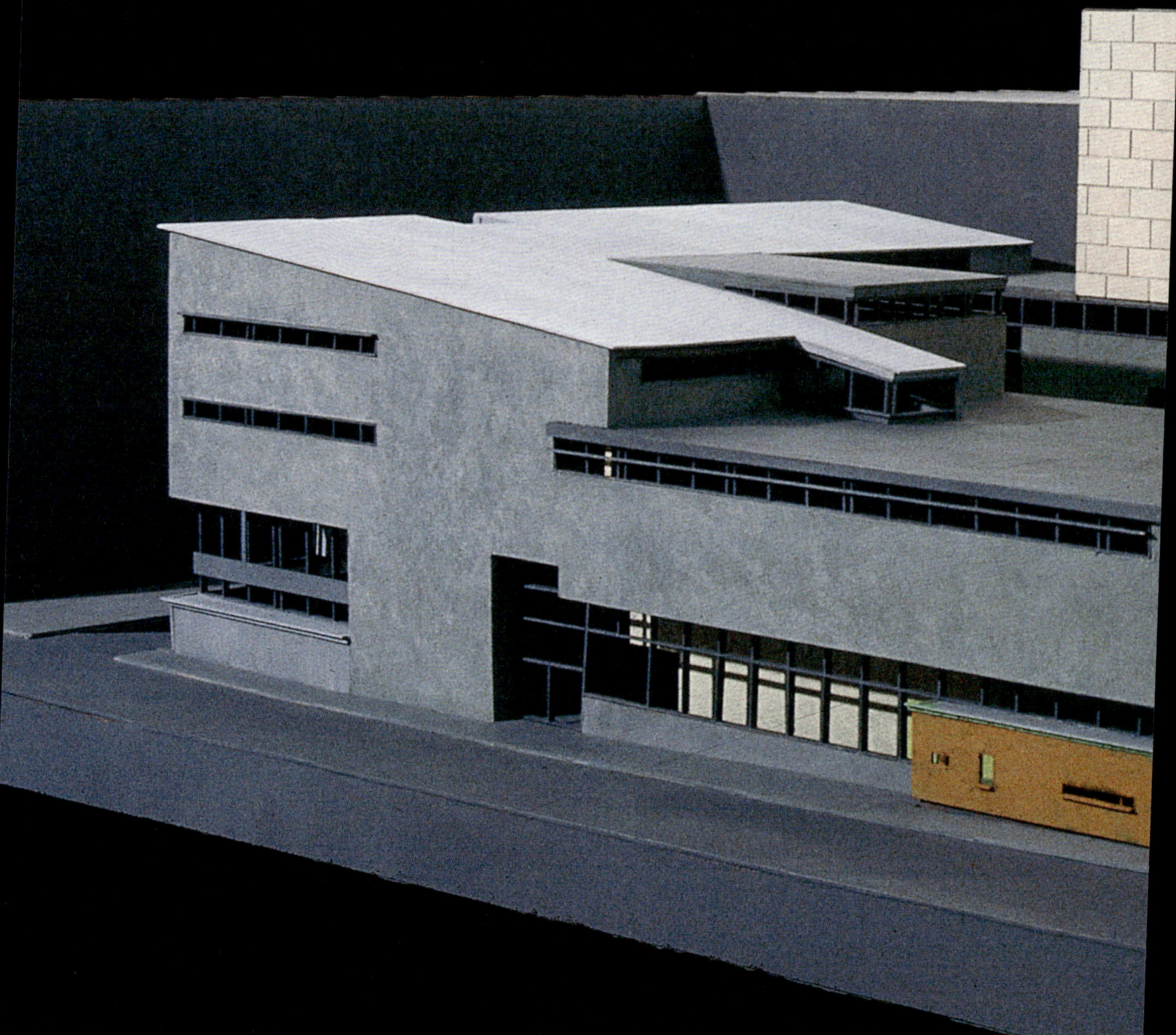

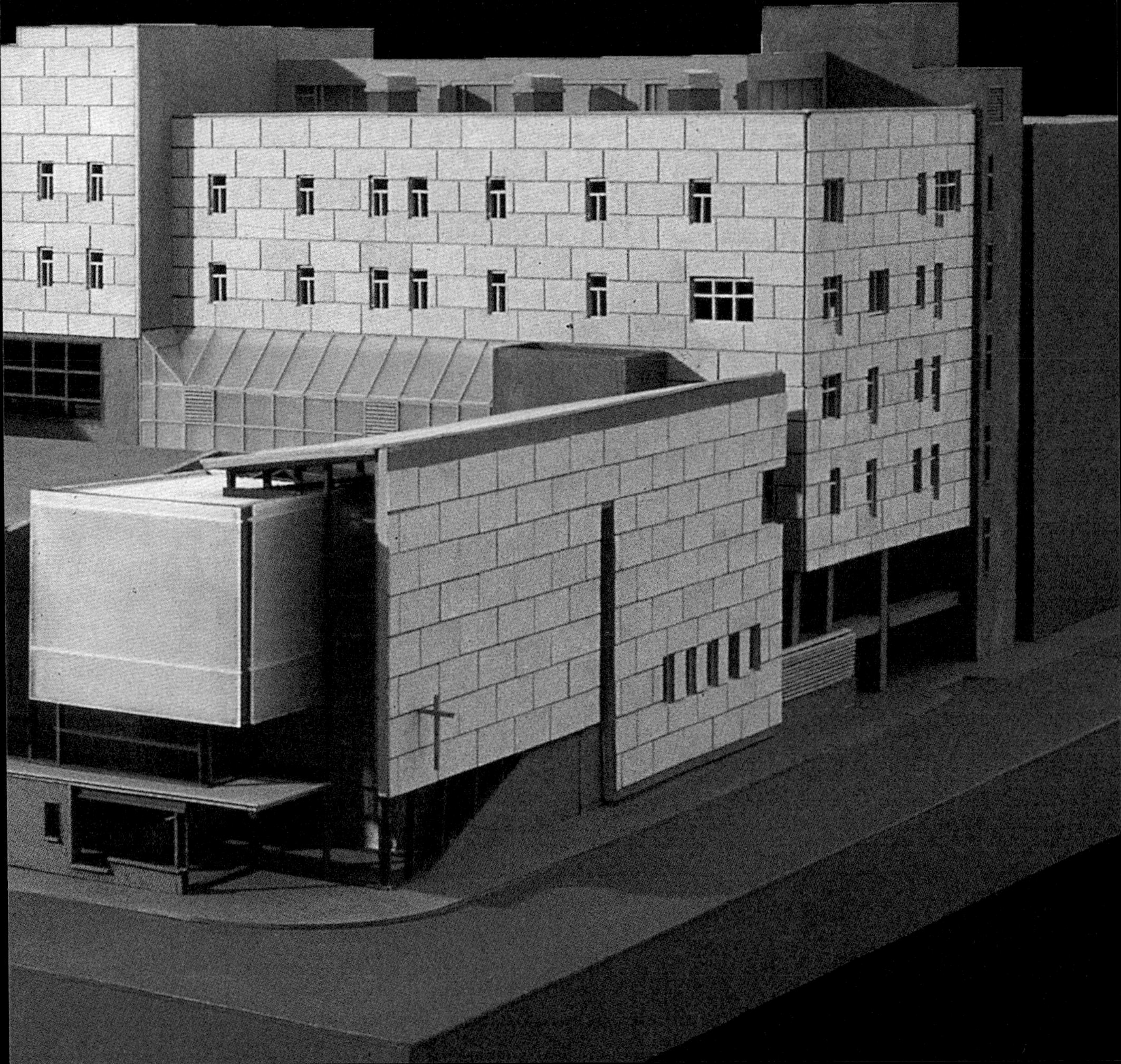

URBAN PREP SCHOOL

Boston, Massachusetts

Don Bosco Technical High School was opened in the 1920s as an all boys' Catholic high school to serve the residents of the Boston area. Don Bosco was operated by the Salesian order based in Rome. Which operates schools throughout the world based on the religious and educational philosophy of Don Bosco.

The school was located on Tremont Street in an area between Chinatown, Bay Village, and the South End of Boston. The school had expanded in both the 1970s and 1980s to complete the edge of the block between Tremont and Washington Streets. There were plans before the Boston Redevelopment Authority to develop the remaining open areas into a cinema complex, residential towers, and a hotel through the proposed sale of land and demolition of some of their facilities. The Salesian order had consolidated the site for the school to 40,000 square feet on the corner of Oak and Washington Streets. The site is located above a portion of the Orange Line of the MBTA Subway System.

Don Bosco Technical High School was trying to take advantage of the development of this area to reconfigure and renovate both their facilities and educational emphasis. In the process, the school had changed from a technical school to a preparatory school. There were 200 students while the new facility anticipated an increase to a co-educational population of 500 students.

The original 1920s building was to be demolished along with approximately thirty percent of the 1970s addition. The remaining structure including the gymnasium would then be encapsulated within the new design. The main entrance would be relocated to the corner of Washington and Oak Streets. The athletic facilities would remain on the lower level while a stair hail would lead up to the classrooms, offices, and chapel. The main classroom level would be located on the third level with an exterior courtyard with the fourth level is dedicated to the science laboratories.

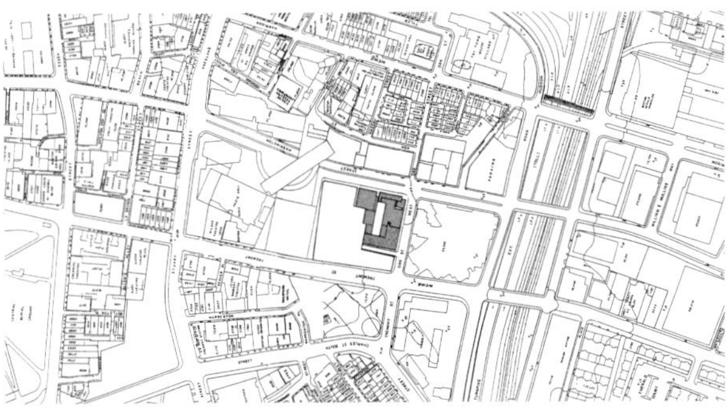

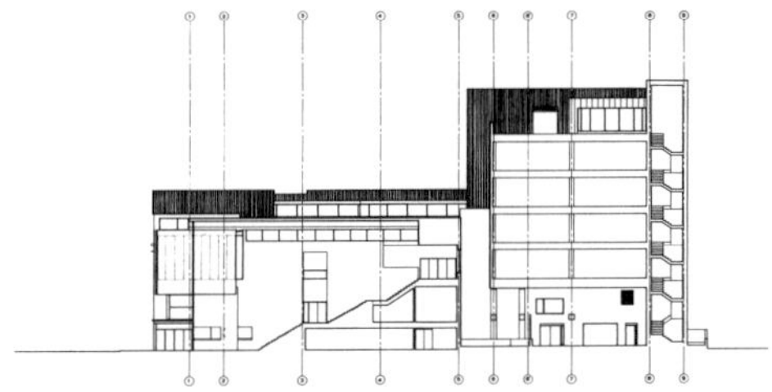

Section - Main stair hall

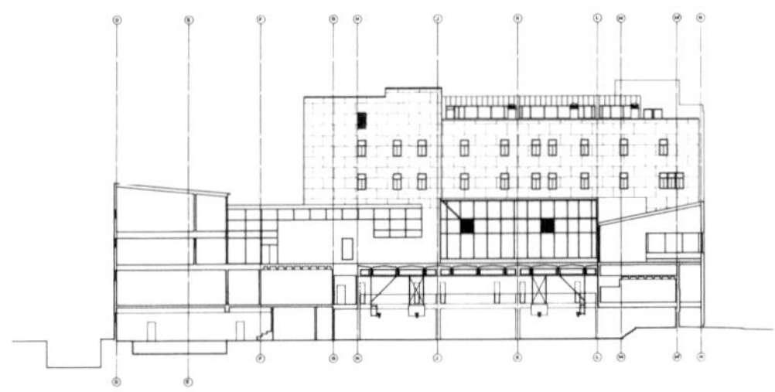

Section through courtyard-pool

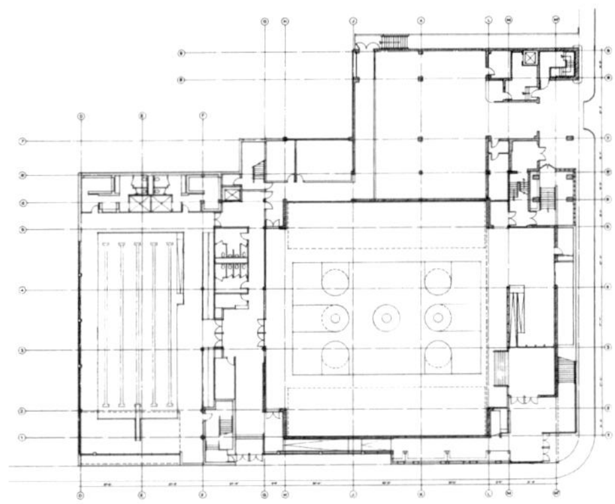

First level plan

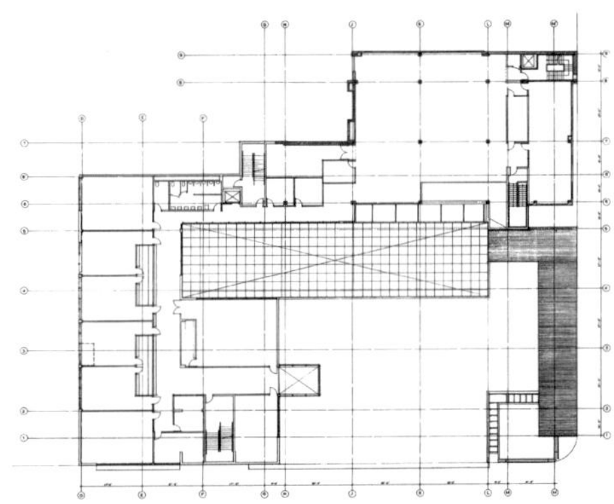

Fourth level plan

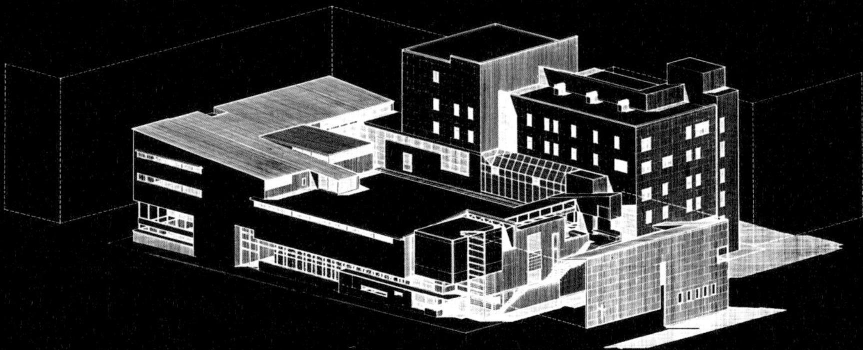

ART COMPLEX

Waltham, Massachusetts

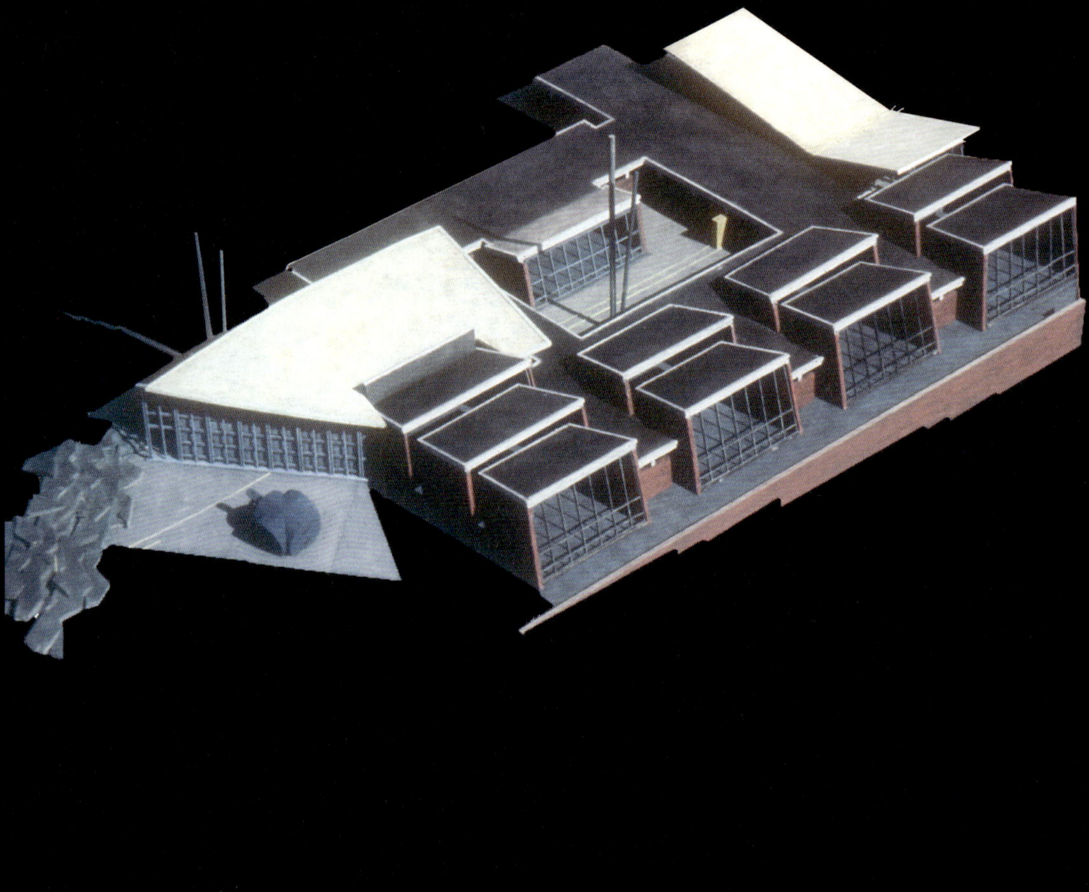

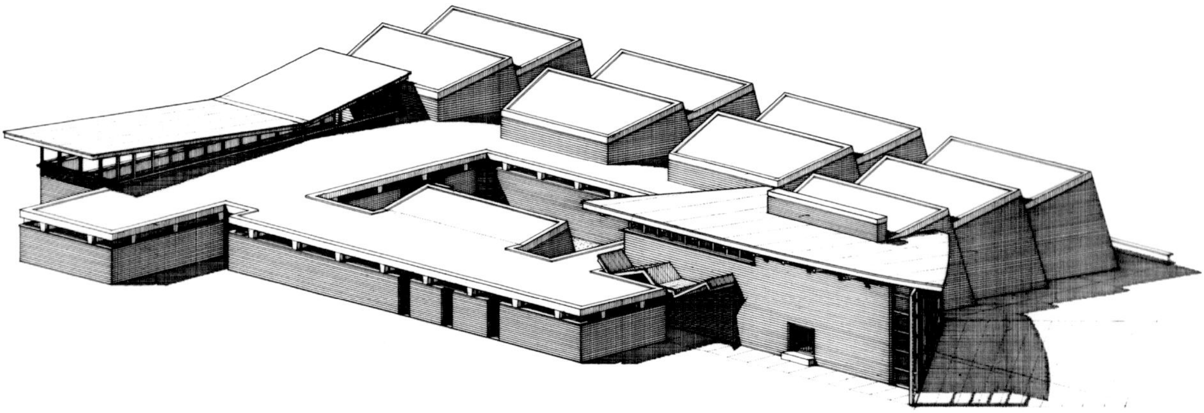

ART COMPLEX

Brandeis University, Waltham, Massachusetts

Harrison and Abramovitz designed the existing Fine Arts Building at Brandeis in 1962. It is isolated in the woods adjacent to the other arts buildings. The program for the renovation involves new gallery and studio space; additional honor studios; and a reconfiguration of the art history department.

The gallery space internalizes the existing courtyard and allows its use for the exterior display of sculpture. The main façade or entry screen of the exhibition space forms an entry court with an existing rock outcrop. It is twisted toward the main campus and the other arts buildings to provide a visual connection and establish a presence within the group. Claes Oldenberg was the recipient of the 1993 Creative Arts Award from Brandeis University and the plug in the model is in honor of that award.

The new entrance relates to the main parking area for faculty and students to the southeast. The main studio and exhibition space will be used for student juries and open workspace. Two pivoting 12-foot panels allow one student to prepare for a critique while another is presenting in the gallery. This space will also be used for the annual exhibition of student work. The courtyard has been redesigned and opened up to internal circulation.

The existing honor studios are currently located in an alcove within this court. They will be relocated to a new pavilion facing the woods to the west. The alcove will become a seminar room open to the courtyard. The renovations of the art history wing will provide a large room for lectures.

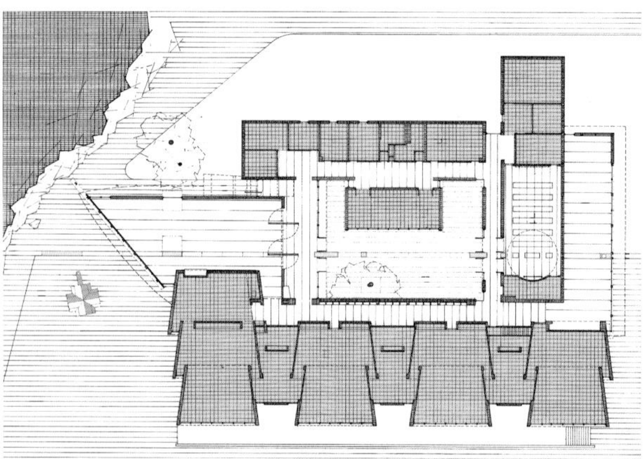

1 New entrance
2 Offices (existing)
3 New entry lobby
4 New studio / Exhibition space
5 Seminar room
6 New lecture room
7 New honors studios
8 Existing studios

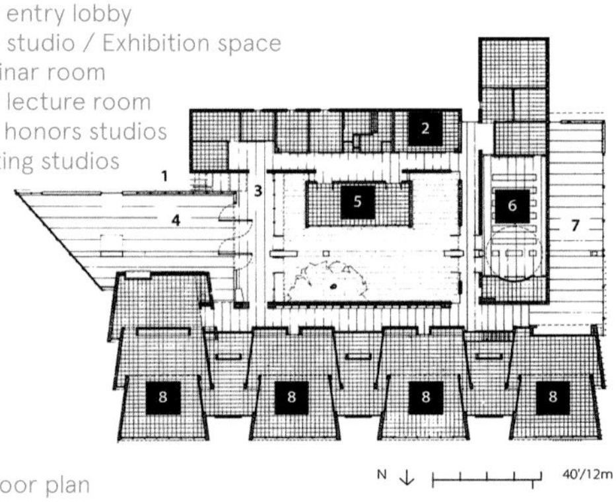

First floor plan

East elevation

West elevation

Section through courtyard looking west

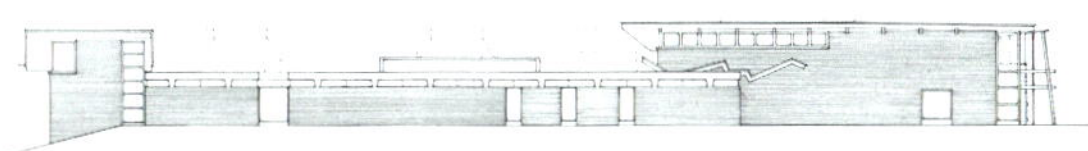

South elevation

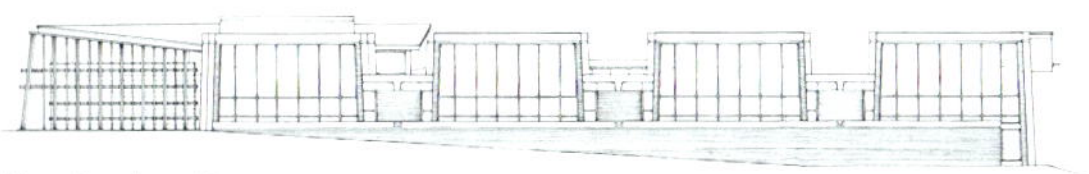

North elevation

PLAN

The gardener understands the nature of a particular site, its climate, soil, shade, and nurtures each plant so that it can become the best possible example of its species. Buildings, with their changing needs and their attachment to site, are more like living trees than inert blocks of stone.

Cesar Pelli

campus and urban regenerations

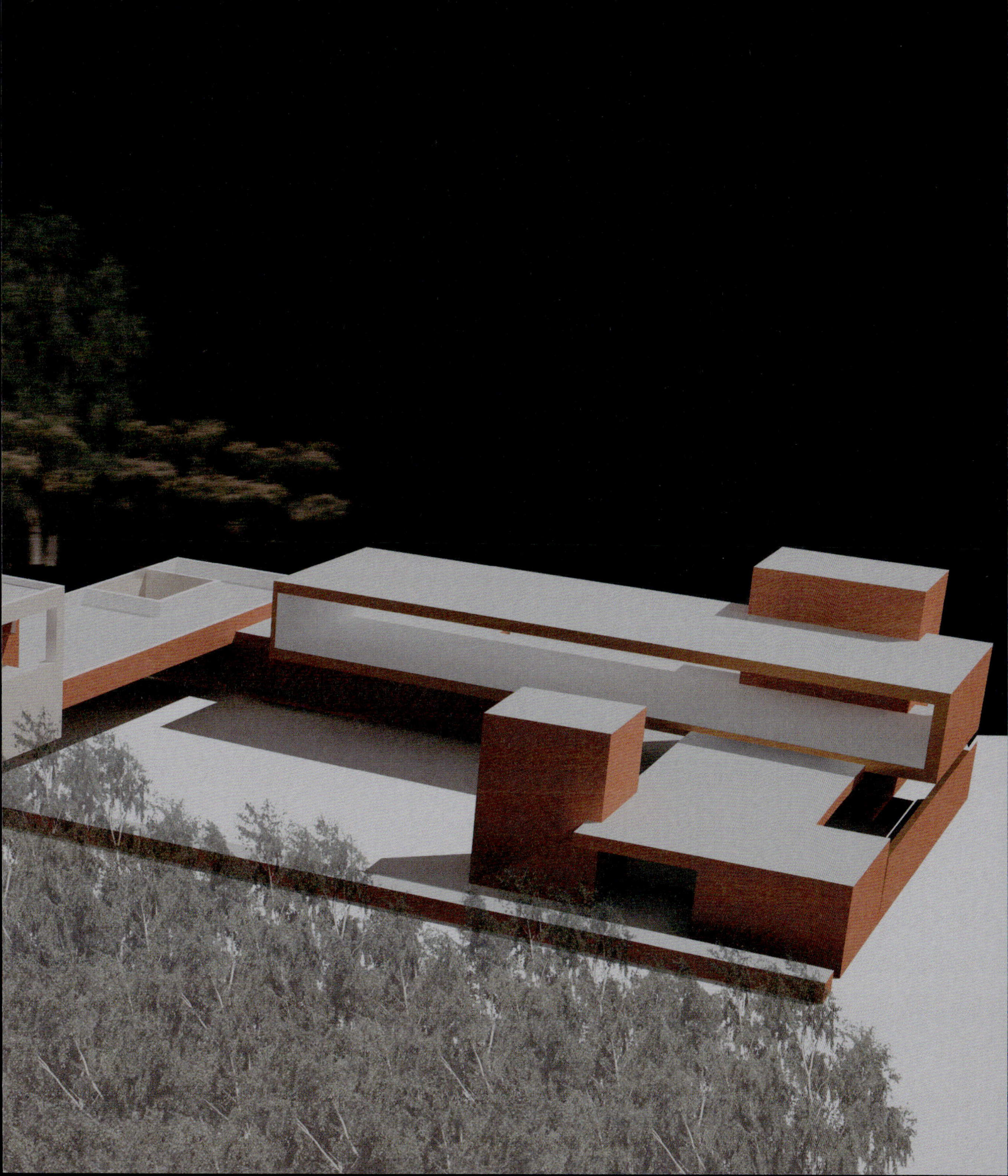

FRAMING PRESENCE

In our world of comfort, simulated excitement and endless images, the role of architecture and the task of the architect remain confused. In the last two hundred years even specialists, critics and architects have had a difficult time differentiating between mere builders of buildings as value-commodities, and architects who are loyal to a more fundamental and long standing historical tradition, who struggle to build meaningfully in our post-industrial cities. Perhaps, part of this confusion arises from a false and ever increasing distance between practice and education. At the core, the question has to do with the way we position ourselves as teachers and architects facing a society and culture that privileges immediacy and specificity; a culture that seems to be at odds with endeavors based on an integration of various modes of cognition.

While the process of "becoming" an architect involves an eventual exposure to a variety of "practices" and professional work, the fundamental questions (intuitions?) are proposed within the context of Architectural Education and continue to unfold during our careers. In a post-industrial world, and paradoxically universalizing culture, in which ultimate truths are no longer instruments for legitimation, and in which diverse modes of practice and teaching co-exist, the ensuing multiplicity (and uncertainty) should accentuate a trend towards responsibility. Uncertainty should increase the ethical weight of choice. So how do we make choices? How do we understand the Architectural Project and the work of the Architect? How do we use our "intuition"?

Through a profound, perseverant, and seriously creative work and teaching, Brian Healy has contributed and continues to contribute to the advancement of the field, profession and discipline of architecture. It seems to me that by sustaining the creative tension and dynamic interaction between education and practice, Brian Healy attempts to bridge and inhabit the distance between critical thinking, design processes and commitment to architectural production. His works at all scales are offerings and acts of translation of ideas to drawings and models, and to those spaces and objects, which can, and do suggest that framing inhabitation is still one of our primary architectural actions. His is not a work of overt or formal representation but of careful attention and loving execution, fueled by a desire to produce a clear and precise architectural work. Prevision, precision, measure, economy of means, clarity of purpose contribute to make intelligent and intelligible works. WORKS that suggest a humble yet stubborn reaffir-

Above left and right Luis Barragan's House and Studio, Mexico City, Mexico (1947)

mation of the values inherent in an architecture understood as a process of transformation of materials and sites into purposeful constructs in place. Values grounded in Architecture's procedures and in its transformative capacity, which include achieving spatial richness through an economy of means, merging and integrating a wealth of resources and "collected materials" (intuitions?) with a clarity of intent. Perhaps, values grounded in an understanding of architecture as medium capable of presenting a limited set of truths in a space located between the questions (intuitions?), the publics and the instruments of our practice/art.

Brian Healy proposes — among other things — a reevaluation of the larger project of modernity, grounded in present realities. It is an attempt to re-socialize modern buildings once again into everyday culture, through multiple dialogues (intuitions?) with the empirical world. Brian Healy's work presents itself as tangible architectural transformations providing frames for everyday life: "Framing presences."

For in between spaces, objects and fields of perception, architecture emerges framing needs and aspirations — to inhabit, to remember, to speak and to act. Framing presences through materiality beyond materiality, through language beyond representation. FRAMING PRESENCES through space and beyond space. In his institutional politics, he has, continues and, I presume, will continue his call for action (perhaps grounded in a quest, a serious quest to regain grounds for making). He has introduced design research, conversations, and many other good ideas to the agenda of the Boston Society of Architects. This political endeavor is hopefully paving the way for others to follow.

Julian Bonder is an architect, designer, artist, and teacher, born in New York and raised in Argentina. He is principal of Julian Bonder + Associates, and partner at Wodiczko + Bonder, Architecture-Art-Design (established as an interdisciplinary firm with Artist and Harvard Professor of Art, Design and the Public Domain Krzysztof Wodiczko in 2003), both in Cambridge, Massachusetts. Bonder's projects include the Center for Holocaust and Genocide Studies at Clark University (recipient of multiple awards); Museo de la Shoah en Buenos Aires; and the Memorial to the Abolition of Slavery in Nantes, France (with Krzysztof Wodiczko), which entails the transformation of 350 metres of the coast of the Loire in downtown Nantes (opened March 2012). Bonder is a Professor of Architecture at Roger Williams University.

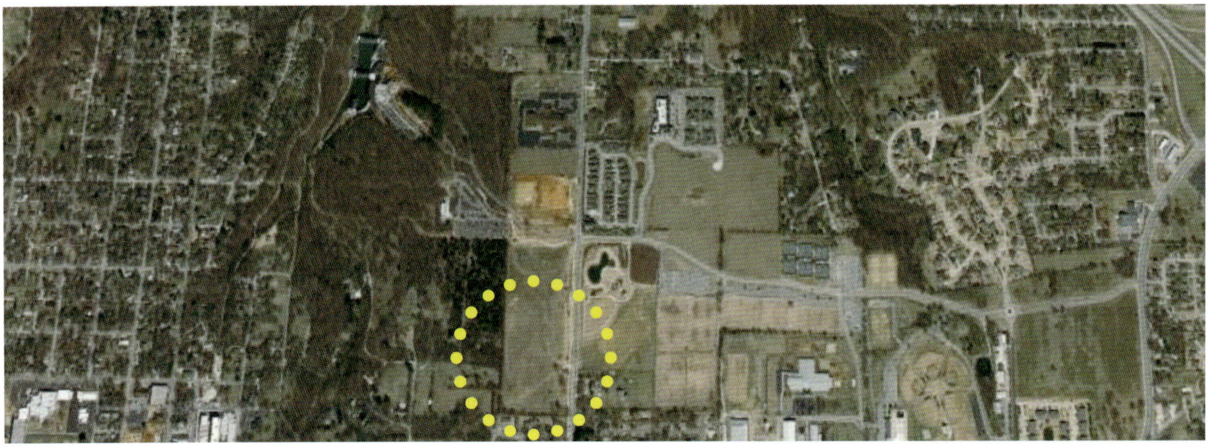

CHILDREN'S ENRICHMENT CENTER

Bentonville, Arkansas

The Helen R. Walton Children's Enrichment Center is part of the Northwest Arkansas Design Excellence Program. The center was to be a newly constructed early childhood environment of approximately 35,000 square feet. It would accommodate and educate 240 children each day in 20 classrooms. The facility would consider the needs of children and their families by including specialty areas for parent resources, extra-curricular activities, therapy space, conferences, and unique educational spaces, common areas that create purposeful connections between the child and parent, and more.

While offering a warm and inviting presence, the facility needs to be a durable, energy efficient, and offer a no maintenance exterior and a low maintenance interior.

The facility would also include a multitude of training rooms, a computer learning lab, and technology to serve remote areas. Additionally, a resource center and library would offer an array of equipment and materials to support teachers throughout the region.

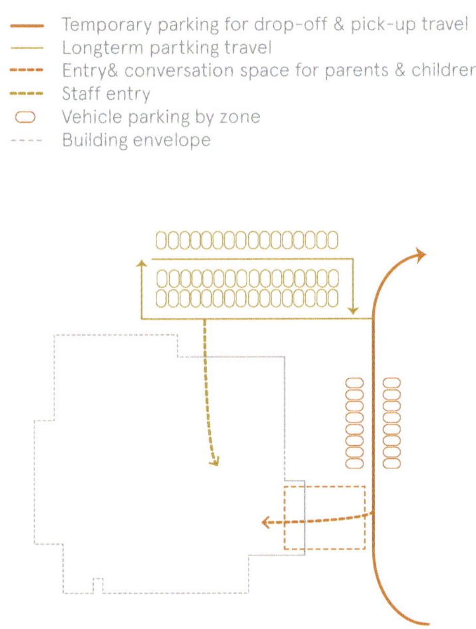

Ideal site circulation

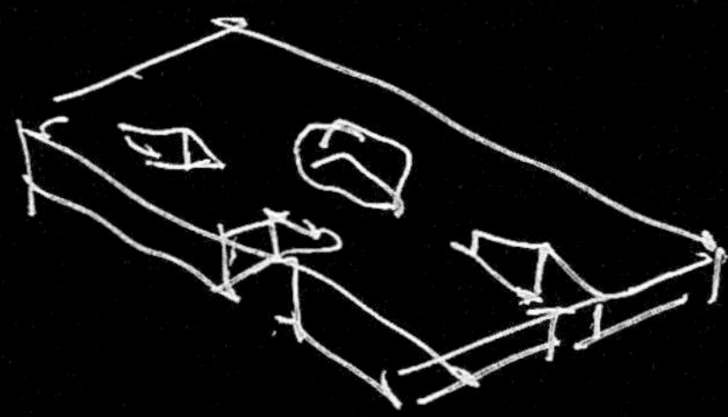

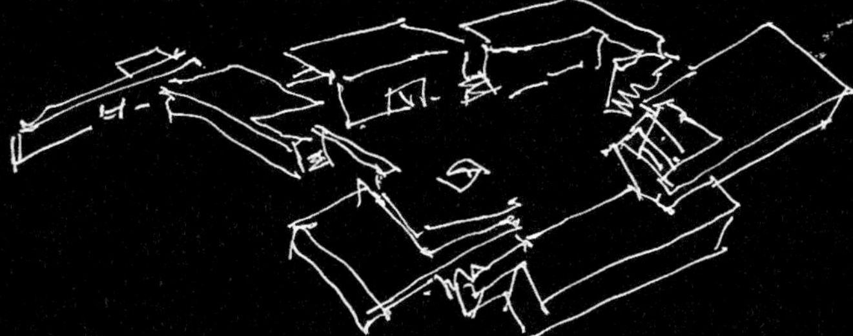

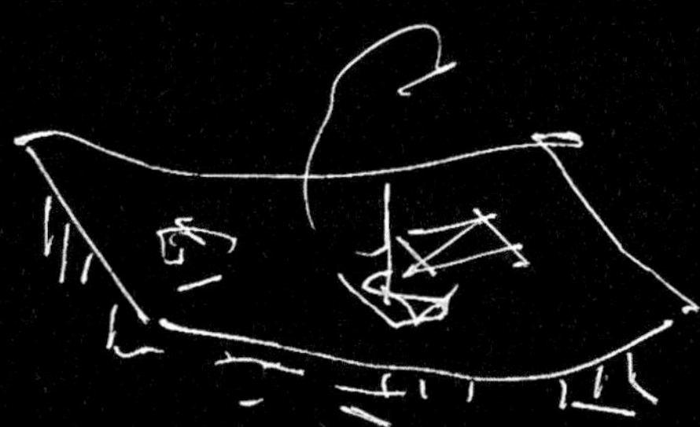

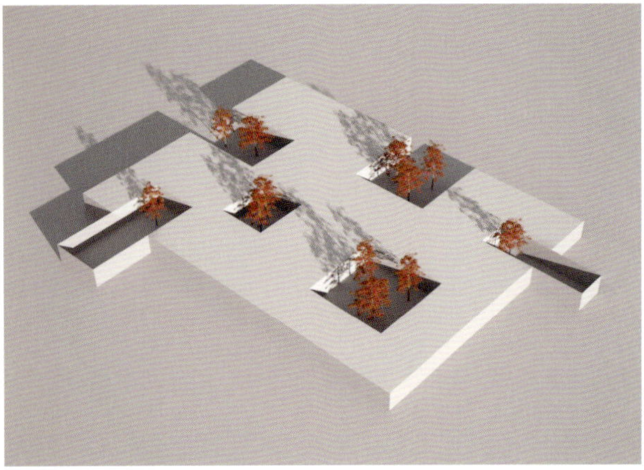

Children need a sense of belonging

Children love to build forts

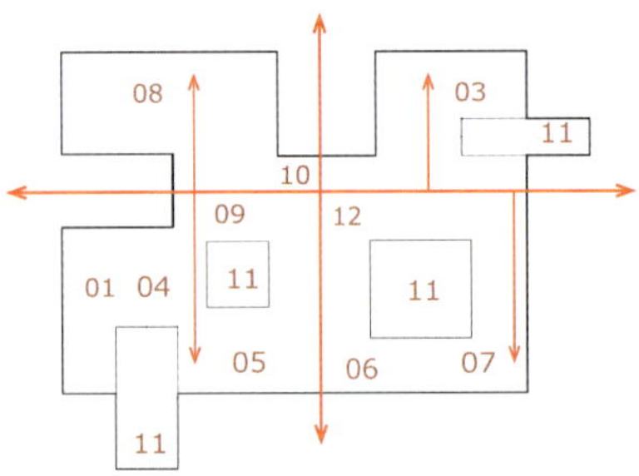

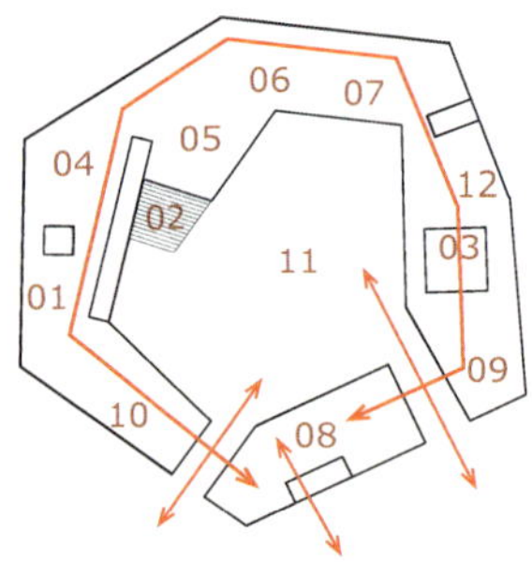

01 Admin/Offices
02 Amphitheater
03 Cafeteria
04 Child service

05 Infant classroom
06 Toddler classroom
07 Pre-K classroom
08 ECIC Training center

09 Entry HWCEC
10 Family service
11 Playscape
12 Storage/Support

01 Admin/Offices
02 Amphitheater
03 Cafeteria
04 Child service

05 Infant classroom
06 Toddler classroom
07 Pre-K classroom
08 ECIC Training center

09 Entry HWCEC
10 Family service
11 Playscape
12 Storage/Support

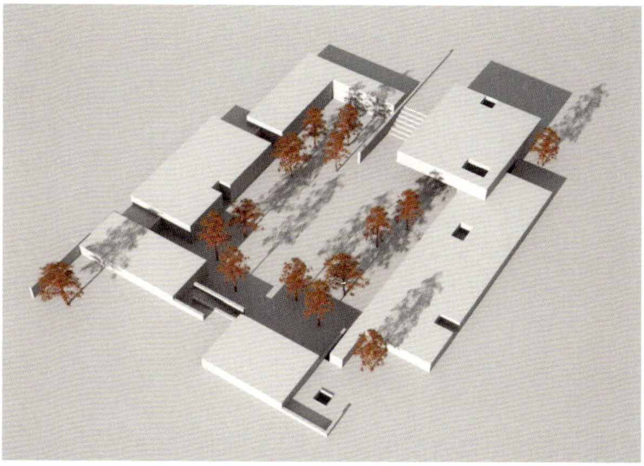

Children love to explore and discover

Children play and dream

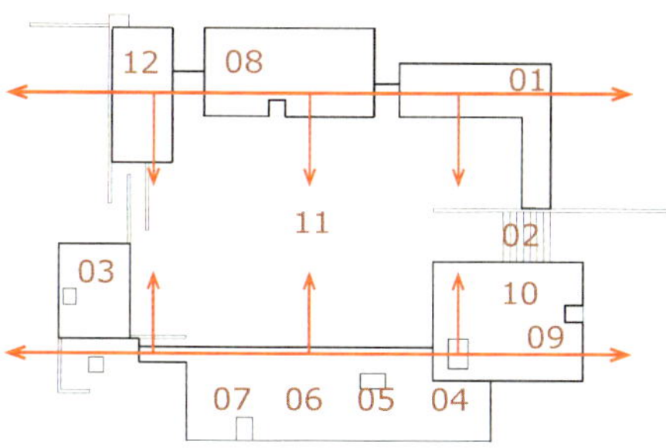

01 Admin/Offices
02 Amphitheater
03 Cafeteria
04 Child service
05 Infant classroom
06 Toddler classroom
07 Pre-K classroom
08 ECIC Training center
09 Entry HWCEC
10 Family service
11 Playscape
12 Storage/Support

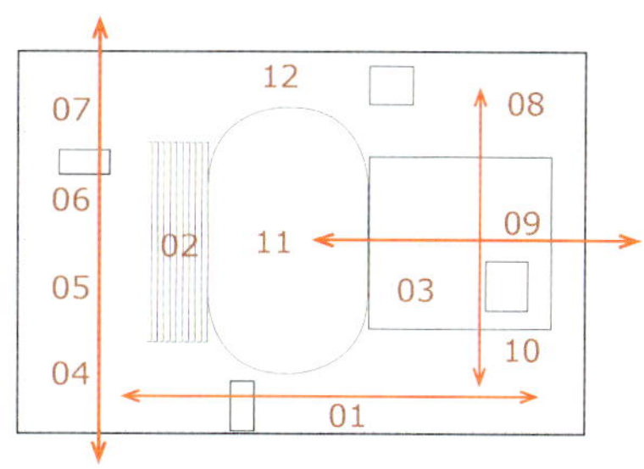

01 Admin/Offices
02 Amphitheater
03 Cafeteria
04 Child service
05 Infant classroom
06 Toddler classroom
07 Pre-K classroom
08 ECIC Training center
09 Entry HWCEC
10 Family service
11 Playscape
12 Storage/Support

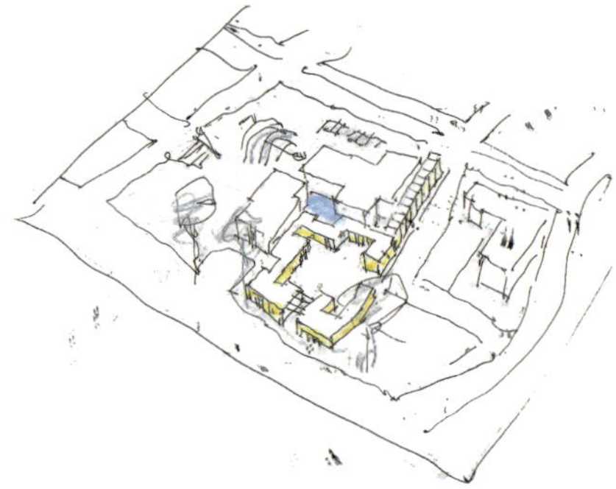

Scheme A

COMMUNITY CENTER

Newport, Rhode Island

With a desire for deeper community connections and social cohesion, including leadership development within the community – along with affordable opportunities for education, skills acquisition, and self-improvement – the Housing Authority of Newport commissioned Edward Mitchell and Brian Healy to help administer the "Community Vision for the Florence Gray Center" project: a collaborative effort of key stakeholders to assess the physical components of the existing center, identify future uses of this site, and develop sustainable business models for programmatic operations. Partners included the Boys & Girls Club of Newport County, Newport Health Equity Zone, Newport Working Cities, Catalyzing Newport, Aquidneck Community Table, local residents, and other public and private institutions.

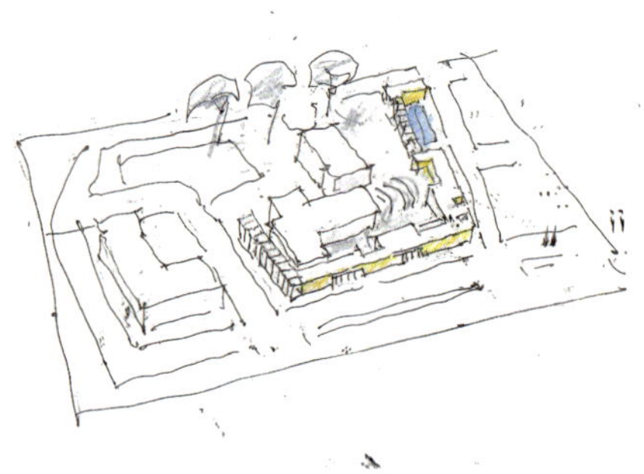

Scheme B

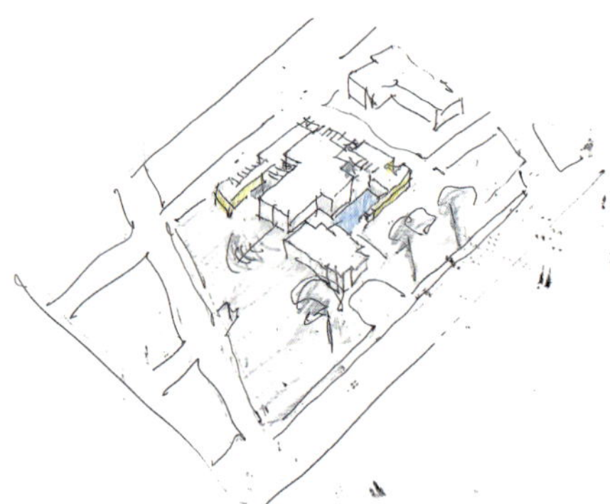

Scheme C

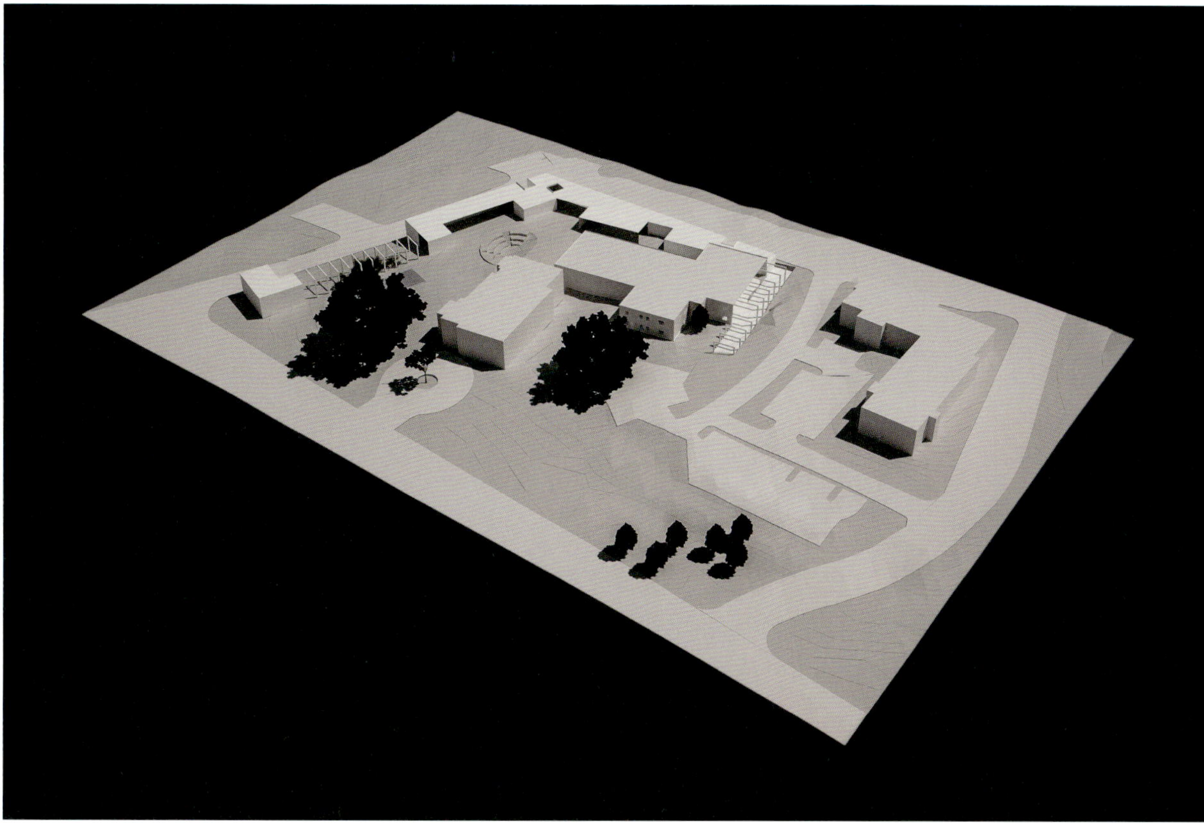

Mitchell and Healy were tasked with conducting a community needs assessment to determine optimal uses of the FGC and ensure a comprehensive community feedback process; develop a strategic plan that includes the costs, benefits and challenges of different financial models (e.g., cooperative ownership, innovative tenant structures for short-term use via popup stores or businesses, public/private partnerships and marketing strategies, etc.) to be matched to a conceptual design strategy; and to create a final schematic model of a future redesigned Florence Gray Center to be presented to the community for community feedback and use in a future fundraising campaign.

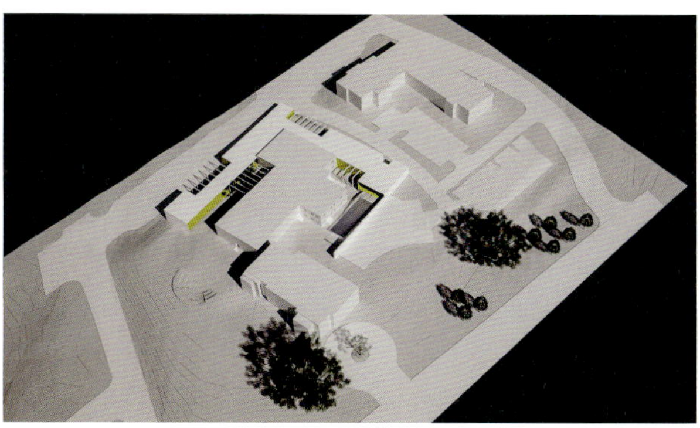

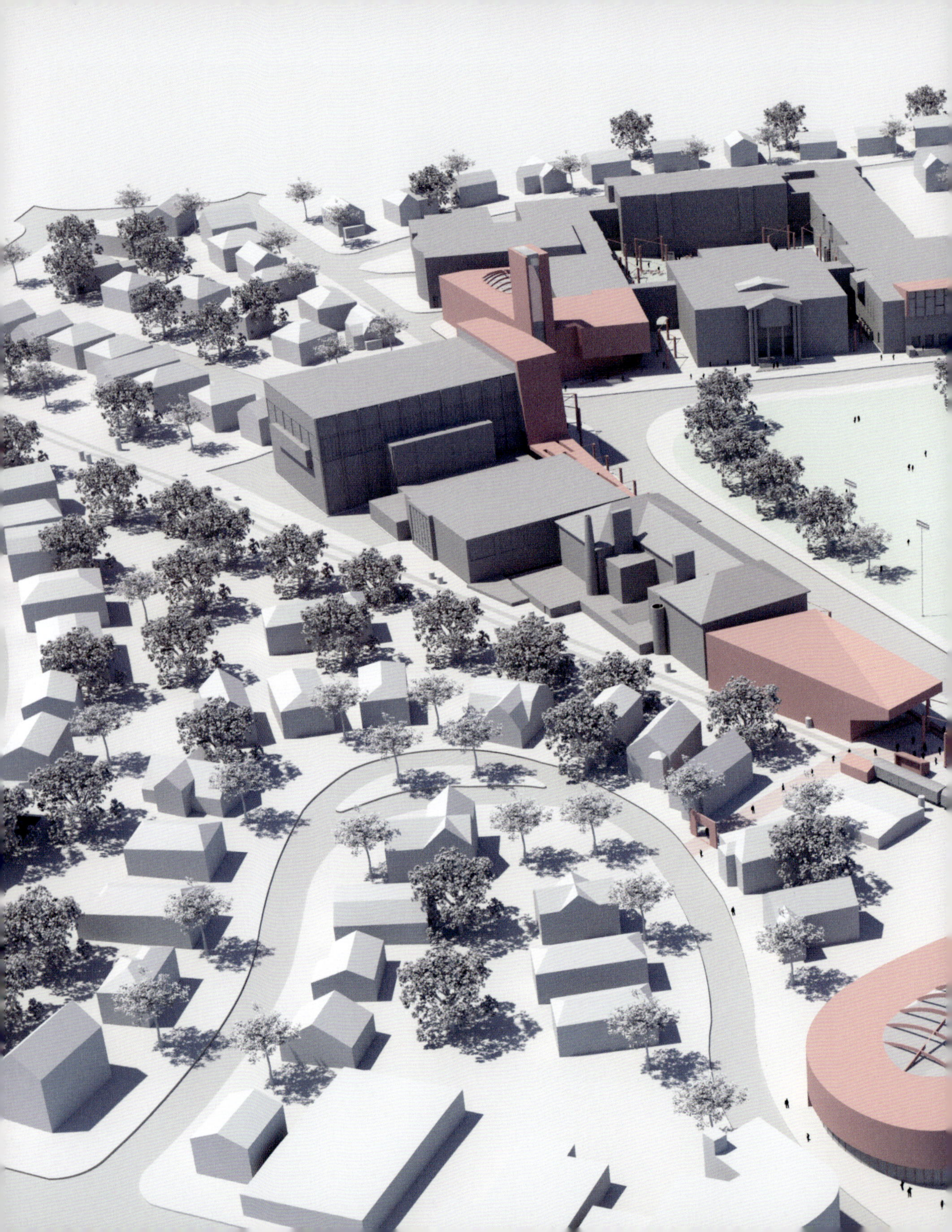

BROOKLINE HIGH SCHOOL

Brookline, Massachusetts

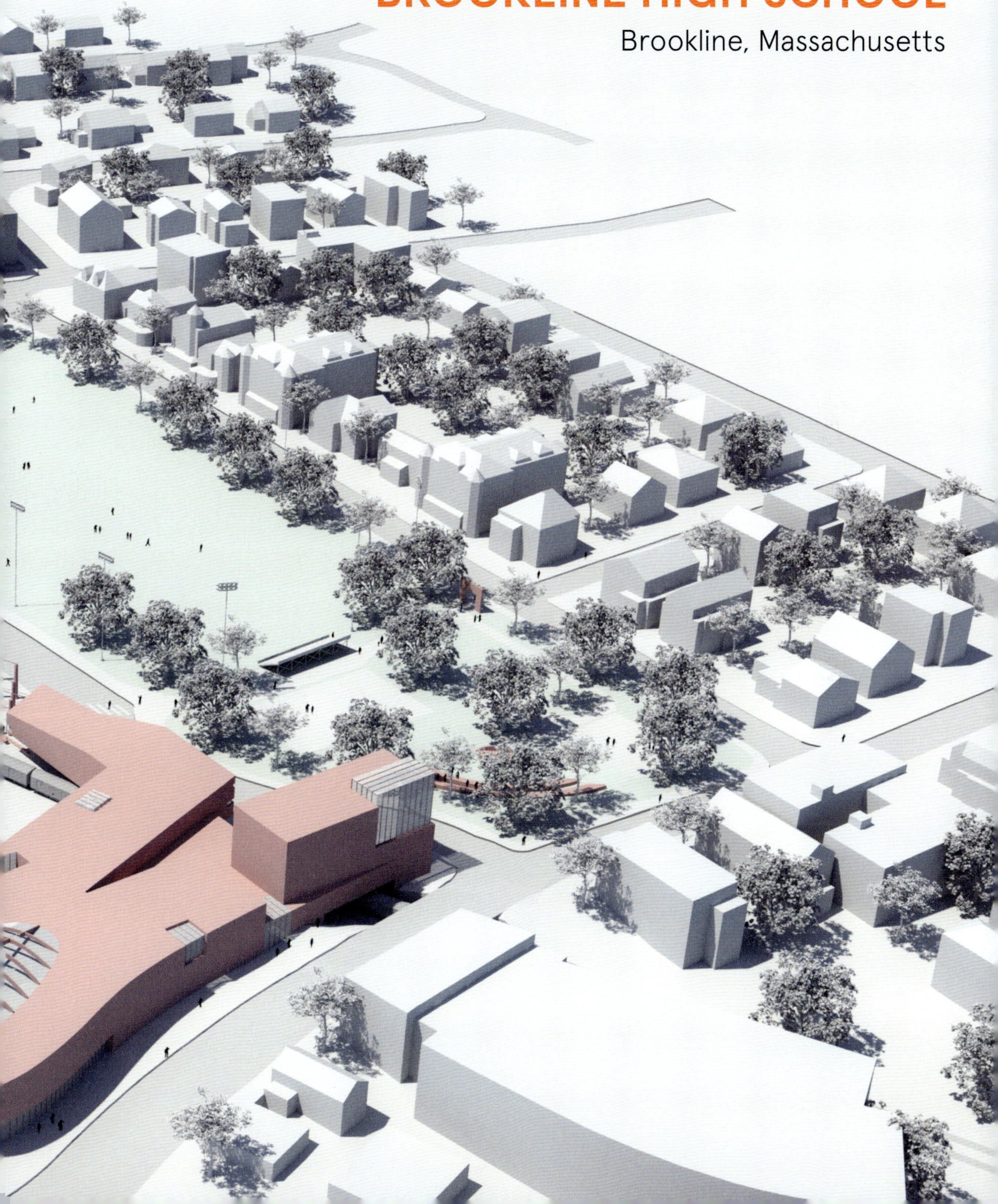

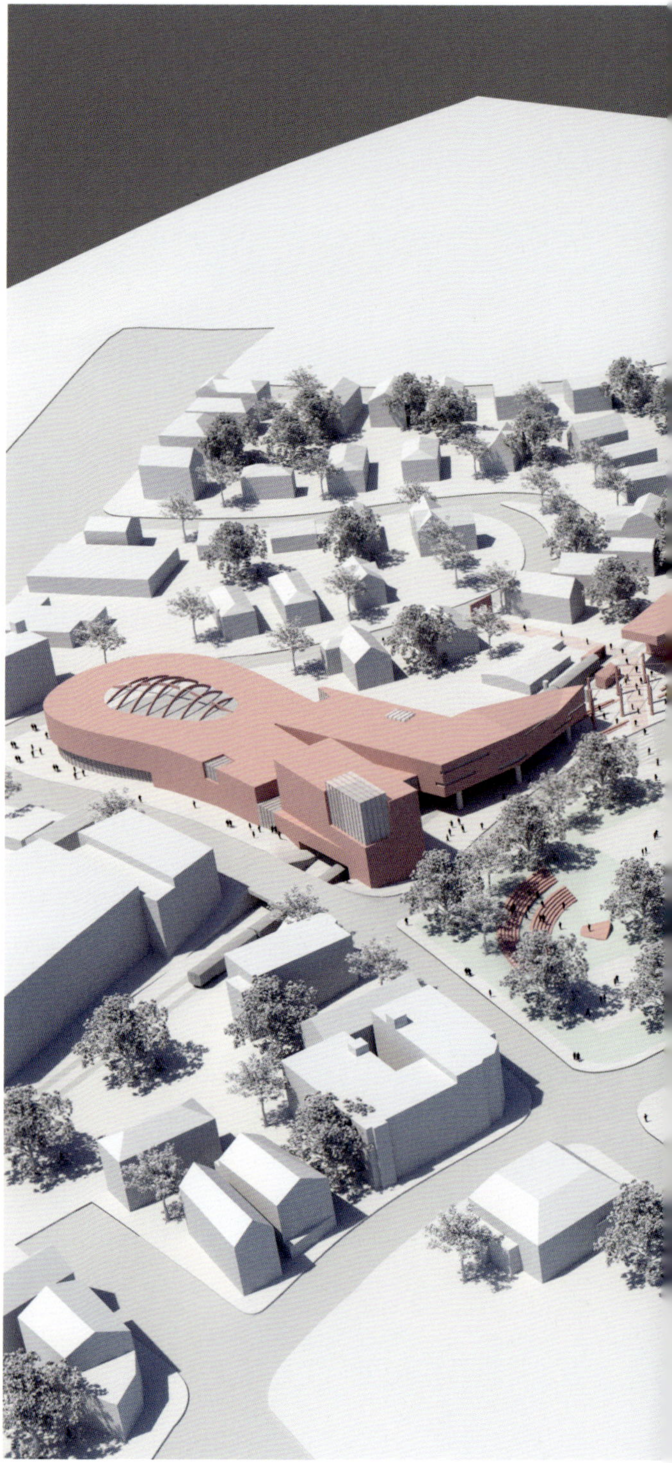

BROOKLINE HIGH SCHOOL

Brookline, Massachusetts

This campus study was conducted in collaboration with George Metzger and his team at HMFH Architects based in Cambridge. They understood that a campus — like the one planned for the Brookline High School — is an ever-changing phenomenon and it needed a commitment to co-creating shared communal places that promote wellness and social interaction.

Their proposal anticipates that the Cypress Building would establish a new entrance point to the BHS campus with an iconic tower at the Cypress Street/Tappan Street crossing. New and existing gate elements connect a series of open campus spaces. Cypress Field is reinforced as a village commons by infilling "missing components" on Tappan Street, marking the heart of campus. And a Science Tower, located at the fulcrum of the two major campus streets, reestablishes the iconic form of the original Brookline High School building while the he Cypress Building's interior "Alumni Court" is a counterpoint to existing BHS quadrangle.

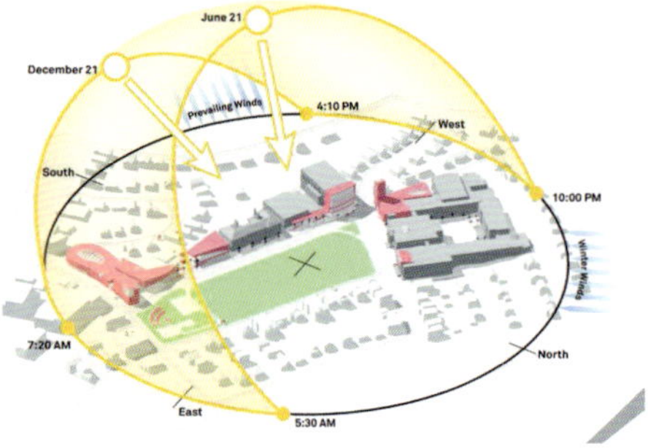

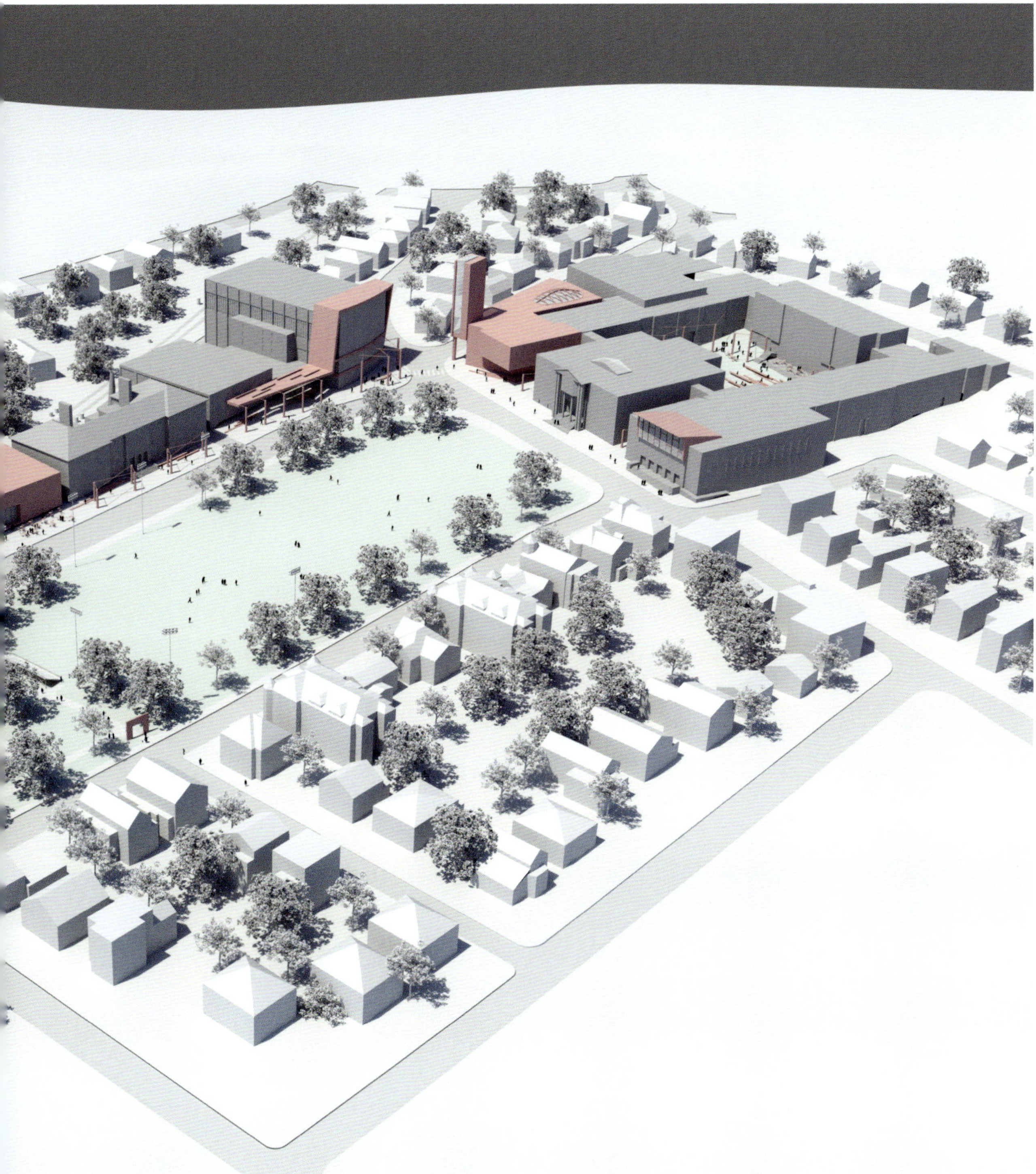

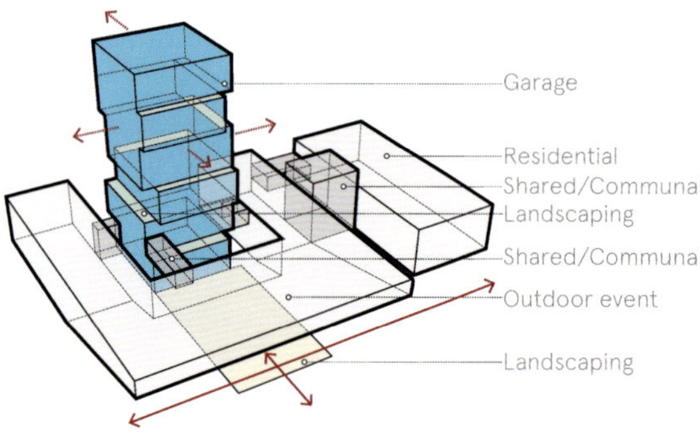

Tower - Site A

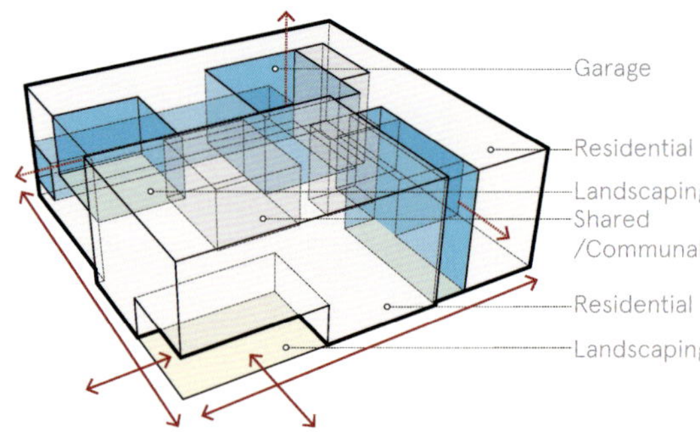

Cluster - Site B

ENTREPRENEUR CENTER

University of Utah
Salt Lake City, Utah

The new Pierre Lassonde Entrepreneur Center at the David Eccles School of Business at the University of Utah is a landmark project, which will advance the learning experience of students through transformative pedagogy for many years to come. Learning models are changing rapidly; this project takes the paradigm of the future, and makes it available now to students at the University of Utah. By bringing the best entrepreneurs and innovators together in a cross-cultural center, many amazing ideas and businesses will emerge. Learning by living and doing will create business leaders and lifelong entrepreneurs who will compete far above current standards. One goal is to enhance recruitment and visually motivate students to develop an interest in the Lassonde Entrepreneur Center.

Second goal is to motivate and recruit more student residents to live on the University of Utah campus. The project aims to accomplish these goals by combining a new Student Entrepreneur Space (Student Garage) with a revenue generating student housing.

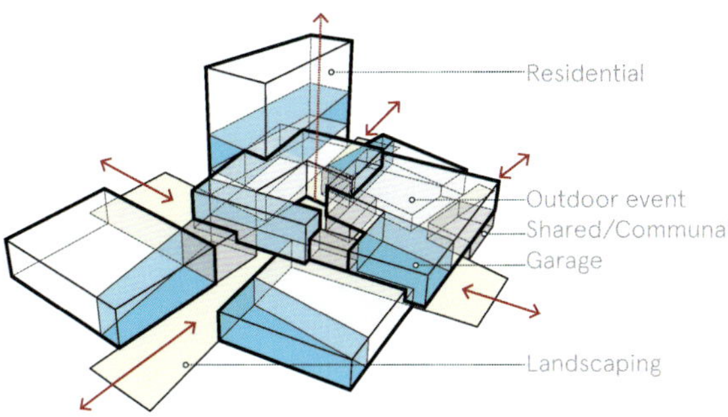

Village - Site C

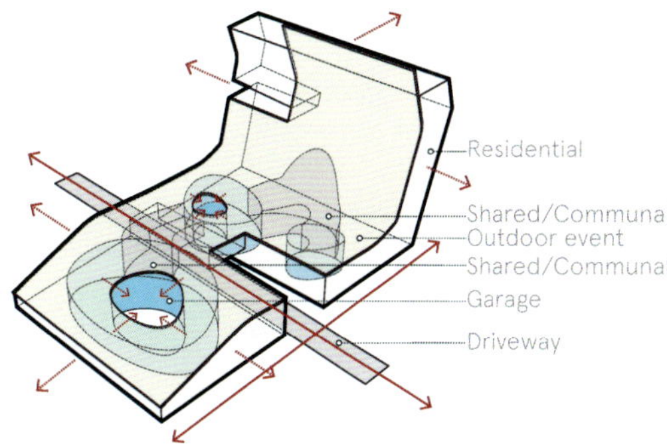

Fold - Site D

MAINE MEDICAL CENTER

Portland, Maine

Maine Medical Center is a 606 bed teaching hospital affiliated with Tuffs University School of Medicine serving the people of Portland and is a major tertiary health care center for northern New England. It provides comprehensive inpatient services in all medical specialties with centers of excellence being developed in cancer care, heart care, children's services as well as other areas.

MMC recently completed its first phase of renovation and expansion projects with the addition of the Women's and Infants Building, an Emergency Department expansion, a new 500 car garage, a new heliport and a new central utility plant designed to accommodate the future growth of the hospital. After completion of this phase, Dennis Kaiser led a team with Healy to study ways to update the master plan for the next phase of the MMC Master Facilities Plan's goals to meet the increasing inpatient demand. Areas of growth foreseen include more inpatient beds, conversion of existing beds to 100% private patient rooms, new state of the art interventional facilities, expanded diagnostic imaging facilities and expanded educational facilities.

As part of the initial analysis, they developed four conceptual proposals of alternative studies for massing and improved site connections.

Aerial view of the site

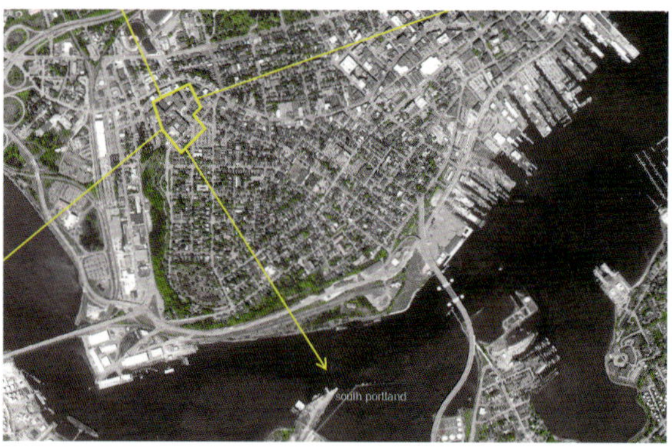

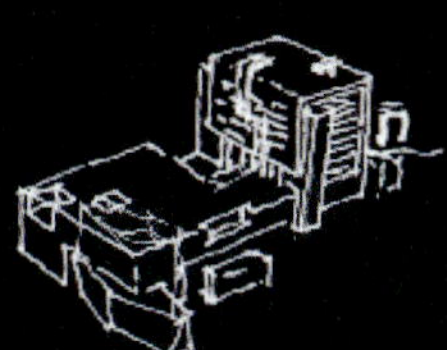

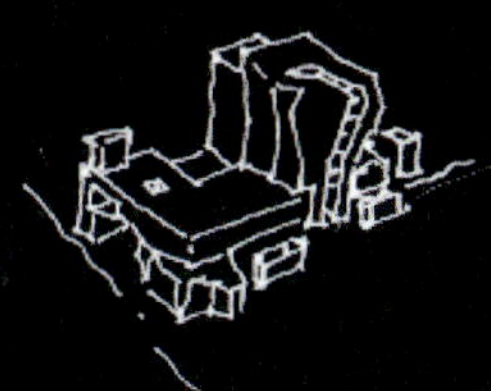

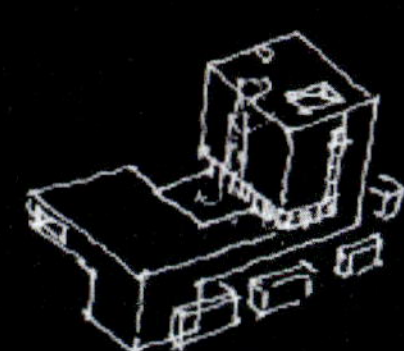

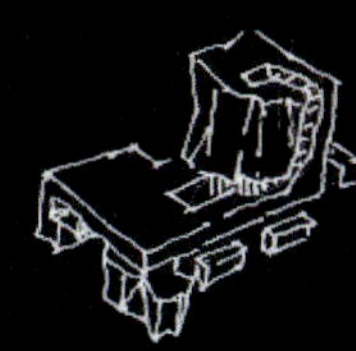

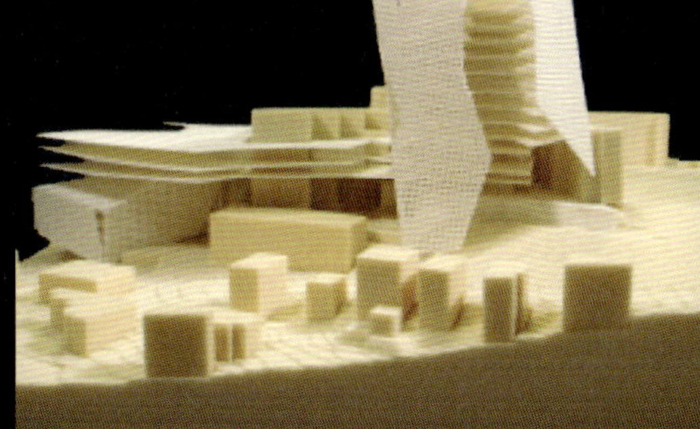

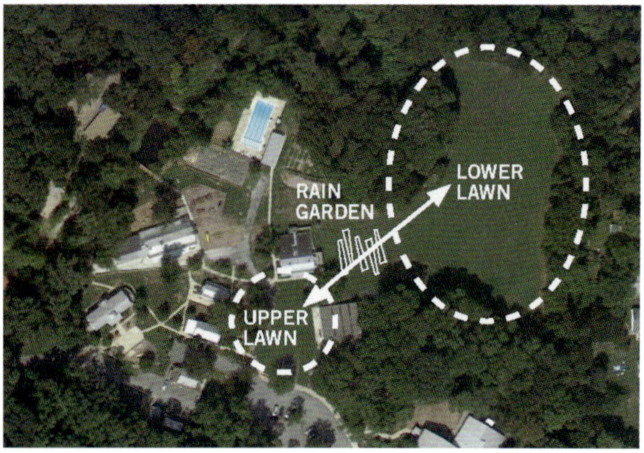

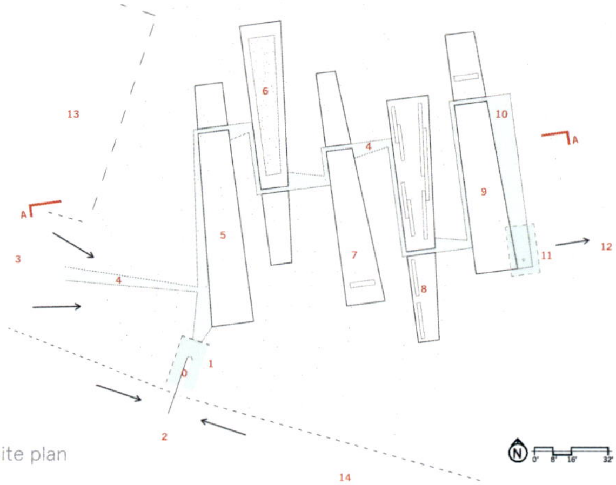

Site plan

COUNTRY DAY SCHOOL

Alexandria, Virginia

Burgundy Farm Country Day School — a pre-Kindergarten to 8th grade independent school — was founded in 1946 on the property of a dairy farm. It is a unique and historic campus spread over 23 acres in the Fairfax County section of Alexandria, Virginia. Its original barn buildings have been renovated over the years, with a number of prime academic buildings added as recently as 1998. The grounds are partially wooded with a small animal barn, pond, and vegetable garden.

It is a campus unlike others in the area and one whose site and features are valued greatly by the campus community and alumni. The grounds of this school are a critical part of the school identity and instrumental to the academic program and mission of the school. The outdoors really are very much an extension of the classroom and in fact are referred to often as "the most important Burgundy classroom".

The is generally described as a new 22,000-25,000 square foot community building, housing a performing arts space, various classrooms, pre-function areas and theater support spaces, to replace the existing auditorium. As part of an invited competition, we developed three schemes simultaneously to compare the relative merits of alternative approaches to integrating a new center into the existing campus — village, tree house, and shell.

0 Scupper
1 Cistern for roof water collection
2 Roof slope to scupper
3 Regrade site to slope to rain garden channel
4 Rain water channel
5 Activity terrace
6 Sandbox terrace
7 Insect colonies terrace
8 Vegetable garden terrace
9 Bird terrace
10 Rain pool
11 Recessed cistern
12 Irrigation for lower lawn
13 Library
14 Community building & campus center
15 Soil stabilizing grasses and meadow plants

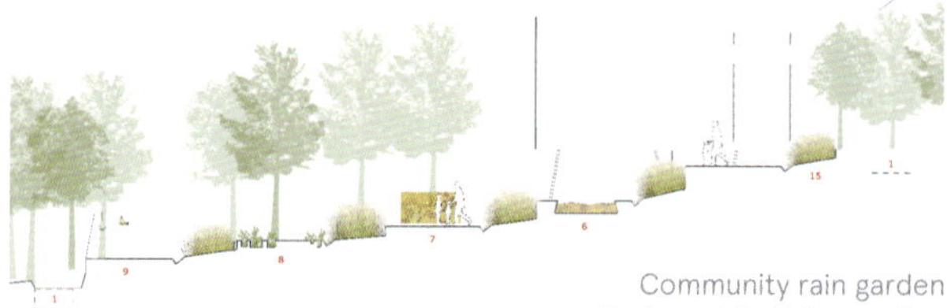

Community rain garden
East-west building section

View into performance hall for the upper lawn

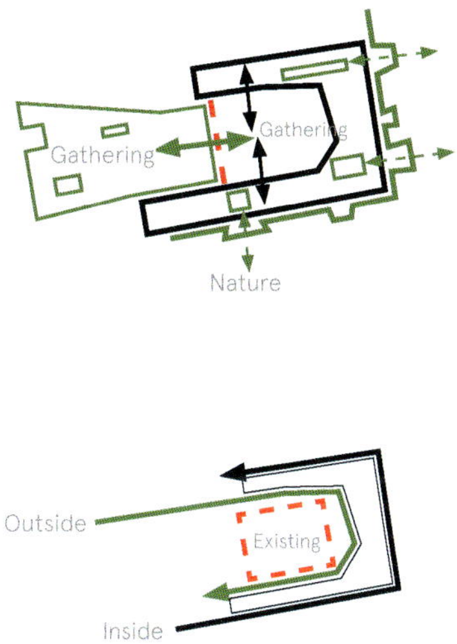

Conceptual spatial diagrams

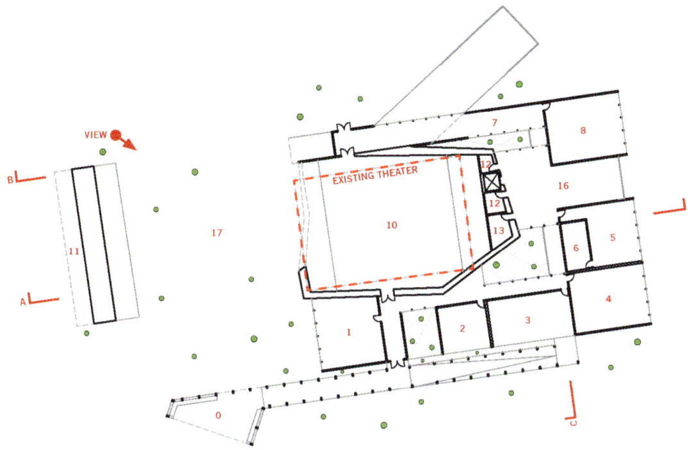

Upper level floor plan

0 Drop-off/Pick-up/Covered wait
1 Gallery
2 Office
3 Art classroom
4 Ceramics
5 Photography
6 Darkroom
7 Dressing/Storage
8 Drama
9 Outdoor classroom/Deck
10 Auditorium
11 Outdoor exhibition
12 Water closet
13 Storage
14 Music
15 Science (below)
16 Lobby/Gallery
17 Upper lawn

Shell
Building sections

View of passageway down to science

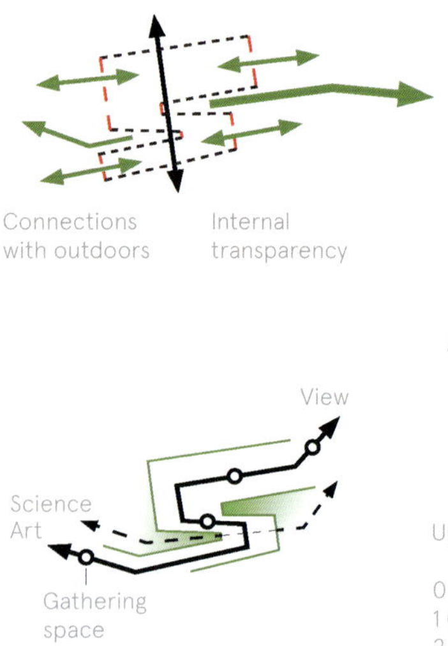

Conceptual spatial diagrams

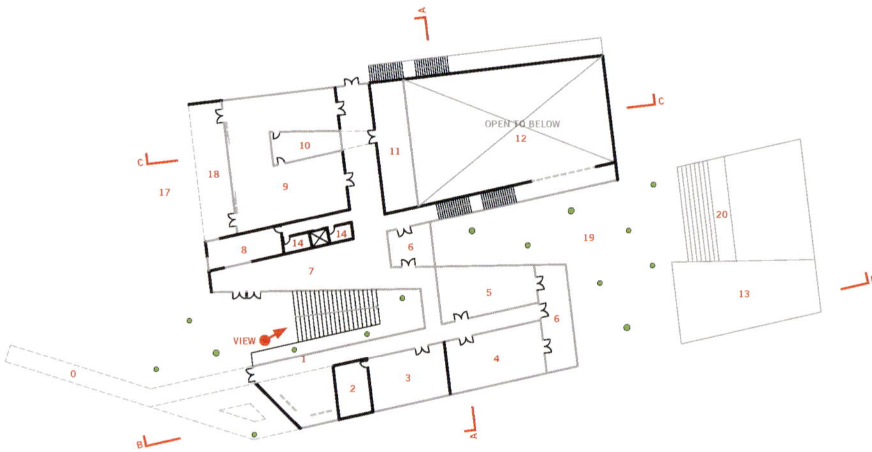

Upper level floor plan

0 Drop-off/Pick-up/Covered wait
1 Gallery
2 Darkroom
3 Photography
4 Ceramics
5 Art classroom
6 Terrace
7 Lobby/Gallery
8 Office
9 Music
10 Courtyard
11 Tech/Mezzanine
12 Auditorium
13 Science (below)
14 Water closet
15 Drama
16 Dressing/Storage/Shop
17 Upper lawn
18 Band shell
19 Science terrace
20 Outdoor classroom

Tree House
Building sections

View of entry atrium and gallery

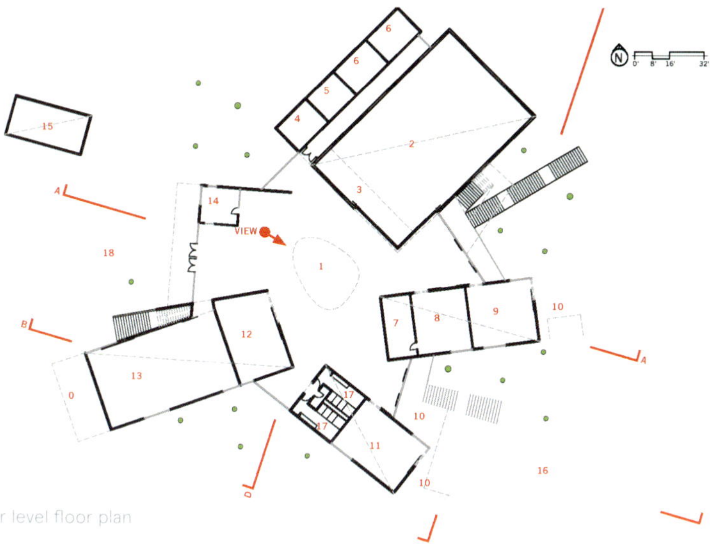

Upper level floor plan

0 Drop-off/Pick-up/Covered wait
1 Lobby/Gallery
2 Auditorium
3 Tech/Mezzanine
4 Storage
5 Shop
6 Dressing
7 Darkroom
8 Photography
9 Ceramics
10 Terrace
11 Art classroom
12 Drama
13 Music
14 Office
15 Pavilion
16 Sciene (below)
17 Water closet
18 Upper lawn

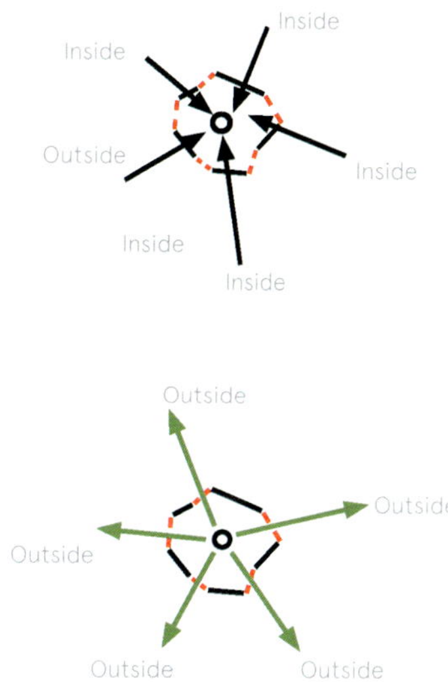

Conceptual spatial diagrams

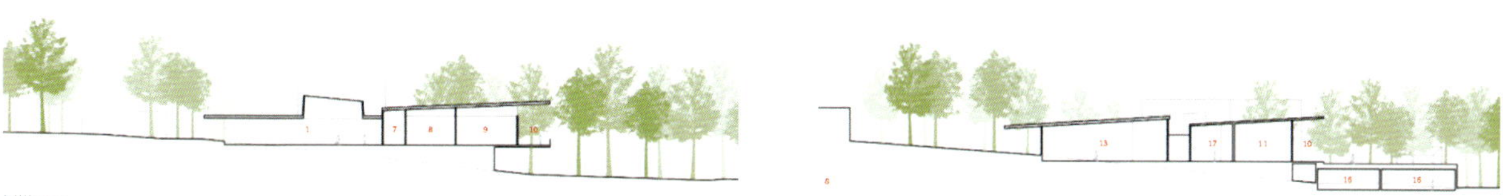

Village
Building sections

INTERGENERATIONAL LEARNING CENTER

Chicago, Illinois

This project was an invited competition – based on the Mayor's imitative – to rebuild neighborhoods one block at a time. It needed to include a senior center, a Head Start Center for preschoolers, and housing for children and their adoptive grandparents – all on a single block. The site was adjacent to a major boulevard, South Michigan Avenue on one side, and smaller side streets in a depressed area of Southside Chicago.

The design team embraced the concept of communal living with its many shared collective spaces. The study models consistently held the edges of the site with a series of internal courtyards, each with a different character, and with various adjacencies and possibilities of interaction. One model, though, posited the possibility that could also give back to the greater community as well. They selected an S-configuration for the site, reserving a large tract of land on the boulevard for everyone's enjoyment. It seemed optimistic – in this scenario – to assume that such a public park would be cared for, but they felt strongly that such optimism was critical when setting up a model community. When rebuilding communities, when setting up a prototype, it's essential to include and feature notions of security, dignity, and confidence in the future.

The family housing consists of a series of private flats organized around communal living space; including study and dining areas, porches, and gardens. Each unit can also be divided into separate units to allow grandparents to remain part of the community when the grandchildren have grown and need to relocate.

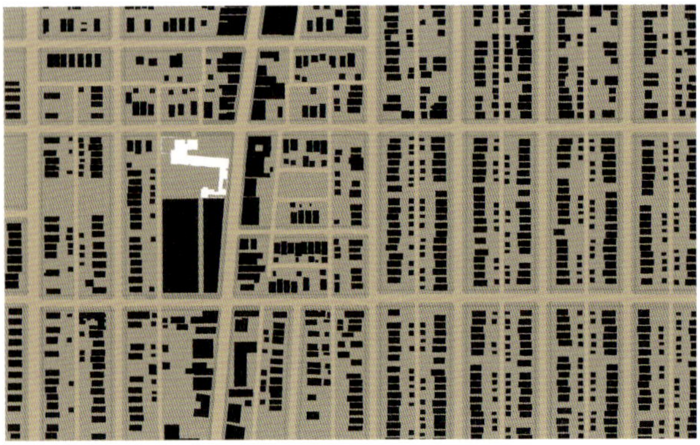

Site plan

First floor plan

Second floor plan

Third floor plan

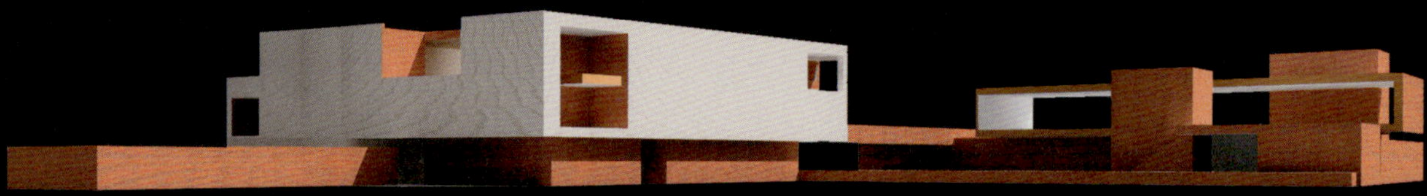

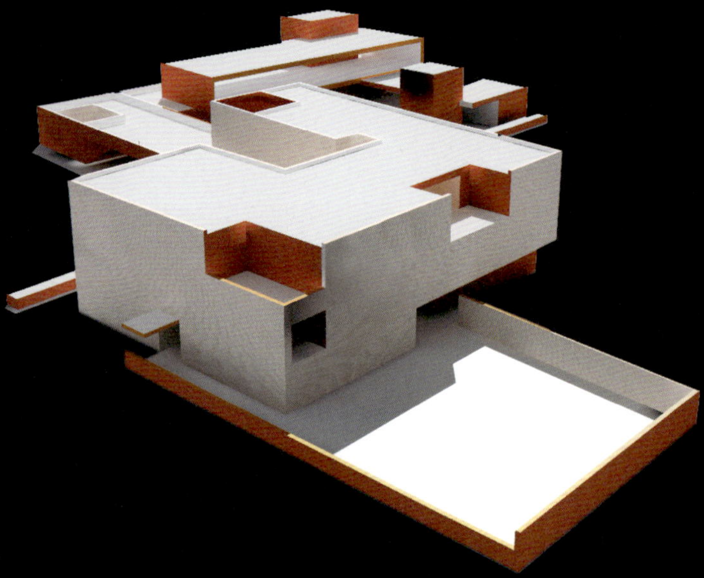

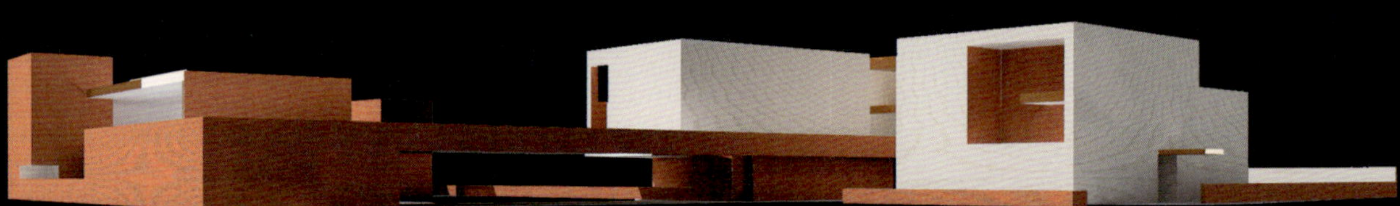

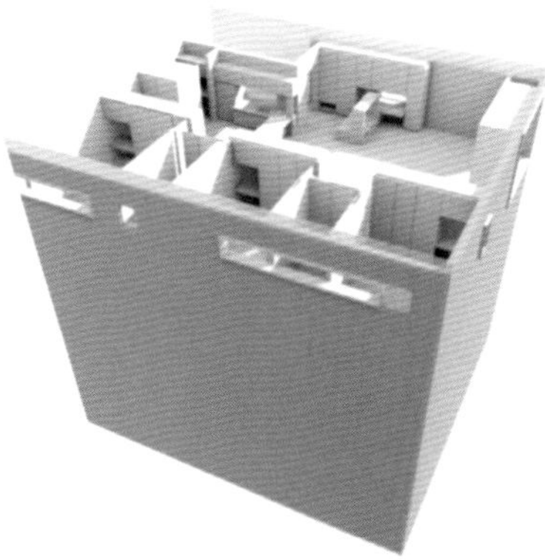

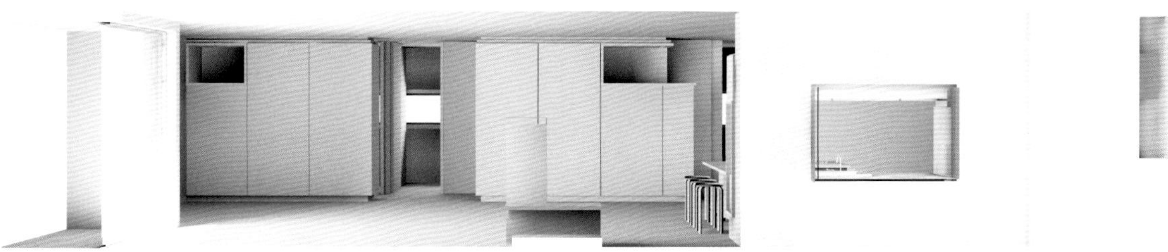

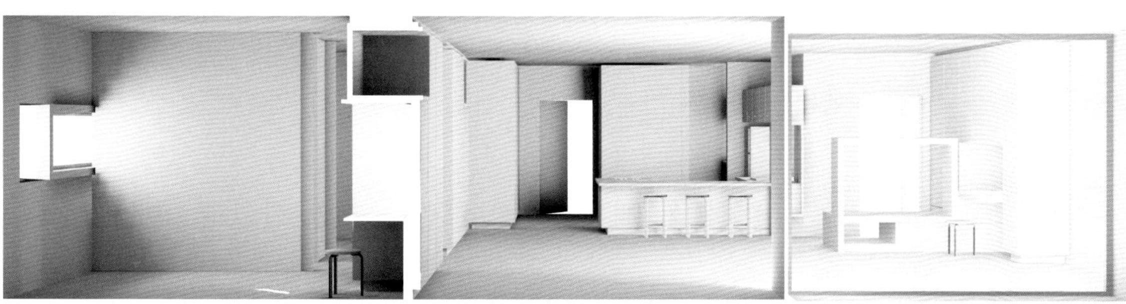

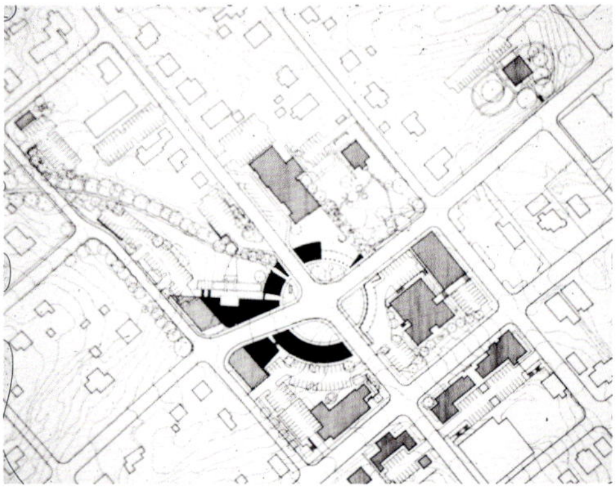

Site plan

TOWN CENTER

Blacksburg, Virginia

An open competition provided the opportunity to explore the potential of developing a social and cultural center at the intersection of two prominent roadways on the outside of downtown Blacksburg.

It was intended as a prototype for social interaction and a back-drop to communal overlaps to allow itself to be used an open air theater or Roman circus with a privileged perch above to observe the events across a typical day, as well as during planned events that may close the streets for a few hours.

A floating halo — or roof structure — provides shade and a comfortable overlook to the activities below, while organizing the disparate parts of the program that line the roadways and sidewalks. These include a theater, retail shops, craft studios, restaurants, bars, coffee shops, and cafes.

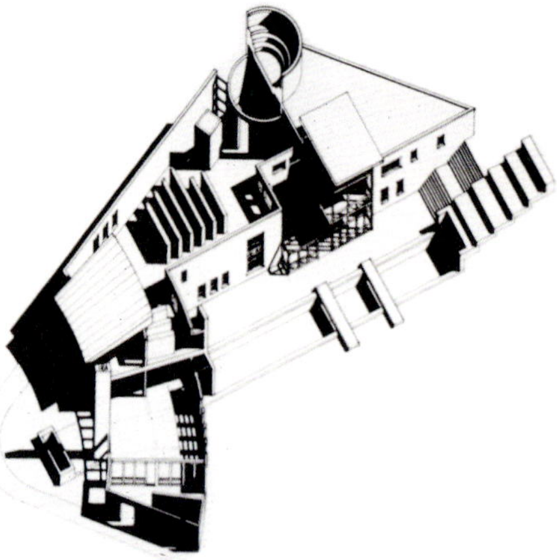

Axonometric

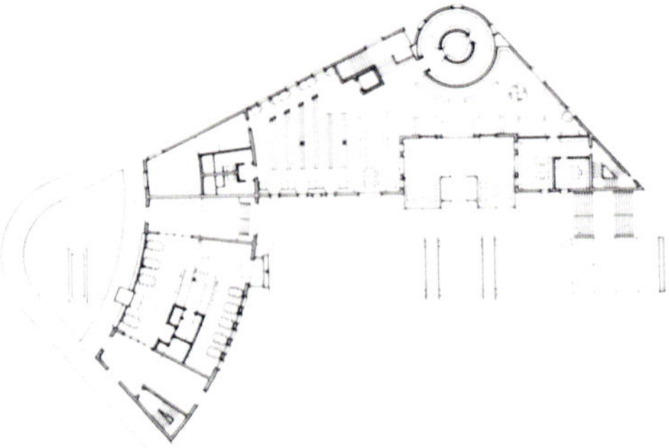

Ground level plan

PRAY

Beauty will save the world.

Fyodor Dostoevsky

religious buildings

ROBERT CAMPBELL

A HOME FOR LIGHT, MUSIC, GOD, AND CHILDREN

One of Boston's best architectural spaces has just opened here in Brookline Village.

"Beauty" isn't a word architects use any more. They think it sounds sentimental, even kitschy. But however they define it, they seek it just the same.

The beautiful new space, if it's OK to call it that, is the children's chapel of the Korean Church of Boston. The chapel is the crown jewel in a recently completed addition to the church and among a series of new additions designed by Somerville-based architect Brian Healy.

Healy's exterior, which features a couple of angular black shapes and a goodly amount of concrete, hasn't been a unanimous hit with the neighbors. But I can't imagine anyone failing to fall in love with the chapel interior, especially on a Sunday morning when it's filled with 60 or 70 enthusiastically singing children.

The chapel is very much a modernist space. It's informal and asymmetrical. Walls and ceilings are pure white. There's no ornament. Even the cross is immaterial: it's made of light, coming through a cutout in the wall behind the altar. More daylight floats in mysteriously from sources you can't see. The effect is magical.

The space of the chapel is loosely arranged, so it can be used in many different ways. Small children can gather up front for stories and older kids can belt out hymns from the high seating rows at the rear. The chapel is like a freely shaped landscape where you can choose to perch almost anywhere.

There's lots of warm-toned oak and bamboo. Big windows keep you in touch with the outdoors and

Above Ceiling within the Children's Chapel at the Korean Church of Boston, Brookline, Massachusetts

its changing seasons and weather. One window deliberately comes to the floor so even the smallest child can see directly out.

The Korean Church of Boston is Presbyterian and was founded in 1953. It draws its members from the entire metropolitan area. All parts of the addition are attached to an older church the congregation has occupied since 1967. It is a handsome red-brick, white-trim building in the traditional style known as Colonial. Nearly all of it has been preserved. Besides the chapel, the new addition includes classrooms, offices, a teen room, outdoor courtyards, and a glass fronted community room that lines the sidewalk like a public storefront. Total cost was $4.1 million.

The new architecture simply weaves its way among the older elements. The result is a complicated place. It's easy to get lost, but in return you discover a wealth of unexpected nooks and crannies.

The Reverend Lee sees the mix of styles as a metaphor for the goals of the church. "The new interpenetrates the old," says Lee. Steve Hahn, an elder of the church who led the building effort, is a retired engineer who used to design blade edges for Gillette. He puts it this way: "The idea of combining the old and the new embodies our vision for future generations."

Healy hadn't built much back in 2003 when the church picked him for the job. But he's long been known as a creative presence in Boston. He's a former president of the Boston Society of Architects and has taught at Yale and elsewhere. An exhibit of Healy's work of the past 10 years opens in New York this week, and the Korean Church will be named one of the best American buildings of 2010 in a forthcoming issue of the national magazine Architecture.

The children's chapel is full of references to icons of modernism. The ceiling, seeming to hang like a hammock overhead, recalls Le Corbusier's great chapel at Ronchamp, France. The daylight, entering from hidden sources, is like that of the American Steven Holl's chapel at the University of Seattle. The indoor-outdoor cross reminds you of noted modern chapels in Japan and Finland. Especially visible as a source is the work of the Finn Alvar Aalto, one of the three or four greats of the 20th century. Healy downplays the influence but admits to a recent tour of Aalto's work in Finland.

As noted, the building's exterior hasn't won any popularity contests among town residents. According to Lee, no one complained when the design was first presented at the Brookline Planning Board. Only when the building was largely built did people begin to groan.

Sometimes, this being literate Brookline, they groaned quite eloquently. One Internet blogger said that the boxy angular chapel, sited among its more traditional neighbors, is "like a big stereo speaker in a room of antique furniture." Another called it "this soul-destroying abomination," and a third predicted: "Wow. Forget any sort of contemporary architecture being welcomed in Brookline for the next 50 years."

There's a law in Massachusetts known as the Dover Amendment, which says that educational institutions, including churches, can more or less ignore local zoning regulations. The Korean Church came under the Dover's safety blanket and the design moved easily though the Brookline approval process.

Much as I love the chapel, I've got sympathy for the naysayers. I wouldn't want to own the house next door to that black exterior. The planning board shouldn't have told Healy what to design, but it could have asked him to reconsider the chapel's cheek-by dark-jowl relationship to the house.

Church members have begun to soften Healy's exterior by planting shrub and flower gardens, replacing the architect's minimalist native grasses. It's a further sign of their wish to reach out to engage the local community. A Korean cultural festival, to be held partly in the new community room, is planned for the spring.

Boston Sunday Globe - November 7, 2010

UNITED PARISH OF WINCHENDON

Winchendon, Massachusetts

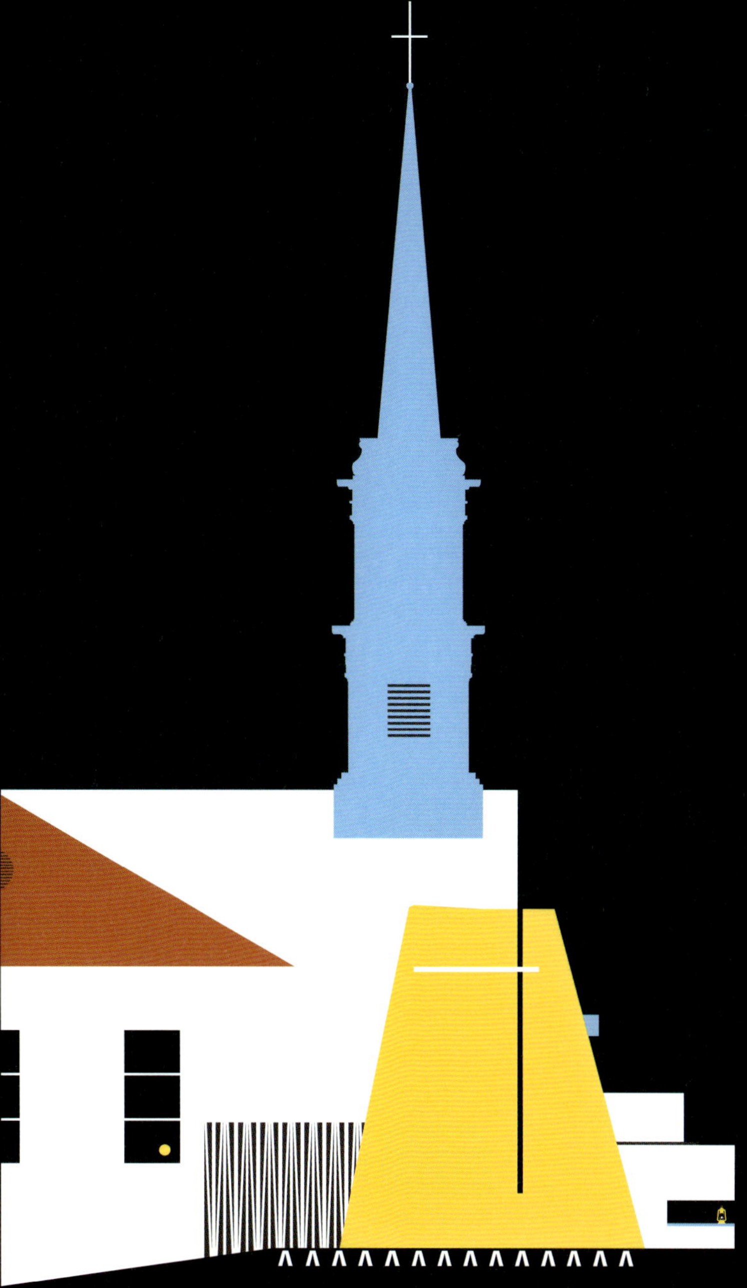

UNITED PARISH OF WINCHENDON

Winchendon, Massachusetts

The existing church, built in 1843, features bold classical detailing and a rigid, axial ordering of space. It also is oriented away from the Town Center. Using it as an anchor, the project seeks to create a campus that reconnects the church to the Town Center while expanding the church's ability to serve an enlarged array of community-oriented functions and constituents.

Christian churches from this era - while beautiful - were insular and exclusive. They were intended to be imposing to those unfamiliar. One needed to be informed that they were welcome and often told - if invited - where to sit.

Today, churches have become more open community centers trying to express their desire to let all know that they are welcome — regardless of creed or background. To find an architectural device that could broadcast that agenda, we looked at ecclesiastic architecture from earlier eras and rediscovered the role of an exonarthex - a forecourt for communal gatherings — like Bernini's colonnade in Rome — or a more modest community porch that serves the same purpose. It becomes a place to meet before and after services, a place for bake sales, wedding receptions, and local performance. We proposed to create a new single story exonarthex for the congregation that extends across the front of the historic church and wraps down into the fellowship hall beneath the sacristy. A head house — a multi-purpose chapel and community room — holds the corner overlooking the main intersection and provides a vivid invitation to everyone in the community.

Site plan

Roof plan

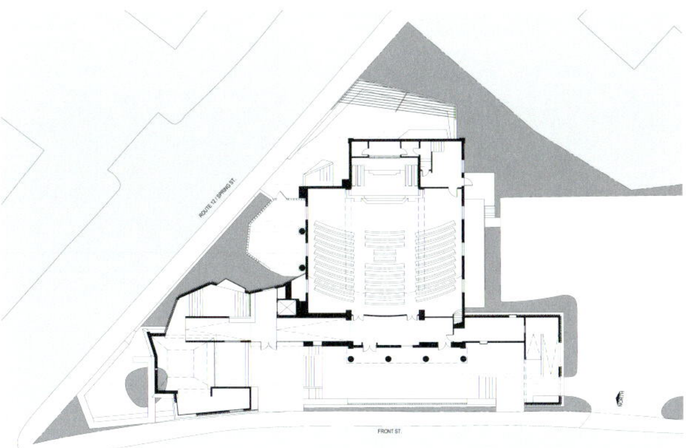

First floor plan

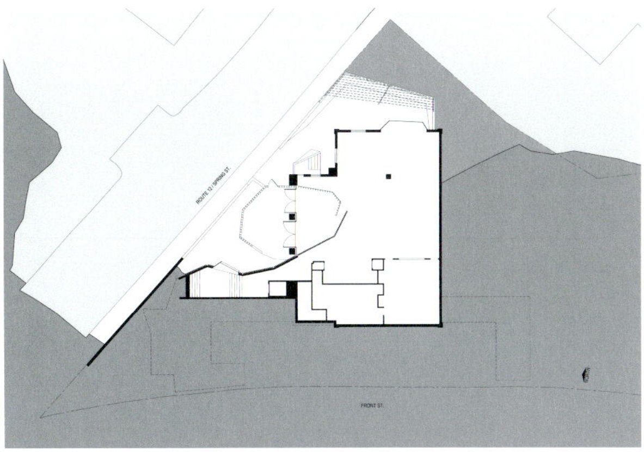

Lower floor plan

Church Studies, 2021

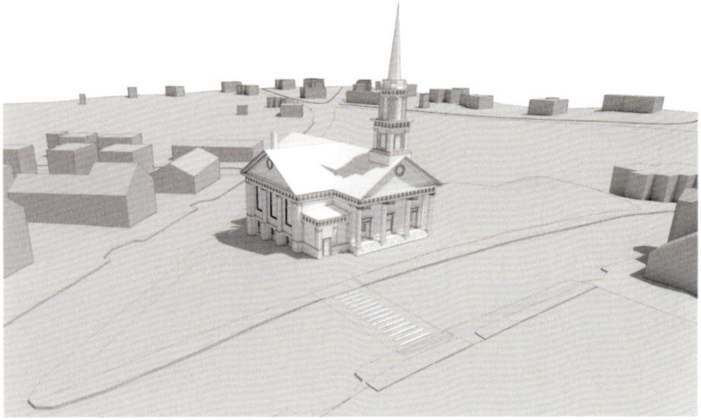

Existing building and site

Proposed addition, aerial view looking east

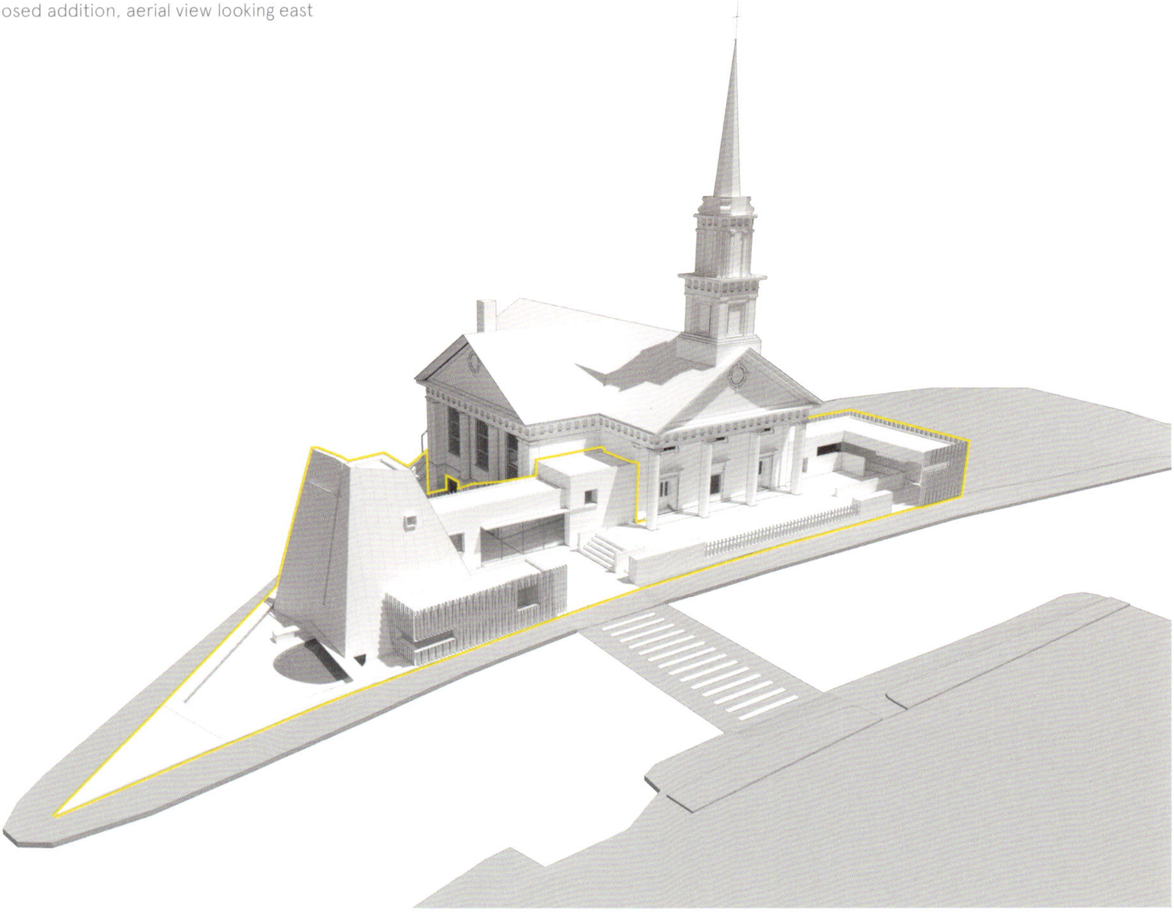

Approach (east)

Approach (west)

Proposed addition, aerial view looking north

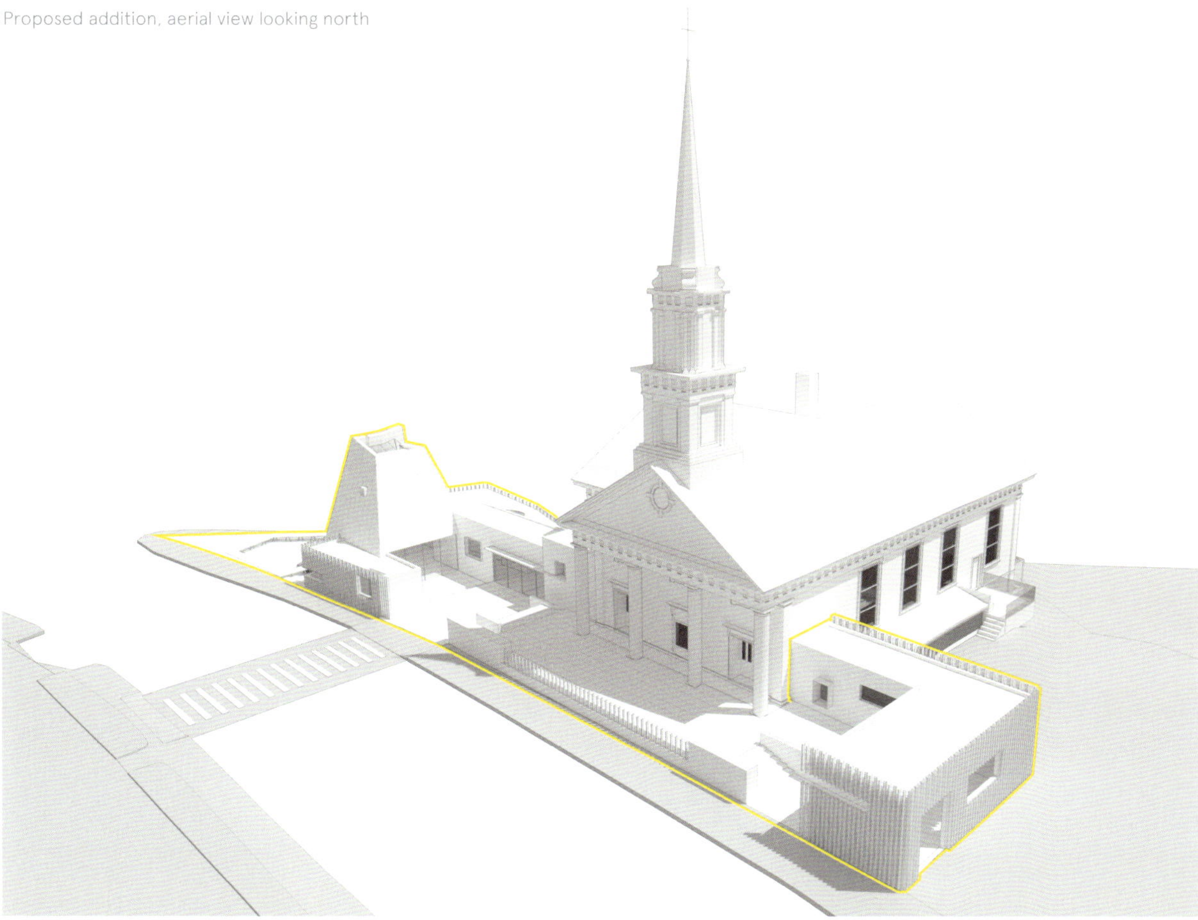

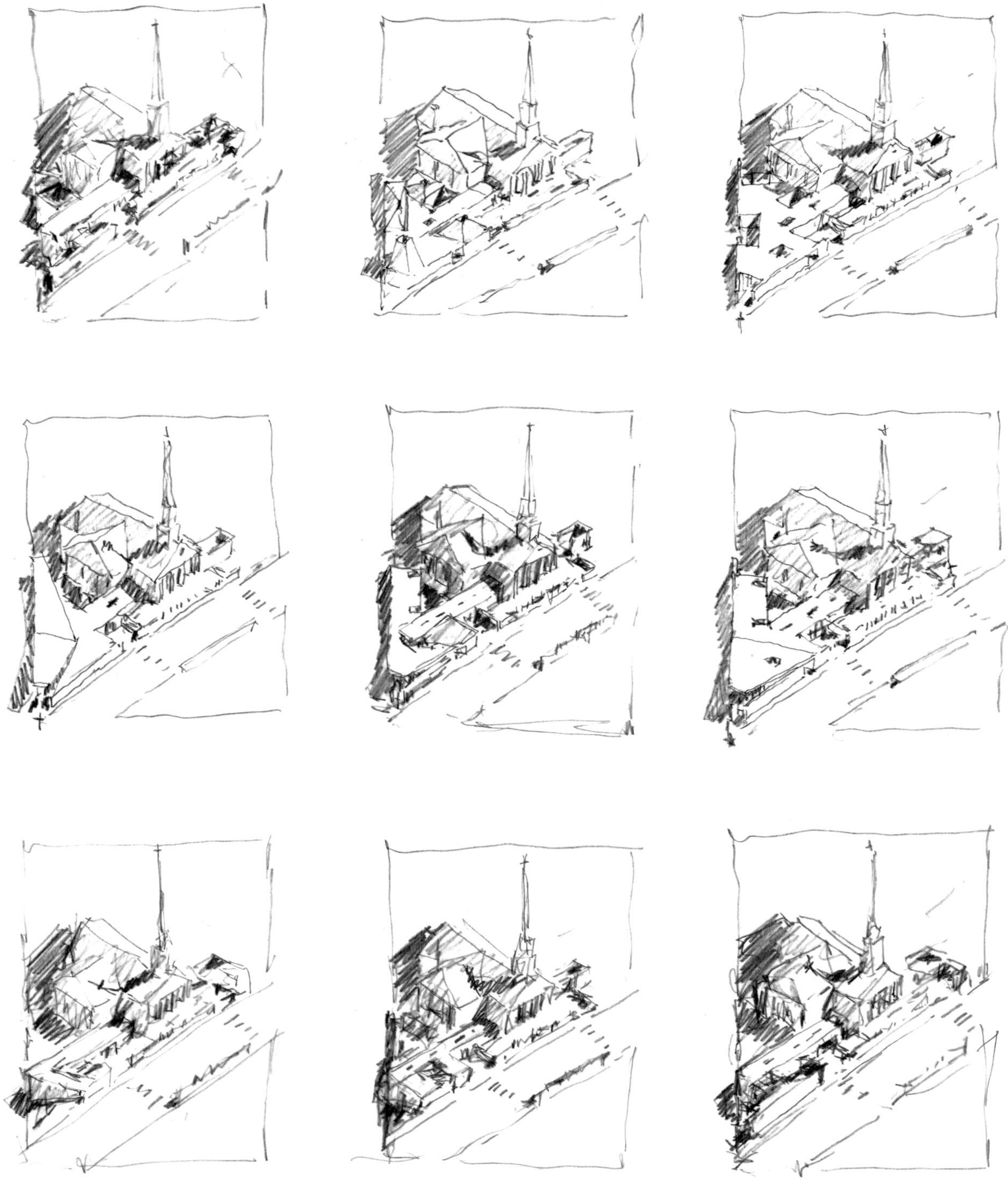

Conceptual design sketches

East elevation

North elevation

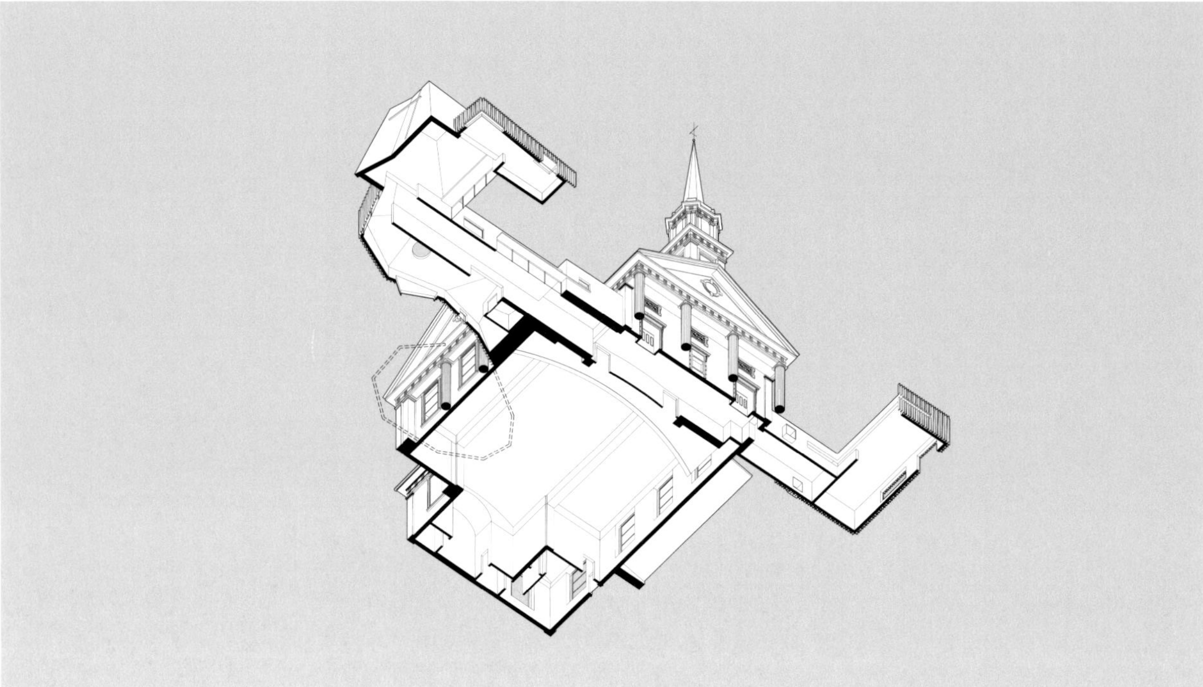

Worm's eye view looking east

Eastern approach – view from Route 12 looking west

Western approach – view from Route 12 looking east

View from church parking lot looking east

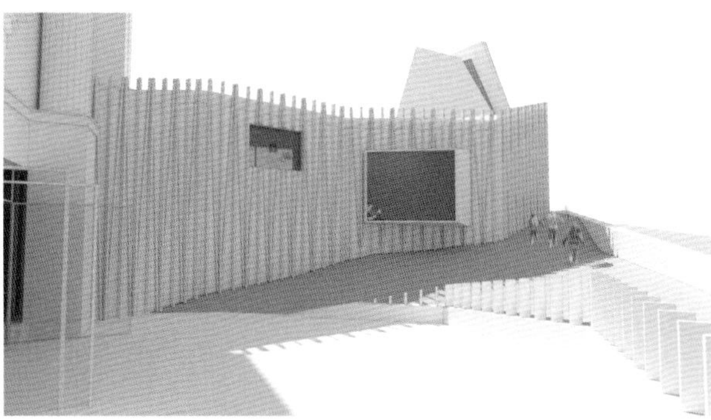

View from new courtyard looking west

View from Exonarthex podium looking north

View from within proposed community room looking south

Section perspective through community room/chapel and exonarthex looking east

View looking north down proposed corridor leading from existing narthex toward new community room

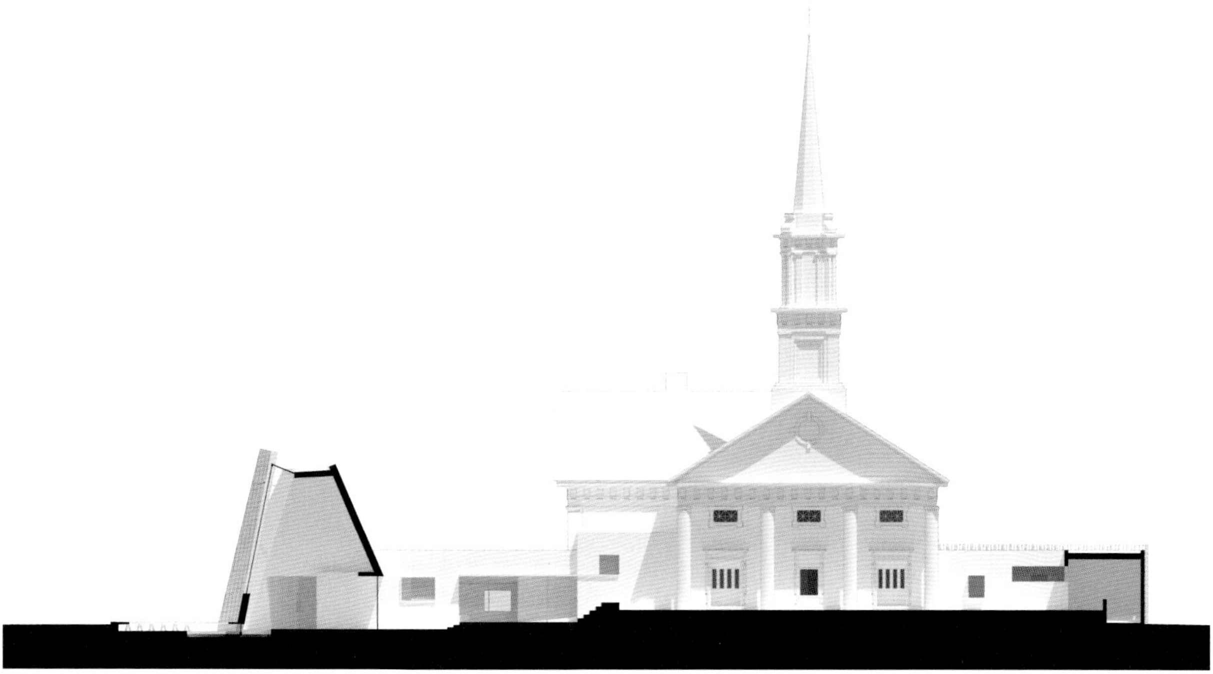

Longitudinal section

Exterior court looking into new multi-purpose room

View along Spring Street upon entry into Winchendon

View of new campus along Front Street

EDUCATION AND COMMUNITY CENTER

Korean Church of Boston
Brookline, Massachusetts

EDUCATION AND COMMUNITY CENTER

Korean Church of Boston
Brookline, Massachusetts

"I think the thing one would do in the beginning of a project like this is completely divorcing the addition – a modest addition – away from a very traditional church. Here, they weave the buildings together and let the architecture come together. From a certain perspective, that was really a brave thing to do."

Progressive Architecture Jury Comments

The congregation of the Korean Church of Boston held an architectural competition in 2003 to celebrate their fiftieth anniversary Jubilee, and they selected Healy's submission for construction. The congregation had decided to honor its third generation members – the children ages five through twelve – by building a new chapel for them next to their existing church in Brookline, Massachusetts. They also decided to provide a teen center with classrooms for seminars and group discussion.

The church campus serves a wide metropolitan congregation and members come from throughout the greater Boston area. Services are held on Sunday morning followed by a community meal. In the afternoon, the children attend classes, their parents gather together into their own study groups, and the elders congregate to discuss church matters. By giving the children a special place of their own in which to worship, play, and study, the congregation recognizes and cultivates the participation of its youngest members. The charge was further animated by the unique qualities of the site and the particular circumstances of this small urban campus that lies between the commercial and governmental areas of Brookline Village. The existing church – constructed in the mid-fifties – is a brick building which turns is back on Harvard Street, the main commercial artery of the area lined with two and three story buildings. The main church and its entry look across Holden Street toward a town green with City Hall, a Library, and Police Station. There is 8,341 square feet of new construction and 2,133 square feet of renovated construction.

The master plan for the sequencing of the renovations and additions address both the campus and its future planning. The Chapel and Education Center was placed parallel to the existing church adjacent to residential buildings that facing the civic institutions of Brookline. The siting also produced a private interior court. Extensive built-in seating throughout the project allows for informal conversations and interaction outside of the classrooms and the chapel.

In order to negotiate the nine-foot height change between Harvard and Holden Streets, the original land was built up as a flat plinth that required a foreboding retaining wall and steep steps along Harvard Street. This plinth was excavated down to grade to create a new park for both the congregation and the public. This park is part of a new Community Center located on Harvard Street and marked by a prominent head house and broad storefront. This center re-establishes the street's edge and provides for a connection to the surrounding community and its active pedestrian traffic.

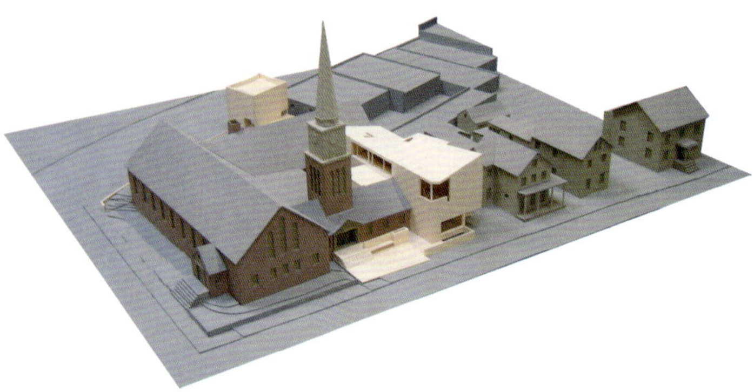

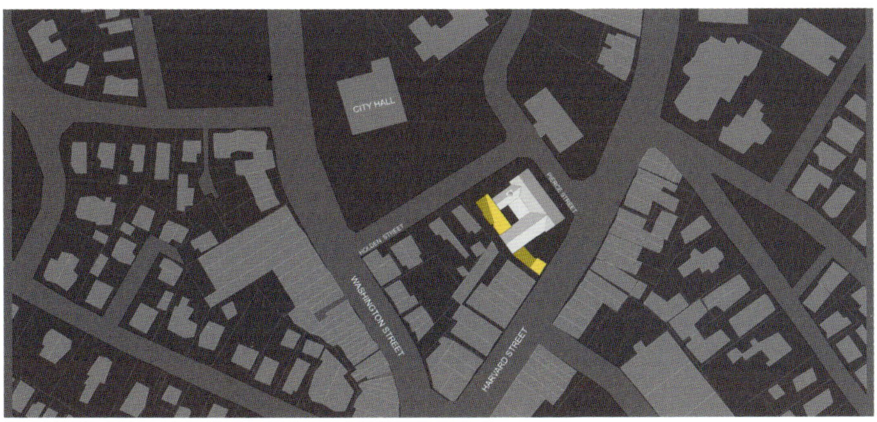
CITY HALL
HOLDEN STREET
PIERCE STREET
WASHINGTON STREET
HARVARD STREET

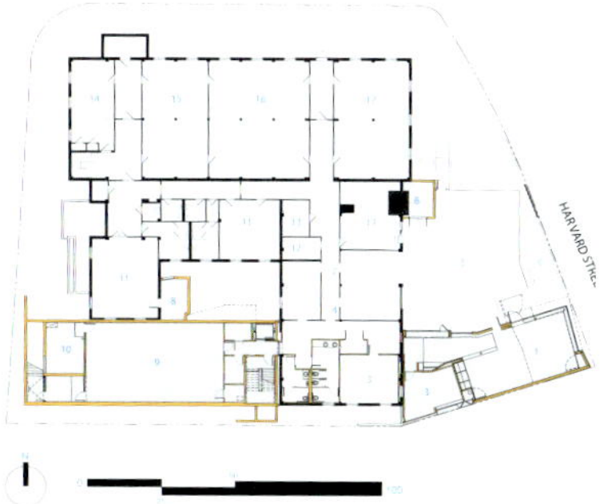

Lower level floor plan

1 Cultural center/ Community hall
2 Kitchenette
3 New classroom
4 Community room
5 Open plaza
6 Planter
7 Passageway
8 Storage room
9 Teen fellowship room
10 Mechanical
11 Existing choir room
12 Existing kitchen
13 Existing storage
14 Existing office
15 Existing student activity room
16 Existing young adult room
17 Existing senior room

First floor plan

1 Parlor
2 New entrance
3 Fellowship hall
4 Classroom
5 Office
6 Existing stage
7 Roof terrace
8 Open to below
9 Plaza below
10 Entry
11 Steeple/Lantern above
12 Foyer
13 Courtyard
14 Existing kitchen
15 Existing office
16 Existing sanctuary
17 Existing altar

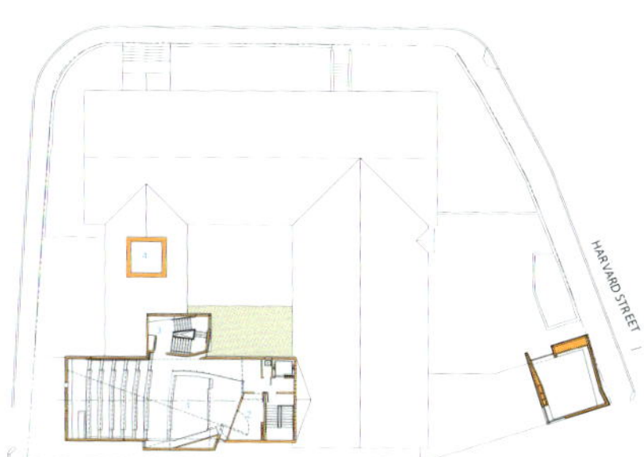

Second floor plan

1 Children's chapel
2 Altar/Stage
3 Entry stair
4 Steeple

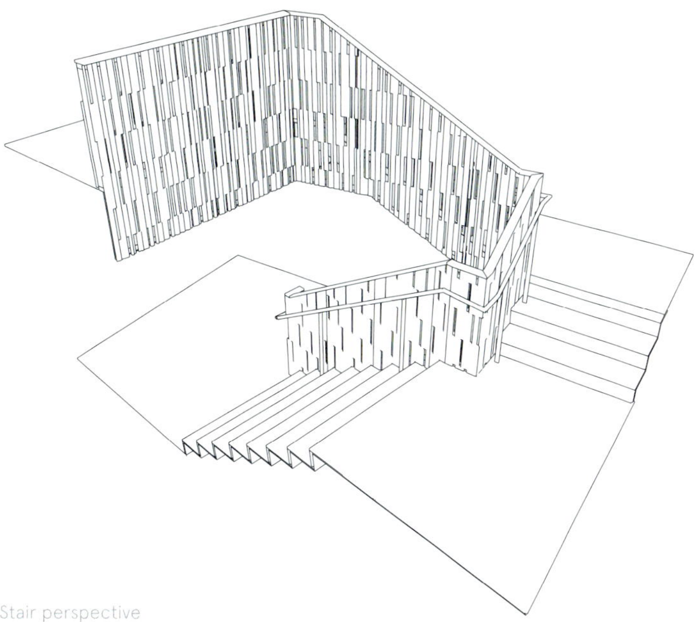

Stair perspective

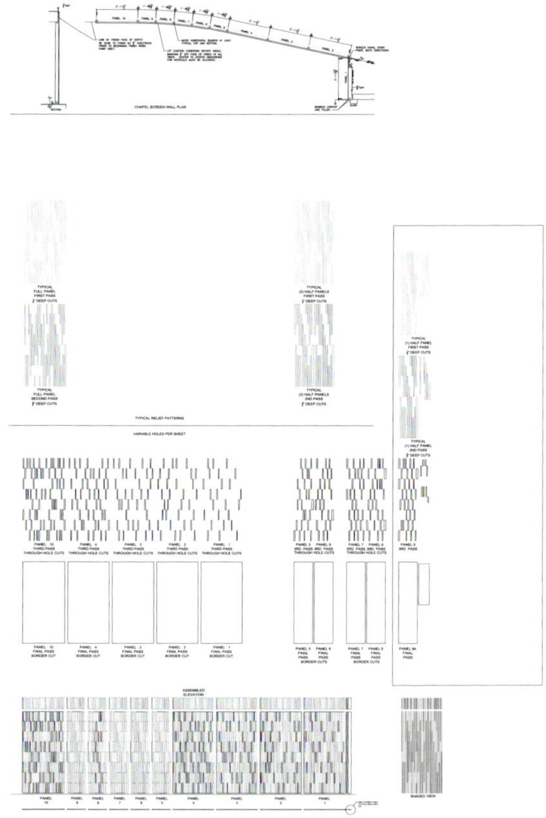

Chapel screenwall

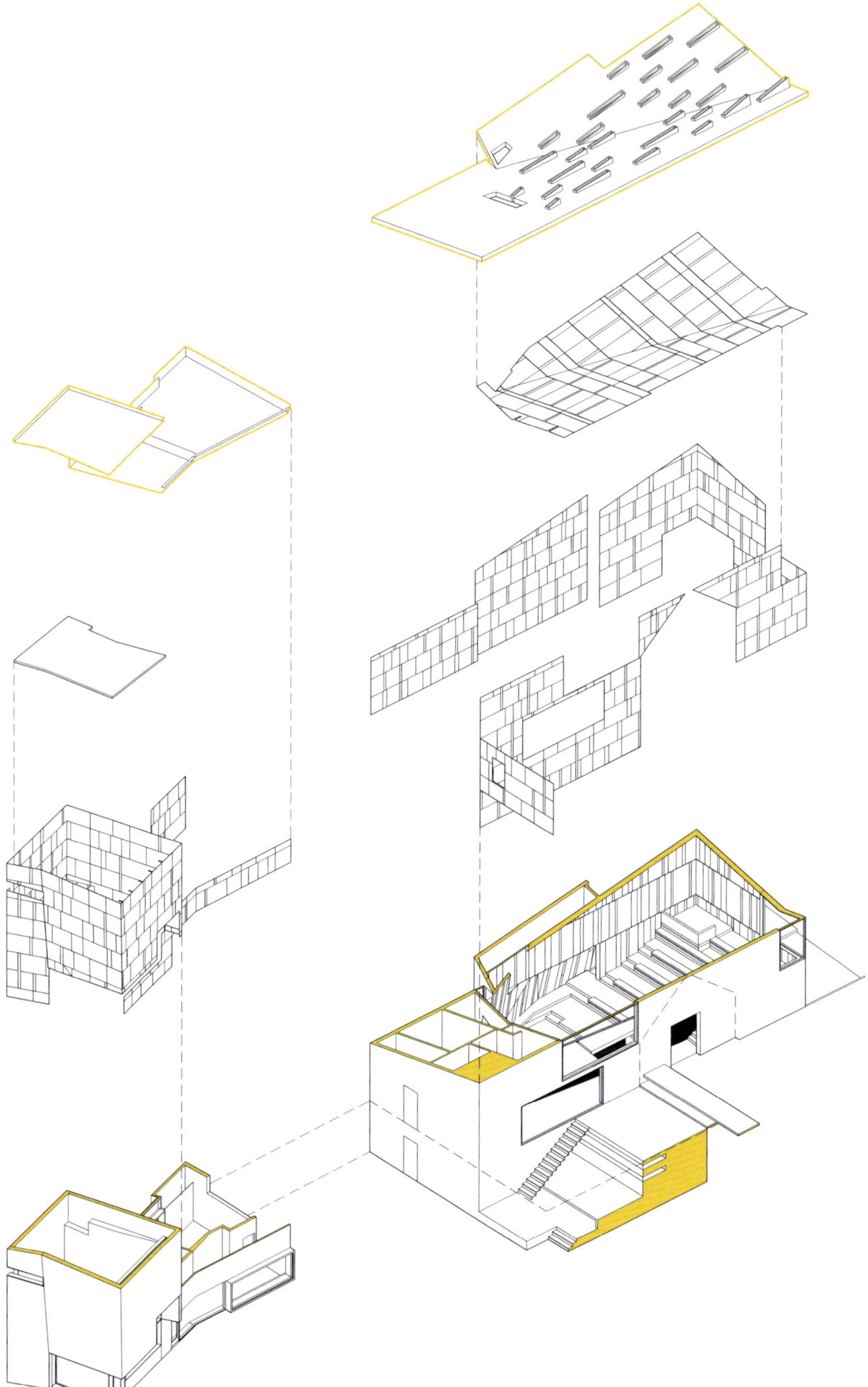

Exploded axonometric

View of chapel from altar

Community Center along Harvard Street

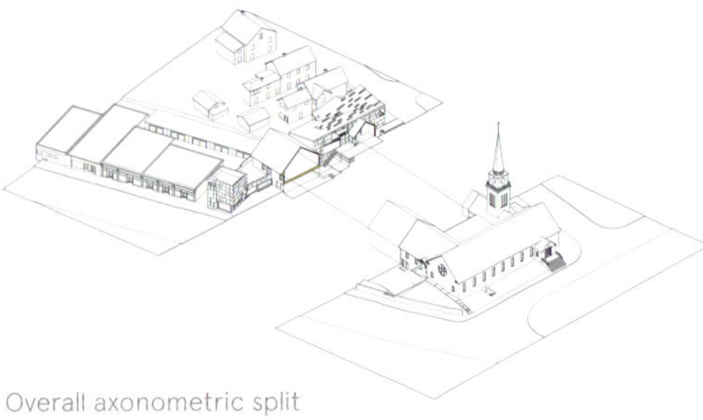

Overall axonometric split

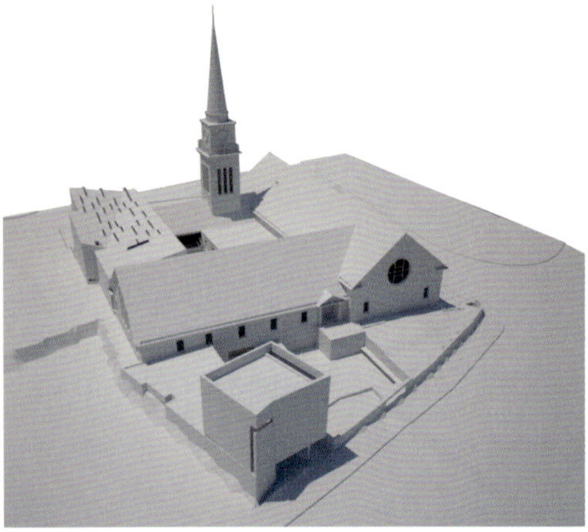

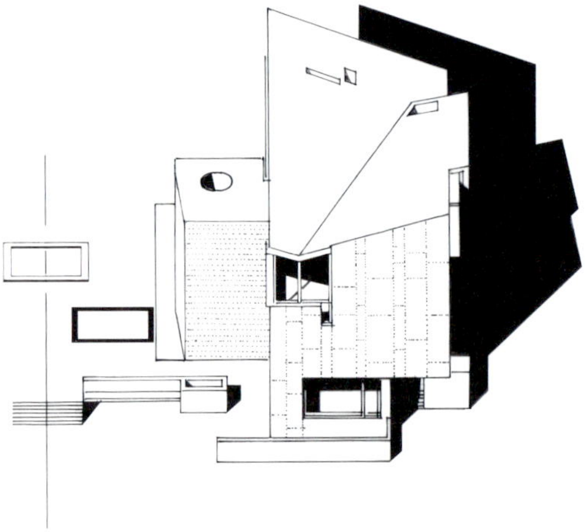

Axonometric from west

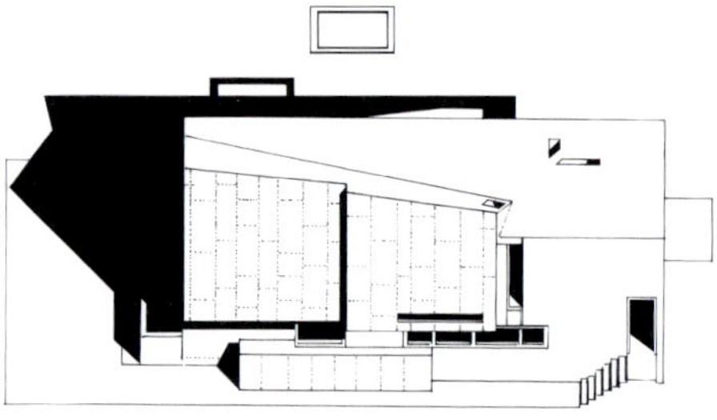

Axonometric from south

LIVE

Ships at a distance have every man's wish on board. For some they come in with the tide. For others they sail forever on the horizon, never out of sight, never landing until the Watcher turns his eyes away in resignation, his dreams mocked to death by Time. That is the life of men.

Now, women forget all those things they don't want to remember, and remember everything they don't want to forget. The dream is the truth. Then they act and do things accordingly.

Their Eyes Were Watching God - Zora Neale Hurston

houses, housing + hotels

ESSAY

Poetry provides the one permissible way of saying one thing and meaning another.

Robert Frost

ROBERT CAMPBELL

IN FLOATYARD, A DESIGN DREAM OF BOSTON HARBOR'S FUTURE

Site Lines

It looks like an enormous cubist bug, heaving itself out of the water of Boston Harbor. Maybe something out of a horror movie? No, it's a proposal for a floating block of residences — a whole floating community, really — on a site in the Charlestown Navy Yard.

When I first saw it, I didn't take it seriously. It seemed like just one more in a stream of sometimes silly fantasies that were being offered by architects and architecture students as solutions to the problem of rising sea levels. But the more you look at it, the more interesting it is. Like a lot of good ideas, this one is just crazy enough to make sense.

It's the brainchild of architect Brian Healy, the director of design in the Boston office of the national firm of Perkins + Will. Healy worked with developer Ed Nardi of Cresset Development, best known for the Liberty Wharf complex in South Boston.

They call their design Floatyard. Recently, it won a prestigious national award for good design from the magazine *Architecture*.

Floatyard is a kind of civic square of residences. Three stories of living units are arranged along the four sides of a central courtyard. You'll get a pretty good sense of Floatyard if you imagine a helicopter hoisting up one of those small residential squares in the South End and dropping it down on the Charlestown waterfront. The entire complex floats, but it remains in place. It rises and falls by sliding up and down on vertical mooring posts, the way a ring slides on a finger.

Floatyard, admittedly, isn't going to be built anytime soon. This is the kind of design that's meant to stir the imagination, not to be immediately practical. The goal is to explore new ideas and stimulate

Above View of Floatyard from Boston Harbor. **Following spread** Porthole and Walkway of Floatyard.

a conversation. Often, in the history of architecture, utopian designs like this have been influential. I hope Floatyard turns out to be one of them.

We live in a city, and in a world, where everyone seems to want to live by the water, but where sea levels and storm surges are predicted to rise to increasingly dangerous levels. There's a need to invent new ways of living with water.

What's so impressive about Floatyard is the breadth of issues it raises. It's just as much about creating a sense of urban community as it is about dealing with changing climate.

The central courtyard, for example, has been imagined as a new kind of space. Like any good city courtyard, it's both a children's playground and an adult meeting place. Overlooked by numerous stairs and balconies, it's a setting for social encounters. But it also contains a water garden that seeks to re-create in miniature the tidal marsh landscape of the original harbor, encouraging the return of native species. This is a place where land and sea meet as friends, not enemies.

Equally inventive is the proposal for construction. New structural materials, such as lightweight concrete, now make floating buildings more practical. But the Floatyard proposal is much more ambitious than that. Healy and Nardi suggest that the building could be fabricated elsewhere and pulled by tugboat across the harbor on barges, as was done with huge sections of the Big Dig tunnels. Much larger chunks of architecture — maybe even entire buildings — can be transported by sea than by land, thus saving costs.

If that concept caught on, they argue, it could stimulate a revival of activity in the Boston seaport's once famous shipyards, now languishing in places like Hull, East Boston, and Quincy. Boston Harbor would be re-industrialized: It would manufacture housing where it once made ships. The water would once again be home to a vital, real-world mix of maritime uses.

As for Floatyard's appearance, nobody's bothered to fuss much yet with the architecture. There are 100-plus living units in several sizes, with ground-floor space for shops and recreational amenities. Nearly all the dwellings enjoy open ocean views, and all are entered from the common courtyard. Some units push out from the facade with angular bay windows, while others recede behind private terraces. The result is to make the building look as if it's inhabited by a diverse population. This is architecture that's doing its job, not shouting for attention.

Floatyard will face plenty of obstacles if and when its creators decide they want to turn some version of the idea into an actual building. Massachusetts waterfronts are heavily guarded by design regulations, a fact we should all be grateful for. The state's Chapter 91 law, which is famous among city planners and dates to 1866, sets out stringent rules for just about everything you'd want to build on or near a waterfront. Floatyard appears to violate it — or let's say challenge it — in more than one way.

But laws and their interpretations evolve in a changing world. And the process is just beginning. Developer Nardi doesn't yet have control of the Navy Yard pier he's selected for this demonstration design. He admits that any future permitting process will be tough. But he thinks it may be possible.

Floating housing has been successful in other parts of the world, notably the Netherlands. And the houseboats in places like Sausalito, in Northern California, are treasured. It doesn't always work. People don't want to feel isolated or surrounded in a world of water. But Floatyard is firmly attached, like a dock, to the land and its utilities. It's just another traditional Boston finger pier that happens to float.

Global warming is a reality and so is the rise of sea levels. Nobody knows how high they'll go. If Sandy had been aimed a few degrees farther north, it would have swamped much of Boston and environs. Someday, another storm surge will do that or worse.

In principle, there are three ways for waterfront cities to respond to rising sea levels. They can pick up and move to higher ground. They can wall themselves off from the water with dikes and barriers. Or they can reach out to welcome the influx of water and, like Venice or Suzhou, China, find ways of living with it and, perhaps, even enhancing the quality of life.

We'll see all three approaches in the coming years. The third is the most interesting and the cheapest. Boston has a long history of reinventing its relationship to the sea, often in radical ways. This is no time to stop.

Is Foatyard a pie-in-the-sky idea? Of course. That's where good ideas begin. My guess is that we haven't seen the last of this one.

Boston Globe - April 27, 2013

TREE HOUSE

Duxbury, Massachusetts

TREE HOUSE

Duxbury, Massachusetts

During the initial phases of design, Healy was permitted to set up a studio and work/live in the existing house on the site for a year. The light – with the spectacular views – changes constantly and those views are framed by an elegant old oak tree that exists along the top of the coastal bank. It reminded the client of his visits to Japanese gardens and provided an inspiration for a new relationship between our proposed internal and external spaces. In fact, they discovered that the entire site can act as a series of frames from the tree lined boulevard through existing mature trees and shrubs, to unlimited views of Duxbury Bay and the Atlantic Ocean. They then designed the compound itself to create another series of frames to compliment the procession through – and within – this existing landscape.

The compound is a retreat for a couple and their family on a 1-acre coastal parcel in Duxbury, a historic community about 35 miles south of Boston. It is located at the tip of a small peninsula and offers views of Clark's Island – the first landing site of the Pilgrims in 1620 – as well as Pilgrim Monument located in distant Provincetown. The home seeks to capture and augment the atmosphere of this place while providing a place of solace and refuge for its owners and their guests.

Vertical planes – sometimes literal, others more transparent – serve as lenses that adjust light and views. The result is an unfolding and layered experience of the site and the new residential compound. The rear façade – conceived of as a kaleidoscope – is composed of large, scattered planes of glass which adjust and alter one's perspective as you move though the house.

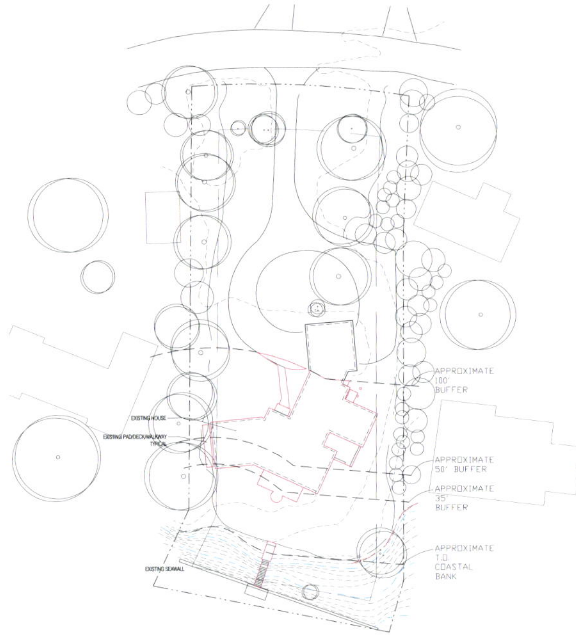

Existing site conditions, coastal buffeer analysis

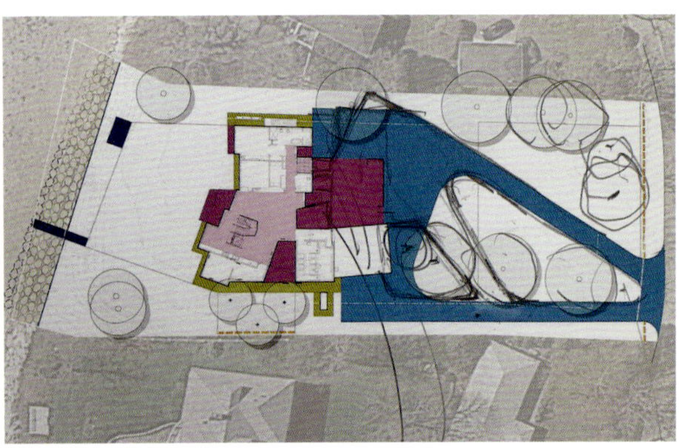

Site plan with new driveway

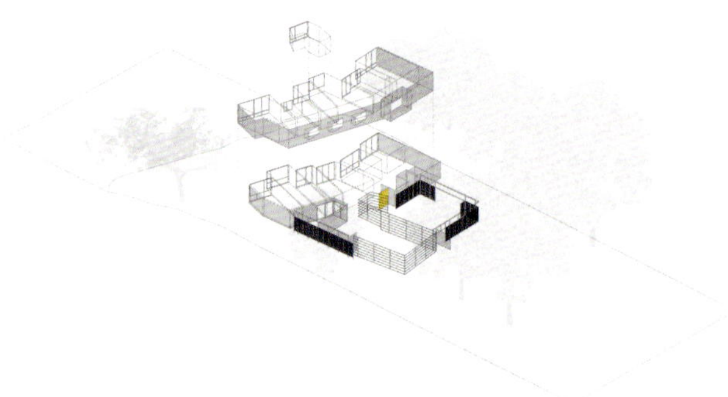

Analytical diagram

Exterior study

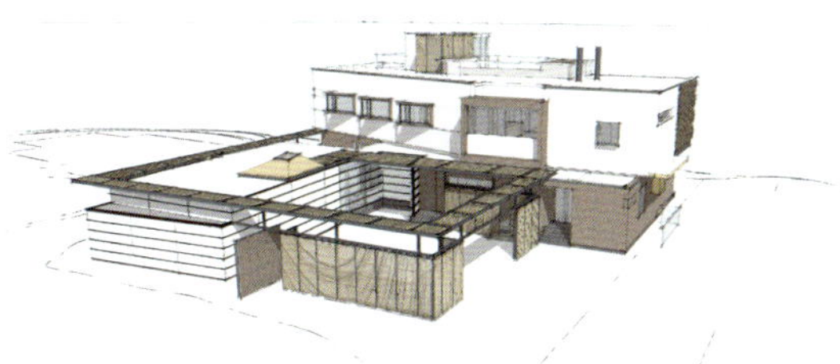

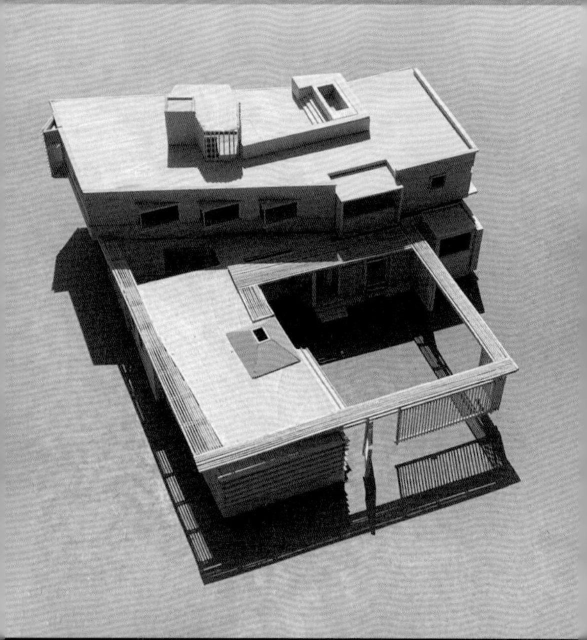

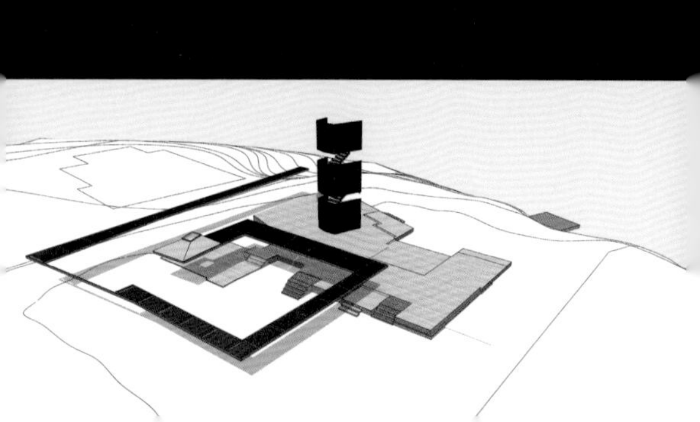

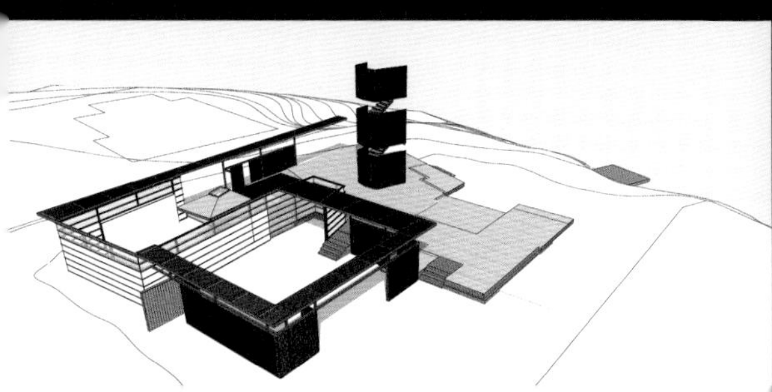

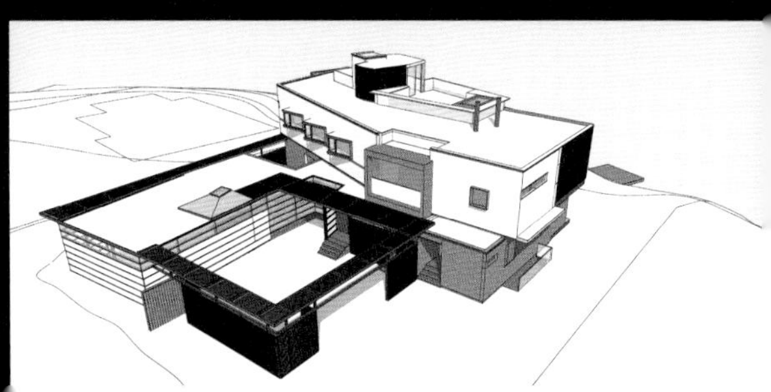

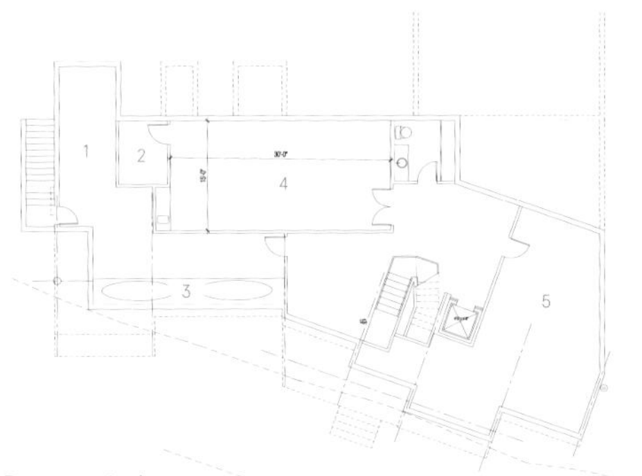

Basement plan

1 Mechanical / storage finished
2 Band storage
3 Paddle board storage
4 Band practice room finished 9′ceiling
5 Unfinished

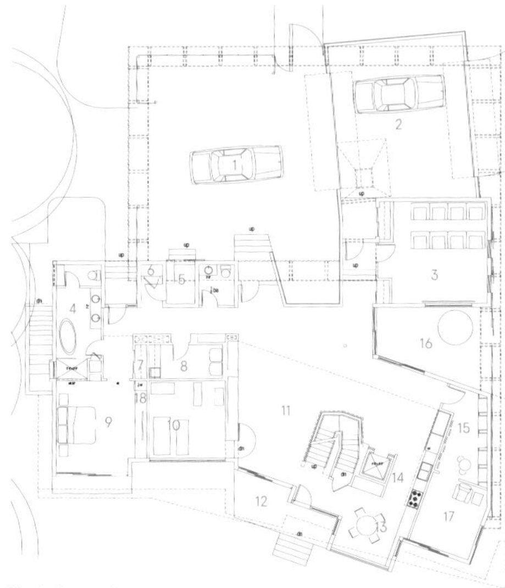

First floor plan

1 Forecourt
2 Two car garage
3 Media room
4 Bath
5 Outdoor shower
6 Storage
7 Clos
8 Laundry
9 Guest bedroom
10 Fitness
11 Family room
12 Outdoor deck
13 Breakfast area
14 Kitchen
15 Equipment
16 Garden
17 Music room
18 Coffee

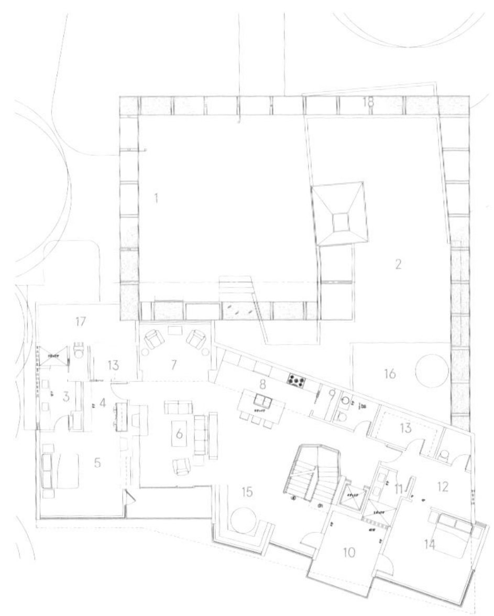

Second floor plan

1 Screen roof below
2 Roof below
3 Bath/dressing
4 Dressing
5 Lisa′s bedroom
6 Living
7 Reading area
8 Kitchen
9 Pantry
10 Porch
11 Bath
12 Dressing
13 Clos
14 Jim′s bedroom
15 Dining
16 Garden below
17 Roof below
18 Skylights below

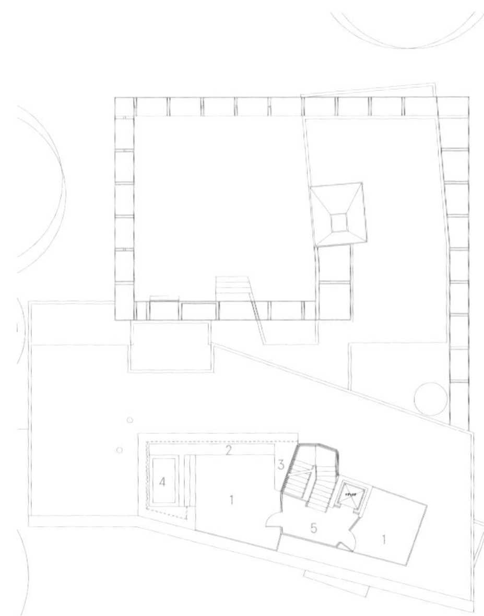

Roof plan

1 Roof deck
2 Storage under bench
3 Bar
4 Hot tub
5 Dn

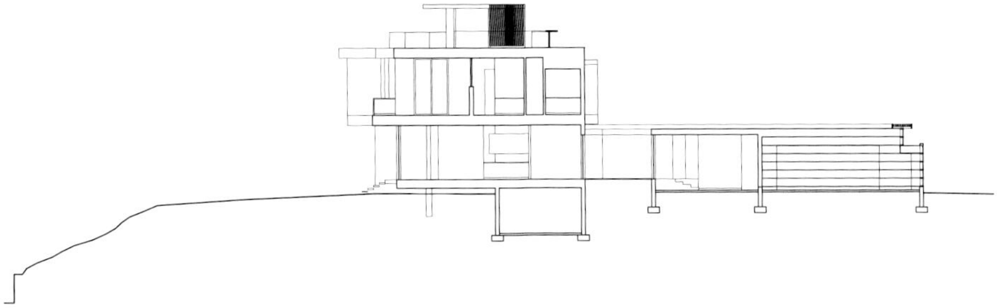

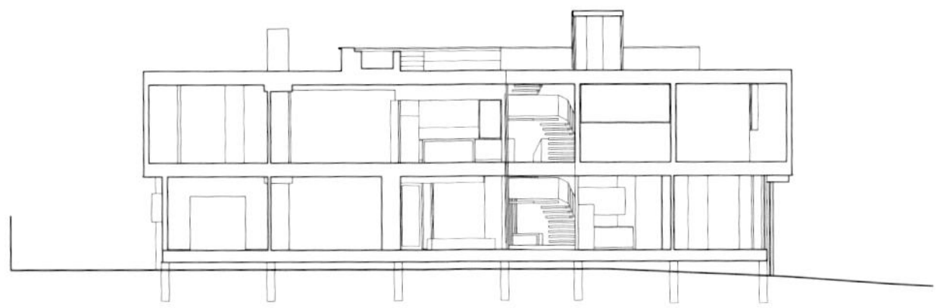

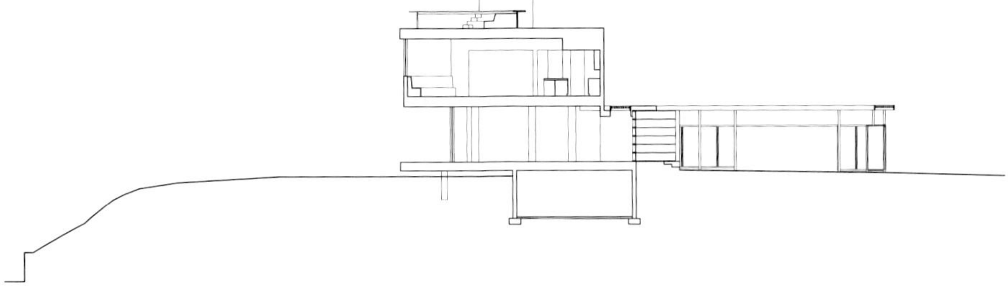

Building sections

76

88 WAREHAM

Boston, Massachusetts

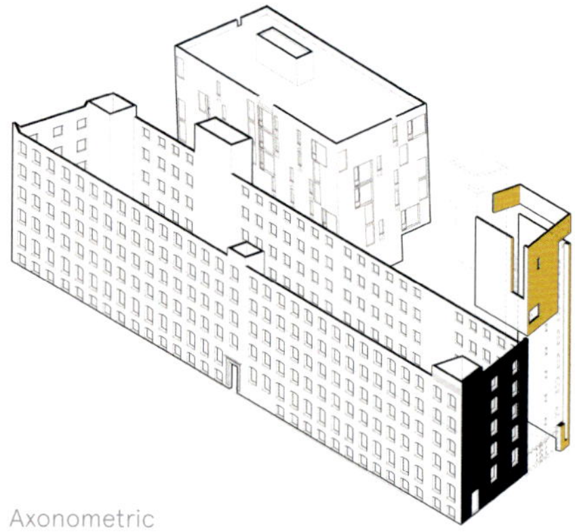

Axonometric

88 WAREHAM

Boston, Massachusetts

After renovating a dozen existing brick warehouses into residential units – including 90 Wareham Street which is directly adjacent to our site in the South End of Boston, the client asked Healy to design a new mixed use building at 88 Wareham that would include 27 condominium units, a retail space, and a fully automated parking structure below. The project also provides the amenity of a shared open roof terrace with extensive views of the Boston skyline.

They had renovated a dozen old brick warehouses across Boston with the client and, accordingly, chose to build upon what they had learned by working with those masonry structures. And sought to construct a 21st century version while incorporated new technologies and systems. They used hand-laid masonry as well but – rather than a repetitious wallpaper of anonymous repetitive windows, we collected the glass openings into singular large floor to ceiling windows – framed in metal – to highlight – and identify – each individual dwelling unit – and by extension – the individuals who reside there.

Each units become unique with floor to ceiling glass – a window to the world – that provides an essential connection between the dweller and the urban streetscape outside with adjacent masonry buildings and metal fire escapes acting as reminder of the others that preceded us.

Given the size and physical constraints of the site, it was not possible to satisfy zoning requirements for parking for the City of Boston. After countless below grade studies revealed inadequate space for adequate parking and traffic circulation, they adopted the automated car parking system to meet the requirements and maintain a viable project. The decision to go with 5BY2 – an automated system from the Netherlands – was the very first of its kind to be approved by the City of Boston.

Axonometric

Lobby

Common standard parcel dimensions:
a 6″
b 10″
c 3″-6″ elongated (lenghts vary)
d 17″x27″
e 20″x20″
f 36″x12″
g 30″x25″
h 30″x15″

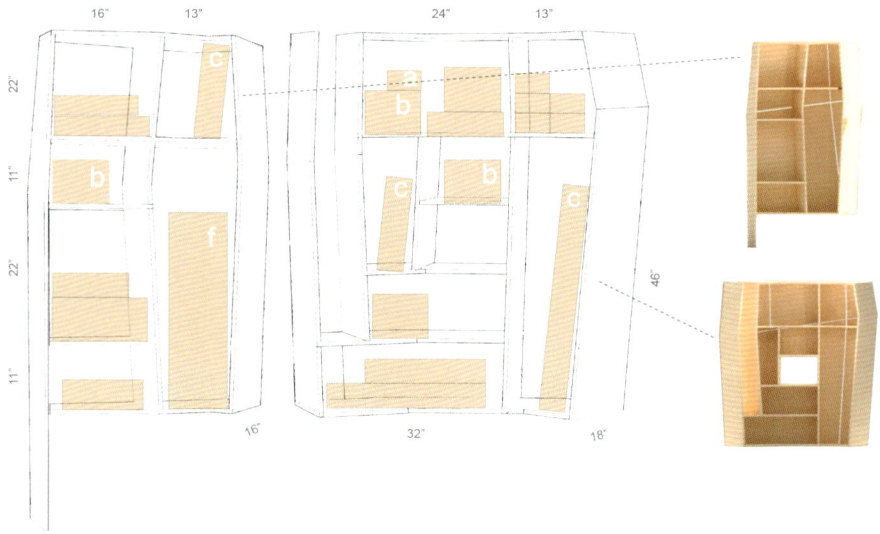

1 Parcel storage

2 Parcel storage

3 Oversized parcel storage

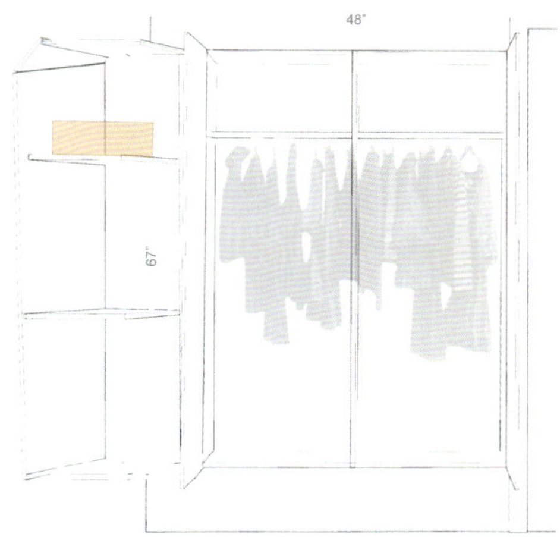

4 Dry-clean delivery

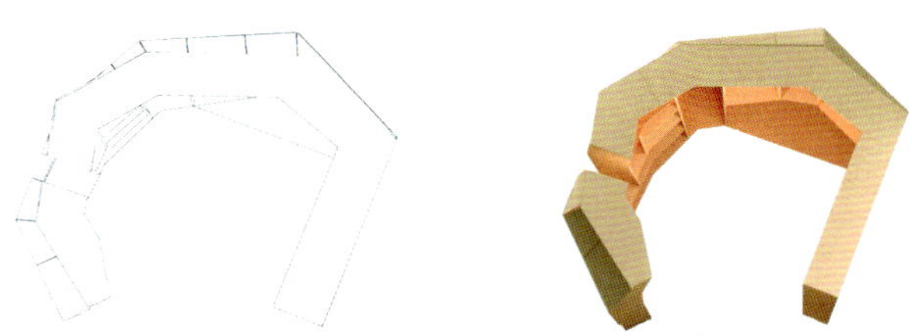

Lobby storage unit

Typical unit - Wood finish

EXIT

Roof terrace overlooking downtown Boston

ZAPATOS

90
WAREHAM
90

DOT COMMON

South Boston, Massachusetts

DOT COMMON

South Boston, Massachusetts

The Boston Society of Architects – with Tim Love as president – invited three local interdisciplinary urban design teams to share their thoughts on the potential development of this vast site along the railroad tracks in the Dorchester Section of South Boston. The open parcel between the tracks and Dorchester Avenue was divided into four sites with new pathways sliced into it to create shared public space that invites people into the heart of the development. In the center, a collective common was created and connected to each site.

The development required storage for 880 automobiles and 678 bicycles. Instead of scattering this requirement across all the parcels, the decision was made to meet that requirement with parking limited exclusively to site D. This allowed us to reduce the number of curb cuts, garage doors, and ground level parking that would preclude an active – interactive – urban streetscape. We utilized a structured mechanized parking system along the rear of the site that anticipates the reuse of the space as the demand for individual automobiles diminish over time. The system could be removed to create new retail or commercial opportunities that would further animate the courtyard and provide future amenities for the neighborhood. Bike parking and tenant storage space is accessed through the courtyard.

The project was envisioned as a microcosm of the city itself with diverse private and public spaces grouped around a shared public common. The complex is 535,000 square feet with the 686 units divided into micro-units, studios, one-bedrooms, two bedrooms, duplexes, and short term rentals similar to hotel accommodations that act as a form of post-graduate housing. In addition to housing, the complex includes amenities that would be shared with the residents of the surrounding neighborhoods including farmer's market, daycare, health club, restaurants, gardens, and terraces. The buildings are oriented to maximize sunlight while blocking the north Atlantic winds and allowing extensive views to the South End and Back Bay on the north and west; and views out to the Harbor to the east and south.

Public and private greens spaces scattered throughout the site – both in plan and section – extend communal space across the site and up throughout the building reinforcing the prominence of the public realm.

Site plan

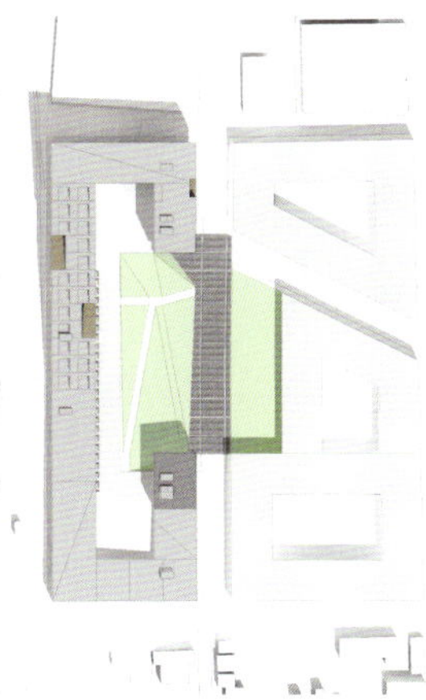
Roof plan

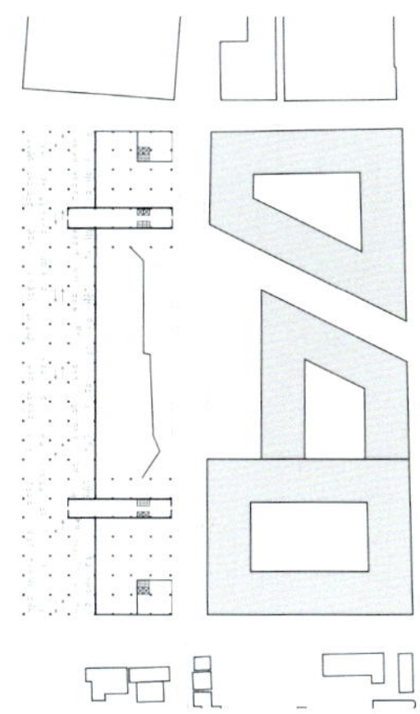
Ground floor plan

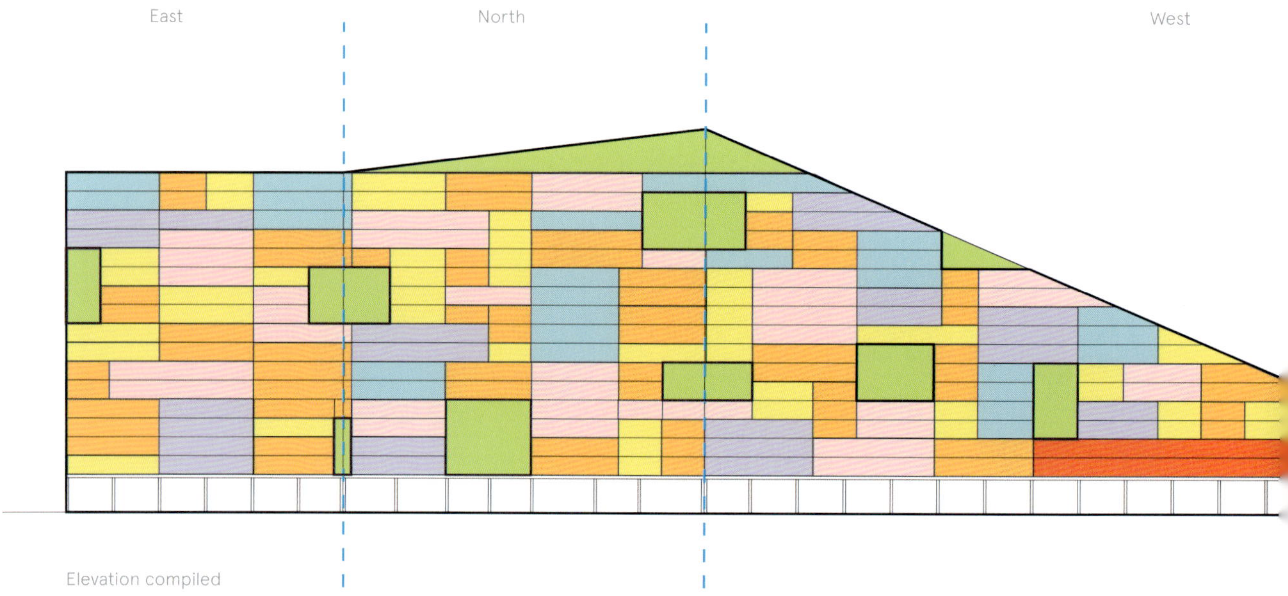

Elevation compiled

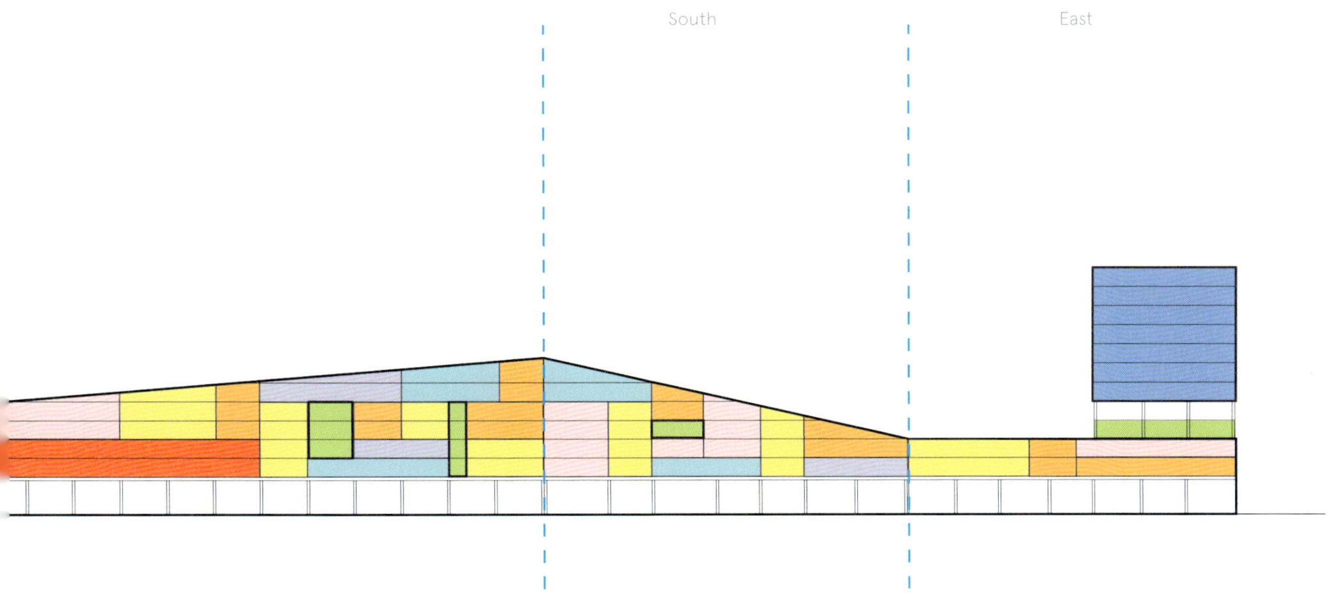
South
East

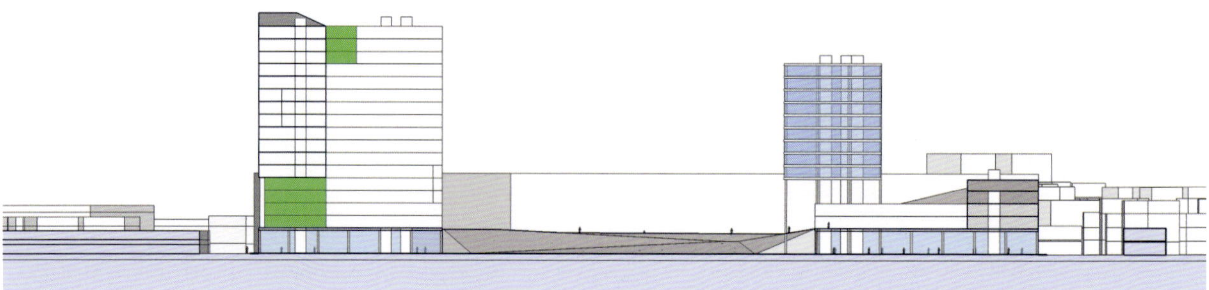

Longitudinal section

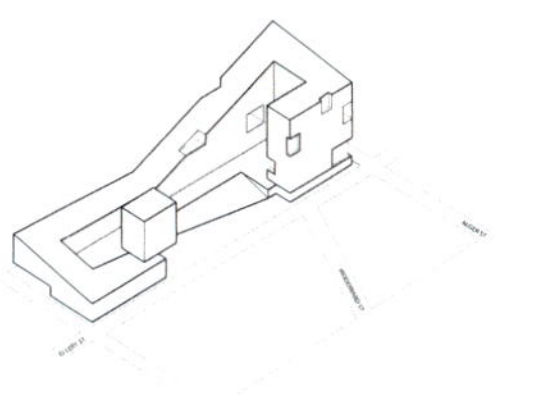

Building an urban microcosm-diversity of lifestyle

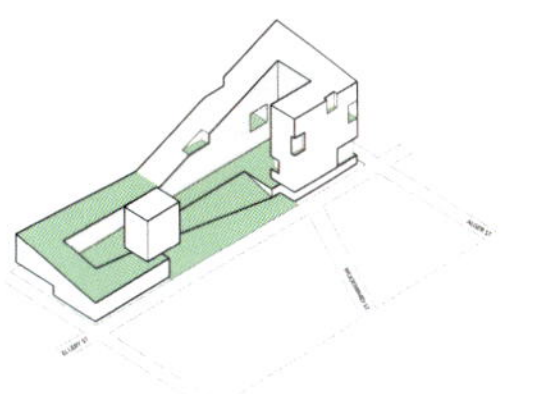

Public and private green space throughtout engages and reinforces the public realm

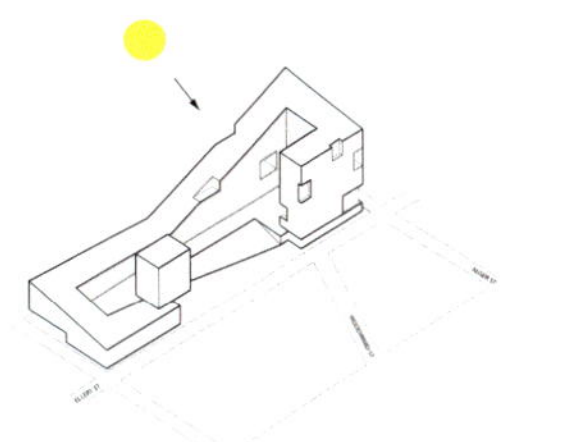

Light filled courtyard creates a comfortable urban space

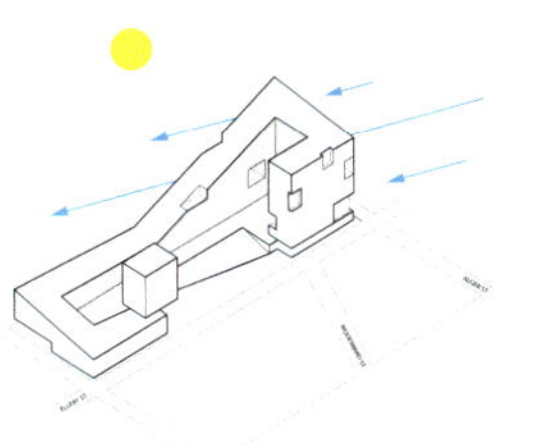

With form that retains winter heat and blocks the Atlantic wind

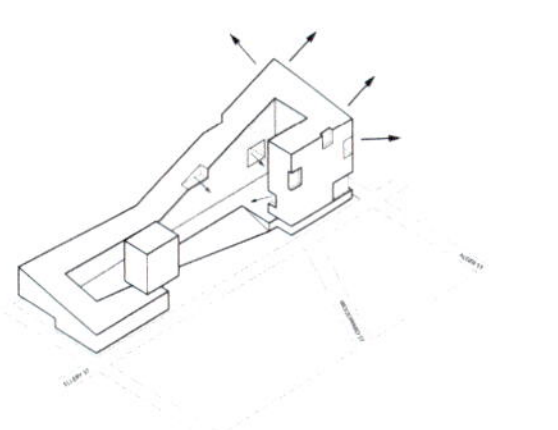

With views inward towards an active realm and outwards to downtown Boston and the sea

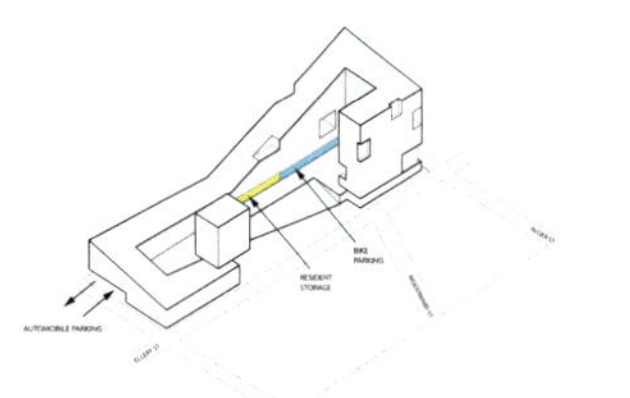

Open air mechanized parking along railroad tracks reduces sound and elevates units for privacy and distant views of South End and Back Bay. Bike parking and tenant storage space accessed through courtyard

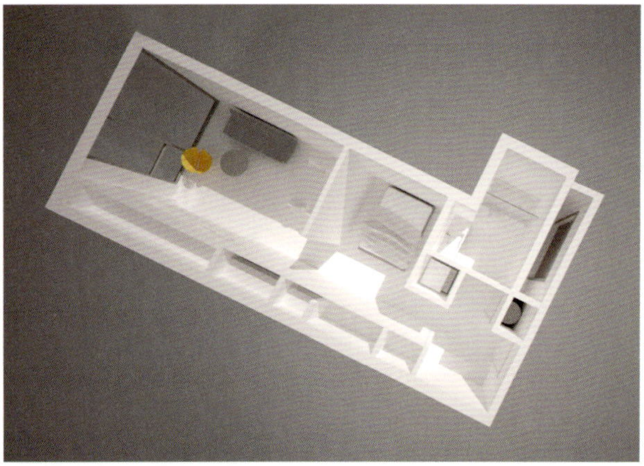

Studio

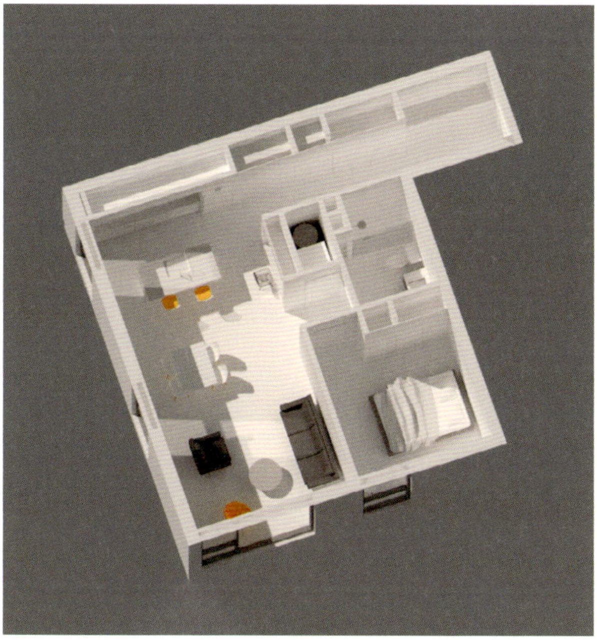

One bed unit

Two bed unit

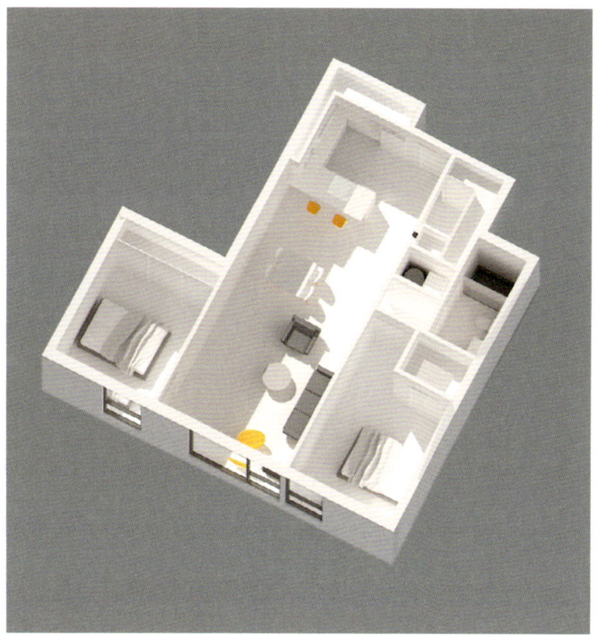

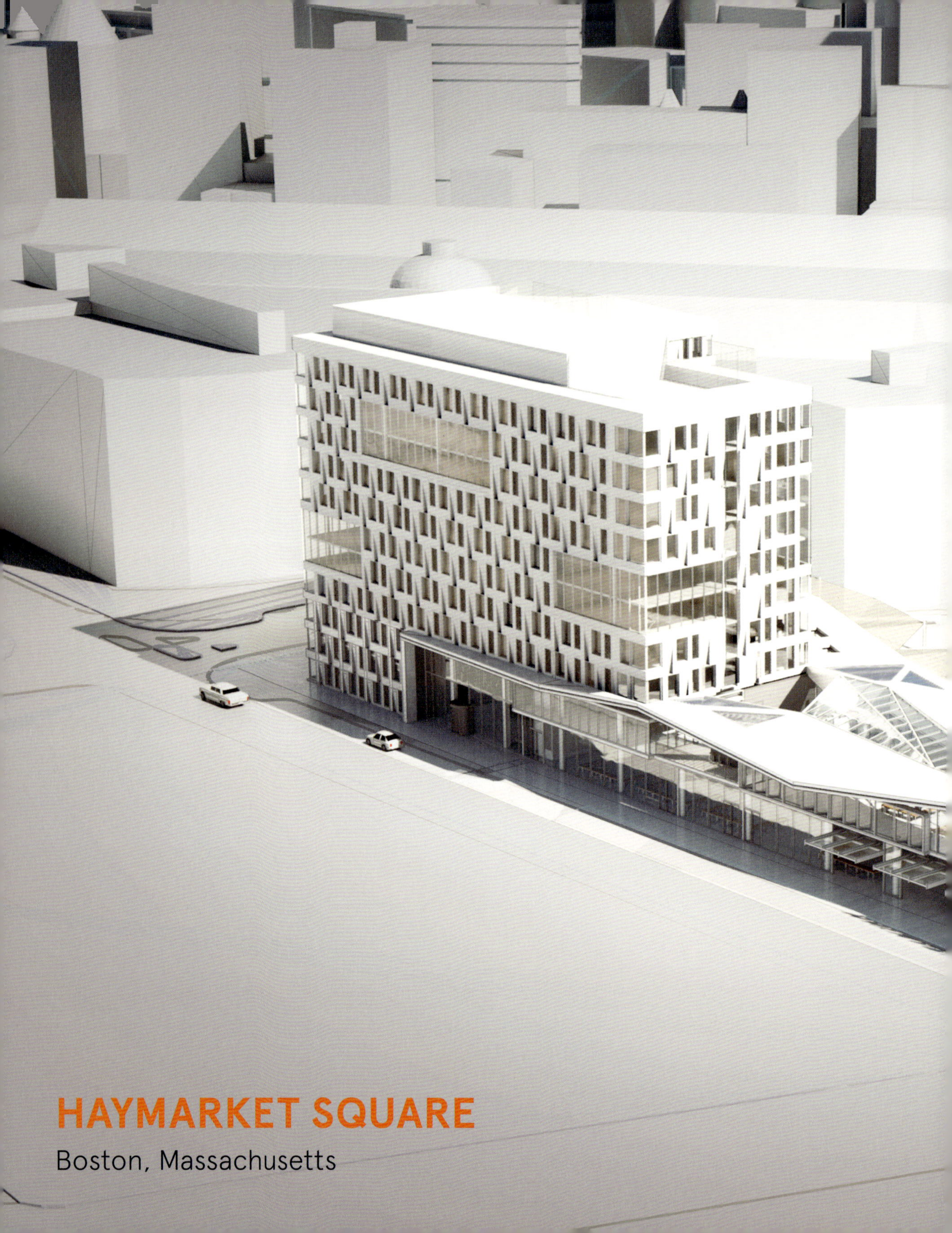

HAYMARKET SQUARE

Boston, Massachusetts

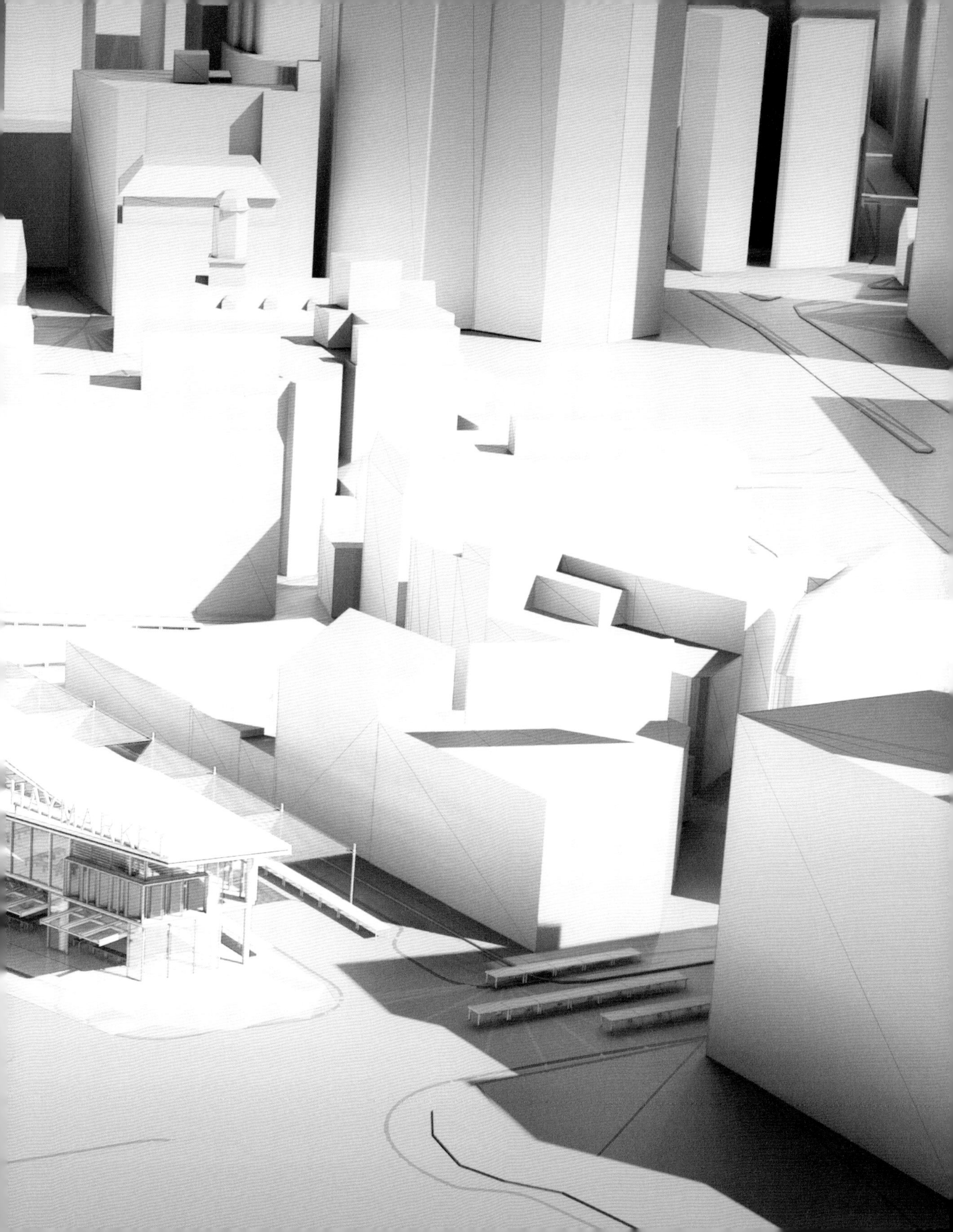
HAYMARKET

HAYMARKET SQUARE

Boston, Massachusetts

Haymarket Square is infamous in Boston for fresh produce, seafood, meats, and an excuse for an early Sunday morning excursion downtown. It is situated along the Rose Kennedy Greenway adjacent to Quincy Market and meets the intersection of Hanover Street – the active main thoroughfare connecting the North End and City Hall Plaza. Across from Hanover Street is the newly renovated Boston Market that dramatically enlarges the reach of Haymarket.

A team formed by Robert Brown – along with Healy and other colleagues at Perkins + Will – developed this proposal for Haymarket Square that upgrades the existing market while providing new venues for display, sales, and entertainment. It also adds a new 180 room hotel with community spaces overlooking the public park supporting the business, tourist, and local family traveler. It acts as a new gateway to the Greenway and knits the park to the city – physically and programmatically – in this vital location. The expanded market district promotes tourist activity of this heavily visited area while affording new opportunities for city workers to gather downtown before, during, and after work hours. By coupling the market with the hotel, the public nature of this territory is amplified with the twenty-four hour activity of the hotel and other public programs. Through this new activity, the south border of the Greenway is recharged and balances the liveliness of the North End that it faces across the park.

Sculptural façade elements articulate individual units in smaller scale, while a series of undulating roof structures span across the marketplace mediating between the markets and park itself. Located next to the Blackstone Block, the complex's ground floor creates a culinary market of cafes, restaurants, and related retail spaces.

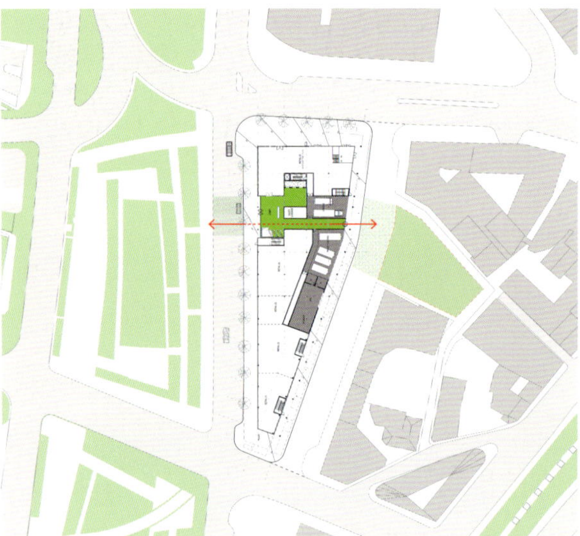

Ground floor - District

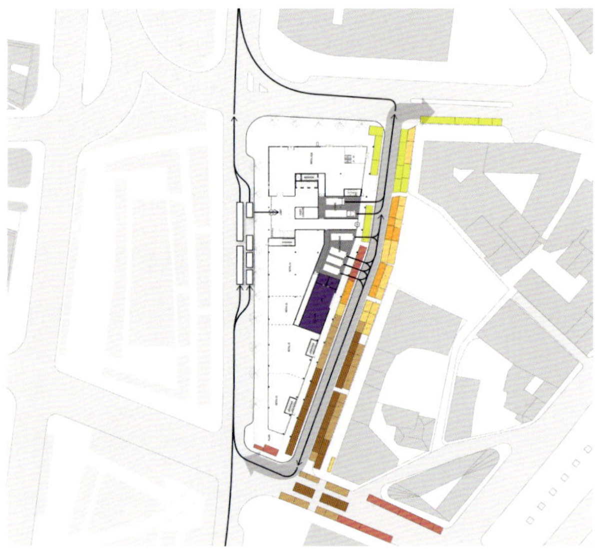

Ground floor - Market

HAYMARKET

Section perspective

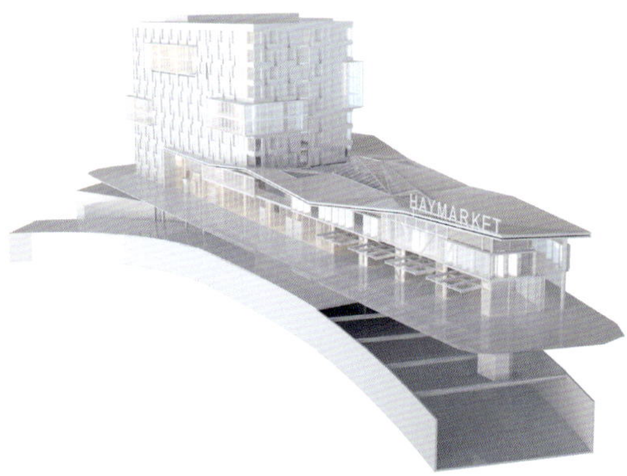

Diagram combined

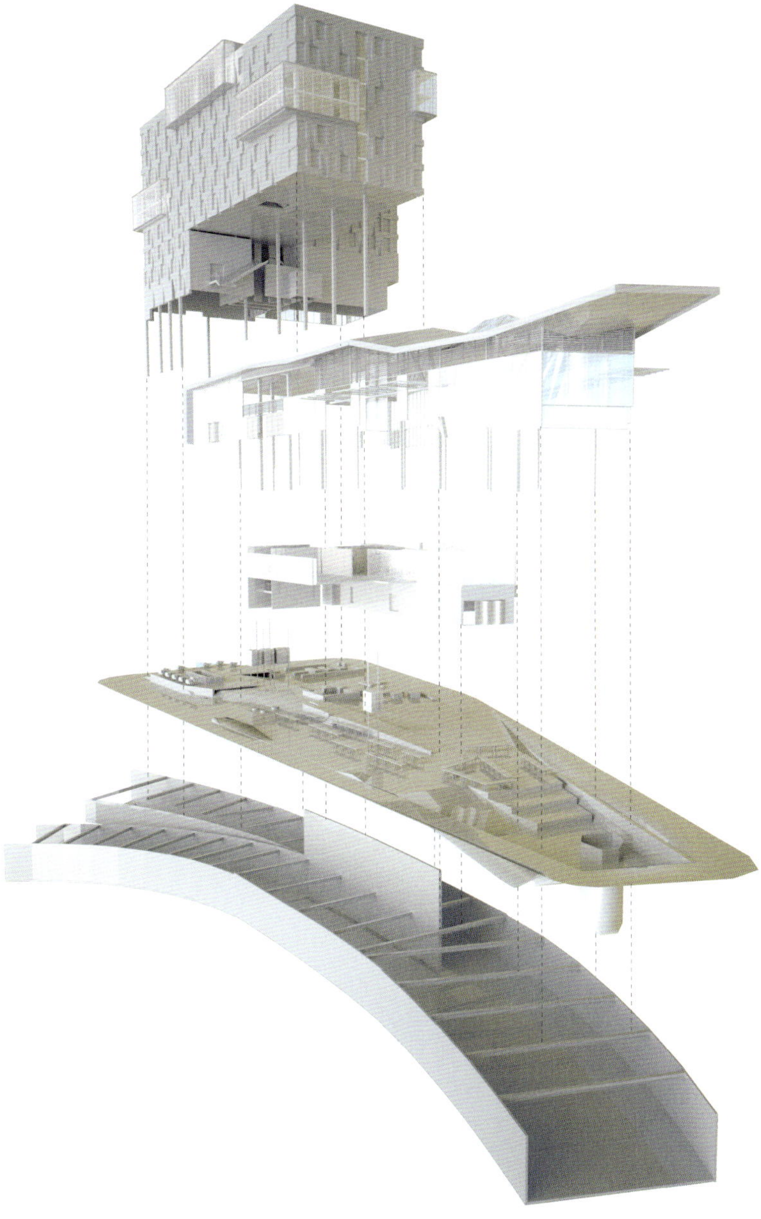

Diagram exploded

Elevation

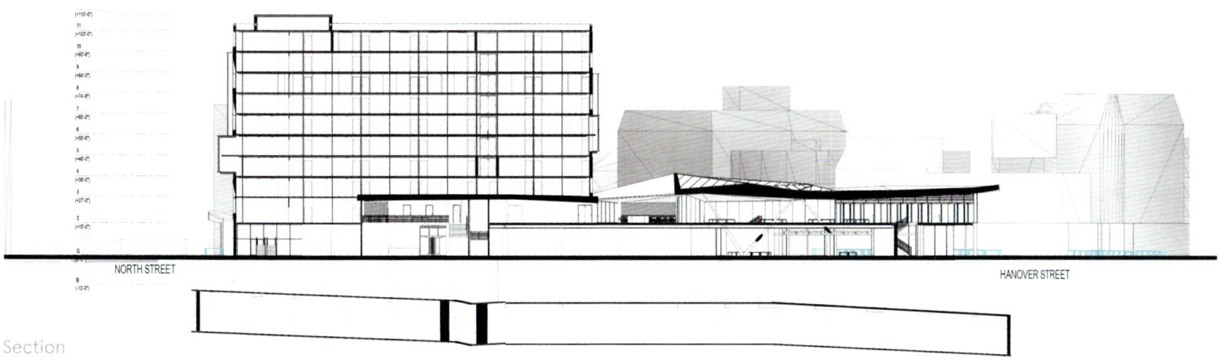

Section

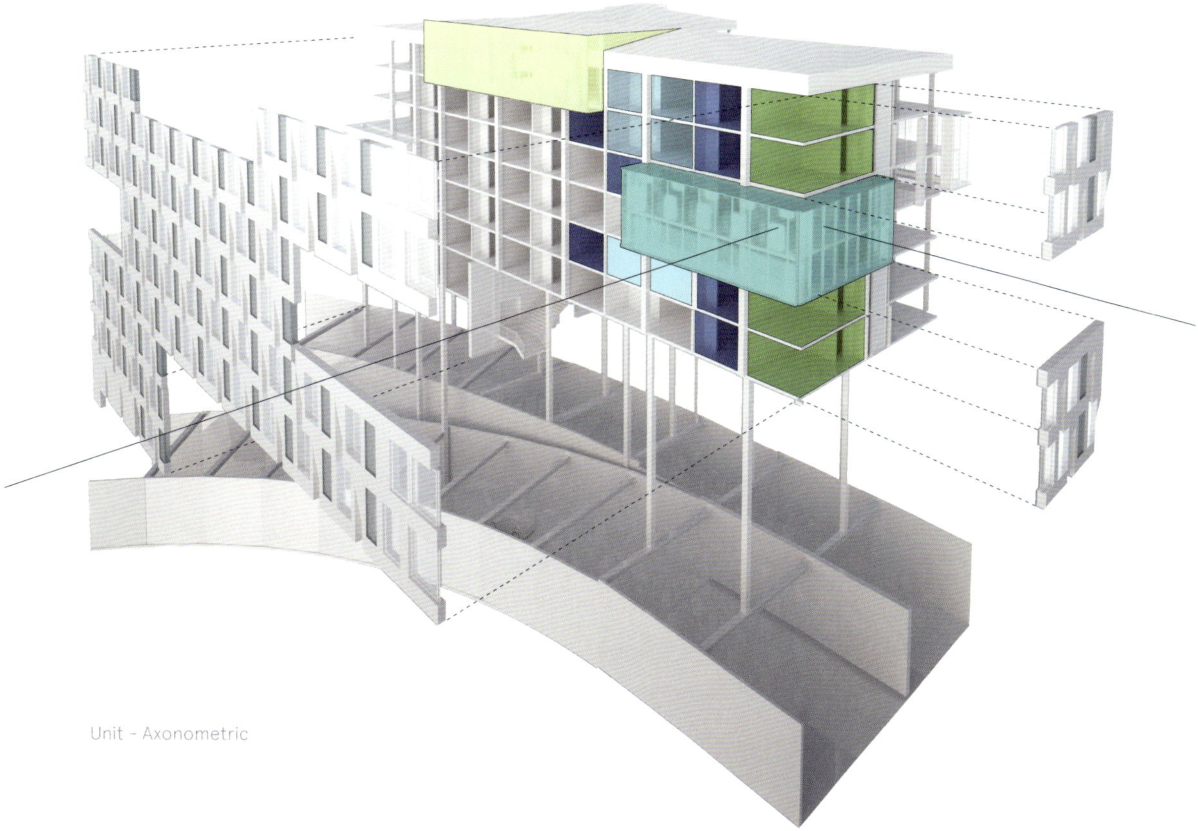

Unit - Axonometric

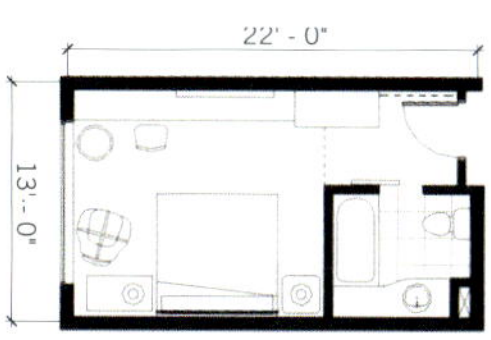

Single room

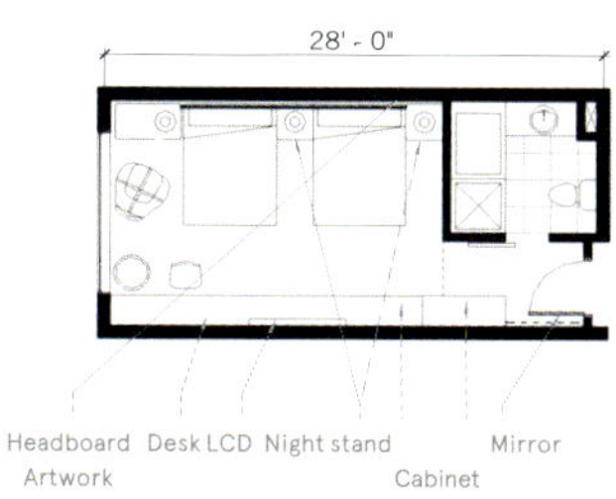

Double room

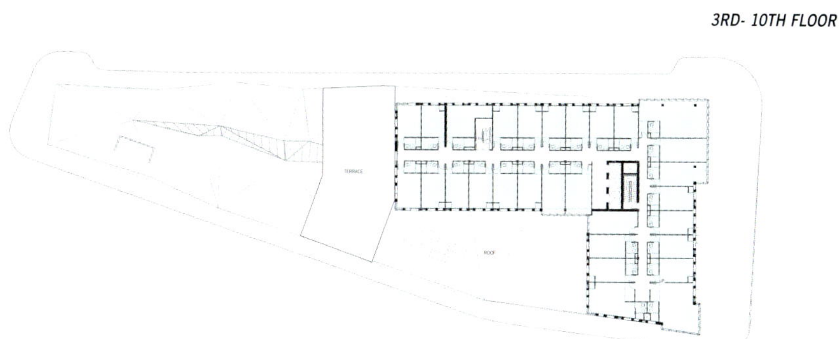

3rd - 10th floor plan

FLOATYARD

Charlestown, Massachusetts

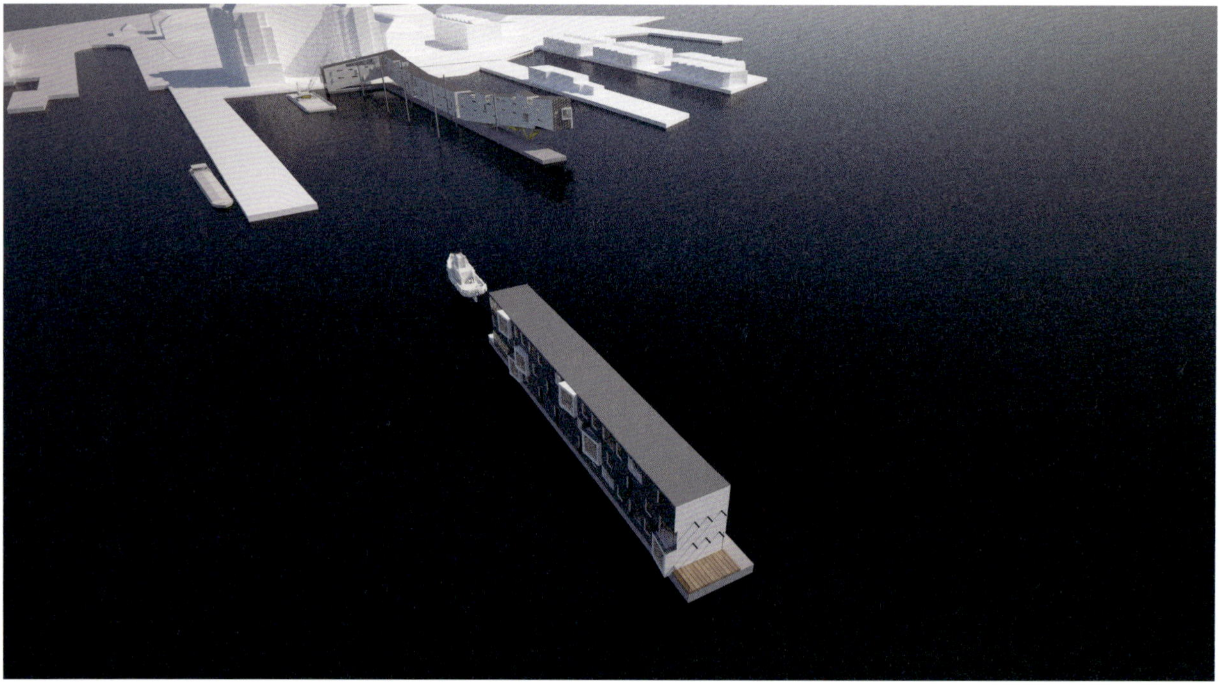

FLOATYARD

Charlestown, Massachusetts

Charlestown is located north of downtown Boston on a peninsula extending southeastward between the Charles River and the Mystic River. The geographic extent of the neighborhood has changed dramatically from its colonial ancestor. Landfill operations have expanded much of Boston, lowering hills and filling existing salt marsh, but there are concerns that the sea will reclaim this land once again when it rises with the tides of global warming.

It is a project that explores the potential to mitigate challenges associated with the rising seas. It is a prototype for a floating residential community in Boston Harbor that was developed as an alternative to restoring the badly damaged pier in Charlestown, Massachusetts. It has been presented to City Hall, the Boston Redevelopment Authority, Editorial Board of the *Boston Globe*, and was as topic for a TEDtalk in Boston. It is a floating development that aspires to solve a number of social, environmental, and economic issues in Boston. The building is capable of generating tidal energy to test the limits of new technologies, including the potential of harvesting energy with pneumatic pistons energized by the rise and fall of the tide. It will host natural wetlands to improve local ecology and re-create the colonial coast of Charlestown and it is programmed to support community recreation. The construction of Floatyard will promote economic growth along the communities of the harbor by activating local underutilized shipyards for construction and transportation. Merging maritime craftsmanship into the construction process will yield a sturdy, waterproof building with a barge-like nature. And, fabricated locally, it would then be towed to the site to erect reducing the costs and complications associated with on-site construction.

Floatyard borrows the basic principles of a traditional centralized court but replaces the ground plane with a water-filled landscape that will become a shifting landscape. This water-court will also support human interaction and waterfront views while hosting a number of waterside activities including kayaking and sailing. The surrounding building will provide protection from Boston's harsh winter weather.

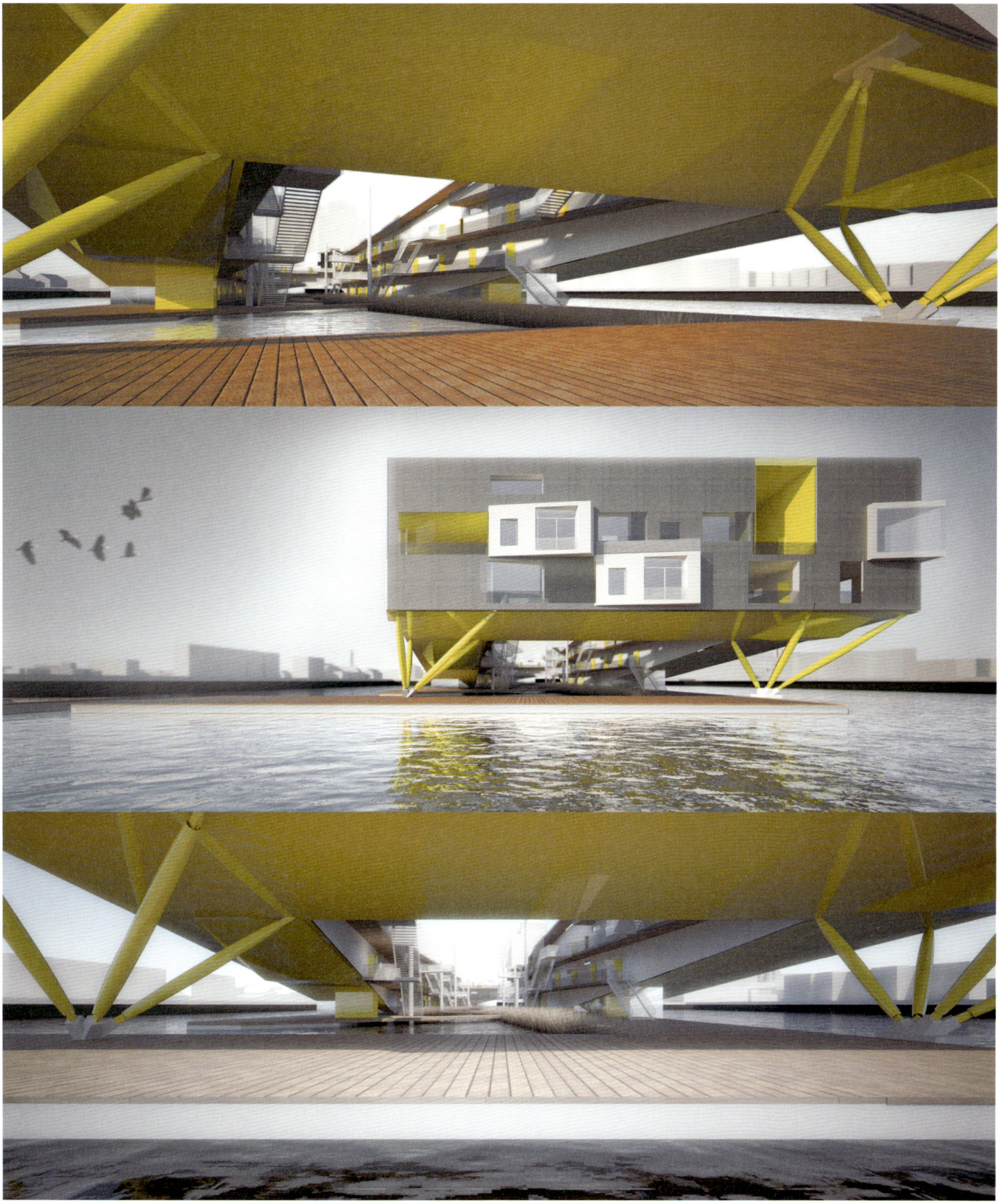

Sitting on the dock of the bay

Floating docks are a common enough sight at Boston Harbor marinas. But these buoyant platforms may be good for more than just securing boats. An entire block of residences could be designed to slide up and down with the tides on vertical mooring posts.

Brian Healy, the director of design in the Boston office of the national architectural firm Perkins + Will, envisions a floating community at the Charlestown Navy Yard that offers ocean views, a communal courtyard, and more than 100 living spaces where residents can float above concerns about global warming and rising sea levels. The concept may seem fanciful, but it's also down-to-earth considering that the alternatives for many people living in vulnerable coastal areas are heading for the hills or cowering behind dikes.

Environmental regulations present major challenges to anyone wishing to build piers, breakwaters, or floats over the state's tidelands. But the sight of shoreline homes washed away in recent storms suggests it is time to give serious consideration to innovative proposals like Healy's plan for a "Floatyard." For added economic benefit, the architect suggests that the components could be manufactured in the area's underutilized shipyards.

Though seemingly only half-serious, the idea has promise. It seems destined to rise and fall, rise and fall, rise and fall in the coming decades.

Boston Globe Editorial Board - May 1, 2013

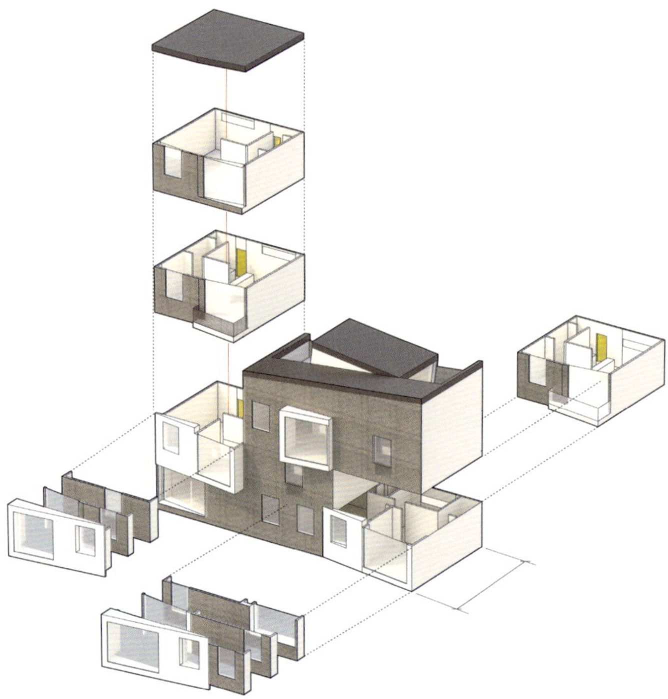

Units - Exploded axonometric

Elevation

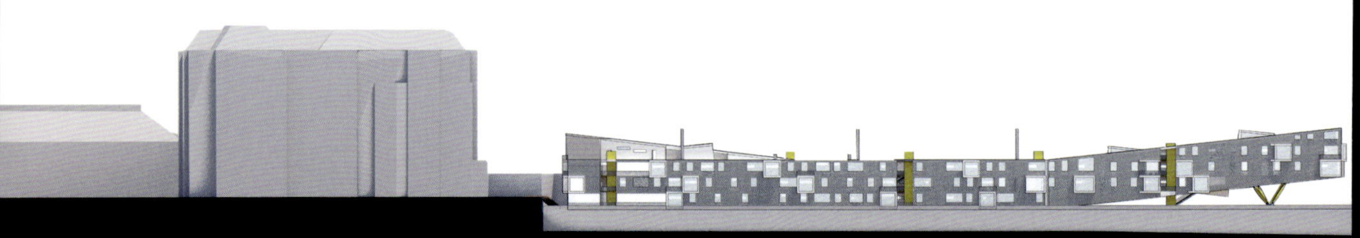

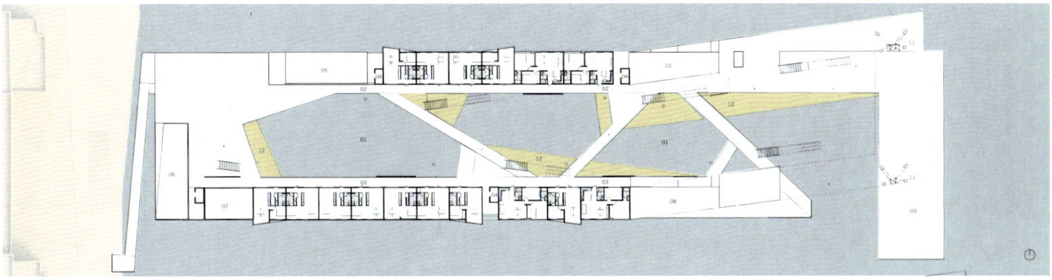

Ground floor plan

01 Courtyard below
02 Central Corridor North
03 Central Corridor South
04 Elevator
05 Cafe
06 Retail
07 Offices
08 Boat Storage
09 Activity Deck
10 Showers/Sauna
11 Support Columns
12 Floating Wetland Island

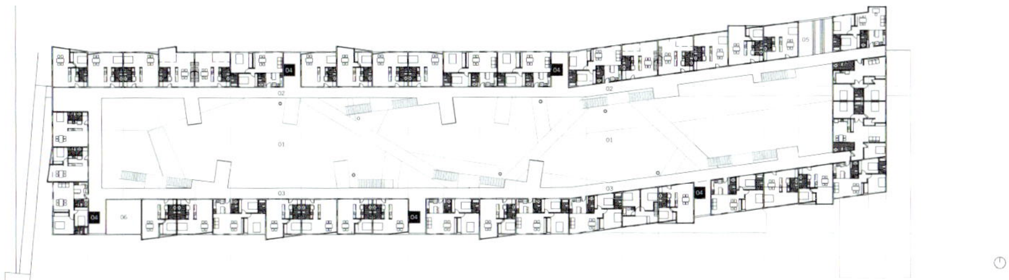

Third level floor plan

01 Courtyard below
02 Central Corridor North
03 Central Corridor South
04 Elevator
05 Meditation Room
06 Laundry Room

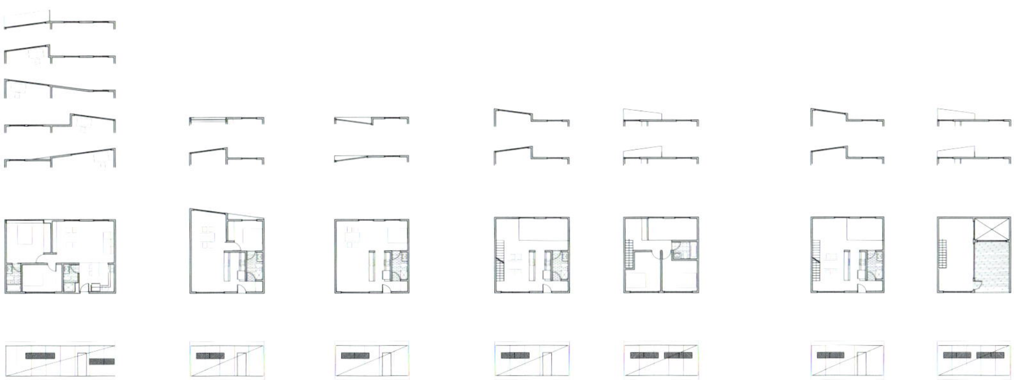

Units a

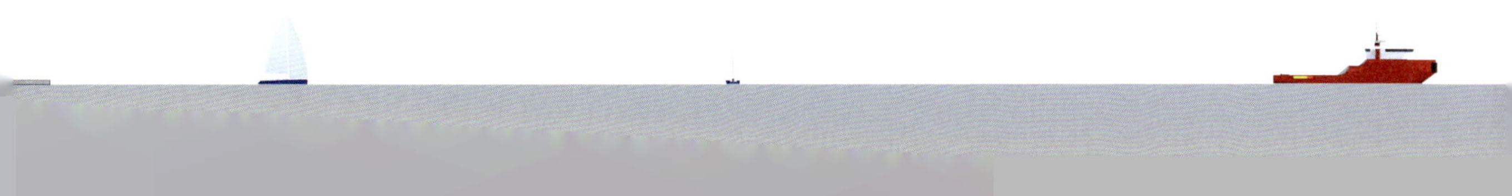

Building section

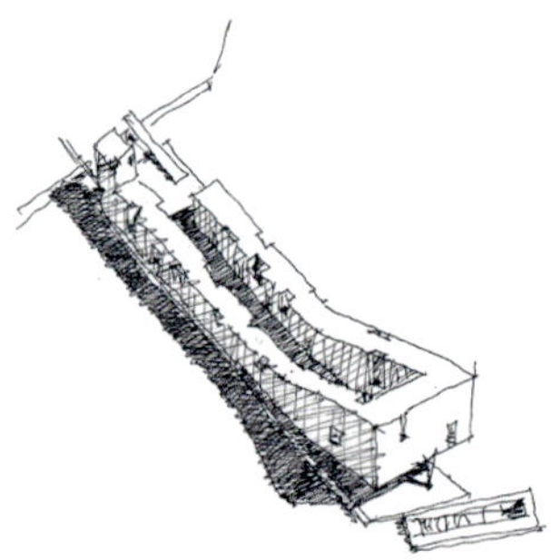

Citizens Bank

Citizens Bank

Citizens Bank

Citizens Bank

KENMORE

Boston, Massachusetts

The new Hotel Buckminster would be in the urban hub of Kenmore Square just a few blocks from the Red Sox and their home at Fenway Park. It sits next to the notorious existing six-story brick hotel and is bounded by Beacon Street, Brookline Avenue and the Massachusetts Turnpike.

The hotel is an efficient vertical slab of rooms that engages a broader base of parking and hotel amenities below. Anticipating the construction of a new eight-story structure over the turnpike to the south, the roof of the parking is set back to be utilized as a raised outdoor amenity terrace with a pool. A new outdoor space between the old and new hotels has been created to permit views and light for the two buildings while amplifying retail frontage and forming a pedestrian plaza that links Beacon Street to Brookline Avenue. The east end of the new hotel is canted to form a compressed threshold to the plaza and an enticement to explore what may be found beyond. The roof terrace is reserved for communal use with a public restaurant and bar overlooking the ballpark.

The exterior of the hotel seeks to reinforce the building form over its parts it uses the plasticity of precast concrete panels to manipulate depth and angles to create a varied, rich texture that will change with the changing angles of the sun and shadows.

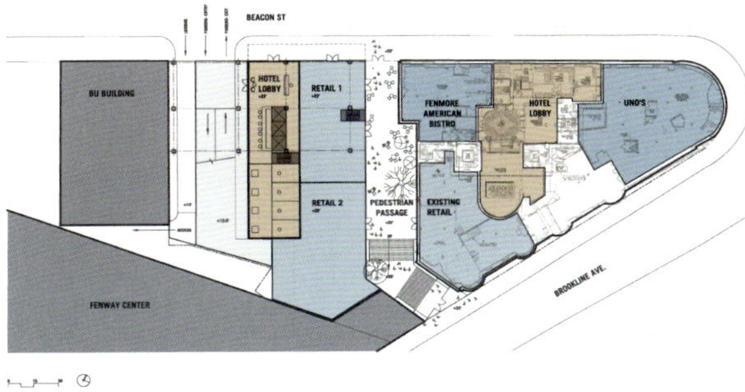

Ground floor plan

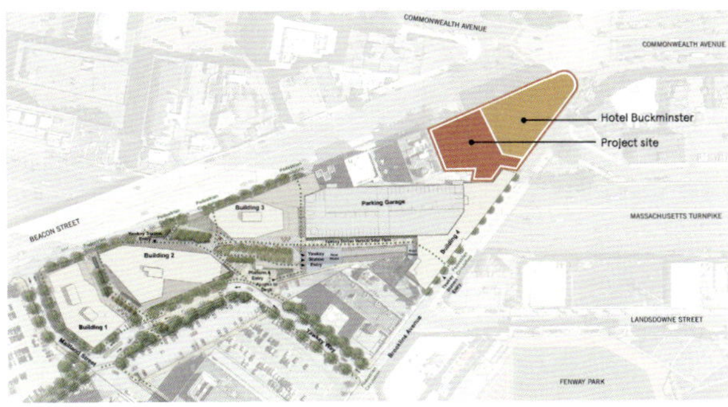

Aerial view of proposed Fenway Center

BOATHOUSE

Essex, Massachusetts

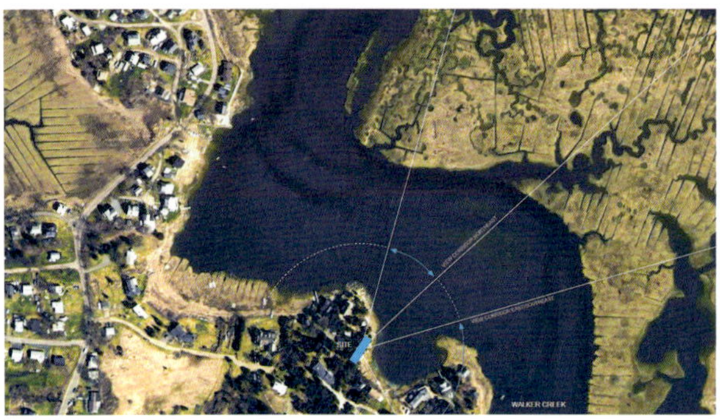

BOATHOUSE

Essex, Massachusetts

This is a small residential renovation of an abandoned boathouse located along Walker Creek in Essex, Massachusetts. It is nestled among a cluster of cedars that frame a view – and allow passage – outward toward Ipswich Bay and the Atlantic Ocean. The original boathouse contained a storage area for boats on the ground level with a one room apartment above. The 1,239 square foot renovation includes new living and sleeping areas as well as a study and library. The existing structure and its sheathing were reused and augmented with a new red cedar rain screen and windows. The windows were inserted with a focus on the views of the adjacent cedars as well as the distant landscape. Skylights illuminate the second floor and populate a roof garden that can be accessed through the library on the third floor.

The house lies directly adjacent to the water which – at low tide – becomes an active year-round clamming flat. At high

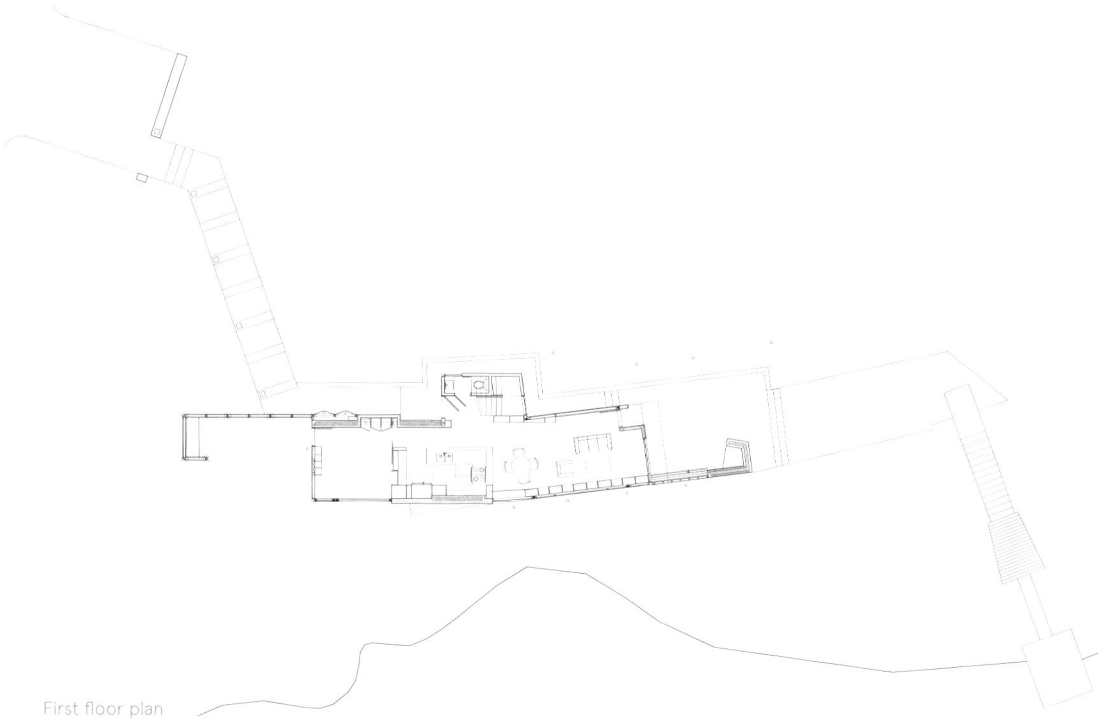

First floor plan

Second floor plan

Attic floor plan

tide, it comes within twenty feet of the house allowing the experience of living in a boathouse.

Because of this proximity to the water, zoning restrictions severely limited the extent that renovations could be made on the existing structure. The new residence could not modify the original footprint or square footage of the existing structure. With this in mind, and with a desire to reuse as much of the existing structure as possible, we emphasized the landscape especially the cedars, the view corridor, and the experience of the house with the adjacent vegetation and the distant vistas.

Just like any building or place, the experience does not begin at the front door. This house is a point of repose — in the woods — along a pathway between the street and the sea; between the boat and the automobile.

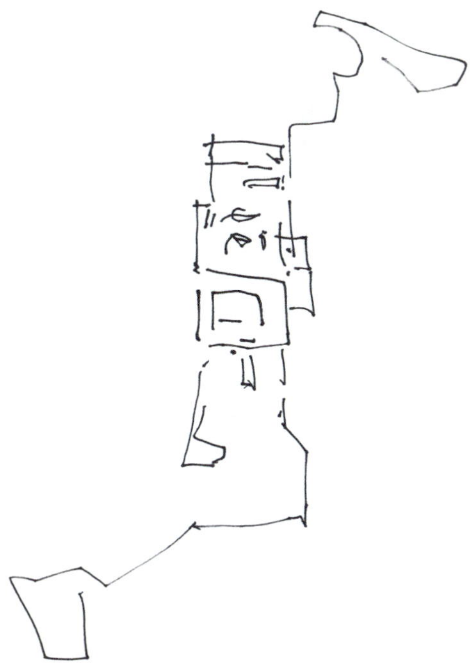

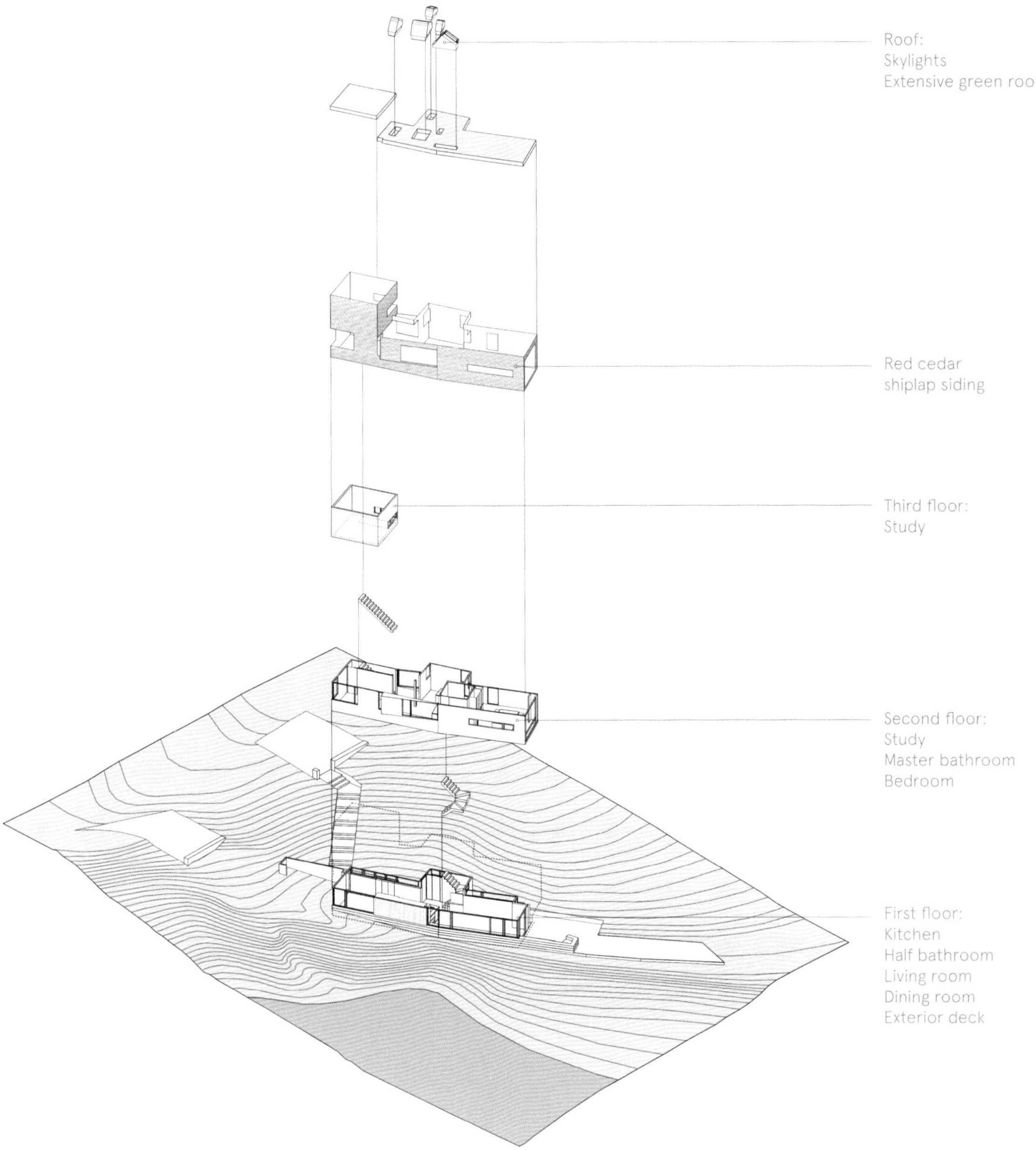

Axonometric

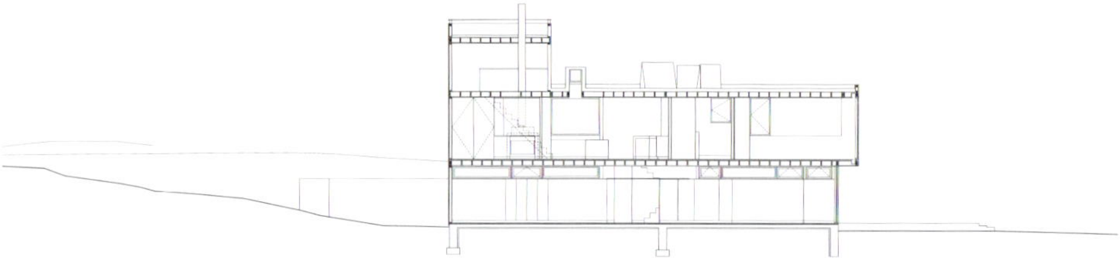

Longitudinal section

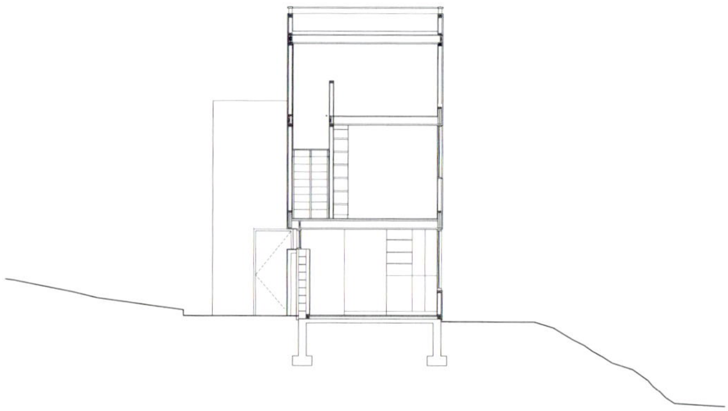

Transverse section

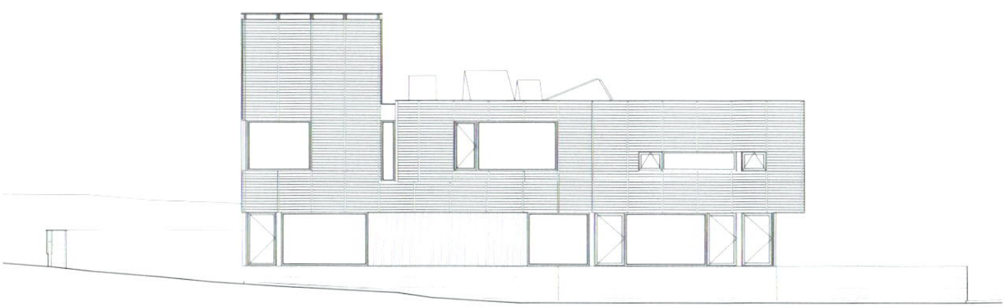

South elevation

West elevation

North elevation

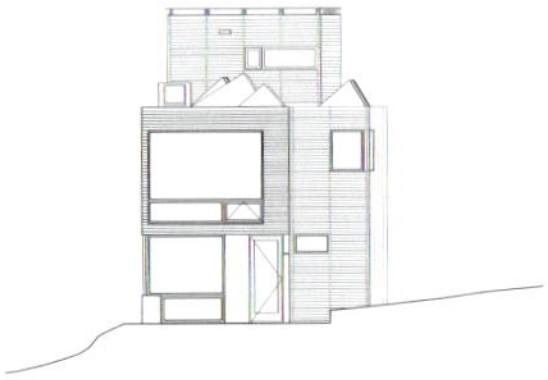

East elevation

SHRIVER GUEST HOUSE

Hyannisport, Massachusetts

SHRIVER GUEST HOUSE

Hyannis Port, Massachusetts

Eunice Shriver was a remarkable woman — funny, tough, and direct. She was also a pleasure to work with developing a small guesthouse on her family compound overlooking Nantucket Sound in Hyannis Port, Massachusetts. The chosen site is nestled into a hill among a cluster of scrub oaks that frame a view outward toward Nantucket and the Atlantic Ocean. It also allows for privacy and distance from the main house. The main house remains the primary focus of the family gatherings but the proposed guesthouse would allow her grown children and their families an isolated respite during their visits. The siting and configuration of this guest housed maintains the tennis court and provides for privacy from shared entry court and the adjacent golf course

The lower level has a game room with mechanical equipment, the main level has the family living areas as well as a bedroom wing off the main entry. The upper level contains a study and master bedroom suite. Exterior gathering areas are located in a morning court behind the house as well as an open roof terrace.

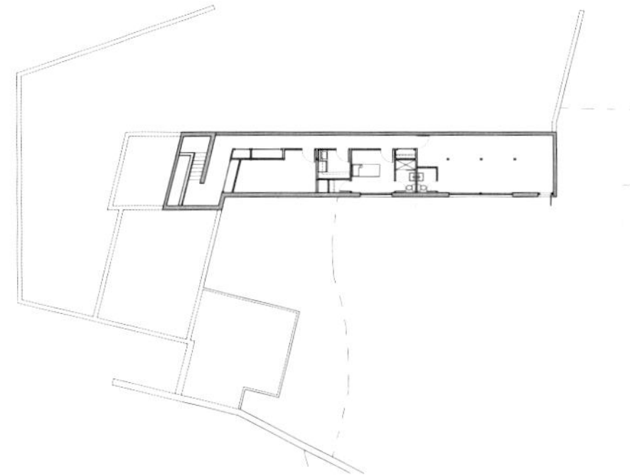

Lower level plan

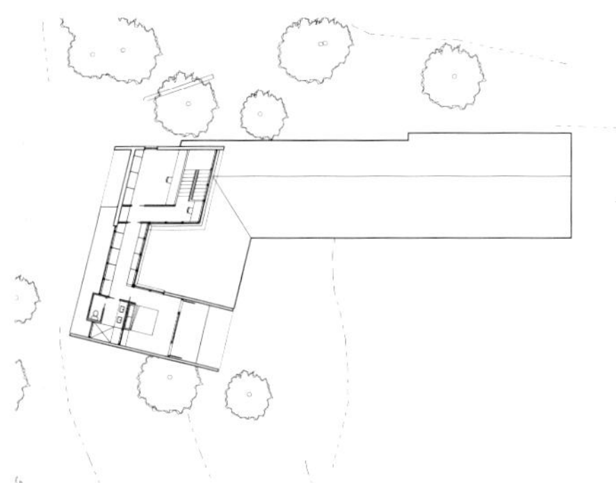

First floor plan

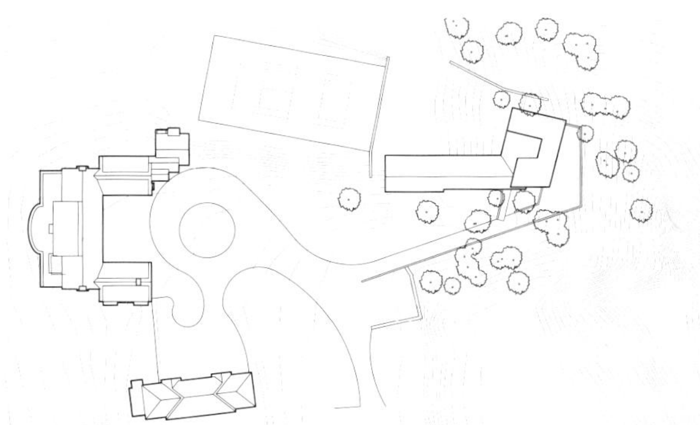

Site plan

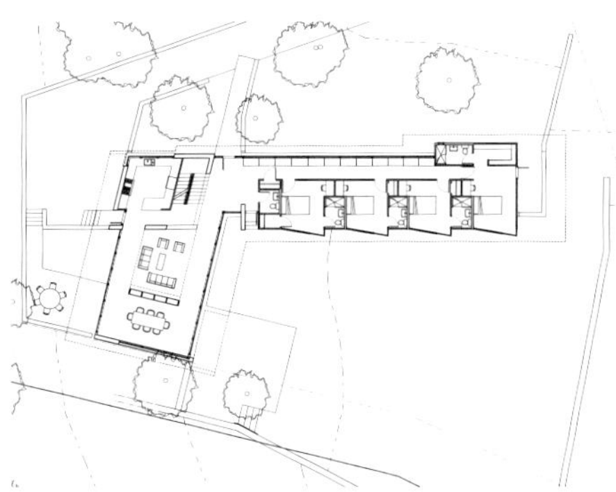

Second floor plan

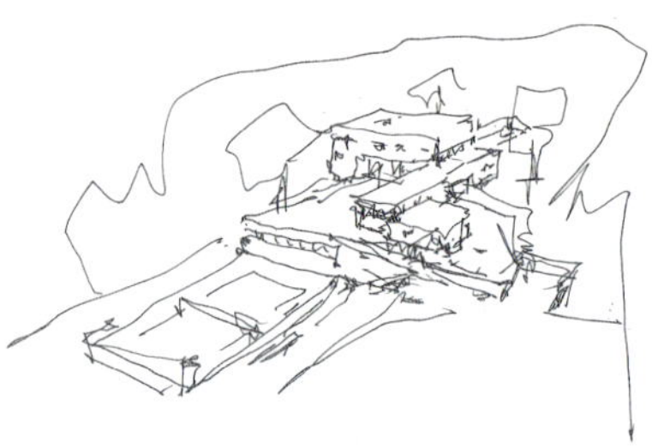

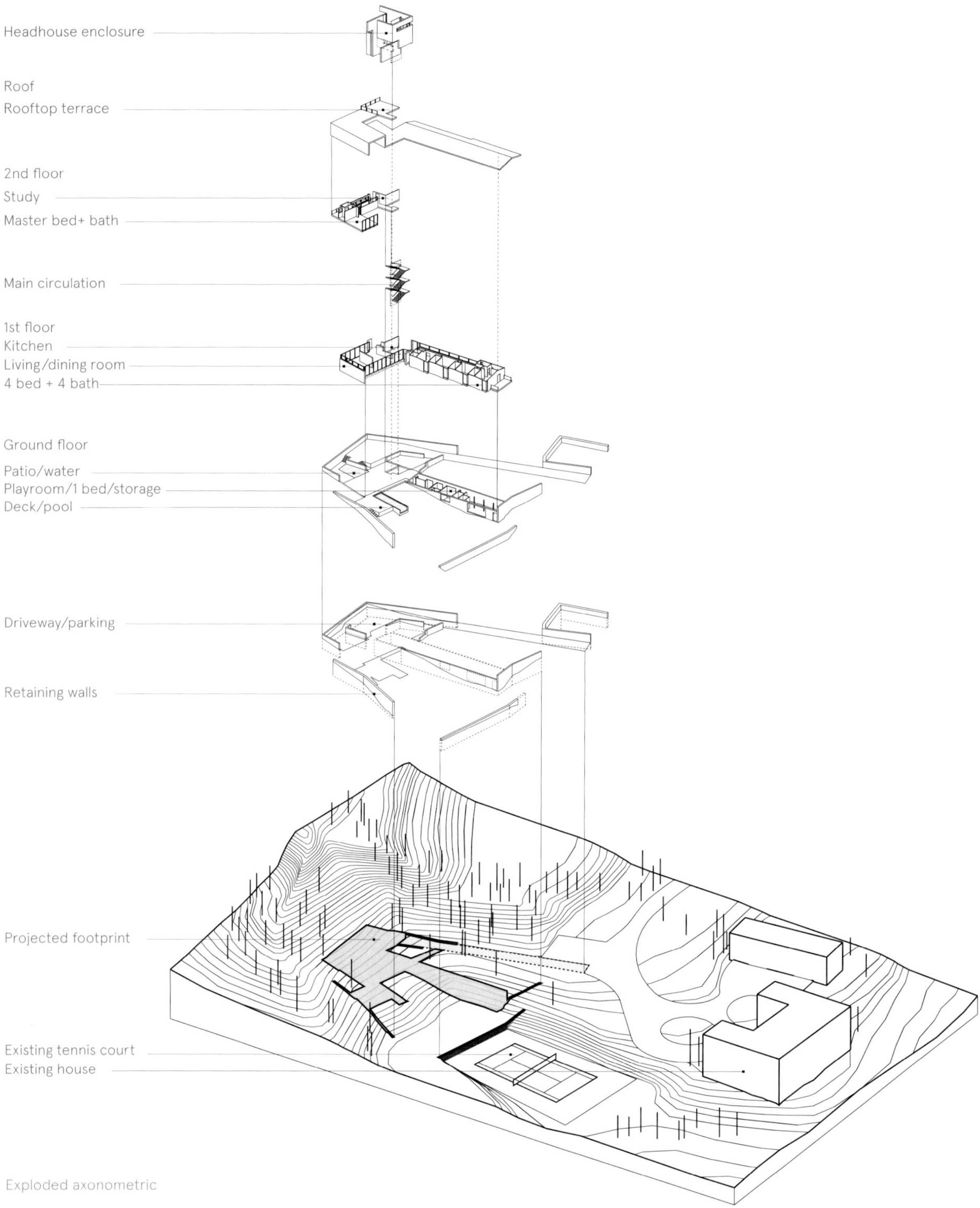

Exploded axonometric

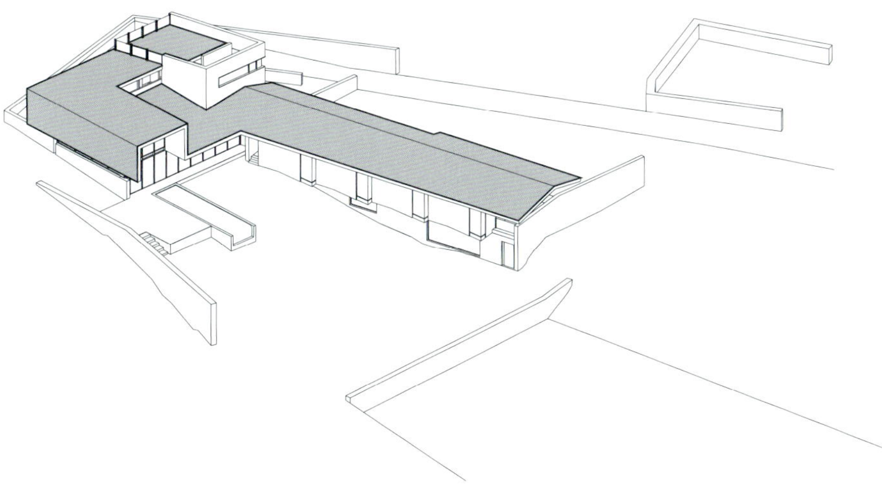

Axonometric

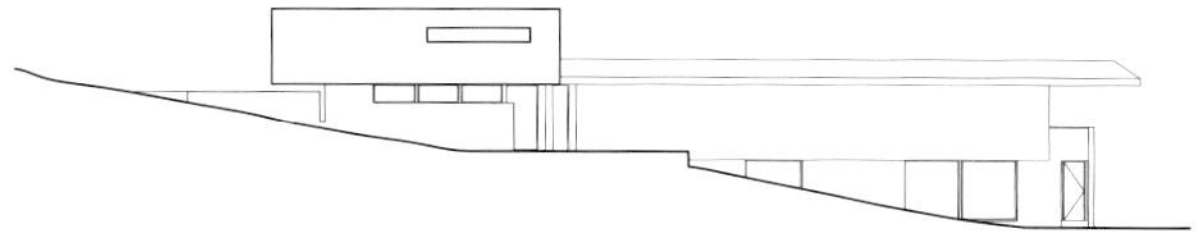

West elevation 1

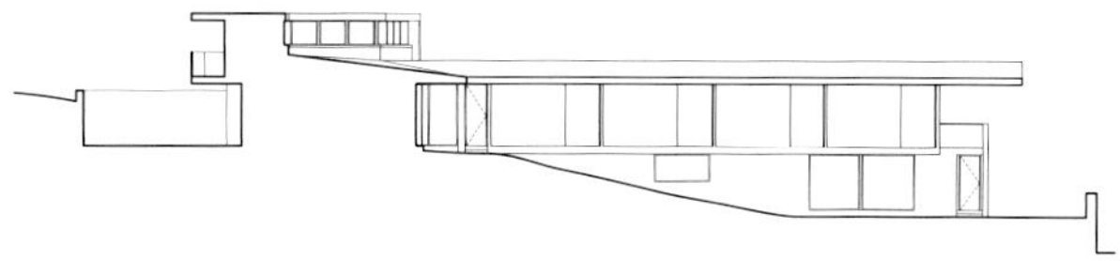

West elevation 2

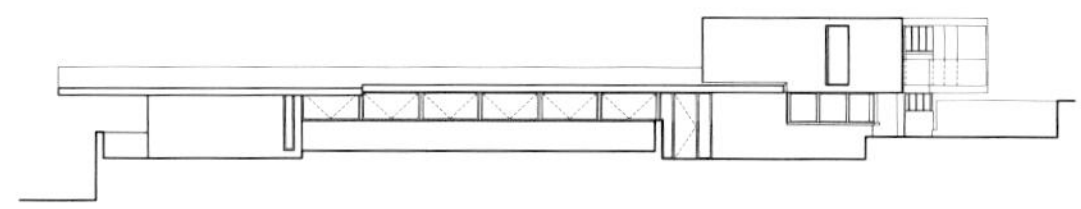

East elevation

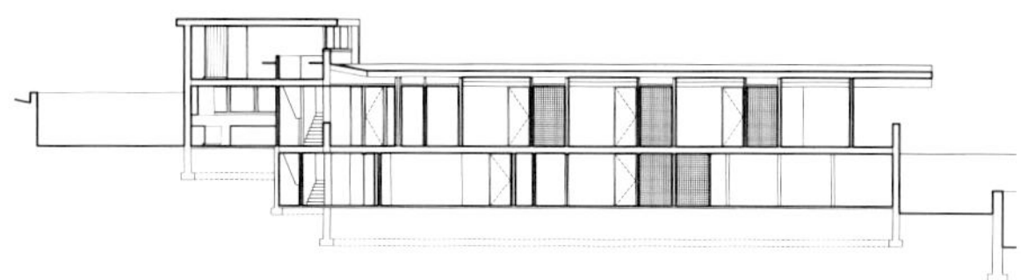

Section longitudinal

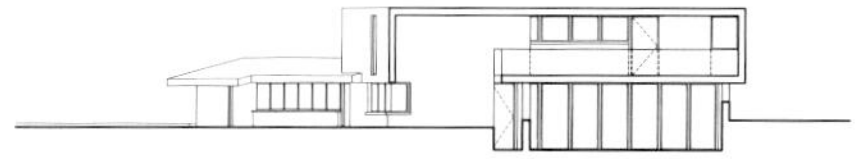

North elevation

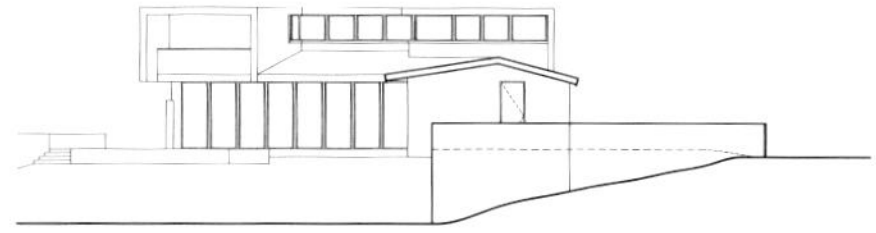

South elevation

HILL HOUSE

Dillon Beach, California

HILL HOUSE

Dillon Beach, California

With the commodification of our homes and the success of shared spaces, our client – a successful itinerant business woman – has asked Healy to develop a small retreat from San Francisco for this site overlooking the Pacific Ocean in Marin County in northern California. While she currently lives in Stockholm, she has homes on Cape Ann in Massachusetts and in Boulder, Colorado. These are all places that she considers her home, places that she returns to frequently.

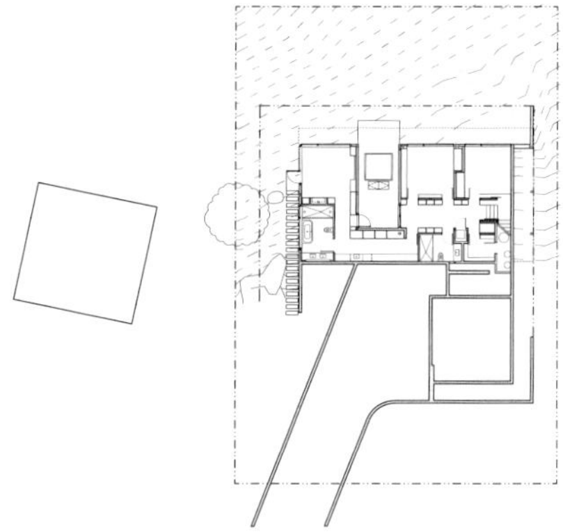

Ground floor plan

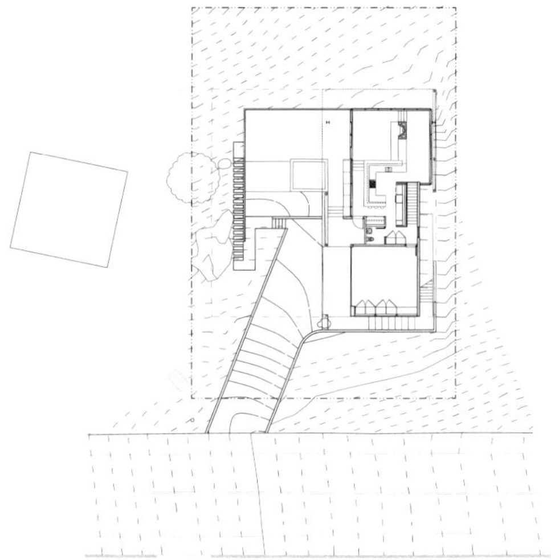

First floor plan

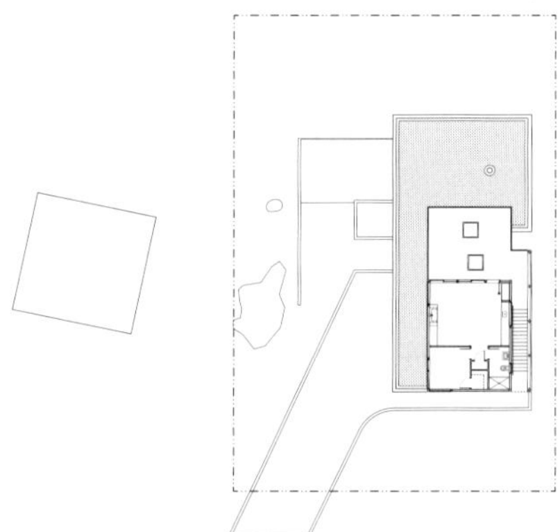

Second floor plan

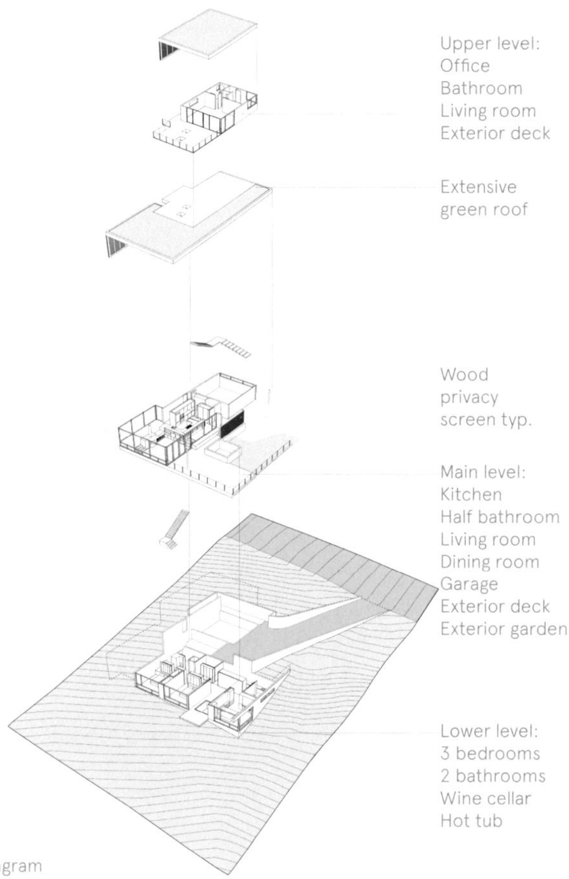

Diagram

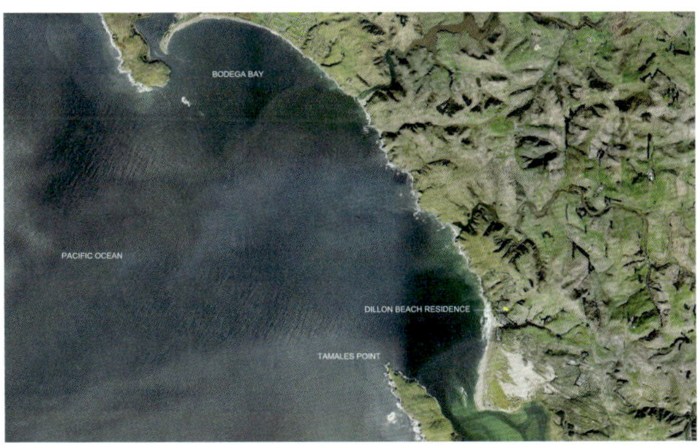
BODEGA BAY
PACIFIC OCEAN
DILLON BEACH RESIDENCE
TAMALES POINT

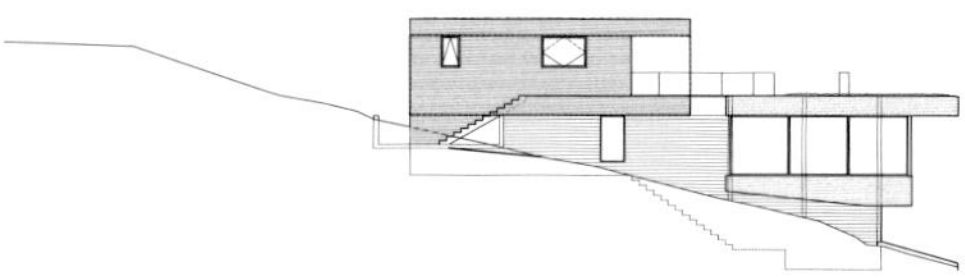

East elevation

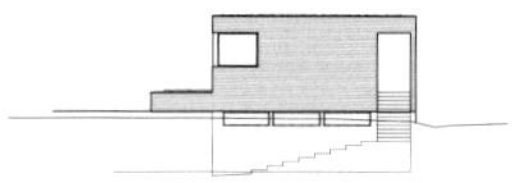

South elevation

North elevation

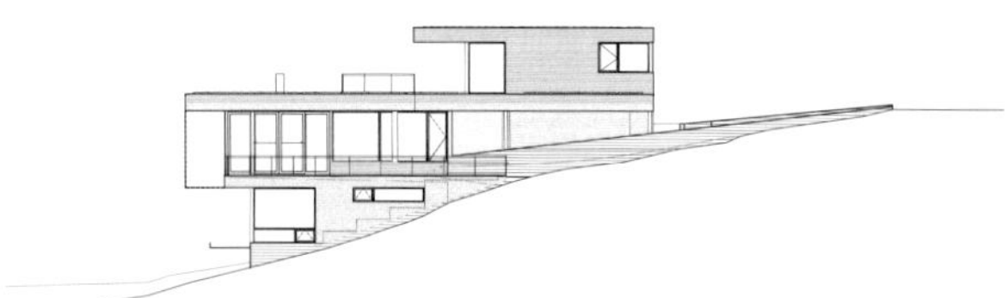

West elevation

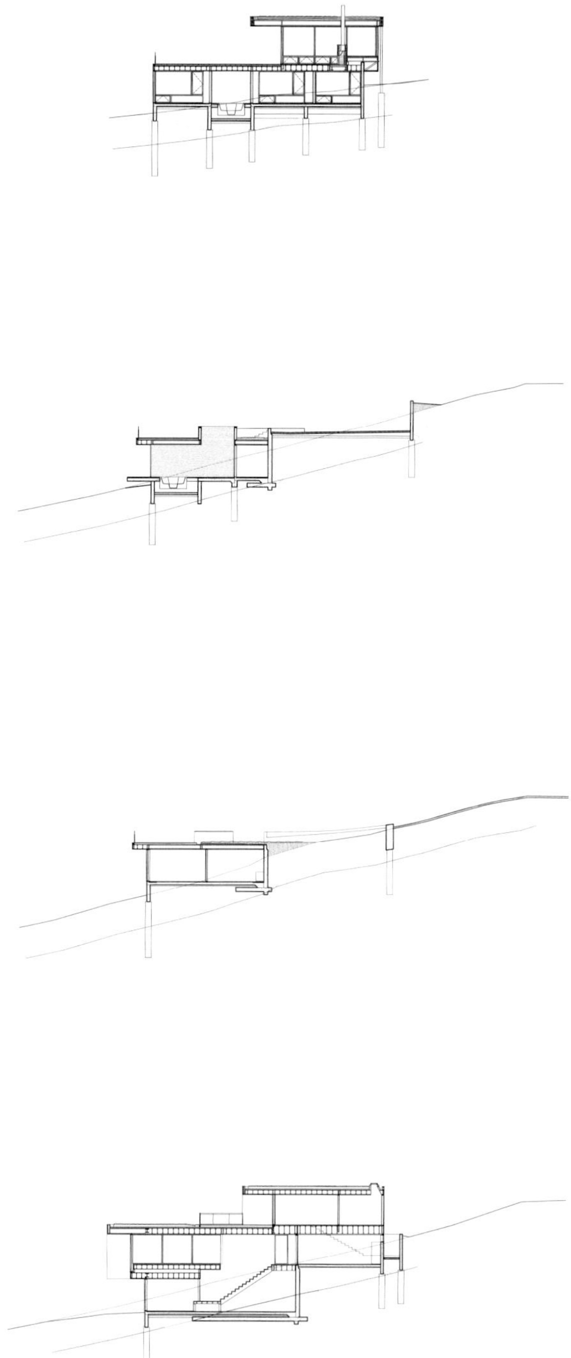

Building sections

Like herself and her colleagues, there is a sense of a restless nomadism with people moving continuously from place to place. She asks if that we imagine – and contribute to – an itinerant design culture that keeps up with this pace of constant movement yet, as we carry ourselves from point to point, we don't need to carry anything else. A culture not dependent on possessions or long term financial commitments.

This project will be located on a hill in Dillon Beach overlooking Tamales Point and Bodega Bay. The parcel of land is at the top of a steep incline of limited development area and surrounded by protected open fields and woods. The house itself nestles into the earth to minimize its presence yet open all interior spaces to the dramatic views. The entire entry level consists of a public lounge serving entertainment, conversation, coffee, food, wine, and spirits. It includes cooking facilities, a dining area, and sitting area with a fireplace. Adjacent to this lounge is an exterior roof terrace overlooking the coast. The lower level is dedicated to the guest rooms including a private suite with private bath. It also includes a laundry, wine storage, and exterior court with a hot tub.

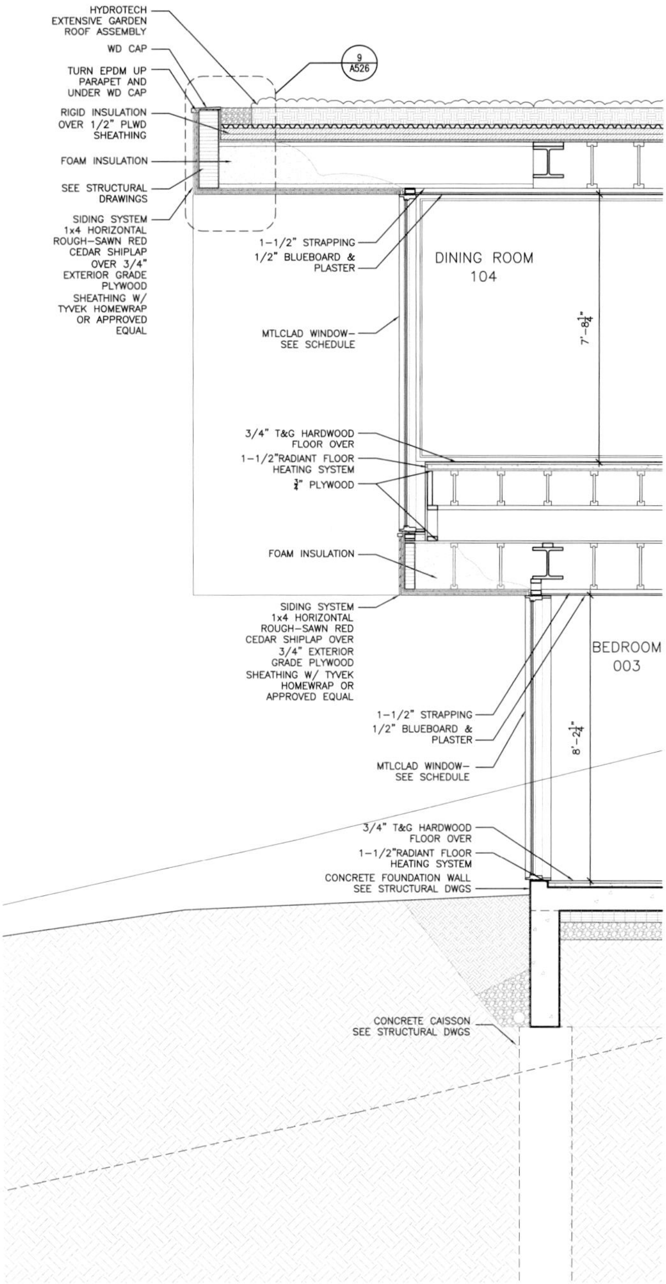

3 ENLARGED WALL SECTION
SCALE: 1/4"=1'-0" | SC01.DWG

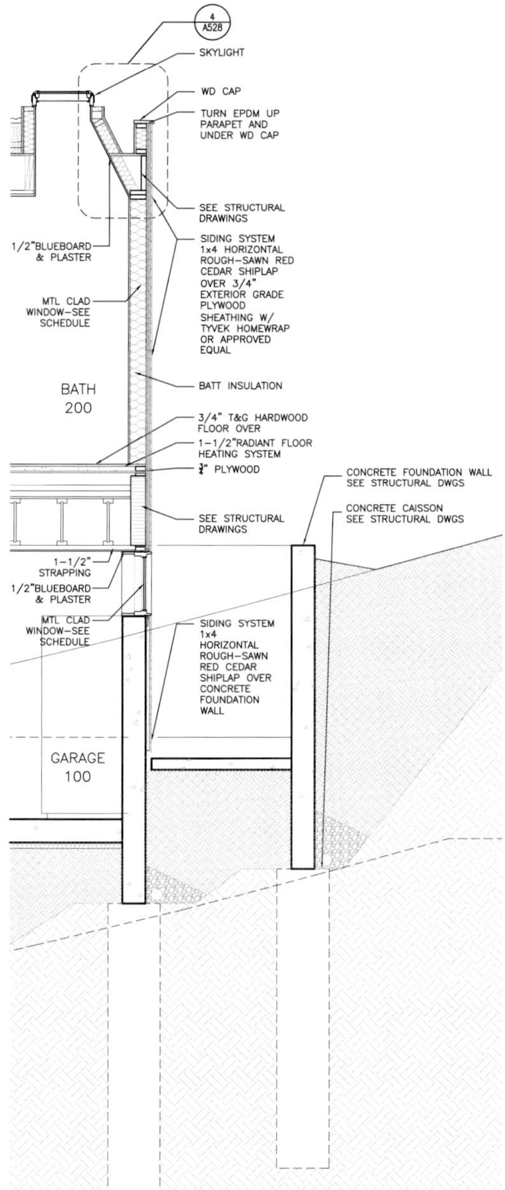

2 ENLARGED WALL SECTION
SCALE: 1/4"=1'-0" | SC01.DWG

Working drawings

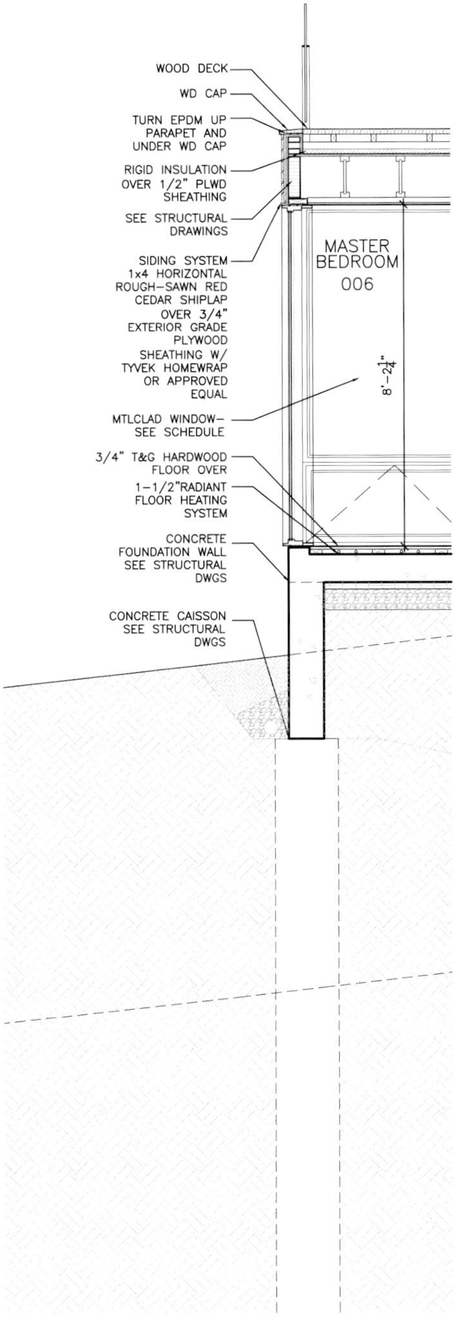

3 ENLARGED WALL SECTION
SCALE: 1/4"=1'-0" SC01.DWG

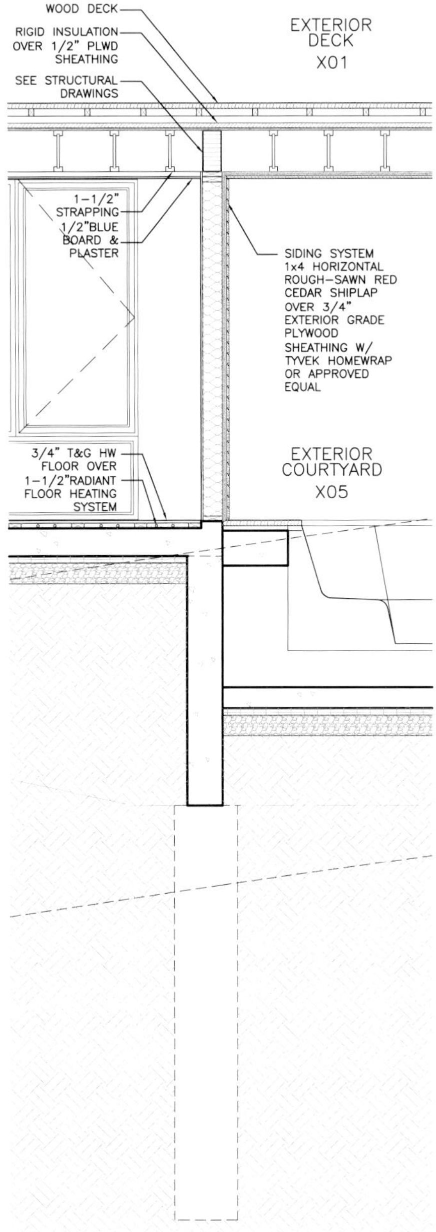

2 ENLARGED WALL SECTION
SCALE: 1/4"=1'-0" SC01.DWG

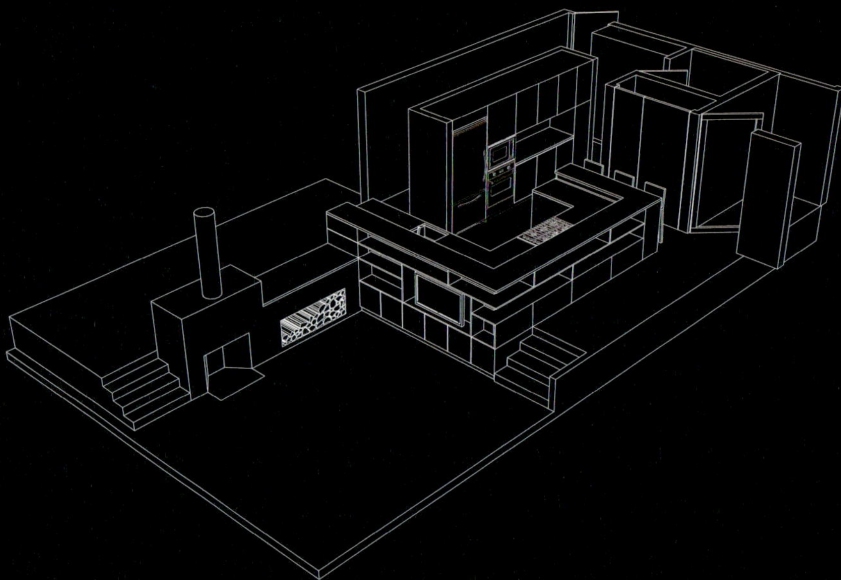

COURT HOUSE

Dillon Beach, California

COURT HOUSE

Dillon Beach, California

This project site is also located on a hill in Dillon Beach overlooking Tamales Point and Bodega Bay, just up the street from the neighboring Hill House. The parcel of land is at the top of a steep incline and surrounded by protected open fields and woods. The house itself nestles into the earth to minimize its presence yet open all interior spaces to the dramatic views. The entire entry level is at grade and limited to the garage and master bedroom suite. The main living areas are one story down off an excavated entry court. This open public area includes a kitchen, a dining area, sitting area with a fireplace and pool on the exterior terrace. The building is constructed primarily with poured in place concrete with a cedar siding with operable shutters to open and close the second floor to the ocean breezes and views.

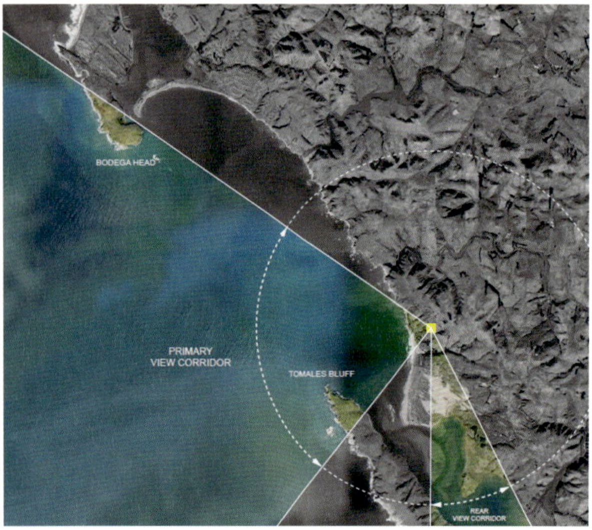

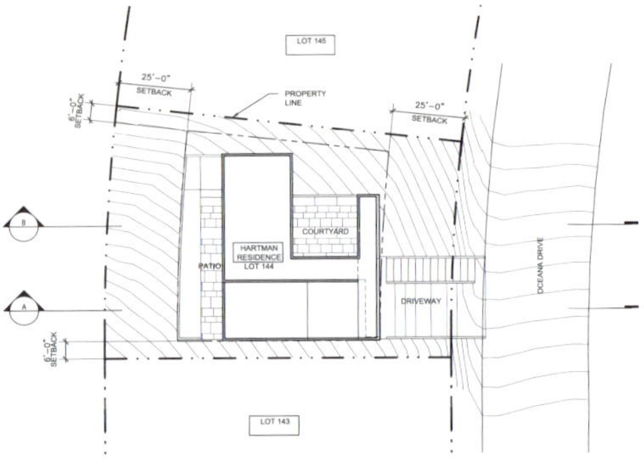

Site plan

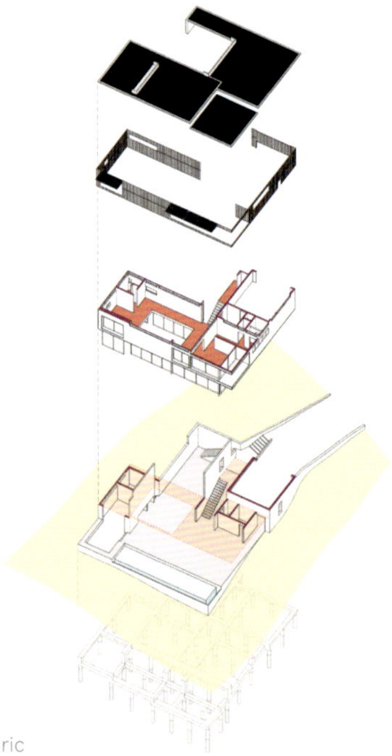

Exploded axonometric

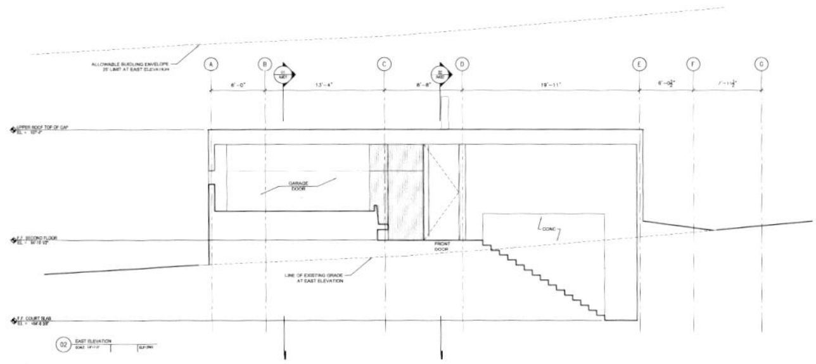

South elevation

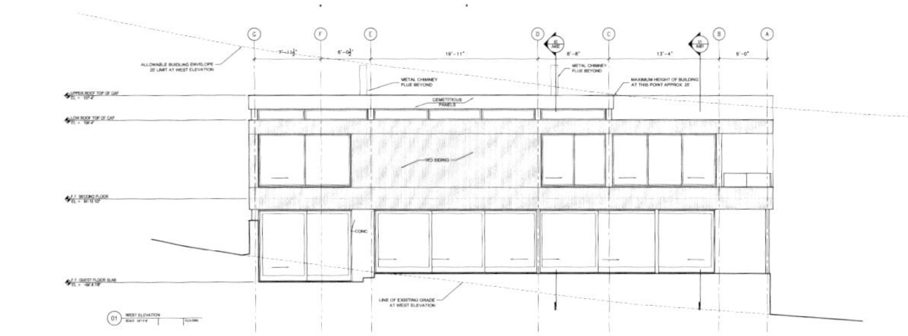

North elevation

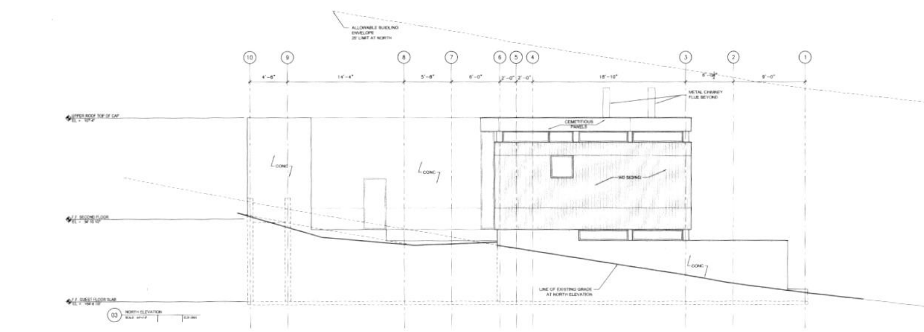

East elevation

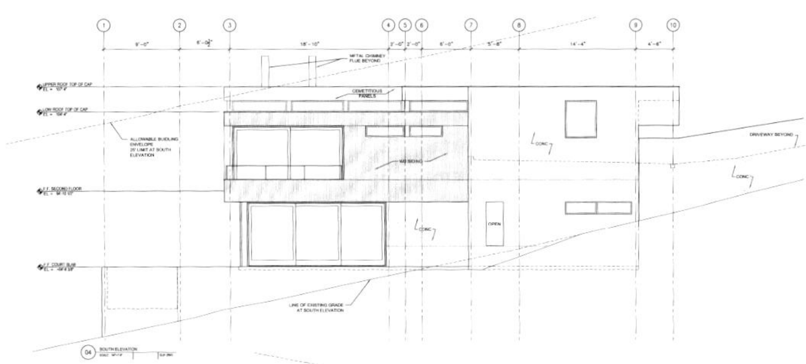

West elevation

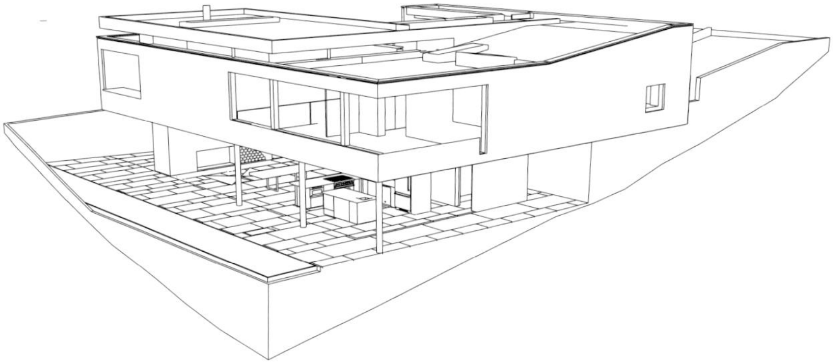

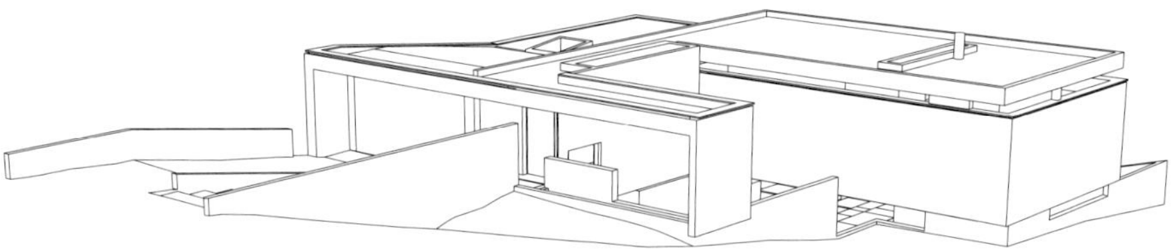

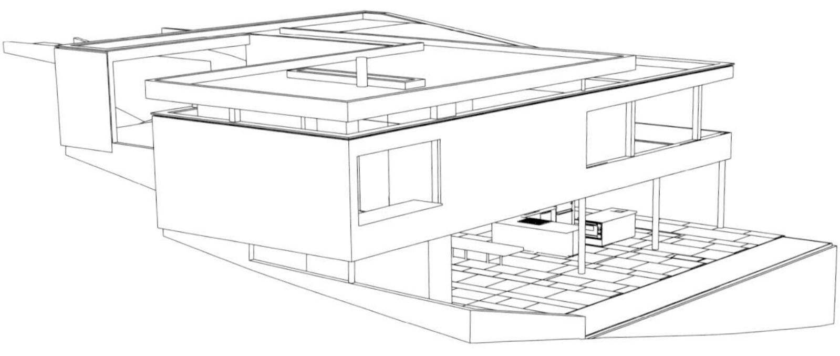

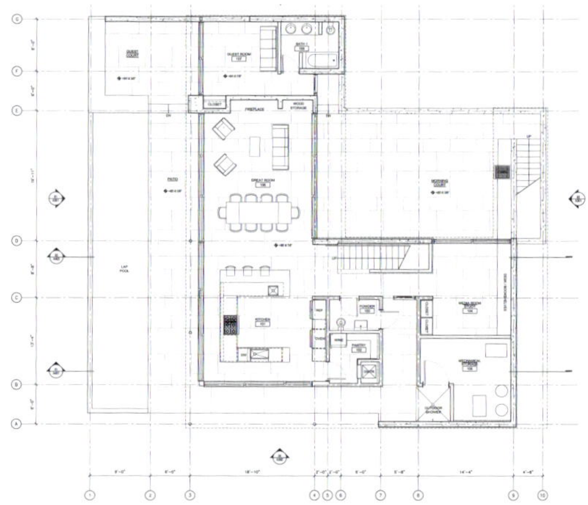

Lower level floor plan

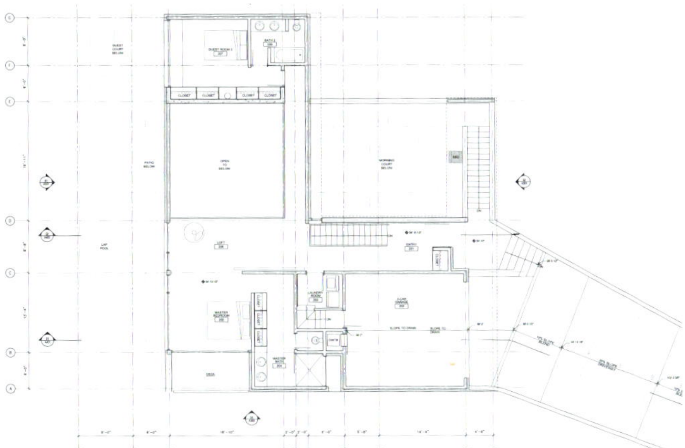

Entry level floor plan

SOUND ADDITION

Charlestown, Rhode Island

SOUND ADDITION

Charlestown, Rhode Island

This is an addition and renovation to an existing beach home for Wendy and Morris in Charlestown, Rhode Island. Located along Charlestown Pond, sweeping views of Ward Island, Governors Island, and the Atlantic Ocean beyond make for commanding views of the waterscape from this home.

Engaged to renovate and add a new dining area, master bedroom suite with terrace, and a private sunroom with roof terrace, a careful insertion took shape to respect the existing context, while revisiting the current uses of the building.

Carving-out of the existing home similar programmatic elements to those requested for the addition, the new central core inserted projects the volume of the spaces forward. Enabling the homeowner to capture framed views of the surrounding lush environment, the addition generates spaces for the owners to relax outdoors while respecting theirprivacy. Beginning to anchor a new architectural language for the home that announces itself to the waterfront and opens itself up to the user to engage their surroundings, this addition highlights a newly integral portion of the home.

The addition is covered with a Douglas fir rain screen along with cedar elements on the interior and punctuated with aluminum windows and doors.

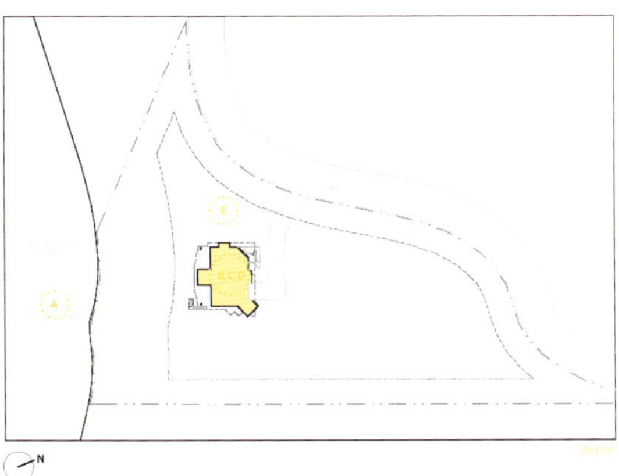

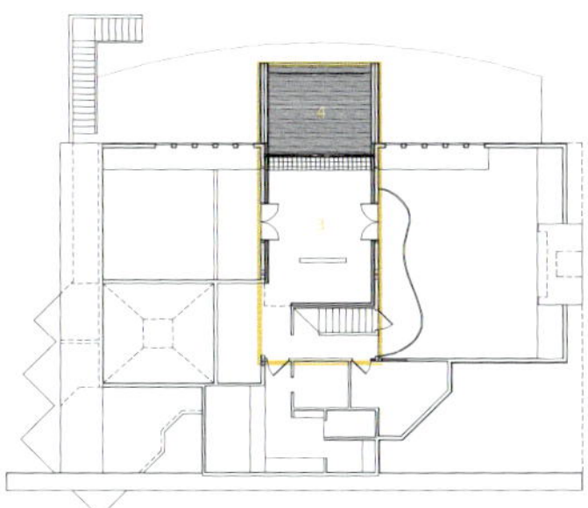

Second floor plan

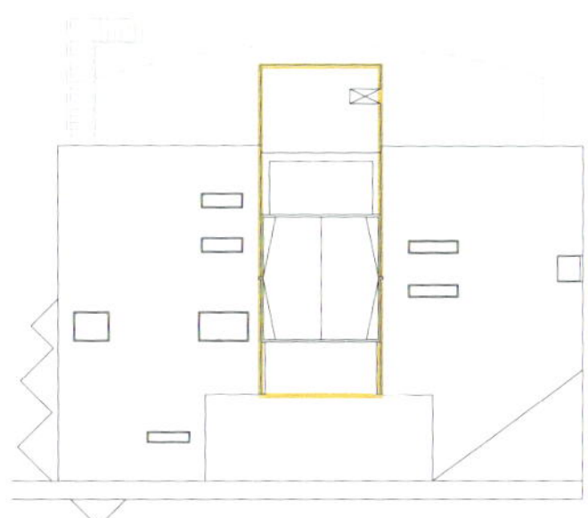

Roof plan

1 Kitchen
2 Dining area
3 Master bedroom
4 Bedroom terrace
5 Private sunroom
6 Roof terrace

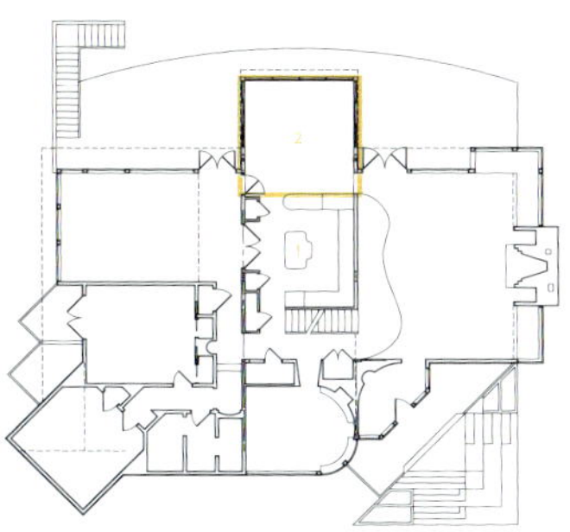

First floor plan

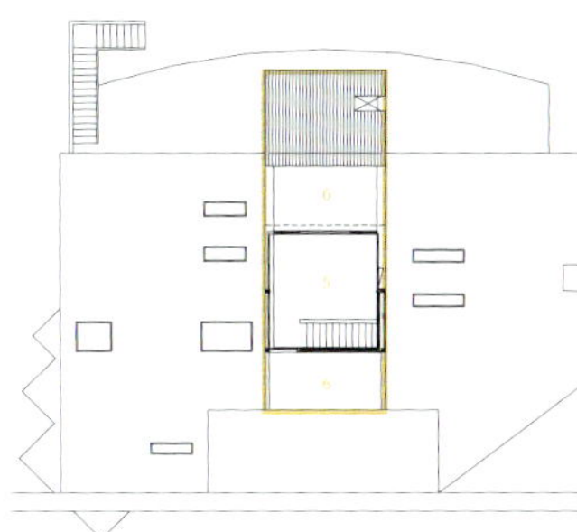

Third floor plan

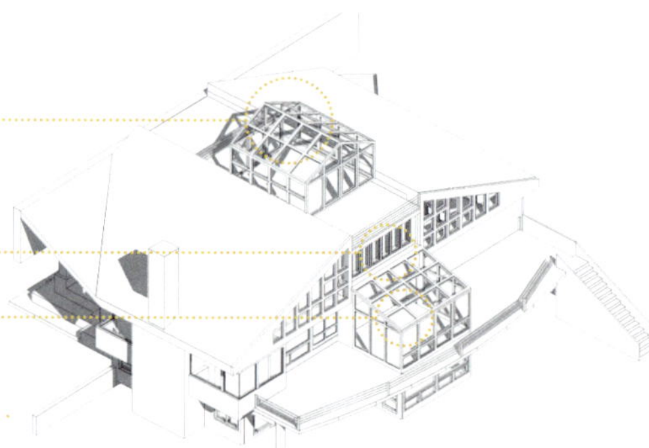

Pre-existing conditions

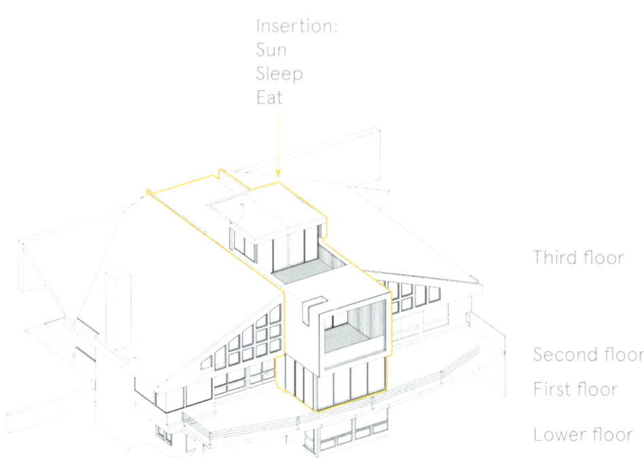
Insertion:
Sun
Sleep
Eat
Third floor
Second floor
First floor
Lower floor

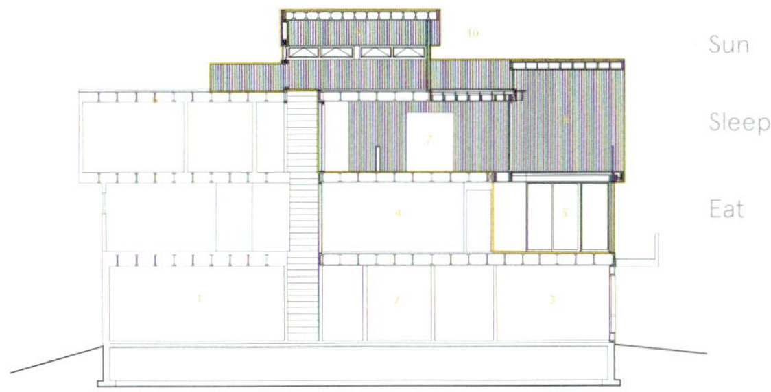

Longitudinal section

1 Family room
2 Bathroom
3 Guest bedroom
4 Kitchen
5 Dining area
6 Closet
7 Master bedroom
8 Bedroom terrace
9 Sunroom
10 Roof terrace

COMMUNITY HOUSING

Long Beach, California

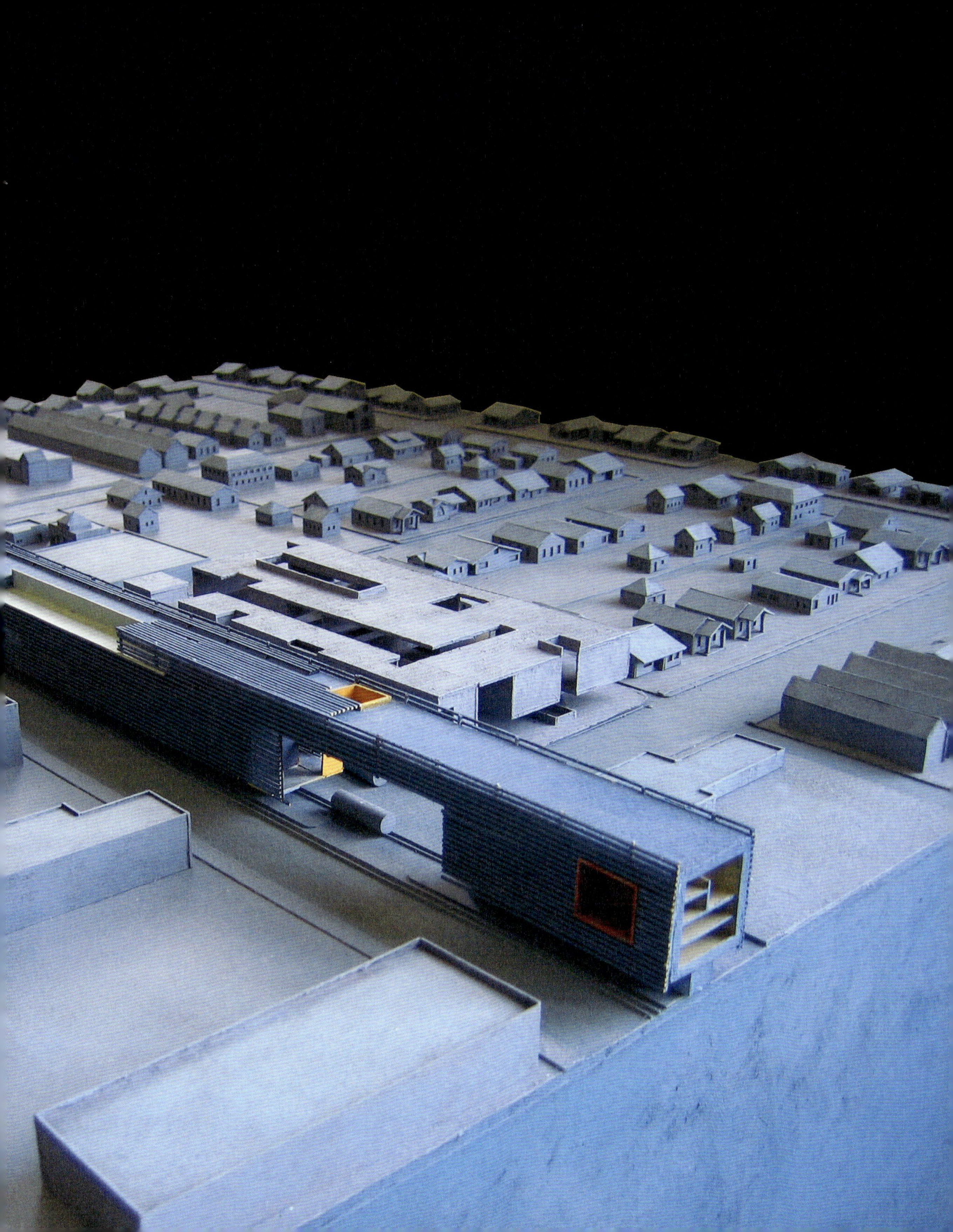

COMMUNITY HOUSING

Long Beach, California

Long Beach was originally developed as a suburb to LA, with residential neighborhoods of bungalows laid out in a grid that could spread in any direction to accommodate the rapidly growing post-war population. It has evolved over the decades from a highly configured bedroom community to a missed use landscape. Many of those bungalows had been neglected or demolished, leaving gaps in the built environment. Ultimately, we approached this project as an issue of density: that the devolution of the fabric had resulted in the loss of a critical mass.

To achieve re-densification, we developed a two pronged approach; the first was to imagine what a housing block should be, given the discontinuous nature of the main boulevard. We turned the housing inward to provide an oasis for its residents, yet hold the block's edges in a way that would anticipate and encourage future growth. But we also felt that a housing block, even an elegantly planned housing block, would not address some of the most critical issues that we had identified through our site analysis. The problem of scale, especially with the extra-wide corroder cutting through the city, needed to be addressed in tandem with the specifics of housing architecture. Further, the drastically under-used blue line metro, which runs the corridor's length, occupied the zone in the middle of that boulevard. The entire spine could benefit from further development if the metro was truly to be used. So, if we developed housing and services along the blue line — in fact, right above it — as a new inhabited corridor, what would reinforce the use of the train and the communities that would arise in its path? We imagined this new spine organizing the entire city, activating the public corridor on both pedestrian and public transportation levels.

This new spine would contain schools, community centers, shops, and loft apartments, all connected by the blue line, and all accessible to the surrounding neighborhoods.

Court interior

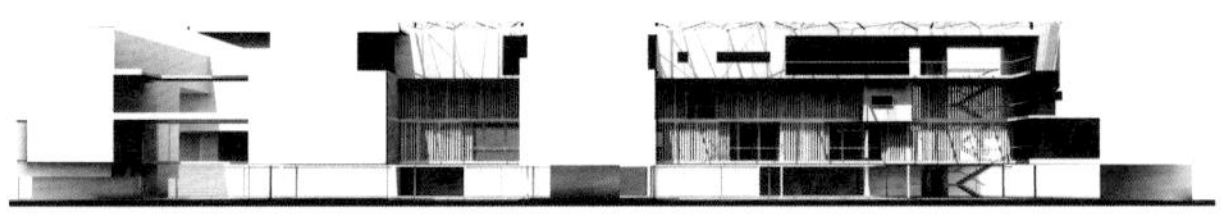

Section

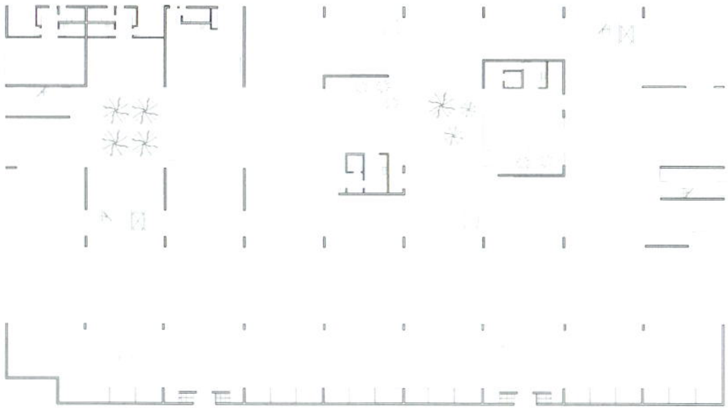

Ground floor plan

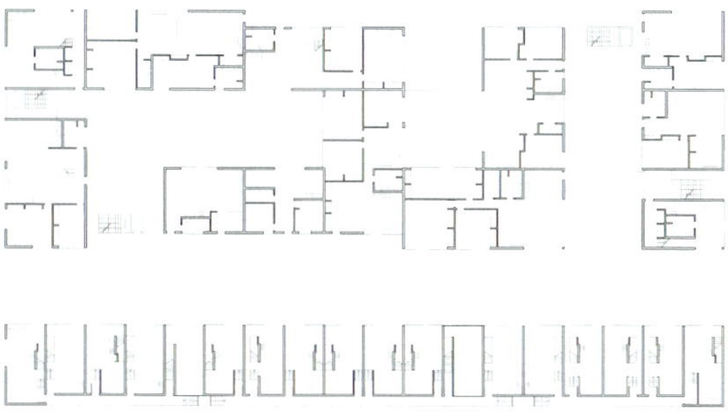

First floor plan

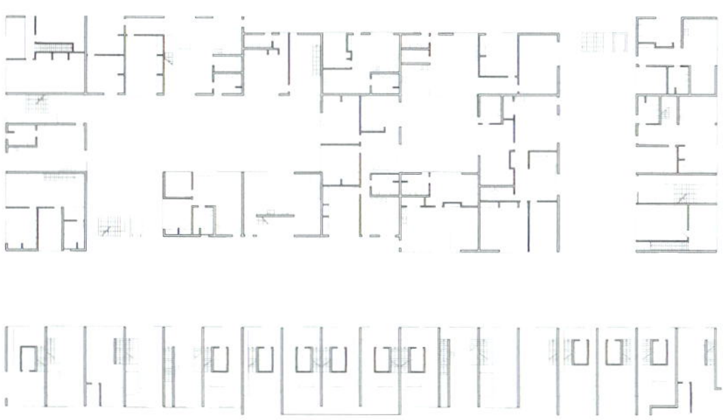

Second floor plan

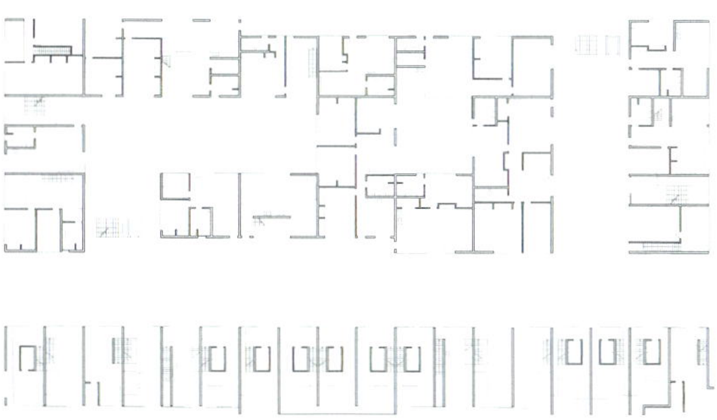

Third floor plan

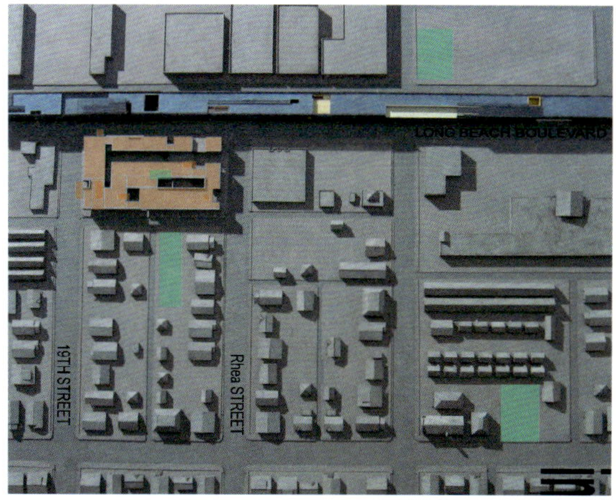

Site plan

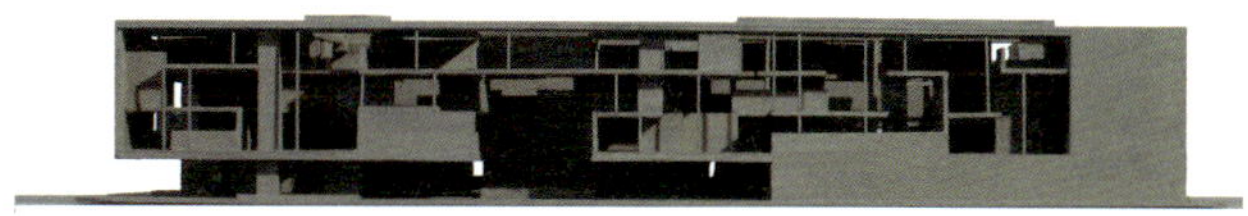

East elevation

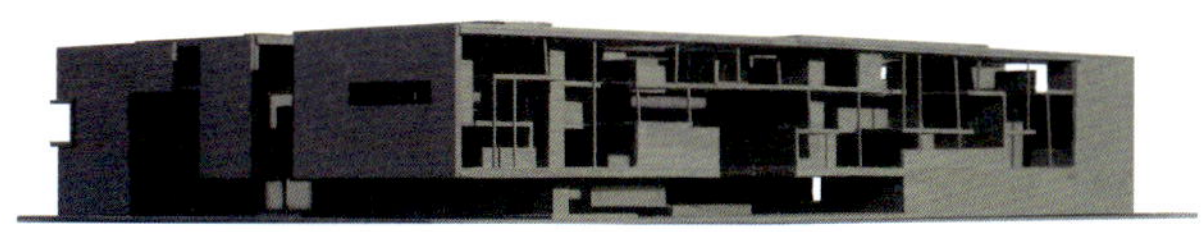

Elevation at southeast corner

South elevation

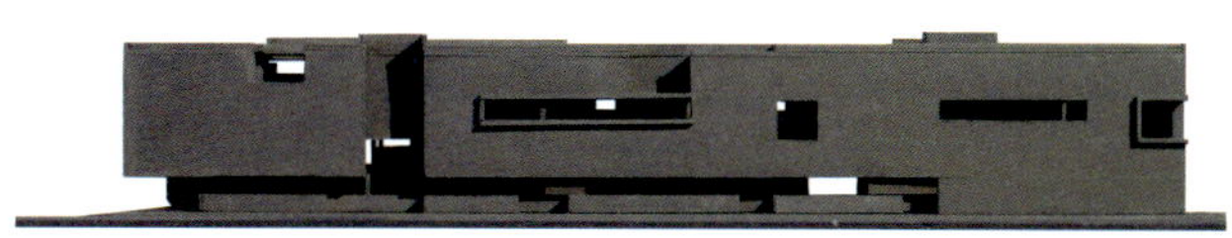

West elevation

Sections

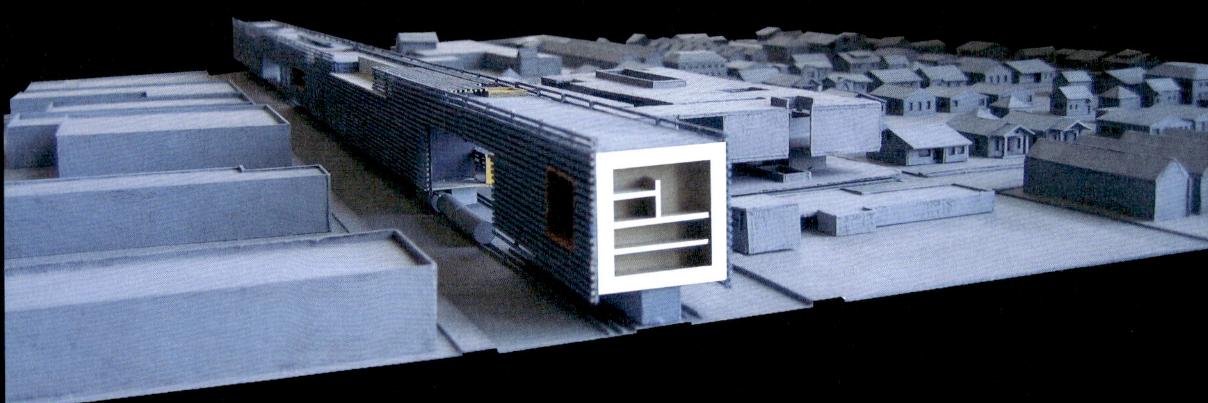

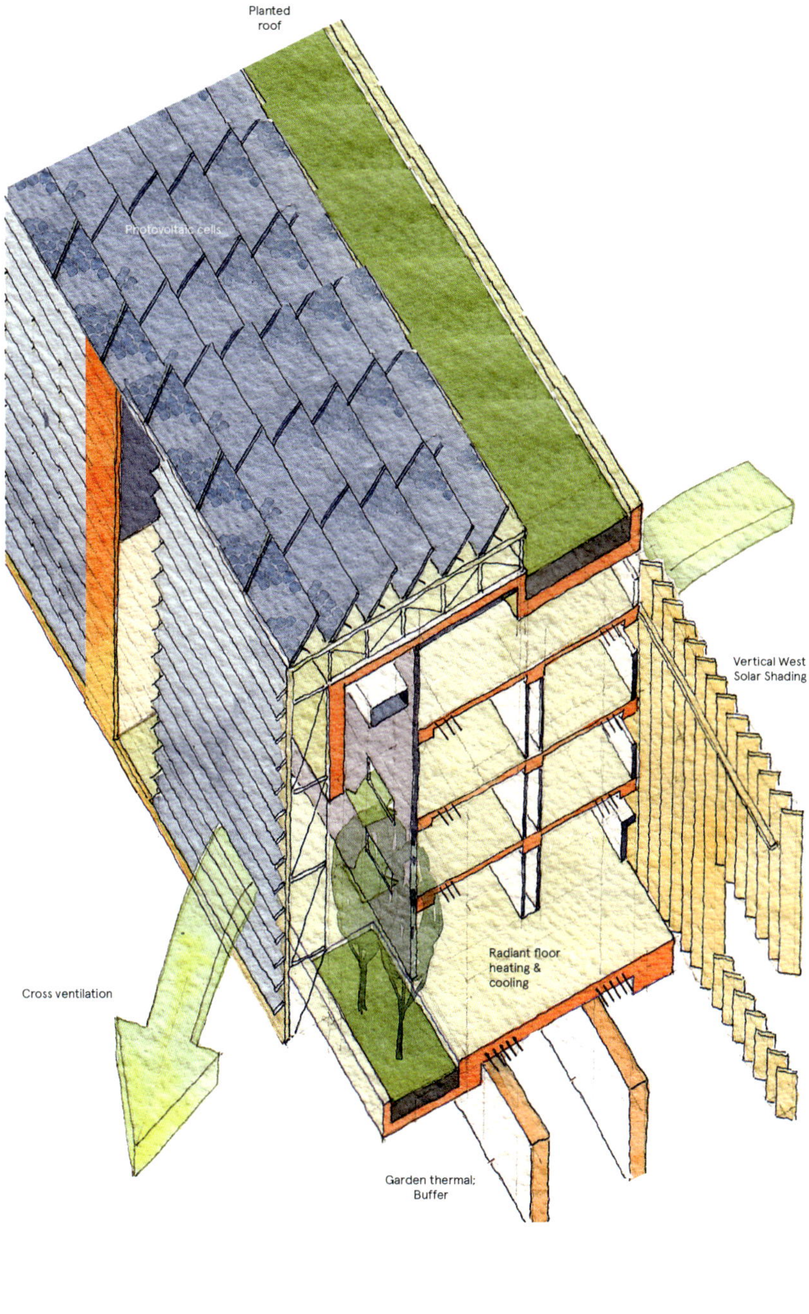

Environmental diversity, working with John Fernandez from MIT

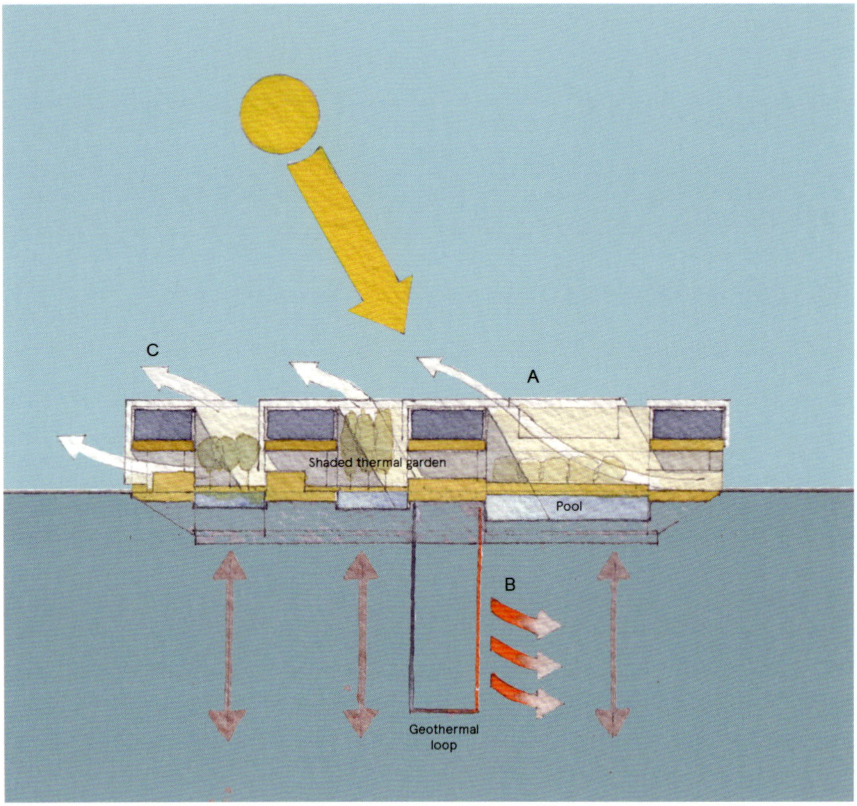

Section - Environmental diversity

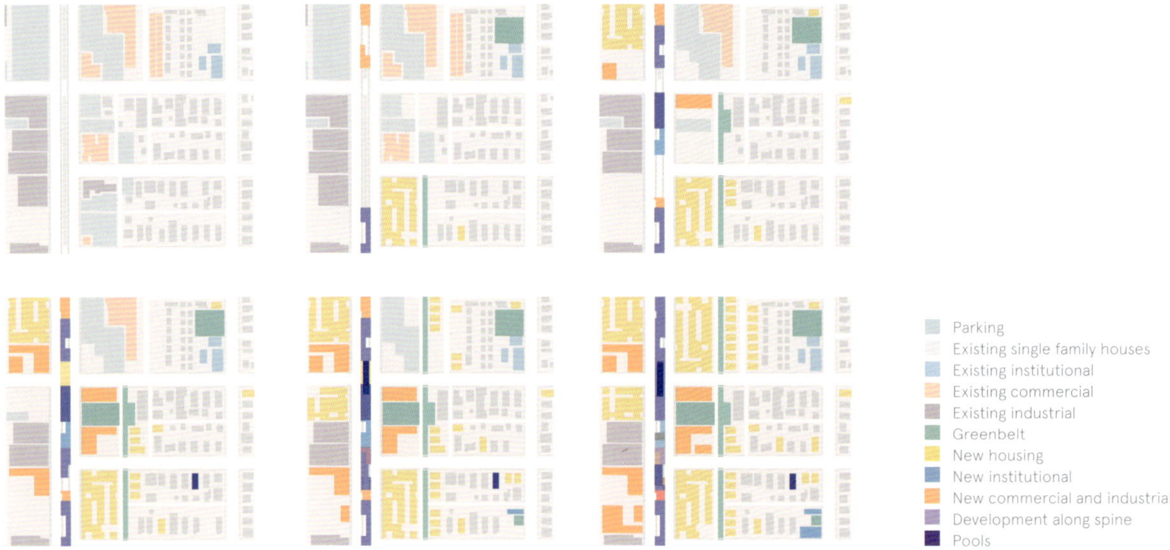

Phasing plans

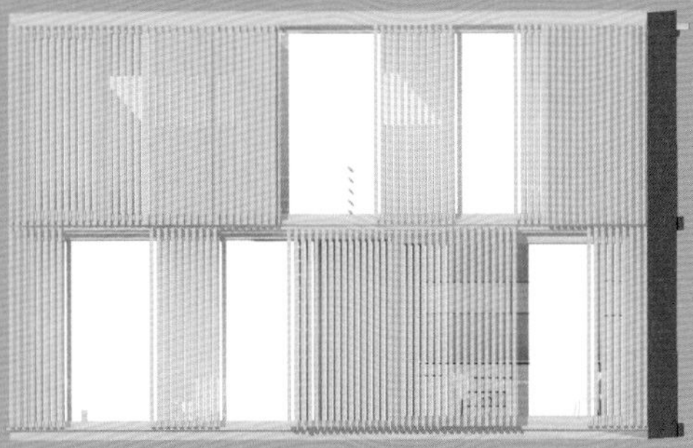

Elevation

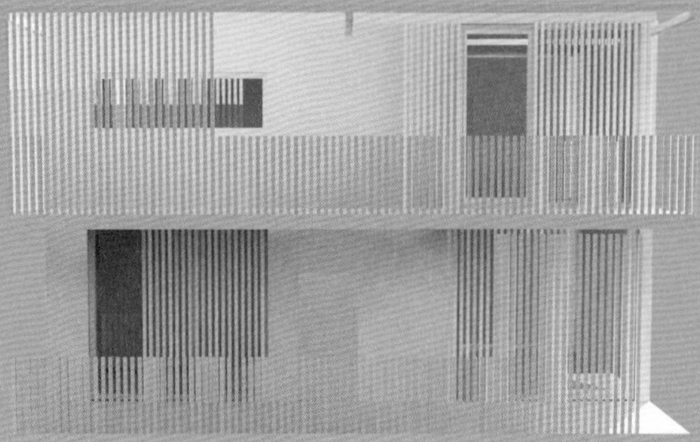

Elevation courtyard

Section dining

Section west

Section east

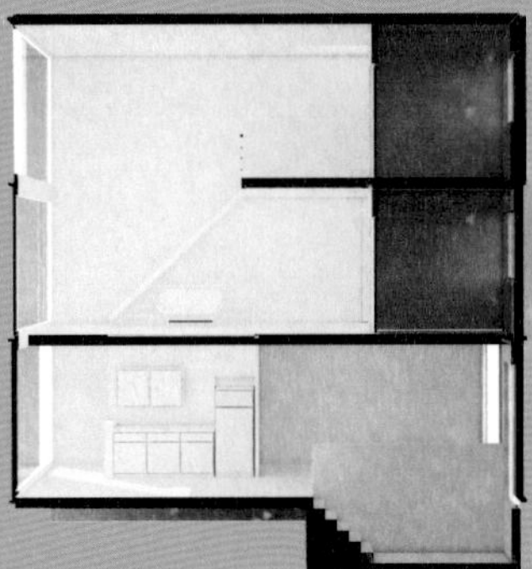

Section kitchen

Section

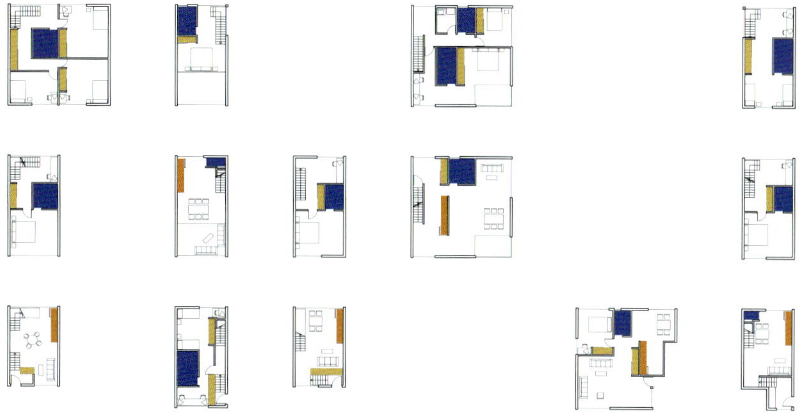

Townhouse diagrams

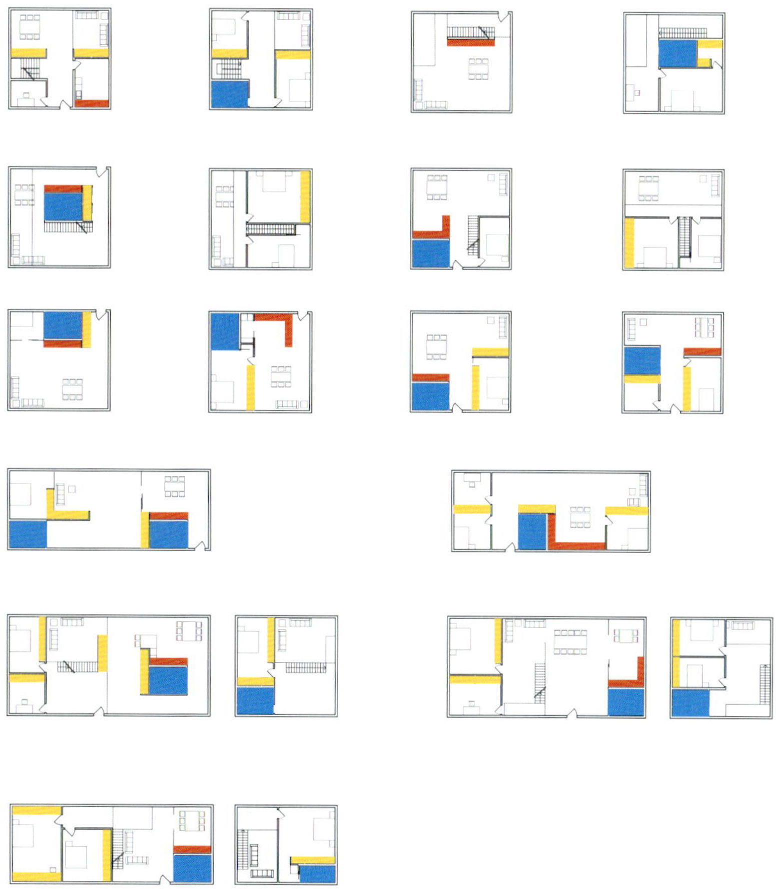

Units diagrams

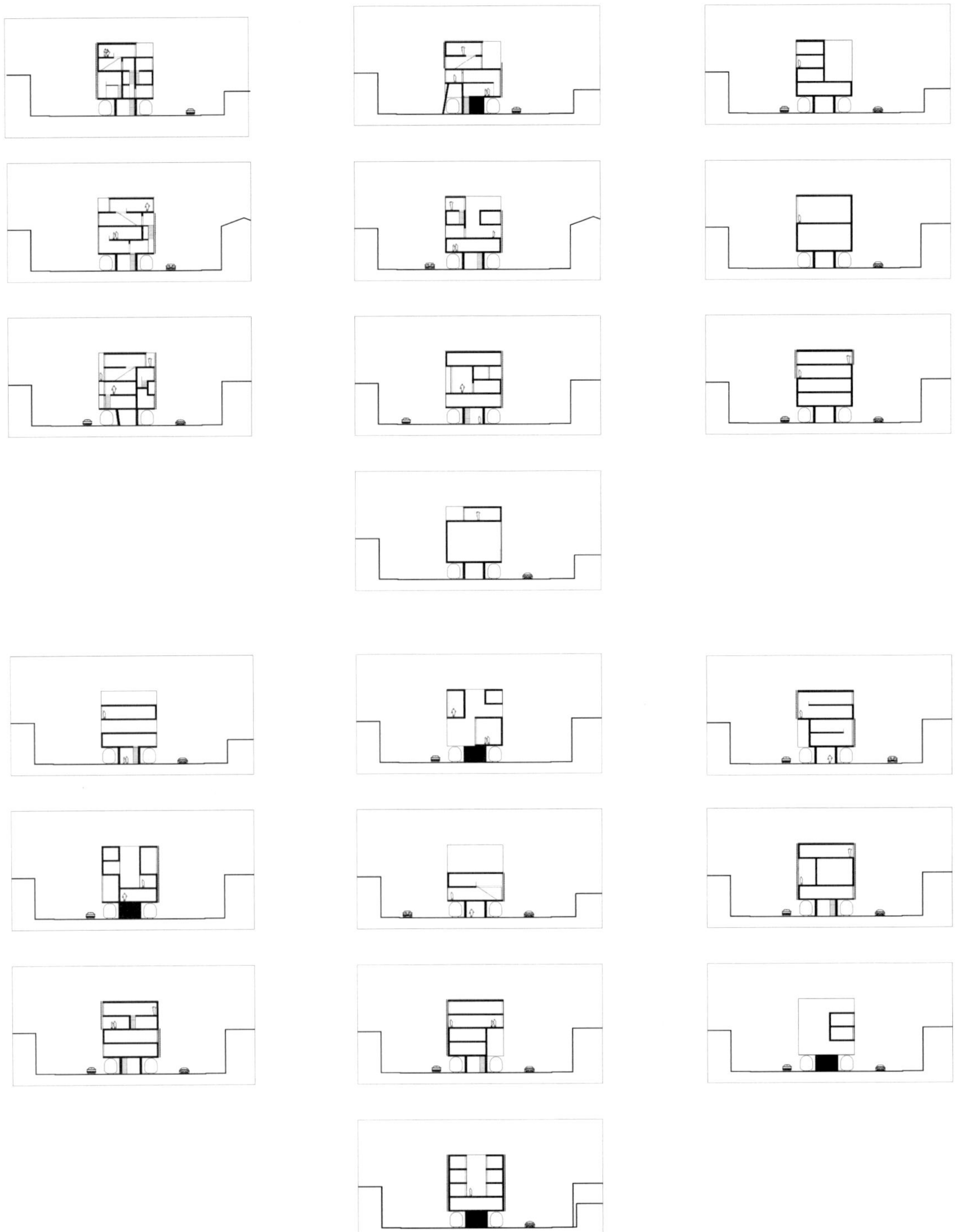

Sections

Living

Entrance

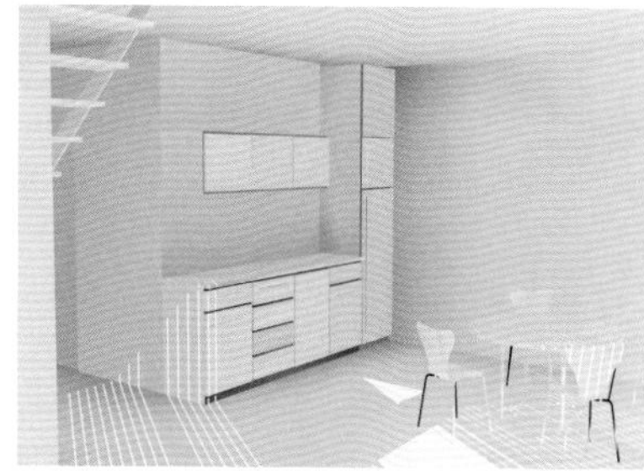
Kitchen

Town kitchen

Bedroom

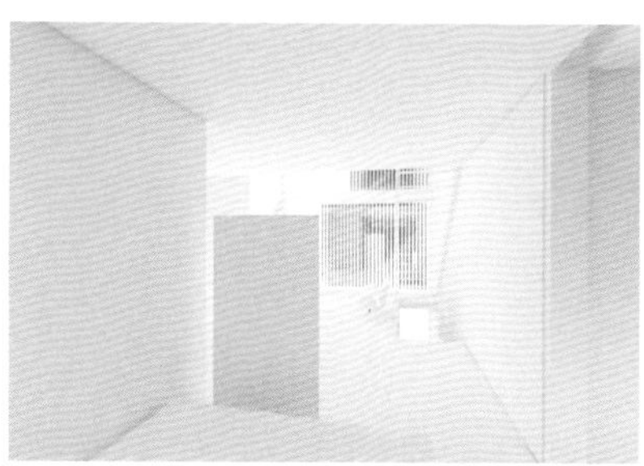
2nd floor living

Dining

VINEYARD HOUSE

Saint Helena, California

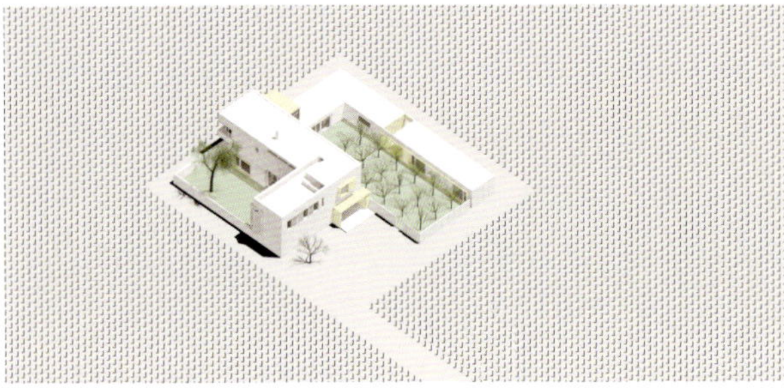

VINEYARD HOUSE

Saint Helena, California

Saint Helena is an agricultural community located in Napa Valley in northern California. The five acre site for this home lies at the edge of Saint Helena overlooking the adjacent vineyards and the rolling hills to the west of the valley. The majority of the site has been planted with vineyards on a five-foot module with the 5,800 square feet house sited within these vineyards directly tied to this spacing.

The clients plan to relocate back to this house after spending the past two decades living in Asia. The home is seen as an internalized repository for the artifacts collected by the clients over these many years abroad. This interior warehouse with display cases floats above the main living room at the intersection between the two external courtyards. It is the most central of a series of furniture-like pieces that focus outward on the vineyards and the distant landscape.

The building itself is also defined by two distinct wings that create the two primary exterior courtyards. One court is off the kitchen and it is intended for exercise and morning use, while the dining room and library define a more quiet and reflective space to the west. The main building is clad in stone while the guest wing is wrapped in red cedar. An exterior roof terrace overlooks the vineyards to the west while a lap pool is located along the northern face of the complex.

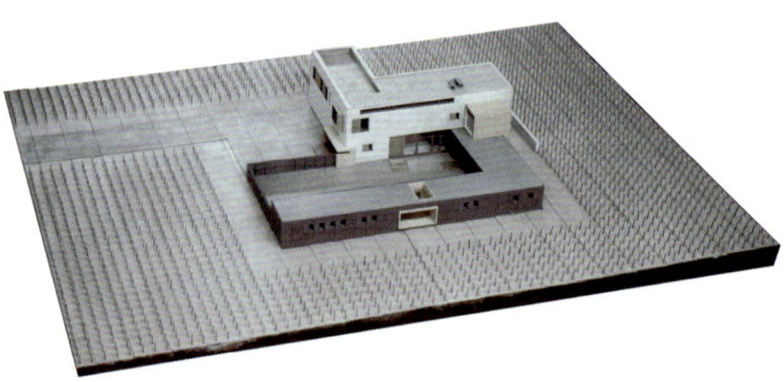

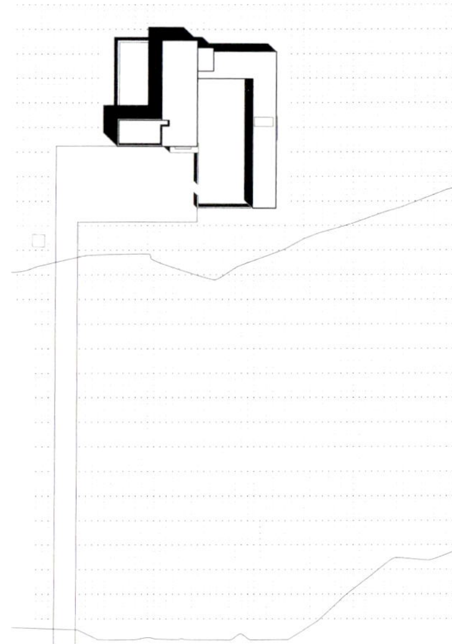

Site plan

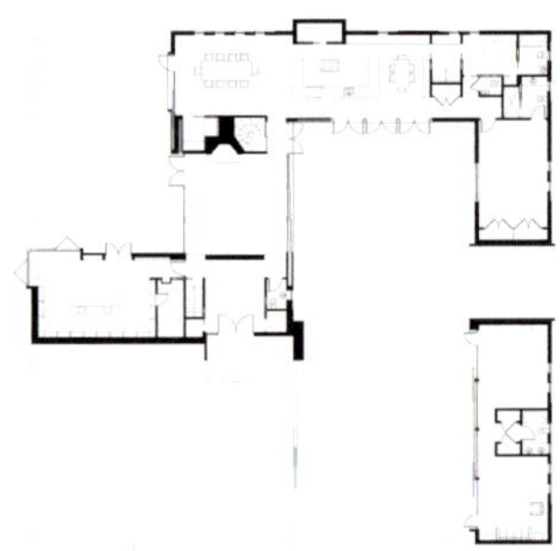

First floor plan

Second floor plan

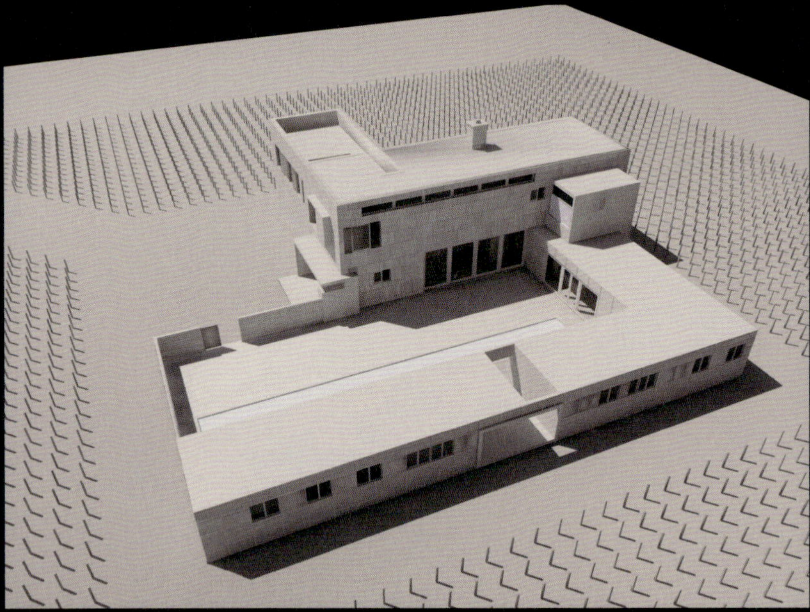

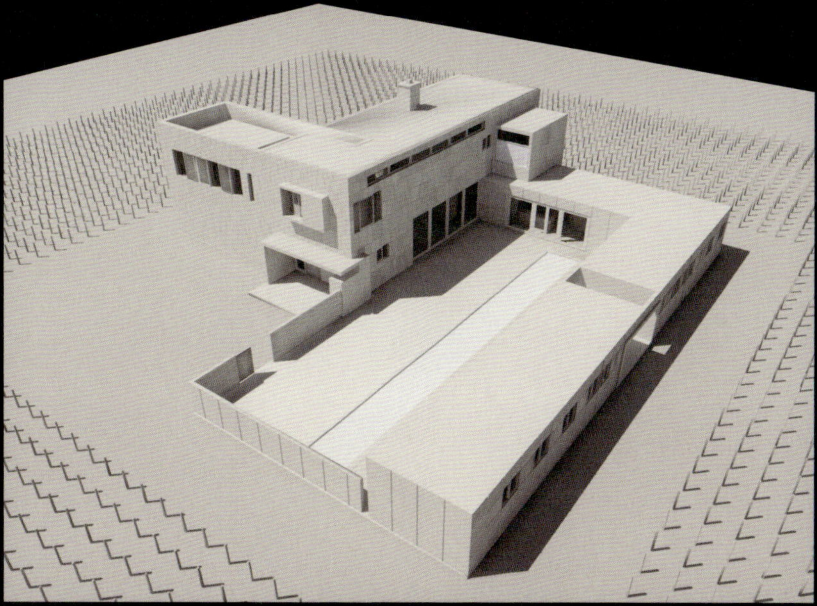

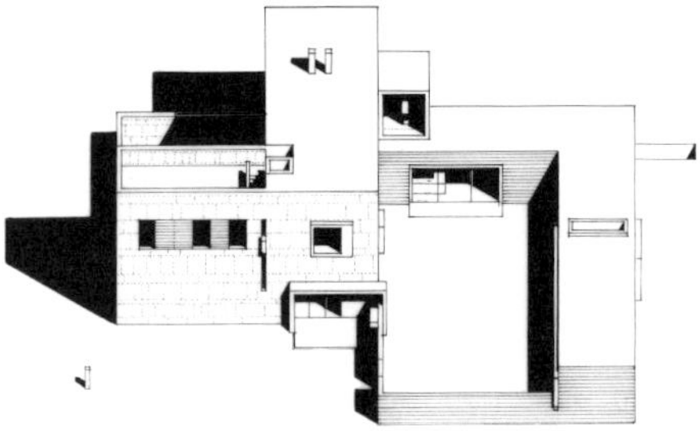

South elevation

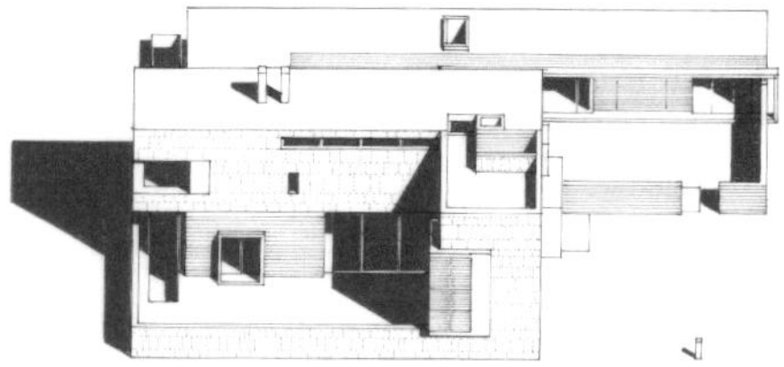

West elevation

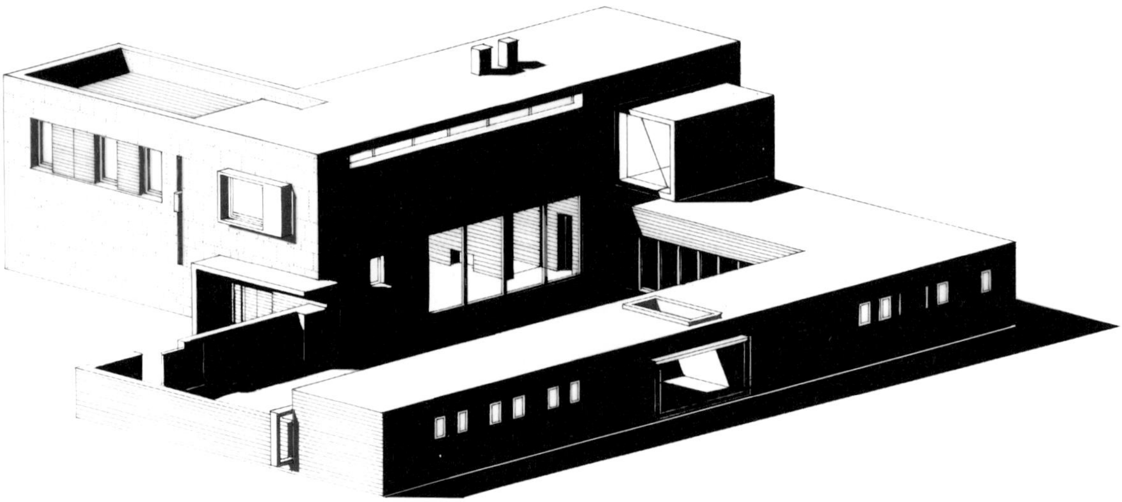

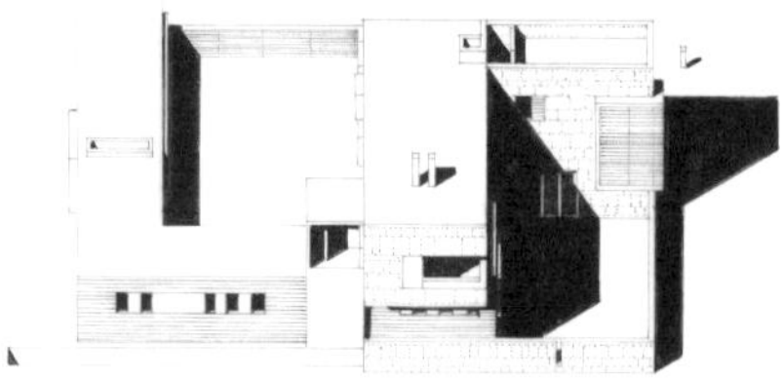

North elevation

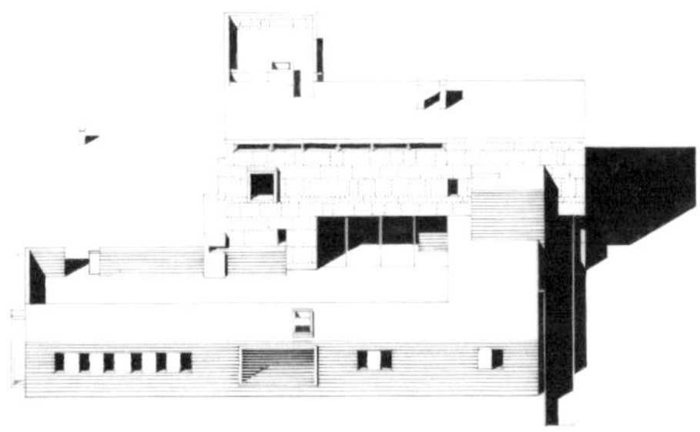

East elevation

East-west section

Central repository

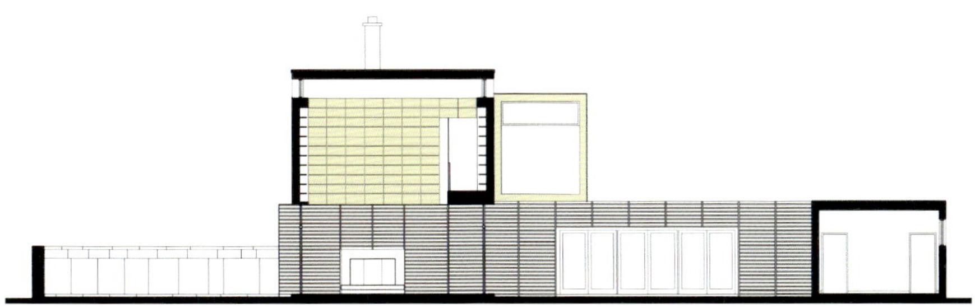

East-west section

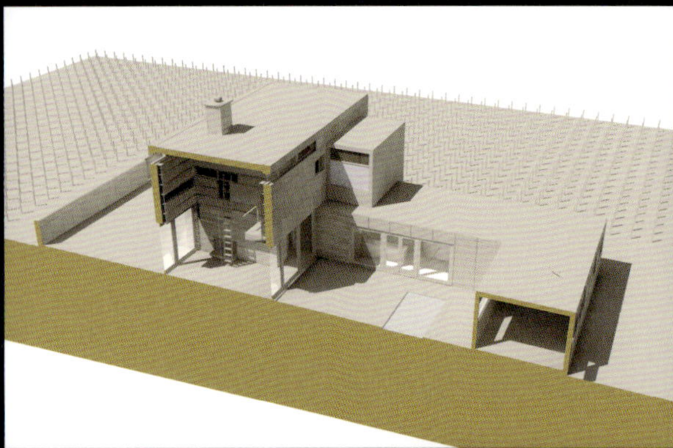

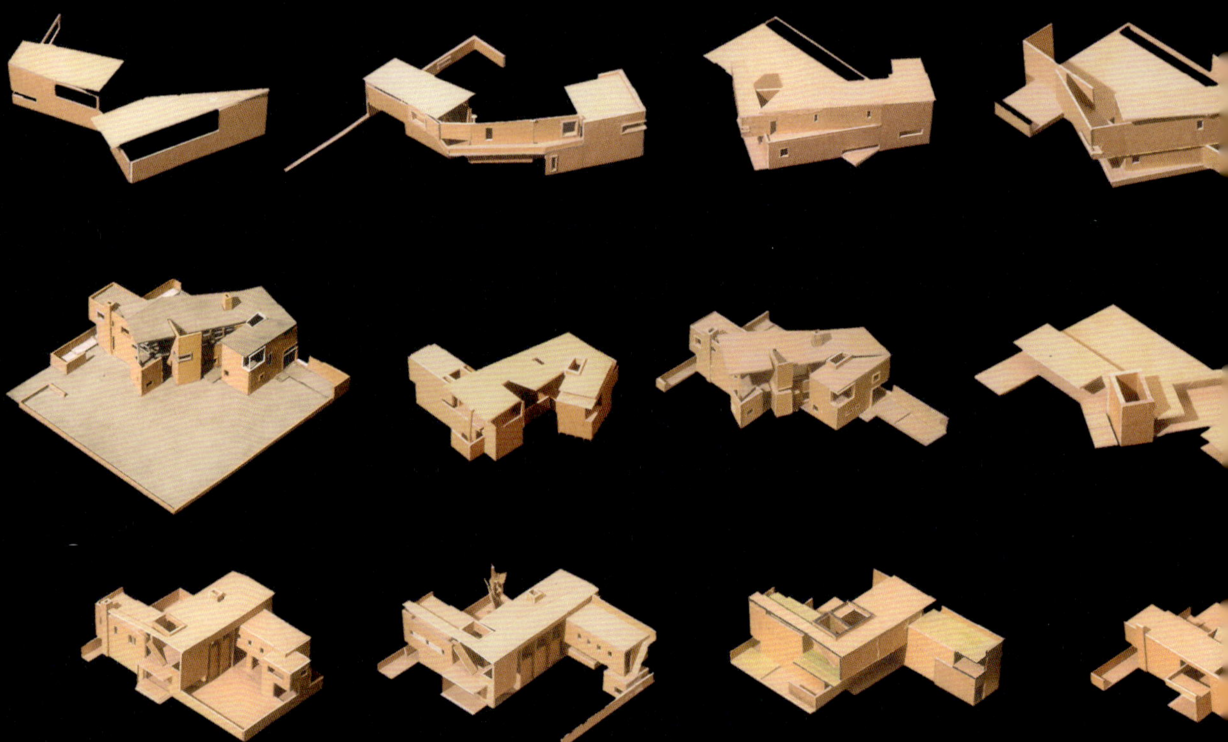

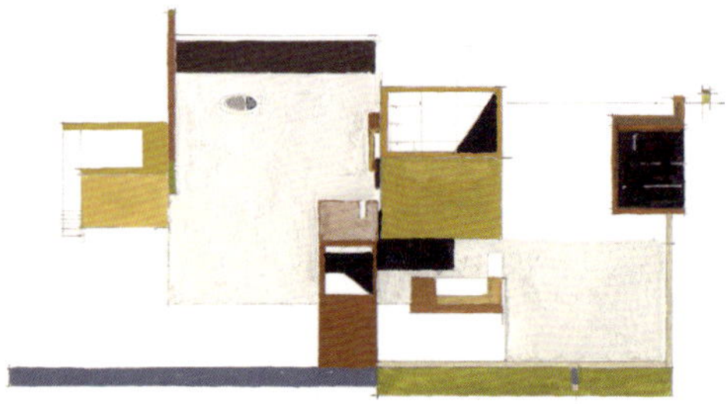
North elevation

South elevation

West elevation

East elevation

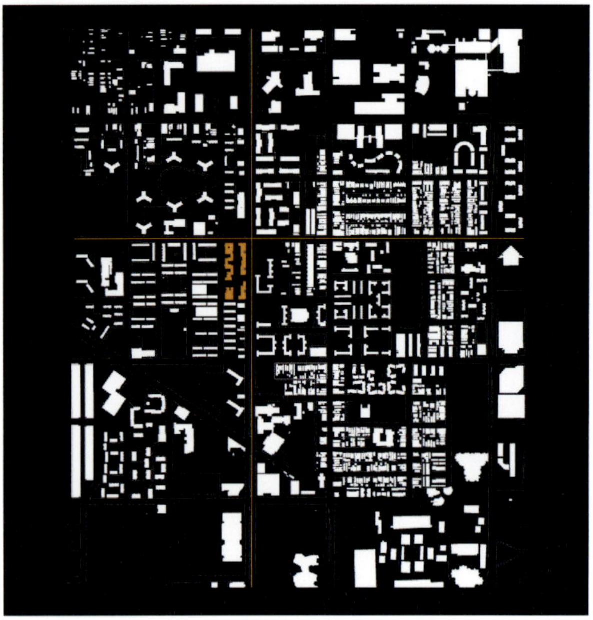

MIXED INCOME HOUSING

Chicago, Illinois

This was a competition sponsored by the City of Chicago and the National Endowment for the Arts as an "Initiative to redefine Public Housing." This proposal was selected by the Jury for development and construction on the Near West Side of Chicago.

The empty lot on the corner of Roosevelt Road and Loomis Street is a prime example of a protean urban landscape. Like the rest of the ABLA neighborhood, its evolution and history are ongoing; its future is being shaped by the Chicago Housing Authority's proposition of holistic redevelopment and mixed-income housing.

Any building can be said to enact a civic role. A well-conceived building gathers together, promotes, and focuses civic energy within itself and along its path. The challenge of this competition is to design housing that will fulfill such a role in the Near West Side of Chicago. That challenge requires a re-imagination of both the city and the urban home. It requires housing units that both fit into the broader context of the neighborhood and meet the needs of public housing residents and private homeowners.

Accordingly, we approach the design of these buildings as a synthesis between complimentary relationships. We choose diversity over strict repetition. We accept the interdependence of communal and personal space and we satisfy the desire for a tranquil interior landscape to balance an increasingly complex urban life. We conceive of the housing and the city block as an open system rather than a closed composition. Our proposal anticipates transformations and permutations. We strive to create fluidity between spaces: between street and garden, entry and home, interior and exterior. The units are emptied out, not partitioned off. We design each home for flexibility of use and evolution rather than for specific tasks and proscribed living arrangements.

—Brian Healy

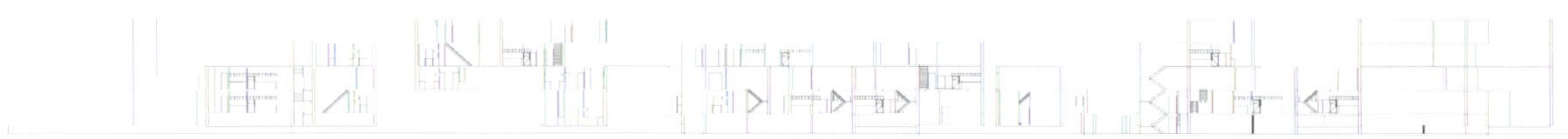

Section

Elevations

ABLA Neighborhood Mixed-Income Housing
Sustainable Strategies

Planted Roof

All roof surfaces of the project will be planted with any number of shallow root plants, depending on the use of the roof. While some of the roofs will be accessible for the residents to enjoy as their own private garden terraces, some public common area and some as a simple roof, all will assist in the insulating, cooling and water management of the project.
The mass of the planted roof is capable of dissipating much of the heat absorbed during the day. The roof uses the edothermic reaction of evaporation to absorb the heat energy and cool the roof. It is also possible for the roof to retain a great deal of water from rain, aiding in stormwater management. Stormwater management becomes critical in urban environments that has such little pourus surface area.

Soft interior

The massing of the building provides a protective thermal buffer around the interior of the block. The interior alley is lined with community gardens, public terraces and tree filled courts. This thermal massing tempers diurnal temperature swings and provides a passive strategy for retaining heat in the winter through the heat storage capacity of concrete and masonry. The exterior space benefits from the massing by existing as a spatially sheltered and enviromentally tempered exterior landscape for use by the residents.

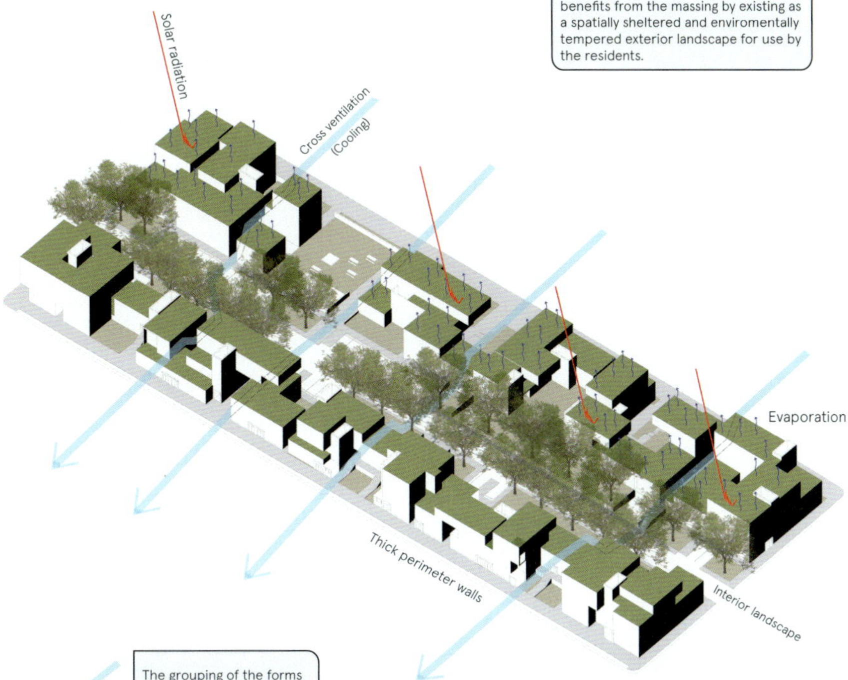

Wind

The grouping of the forms taps into the prevailing energy flows of the sun and wind to provide for a portion of the heating and cooling needs of the residents while providing for a diversity of microclimates and spatial conditions. The prevailing winds provides the necessary cooling to lower the need for mechanically driven air conditioning and provides a link between the environment and the large volumes of the individual units. During hot, humid summer months, the complexity of the form allows for numerous through-mass paths for cross ventilation.

Infrared

Solar infrared radiation provides for solar heat gain and the large openings carved into the building volumes shades the interior environment on warm days while allowing the lower winter sun to penetrate the spaces, reducing the load for mechanical heating. Much of the unwanted infrared radiation is absorbed and dissapated by the mass of the planted roofs.

Plans

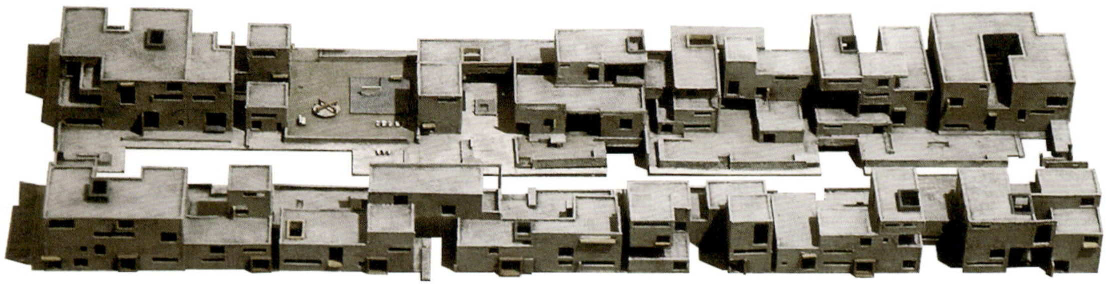

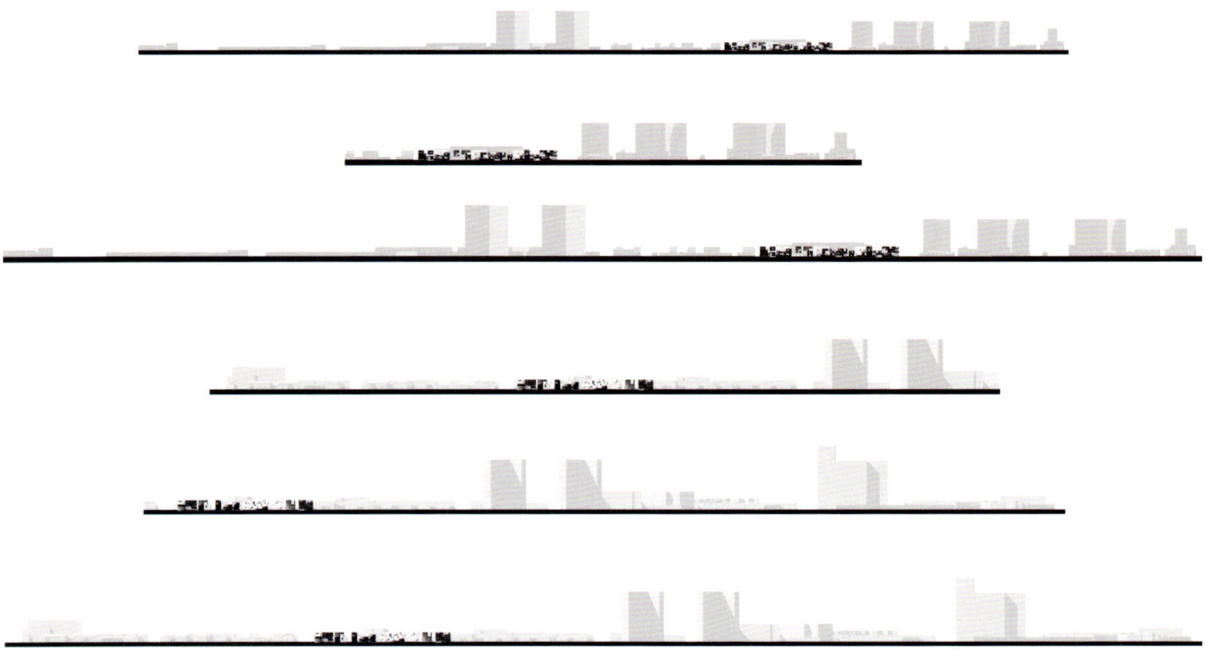

Site sections

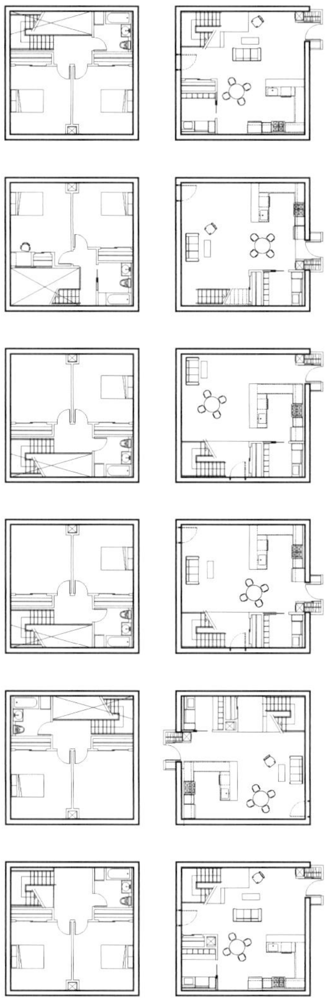

Permutations of living units

Three bedroom unit

Two bedroom unit

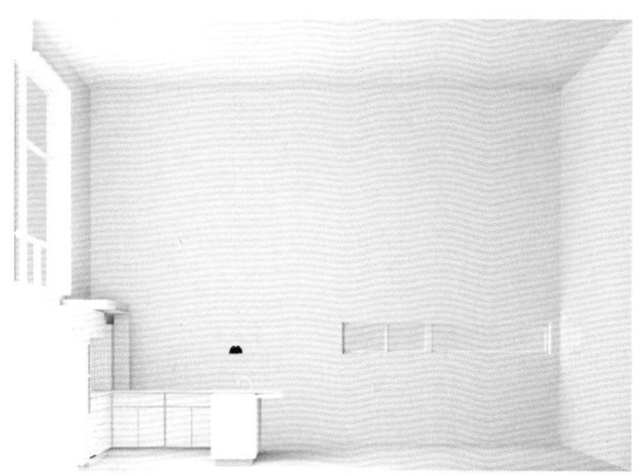

One bedroom unit

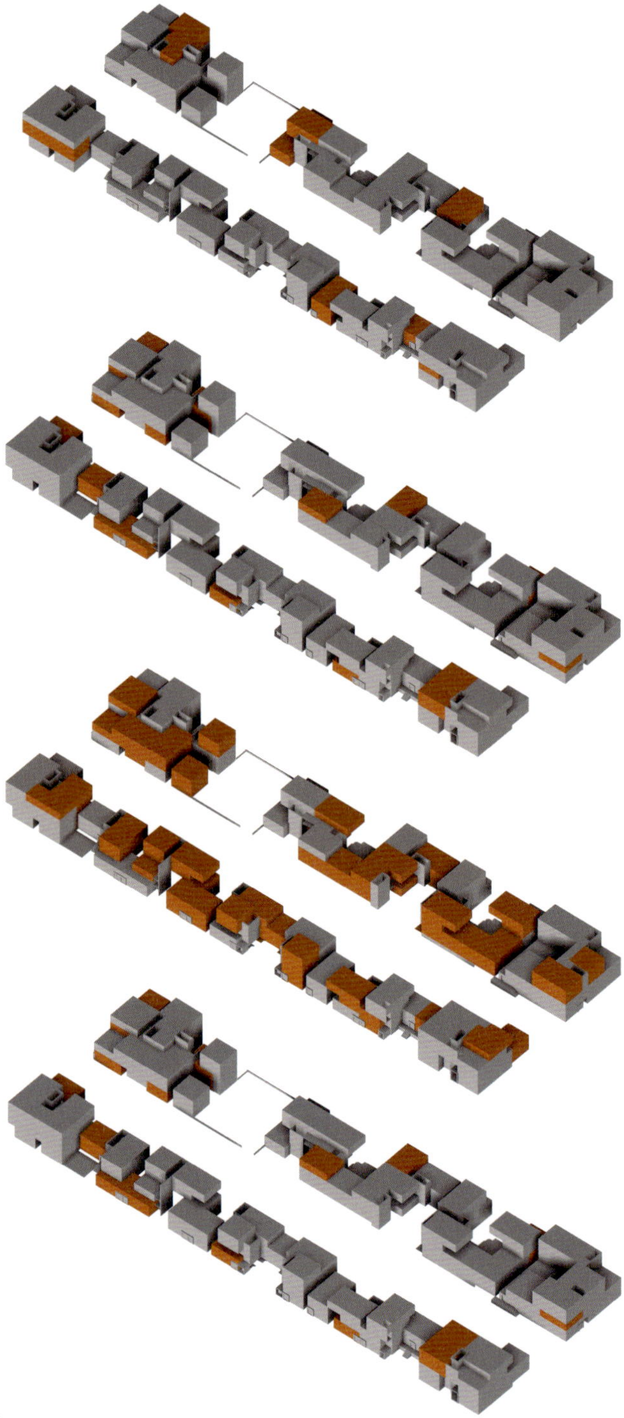

Four bedrooms

Three bedrooms

Two bedrooms

One bedroom

Bedroom distribution axonometric

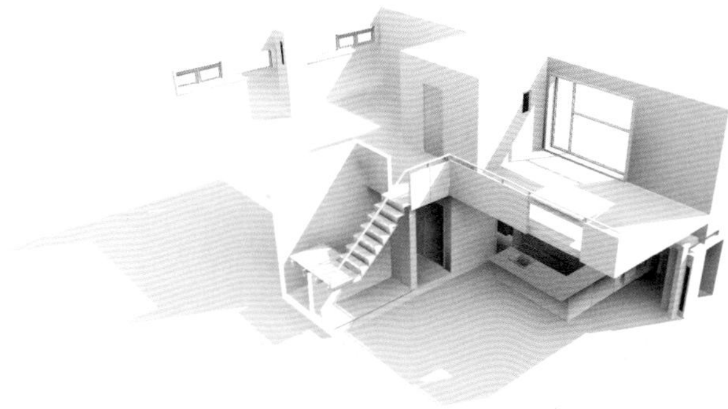

Three bedroom unit

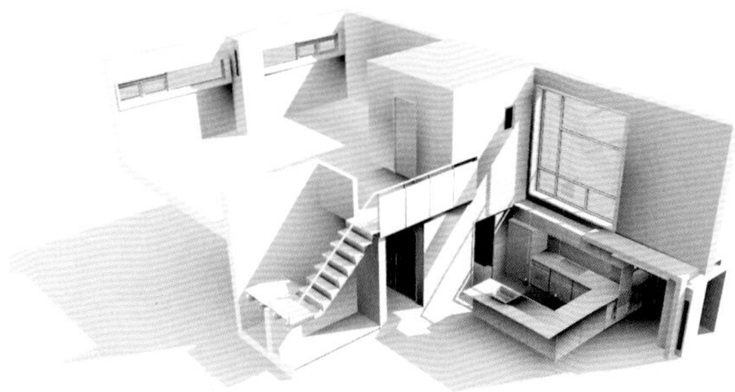

Two bedroom unit

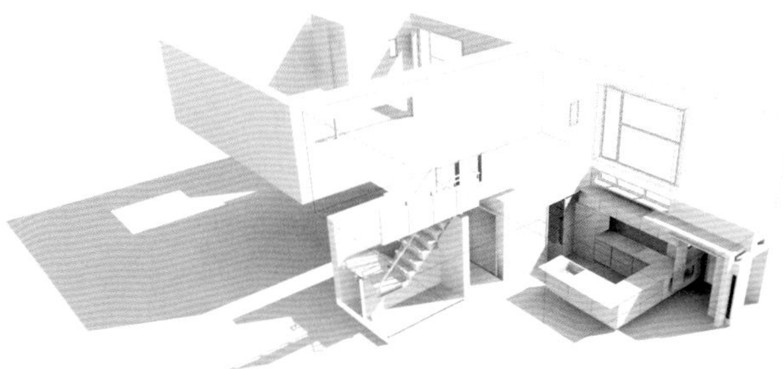

One bedroom unit

APARTMENT BUILDING

Chicago, Illinois

APARTMENT BUILDING

Chicago, Illinois

After being selected in the Chicago Housing Authority's Competition for Mixed Income Housing, BHA was commissioned by the designated developer to design a series of 12 and 15 apartment buildings along Roosevelt Road in the Near West Side of Chicago.

Rather than import more ideas into the neighborhood, they began to imagine what these housing blocks could be if they engaged with parts of the existing neighborhood. Because this area had been a low-income part of the city for some time, there were plenty examples of bad housing strategies that had been tried over the past century. At the time, several large housing projects were in severe disrepair, abandoned, or slated for demolition, and other "models" of their day were depressing masses that turned their backs on the life of the street as well as to each other.

Searching for some positive context, they were drawn to the scale and complexity of the original blocks that held the street edge as a wall, setting up a vocabulary of openings, stoops, and street furniture. The three story masonry buildings include brick with cedar cladding in the open porches.

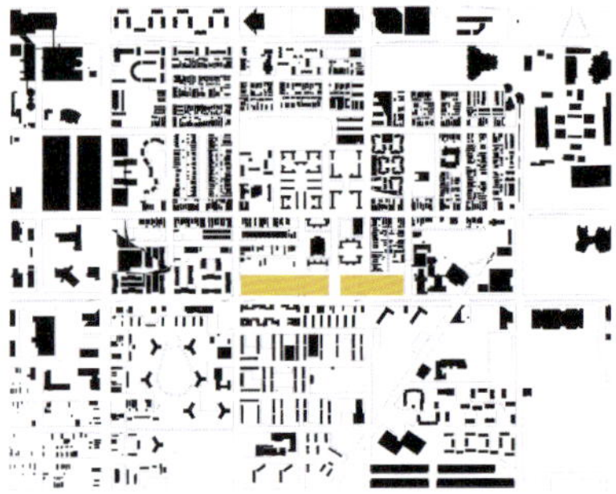

Site plan

Plan

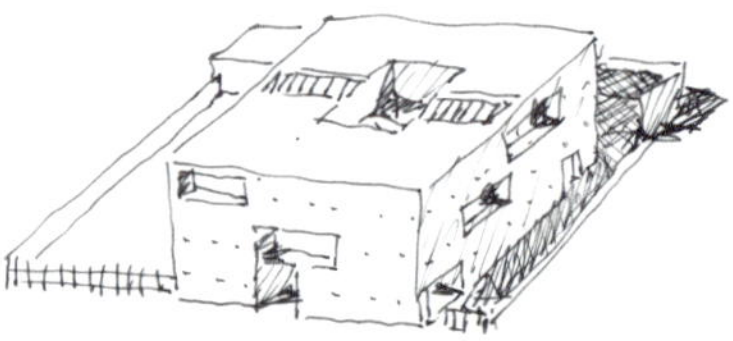

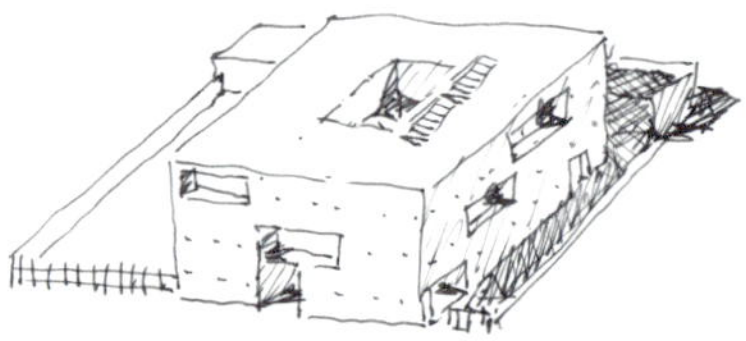

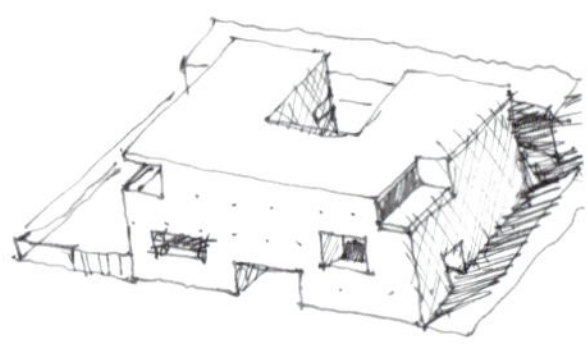

Third floor plan

Second floor plan

Ground floor plan

SAG HARBOR HOUSE

Sag Harbor, New York

SAG HARBOR HOUSE

Sag Harbor, New York

A brother and sister living in New York City were the clients for this summer home on Long Island. It is located in Sag Harbor at the junction of the northern and southern forks of eastern Long Island. The site itself sits between Peconic Bay to the east and protected wetlands to the west. It is located at the end of a small lane that also serves as a public boat launch. The site provides spectacular views of Morgan Nature Refuge, Shelter Island, and Sag Harbor.

The project essentially has two front yards: one facing the bay and the other overlooking the wetlands. It also has two independent clients. The building is shaped by these dualities as well as those inherent to a residential program (open/closed-public/private).

The main living areas, both internally and externally, are aligned along an existing storm wall running parallel to the waterline. These spaces hover above the wall and high water mark allowing for cross breezes and distant views. The building has a wood frame with red cedar and concrete panel siding.

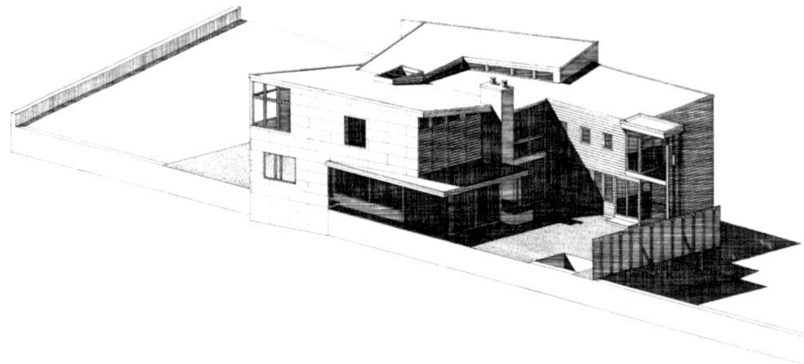

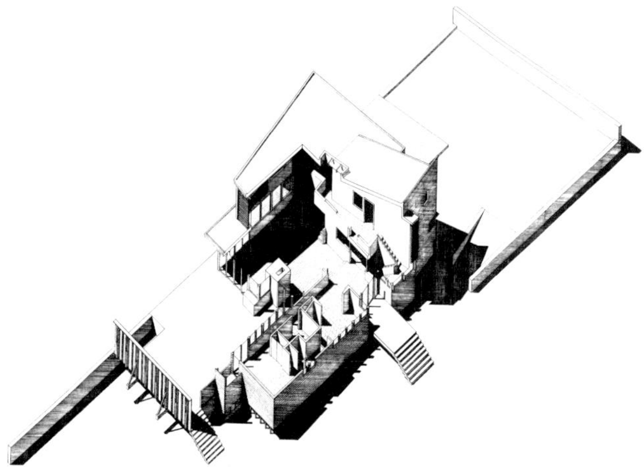

Axonometrics

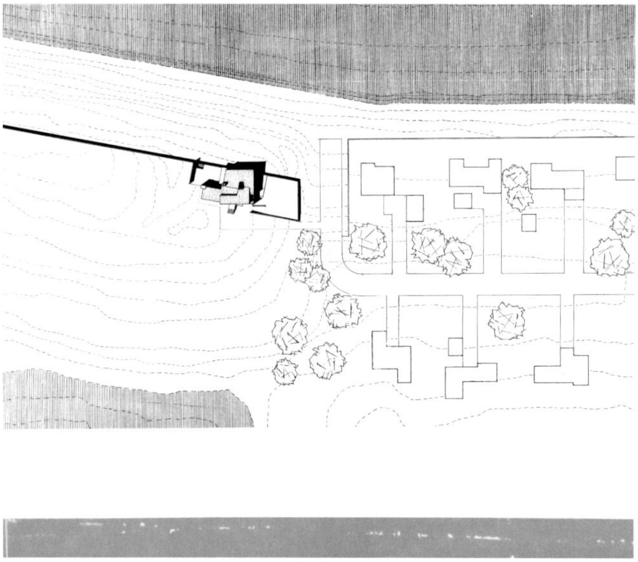

Site plan

South elevation

North elevation

West elevation

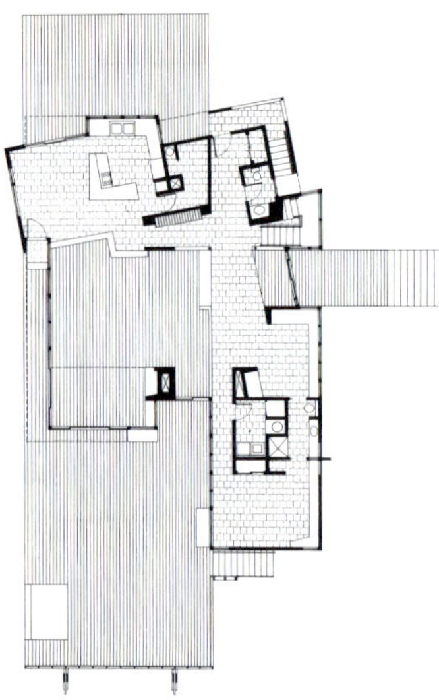

Entry level plan

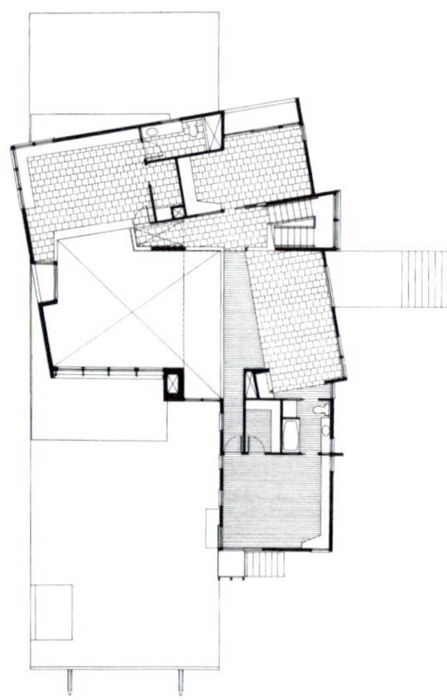

Upper level plan

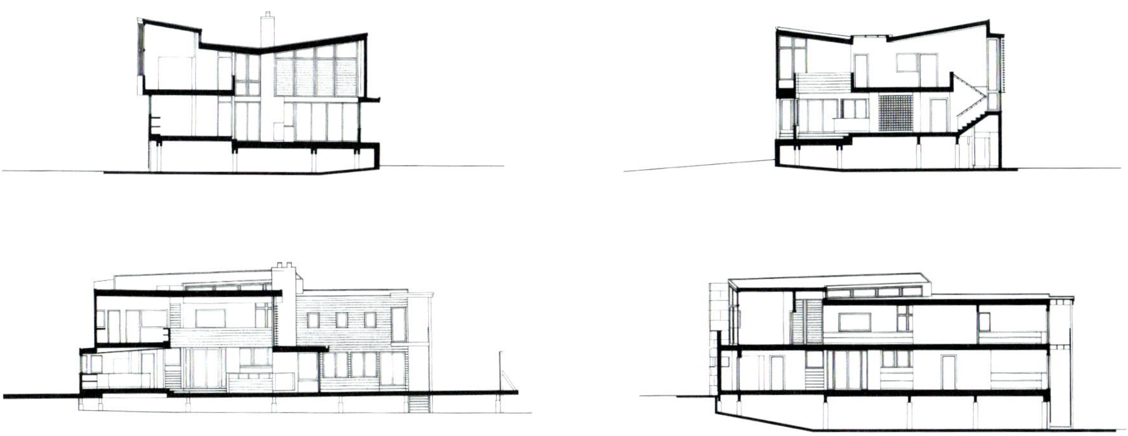

Building sections

ONTEORA TOWER

Tannersville, New York

ONTEORA TOWER

Tannersville, New York

Onteora Park was established in 1896 as a remote artist colony in the Catskill Mountains and it was an integral part of the Arts & Crafts movement of that time. Based on a connection to nature and a blurring of traditional boundaries between the work of fine artists and artisans, over seventy-five houses and cottages supported writers, painters, actors, musicians, fabric weavers, etc. The clients were a young couple and their family who purchased the property with the intention of re-establishing its use as an artist retreat removed from New York City. He is a writer and she is a painter.

The ten-acre site is located along Greene County Route 25. The main house was designed by George Reid in 1898, and includes a series of large murals that he painted depicting seasonal views of the Onteora landscape. The site also includes a number of outbuildings inter-connected by pathways and gardens. These include a water tower, greenhouse, pump station, and stable. The 85-foot tall water tower was constructed in 1920 and provided service to neighboring houses and gardens.

Since the water tower is no longer in use, the clients elected us to renovate it for their personal use as painting and writing studios. The design responds to several site-specific conditions including the myriad pathways across the site, the physical overlap of spaces and activities, and the seasonal variations of light and color.

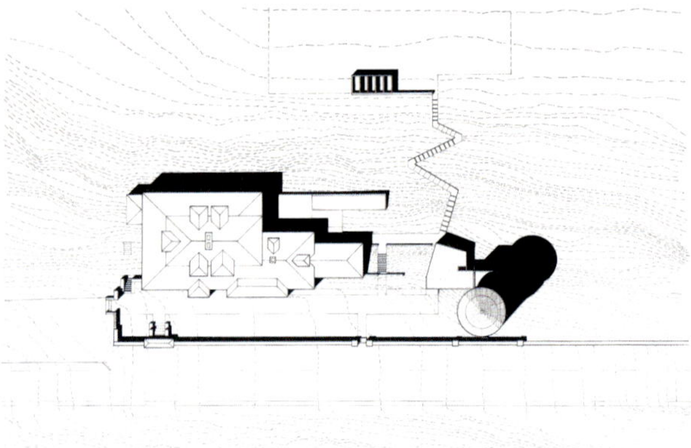

Site roof plan

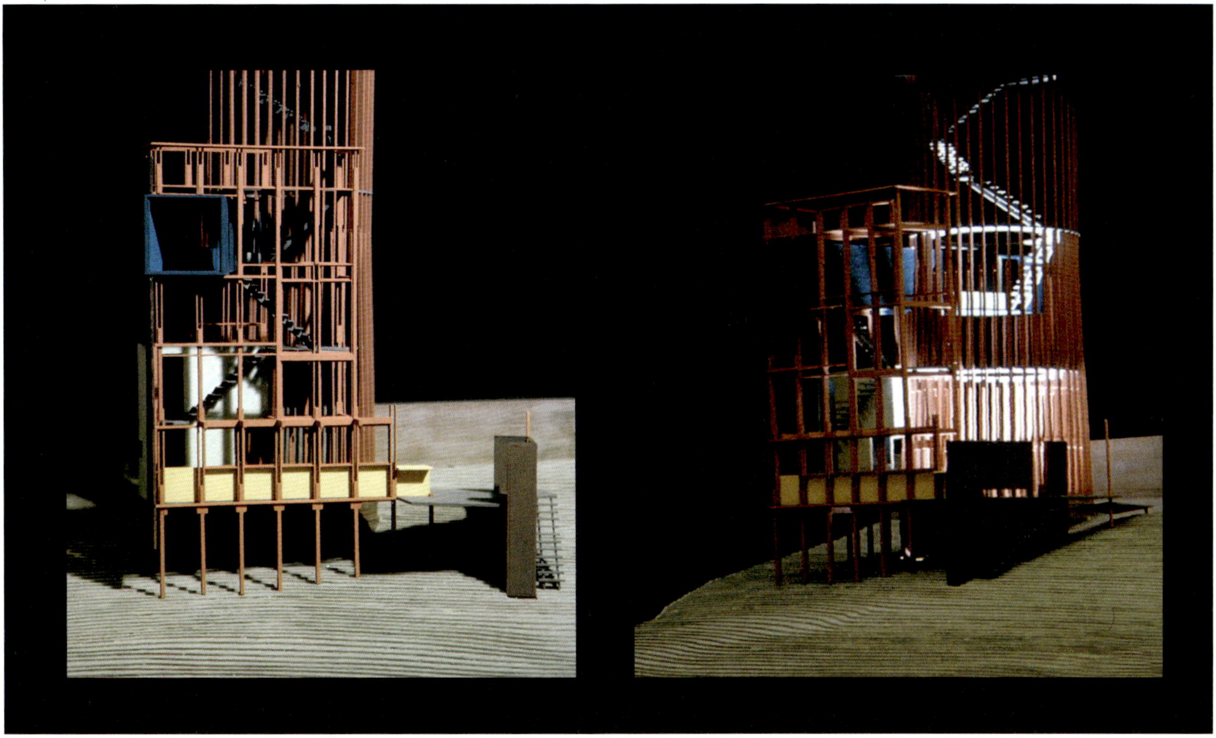

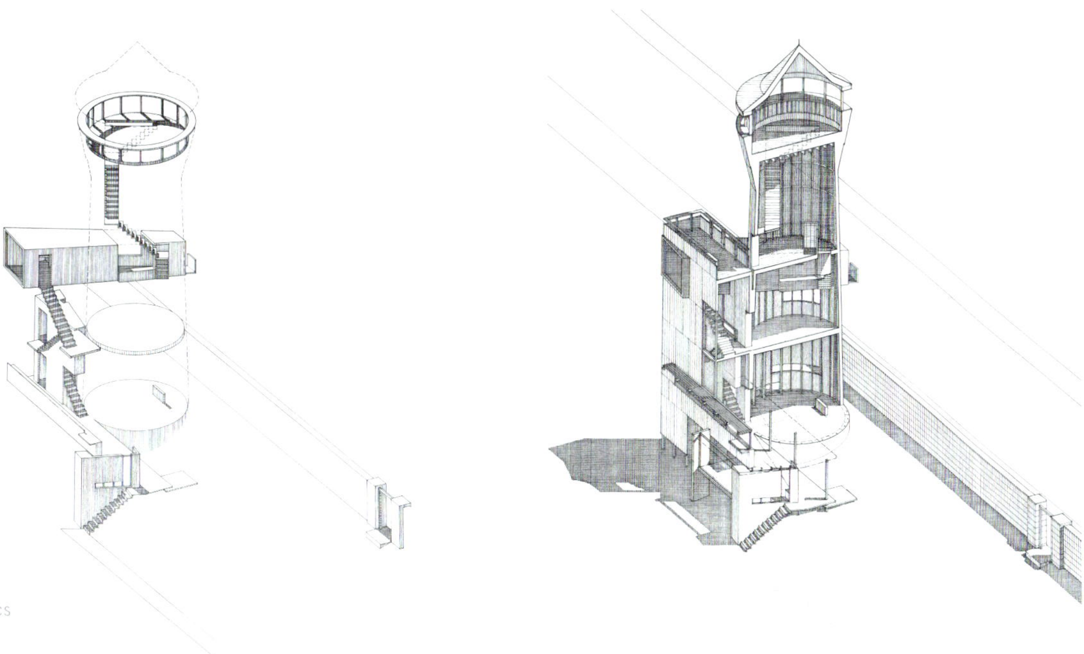

Axonometrics

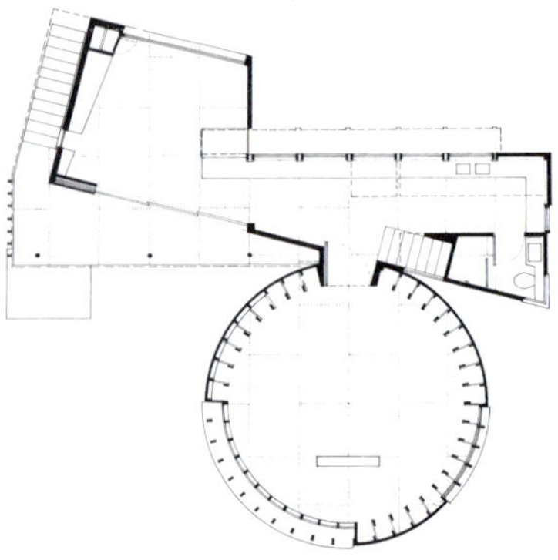

Plan at grade

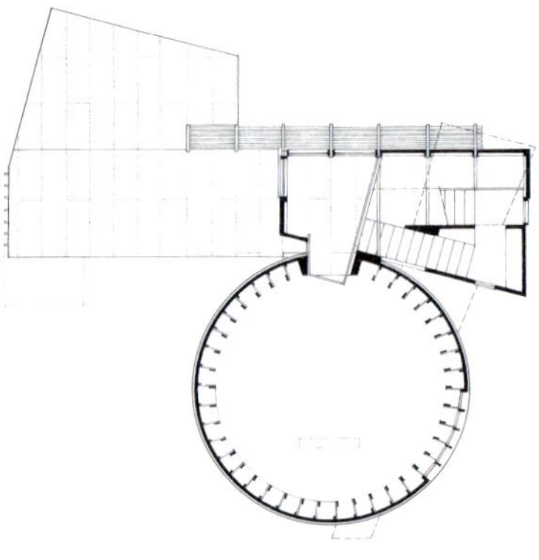

Plan at 8 feet above grade

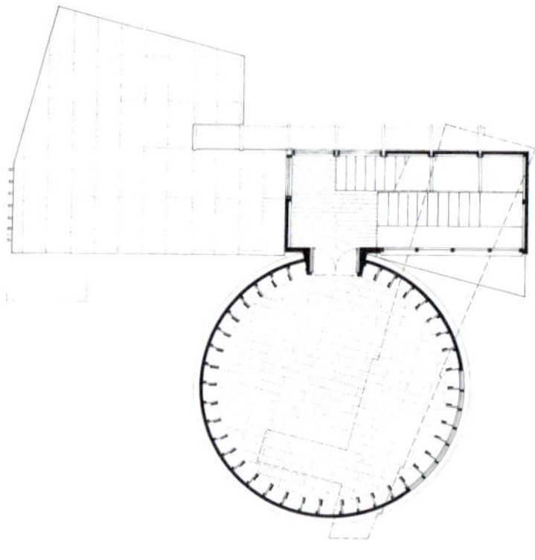

Plan at 16 feet above grade

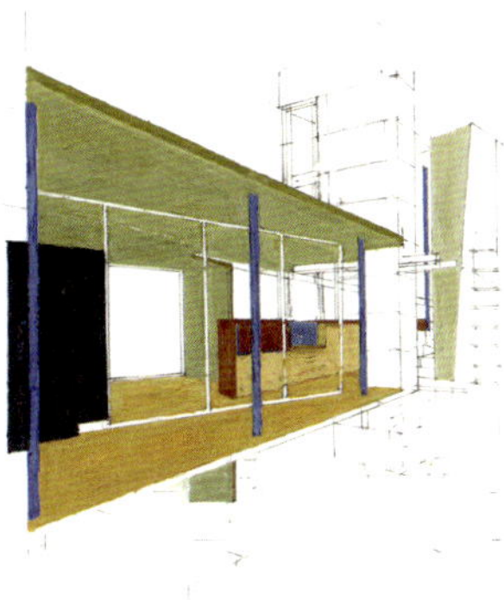

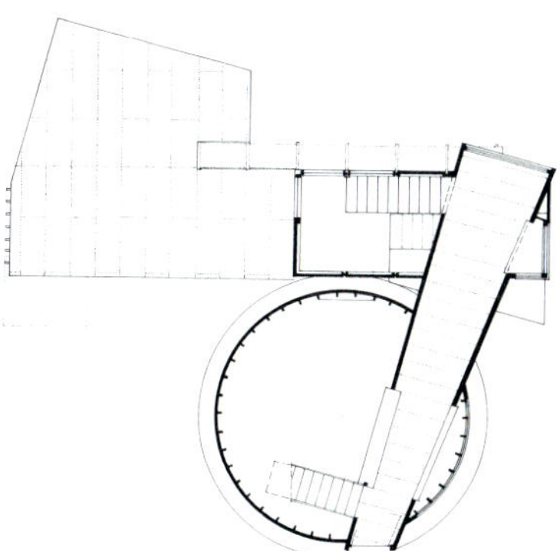

Plan at 24 feet above grade

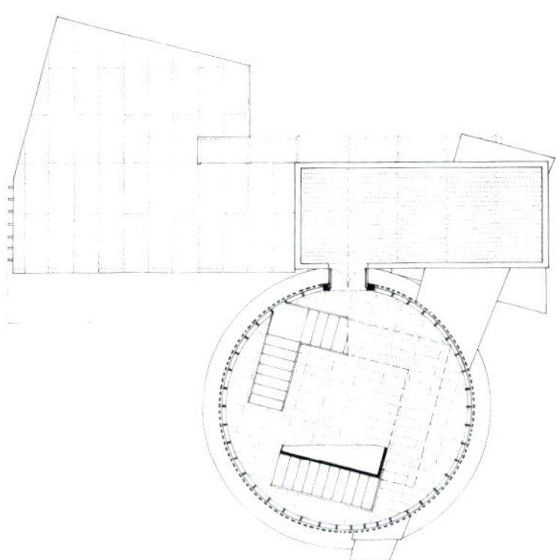

Plan at 32 feet above grade

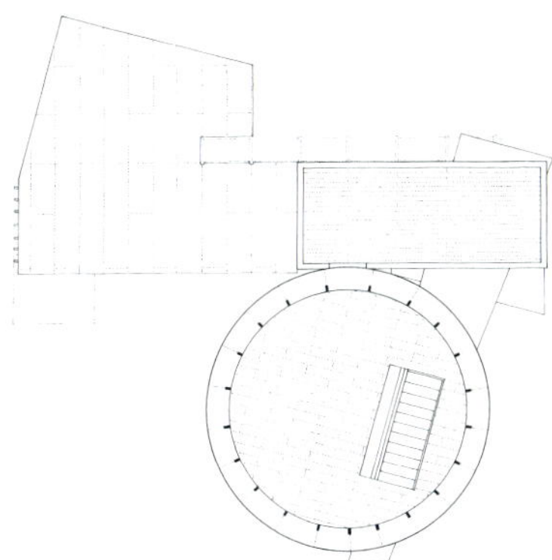

Plan at 56 feet above grade

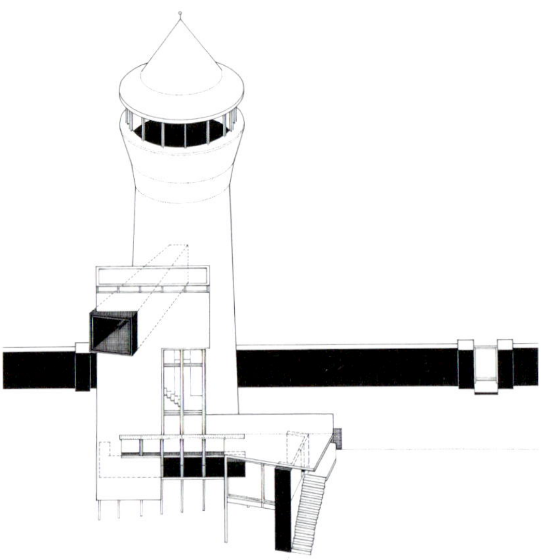

South elevation

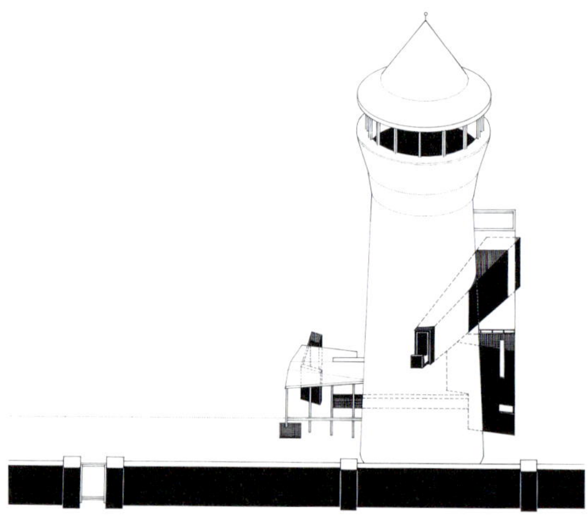

North elevation

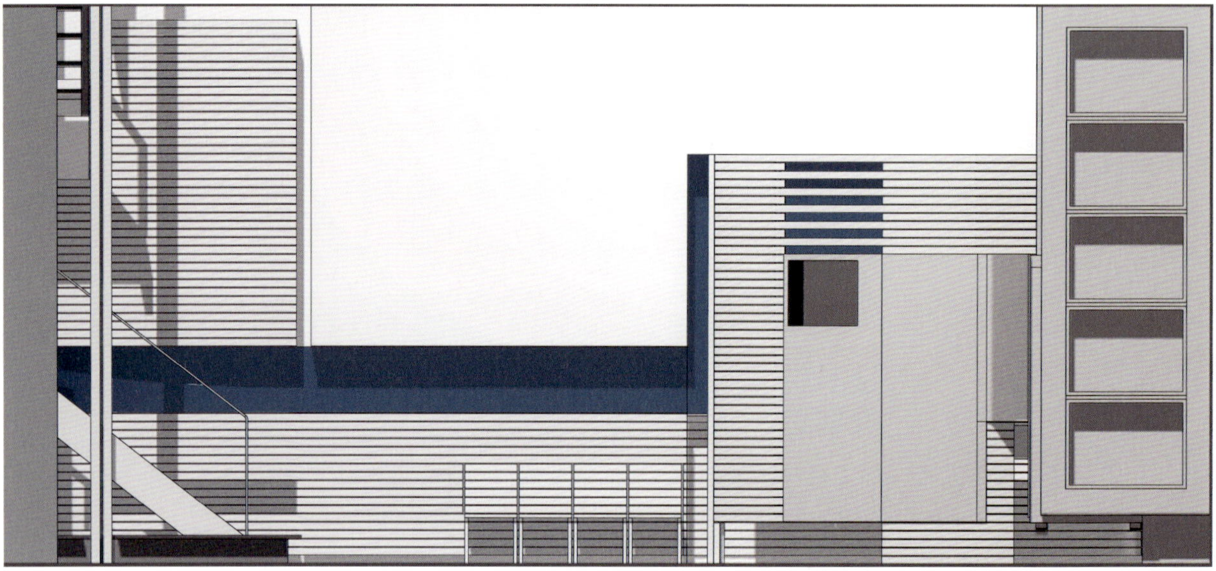

Elevation

CHELSEA LOFT

New York, New York

While working on the rural retreat – that included a prominent water tower – in the Catskills, the clients also requested the renovation of a penthouse unit in a converted warehouse on the far western edge of 22nd Street in Chelsea. Chelsea is a neighborhood on the west side of Manhattan that has become home to numerous institutions, restaurants, and major art galleries. This particular site is adjacent to Dia Art Foundation and would have overlooked the existing sculpture garden on the roof.

The 3,250 SF loft is located on the fifth and sixth floors of the warehouse. The lower floor consists of 2,500 square feet and serves as the main living area including: entry, private office, media room/guest room, lounge, kitchen, dining, and master bedroom suite.

The upper level is also the roof of the building. It has 750 square feet of interior space including a private study and a lounge/guest room. The roof also includes a 1,250 square foot exterior terrace with pools and sauna. It contains a privacy screen on the west and south that can be raised or lowered as desired. The main terrace focuses on the skyline of Manhattan while a small upper terrace overlooks the Hudson River.

Satellite

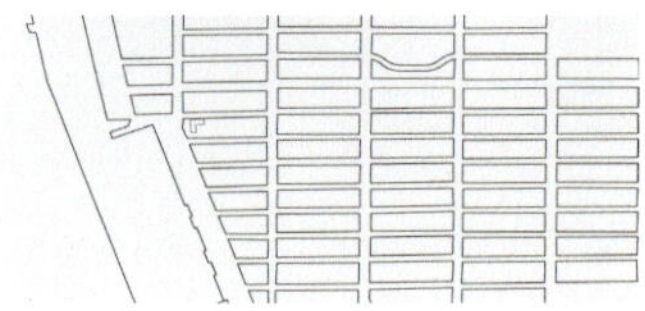

Site plan

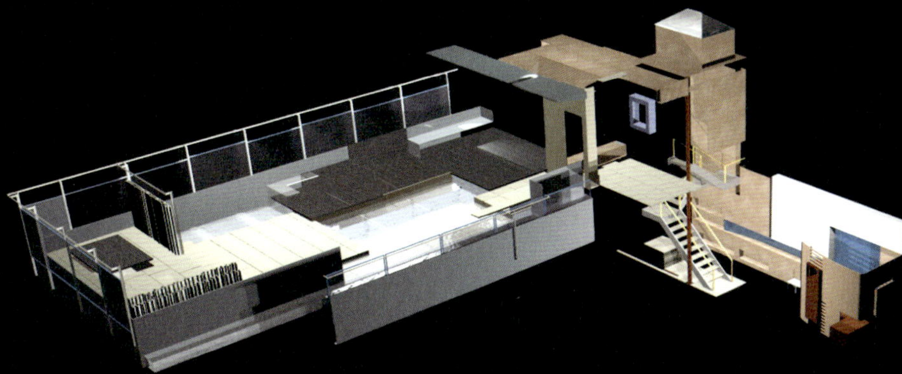

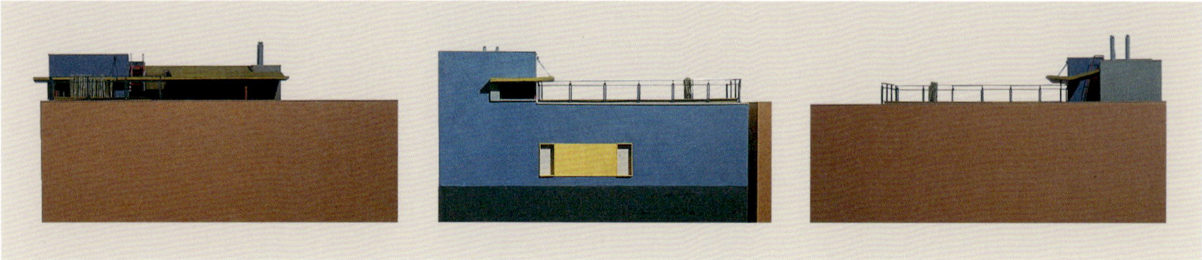

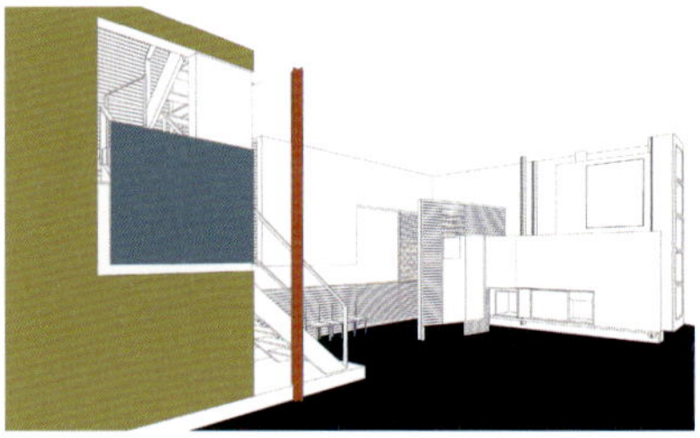

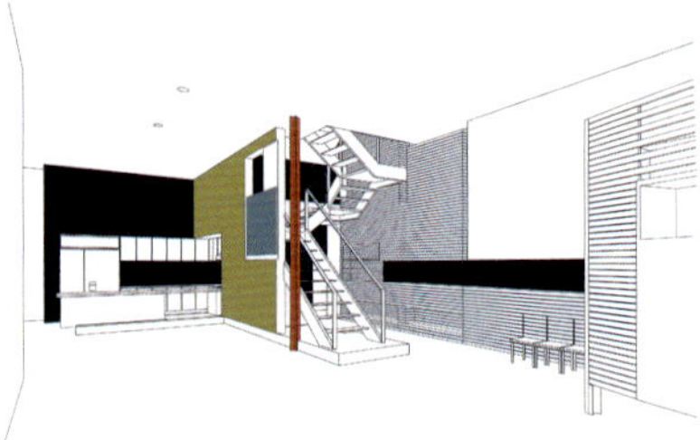

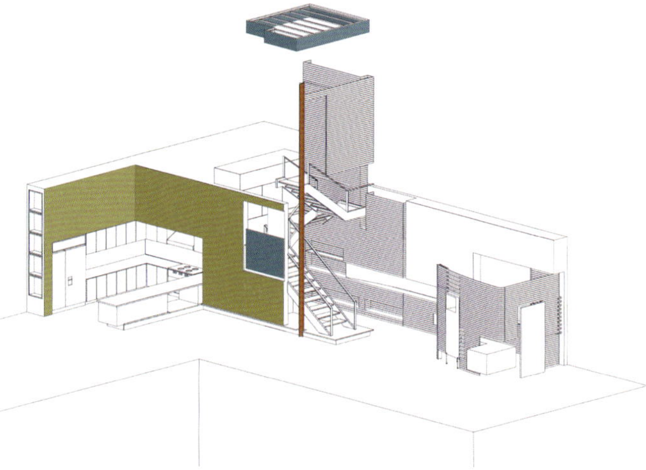

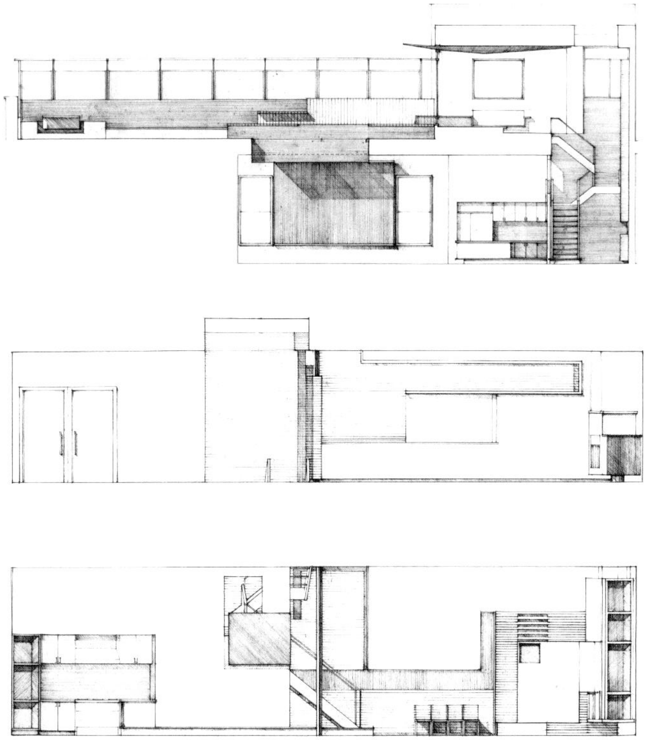

Sections

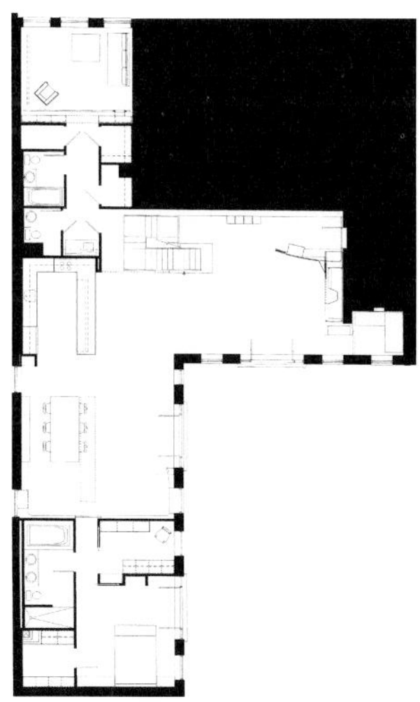

Fifth floor plan

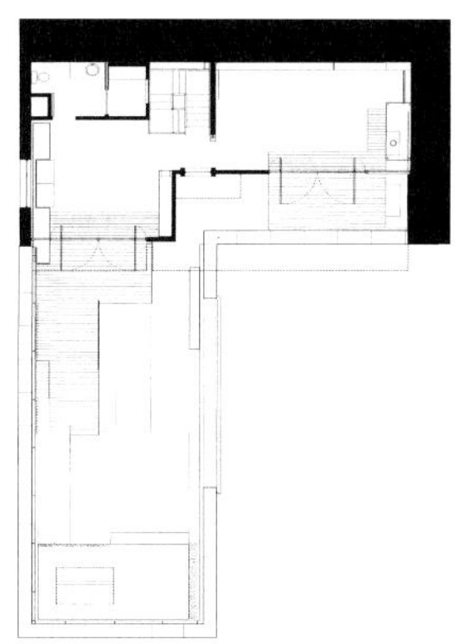

Sixth floor plan

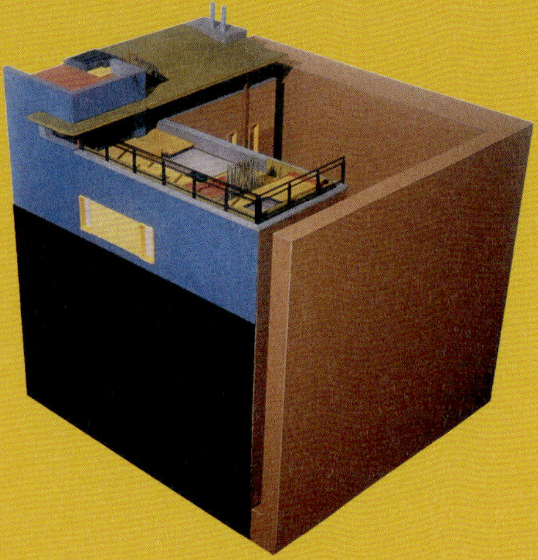

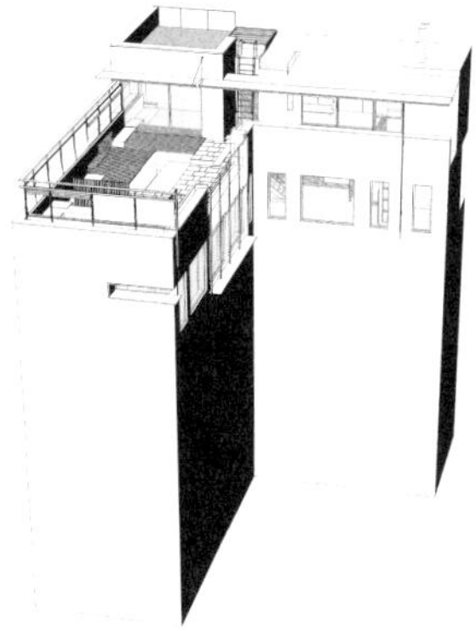

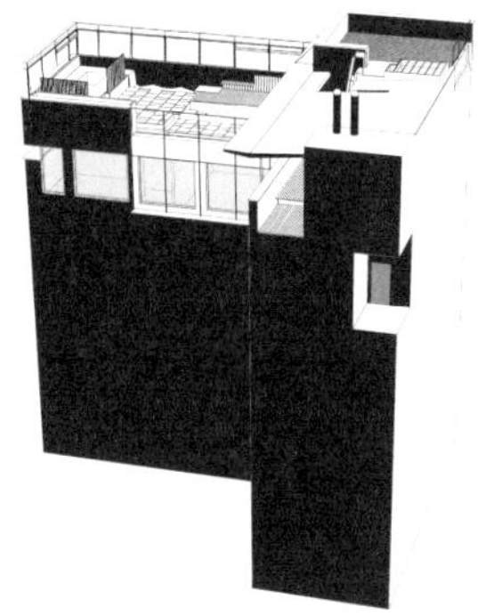

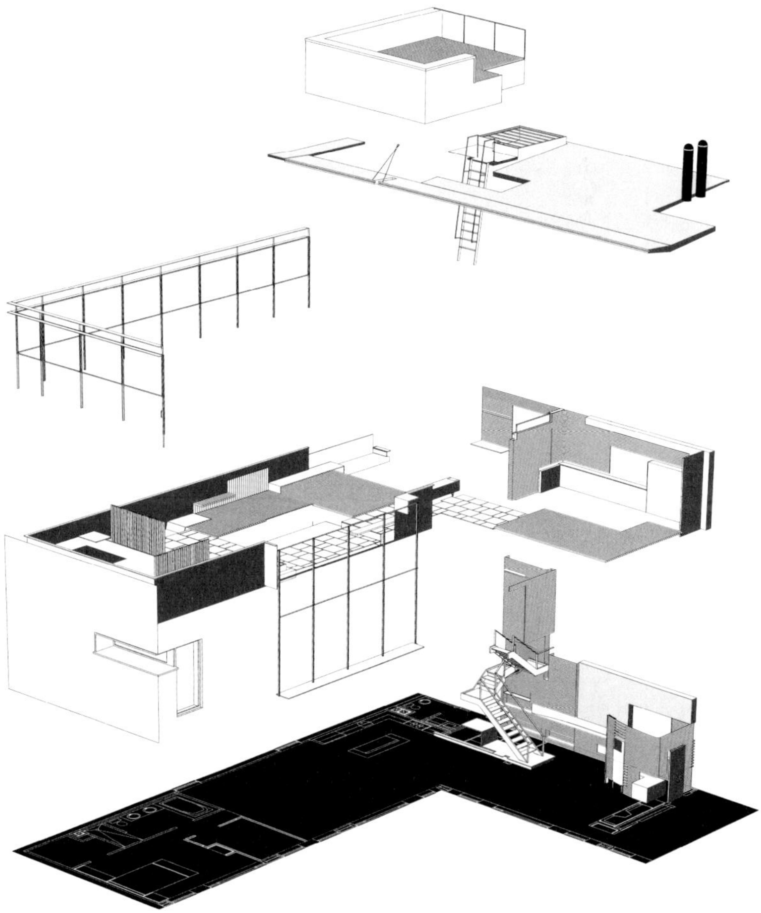

Exploded axonometric

CAMBRIDGE CONVERSION

Cambridge, Massachusetts

In a city like Cambridge, each street forms its own separate identity and distinct community within a neighborhood. The street and sidewalks become shared public spaces connecting with other streets knitting neighborhoods together into a city.

This single-family home is the primary residence for a family composed of a couple with two young children. Although the family has lived in the house for several years, the clients were unhappy with the layout and aesthetics of their home. Initially, they had preferred to purchase an open lot and build a new modern house, but their overriding consideration was the quality of life their children had found along this particular and familiar street. So, instead of starting over, they sought to re-imagine their home and their place along that street. They specifically asked if we could convert their traditional developer tract house from the middle of the century into a modern home.

The primary goal of the transformation was to make explicit the connection between interior and exterior spaces. In the reconfigured design, the first floor becomes an open porch or pavilion mediating between the primary exterior spaces: the public street and the private garden. Transparent sliding glass panels define each porch and allow for unobstructed passage from front to back. The southern wall along the driveway is re-skinned with structural plastic and glass panels on steel frames. These translucent panels allow light to enter while obscuring views of the adjacent drive and neighboring house. The second floor retains its function as the private family quarters.

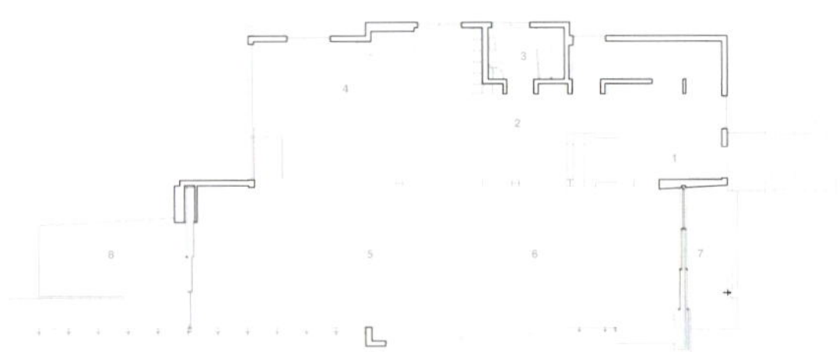

Lower level plan

1 Entrance
2 Office
3 Bathroom
4 Kitchen
5 Dining room
6 Living room
7 Front proch
8 Back porch

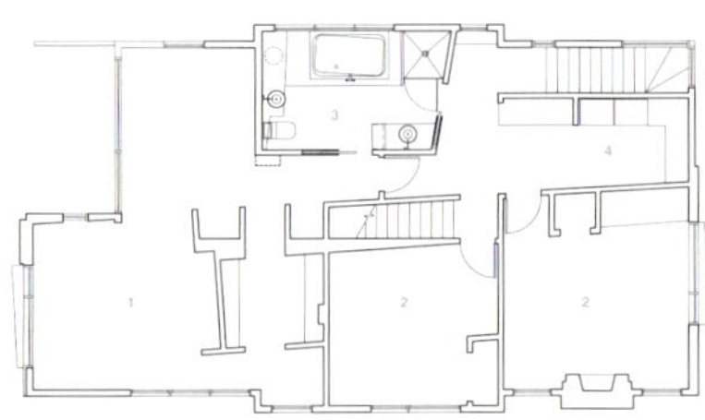

Upper level plan

1 Master bedroom
2 Bedroom
3 Bathroom
4 Laundry

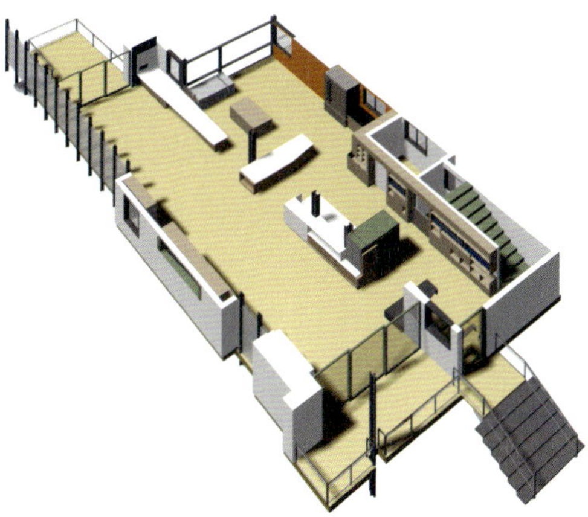

East elevation

West elevation

South elevation

POOL HOUSE

Media, Pennsylvania

POOL HOUSE

Media, Pennsylvania

The seven-acre site in southeastern Pennsylvania is heavily wooded with a gentle slope leading down to a stream. The house was sited at the property's southern edge to allow long views into the woods and to preserve the integrity of the land as much as possible.

The plan is a simple bar divided into three distinct volumes. The central volume is the primary shared communal space and it includes the living area and kitchen It is entirely glazed on the north side — orienting the house toward the woods beyond — providing ambient light throughout the day. The southern elevation features an oversized, framed portal to the patio and the pool.

The two-story master suite sits on one end of this double-height volume, with the bedroom and bath on the first floor. A sitting loft, deck, and exercise room are above; integrated with the central volume under the canopy of the roof.

The guest wing is on the second floor across the central volume from the master suite, above the garage and main entry. It is oriented north and south, consciously separate from the main living space — to give maximum privacy to guests — while affording them generous views of the surrounding landscape.

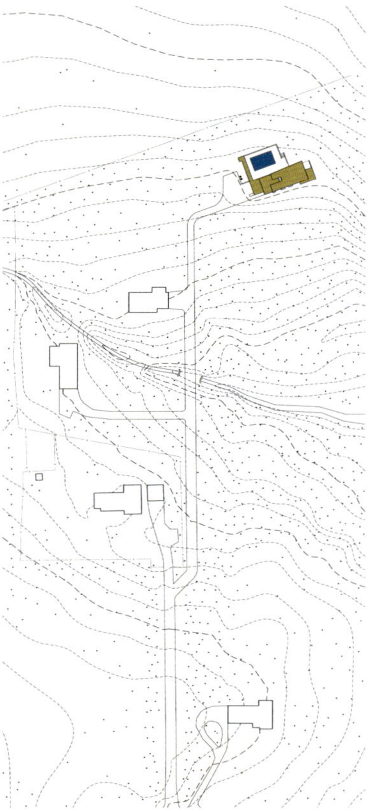

Site plan

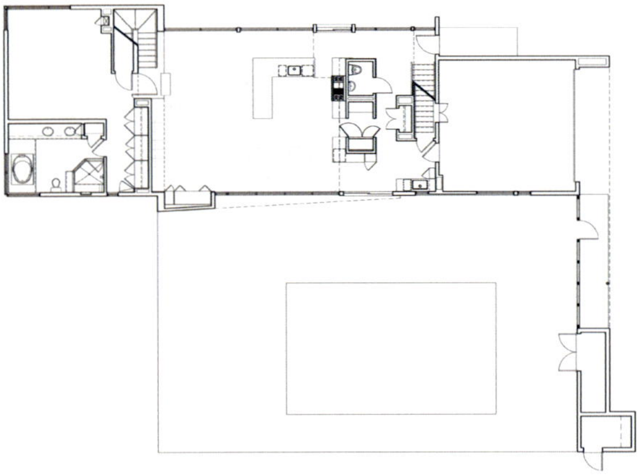

First floor plan

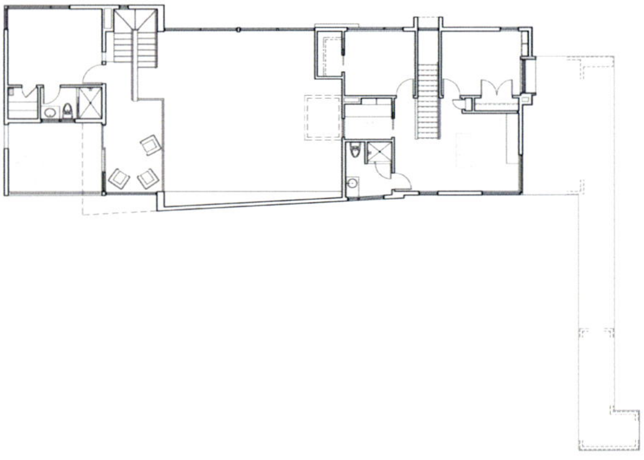

Second floor plan

Axonometric views

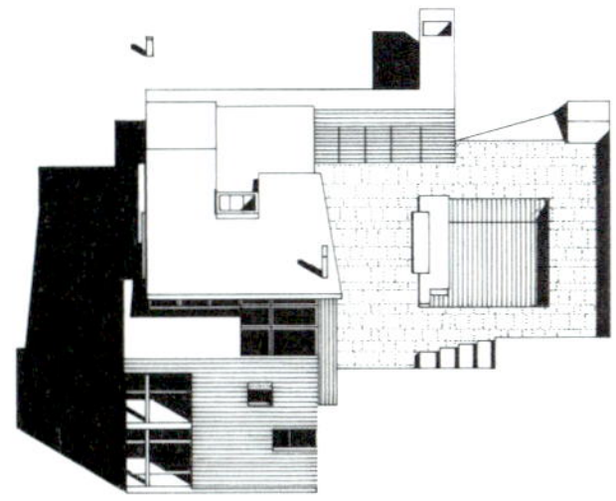

West

North

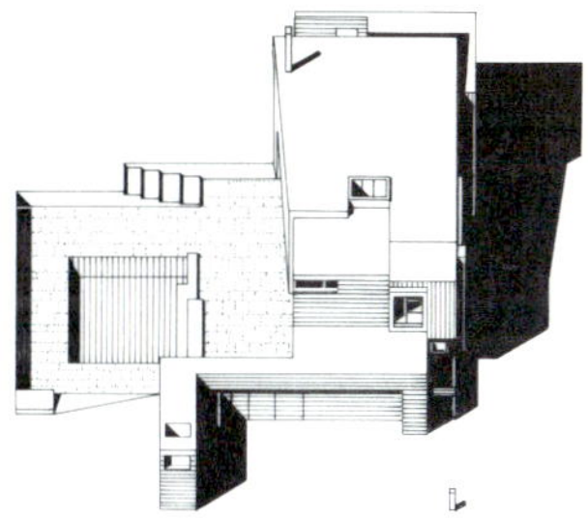

East

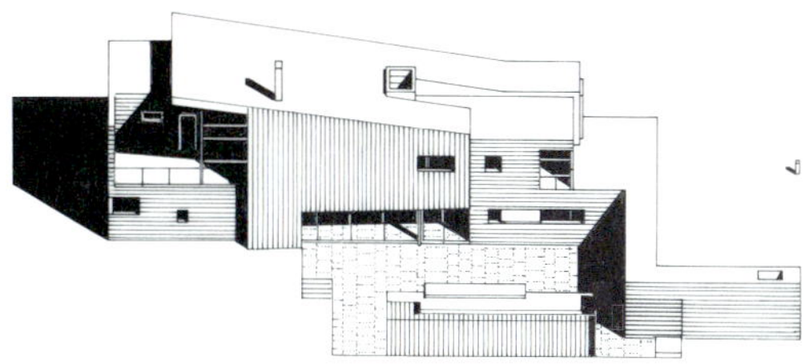

South

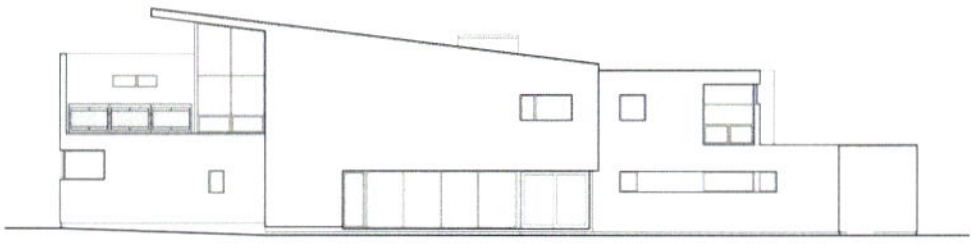

South elevation

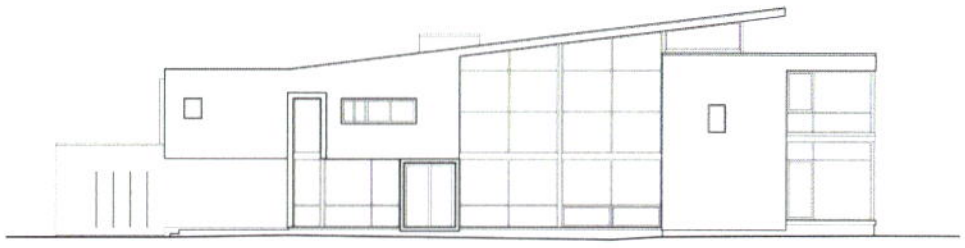

North elevation

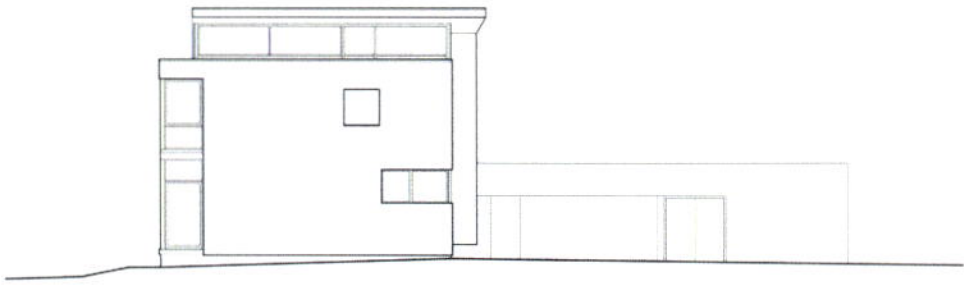

West elevation

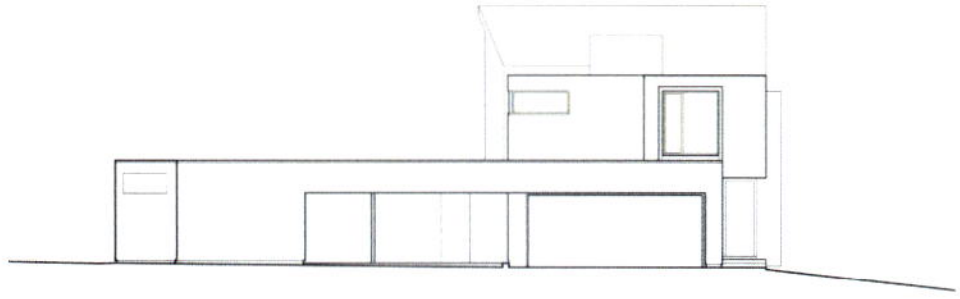

East elevation

Building section

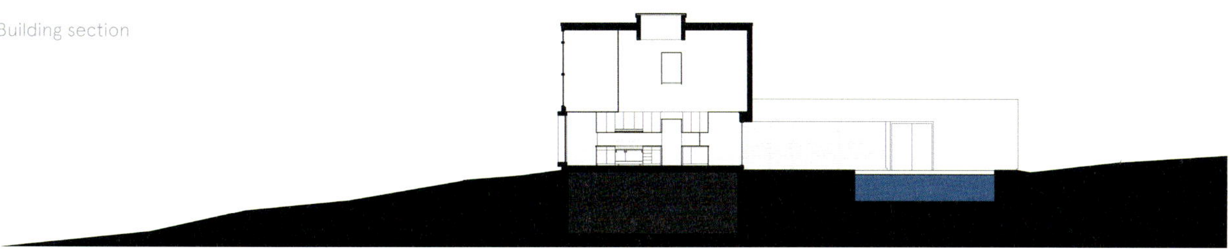

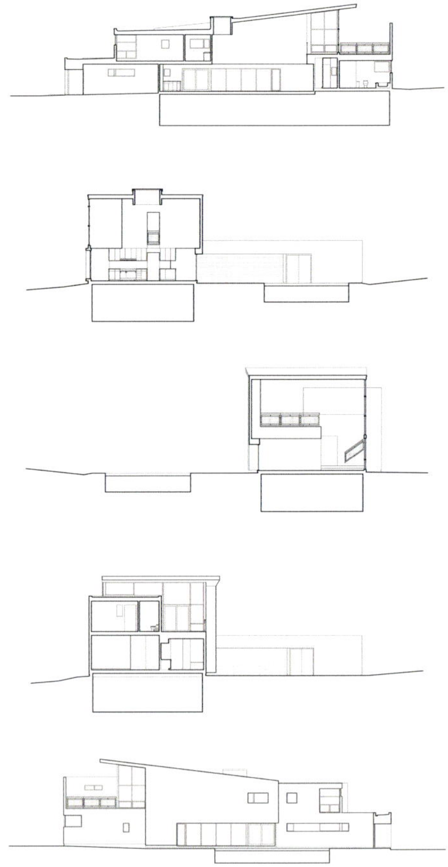

Building section

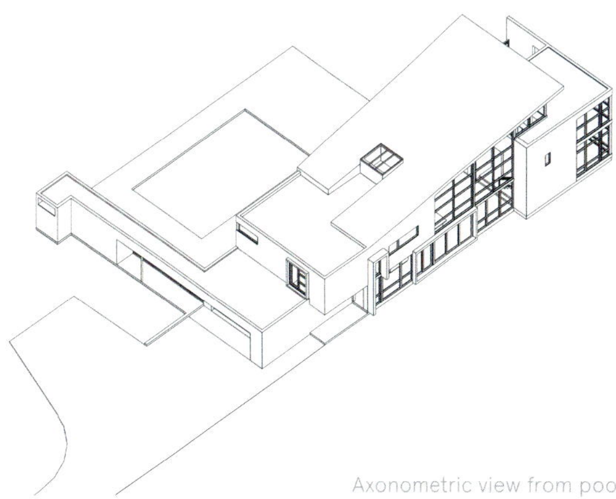

Axonometric view from pool

SUMMER COMPOUND

Barnegat Light, New Jersey

SUMMER COMPOUND

Barnegat Light, New Jersey

Barnegat Light is a year-round fishing community located at the northern tip of Long Beach Island. The site is on a cul-de-sac overlooking Barnegat Bay with views of Island Beach State Park and the Barnegat Lighthouse. The compound was designed as a summer residence for three generations of the Deixler Family.

The multi-generational program — developed with Michael Ryan and Randee Spelkoman — suggested a village-like arrangement to allow both private and common spaces. Each family has a distinct volume of bedrooms and bathrooms within the compound, and the moments of volumetric overlap create the shared spaces: kitchen, dining, and main living areas.

The first generation's building has two levels. The ground level contains the kitchen, dining areas, and screen porch. The loft-like second floor contains dressing area, bathroom, outdoor shower, study and bedroom overlooking the main living room.

The second generation's building has four levels. The ground level has a playroom, storage, mechanical room, laundry, and outdoor shower. The second and third level contains living quarters for the second generation with bedrooms, baths, and studies. The upper level is a communal roof deck.

The third generation's building has three levels. The ground level has a toilet room and storage area. The upper two levels have bunkrooms with bathrooms and sleeping lofts for the grandchildren. The main living room is a glazed pavilion — angled to achieve the best view of the historic lighthouse — adjacent to a series of exterior decks with pools and docks for boating and windsurfing.

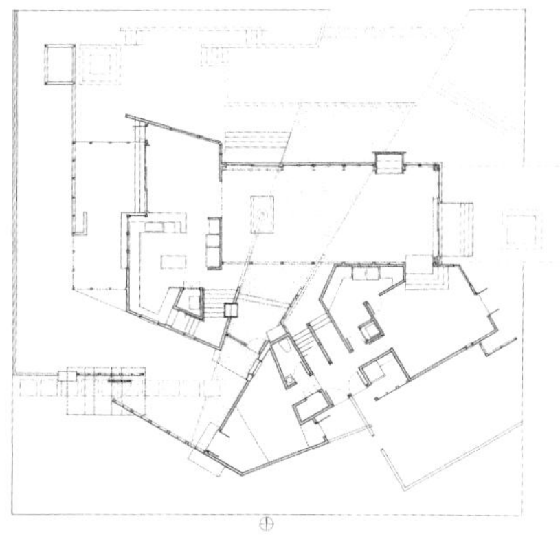

Ground floor plan

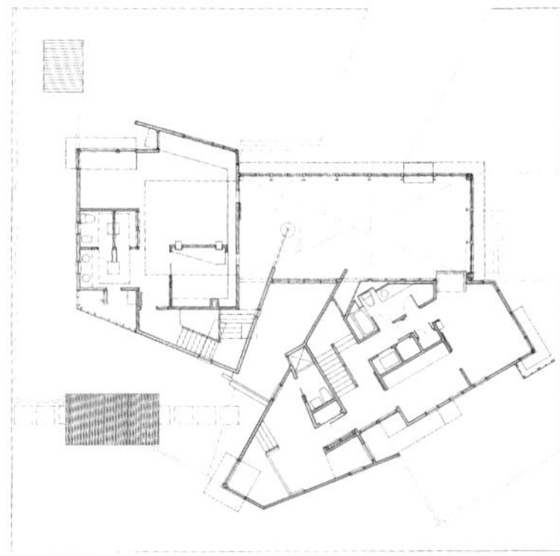

First floor plan

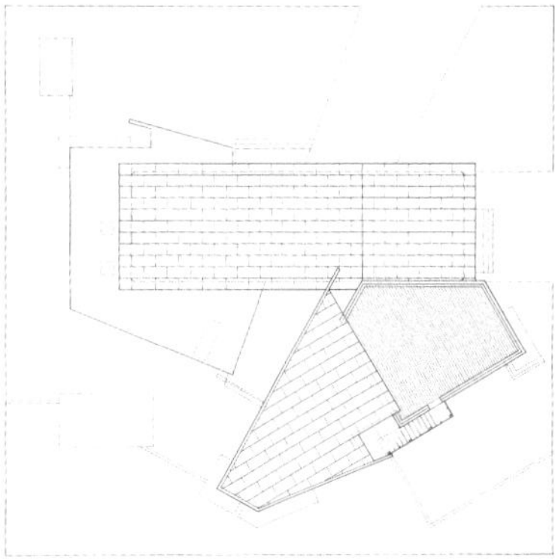

Roof plan

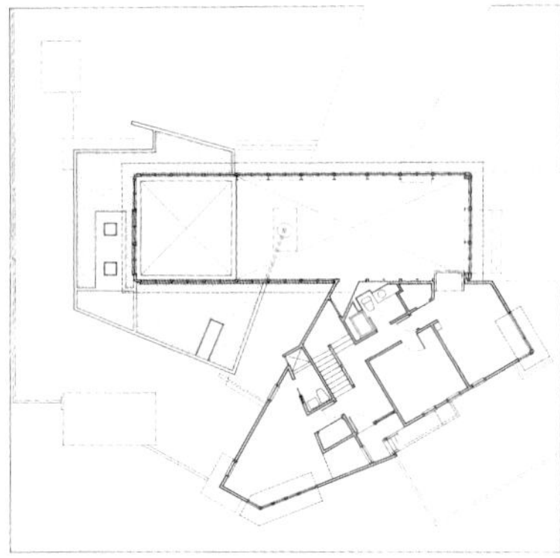

Second floor plan

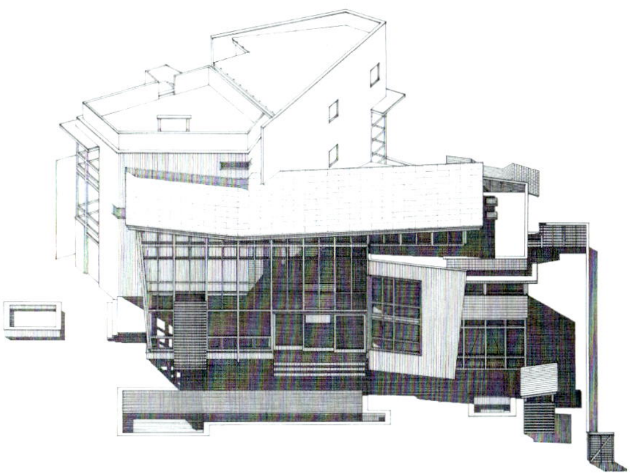

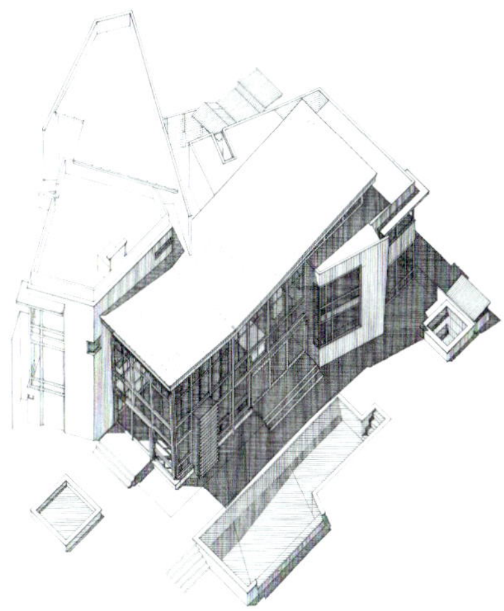

Axonometric from bay

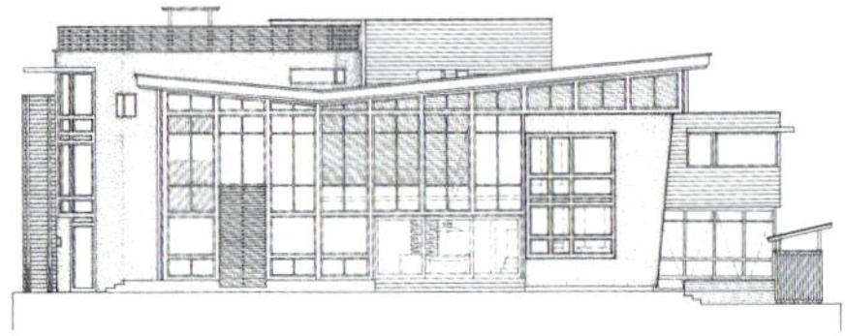

North elevation from Barnegat Bay

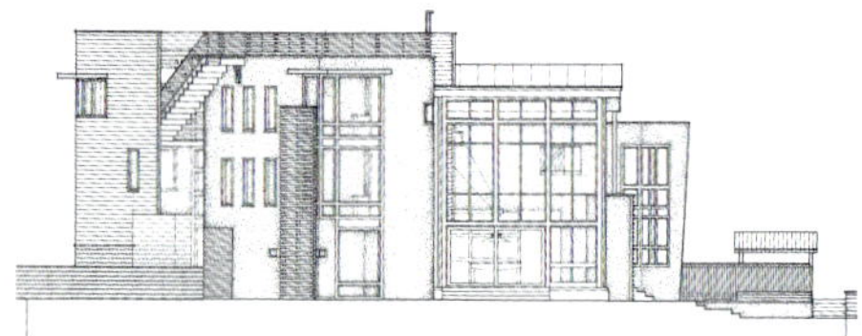

East elevation from Allison Cove

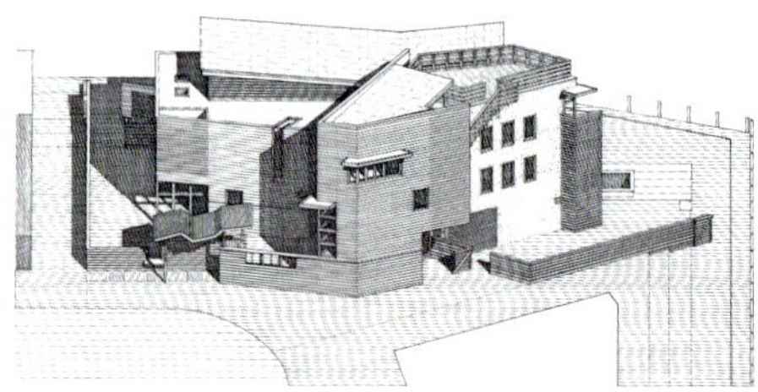

Axonometric

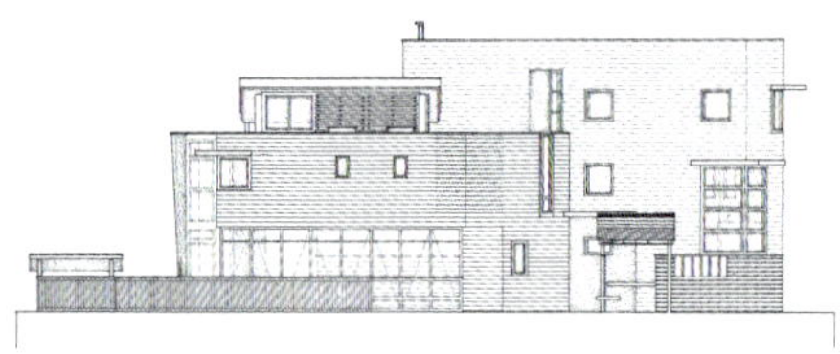

West elevation

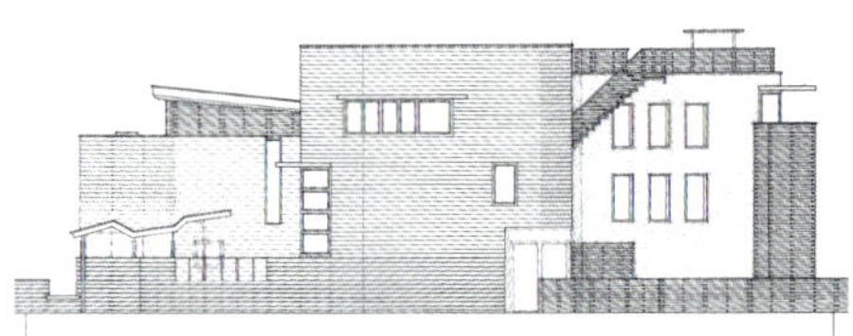

South elevation from the Cul-de-Sac

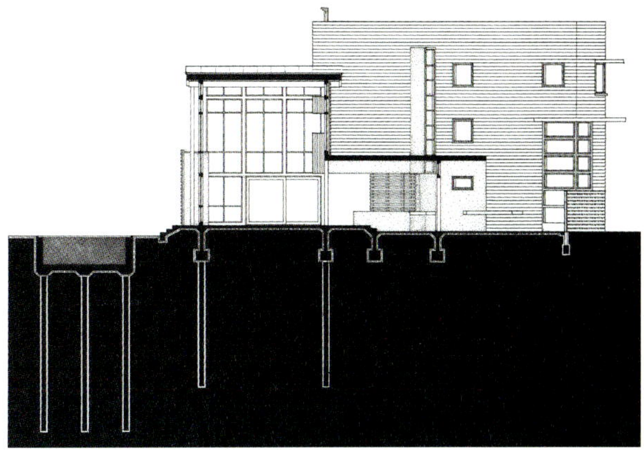

Section through entry and main living area looking east

Section through entry and main living area looking west

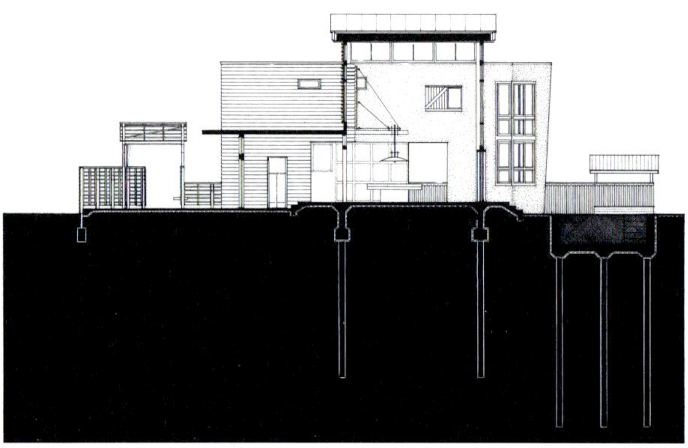

Section through main living and bedroom areas looking south

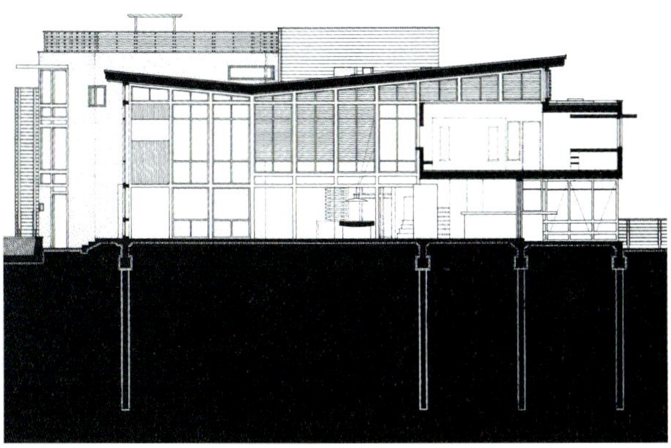

Section through main living and bedroom areas looking north

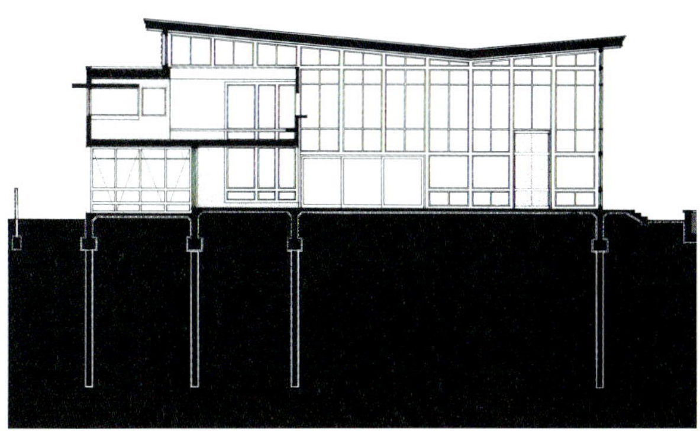

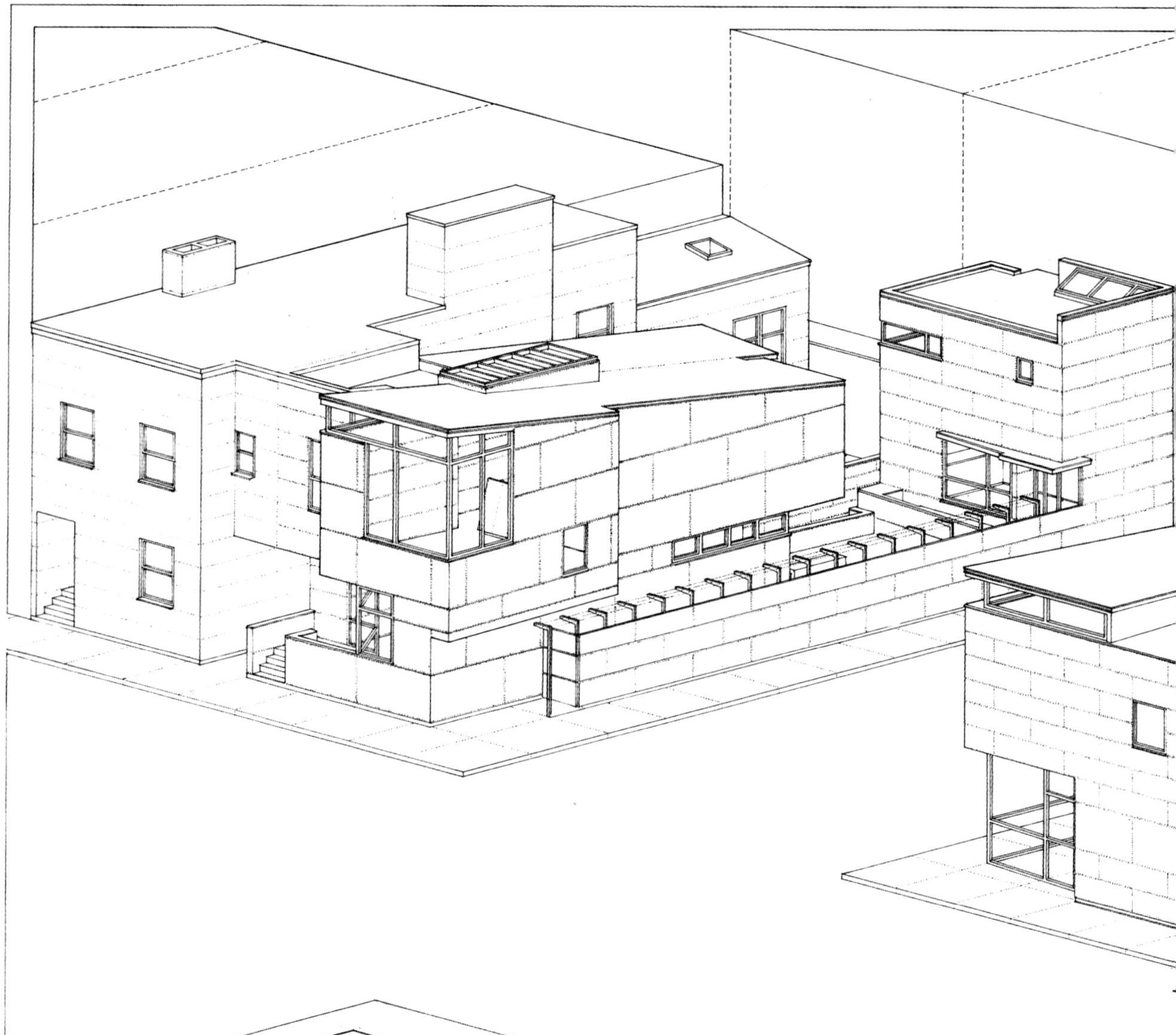

HOUSING PROTOTYPES

Atlantic City, New Jersey

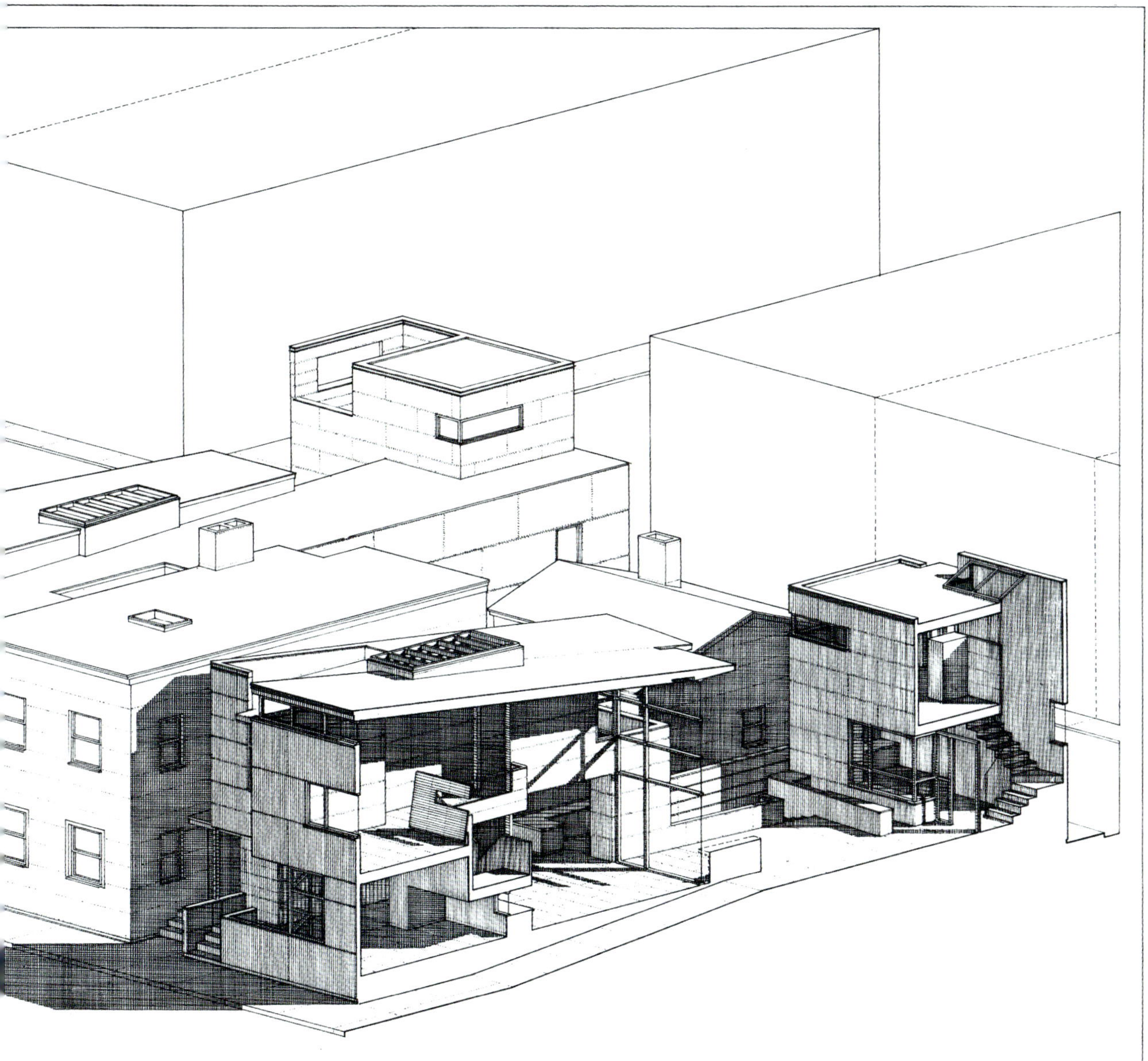

HOUSING PROTOTYPES

Atlantic City, New Jersey

The architect took this as a very serious investigation of the quality of the living units, which should be a lot of what housing is about....these units could work. The architect ingeniously seeks ways to reconfigure circulation, edges, and overlaps of the row condition to create more interesting, rich spatial conditions.... It's almost a classical solution for the urban texture....
- Progressive Architecture Jury Comments

If you drove into this part of Atlantic City in the early nineties, you would probably want to leave. It appeared to be abandoned and the emptiness was uncomfortable. But if you got out of the car and you walked around, you'd find that the important pieces that could be used to return this place to a active neighborhood were still there. The sidewalks, the porches, and the alleyways – the small things that make a city vital – still held this place together.

This project was for a competition held by Atlantic City to try to establish a more stable neighborhood through home ownership. Providing this opportunity for people of all income levels was understood to be a prerequisite for creating a viable urban environment and there were approximately eighty empty sites within the Northeast Inlet area of the city that could provide opportunities for the construction of new in-fill housing.

Protoype elevations

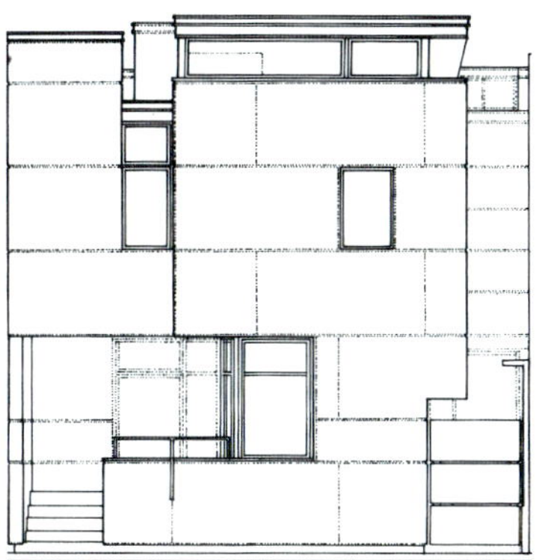

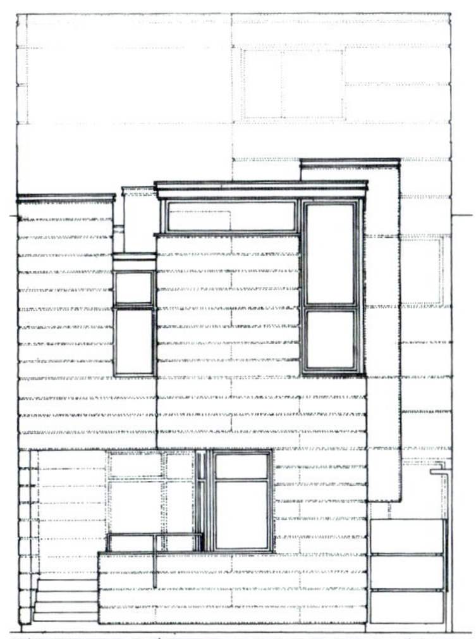

The neighborhood conformed to a traditional understanding of a city as a series of interlocking and interconnected spaces. The prototypes maintain a balance between the public and private realms of urban life while respecting the modest nature of the community. They re-imagine a modest single and two-family home as an established precedent to intertwine the personal with the communal by reinforcing both the street and the back alley.

Internally, the homes also recognize that many lives no longer conform to a traditional separation of work and home. Each unit is divided along a line that further separates the communal areas of the house from those more private. The communal rooms are open and flexible, while the more private parts of the house are specific and compact. The front room, for instance, could be used as a home office, an extra bedroom, a small formal living area, or a den for children.

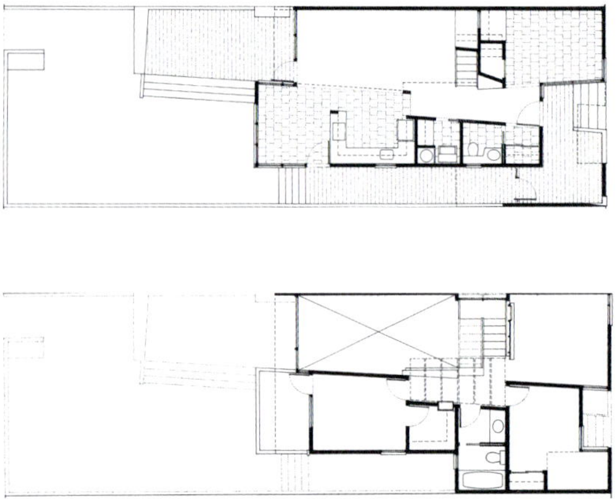

Protoype a plan

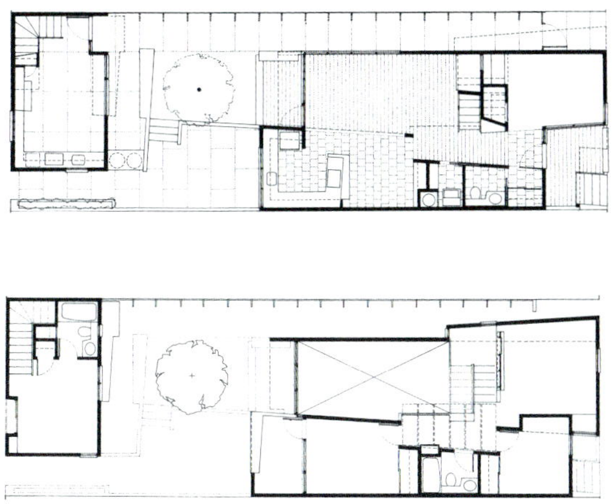

Protoype b plan

Protoype c plan

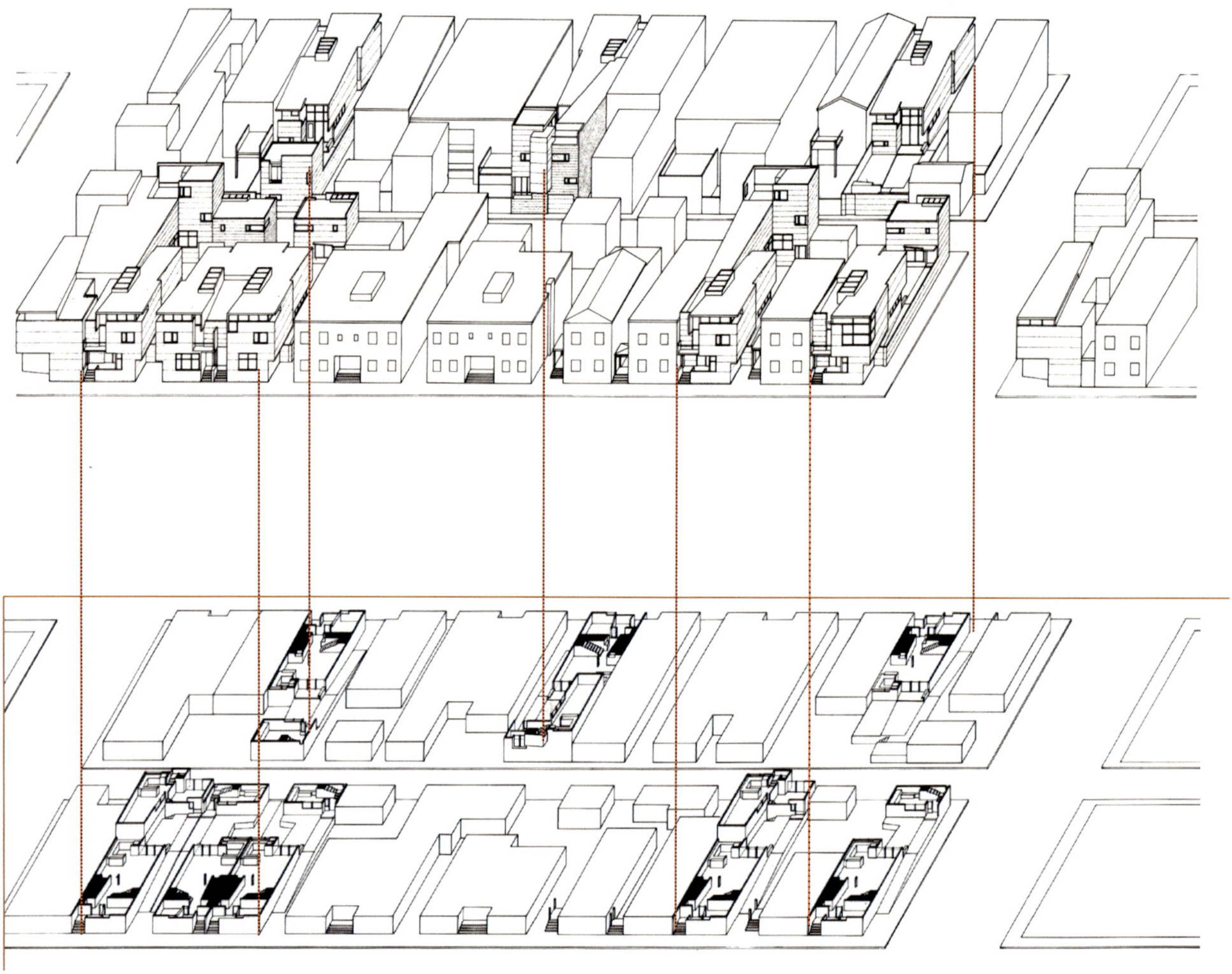

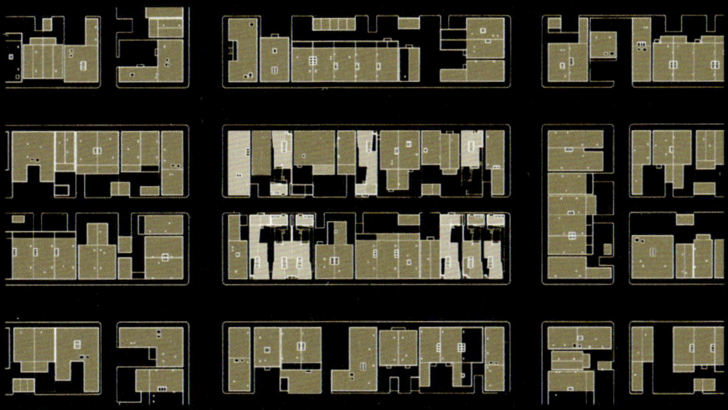

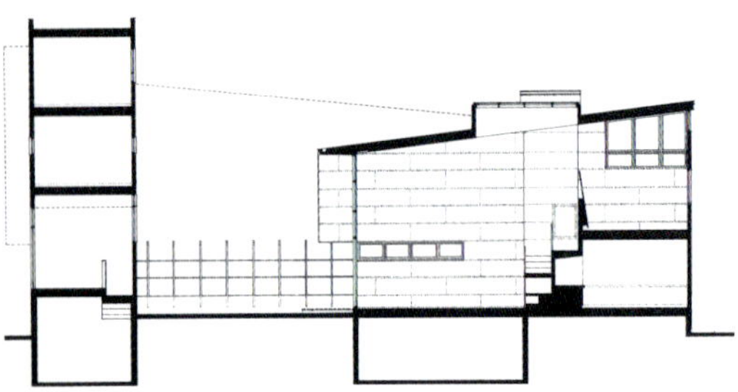

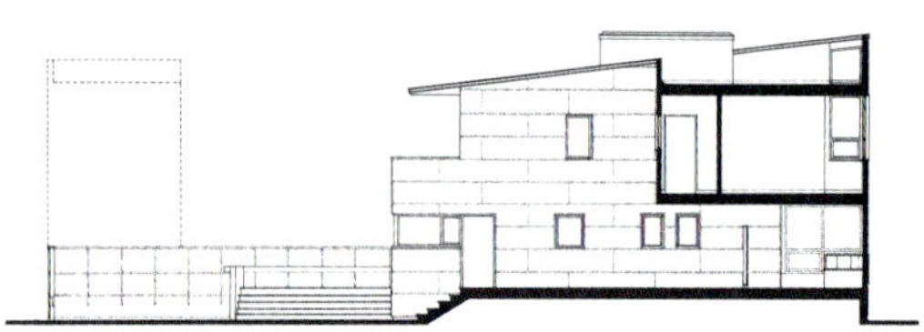

Building sections

BEACH HOUSE

Loveladies, New Jersey

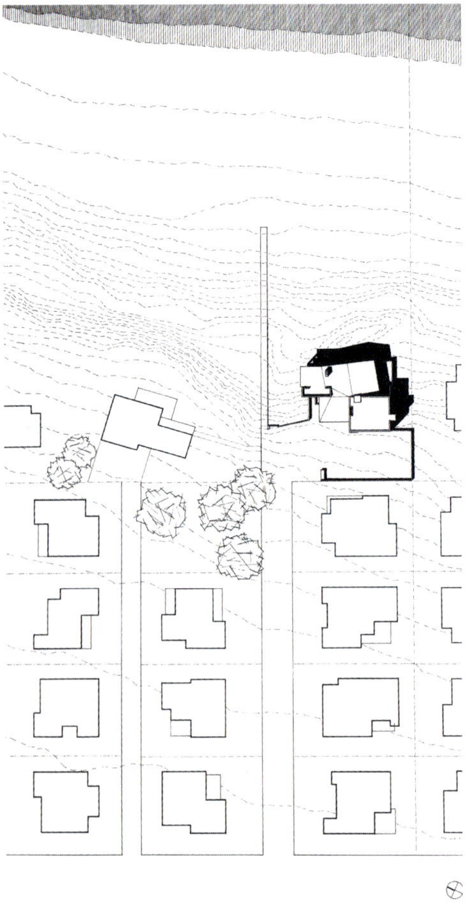

Site plan

BEACH HOUSE

Loveladies, New Jersey

The Healy family spent their summer vacations on Long Beach Island along the central coast of New Jersey. It is a thin barrier island used primarily as a summer resort. With the exception of an active commercial fishing fleet, there is little year round activity. But LBI is also a string of neighborhoods — almost urban — connected by the boulevard, the streets, and the sidewalks that we rode our bikes on. These elements define the place almost as much as the main shared public space of the island — the beach.

This house is one of a series of summer homes that were designed and built with Michael Ryan and Randee Spelkoman along the waterfront of Long Beach Island. Each of these houses explores the dual nature of the place and attempts to mediate between the vertical wall of the street and the strong horizontal of the water. In the process, they challenge the autonomy of adjacent suburban homes by acknowledging and reinforcing the collective edges of the street and waterfront.

The site for this house is located at the end of a road leading to the ocean along the northern edge of the island. It is at a natural curve of the beach that offers distant views up the coast. Summer breezes arrive from the southeast.

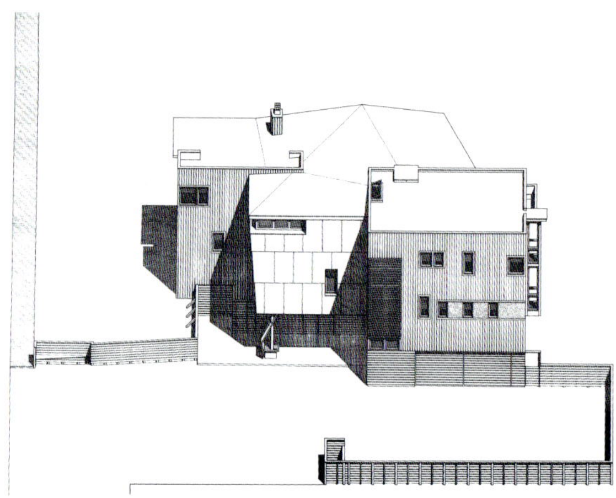

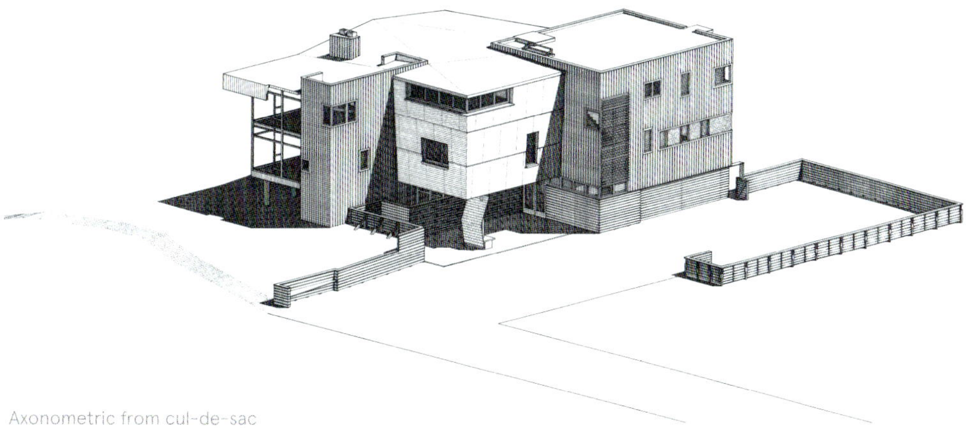

Axonometric from cul-de-sac

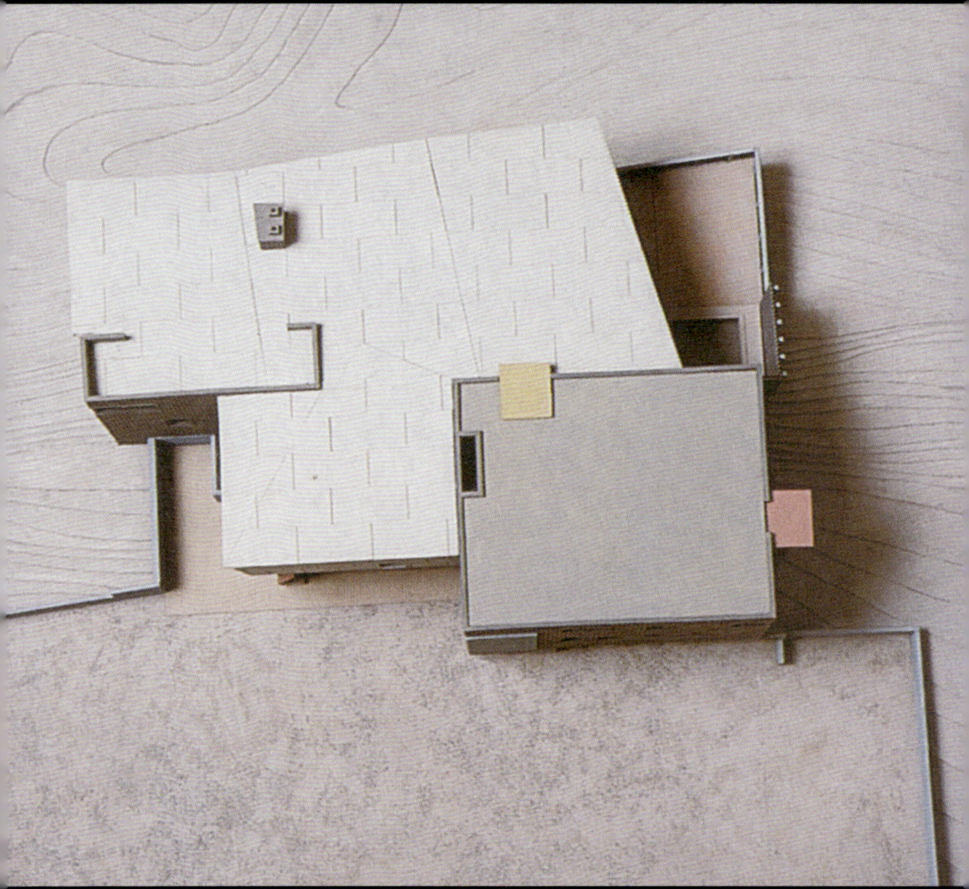

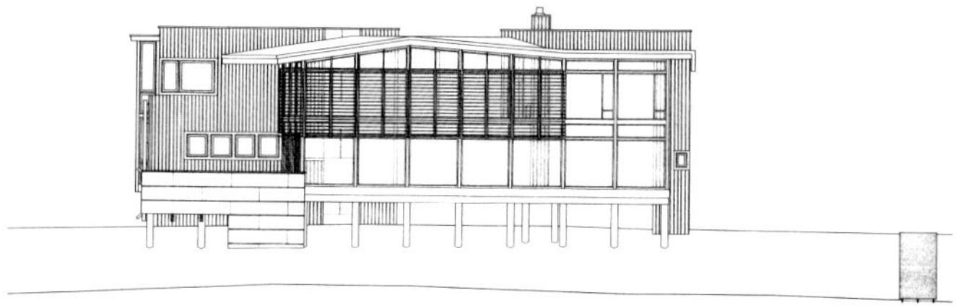

East elevation

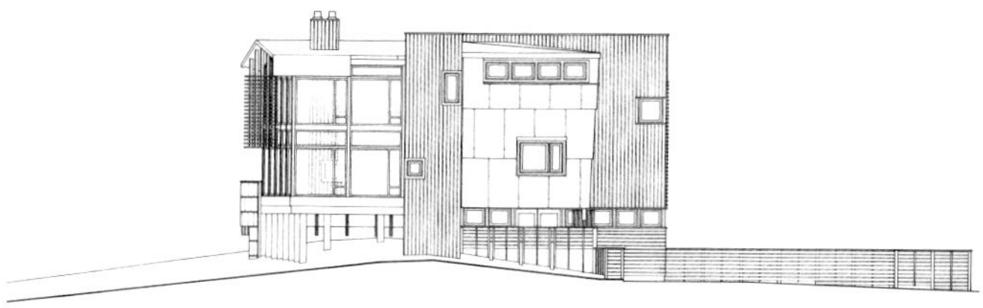

North elevation

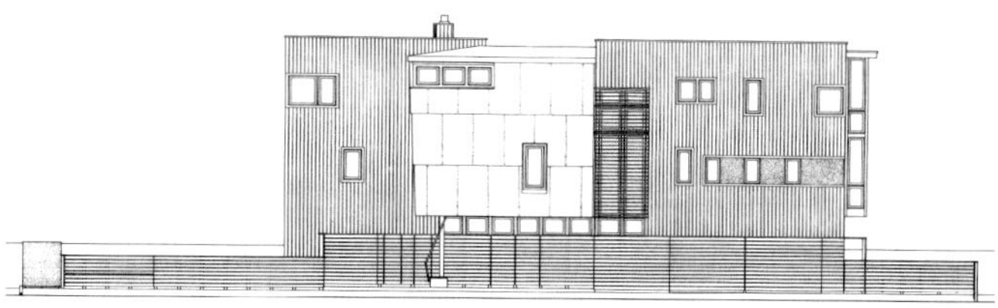

West elevation

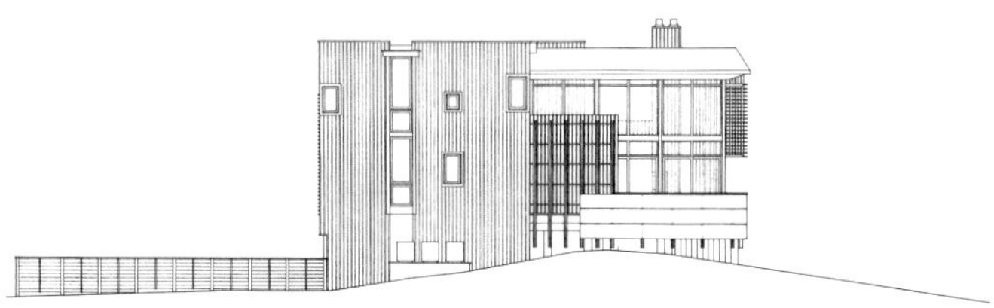

South elevation

Gourmet

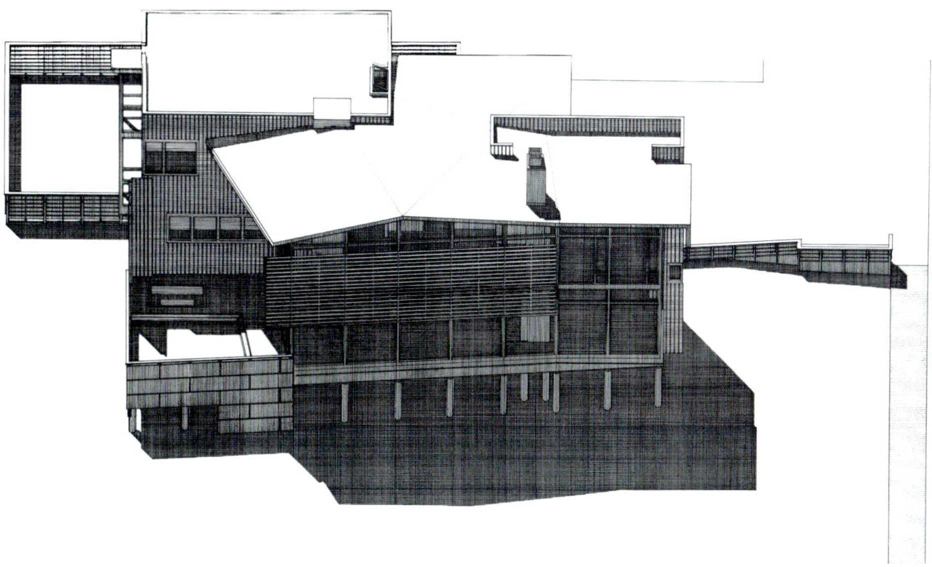

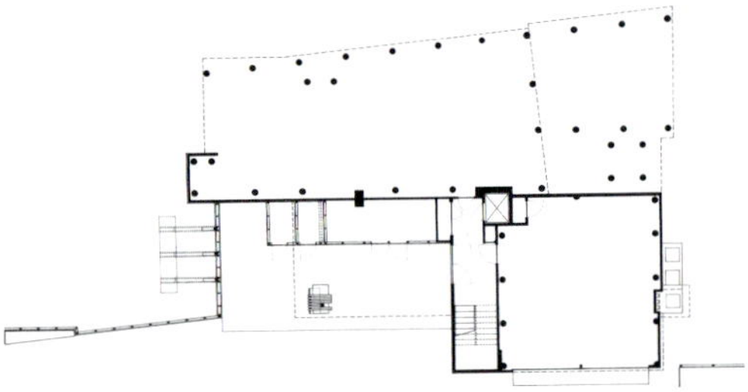

Ground floor plan

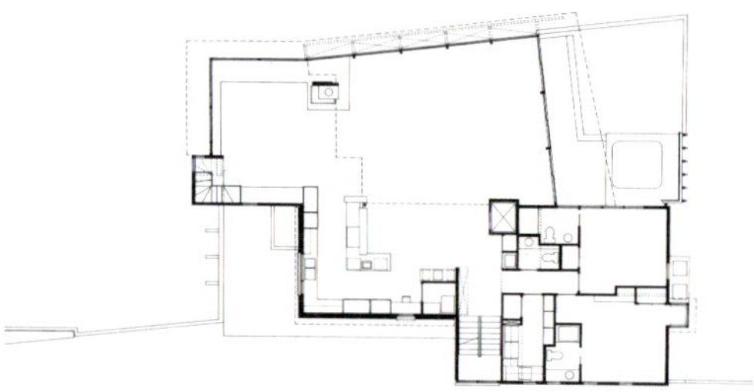

First floor plan

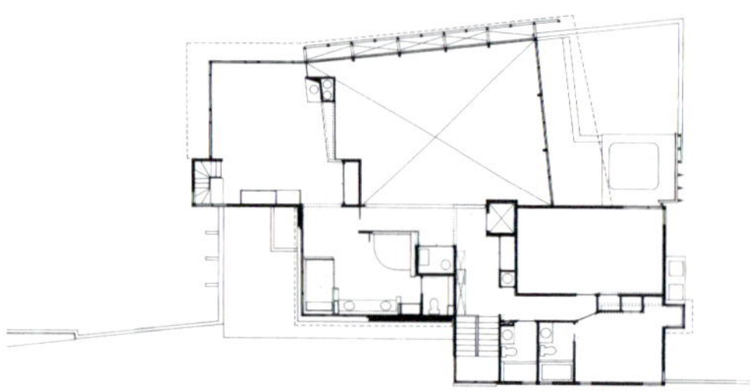

Second floor plan

AMERICA BY DESIGN
PIERRE CHAREAU

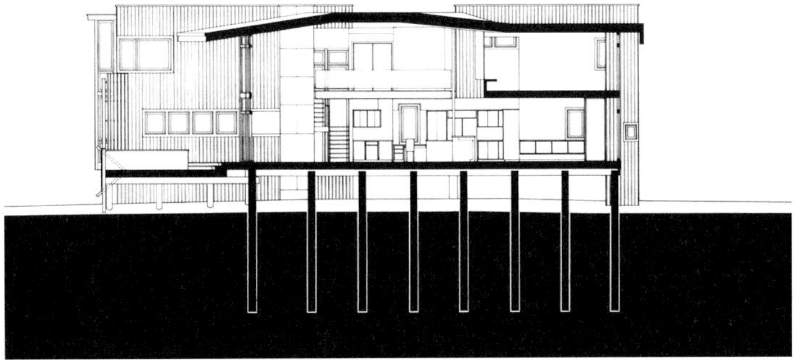

Section

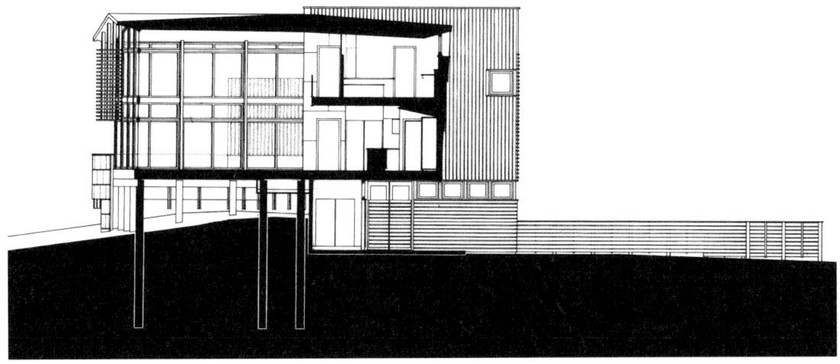

Section through main living area and kitchen looking south

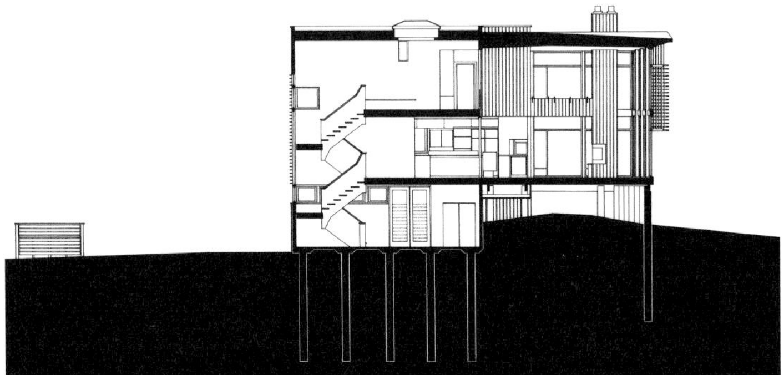

Section through stair and living room looking north

BAYSIDE HOUSE

Beach Haven, New Jersey

The site is located on Little Egg Harbor between Long Beach Island and the central coast of New Jersey. Beach Haven, one of the older communities on the Island, has a somewhat suburban character. The homes have formal simply ordered façades, green lawns, trees, and sidewalks. This site is located at a point where the bulkhead jogs into the bay opening vistas along the waterfront.

In order to take advantage of the peculiar shape of the property, the building – designed with Michael Ryan and Randee Spelkoman – was divided into two distinct elements; the main house and a separate screened-in pavilion. The exterior walls of these two structures extend beyond themselves to define and provide privacy for an exterior deck area.

In keeping with the neighborhood, the main building has a formal presence on West Street. Internally, it is separated into four distinct levels. The formal entry and the garage are on the ground level. The main living level is a few steps up from the pavilion and exterior deck. It contains the living, dining and kitchen areas. A study with a bath overlooks this lower level. The upper level contains the family bedrooms, baths, and a sitting room. The main bedroom is situated behind the window wall facing the bay.

The screened-in pavilion was placed directly on the Bay along Norwood Avenue. It is equipped with a toilet; shower; and kitchenette.

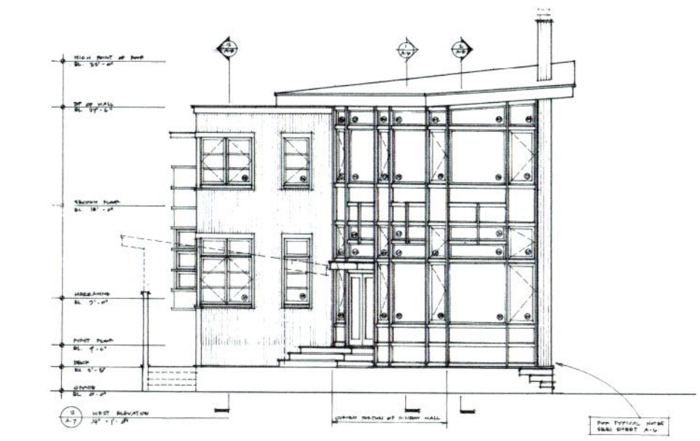

West elevation

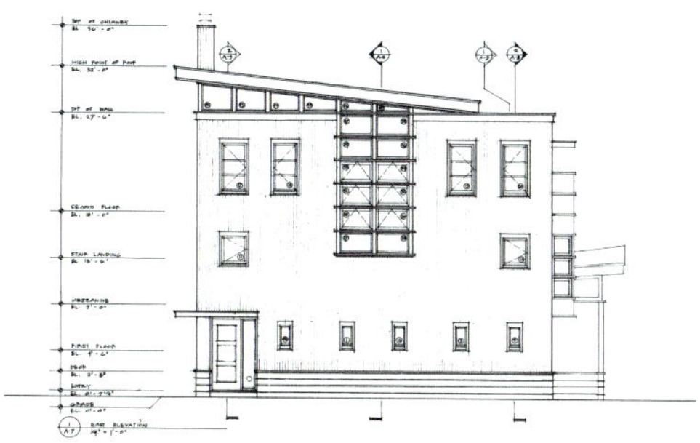

East elevation

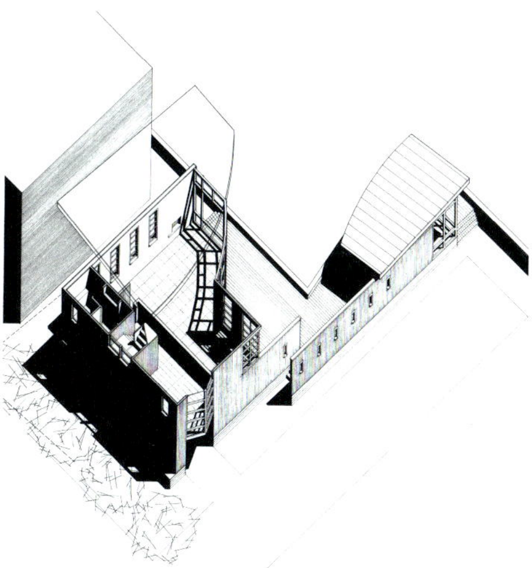

Site plan

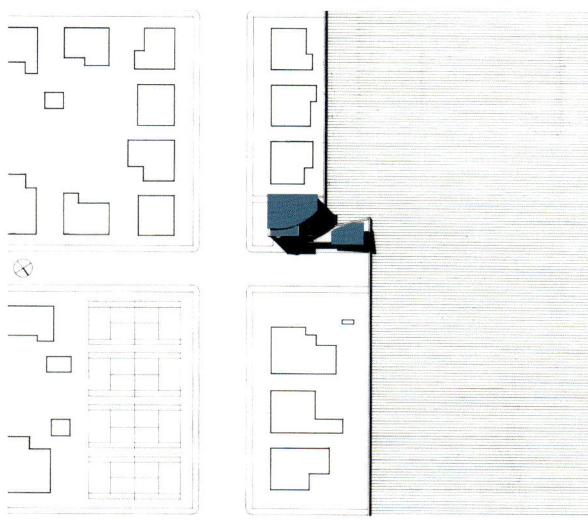

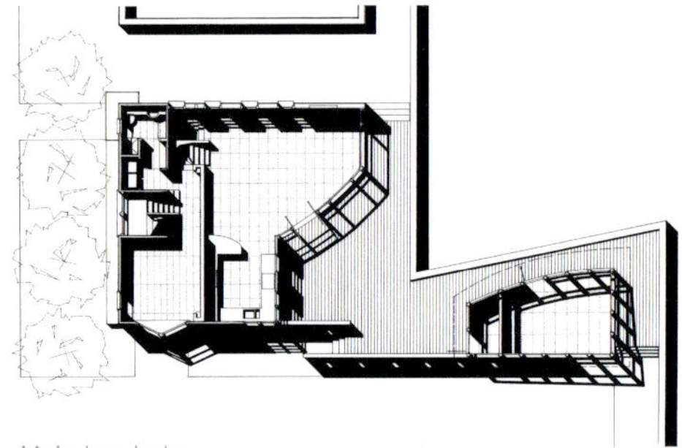

Main level plan

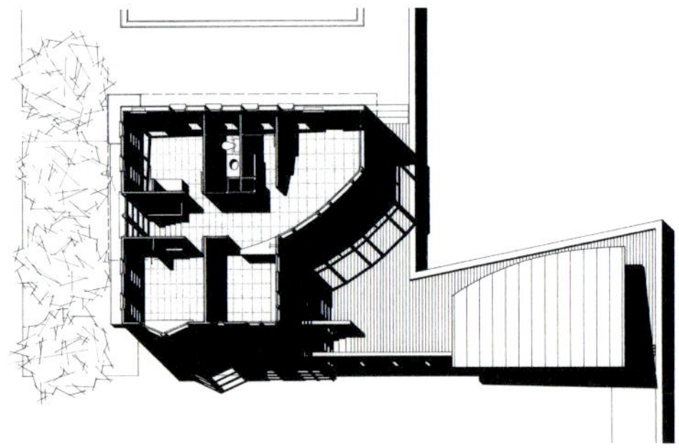

Upper level plan

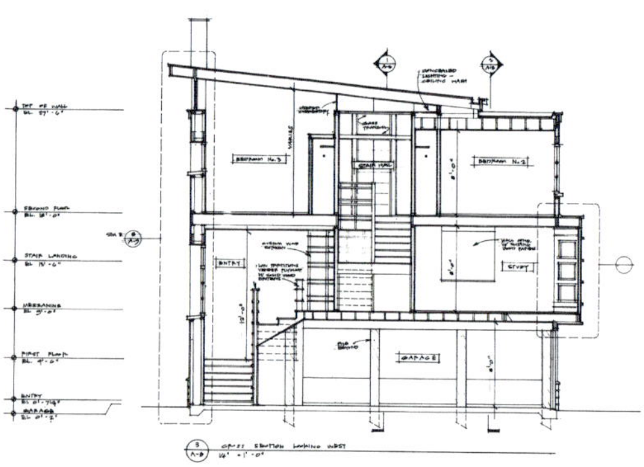

Building section looking east

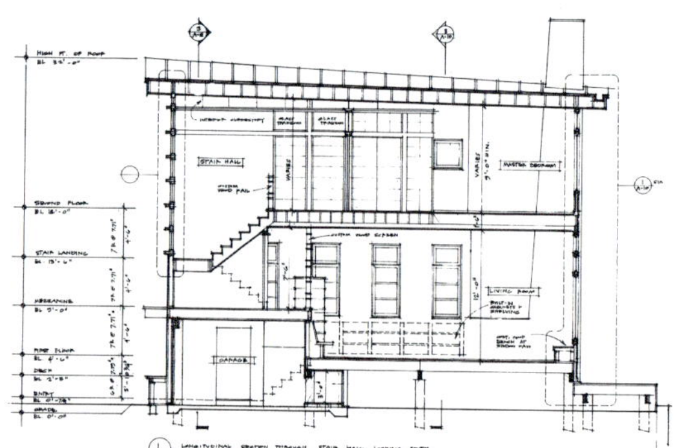

Building section looking south

SANDY COVE

Loveladies, New Jersey

This is another summer home designed on Barnegat Bay on Long Beach Island. In this case, though, it was commissioned on a speculative basis for this particular site. The owner intended to sell the two as a package and supervise construction of the house.

The site is at the tip of a peninsula which is bound by the bay to the west; a large cove to the north; and protected wetlands to the south. It is the last of a string of narrow lots that extend from the boulevard to the bay. The house is sited at a prominent location as seen from either the island or the bay. It can be seen from Long Beach Island Boulevard across the wetlands to the south and acts as a terminus to Sandy Cove Road. From the Bay, it serves as a marker for entry by boats into the cove to the north.

The building responds to these conditions in different ways. A reserved presence is maintained on the east and south as approached by car or bike. The building then opens up to the Bay on the north and west. The house is divided programmatically as well. The main pavilion contains kitchen, dining, and living spaces on the lower level with the main bedroom areas above. The entry wing contains guest quarters, exercise room, and bedrooms for the children.

An exterior deck is provided along the curved glass wall to the southwest. It contains a shallow wading pool that reflects light into the main living areas. A dock extends into the cove for fishing, boating, and windsurfing.

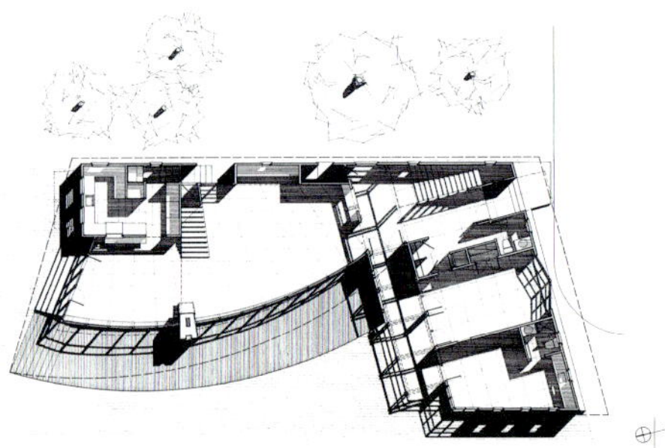

Ground floor plan

First floor plan

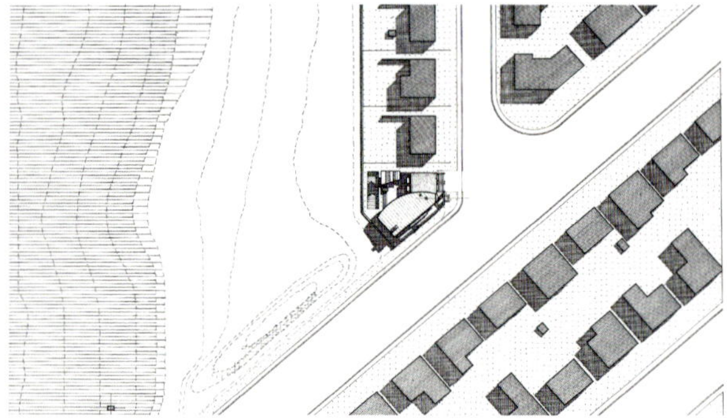

Site plan

JETTY HOUSE

Longport, New Jersey

Longport is located on the southwest corner of Absecon Island, along with Margate City, Ventnor City and Atlantic City to the northeast. This property is at the end of a road overlooking a stone jetty and the Atlantic Ocean. The jetty – while acting as a breakwater for incoming tides – is also a popular fishing destination. The house, designed with Michael Ryan and Randee Spelkoman, unfold to open to the views of the ocean and conforms to the non-orthogonal relationship of the abutting streets. The intersection of the two angles marks the entry pavilion – a round stair hall.

The house itself is divided into two wings. The main contains the primary living spaces on the entry level with a master bedroom suite above. The secondary wing contains bedrooms for the family and guests. An exterior terrace contains a pool, bar, and sitting areas overlooking the jetty.

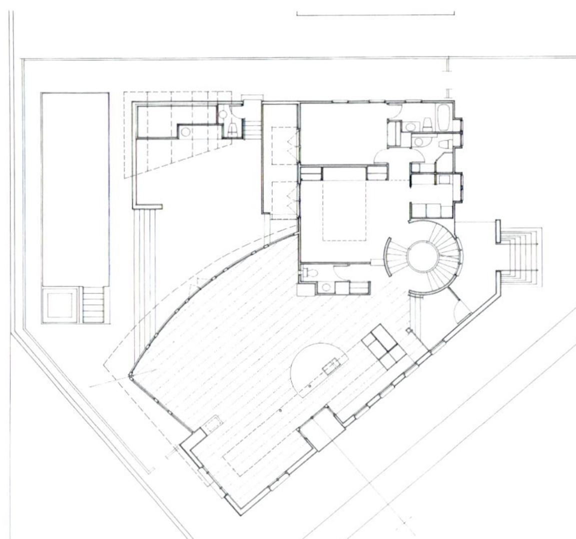

Ground floor plan

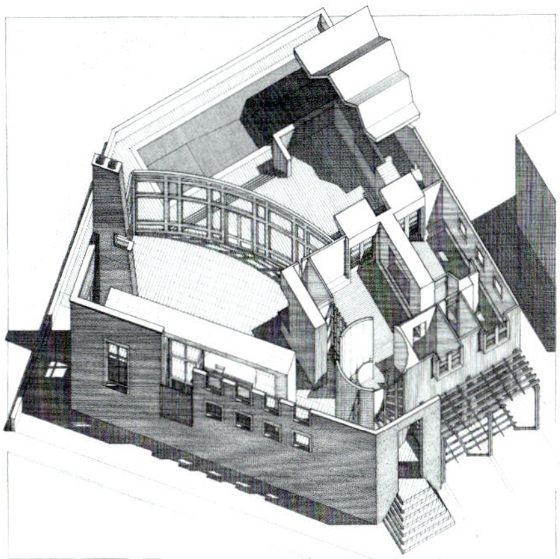

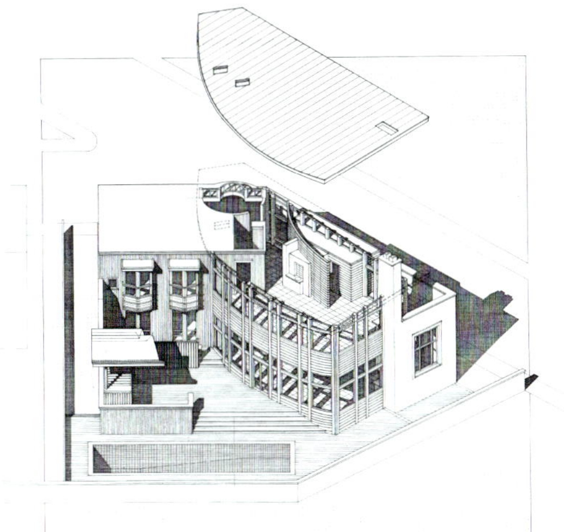

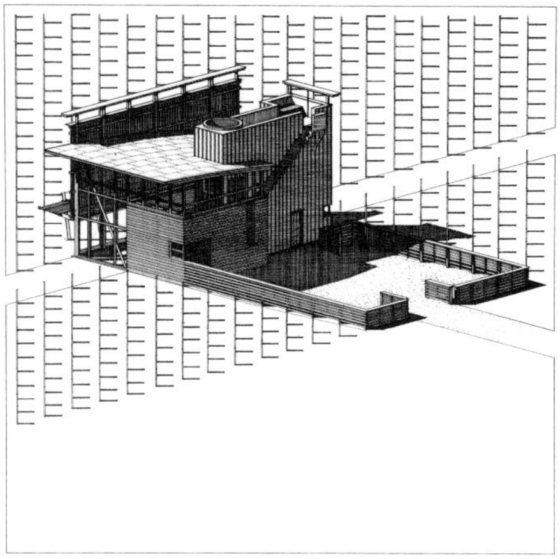

Axonometric

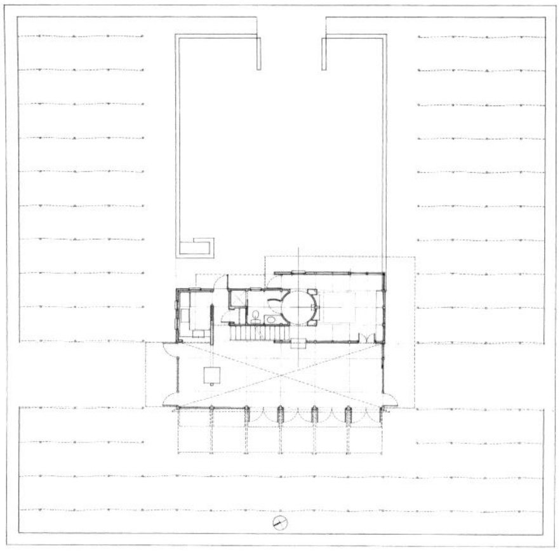

Lower level plan

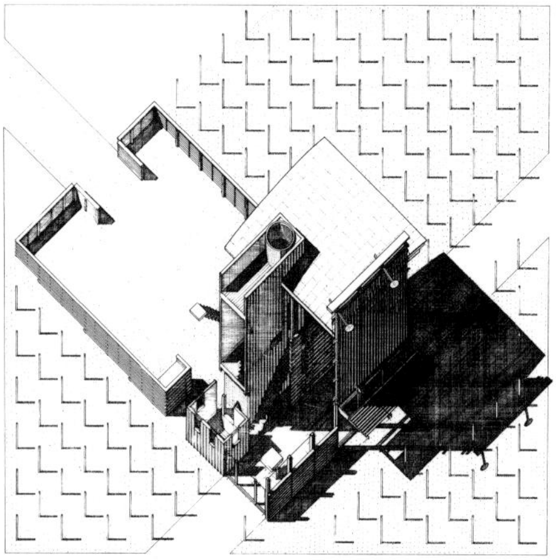

Axonometric

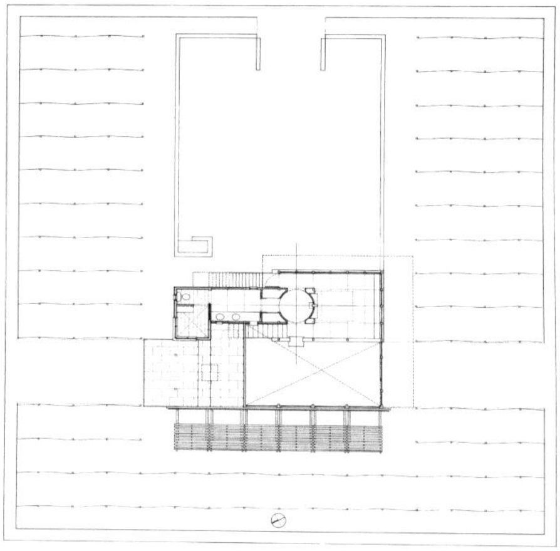

Upper level plan

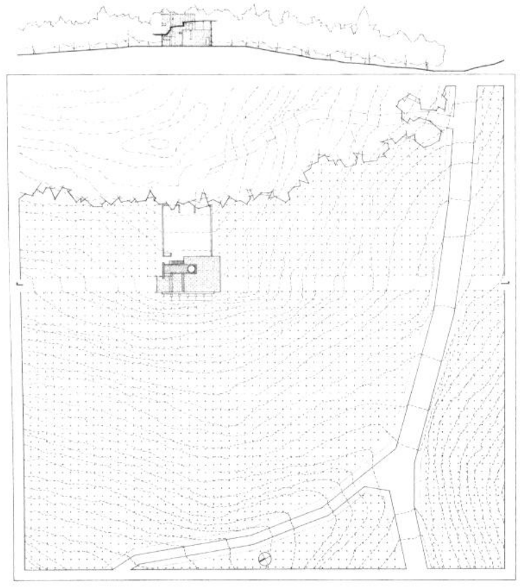

Elevation and site plan

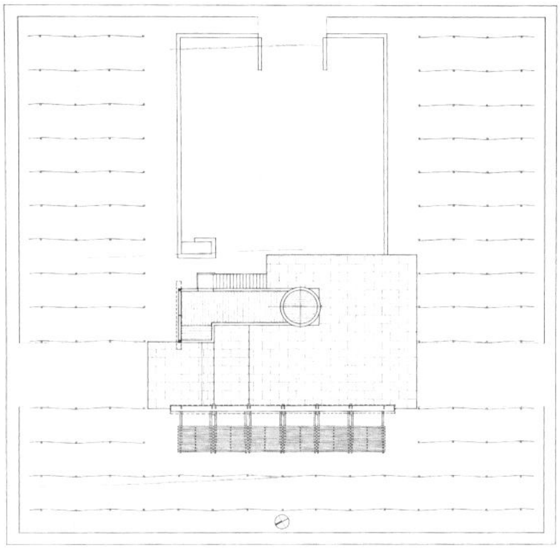

Roof plan

SMALL LODGE

Saint Helena, California

The light in some of the spaces will be extraordinary... the billboard is a witty reinterpretation of a highway vernacular.... appreciate the way the building sits lightly on the landscape and will age with just the right amount of romantic decrepitude for an agricultural building....one of the few projects we have seen that doesn't use a clichéd vocabulary. The lodge is inventive and very controlled.
– Progressive Architecture Jury Comments

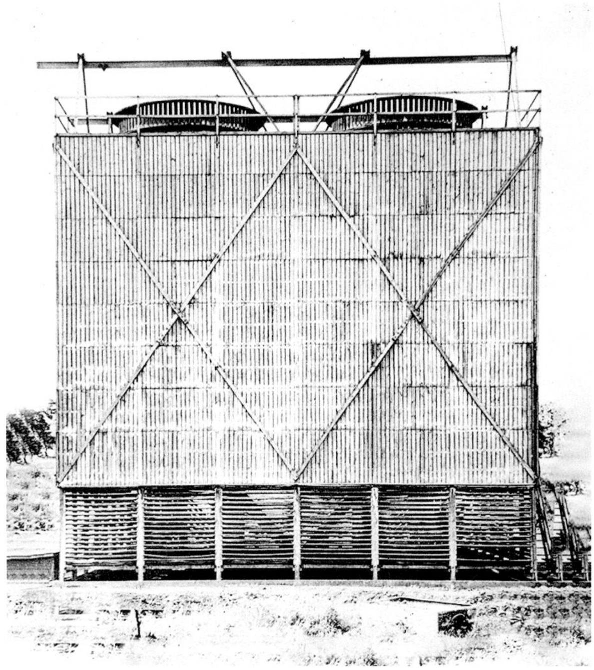

The building sits along the main road that connects Napa and Sonoma Counties in Northern California. It includes eighteen acres of vineyards in the hills overlooking the valley and an adjacent mountain range.

The clients leased the land to an adjoining winery with the intention to also construct a small inn or a lodge on the site. The rural route along the site offers a context with which to connect the building to tourism and agrarian life. Accordingly, the building pays respect to the artifacts found along that highway such as fences, barns, and billboards. Like those buildings, it acts as a marker in the field; both during the day and at night when illuminated by floodlights and the headlights of passing cars.

The building is placed at the edge of the field and it aligns itself with an existing service pathway that runs through the vineyard. The primary access for guests is through the existing grove of trees and into an entry court. The building provides separate residential quarters that can operate independently from each other.

The layout of the structure of the house relates directly to the spacing of the supports for the adjacent vines. Overhangs and wooden slats provide solar protection with vertical slats protecting against the afternoon sun. Overhangs and horizontal slats shade the interior spaces during the summer months.

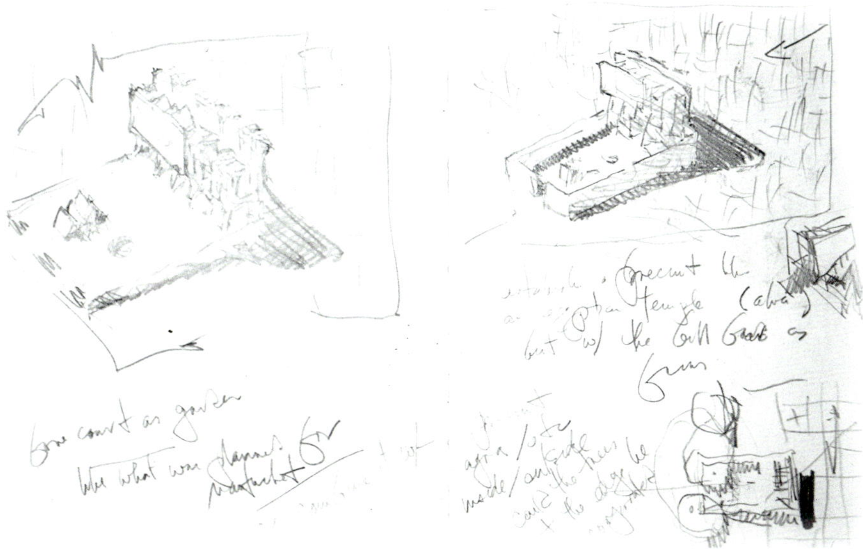

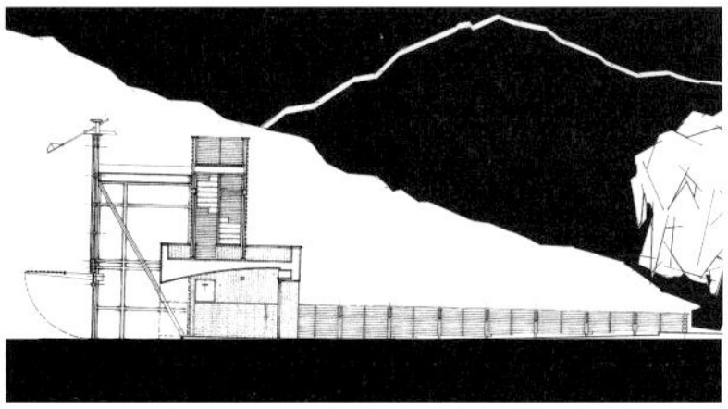

Southwest elevation

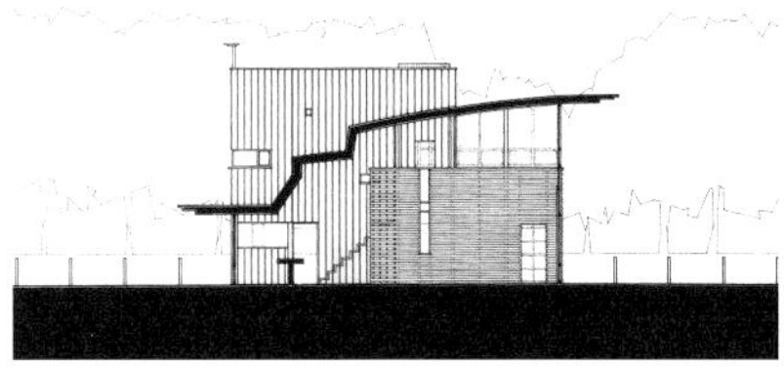

Section through main living area

Section through guest rooms

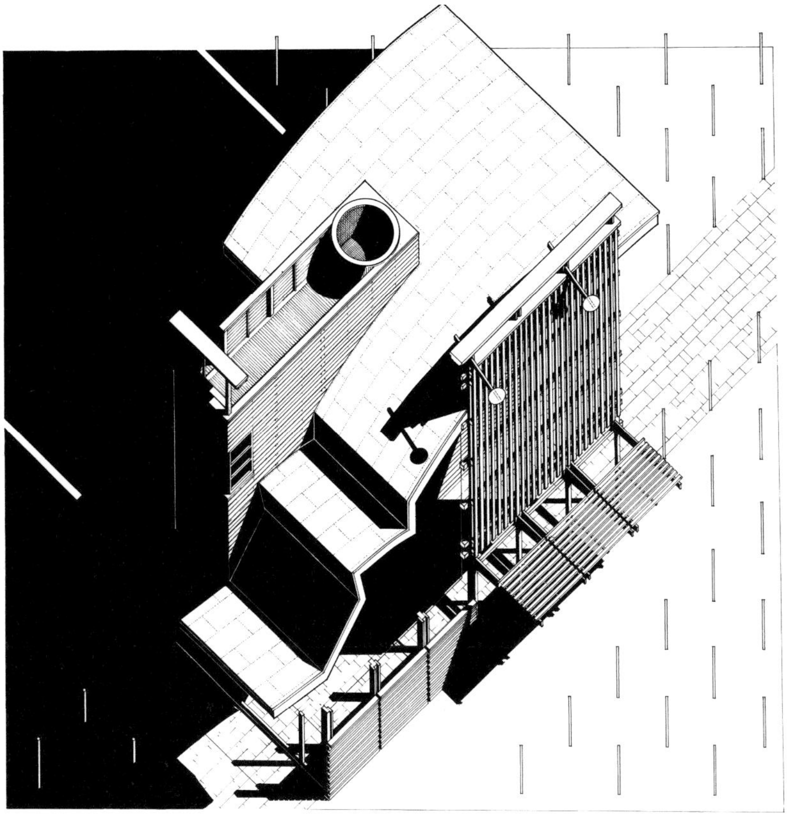

Axonometric-section from north

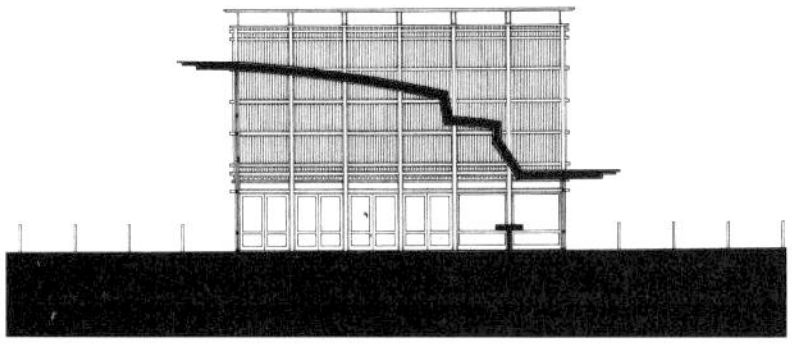

Section through main living area

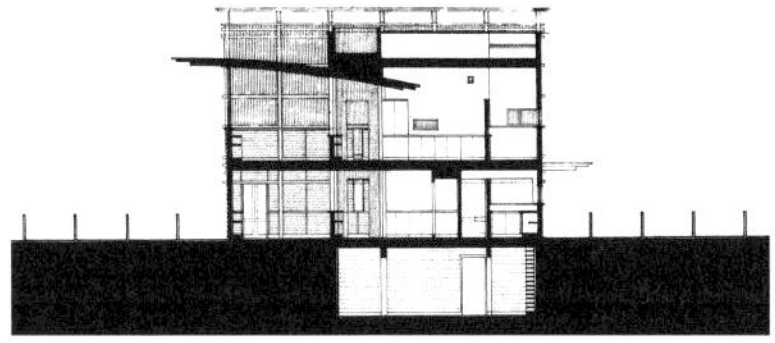

Section through guest rooms and kitchen

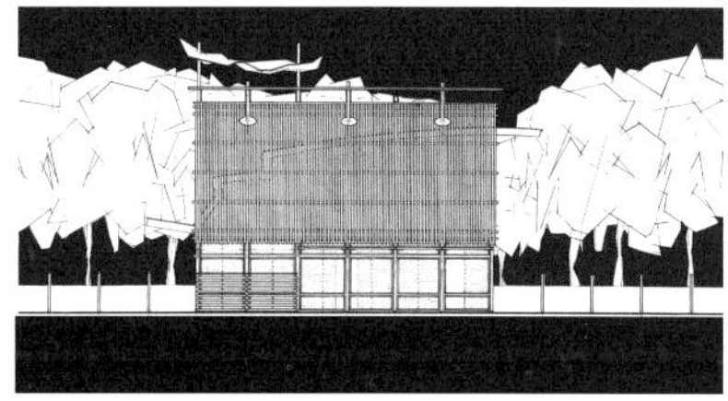

Northwest elevation

HOUSE ON BUZZARDS BAY

South Dartmouth, Massachusetts

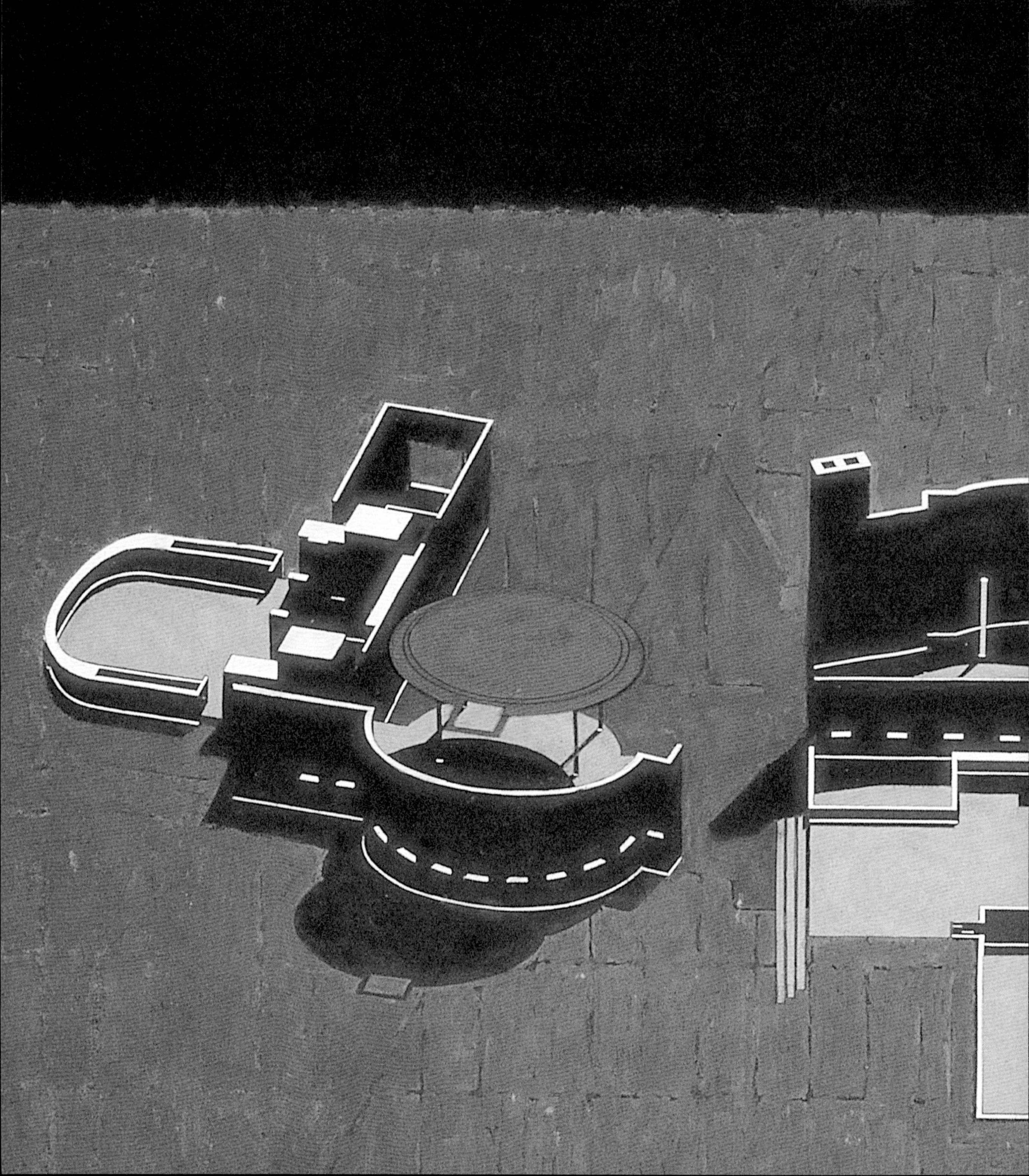

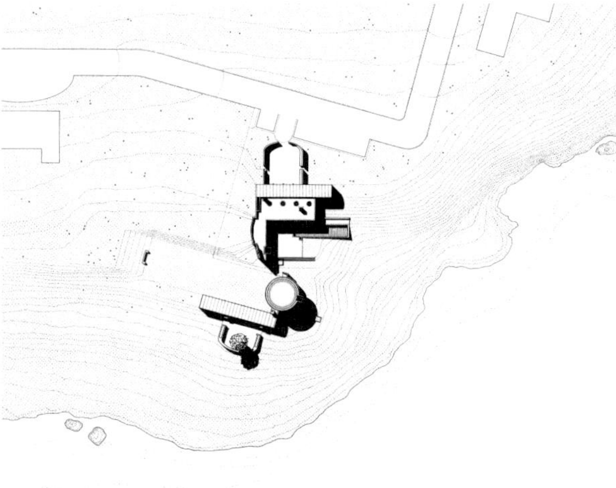

Site plan

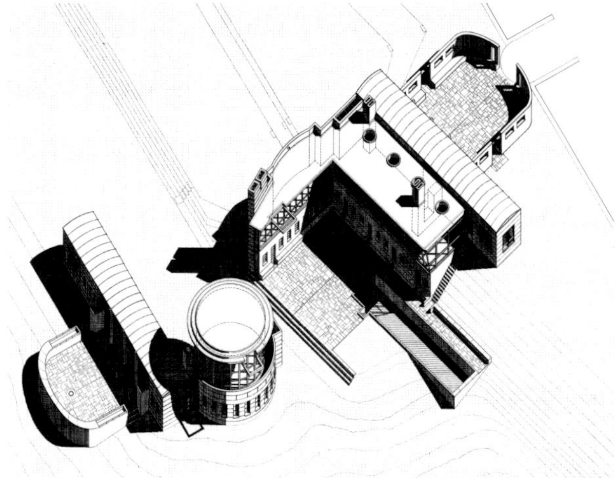

Axonometric

HOUSE ON BUZZARDS BAY

South Dartmouth, Massachusetts

Sited on sloping wooded lot overlooking Buzzards Bay in Southern Massachusetts, the house contains an upper wing for the family's children and their guests, and a lower wing for the owners and their guest. A series of three outdoor courts, beginning with the entry court providing sequencing and privacy between wings provide increasing levels of privacy as one moves through the site.

In the upper wing, bedrooms are placed below the L-shaped upper level living spaces — lined with floor to ceilings windows, and the lower drum-like structure is a two-story with an attached rectangular wing which contains the master bedroom suite.

The structures are clad in board and batten cedar with standing seam roofing.

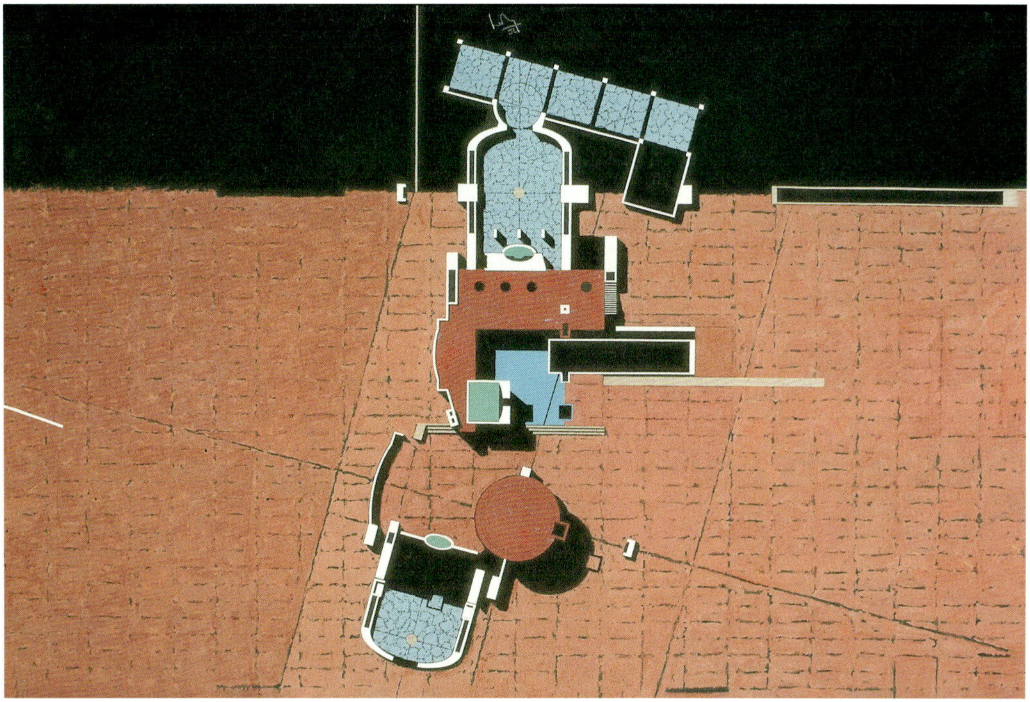

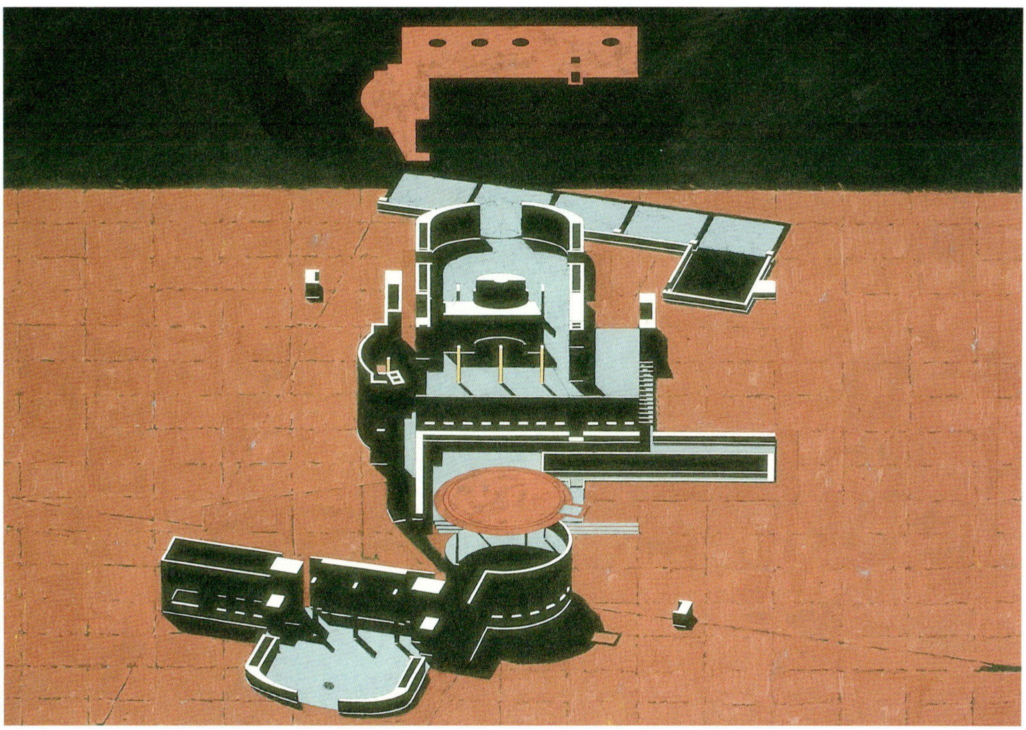

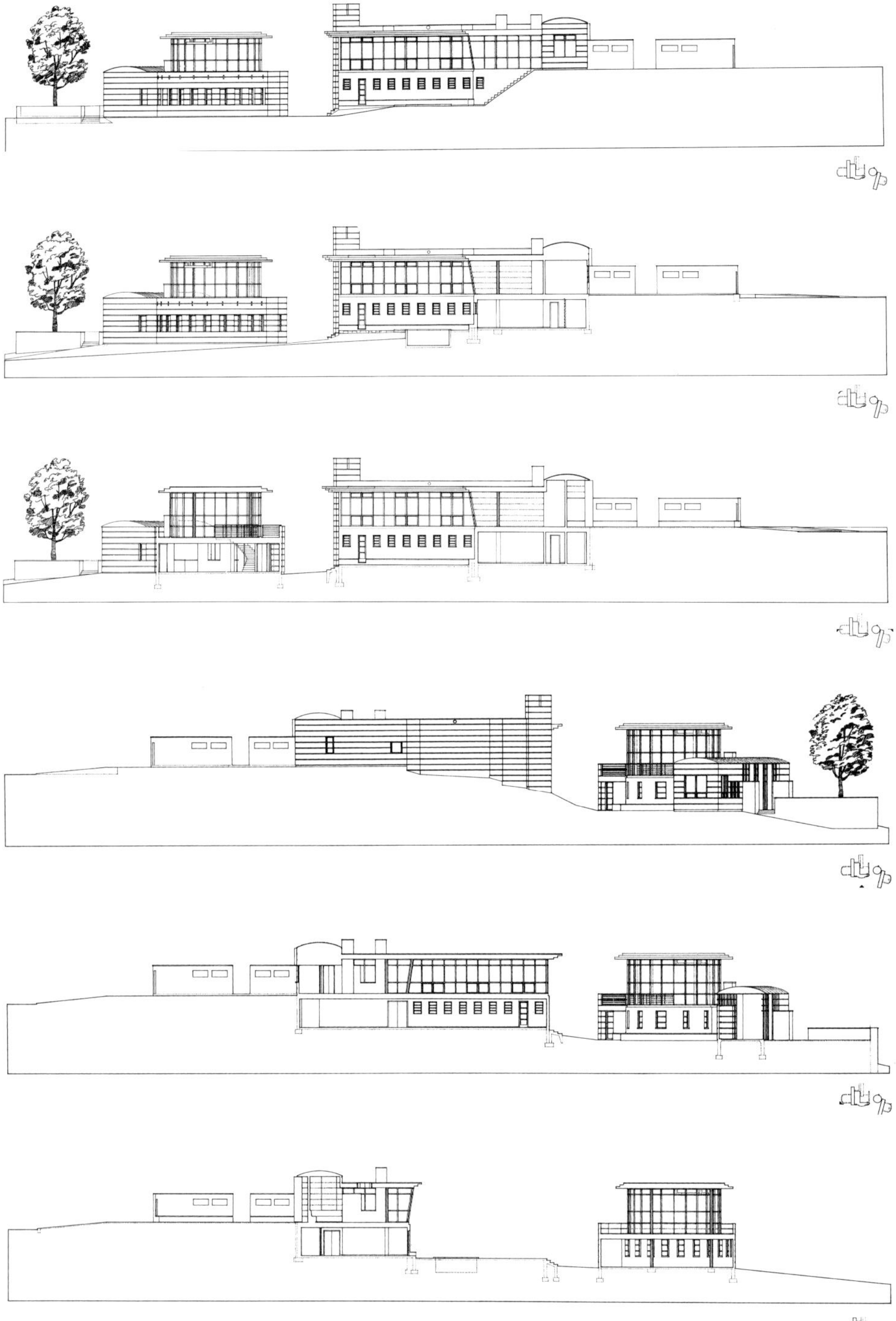

Section and elevations

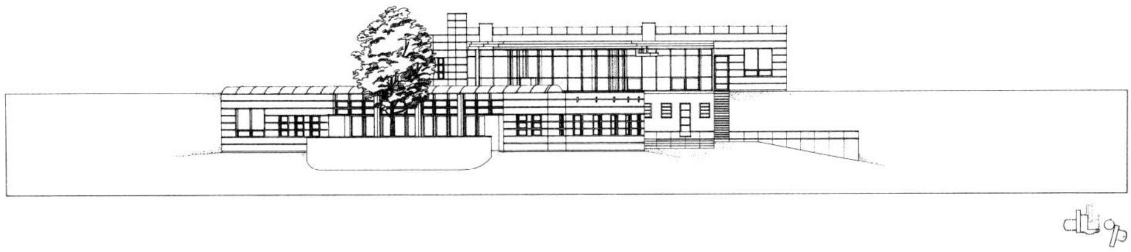

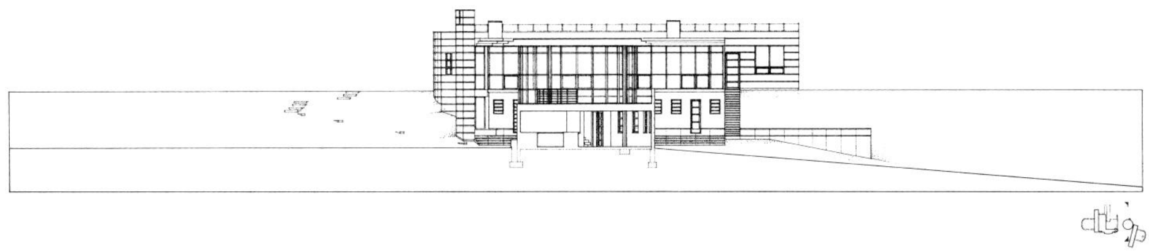

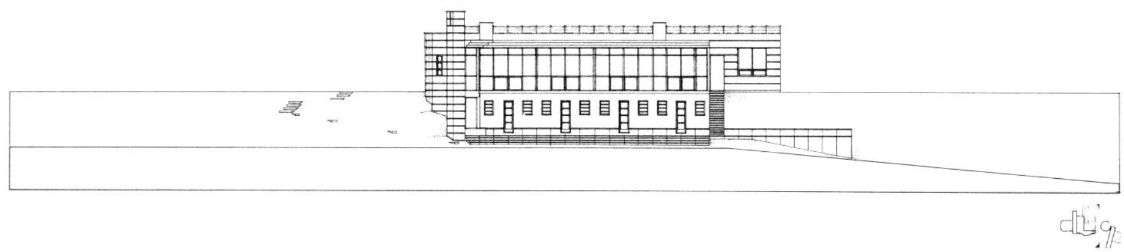

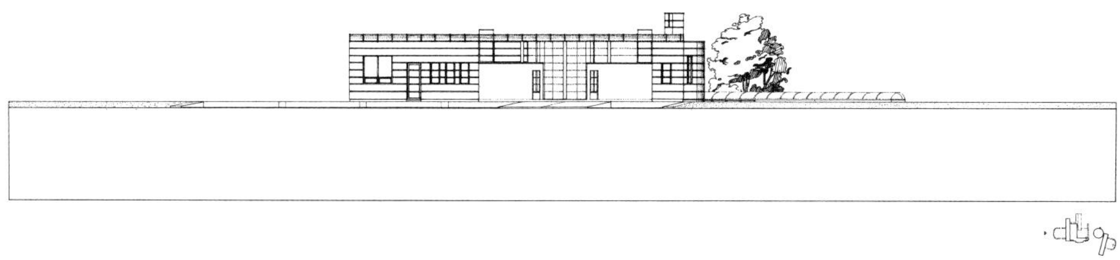

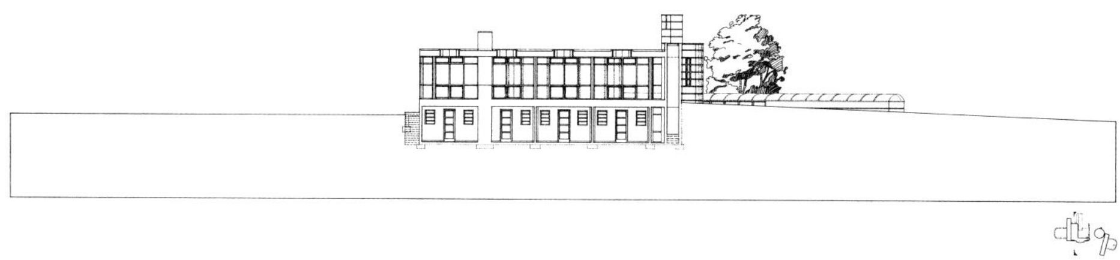

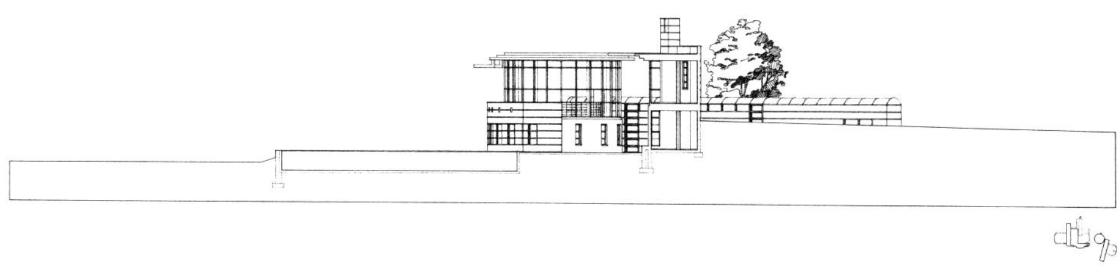

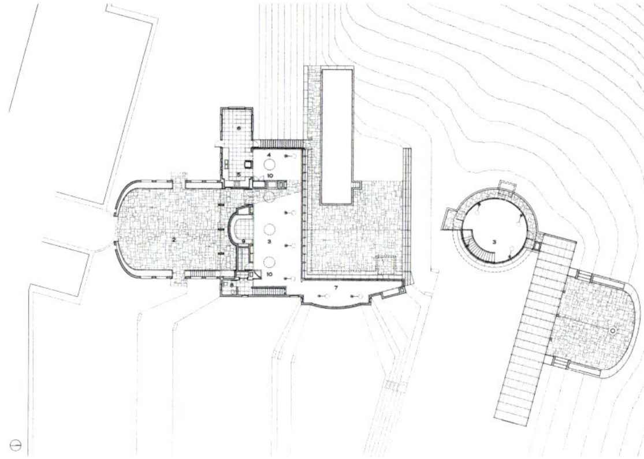

Lower floor plan
1 Parking area
2 Entry courtyard
3 Family living area
/Veranda
4 Dining area
5 Kitchen
6 Breakfast area
7 Study/Den
8 Toilet room
9 Reading alcove
10 Fireplace

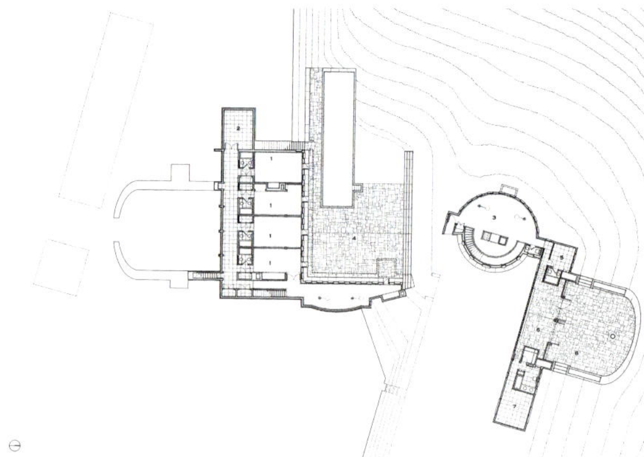

Upper floor plan
1 Bedroom/Bathroom
2 Laundry/Storage
3 Kitchen/Dining area
4 Upper terrace
with pool
5 Study/Bedroom
/Bathroom
6 Sun room
7 Master bedroom
/Bathroom
8 Lower terrace

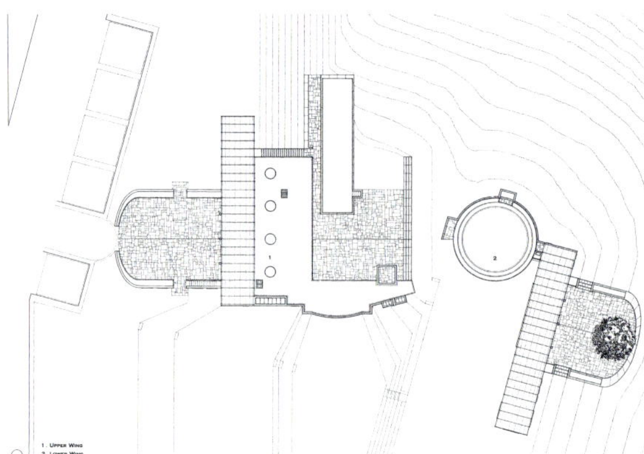

1 Upper wing
2 Lower wing

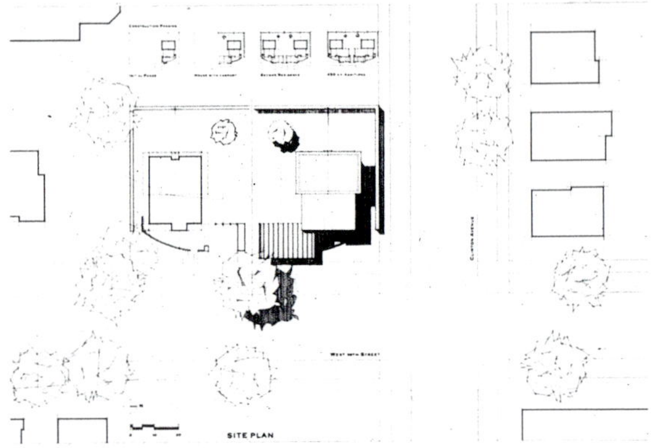

Site plan

URBAN DUPLEX

Watertown, Massachusetts

The residential communities – outside of Boston proper – which define the larger metropolitan area are filled with housing stock defined by two and three family wooden frame structures. This projects looks to develop a prototype for two adjacent homes that co-exist on a single site. Each has its own identity, entry porch, drive, and back yard. Constructed of a wood frame with cedar plywood siding and horizontal battens, each house is inward focused around a central interior space illuminated by a continuous clerestory at the roofline. The main lining areas are on the entry level with bedrooms on the upper level.

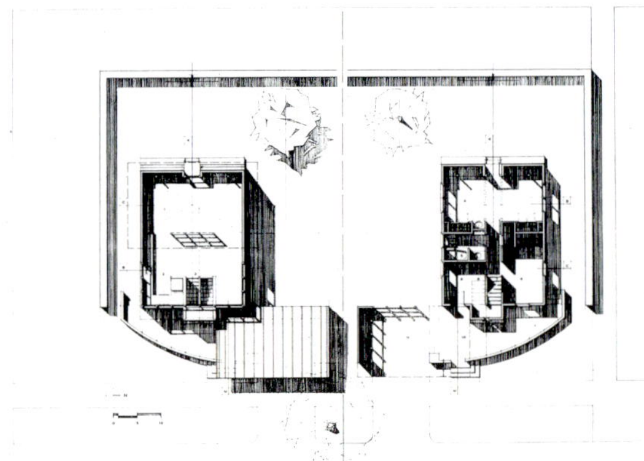

Upper level plan Lower level plan

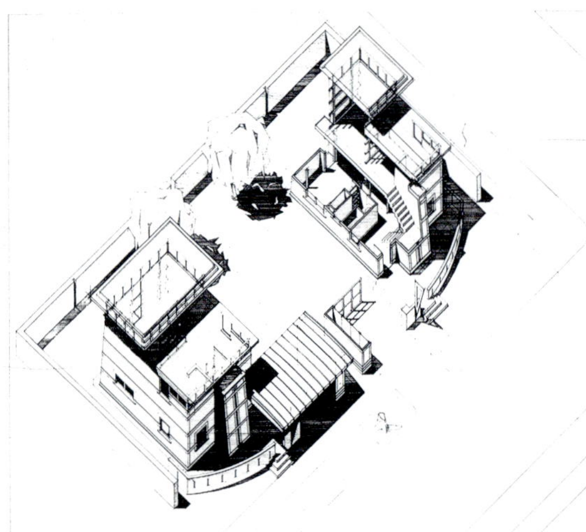

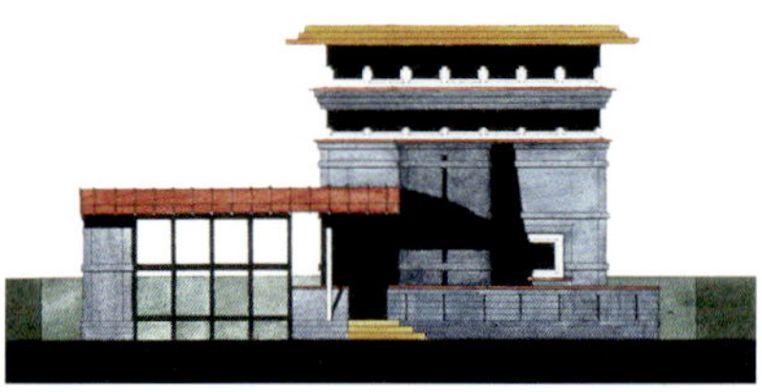

Section and elevations

WALL HOUSE

Saint Helena, California

The hills surrounding Napa Valley in Northern California are thickly wooded or cleared for vineyards. The eighty-acre site for this building is in a particularly dense wooded area at the edge of a ridge overlooking the valley. The house is concealed upon approach from the northwest. Entry is on foot through a trellis that frames a view of the adjacent vineyards. The exterior wall of the house unravels down the slope to form a courtyard open to views of the valley. Exterior paving is limited to the entry while natural ground cover is brought along the pool and into the court. The exterior walls are concrete and masonry with heavy timber framing and metal roofs.

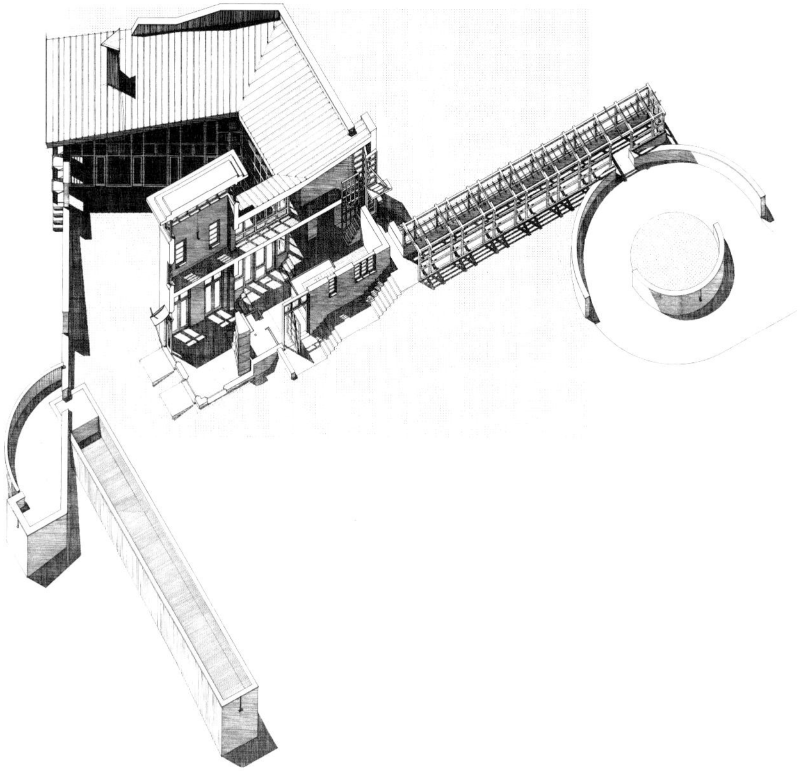

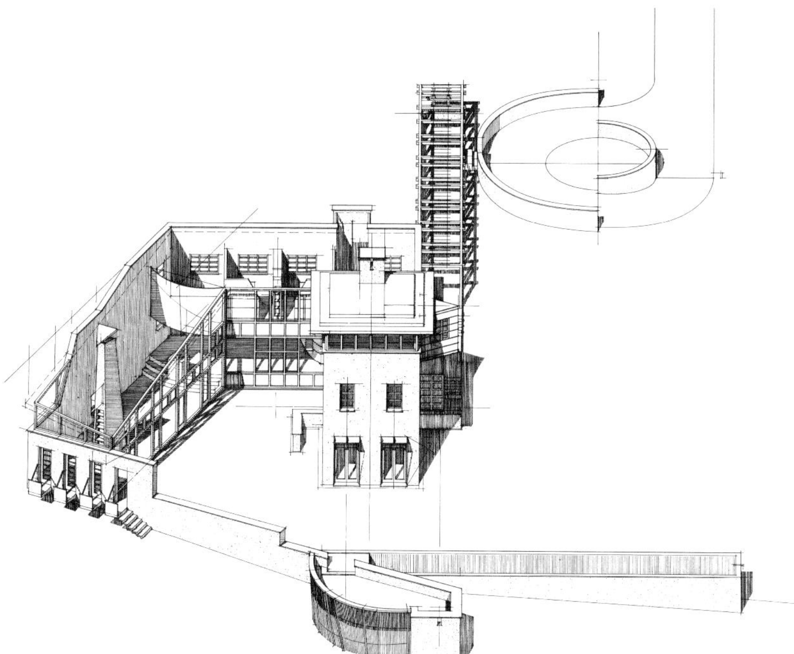

Axonometrics

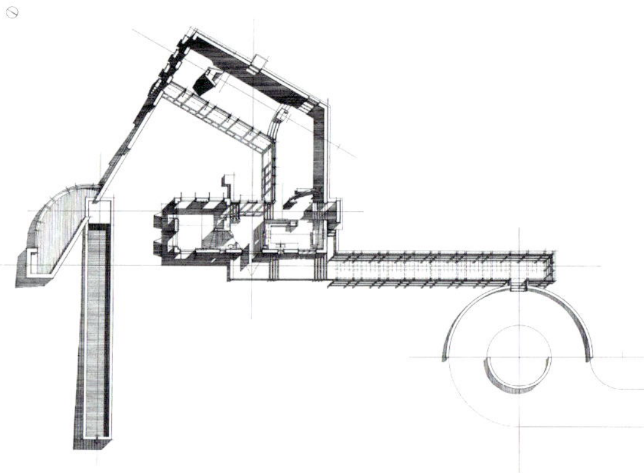

Ground level plan

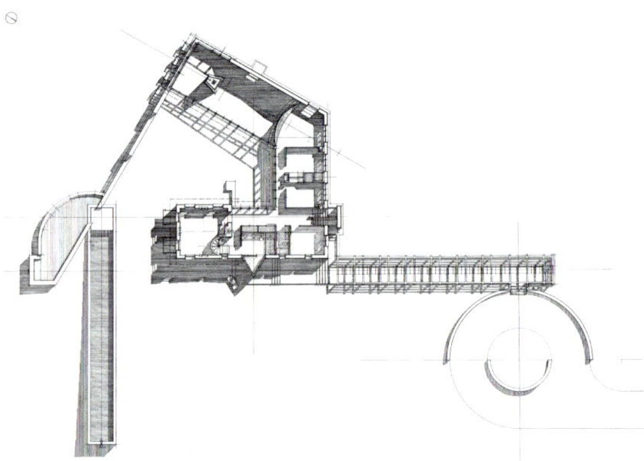

Upper level plan

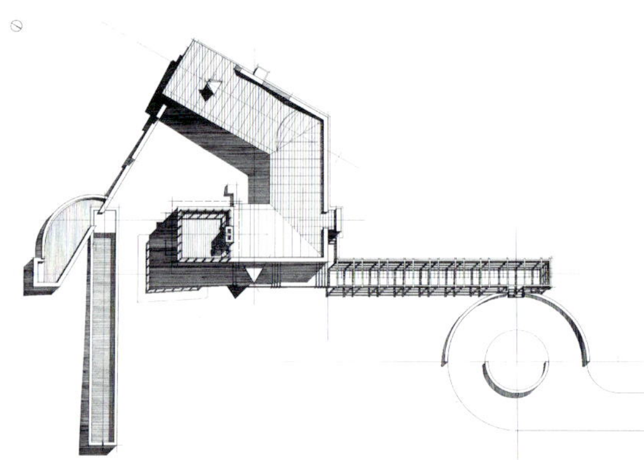

Roof plan

RIVER HOUSE

Alva, Florida

RIVER HOUSE

Alva, Florida

The site is located at a bend in the Caloosahatchee in Southwest Florida. The natural vegetation consists of live oaks and palmetto palms surrounded by citrus groves. The primary access to the site is by boat.

In a manner similar to other homes located along rural routes, this small studio in Alva both acknowledges and responds to the vehicles moving along the waterway. It serves as a marker at the bend while paying respect to the industrial artifacts found along the river.

The program consists of a small rural residence and studio for two artists; a ceramist and a printmaker. The 1,400 square foot house establishes a public presence on the river while maintaining a private enclosed exterior court behind the house. Living and studio space is located on the second level. Bedrooms and baths are on the ground level. A detached work shed is provided for tending to the boat and fishing equipment.

The walls of the building and shed are smooth stucco on block with coquina sills and coping. The interior surfaces include stucco, plywood, and slate. The metal framed stair enclosure is covered with copper. The exterior paving is random slate with a stained cedar dock.

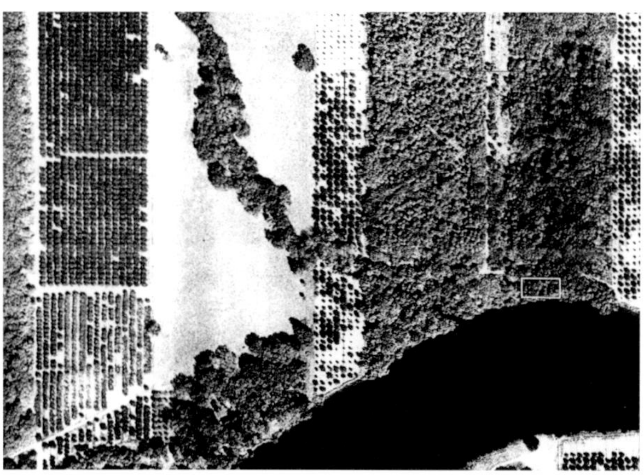

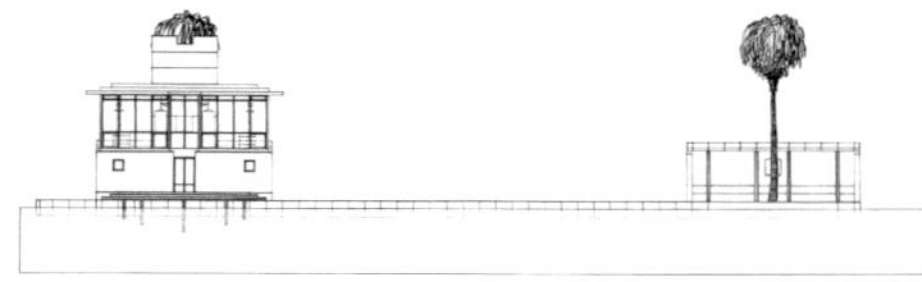

West elevation

East elevation

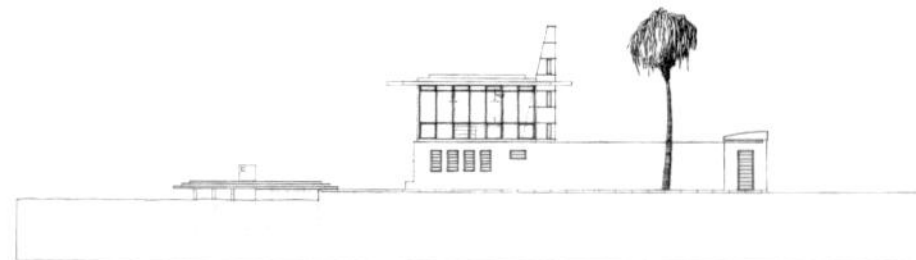

South elevation

North elevation

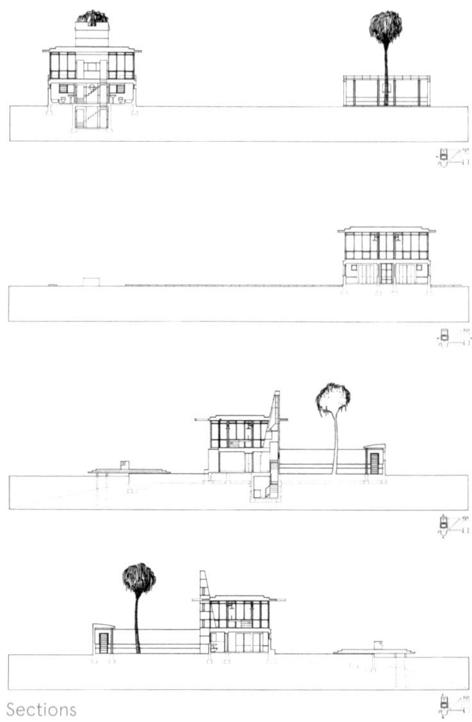

Sections

Aerial view along Caloosahatchee River

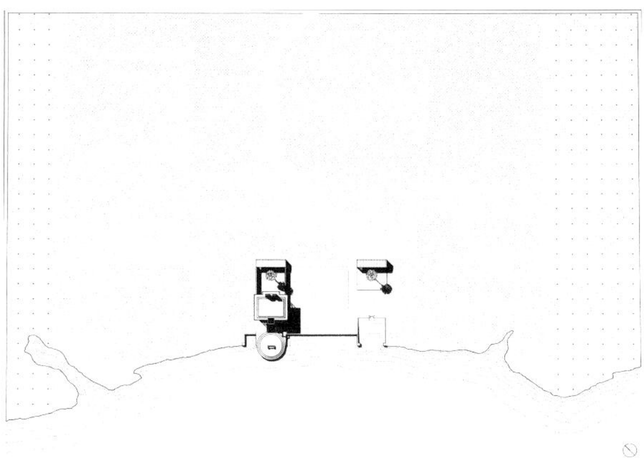

Site plan

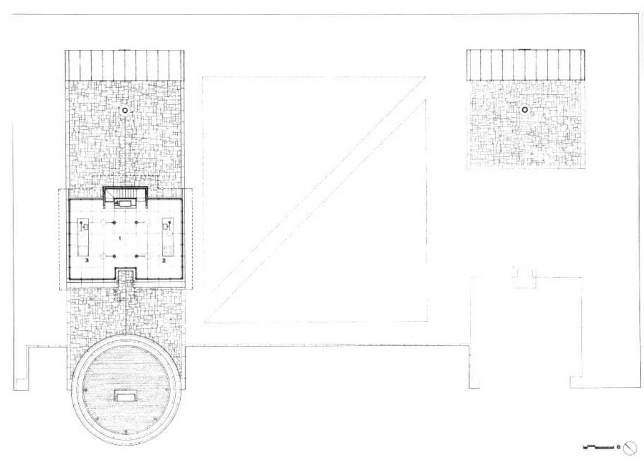

Second level plan

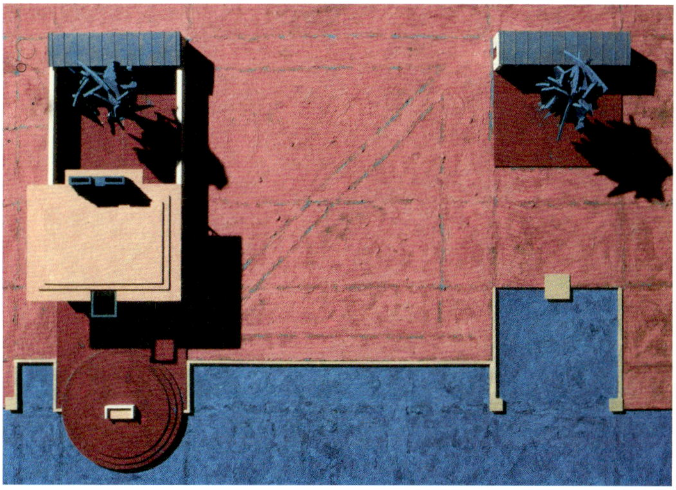

OPEN HOUSE

Estero, Florida

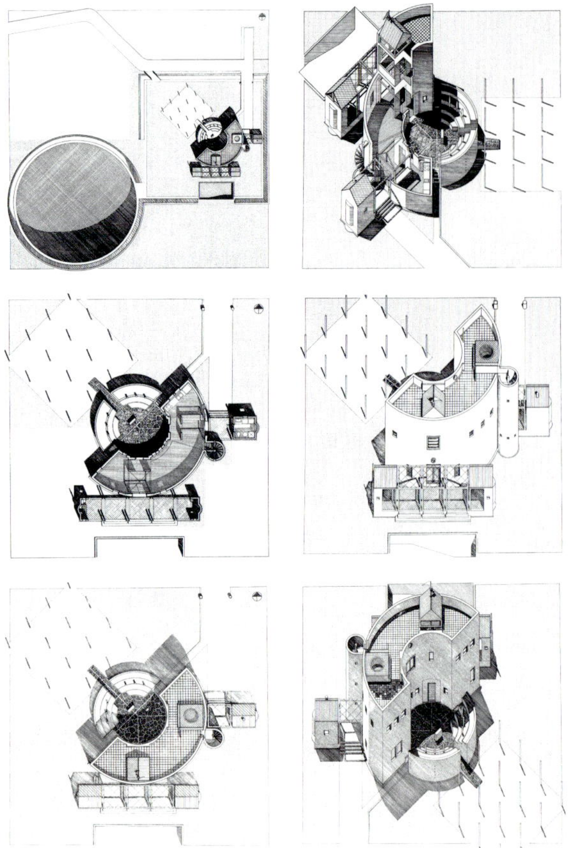

OPEN HOUSE

Estero, Florida

The house makes a gesture, like being a little theater. The house can be an object of art. It doesn't just organize functions or provide for shelter, but goes beyond to make a very formal king of living. You can act in this house as your own actor. Lots of people want to identify themselves with a house asd they identify themselves with a suit, a motor car, or whatever. They want to live a certain formal life. This is what makes the urbanity of that little piece: it's a stage set in front of which he and his guests can act.
– Progressive Architecture Jury Comments

The original house, designed in 1984, is a small rural retreat built around an outdoor amphitheater that acts as a backdrop for the client, his guests, and his plants. He was an avid horticulturist intent on his home being consumed into his nursery. The client lived in the home for 35 years before falling ill and the house fell into disrepair.

The proposed renovations and additions tried to imagine the creation of a backstage for the day-to-day interactions of the client and his guests while the front court remains the primary focus for collective gatherings. The new complex, including a master suite, 4 guest rooms, an art studio/garage, and enclosed pool seeks to complement the existing home: an asymmetrical, rectilinear geometry contrasts the original symmetrical, curved massing; and a delicate and articulated frame contrasts the smooth bold stucco surfaces of the original structure. The fenestration and spatial ordering of the proposed is dynamic and indeterminate, while the original is highly ordered and fixed. These distinctions create a rich open stage that expands the possibilities for formal and informal life at his nursery.

The original house was masonry construction with stucco finish. While this component of the compound will be upgraded, the new addition will be an open wood frame with cedar siding, louvers, and sliding panels.

NOMAD EXQUISITE

As the immense dew of Florida
Brings forth
The big-finned palm
And green vine angering for life,

As the immense dew of Florida
Brings forth hymn and hymn
From the beholder,
Beholding all these green sides
And gold sides of green sides,

And blessed mornings,
Meet for the eye of the young alligator,
And lightning colors
So, in me, comes flinging
Forms, flames, and the flakes of flames.

Wallace Stevens

East elevation

North elevation

West elevation

South elevation

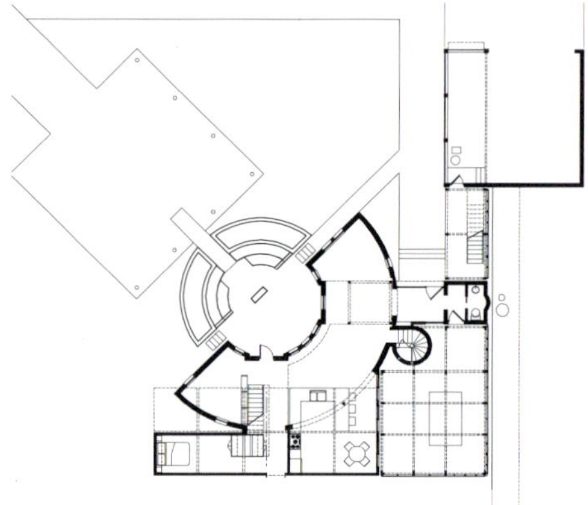

Renovation of first floor plan

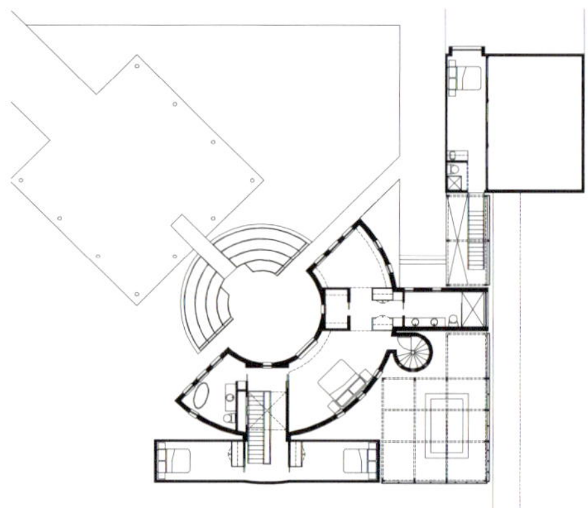

Renovation of second floor plan

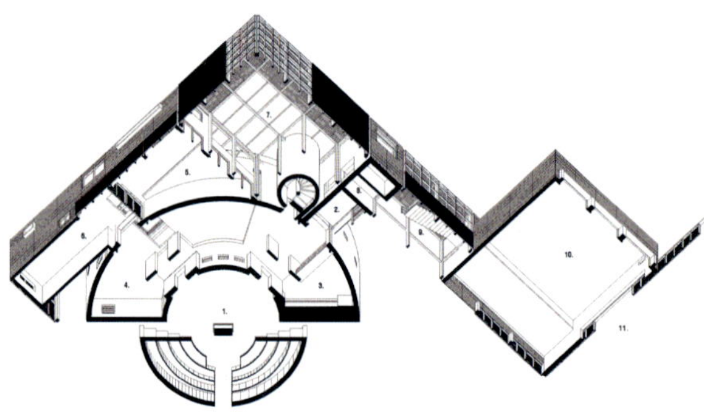

1 External amphitheater
2 Entry
3 Study
4 Sitting room
5 Kitchen / Dining
6 Bedroom
7 Enclosed pool
8 Bath / Shower
9 Stair to guest suite
10 Garage / Art studio
11 Driveway

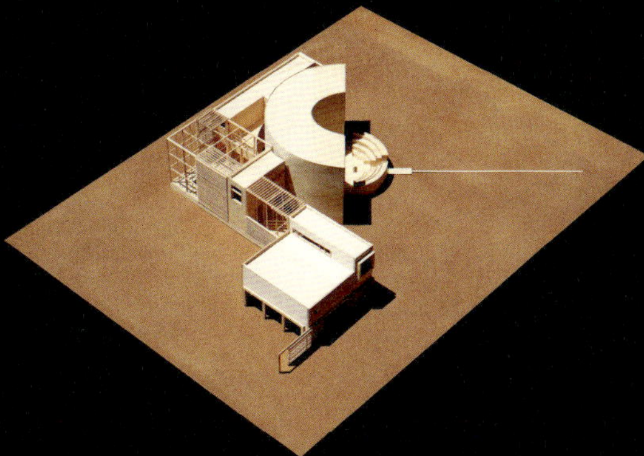
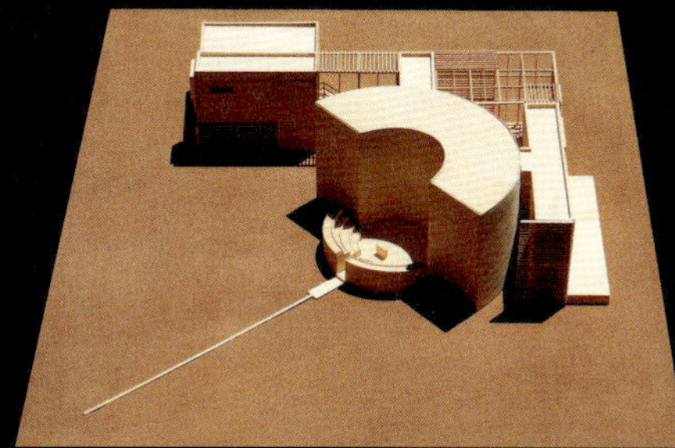
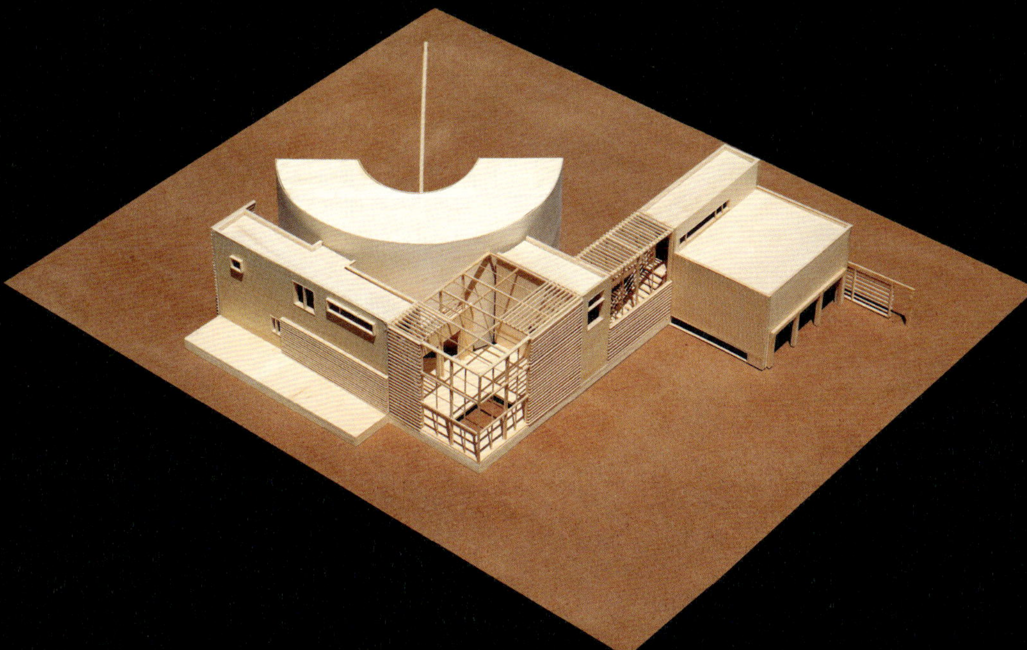
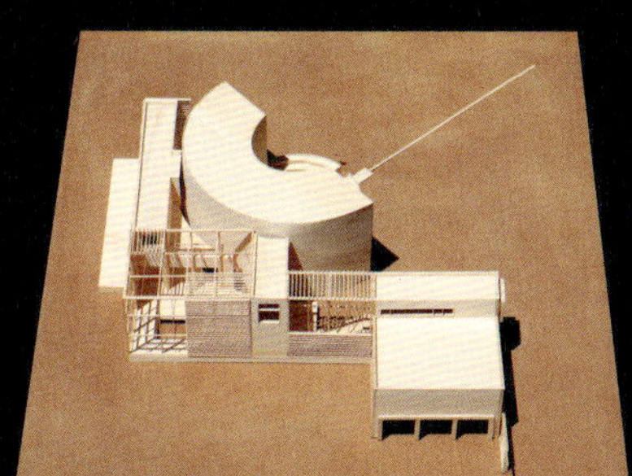

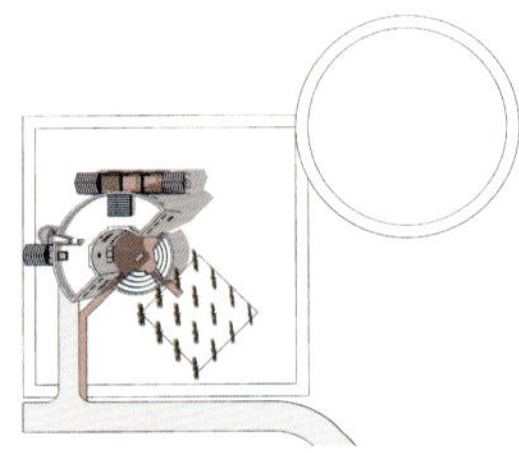

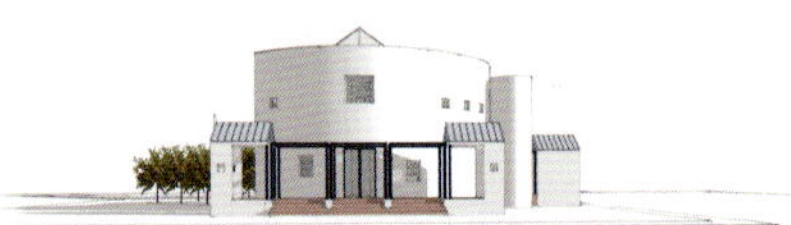

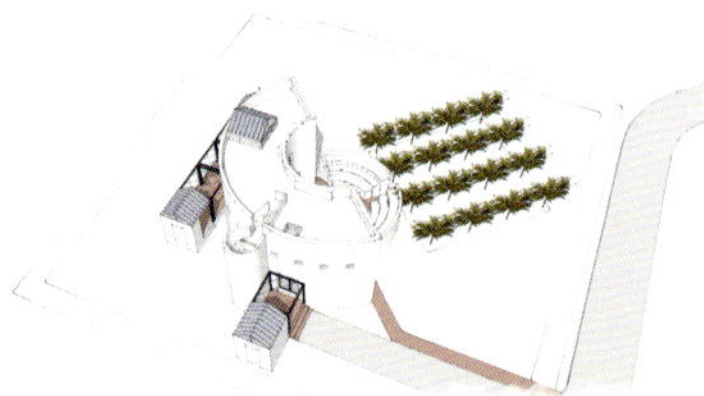

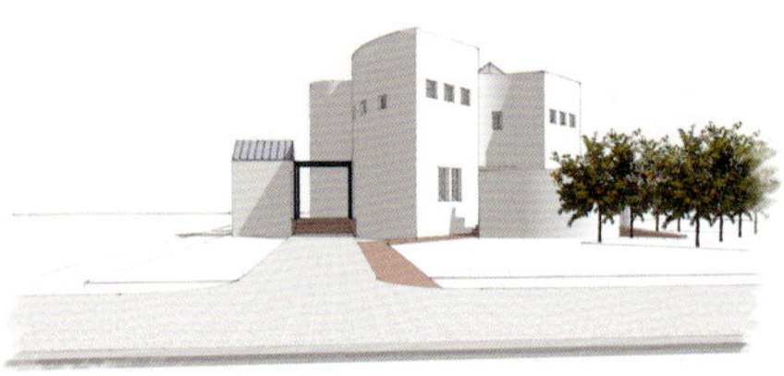

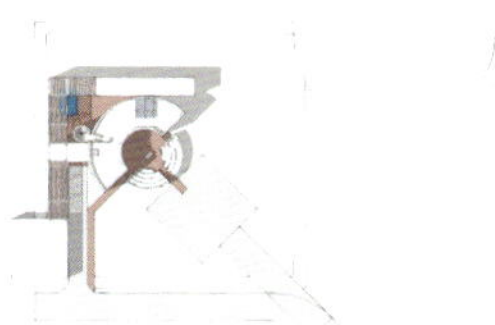

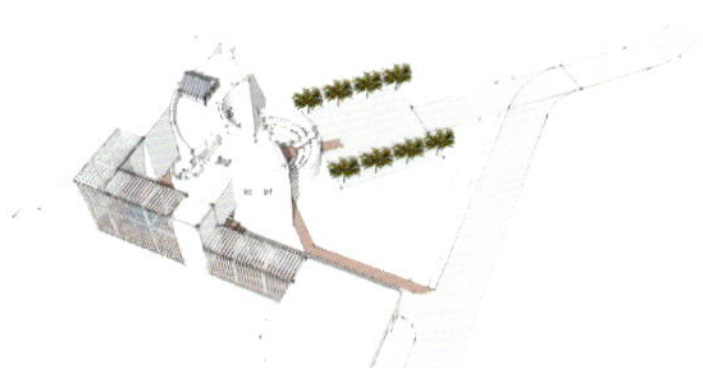

VLADIMIR BELOGOLOVSKY WITH BRIAN HEALY

INTERESTING THINGS HAPPEN IN THE SHADOWS

In Conversation with Brian Healy December 17, 2020

Brian Healy: ...I think the fixation in our profession on the business of architecture should be superseded by what architects such as John Hejduk have called a poetic reinterpretation of how we might live. The two are not mutually exclusive, but somehow the latter seems to have been abandoned. There are, of course, many great schools out there — and a few practices — that share this perspective, but increasingly, it seems like market forces are ruling the day.

When I decided to become an architect, it wasn't in an attempt to save the world. I simply could not think of something more potent than to create environments where other people would live. Architecture has the potential to set up opportunities for people to renew and refresh their lives. I always cared for that aspect of our profession.

My education allowed me to see architecture as more than just pursing career opportunities and as a way of understanding how we live and how what we do impacts the lives of others, hopefully, in a positive way. Education is supposed to be liberating and aspirational. We should be civic leaders, not just service providers. I find that a lack of pragmatism often exposes other possibilities which should to be explored and pursued. If we focus exclusively on the business of architecture, we can miss the potency of architecture and how it might be useful.

Vladimir Belogolovsky: I agree with you. At the same time, saying that the lack of pragmatism opens possibilities can make many clients pretty nervous, no?

BH: I don't think that our day-to-day efforts should be exclusively about obtaining the next project or commission. It's important to me that people get what they want out of a project or building. And if I can help them get it, nothing makes me happier. I do not wish to impose my particular viewpoint on anyone. I care for how people live in these buildings and want them as open and accessible as possible.

Above Study for proposed amphitheater in Dewey Square along the Rose Kennedy Greenway

VB: I came across a passage, in which you described architecture as "making poetic vacancies and poetic imaginings." Could you elaborate on that?

BH: Well, it should go without saying that what we do is complicated and difficult to both conceive and construct. I'm very fond of an old Tao meditation that notes that "life is too ugly, too violent, that we need something delicate to care about"... I think that architecture can help with that.

VB: Then perhaps you could tell me why you got into architecture in the first place.

BH: My father was born in Harlem and we were told that my great grandfather worked on the stained-glass windows in St. Patrick's Cathedral in midtown New York. I remember going there with him and my brothers and — while my younger brothers were all racing around the building, trying to figure out just which window he made — all I could think of was "Wait a minute, somebody actually made this place?" It was probably the first time that it occurred to me that buildings and places as grandiose as that were, in fact, designed and built by human hands. I was about ten years old then and my family had just bought a couple acres in a field on Greene's Farm in Bucks County, Pennsylvania where we built a new home. It was a neo-colonial wooden structure with a stone façade and a nice place to grow up with my six brothers.

It was there that I also learned to appreciate the beauty of barns, outbuildings, farmhouses, and the local, modest vernacular architecture like road-side billboards and farm stands. These experiences influenced my decision to study architecture. I certainly never looked back. It also reinforced a belief that architecture is not only found in the extraordinary world of a St. Patrick's, but also in the ordinary world that is around us every day. The ordinary and extraordinary blur. I don't think architecture should be limited to select structures or those found in history books. The commonplace also has its own potential to be architecture. To go back to your earlier question, as architects, we only make the places and the buildings. We don't always live in them. When I design a home, or a lab, or a church, I speculate on how someone else – or some group — might occupy it and relate to it. That's what I mean when I describe architecture as making poetic vacancies. We can suggest how a place can grow by adding to it. In the end, every decent building needs to be an appropriate addition to what is already there — not as a foil or compliment — but an indication of how that place can evolve and grow.

VB: In early 1980s, after Yale you worked for some of the leading architects who were at their prime then, including Richard Meier who was just awarded the Pritzker Prize then and Cesar Pelli, the Dean at Yale at the time. Before that you also worked at the office of Charles Moore. I wonder how was your experience working with him and what did you learn from him?

BH: Charles was my first design instructor at Yale, and he wanted everyone to know that architecture could be fun. It could be ironic, even silly. It could be enjoyed in its making and enjoyable in its use and make people happy. That's my most significant lesson from him. Coming to Yale, it was something new to me because so many other professors were pretty uptight. [Laughs.] It was not his only agenda, of course. He was a larger than life guy and he would take the class up to his place in Newport. If people didn't like his work, it was fine with him. He was very approachable and open to discussion with anyone, whereas some other professors would say, "This is not architecture, and there is nothing to talk about here." But Charles didn't want to define — or limit — what "architecture" was; he didn't want us to either. He did not want us — as students — to feel pressure for a perfect definition of what architecture is — or could be. In fact, what was wonderful about my education at Yale was that all the great educators who I encountered there — Stirling, Scully, Hejduk, Pelli, Kubler, Millard, Purves, Livesey — nobody presumed that what they just said was the end of the discussion. It was the beginning and it was an opening to everybody to make new conclusions — or at least, present an alternative proposition. What seemed important was to have an open dialogue that leads somewhere to a critical point. I've tried to carry that forward but, I am sorry, the client isn't always right, or the consultants. [Laughs.] If I disagree, I will say so.

VB: It was said about you that you are mixing architecture with art. If you could touch on your design process? What are your typical inspirations and what are your initial steps?

BH: I like to draw and paint. I do so literally to put light on an idea, to illuminate a thought, and make it tangible, maybe legible. I am not interested in making an illustration or a documentary. But it is important to acknowledge that — when at Yale — we all worked in the A+A — the Arts and Architecture Building — with art studios on floors 4 and 5 and the architecture studios on 6 and 7 — with unbelievable art galleries and an incredible art history department right across the street. We would be riding the elevator and sharing the coffee shop with painters and print makers, it was intense. Making art is an ongoing aspiration and making architecture is very difficult. It involves vulnerabilities that most people are not comfortable with. Painting is something that I do all the time, and I often paint something entirely unrelated to my projects or to specific thoughts on architecture. Yet, these paintings inevitably become architectural. I may paint how a building sits in the landscape or dissolves into the city or sky. These paintings are frequently like collages of anticipated buildings. But working on a project always starts the same — by meeting the client — and studying what the site might allow. I then simply need to spend some time in my studio to gather my thoughts.

VB: Alone?

BH: Yes, of course. I will — naturally — share my ideas with colleagues and each are welcome to critique and challenge those ideas — to analysis and probably improve them. That is the best part of a collaborative process. But what we need as a design team is a focus — a defined beginning. So, yes, I need to start a project alone. That's how I initiate every project. I never ask for ideas from others in my office at the very beginning. I think an architect's idea should be fully developed in his or her head before asking others what they think. That's my feeling. Of course, we don't have to agree, but that's how I gather my thoughts.

VB: Would you then call yourself an author?

BH: Well, I'm not comfortable with that word because I think our profession has been much too obsessed with authorship. An editor might be more appropriate. I don't believe Wright when he said that he "shakes them out of his sleeve." Of course, he was a great architect. But our profession is collaborative, and the work has many fingerprints on it. It should and it does. So, sure, it is the lead architect who picks one path out of many. But there is always a team to bounce ideas off, to adjust direction, and dig deeper and deeper. Some clients or teachers may say, "That's a great idea! Now, give me two more." I don't understand that concept. If it's a great idea, then let's dig deeper and see what the potency of that idea is? Why start out by getting distracted by another idea? Some people think it is restrictive, but I prefer to think of it as focused. The beginning is key, and you must decide — after some analysis — which path are you taking.

VB: And it is you who will make that decision, right? You would not bring two-three ideas to a client and ask for direction, right?

BH: No! Why would I do that? Of course, when we work on our designs in the studio, we develop two or three options simultaneously. Many times, more with an iterative string of study models and planning diagrams.

VB: But it is up to you to decide what to show to the client.

BH: Of course! Who else? We inevitably come to a consensus, but I make the call.

VB: Many architects want the client to make that choice because they want the client to be happy, and more importantly – responsible.

BH: That's ridiculous. I can't even imagine a situation like that... then I am just a service provider, or a vender peddling wares? We are hired as professionals with experience, let's not forget.

VB: Exactly.

BH: I think our profession is challenging enough. Well, no, I don't do that.

VB: Robert McCarter suggested that Wright's Usonian Houses are perhaps closest in spirit to your buildings. Could you talk about some of your strongest influences?

BH: It is very nice of Robert to say that. It was taken as an enormous compliment and challenge. He is a teacher of teachers, as well as students and other architects, and — at the University of Florida — was one

of the first to invite me to teach a design studio. I probably visited two dozen of those Wright homes across the country. What I think Robert meant was that a parallel path between Wright's Usonian houses and mine exists that includes and incorporates a sense of shelter, domesticity, scale, proportions, fragility, materiality, and so on. My grandparents grew up in Oak Park, where everyone was aware of Wright, of course. He was always a strong reference for me. Yet, despite the fact that his work is so public, so vast, and so incredible, I don't remember his name ever being mentioned during my years at Yale. There was more focus on European modernists, such as Aalto, Schindler, Neutra, Breuer (all practicing here), and American architects such as Kahn, Sullivan, and Rudolph. These are the architects that deeply influenced me as, of course, Wright did. All these architects were making architecture as they saw fit — for that place and time — and it did not seem prescribed or formulaic to me.

A contemporary architect whose work I admire greatly is Alvaro Siza. Yet, I have to say that all these architects create the kind of work that cannot be taught. What I mean by that is that it is intuitive, visceral, and very personal. And it being personal can make some people uncomfortable because — if it is personal then it is individual — and it cannot be promoted as a methodology or a system. It seems to me that individualism and a healthy disregard of preordained paths feed art and it should fuel design. But I haven't seen it recognized — or encouraged — in either our schools or our professional offices. When I talk about individualism, I am not promoting mindless expression or dismissing precedents. I am talking about reinvention, reexamining, rediscovering, and illuminating some fundamental values that were articulated by those who preceded us — and a few currently working alongside that still do. What's important to me is to acknowledge that great architecture comes from the study and experience of other buildings and places, whether vernacular or heroic. It is critical to rethink old questions within each new circumstance.

VB: I read that you get more pleasure from looking at paintings rather than architecture. Could you talk about that?

BH: That is true if the emphasis is on looking rather than experiencing. If I had to sit in a lawn chair in front of a building then, yes, I would rather sit in front of a painting. I find paintings often challenging and inspirational. Architecture can do the same, but you must get out of that chair. You must move around. Architecture is not a static thing. It is dependent on the weather, the season, the time of day, aging, and on and on. When I was at school those experiential factors, were also "out there," not just in the studio. I guess you could say that we also needed to get off the stool in the studio — or the nearby bar stool — and walk around. Conveniently, New Haven has many great buildings and spaces to explore — many good places to get lost.

VB: You also paint on the side. What kind of paintings are they?

BH: I would not call it "on the side" — it is integral. My paintings are not directly related to the projects. The collages are, I suppose, as I work on them to study the projects — working on composition, proportion, texture, etc. But when I look at my paintings over the years, even if they are unrelated to my projects, they are usually paintings of various buildings. As we speak, and I look around the studio, I see the Pyramids in Giza, a house on Key West, a Shaker village, and a dozen or so new studies of a little chapel that I love up here in New Hampshire caught in a storm.

VB: Are these paintings abstract reinterpretations? You don't paint what you see, right?

BH: [Laughs.] Well, that's a good and provocative question! I paint what I see. You may think it is abstract, but I paint what I see.

VB: You paint what you see. But what you see is not what everyone else sees. Is that what you mean?

BH: That's another good question. And I don't know the answer to that. Again, I paint what I see. But when I am done, I am curious whether others understand my particular view. People who are familiar with what I paint will recognize it. But, of course, my paintings are interpretative and how I think about what I paint is personal. As with architecture in general, if you want to engage architecture, you need to make it personal. If you ask me to work on your project, I will let you know what I think, and I wouldn't want to have a client — or colleague — who doesn't want to know what I think. But then we also often disagree, and I can change my opinion if a better alternative is presented. New propositions can always be made but I ask for some openness and an honest exchange of ideas.

VB: Could you talk in more detail about one of your projects, Harbor House in Sag Harbor, New York? The reason I picked it is because it appears to be a very sculptural and abstract work, perhaps inspired by some cubist paintings. Irrespectively of how it works, what's the context, and what life goes in it, I like its abstract nature and a potential for inhabiting it. It also appears to be a part of a series, a pursuit of a sculptural idea, meaning it goes beyond its program. And your houses seem to share a common language, they are a family.

BH: I never thought of it that way, but I can see that — each house has its own history — but they could also be seen as an extended family. The house on Long Island came out of many conversations with that particular client. CJ is a movie producer who would ride his motorcycle up from New York to Boston for our meetings. He said that he needed the time to get ready for our discussions. For him, like everything else, the house was an adventure. It was going to be his second home, not a primary residence, but he wanted something special and he believed that I was the right person to help him. As you mentioned, it is similar to other houses that we have built. It is perhaps a bit simpler than some houses in California, Pennsylvania, or New Jersey. But it was special for me to be working with him on such a beautiful site. There is a twist in the geometry that I think adds intimacy to the common areas and allows it to be less static. There is also a shift in that building that turns in on itself protecting inside and looking out onto the harbor that adds a sculptural element as well. That was a strategic move to make the interior more intimate.

VB: Is there one manifesto project in your work that pointed to a certain direction for you? In other words, was there an epiphany moment in your practice that suddenly gave you a new sense of direction?

BH: I think the path meanders and it is very much about change and evolution. I am interested in discovering a new potential for each place rather than applying something or projecting my own meaning and style. I enjoy exploring those potentials. I taught architecture for many years and I think — in school — that it is important to empower students by letting them explore what they are interested in - new worlds that they can discover. I get tired of listening to faculty who are always telling students what they are supposed to be doing. As educators, we should allow students to explore and express what they think their place in the world is. Granted, there is a long list of criteria to evaluate that from, but they should be allowed to initiate the discussion in studio.

VB: You just mentioned about your teaching experience. What is it that you like about it most and what is your favorite assignment for students?

BH: I always encourage students to begin by looking at great precedents such as a house by Barragan, Schindler, Aalto, Corb, Nishazawa, or Zumthor. To build a new model by hand of that project, in order to study and understand the setting and the drawings it generated. The idea is to establish a methodology — how do you get from nothing to something. You need to identify a design path for yourself. Once you study a particular work in depth — by making a model and reconstructing drawings — it gets into your blood — and you start relating to it — you start wanting to change it. We are not making things up; we are building our ideas on the shoulders of other people who have done great work. And, for me, that's what architecture is about — we never start from nothing, we continue what others have already begun — intellectually, compositionally, socially, and philosophically.

VB: And what happens after the analysis?

BH: After a couple of weeks of analyzing a certain precedent, I would ask students to design another building type in a particular part of a city. It's interesting, though, that once they studied a particular work, I've often found that there is an unavoidable dialogue between what they studied and the development of their own design project. The analysis had set a standard, if you will. They now understand what a plan is, what a section is, what a building may look like. It opens avenues into new ways of thinking. It also creates a great starting point for their own individual analysis and design. It is not about how to dream up something completely new, but about asking fundamental questions such as a place having its own history. In a way, this method is arbitrary, but it is also evocative and often influential. The students may not know the difference between a concrete building and a wood structure, but once they analyze the particular materials and their characteristics, they start to understand how the selection of material — or construction system — or detail — will lead to completely different conclusions.

VB: You said, "Architecture is not just about forms and materials, it is a social act." Did you refer to your floating residential community project on the water in Boston Harbor?

BH: Yes, and others, but Floatyard is a great experiment. Ed Nardi commissioned this project a few years back. We had worked together on several projects in the city before this one. He had a speculative and provocative idea to reenergize Boston Harbor and animate its edges. He wondered if a building could float. He asked simply ... "what if we make a new site instead of finding one?"

He was thinking about the abandoned piers along the coast of Charlestown and the Boston Harbor, which used to be the center of the city. It was an industrial zone, but now was being repurposed and animated with structures in place of coastal shipyards. Of course, it was right on the water. We found precedents in cities like Amsterdam and the idea is not as novel as it first seemed. As far as a social agenda, it is not just going to be limited to people who live there; it is about bringing the city to the water — and the harbor back to the shoreline. In our housing design, we relied on a classic courtyard model and studied different forms of communal living in various cultures to propose something special, even delicate. We also addressed the issue of rising sea levels and proposed using pneumatic pistons that would adjust the building's level along with the rising tide and generate energy. It is a speculative project, still ongoing, but with a lot of potential. Both former and current mayors expressed support for the project, and it received strong support in the press. I am confident that something like it will happen one day in Boston Harbor. Hopefully, it will be with our involvement.

VB: What are the key intentions of your work?

BH: Most importantly, I believe that we need to create beautiful places for people to live and to share with others.

VB: And your friend Marlon Blackwell wrote that you have a deep love for ordinariness. What do you think he meant?

BH: Marlon likes to talk about architecture as being "a matter of inches." I suppose that he means the everyday — the chores, the groceries, the cooking, food, drink, maybe your pillow. I want to do a kind of architecture that's accessible and legible, that is relevant to its place. I don't think it is magic, but it does require thought and study. Great buildings — and not so great buildings — are all achieved through hard work. Anyone can understand a great work of architecture, but it needs beauty and a good plan. It isn't magic — it's inches, not feet.

VB: Yet, you have traveled the world; wouldn't you agree that there are masterpieces out there so powerful that they come pretty close to being magical?

BH: Magical? Yes, but they don't come from magic. There's no pixy dust that I know of. They come from intuition, study, patience, culture, and hard work — probably with many subliminal connections that we chose to overlook. After graduation, I used traveling scholarship money from Yale, the Van Allen, and AAR to travel around the world by myself for a year, exploring ancient ruins in Britain, Italy, Greece, Crete, Egypt, India, Nepal, and Thailand. The Taj Mahal was out of this world but so were the caves at Ajanta and Ellora.

VB: Jujani Pallasmaa said, "The door handle is the handshake of the building." Could you talk about how you approach some of the smallest details in your work? What are your priorities? What do you pay most attention to?

BH: I love Juhani's many great observations, but I do not think his intention was that we all start designing doorknobs. I prefer other reflective notions such as "the patience of a tree." I recall a special visit with him in Helsinki — arranged by Peter MacKeith — with a few other American architects and educators back in 2006. He is a kind and generous soul who is open to sharing and hearing other thoughts. It seemed the sensory and auditory aspects of architecture were very important to him such as the resounding footfall that announces your entry into the beautiful country church in Petajavesi. I agree that sounds are crucial to experience. But again, what we do as architects is set up these poetic opportunities for other people to enjoy with their own experiences. We don't need to dictate anything one way or another. If I design spaces where people can enjoy themselves, I am happy. Of course, there are masterpieces that are beyond just providing these opportunities. They are unique on their own. I also recall spending time at the Villa Mairea while in Finland. That work is beyond explanation or rationalization. It is a place of pure joy on the level of other buildings such as either Taliesin by Wright in Spring Green or Scottsdale, Siza's Boa Nova Tea House in Porto, or Barragán's House and Studio in Mexico City. We need to absorb those sensations, but it doesn't mean that all architecture needs to even aspire to reach that level. There is always a role for the commonplace — but to ignore the potency of any precedent is a mistake.

VB: In many years of practice what are some of the key lessons you learned about practicing architecture that you would like to share?

Pages 796-797 Summer Compound façade. **Above left** Petajavesi Old Church, Petajavesi, Finland (church 1763 + bell tower 1821). **Above right** Entry court at Taliesin West, Scottsdale, Arizona. **Opposite page** Detail of Lincoln Street Garage in Boston.

BH: Engaging architecture requires a multitude of experiences and a real need for opportunities. It is a difficult process and a difficult profession, but I would not choose anything else. I can also say that I have never been bored with it. But you really need to love it and, in order to love it, you need to come to your own understanding of its role in your life and the lives of others. It is not preordained — or neutral — or static — or limited to preconceptions that are either your own or those of others. You get to determine what your time is worth, while - constantly — acknowledging that what others are doing is probably not worth thinking about.

VB: What single term words or short phrases would you use to describe your work or the kind of architecture that you try to achieve?

BH: I love that architecture is specific. It is always someplace; it can't be anyplace. A good building is always an addition to its place, to what is there. Nothing is ever new, and one needs to understand what is there before adding to it. I think good architecture is about integrity, beauty, compassion, how it sits on the site, and about a commitment to its neighbors. As a counterpoint, I would use the word "unfortunate" to describe most of the buildings that we see around us every day. The lack of thought — or effort — is openly apparent. But, still, every now and then we discover a glimpse of inspiration out there. While the profession — and a large portion of the general public — seem unconcerned about social unrest, a looming ecological crisis, and an unsettled political landscape, we do have individuals and groups attempting to affect positive change which is always encouraging. We just need to do more and do so more vocally.

VB: Do you think about progress in your work? Do you consciously think about a particular progression from project to project?

BH: I find satisfaction in the work itself. And I am very happy working out of the spotlight. Interesting things happen in the shadows. Of course, I am the same person. I ask similar questions - or maybe the same question, over and over - never sure. People often tell me that my work has been consistent over the years. Depending on who tells me this, it could be thought of as a criticism or a compliment. [Laughs.] Thanks, Vladimir, I appreciated the opportunity to have this conversation.

ESSAY

Like a convalescent, I took the hand
stretched down from the jetty, sensed again
an alien comfort as I stepped on ground
to find the helping hand still gripping mine,
fish-cold and bony, but whether to guide
to be guided I could not be certain...

...Your obligation
is not discharged by any common rite.
What you must do must be done on your own
so get back in harness. The main thing is to write
for the joy of it. Cultivate a work-lust
that imagines its haven like your hands at night
dreaming the sun in the sunspot of a breast.
You are fasted now, light-headed, dangerous.
Take off from here. And don't be so earnest,
let others wear the sackcloth and the ashes.
Let go, let fly, forget.

Station Island XII - Seamus Heaney

BRIAN HEALY

NOTES ON EDUCATION AND INTUITION

As educators and designers, we often try to formalize a method for getting from nothing to something. These exercises are designed to draw ourselves, our clients, and the community into the project, and eventually, to own an attitude about its site and assemblage. But formulaic methods ignore the possibility that those involved already have a sense of what should be there.

How you value architecture determines where you first go when you begin to design. If you start in your head, for example, architecture is an intellectual pursuit. If you start in your hands, architecture is both craft and sculpture. If you start with a theory, architecture is a mathematical proof. If you start with history, architecture is a continuation. And if you begin with poetry, architecture can become a dream.

Regardless, the beginning is critical. Once you adopt your generative tool, once the objectives have been drawn and the lines are hardened in pixels or graphite, the project has shape and direction, a genetic code. You may conscientiously acknowledge the code, or you may suppress it, but no amount of cladding can conceal the bones of the idea.

Everyone of a certain age – whether undergraduate or graduate student — has been living and interacting with buildings and places for decades. If we've kept our eyes open, we already have a sense of place. This is what I call architectural instinct. Instinct is an innate pattern of behavior, a response to specific environmental stimuli. You put your hand up to block a punch; or extend an arm to protect yourself from a fall. I've taken some liberties to apply it to spatial understanding, but I think it's an easy extension of the idea. Instinct is what we know works and what doesn't work, architecturally, spatially, just from living in this particular world, constrained by gravity, building methods and materials. Instinct tells us that stairs lead us up, and stairs lead us down. A door is an opening to another room. A window offers light, air — and sometimes — a view. Floors can usually carry our weight, and

Above left and right Steeple Studies 2020

walls separate one space from another. Instinct helps us navigate through unfamiliar space. All sentient humans have these instincts.

So what does an architectural training add to this knowledge? How does an architect's solution differ from an untrained designer? What is there to learn? My answer is intuition. Intuition is the essential ingredient in the teaching and expression of creativity. And — in design studios and seminars — I like to explore an architect's intuition, how it is developed, and how we can listen to it; how it can lead us from nothing to something. How acknowledging it and nourishing it can result in design excellence.

First, let's look a little closer at intuition. Intuition is a direct or immediate apprehension, an understanding that excludes all inference, all discursive reasoning, which is an indirect, rather than a direct, mode of apprehension. But unlike other methods of apprehension, intuition is the result of training and education.

I will explain this by using the 17th century philosopher, Spinoza, to help set up the argument. In Spinoza's work, he defines the three ways that we think, and sets them hierarchically. The first is a kind of crude, basic sensory-perception, which we don't need to discuss here. The second, higher stage is a rational understanding of things, based on empirical evidence. We've discussed that above, and termed it instinct. You've seen stairs before, so you know how to use them.

The highest level of thinking is what Spinoza calls "intuitive knowledge." Intuitive knowledge is based on seeing the connectedness of all things, recognizing the complex patterns that make up our universe. It's knowing that streets connect with other streets, and highways, and cities, and states. It's looking out to sea and understanding that the horizon is not the edge of the earth. Intuition is based on both

what one has experienced, and what one has learned, but not directly experienced. Intuition allows us to understand that the earth is round, even though its radius is too great for us to directly perceive. Intuition allows us to imagine a construction similar, though not exactly the same, as a construction we have already seen. Intuition allows us to expand on ideas, taking them a beyond what is known. Intuitive knowledge is at the heart of any intellectual and creative endeavor.

Armed with a strong intuitive sense of space and its components, an architect can move beyond derivative design, recognize good ideas, and pursue them. Honing intuition, and learning to trust intuition, I believe, is the greatest gift an educator can give, but it is also the most difficult process to develop, and not everyone is capable of reaping its rewards. Unlike instinct, we are not born with the ability to intuit good design. We must develop our intuition through hard work and conscious application.

So, how does an architect get from nothing to something? How does an architect develop an intuition that is strong, capable, and unique? That specific method is determined by the architect's deepest understanding of the responsibility of architecture.

In my practice and the studios that I conduct, architecture has four unquestionable duties:

1. Architecture has the responsibility to function in plan, so that one can use instinct to find one's way around. All plans reflect a social organization; they imply a complex structure of interrelatedness between space and the program. How wisely a plan functions depends on the architect's understanding of human movement. An architect learns how people move through and occupy space by watching, by walking, by listening. I walk through cities. I walk through plans, and I walk through buildings. Architecture should not dictate human movements; it should facilitate them.

2. Architecture has the responsibility to be beautiful, to have a sense of proportion, scale, and materiality. And this is important: beauty doesn't come from a vacuum. The eye requires constant training, through study of fine art, architecture, and the articulation of building components. We constantly learn from what preceded us — there is nothing completely new.

3. Architecture has the responsibility to connect to the site, to be a catalyst in a positive transformation of place and an appropriate addition to what that place is becoming. As one understands the architecture of a place as the complex connection of materials and spaces, sidewalks and streets, there is little room left for heroics or monumental moves.

4. We move at a specific speed, and our dimensions vary within small increments. Our experience is bound by the walls and portals and apertures, the scale of things. These are the variables that we work with in the studio: the materiality of walls and scale of apertures within reach that relate directly to the human form. It seeks to become a celebration of humanity — of all things human.

Opposite page Brian Healy, *Key West*, 1998

CHRONOLOGY

BUILDING PROJECTS / STUDIOS / TEACHING POSITIONS

Building Projects
Florida
Estero
- Open House – 1982, 1994, 2018
- Rural Nursery - 1983

Alva
- River House - 1986

California
Lake Elsinore
- Civic Center - 2007

Ross
- HZ West - 2002

Dillon Beach
- Hill House - 2009
- Court House - 2010

Long Beach
- Community Housing - 2004

Saint Helena
- Vineyard House - 2002
- Small Lodge - 1994
- Wall House - 1991

Massachusetts
Boston
- Pier 7 - 2014
- Innovation Center - 2013
- E.M. Kennedy Institute - 2008
- Downtown Crossing - 2003
- Lincoln Street Garage - 1999
- Enfold -2012
- BAC Installation - 2009
- Rose Kennedy Greenway - 2008
- Urban Prep School - 1996
- 88 Wareham - 2016
- DOT Common - 2017
- Haymarket Square - 2012
- Floatyard - 2013
- Kenmore - 2014

Brookline
- Brookline High School - 2019
- Education and Community Center - 2010

Cambridge
- Harvard SEAS - 2007
- Boston Film - 1988
- Cambridge Conversion - 2002

Lowell
- Student Center - 2014

Amherst
- Stadium Additions - 2014

Waltham
- Art Complex - 1992

Winchendon
- United Parish of Winchendon - 2020

Duxbury
- Tree House - 2019

Essex
- Boathouse - 2008

Hyannisport
- Shriver Guest House - 2009

Dartmouth
- House On Buzzards Bay - 1988

Watertown
- Urban Duplex - 1990

Siasconset
- HZ East - 1991

New Jersey
Long Beach Island
- Summer Compound - 1994
- Beach House - 1996
- Bayside House - 1992
- Sandy Cove - 1993

Atlantic City
- Housing Prototypes - 1998

Longport
- Jetty House - 1991

North Carolina
Hendersonville
- Mill Center for the Arts - 2004

Boone
- Rural Pool Hall - 1995

Illinois
Chicago

Intergenerational Learning Center - 2003
Mixed Income Housing - 2000
Apartment Building - 2001

New York
Buffalo
FLW Visitors' Center - 2002
Sag Harbor
Sag Harbor House - 1998
Tannersville
Onteora Tower - 2001
New York
Chelsea Loft - 2002

Pennsylvania
Media
Pool House - 2002

Rhode Island
Providence
Grant Recital Hall - 2006
Fulton Concert Hall - 2007
Newport
Community Center - 2019
Charlestown
Sound Addition - 2007

Maine
Portland
Maine Medical Center - 2012

New Hampshire
Jackson
Jackson Fire - 2020
Ellis River Studio - 2020

Connecticut
Farmington
Jackson Lab - 2013

Virginia
Alexandria
Country Day School - 2012
Blacksburg
Town Center - 1988

Utah
Salt Lake City
Entrepreneur Center - 2014

Arkansas
Bentonville
Children's Enrichment Center - 2017

Studios
Fort Myers, Florida: 1982-83
Brooklyn, New York: 1984
Boston, Massachusetts: 1985-96
Peterborough, New Hampshire: 1994
East Cambridge, Massachusetts: 1996-2000
Temecula, California: 1999
Boston, Massachusetts: 2000-2008
Amherst, Massachusetts: 2007
Somerville, Massachusetts: 2008-
Montreal, Quebec: 2009
Jackson, New Hampshire: 2017-

Teaching Positions
Rhode Island School of Design: 1988
Pennsylvania State University: 1991-92
University of Virginia: 1992
New Jersey Institute of Technology: 1996, 1999
University of Florida: 1996
Dartmouth College: 1997
University of Michigan: 1997
University of Pennsylvania: 1997, 1998, 1999, 2000
Yale School of Architecture: 2001, 2002, 2003, 2004, 2005
Massachusetts Institute of Technology: 2001, 2002, 2003
Harvard Graduate School of Design: 2004, 2012
Washington University in Saint Louis: 2005,
University of Arkansas: 2006
Amherst College: 2007
Roger Williams University: 2007, 2008, 2013
Middlebury College: 2008
Boston Architectural College: 2009
McGill University: 2009
City College of New York: 2010, 2014
University Of Cincinnati: 2018

Academic Positions
Building Projects
Lectures + Exhibitions

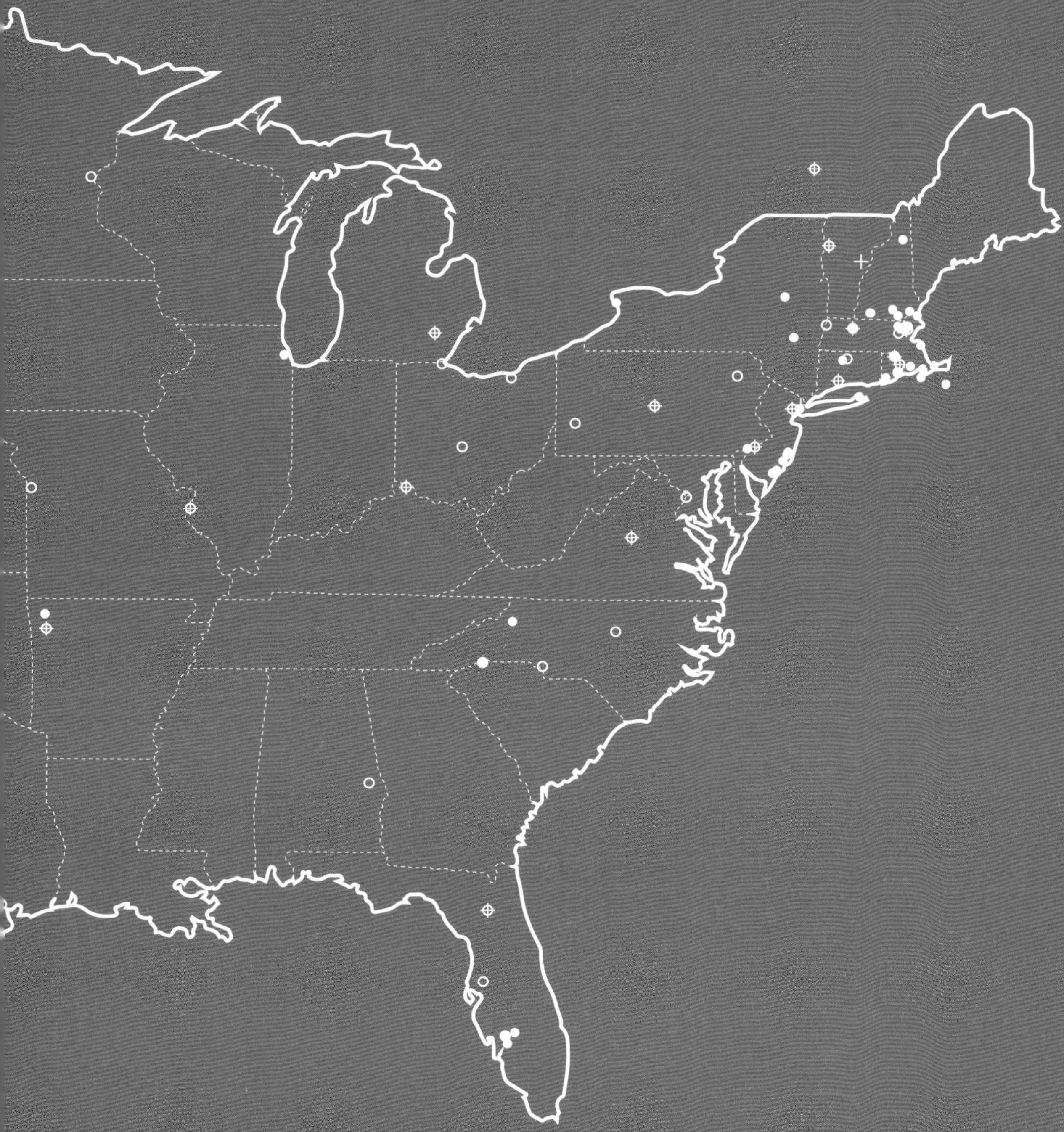

Marlon teaches, as do I, because of the great sense of responsibility to add a measure of reality to the education of architectural students while also supporting the theoretical or less pragmatic aspects of their education.

Thom Mayne

MARLON BLACKWELL

A SONG NEEDS AN ADDRESS

Marlon Blackwell with Jonathan Boelkins

Brian Healy is a storyteller. While he can tell a great story in person, far greater are the stories his buildings tell through the language of architecture, an act reminiscent of how traditional storytellers use unique dialogue and personal interaction with an audience to create a living art. Brian's stories are his buildings, each telling the history of their place, their climate, their building traditions. Such an approach is inherently tectonic and elemental, relying on articulation and materiality to communicate, and while scale varies dramatically, the underlying message is consistent and ever-present.

Having practiced initially in Boston, I have a specific appreciation for Brian's ability to create such a distinct and distinguished body of work in what is arguably America's oldest city. Boston's medieval streets and steeped traditions hardly lend themselves to modern interpretation and more often suffocate them. It's precisely this context that reveals an audacity, a willingness to adapt, to mix and combine the local and the universal.

Perhaps my favorite story of his comes from his college days at Yale. Almost offhandedly he recounted how as a first-year architecture student, he would, uninvited, bring his design work to the offices of the storied senior faculty for review. Without fear and without appointment, he would knock on the door of Vincent Scully, once described by Philip Johnson as "the most influential architectural teacher ever," for an impromptu review. At some point, Brian laughed as he told the story, looking down into his drink as if looking back in time, realizing both the naivete this took and the formative value that resulted. When asked how he had such audacity, he simply said, "pretension precedes profession."

Brian and I share many things, the first being a willingness to knock on doors uninvited, doors literal and figurative, doors mythical and mundane. In my case, I was selling Bibles across the Deep South to people who already had them, paying my way through architecture school and getting another education entirely. We didn't know each other in college, but together we were engaging culture at opposite ends of the

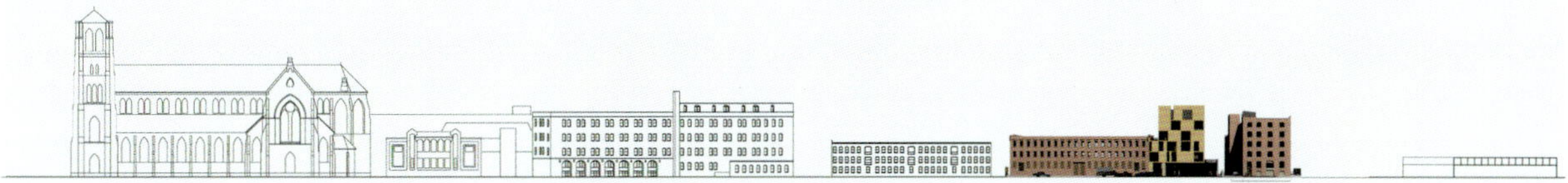

Above Elevation of Wareham Street in the South End of Boston. Above Axonometric of Open House.

spectrum, high culture and low culture, immersing ourselves in the ideal and the real. We both recognized the remarkable source of inspiration we had found, but also intuitively understood their limitations. Coming from seemingly opposite directions, we arrived at the same conclusion, that, as Alvar Aalto said, "Even the smallest daily chore can be humanized with the harmony of culture."

For me, I needed the counterweight of the universal, of the ideal. Brian needed the immediate and the ordinary as a way to humanize and transform the ideal, knowing that, in the words of Tom Waits, "A song needs an address." Though we departed from seemingly opposite conditions and directions, we arrived as fellow travelers with a profound appreciation of the potency of the ordinary and its ability to transform into the extraordinary, for seemingly low culture to be injected with dignity and become high culture. It should go without saying that this isn't easy. This kind of practice is demanding, requiring every last bit of willpower and curiosity, adhering to principles rather than any kind of stylistic de rigueur. Every project is born instead out of the combination of the particularities of place while inviting in the timeless oeuvre of architecture.

This is something that Brian and I share at the most fundamental level, a love for what I like to call the architecture of architecture: details, articulation, transition, elements like columns, doors, windows, stairs. These elements are the mediating scale between the scale of building and the scale of the hand; taken individually they often provide the most direct experience, the places where we actually come into physical contact, but together they aggregate to form patterns and fields, the very texture of our streets and cities. It is in the articulation and organization of the elements that the diagram is transcended, that architecture becomes Architecture of the highest aspirations.

There is an inherent challenge in this as every project must be considered anew. While some lessons endure, each new site, client, and program demand a reconsideration of everything before. What emerges, to paraphrase Peter Eisenman, is the project and The Project. The project is the one at hand with all its immediacy; The Project is the entirety of practice, its direction, its meaning, its value. As much as we both value and hold dear our built works, it is affirming to see so many unrealized projects included here, deposits in a spiritual savings bank that we draw from more often than anyone knows.

Another commitment that Brian and I share is an equal dedication to teaching and practice, and an understanding of how they resonate and reverberate. Teaching and creative practice are truly inseparable for our kind of practice, where lessons from each solve challenges in the other. Teaching establishes the expectation that such a practice operates at a very high level because it is held out for our students to see. Put simply, we practice what we preach: rigor, iteration, craft, discipline. Teaching provides another way through which ideas are filtered, a laboratory where theories are tested, refined, and tested again, all in the hopes that they too graduate and move into the real world.

Whether in teaching or practice, ideas get nurtured in the shadows, not in the spotlight. It is rare for anything of value to simply burst forth, contrary to the creative genius myth, so efficiently dismissed by Chuck Close, who says, "Inspiration is for amateurs. The rest of us just show up and get to work." While the quality and quantity of Brian's work is evident in the heft of the book itself, there is an even greater body of work — *The Work* — that isn't seen, produced by a relentless commitment to turning a problem over and over and over, to moving successively closer to solutions, to teasing truth out of endless models and mockups, out of late nights and weekends, out of drawing on anything and everything.

For practices like ours, there is no more efficient spoon with which to stir than a good pencil. Our offices are overwhelmingly digital, but nothing replaces the need for drawing, preferably with a big, soft lead, but even a good, yellow 2B pencil will do the job when put to a fresh roll of canary yellow trace, a new page of a Moleskine sketchbook, or even the cliché of a cocktail napkin. Nothing allows us to work as quickly, to record impressions and absorb influences, to mix the local and the universal as a drawing. The immediacy and tactility of drawing allows ideas to flow in a way that is simultaneously ancient and modern. Pencils offer simpler beginnings as they require so little from us, important because the beginnings are critical even though they are often ordinary.

But from these humble beginnings and a deep love for ordinariness, Brian has built a distinct and distinguished body of work. His work is that of a citizen architect, deeply committed to architecture's lofty role in creating culture but in a way that is born out of creating beloved spaces that are filled with natural light and tactile materials. Eschewing the default position of glass boxes with perforated panels or louvers, or "screens and things" as I disparagingly refer to them, walls thicken once more, rich materials catch the zenithal light that drifts in, and we are transported. This is the opposite of what we tend to get today: the thin, fast and explicit work that is more shape than form.

Form is important to Brian, but it is his dedication to articulation that really drives the work and bears witness to what he believes architecture is. Volumes and materials are equally interlocked and interwoven, regardless of scale, like the most powerful of still lifes. I wish there was a Brian Healy building I could cut through on my walk to work, so I could sit along an edge and watch the light change, illuminating crisp joints and subtle grains. I'd like to sit in the window and watch the life on the street, to sit there and draw for a while, to feel like I am a part of the story he tells, one of the patient search for true things, of hope and possibility.

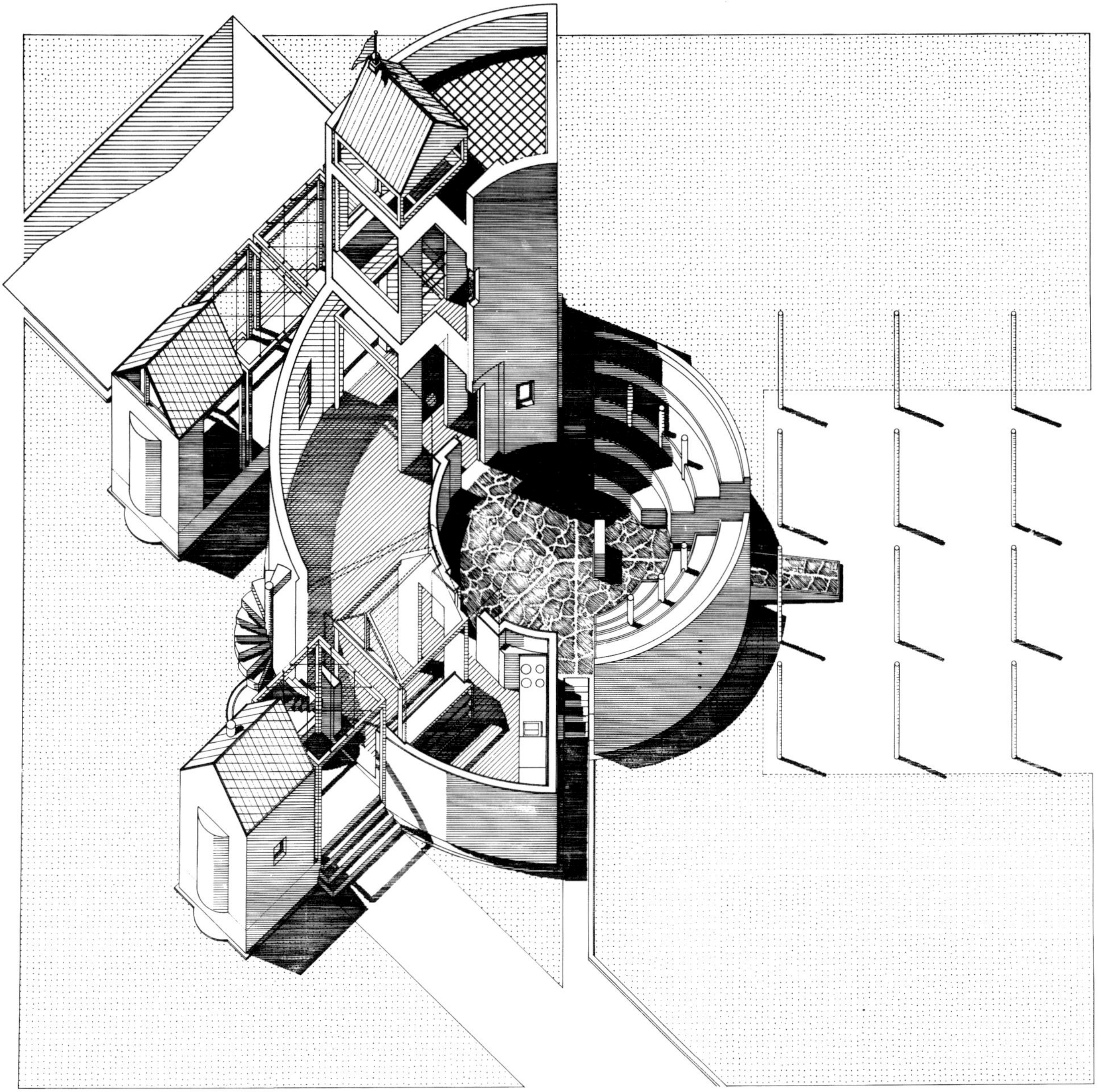

Marlon Blackwell, FAIA, is a practicing architect in Fayetteville, Arkansas, and serves as the E. Fay Jones Distinguished Professor at the Fay Jones School of Architecture and Design at the University of Arkansas. Blackwell is the recipient of the 2020 AIA Gold Medal. He was a 2019 Resident Fellow of the American Academy in Rome, inducted into the 2018 National Academy of Design, and selected as a 2014 United States Artists Ford Fellow. Work produced in his professional office (MBA), has received national and international recognition with significant publication in books, architectural journals and magazines and more than 140 domestic and international awards. MBA received the 2016 Cooper Hewitt National Design Award in Architecture. **Jonathan Boelkins** is an architect and writer who teaches at the Fay Jones School of Architecture and Design at the University of Arkansas. Formerly the Studio Director at Marlon Blackwell Architects, he made significant contributions to numerous award-winning projects including the Ruth Lilly Visitor's Pavilion at the Indianapolis Museum of Art, the Saint Nicholas Eastern Orthodox Church, and Shelby Farms Park. As a writer, he captures the essential qualities and aspirations of architecture, and his work has been featured in several books.

ACKNOWLEDGE

WHEN WE SCAN THINGS FOR THE SHAPE OF THE PAST, everything about them deserves our attention. Yet this conclusion, which is self-evident once we recognize that things alone allow us to know the past, is generally ignored under the demands of specialized study. Archaeological studies and the history of science are concerned with things only as technical products, while art history has been reduced to a discussion of the meanings of things — without much attention to their technical or formal organization. The task of the present generation is to construct a history of things that will do justice both to meaning and being, both to the plan and to the fullness of existence, both to the scheme and to the thing. This purpose raises the familiar existential dilemma between meaning and being. We are discovering little by little all over again that what a thing means is not more important than what it is; that expression and form are equivalent challenges to the historian; and to neglect either meaning or being, either essence or existence, deforms our comprehension of both.

***The Shape of Time* - George Kubler**

TEACH + RESIDE

Yale Building Project / Studios + Seminars

Dean Stern invited Healy to join the faculty at the Yale School of Architecture to work with Paul Brouard, Alan Organschi, Adam Hofner, and other faculty members – for five years – on the First Year Building Project at Yale. This studio presents a powerful opportunity for young architects and designers to engage in responsible construction techniques and recognize our obligations to community involvement. Architecture students have become increasingly more interested in how they can play an active and positive role in the development of their communities and how they can participate in the protection and appropriate use of the broader environment. A fundamental mission for an education in design – and in our collective design culture – should be to support curricular and extra-curricular activities that nurture this social responsibility within our students as they begin to anticipate their professional lives.

For the past thirty years, Healy has taught architectural design at twenty-one of the most accomplished design institutions in the North America. This teaching experience involved both undergraduate and graduate-level design studios and seminars establishing the essential connections between a built environment and its place in the world. Other academic leaders who have invited Healy to teach in their programs include: Peter Magyar, Ken Schwartz, Robert McCarter, Richard Wesley, Stanford Anderson, Toshiko Mori, Cynthia Weese, Peter MacKeith, Marlon Blackwell, Urs Gauchet, Tim de Noble, Ed Mitchell, and others.

Of particular note, Deans Ranalli and White have extended multiple appointments for Healy to teach at the City College of New York and Roger Williams University, as well as support extensive exhibitions of his work in their galleries. These exhibitions provided essential opportunities to organize and develop the work presented in this book.

Residencies

Graduating from Yale School of Architecture, Healy received the William Wirt Wincester Travelling Fellowship which – when combined with the Dinkleloo Traveling Fellowship in Architecture from the Van Allen Institute – afforded him the opportunity to take a year and travel alone around the world. The fellowship also included a residency at the American Academy in Rome (2005). Other residencies included studio time at the MacDowell Art Colony in Peterborough, New Hampshire (1994), and the Dorland Mountain Art Colony in Temecula, California (1998). Residencies associated with teachings studio and organizing a public exhibition include being the Artist in Residence at Amherst College (2007), the Cameron Visiting Architect at Middlebury College (2008), and the Gerard Sheff Visiting Professor in Architecture at McGill University in Montreal, Quebec (2009).

Teaching Positions

Rhode Island School of Design, Pennsylvania State University, University of Virginia, New Jersey Institute of Technology, University of Florida, Dartmouth College, University of Michigan, University of Pennsylvania, Yale School of Architecture, Massachusetts Institute of Technology, Harvard Graduate School of Design, Washington University in Saint Louis, University of Arkansas, Amherst College, Roger Williams University, Middlebury College, Boston Architectural College, McGill University, City College of New York, University Of Cincinnati.

Opposite page further left Yale School of Architecture - with Stern and other guest reviewers
Opposite page left MacdDowell's Studio
Right Frank Furness Fisher Library - UPenn
Further right American Academy in Rome

LISTEN

Just after Brian Healy opened his studio in Boston, *Robert Campbell* saw his drawings on a jury review and asked if he could stop by for a visit. One cannot overstate the positive influence that Robert has had in Boston and across the region in his dissection and analysis of numerous works of architecture – particularly as they related to the public realm. Campbell's connection to the history of the place is highlighted in his book – *Cityscapes of Boston: An American City through Time* - which he did with *Peter Vanderwarker* – as well as his many weekly columns for *The Boston Globe*.

That was back in the late eighties, and Robert and Brian have shared lunches, stories, poetry, and conversations on the state of architecture since that meeting. Campbell has a keen understanding of how architects think and how their efforts affect "non-architects" and the evolution of the city. One does not need to always agree with his observations but they will leave one energized by a need to rethink a project – or re-read a poem. Several of the articles that Campbell wrote about Healy's work in the *Boston Globe* are included in this book as well as the following excerpt, which was published in the *Globe Sunday Magazine* after that initial encounter in East Cambridge.

ARTYTECTURE : Forced by a sluggish economy to rechannel their creativity, young architects are inventing new art forms
Robert Campbell

They always seem to work somewhere on the margin of the city – in a half empty warehouse in east Cambridge, a sweatshop in the North End, an abandoned schoolhouse in Newton. They're architects, they're 30-something, and they can't get work. Not enough, anyway, to survive on. Not in this recession. So they've invented a new kind of career: they're mixing architecture and art.

Furhetr left View behind East Cambridge Studio
Left Rembrandt's 'Artist in his Studio'
Opposite page right Point Reyes in Northern California
Opposite page further right Tomales Point -NL Historic Ranch

They all have one thing in common: a love affair with the city and, especially, with the relics of the city's industrial past – the evocative rusting bridges and abandoned rail lines and empty waterfronts. They all seem to know one another, but they do not look at themselves as a group. 'We're not a movement, we're just a conversation' one says. Still they need a name. Let's call them artytects. We'll talk to four *(including Wellington Righter, Frano Violich, Sheila Kennedy, and Brian Healy)* ....

Brian Healy is my third and last stop. Healy doesn't quite fit in, a characterization that would probably delight him. He's the nearest thing to a traditional architect among the four. But he works in the same kind of space. His office occupies the end of a vast area on an upper floor of a largely abandoned warehouse on the Monsignor O'Brien Highway in east Cambridge. His little group of tables and chairs and bright drawings and models looks, in this barren space, like a picnic in the desert.

"I'm on the edge of town," he agrees. He takes a visitor to a high window, pointing out over the industrial scene on the Cambridge-Somerville border, a desolate but visually powerful landscape of railroad yards and a concrete batching plant. You feel as if a European grandee were taking you to a castle window to display his estates."The industrial age is something we should all look at with deference", Healy says, "I don't have any problem with being romantic about it."

Healy designs house, mostly, often on rural sites. The office is full of them. Represented by rough but elegant little models and by small oil paintings. The paintings are works of art. They're done in a style that Healy seems more or less to have invented, combining the lush color and thick oil of the West with a flattened, Asian kind of perspective....

LISTEN

His office is a kind of three-medium museum: art reproductions from every era paper the walls, rock, jazz and classical tapes line the shelves. He's a special fan of Wallace Stevens, citing a poem called "Men Made of Words":

Life consists
Of propositions about life.
Revery is a solitude in
Which
We compose these
Propositions, torn by
Dreams.

He admires Steven's obscurity: "You know you're not quite going to get it." And he's obsessed with art. He likes early American modernists – Marsden Hartley, Milton Avery, Arthur Dove, Stuart Davis – admiring them for what he calls their "awkward groping," for "not being glib," for being unwilling to defer too easily to the more accomplished European modernism of Picasso and Matisse. He likes the sense of a grainy American self — reliance. He also singles out a self-portrait by Rembrandt in Boston's Museum of Fine Arts, of the painter standing at his easel. Healy imagines Rembrandt saying: "I stand here and I make these paintings, and people either buy them or they don't." Obviously, he is thinking of himself and his own stubborn independence....

He's the most poetic and verbally evocative of the group, though his words can sometimes be cloudy. He tries again to define architecture: "All we do as architects is set up the poetics. We make poetic imaginings, and someone else fills them in with living." Then he hits a bull's-eye. "Architecture," says Healy, as if speaking for all the artytects, "is making poetic vacancies."

Boston Globe Sunday Magazine, 5 December 1993

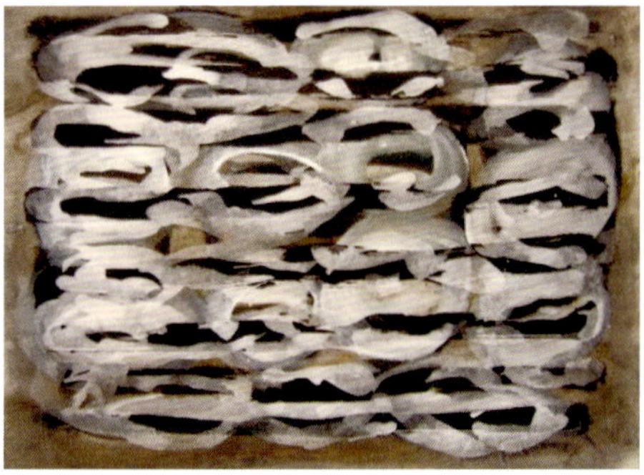

Opposite page from left to right Robert Campbell; Marilyn Ranker - *Passing* - 2007
Right Drawing detail from Rural Pool Hall

LISTEN

"Architects and educators are not defined solely by our professional efforts, or our commitments within the studio and classroom. We also have a civic responsibility to participate in the evolution of our communities — social and cultural — local and global — by volunteering our time." *Brian Healy*

Brian Healy was selected to develop and edit *Perspecta 19: The Yale Architecture Journal* as a graduate student in New Haven. He also served for five years on the *Board of Directors of the Boston Society of Architects* — the largest chapter of the American Institute of Architects — including two years on the Executive Committee and one year as the BSA president. Brian also served as the *Director of Design* between 2011 and 2014 at Perkins+Will — here in Boston - which included a role as a National Director of the ***Social Responsibility Initiative*** which P+W formed to provide pro bono services efforts for non-profit organizations across the country and creates a chance to "contribute to our communities in more personal ways."

Perspecta 19

Perspecta is a prominent academic journal that is published by the *School of Architecture at Yale* with editors being selected on an annual basis by the faculty and administration. This issue was representative of the Class of 1981, and edited by Healy with Nate McBride and Jane Murphy. The graphic design was done by Lorraine Wild.

The journal included interviews with *Cesar Pelli* and *Kevin Roche*, original essays by *Richard Serra, John Hedjuk, George Kubler, Karsten Harries. Alexander Purves, Denzel Hurley, Jay Fellows, Rainer Crone, Peter Millard, and Raymond Abraham.* It also included a lecture by *Louis Kahn* and an essay by *T.S. Eliot.*

Boston Society of Architects

Richard Fitzgerald, as Executive Director, ran the Boston Society of Architects during Healy's involvement with the organization, along with Nancy Jenner. Their focus was on promoting inclusivity and presenting an honest assessment of our responsibilities and obligations as architects and citizens. Healy served on the Executive Board from 2000-2005 and was President in 2004. During that time, he worked with Richard and Nancy, along with Carol Burns, to develop a *Research Grant Program* that distributed supporting funds to individuals and organizations across the country. They also re-energized a popular program *Conversations On Architectur*e that brought practioners, along with academic and civic leaders from across the nation, to talk about their current concerns.

The invited provocateurs with the program included *Ada Louise Huxtable, Michael McKinnell, Robert Campbell, Mitchell Joachim, Peter MacKeith, Carlo Ratti, Brian MacKay-Lyons, Neil Denari, Michael Jones, Mack Scogin, William Mitchell, Ed Mitchell, Nader Tehrani, Robert McCarter, Paul Nakazawa, Rahul Mehrota, Adele Santos, Jonathan Segal, Robert Silver, Ed Schlossberg, Marion Weiss, Ann Beha, Joel Sanders, James Cutler, Kevin Daly, Studio Luz, Hilary Sample, Stefan Behnisch, Hashim Sarkis, Stephen Keiran, Michael Meredith, Ann-Pendleton Julian, Michael Boucher, Brian Healy, Robert Campbell, Yung Ho Chang, Jane Weinzapfel, Andrea Leers, Tim Love, Alex Anmahian, Meejin Yoon, Bill Rawn, Peter Rose, Marc Goulthrorpe, SHIFTBoston, Chris Reed, Maryann Thompson, Doug Reed, Preston Scott Cohen, Ken Greenberg, Rudolfo Machado, Jorge Silvetti, Sheila Kennedy, Frano Violich, Sarah Whiting, Ron Witte, Jonathan Levi, John Fernandez, Merril Elam, Stanford Anderson....*

Opposite page Brian Healy at Ted Talk
Right Richard Fitzgerald and Nancy Jenner
Further right BSA offices at 52 Broad Street, Boston

COLLABORATE

Michael Ryan
Ryan and Healy met during their first day of classes at Penn State back in 1978. When Professor Corbelletti was introducing the program to the incoming freshman, he casually informed them that "only two of you will ever become practicing architects"…. Healy immediately stood up and, when he looked around, Mike was the only other classmate standing. They acknowledged each other from across the room and have been friends ever since. They were also dorm mates at Beam Hall – the A+A dorm on campus – with a theater major, Randee Spelkoman. Mike and Randee met there, fell in love, and have been partners ever since. The built work in New Jersey that has been included in this book was done in collaboration with Mike and Randee, along with Andrew Wilkinson, Michael Meggitt, Chris Jeffrey, and Keith Burns.

Edward Nardi
Nardi and Healy met while wind-surfing in Cataumet down on Cape Cod in 1986, just as Healy was moving to Boston. Nardi was a furniture builder, painter, contractor, and aspiring developer. They have worked on dozens of projects together and many of those projects – included in this book – were done in collaboration with Ed and his partners at *Cresset*, Bill Curtis and John Baxter along with Andrew Castraberti. The projects include *Floatyard, Pier 7, 88 Wareham, 30 Winter Street, Don Bosco, Watertown Duplex, Lincoln Street Garage*, as well as their offices on Water Street in downtown Boston, and his home in Lincoln.

Far left Michael Ryan and Randee Spelkoman
Left 'Drawing a Line' - Ryan+Healy on Penn State's Campus 1978
From left to right Office of P+W Boston; Ed Nardi; Tom Rourke's Studio

Robert Brown

Brown and Healy served together on the Executive Committee and Board of Directors of the *Boston Society of Architects*. Robert was the BSA President in 2003 and Healy followed him as President in 2004. Years later, when Brown was selected as *Managing Director* for the Boston Office of *Perkins + Will*, a prominent international design practice with a strong commitment to both environmental and social responsibility, he asked Healy to join him as *Design Director*. Along with Phil Harrison and fellow Boston principals – Dana Anderson, Sherwood Butler, Jeannine Campbell, David Dymecki, Dennis Kaiser, Tim Marsters, and Gary Shaw – and a large supporting cast of designers and professionals, they sought to develop a new path of organizing and growing a progressive office overlooking Post Office Square and the harbor in downtown Boston.

Tom Rourke

Tom was Design Director at *Wallace Floyd Associates*, a firm founded with Buckminster Fuller to design and build such signature projects as the United States Pavilion at Expo 67. As director, Rourke led a team in charge of the design for prominent civic projects such as the subway station at Logan Airport. While returning to his own practice, he also joined BHA as a senior associate to help on the development of selected projects including the *Korean Church of Boston*, the *Civic Center at Lake Elsinore*, and the *Essex Boathouse*. More recently, Tom and Brian have continued to collaborate on new projects such as *374 Somerville Ave* in Somerville, the *Tree House* in Duxbury, as well as a new fire station and design studio up in Jackson, New Hampshire.

ORGANIZE

Design Panel for Interim Programming

As president of the BSA, Healy joined Ed Schlossberg on *The Mayor's and MTA Design Advisory Panel* for The Rose Fitzgerald Kennedy Greenway. The greenway was a new open, public, urban space that was being created by the removal of the central artery that used to run through downtown Boston. Believing that programming was an essential key to understanding and developing useful places in the public domain, they were asked by the *RFK Conservancy* to create — along with Linda Jonash — a separate committee of local design professionals to form a *Design Panel for Interim Programing* to look at the potential of uses of the parcels adjacent to *South Station* and *Dewey Square* and to develop guidelines for it potential future use. Those panel members included: *Schlossberg (ESI) + Healy (BHA)* as co-chairs along with *Matt Coogan, Matt Johnson (SGH), Laura Solano (MVVA), Linda Wheelock, and Meejin Yoon (HYA).* Some of that work — and selected recommendations for those parcels — are included in this book.

SHIFTboston

Kim Poliquin founded SHIFTboston as a professional organization within the *Boston Society of Architects* to promote the advancement of design-in-practice and in the urban-environment through interdisciplinary design challenges. They created a place for industry professionals to gather, connect, and inspire while generating awareness of the importance of design excellence in architecture, urban planning and technology by hosting inspirational exhibitions, forums and events. They remain committed to the ideas of those who are pushing our profession forward, and expanding progressive thinking in the urban realm.

SHIFTboston hosted 6 design challenges to date that have stretched beyond Boston reaching design professionals around the world. The competitions *"Why not," "moon capital," "float," "why stop,"* and *"glow"* have brought together fascinating minds in — and beyond — our industry. Healy served as jury chair hosting a fleet of outstanding practitioners and thinkers including architects *Thom Mayne, Hillary Sample, Amanda Levete,* and *Stefan Behnisch;* educational leaders *Sarah Whiting, Michelle Addington,* and *Kathryn Dean;* renowned space engineers *Kris Kennedy* and *Brent Sherwood;* and urban innovators *Michael Sorkin* and *Mitch Joachim.*

Left Hands On Enfold
Opposite page above ICA Forum
Opposite page from left to right Milton Avery Etching; Kim Poliquin; Greenway Stadium entry at night; Ed Schlossberg

Milton Avery

TALK

Public Lectures

University of Cincinnati, City College of New York, AIA Colorado Design Conference, Wentworth Institute of Technology, Boston Architectural College, TEDx Boston, Roger Williams University, AIA Toledo, Marywood University, Washington University in Saint Louis, Boston Society of Architects, McGill University, Raleigh/Durham/Chapel Hill AIA, Middlebury College, Kansas State University, Harvard University Graduate School of Design, Amherst College, Keynote Speaker: AIAS Forum 2006, XV Quito Architecture Biennale, University of Arkansas, Boston Public Library, Albright Knox Art Gallery, University of North Carolina, University of Florida, Chicago Cultural Center, Chicago Architecture Foundation, Central States AIA, Tyler School of Art, Rhode Island School of Design, The Architectural League of New York, Northeastern University, University of South Florida, University of Pennsylvania, Dartmouth College, University of Michigan, Yale School of Architecture, Ohio State University, University of Virginia, The Pennsylvania State University

Academic Juries

Amherst College, Boston Architectural College, California College of the Arts, City College of New York, Dartmouth College, Harvard University Graduate School of Design, Massachusetts Institute of Technology, McGill University, Middlebury College, New Jersey Institute of Technology, Northeastern University, North Carolina State University, Ohio State University, Pennsylvania State University, Princeton University, Rhode Island School of Design, Roger Williams University, Syracuse University, Temple University, University of Arkansas, University of California, University of Cincinnati, University of Florida, University of Massachusetts, University of Michigan, University of Pennsylvania, University of South Florida, University of Toronto, University of Virginia, Washington University in Saint Louis, Wentworth Institute, Yale University School of Architecture

Professional Juries

AIA Raleigh/Durham/Chapel Hill Design Awards Program (2011); AIA Minnesota Honor Awards Program (2011); SHIFTboston BARGE Design Competition (2011); SHIFTboston MOON CAPITAL Design Competition (2010); AIA

New York Architecture Design Awards Program (2009); SHIFTboston International Design Competition for Boston (2009); Architectural Research Grant Program, Boston Society of Architects (2004-2009); AIA Raleigh/Durham/Chapel Hill Design Awards Program (2009); AIA Chicago Honor Award Program (2008); AIA Central States Honor Awards Program (2007); Louisiana AIA Honor Awards Program (2007); XV Quito Architecture Biennale, Quito, Ecuador (2006); 52nd Annual Progressive/Architecture Award Program (2006); AIA Seattle Honor Awards Program (2006); National Parks Service Competition, Boston Islands Visitor Center (2006); National Endowment for the Arts Design Competition, Robbins School (2005); Rotch Traveling Scholarship (2003); Rotch Traveling Studio (2003-2004); AIA Central Sates Honor Award Program (2003); AIA Arizona Honor Award Program (2002); AIA South Carolina Honor Awards Program (2001); Lyceum Fellowship (2000)

Studios + Seminars

Rhode Island School of Design: 1988; Pennsylvania State University: 1991-92; University of Virginia: 1992; New Jersey Institute of Technology: 1996, 1999; University of Florida: 1996; Dartmouth College: 1997; University of Michigan: 1997; University of Pennsylvania: 1997, 1998, 1999, 2000; Yale School of Architecture: 2001, 2002, 2003, 2004, 2005; Massachusetts Institute of Technology: 2001, 2002, 2003; Harvard Graduate School of Design: 2004, 2012; Washington University in Saint Louis: 2005; University of Arkansas: 2006; Amherst College: 2007; Roger Williams University: 2007, 2008, 2013; Middlebury College: 2008; Boston Architectural College: 2009; McGill University: 2009; City College of New York: 2010, 2014; University Of Cincinnati: 2018

Opposite page Studio at 374, Brian Healy at Montreal Studio
Right Duxbury Studio
Furthet right Studio at 193

374
SOMERVILLE AVENUE
SOMERVILLE
OPEN
HOUSE
6PM
FRIDAY
04.03.09
BRIAN
HEALY
ARCHITECTS

Left Poster with Shephard Fairey Mural on 374
Opposite page above Paxton, Silvia, and team at Melcher Street studio
Opposite page right Studio at 374

Exhibitions

Yale School of Architecture, The Canterbury Shaker Village, National Building Museum, Roger Williams University, Portland Society of Architecture, SPACE, Pennsylvania State College of Arts and Architecture, Maywood University, Woodbury University Hollywood Gallery, Spitzer School of Architecture, City College of New York, McGill University, Moscow Institute of Architecture, Boston Architectural College, Middlebury College, Harvard University Graduate School of Design, Harvard University, Brickbottom Gallery, Amherst College, University of Minnesota, University of North Carolina, Heinz Architectural Center, Chicago Architecture Foundation, Chicago, Illinois, University of California Los Angeles, Albright Knox Art Gallery, Massachusetts Institute of Technology, Max Protetch Gallery, Dartmouth College, University of Pennsylvania, Lionheart Gallery, Northeastern University, Milan Triennale, University of Florida Gallery, The Berkshire Museum, Spaces Gallery, Steelcase Design Partnership, Emmanuel College, Boston Center for the Arts, Rhode Island School of Design, Museum of Fine Arts, University of South Florida, American Academy in Rome.

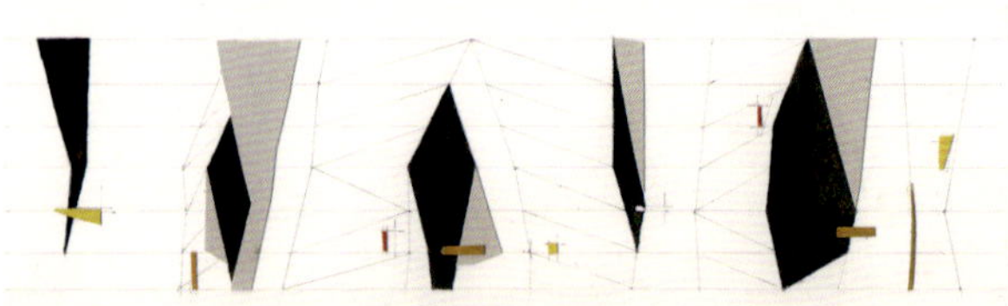

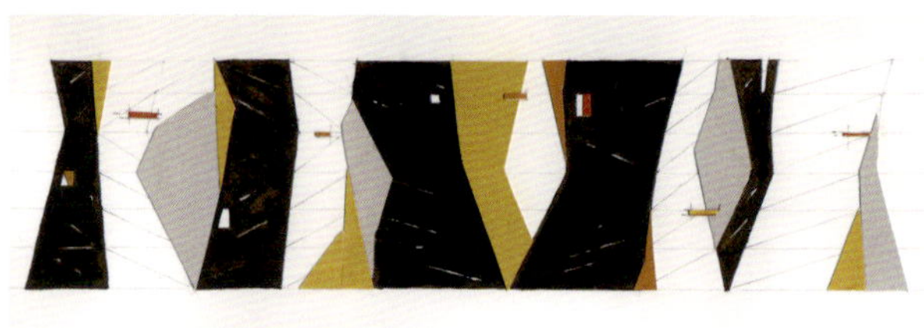

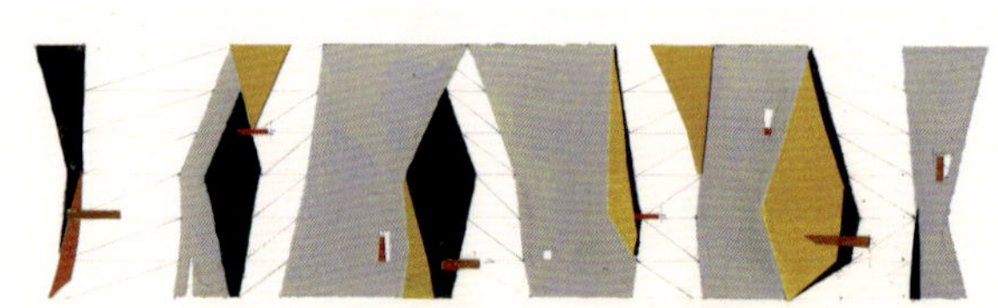

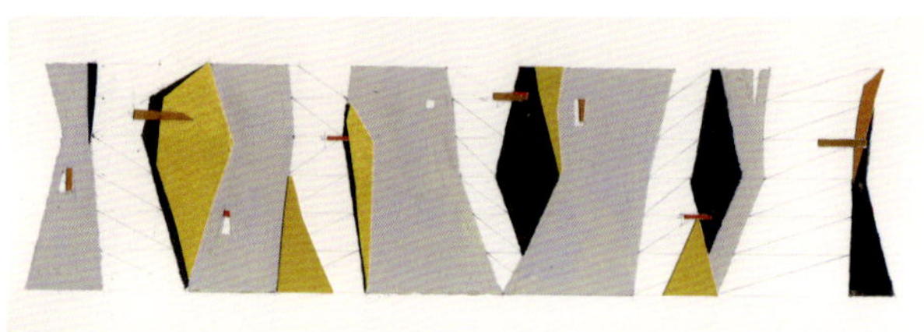

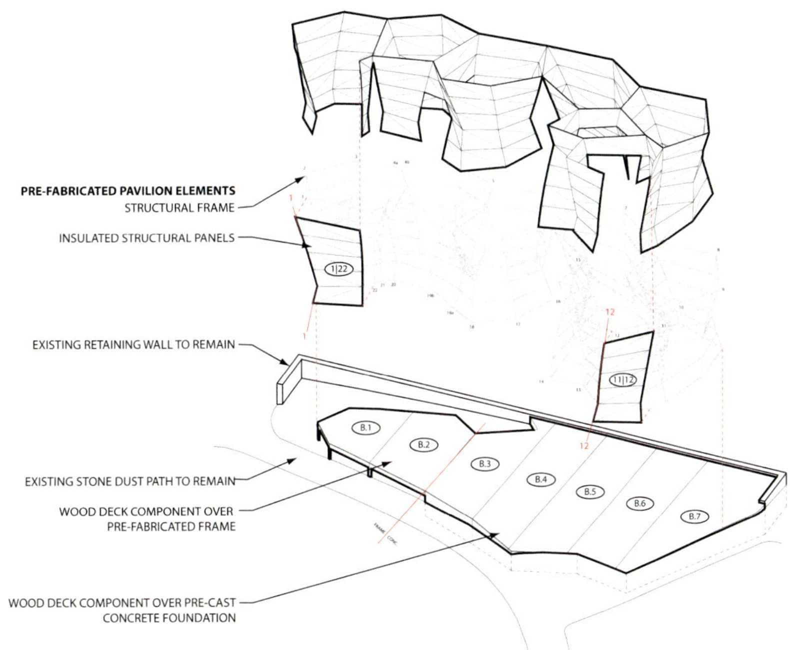

Opposite page Pavillion studies
Right above Pavillion, exploded axonometric
Right Pavillion study model

Opposite page above Studio in DUMBO, Brooklyn, NY - 1983
Opposite page right Giza, Egypt
Right Another Day in Jackson - 2021

DESIGN

Brian Healy Architects

Associates: Paxton Sheldahl, Greg Burchard, Tom Rourke. Collaborators: Kim Poliquin, Edward Mitchell, Garrett Rauck, Rick Jones, Elona Habipi, Gyung-Dong Lee, Trenton Bradford, Elijah Wood, Sean Lawler, Gerry Gutierrez, Elizabeth Kostojohn, Bohseung Kong, Silvia Illia , Julie Chen, Esra Enhos, Eric Jonash, Dan Bonham, Stani Ionadonna, Alec Templeton, Justin Hedde, Lu Yi, Tala Klinck, Jeff Butcher, Anna Matteson, Amy Campos, Greg Schmidt, Tamara Metz, Rachel Levitt, Elizabeth Whittaker, Jennifer Taylor, Heike Braungardt, Paul Schlapobersky, Akira Sasaki, John McDonald, Duy Ho, Matt Pierce, Chris Muskopf, Steve Mayer, Karl Munkelwitz, Amelia Stephenson, Jennifer Mack, Andrew Powell, Edward Palushock, Rosemary Olson, Lee Peters, Bob Gillig, Joe Haskett, Chris Grimley, Maiya Dos, Betsy Walker, Christine Cuttitta, Michael Sparkman, Jill Annarino, Mark Sanderson, Sandra Venus , Karin Tehve, Craig Scott, Antonello Magliozzi, Andrew Burgess, Joel Schmidt, Francesco Guttierrez, Lisa Iwamoto, Heather Crichfield, John Noble, Allison Walker, John Sheehan, Kevin Thornton, John Upton, Chantelle Gutzwillter, Amy Howard Klee, Marilyn Ranker, Charles Crowley

Perkins + Will Boston

Principals Robert Brown: Managing Director, Brian Healy: Design Director, Dana Anderson, Sherwood Butler, Jeannine Campbell, David Dymecki, Dennis Kaiser, Tim Marsters, Gary Shaw Associates and Collaborators John McDonald, Matthew Pierce, Kimberly Poliquin, Jiseok Park, Alec Templeton, Xi Liu, Patrick Cunningham, Emily Lammert, James Forren, Yanel de Angel, David Damon, Tom Grimble, Chris Karlson, John Nelson, Andrew Grote, Susanna Baker, Alec Zebrowski, Michael Bongiorni, Deborah Rivers, Derek Johnson, Andrew Goetze, Christina Long, Christine DiLallo, Alan Estabrook, Jennifer Rheaume, Jessie Greenberg, Jeff Lewis, Kate Hriczo, Anthony Paprocki, Sandra Smith, Rashid Ashraf, Christopher Lockery.

The projects in this book with Brian Healy as *Design Director at P+W* include *UMASS Lowell, UMASS Amherst, Maine Medical, Utah, Haymarket, and ENfold. Floatyard, and Pier 7. Wentworth, Jackson Lab, Floatyard, and Pier 7* began as schematic designs at *P+W* and have been further developed in the offices of *Brian Healy Architects.*

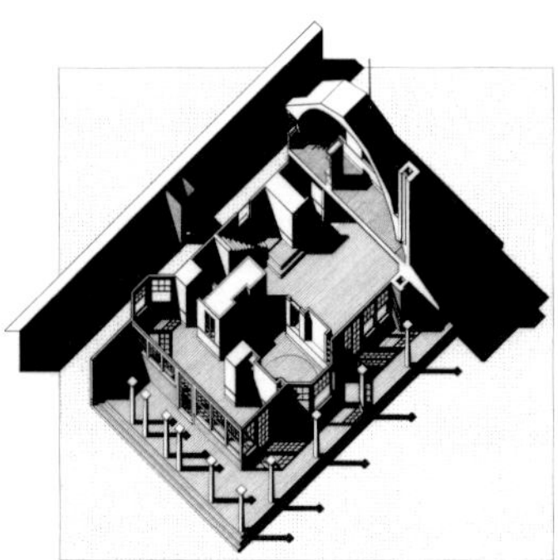

Left HZ House axonometric
Opposite page above Vaulted ceiling
Opposite page form left to right HZ House Siasconset; HZ bedroom vault; Walker Guest House, Sanibel, Florida

PUBLISH

Books

Common Wealth, Edited by Edward Mitchell, Yale School of Architecture, *'Listening to Squares: Keys and Counterpoints'*, Brian Healy (2016); *Thirty Years of Emerging Voices: Idea, Form, Resonance*, Architectural League of New York, Princeton Architectural Press (2015); *Car Parks - Lincoln Street Garage, Song Jia*, Art Power International Publishing Co., Hong Kong (2014); *The Ageing of Aquarius: Designing New Housing Solutions for Australia's Baby-Boomers; Housing Prototypes for Atlantic City,* Shane Murray, University of Western Australia Press, (2010); *AIA Guide to Boston, Lincoln Street Garage,* Susan and Michael Southwick (2008); *Commonplaces: Thinking about an American Architecture,* Brian Healy, ORO Editions: San Francisco – Hong Kong (2008); *The Architecture of Parking,* Simon Henley (Thames & Hudson), *Lincoln Street Garage* (2007); *Proceed and Be Bold: Giving Shape to the Arts,* Design Competition for the Mill Center for the Arts; Edited by Brenda Coates, *The Mill Center for the Arts* (2006); *On Wright: Frank Lloyd Wright's Darwin Martin Visitor's Center Competition*, Edited by Kent Kleinman and Eric Jackson-Forsberg, University of Buffalo (2005); *Materials: Architecture in Detail,* Oscar Riera Ojeda and Mark Pasnik, Rockport Publishers, Gloucester, Massachusetts (2003); *Elements: Architecture in Detail,* Oscar Riera Ojeda and Mark Pasnik, Rockport Publishers, Gloucester, Massachusetts (2003); *100 of the World's Best Houses,* Catherine Stessor, *Beach House*, Images Publishing Australia (2002); *Beach Cottages*, Haike Falkenberg, *Beach House and Summer Compound*, Loft publications, Harper Collins International (2002); *New Coastal Houses, Beach House and Summer Compound*, Links Publications, Barcelona, Spain (2002); *New Coastal Houses* by Arian Mostaedi, *Beach House,* Carles Broto I Comerma, Barcelona, Spain (2001); *New American Houses 2 – Country, Sea, & Cities* by Matteo Vercelloni, *Beach House*, Edizioni L'Archivolto: Milano, Italy (2001); *The Best of American Homes,* Edited by Oscar Riera Ojeda, *Beach House,* Kliczkowski, Barcelona, Spain (2000); *Brian Healy* – Edited by Oscar Riera Ojeda, CASAS International, Kliczkowski, Barcelona, Spain (2000); *Built In Boston: City and Suburb 1800-2000*, Douglass Shand-Tucci, University of Massachusetts Press (2000); *The Best of American Houses*, Edited by Oscar Riera Ojeda, Beach House, Kliczkowski, Barcelona, Spain (2000); *Housing*, Edited by Bianca Bottero, *Housing Prototypes for Atlantic City*, Laboratorio ABITA Milano, Politecnico di Milano (1999); *40 Under 40,* 'Context Matters', Beverly Russell, Vitae Press, Grand Rapids, Michigan, Jurors: Robert AM Stern, Frances Halsband Walter Chatham (1996); *Architectural Design: Drawing Types and Methods,* Rendow Yee, *Healy House in Estero*, John Wiley & Sons, New York (1996); *Architectural Drawing: Options for Design,* Paul Laseau, Florida Residence and Nursery, McGraw Hill (1995); *Ottagono*, *Young Architects: Eastern USA, September, the analogous and the anomalous: architecture and the everyday*, Andrew Bartle and Jonathan Kirschenfeld, Milan, (1987); *Design Simulation,* Ernest Burden, *Healy House in Estero*, Wiley & Sons; New York (1985).

Journals

Manifest: A Journal of American Architecture and Urbanism: Kingdoms of God, Korean Church of Boston, Manifest Journal, New York, NY, (2016); *Competitions*, Winter, *'The Lake Elsinore Civic Center Competition',* Stanley Collyer (2007); *CONCEPT 80: International Magazine of Competition, 2005.12, Brian Healy Architects: Lincoln Street Garage and Beach House (2005); CONCEPT 79: International Magazine of Competition, 2005.11, The Mill Center for the Arts (2005); Competitions, Fall- 2006, Hendersonville: Why Settle for*

Less?, An Arts Center Competition in Appalachia, *The Mill Center for the Arts,* Stanley Collyer (2006); Competitions, Summer - 2004, *Livable Places - Moving to the Head of the Class'*, Larry Gordon (2004); *GA Houses 74: Projects 2003* Global Architecture, Tokyo, Japan, *Patrizio Residence* (2003); *GA Houses 70: Projects 2002 Global Architecture,* Tokyo, Japan, *House in Napa Valley* (2002); *Praxis 3: journal of writing and building,* housing tactics, *Chicago Housing Competition*, Ben Gilmartin (2002); *Praxis 3: journal of writing and building,* housing tactics, *Is Chicago Merely History?*, Robert McAnulty (2002); *Competitions, Volume 11, No.4*, Penance for Projects Past: Chicago Housing Authority Competition, Rosemarie Buchanan (2002); *Chicago Journal,* August 30, Not Raw, but True, Lydialyle Gibson (2002); *GA Houses 63: Projects 2000 Global Architecture,* Tokyo, Japan, *Tower at Onteora* (2000); *GA Houses 55: Projects 1998 Global Architecture,* Tokyo, Japan, *Follini Residence* (1998); *GA Houses 52: Projects 1997 Global Architecture,* Tokyo, Japan, *Housing Prototypes for Atlantic City* (1997); *GA Houses 52: Projects 1997 Global Architecture,* Tokyo, Japan, *Beach House* (1997); *Dimensions v.11,* Journal of the College of Architecture + Urban Planning; University of Michigan, *Poetic Vacancies,* Brian Healy (1997); *GA Houses 45: Projects 1995* Global Architecture, Tokyo, Japan, A Small Lodge (1995); *GA Houses 45: Projects 1995* Global Architecture, Tokyo, Japan, *Three Family Cooperative* (1995); *Fusion Planning*, No. 37, *Brian Healy,* Tokyo, Japan (1992); *Perspecta 19: The Yale Architectural Journal,* Edited by Brian Healy, MIT Press, Cambridge, Massachusetts (1982)

Magazines

Abitare, ArchDaily, Architect, Architect Annual Design Review, Architectural Record, Architecture, Architecture Boston, Art New England, Boston Globe Magazine, Boston HOME, Dwell, Home and Garden. I.D. Magazine, Interiors, LIFE, New England HOME, New England Real Estate Journal, NYARTS, Residential Architect, Progressive Architecture, Streetwise, Tasarim

Press

Boston Globe, Boston Herald, Chicago Tribune, New York Times, Henderson-Times News, The Dartmouth

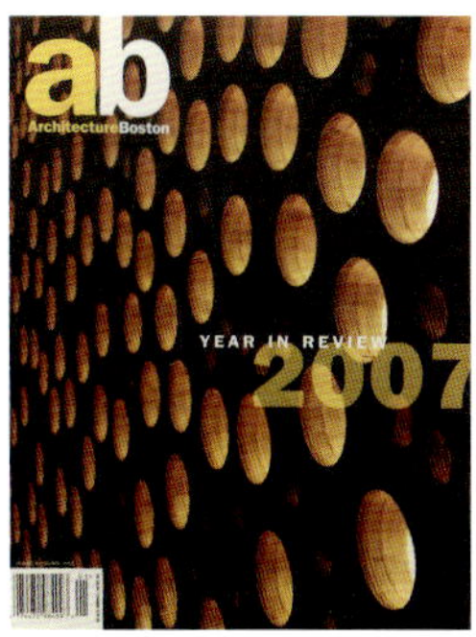

From left to right "Casas" Cover, "Architecture Boston" Cover, "COMMONPLACES I - Thinking about an american architecture" Cover

RECOGNIZE

Design Awards

Harleston Parker Medal: City of Boston and Boston Society of Architects, Education and Community Center, Korean Church of Boston (Finalist - 2016); Progressive/Architecture Award Program, Floatyard (Award for Design Excellence - 2014); World Architecture Festival Award, Future Projects Residential Category, Floatyard (Finalist with PW- 2014); The Interfaith Forum on Religion, Art and Architecture, Children's Chapel and Education Center (Merit Award - 2014); Unbuilt Architecture, Boston Society of Architects, Floatyard (Honor Award -2014); Unbuilt Architecture, Boston Society of Architects, ENfold (Honor Award with PW- 2012); Boston Society of Architects, Essex Boathouse (Honor Award for Design Excellence – 2011); New England AIA, Education and Community Center, Korean Church of Boston (Honor Award for Design Excellence- 2011); Harleston Parker Medal: City of Boston and Boston Society of Architects, Education and Community Center, Korean Church of Boston (Finalist – 2011); New York AIA and Boston Society of Architects, Education and Community Center, Korean Church of Boston (Educational Facilities Design Award – 2011); Architect Magazine, Children's Chapel and Education Center, Korean Church of Boston (Award – Annual Design Review – 2010); Boston Society of Architects, Children's Chapel and Education Center, Korean Church of Boston (Honor Award for Design Excellence – 2010); Boston Society of Architects, Grant Recital Hall, Brown University (Higher Education Design Award – 2009); Progressive/Architecture Award Program, Children's Chapel and Community Center (Award for Design Excellence – 2008); Educational Facility Design, Grant Recital Hall, Brown University (Merit Award – NY AIA Building Type Award – 2008); Interior Design, Boston Society of Architects, Grant Recital Hall, Brown University (Honor Award – 2008); Boston Society of Architects, Grant Recital Hall, Brown University (Honor Award for Design Excellence – 2007); New England AIA, Grant Recital Hall, Brown University (Honor Award for Design Excellence – 2007); New England AIA, Patrizio Residence/Pool House (Honor Award for Design Excellence – 2005); The Boston Society of Architects, Patrizio Residence/Pool House (Honor Award for Design Excellence – 2004); NY AIA/Boston Society of Architects, Patrizio Residence/ Pool House (Honor Award for Design Excellence – 2004); New England AIA, Lincoln Street Garage

Left Mill Center with model in Hendersonville, NC
Opposite page Shaker Dance, Canterbury at Dusk and Shaker Dance, Canterbury at Dusk

(Honor Award for Design Excellence – 2002); Progressive/Architecture Award Program, Mixed Income Housing, Chicago, Illinois (Citation for Design Excellence – 2002); Boston Society of Architects, Lincoln Street Garage (Honor Award for Design Excellence – 2000); I.D. Magazine's 46th Annual Design Review, Revisiting Lincoln Street Garage (Design Distinction- 2000); Boston Society of Architects, Beach House (Honor Award for Design Excellence - w/ Michael Ryan 1999); New England AIA, Beach House (Honor Award for Design Excellence - w/ Michael Ryan 1998); New Jersey AIA, Beach House (Honor Award for Design Excellence - w/ Michael Ryan 1998), Boston Society of Architects, Beach House (Honor Award for Housing Design w/ Michael Ryan – 1998): Boston Society of Architects, Beach House, Long Beach Island, NJ (Honor Award for Design Excellence w/ Michael Ryan - 1998); Progressive/Architecture Award Program, Housing Prototypes, Atlantic City (Citation for Design Excellence – 1997); Boston Society of Architects, Summer Compound (Award for Design excellence with Michael Ryan - 1996); New Jersey AIA, Summer Compound (Award for Design excellence with Michael Ryan – 1996); Boston Society of Architects, A Rural Pool Hall (Award for Design Excellence – 1995); 41st I.D. Annual Design Review, Boston Film Company (Honorable Mention – 1995); New Jersey AIA, Three Family Co-operative, Barnegat Light, New Jersey (Award of Merit with Michael Ryan - 1995); Progressive/Architecture Award Program, A Small Lodge (Citation for Design Excellence – 1994); Boston Society of Architects, Additions to the Fine Arts Building at Brandeis University (Citation for Design Excellence – 1994); Boston Society of Architects, A Small Lodge (Honor Award for Design Excellence – 1993); Boston Society of Architects, River House (Honor Award for Design Excellence with Charles Crowley- 1993); Boston Society of Architects, Residence on Spring Mountain/Wall House (Award of Merit – 1992); Boston Society of Architects, Sandy Cove Residence (Award of Merit with Michael Ryan – 1991); New Jersey AIA, Sandy Cove Residence (Award of Merit with Michael Ryan – 1990); Progressive/Architecture Award Program, Florida Nursery & Residence (Citation for Design Excellence – 1985); Progressive/Architecture Award Program, Healy House (Citation for Design Excellence – 1984)

Professional Honors

National Director: *Social Responsibility Initiative,* Perkins+Will (2012-2014); College of Fellows: American Institute of Architects (2013); LEED AP Neighborhood Development (2013); President: The Boston Society of Architects (2004); Board of Directors: The Boston Society of Architects (2000-2005); EMERGING VOICES: The Architectural League of New York (1999); Alumni Achievement Award: School of Arts & Architecture, Pennsylvania State University (1997); 40 UNDER 40: Jury Members: Robert Stern, Frances Halsband, and Walter Chatham (1996); YOUNG ARCHITECTS: *Progressive Architecture Magazine* (1990); National Register of Peer Professionals, General Service Administration Design Excellence Program (Member - 2004-2009); The Dinkeloo Traveling Fellowship in Architecture, Van Allen Institute/American Academy in Rome (1982); Editor: *Perspecta 19: The Yale Architectural Journal*, MIT Press, Cambridge, Massachusetts (1982); The William Wirt Winchester Traveling Fellowship, Yale School of Architecture (1981); The H.I. Feldman Prize in Design, Yale School of Architecture (1981)

Competitions

P+W BIENNALE – Miami (Finalist - 2014); *World Architecture Festival Award, Future Projects Residential Category* (Finalist – 2013); Design Competition; *Senator Edward M. Kennedy Institute for the Senate,* Boston, Massachusetts (Finalist – 2008); *National Endowment for the Arts Design Competition; Lake Elsinore Civic Center,* Lake Elsinore, California (Finalist – 20007); *National Endowment for the Arts Design Competition, The Mill Center for the Arts,* Hendersonville, North Carolina (First Place – 2005); *Derby Line Border Station, Derby Line,* Vermont, General Service Administration Design Excellence Program (Finalist – 2005); *Competition for an Education Center and Children's Chapel for the Korean Church of Boston,* Brookline, Massachusetts (First Place – 2004); *National Endowment for the Arts Design Competition, Inter-Generational Learning Center,* Chicago, Illinois (Finalist – 2003); *National Endowment for the Arts Design Competition, Innovations in Community Design and Housing for Livable Places,* Long Beach, California (Finalist – 2003); *Visitor's Center for the Frank Lloyd Wright's Martin House,* Buffalo, New York (Finalist – 2002); *National Endowment for the Arts Design Competition, Chicago Housing Authority's Design Competition for Mixed Income Housing,* Chicago, Illinois (First Place – 2001); *Atlantic City Housing Design Competition,* Casino Development Authority (Award of Merit -1996)

Further left Brian Healy and George Ranalli at CCNY Exhibition
Opposite page Exhibition of the work of Brian Healy and his firm at the City College of New York

Yankees

CREDITS

Photography Credits

Bruce Martin (2, 3, 136, 139-144); John Horner (8, 9, 136, 137, 139, 144, 146, 147, 178-189, 212, 235, 362, 366, 370-375, 384, 388-394, 418-445, 490-495, 548-563, 649, 810); Paxton Sheldahl (12, 13, 238-245, 252, 256, 262, 263, 274, 275, 321, 328, 329, 333, 364, 368, 376-383, 496, 519, 521, 523, 533, 564, 567); Kevin Crawford (14, 15); Kim Poliquin (18, 68, 69, 386, 822, 850, 861); PaulWarchol (24, 25, 160, 161, 162, 163, 164, 165, 168, 169, 171, 172, 174, 175, 176, 177, 654-659, 661-667, 668-685, 696-715, 716-725, 796, 862); Brian Healy (28, 29, 60, 61, 62, 63, 64, 65, 70, 71, 148, 149, 152, 153, 155, 283, 285, 289, 290, 304, 315, 316-319, 324, 410-41, 488, 498-514, 580, 584, 584-595, 610, 632-646, 651, 660, 693, 685, 700, 727, 732-739, 770, 774-777, 816; Dan Bibb (140, 142, 143, 146, 803, 865); Peter Vanderwarker (190-205); Silvia Illia (206-210, 236, 237, cover); Harris Allen (606-609, 613-631, 804); Kimberly Holcombe (750, 753-755, 758, 764-767, 771-773, 859)

Illustration Credits

all drawings by BHA and PW except:
Charles Crowley (748, 753, 764, 767); MIR (408, 411, 420); NEAT Agency; (32, 33, 38, 39, 40, 41,42, 43, 44, 45, 46, 48, 49, 72, 73, 75, 76, 77, 79, 82, 83, 84, 85, 87, 88, 90, 91, 92, 93, 94, 95, 97, 98, 101,102, 103, 128, 129, 131, 132, 133, 134, 135, 335, 342-343, 347, 350, 354-358, 768, 778, 782-791, 856); ARCHVIZ-STUDIO (50, 51, 56, 57)

Professional credits

Structural Engineers - Richmond So Associates (6,12, 216-249, 332-337, 366-399, 408-421, 492-518, 552-557, 580-591); MEP – Allied Engineering (408-421, 492-518, 552-557) Acoustics – Kierkegaard Associates (216-249, 250-263, 332-337, 366-399); Cavanaugh Associates (422-499); Lighting – LAM Partners (164-180, 216-249, 332-337, 366-399, 408-421, 492-518); Landscape Architects – Reed Hildebrand LA (250-263); Michael Boucher LA (408-421); GROUND LA (422-449)

SUPPORT

Family
Claire Healy
James Thomas + Jean Claire Healy
Dennis, Kevin, Tim, Brian, Michael, Mark, Jim Jr.

Clients
Jim and Lisa LaTorre, Cresset Group, Edward Nardi, William Curtis, John Baxter, Korean Church of Boston, United Parish of Winchendon, 374 Somerville Avenue LLC, Michael Ryan Architects, The Shotwell Family, The Deixler Family, The Heikemian Family, The Peron Family, CJ Follini, Seth Harrison, Wendy and Morris Evans, Helen Hobart and David Zorensky, Leah Maher, Amy and Andrew Hartman, Hsueh-Ming Wang and James Healy, Perkins + Will Boston, Wentworth Institute of Technology, Jackson Labs, Maine Medical Center, University of Massachusetts Lowell, University of Massachusetts Amherst, Intercontinental Development, Bob Palandjian, Mark Healy, Mark and Amanda Harmeling, The Forman Family, Chicago Housing Authority, City of Lake Elsinore, Atlantic City Casino Redevelopment Authority, Ellen Kurz and Tom Cosgrove, Ed and Bean Nardi, The McLaughlin Family, Boston Film Company, Amin Khoury, The Florence Grey Community Center, The Walton Family, Fenway Alliance, Boston Architectural College, Boston Society of Architects, Long Beach Community Housing, Steve and Judy Patrizio, Brown University, Harvard University, Eunice Shriver, The Rose Kennedy Greenway, Kennedy Institute for the Senate, Tim Healy

Sponsors
This book is made possible by the generous support of *Dean Gregory Call* at Amherst College, *Dean George Ranalli* at the Bernard & Anne Spitzer School of Architecture at the City College of New York, and *Dean Gregory Hunt* at Marywood University in Scanton, Pennsylvania.

Editor
Oscar Riera Ojeda and *Brian Healy* have worked together over the past twenty years on six separate books. It is important to recognize and acknowledge Oscar's essential guidance, encouragement, and support in the development of this version of ***COMMONPLACES***.

Left Global Sketch by Claire Healy
Opposite page above Pashupatinath Temple, Kathmandu - 1983
Opposite page Brothers at the construction site of Tim's House in Estero, Florida - 1983; Claire at Wadi Rum in Jordon 2020; Sippewisset - Tim and Jim, 1986

DEDICATE

FOR **JIM + JEAN CLAIRE**

1922-1995 + 1928-2018

This body that clothes the spirit, that moves with grace and boldness, that knows love, that is apt for self-sacrifice – no one now so much as thinks of giving it a decent burial. I thought of our respect for the dead. I thought of the white sanatorium where the light of a man's life goes quietly out in the presence of those who love him and who garner as if it were an inestimable treasure his last words, his ultimate smile. How right they are! Seeing that this same whole is never again to take shape in the world. Never again will be heard exactly that note of laughter, that intonation of voice, that quality of repartee. Each individual is a miracle. No wonder we go on speaking of the dead for twenty years."

Antonine De Saint-Exupery

+ TIM

1957-2018

APPENDIX

As an architecture student at Yale University in the early 1980's, I wandered many mornings onto the roof terrace of the Art and Architecture Building, exhausted, and watched the sun rise after a night at my drafting table. If I found any consolation during these interludes, it did not lie with the drawings I left behind, but in the street below.

Strange Details – Michael Cadwell

BRIAN HEALY ARCHITECTS

Born in Gary, Indiana, Healy moved to the east coast with his family to northern New Jersey and then Bucks County in southeastern Pennsylvania. He was educated at the Pennsylvania State University (1978) and the Yale School of Architecture (1981) where he was Editor of *Perspecta 19: the Yale Architectural Journal*. He worked with some of the industry's most renowned design firms including Charles Moore, Cesar Pelli, and Richard Meier prior to establishing his own architectural practice in Boston in 1985, where he compiled a distinguished record of creative activity, community service, and professional achievement.

The architectural projects produced by his office have received over fifty national and regional design awards including seven within the Progressive Architecture Award Program. He was selected as an *Emerging Voice* by the Architectural League of New York and included in *Forty under Forty* and P/A's issue focusing on *Young Architects*. His firm won first place in international design competitions including *Chicago's Initiative to Redefine Public Housing* and the *Mill Center for the Arts* in Hendersonville, North Carolina. His work spans a diverse range of scales and settings – from installations to urban design – and his projects have been extensively published and exhibited both here and abroad. His 2009 monograph *Commonplaces: Thinking of an American Architecture* documents his appreciation of the inherent links between each place and its unique landscape.

Healy was on the Board of Directors of the *Boston Society of Architects* for five years including two years on the Executive Committee and one year as the 2004 BSA president. He was elevated to the College of Fellows at the American Institute for Architects in 2015 and was the Design Director in the Boston office of Perkins+Will from 2011-2014.

For the past thirty years, Healy has also been consistently active in teaching architectural design studios and seminars at many college and universities across North America including the Yale School of Architecture, the Graduate School of Design at Harvard, Massachusetts Institute of Technology, University of Pennsylvania, Dartmouth College, Middlebury College, Washington University, University of Virginia, University of Florida, University of Michigan, University of Arkansas, and the Pennsylvania State University. He was the Hideo Sasaki Distinguished Visiting Critic at the Boston Architectural College, and Visiting Distinguished Professor in Architecture at The City College of New York and Roger Williams University in Bristol, Rhode Island.

He has received fellowships for residency at the American Academy in Rome, the MacDowell Art Colony in Peterborough, New Hampshire, and Dorland Mountain Art Colony in Temecula, California. He received the Dinkeloo Traveling Fellowship from the Van Allen Institute and the William Wirt Winchester Traveling Fellowship from the Yale School of Architecture. He was the Visiting Artist in Residence at Amherst College, the Cameron Visiting Architect at Middlebury College, and the Gerald Sheff Visiting Professor in Architecture at McGill University in Montreal.

Right above Studio at Melcher street - Fort Point Channel - Boston
Right Brian Healy

BOOK CREDITS

Art Director: Oscar Riera Ojeda
Graphic Design: Lucia B Bauza

OSCAR RIERA OJEDA
PUBLISHERS

ISBN 978-1-946226-37-2
Published by Oscar Riera Ojeda Publishers Limited
Printed in China

Oscar Riera Ojeda Publishers Limited
Unit 1003-04, 10/F.,
Shanghai Industrial Investment Building,
48-62 Hennessy Road, Wanchai, Hong Kong

Production Offices
Suit 19, Shenyun Road,
Nanshan District, Shenzhen 518055, China

International Customer Service & Editorial Questions: +1-484-502-5400

www.oropublishers.com | www.oscarrieraojeda.com
oscar@oscarrieraojeda.com

The
MACAL

THE ARCHIVA

FOLI
7